Ways of Reading

AN ANTHOLOGY FOR WRITERS

TENTH EDITION

David Bartholomae
UNIVERSITY OF PITTSBURGH

Anthony Petrosky
UNIVERSITY OF PITTSBURGH

Stacey Waite
UNIVERSITY OF NEBRASKA–LINCOLN

BEDFORD/MARTIN'S
BOSTON ◆ NEW YORK

For Bedford/St. Martin's

Publisher for Composition: Leasa Burton
Executive Editor: John E. Sullivan III
Developmental Editor: Regina Tavani
Senior Production Editor: Bridget Leahy
Production Supervisor: Samuel Jones
Marketing Manager: Emily Rowin
Editorial Assistant: Brenna Cleeland
Copy Editor: Jeannine Walls Thibodeau
Photo Researcher: Linda Finigan
Senior Art Director: Anna Palchik
Text Design: Tom Carling
Cover Design: Marine Miller
Cover Art: Vector, by Doug Beube. Used by permission of the artist.
Composition: Jouve
Printing and Binding: RR Donnelley and Sons

President, Bedford/St. Martin's: Denise B. Wydra
Editorial Director, English and Music: Karen S. Henry
Director of Marketing: Karen R. Soeltz
Production Director: Susan W. Brown
Director of Rights and Permissions: Hilary Newman

Manufactured in the United States of America.
8 7 6 5 4 3
f e d c b a

For information, write: Bedford/St. Martin's, 75 Arlington Street, Boston, MA 02116
(617-399-4000)

ISBN 978-1-4576-2685-2

Acknowledgments
Acknowledgments and copyrights are continued at the back of the book on pages 513–517, which constitute an extension of the copyright page. It is a violation of the law to reproduce these selections by any means whatsoever without the written permission of the copyright holder.

Preface

Ways of Reading is designed for a course where students are given the opportunity to work on what they read, and to work on it by writing. When we began developing such courses, we realized that the problems our students had when asked to write or talk about what they read were not "reading problems," at least not as these are strictly defined. Our students knew how to move from one page to the next. They could read sentences. They had, obviously, been able to carry out many of the versions of reading required for their education — skimming textbooks, cramming for tests, strip-mining books for term papers.

Our students, however, felt powerless in the face of serious writing, in the face of long and complicated texts — the kinds of texts we thought they should find interesting and challenging. We thought (as many teachers have thought) that if we just, finally, gave them something good to read — something rich and meaty — they would change forever their ways of thinking about English. It didn't work, of course. The issue is not only *what* students read, but what they can learn to *do* with what they read. We learned that the problems our students had lay not in the reading material (it was too hard) or in the students (they were poorly prepared) but in the classroom — in the ways we and they imagined what it meant to work on an essay.

There is no better place to work on reading than in a writing course, and this book is intended to provide occasions for readers to write. You will find a number of distinctive features in *Ways of Reading*. For one thing, it contains selections you don't usually see in a college reader: long, powerful, mysterious, and difficult pieces like John Berger's "Ways of Seeing," Judith Butler's "Beside Oneself: On the Limits of Sexual Autonomy," Susan Griffin's "Our Secret," Edward Said's "States," John Edgar Wideman's "Our Time," David Foster Wallace's "Authority and American Usage," or Michel Foucault's "Panopticism." These are the sorts of readings we talk about when we talk with our colleagues. We have learned that we can talk about them with our students as well.

When we chose the essays, we were looking for "readable" texts — that is, texts that leave some work for a reader to do. We wanted selections that invite students to be active, critical readers, that present powerful readings of common experience, that open up the familiar world and make it puzzling, rich, and problematic. We wanted to choose selections that invite students to take responsibility for their acts of interpretation. So we avoided the short set-pieces you find in so many anthologies. In a sense, those short selections misrepresent the act of reading. They can be read in a single sitting; they make arguments that can be easily paraphrased; they solve all the problems they raise; they wrap up life and put it into a box; and so they turn reading into an act of appreciation, where the most that seems to be required is a nod of the head. And they suggest that a writer's job is to do just that, to write a piece that is similarly tight and neat and self-contained. We wanted to avoid pieces that were so plainly written or tightly bound that there was little for students to do but "get the point."

We learned that if our students had reading problems when faced with long and complex texts, the problems lay in the way they imagined a reader—the role a reader plays, what a reader does, why a reader reads (if not simply to satisfy the requirements of a course). When, for example, our students were puzzled by what they read, they took this as a sign of failure. ("It doesn't make any sense," they would say, as though the sense was supposed to be waiting on the page, ready for them the first time they read through.) And our students were haunted by the thought that they couldn't remember everything they had read (as though one could store all of Judith Butler's "Beside Oneself: On the Limits of Sexual Autonomy" in memory); or if they did remember bits and pieces, they felt that the fragmented text they possessed was evidence that they could not do what they were supposed to do. Our students were confronting the experience of reading, in other words, but they were taking the problems of reading—problems all readers face—and concluding that there was nothing for them to do but give up.

As expert readers, we have all learned what to do with a complex text. We know that we can go back to a text; we don't have to remember it—in fact, we've learned to mark up a text to ease that reentry. We know that a reader is a person who puts together fragments. Those coherent readings we construct begin with confusion and puzzlement, and we construct those readings by writing and rewriting—by working on a text.

These are the lessons our students need to learn, and this is why a course in reading is also a course in writing. Our students need to learn that there is something they can do once they have first read through a complicated text; successful reading is not just a matter of "getting" an essay the first time. In a very real sense, you can't begin to feel the power a reader has until you realize the problems, until you realize that no one "gets" Appiah or Butler or Wideman all at once. You work on what you read, and then what you have at the end is something that is yours, something you made. And this is what the teaching apparatus in *Ways of Reading* is designed to do. In a sense, it says to students, "OK, let's get to work on these essays; let's see what you can make of them."

This, then, is the second distinctive feature you will find in *Ways of Reading*: reading and writing assignments designed to give students access to the essays. After each selection, for example, you will find "Questions for a Second Reading." We wanted to acknowledge that rereading is a natural way of carrying out the work of a reader, just as rewriting is a natural way of completing the work of a writer. It is not something done out of despair or as a punishment for not getting things right the first time. The questions we have written highlight what we see as central textual or interpretive problems. These questions might serve as preparations for class discussion or ways of directing students' work in journals. Whatever the case, they both honor and direct the work of rereading.

Each selection is also followed by two sets of writing assignments, "Assignments for Writing" and "Making Connections." The first set directs students back into the work they have just read. While the assignments vary, there are some basic principles behind them. They ask students to work on the essay by focusing on difficult or problematic moments in the text; they ask students to work on the author's examples, extending and testing his or her methods of analysis; or they ask students to apply the method of the essay (its way of seeing and understanding the world) to settings or experiences of their own. The last assignments, "Making Connections," invite students to read one essay in the context of another, to see, for example, if Mary Louise Pratt's account of the "literate arts of the contact zone" can be used to frame a reading of Gloria Anzaldúa's prose or Paulo Freire's or Richard E. Miller's account of education. In a sense, then, the essays are offered as models, but not as "prose models" in the strictest sense. What they model is a way of seeing or reading the world, of both imagining problems and imagining methods to make those problems available to a writer.

At the end of the book, we have included several assignment sequences. A single sequence provides structure for an entire course. (There are a number of additional sequences included online in the e-Pages and in the Instructor's Manual.) Most of the sequences include more than one essay in the anthology and require a series of separate drafts and revisions. Alternative essays and assignments are included with the sequences. In academic life, readers seldom read single essays in isolation, as though one were "finished" with Judith Butler after a week or two. Rather, they read with a purpose — with a project in mind or a problem to solve. The assignment sequences are designed to give students a feel for the rhythm and texture of an extended academic project. They offer, that is, one more way of reading and writing. Because these sequences lead students through intellectual projects proceeding from one week to the next, they enable them to develop authority as specialists, to feel the difference between being an expert and being a "common" reader on a single subject. And, with the luxury of time available for self-reflection, students can look back on what they have done, not only to revise what they know, but also to take stock and comment on the value and direction of their work.

Because of their diversity, it is difficult to summarize the assignment sequences. Perhaps the best way to see what we have done is to turn to the back of the book and look at them. They are meant to frame a project for students but to leave open possibilities for new directions. You should feel free to add or drop readings, to mix sequences, and to revise the assignments to fit your course and your schedule.

You will also notice that there are few "glosses" appended to the essays. We have not added many editors' notes to define difficult words or to identify names or allusions to other authors or artists. We've omitted them because their presence suggests something we feel is false about reading. They suggest that good readers know all the words or pick up all the allusions or recognize every name that is mentioned. This is not true. Good readers do what they can and try their best to fill in the blanks; they ignore seemingly unimportant references and look up the important ones. There is no reason for students to feel they lack the knowledge necessary to complete a reading of these texts. We have translated some foreign phrases, but we have kept the selections as clean and open as possible.

We have been asked on several occasions whether the readings aren't finally just too hard for students. The answer is no. Students will have to work on the selections, but that is the point of the course and the reason, as we said before, why a reading course is also a course in writing. College students want to believe that they can strike out on their own, make their mark, do something they have never done before. They want to *be* experts, not just hear from them. This is the great pleasure, as well as the great challenge, of undergraduate instruction. It is not hard to convince students they ought to be able to speak alongside of (or even speak back to) Judith Butler or Edward Said. And, if a teacher is patient and forgiving—willing, that is, to let a student work out a reading of Butler or Said, willing to keep from saying, "No, that's not it," and filling the silence with the "right" reading—then students can, with care and assistance, learn to speak for themselves. It takes a certain kind of classroom, to be sure. A teacher who teaches this book will have to be comfortable turning the essays over to the students, even with the knowledge that they will not do immediately on their own what a professional could do—at least not completely, or with the same grace and authority.

In our own teaching, we have learned that we do not have to be experts on every figure or every area of inquiry represented in this book. And, frankly, that has come as a great relief. We can have intelligent, responsible conversations about Appiah's "Racial Identities" without being experts on Appiah's work or current work on race and identity. We needed to prepare ourselves to engage and direct students as readers, but we did not have to prepare ourselves to lecture on Foucault or Butler, on poststructuralism and gender theory. The classes we have been teaching, and they have been some of the most exciting we have ever taught, have been classes where students—together and with their instructors—work on what these essays might mean.

So here we are, imagining students working shoulder to shoulder with Said, Butler, and Foucault, even talking back to them as the occasion arises. There is a wonderful Emersonian bravado in all this. But such is the case with strong and active readers. If we allow students to work on powerful texts, they will want to share the power. This is the heady fun of academic life, the real pleasure of thinking, reading, and writing. There is no reason to keep it secret from our students.

NEW TO THE TENTH EDITION

Nearly half of the selections in the tenth edition of *Ways of Reading* are new. Our principle of selection remained the same—we were looking for "readable" texts, pieces that instructors and students would find challenging and compelling, pieces that offer powerful readings of ordinary experiences, pieces worth extended work.

In the print book, there are new chapter-length selections by Kwame Anthony Appiah, Judith Halberstam, Joshua Foer, Kathleen Jamie, Jonathan Lethem, and Kathryn Schulz. Along with many other chapter-length pieces, we've kept the briefer selections by Anne Carson and Brian Doyle introduced in the ninth edition. These shorter selections offer students opportunities to see how substantial intellectual and analytic work can be taken on with just a few pages or lines. These, like the longer selections, offer students the possibility of articulating the complex and exploring the connections between the experimental and the critical. We have, for the first time, also included a selection of graphic memoir, a chapter from Alison Bechdel's most recent book, *Are You My Mother?*, to give students an opportunity to engage with a visual project.

Bedford Integrated Media. Many selections in the tenth edition are located in the book's Integrated Media: e-Pages that give the book a rich array of assignable selections, some with multimodal content. Here we've reintroduced classic essays from Ralph Waldo Emerson and James Baldwin available in previous edition of *Ways of Reading*, as well as engaging video content, including interviews with Judith Butler and Errol Morris and the first episode of the *Ways of Seeing* television series from the BBC. Selections in the e-Pages include the same types of assignment questions offered with selections in the print text.

Students access the online e-Pages through the Bedford Integrated Media page for *Ways of Reading* at **bedfordstmartins.com/waysofreading**. They receive automatic access to e-Pages with the purchase of a new book. (Students who buy a used book or who rent a book can purchase access at this same site.) The e-Pages format makes it easy for instructors to see and evaluate what students are doing and gives new options for readings and assignments.

We have also added more examples of student work, including two essays that respond to the Brian Doyle selection. Rather than offering these essays as student samples, as an exhortative *You can do it, too!* we ask that students work with these essays *as* essays, as thoughtful responses to the Miller and Doyle readings, as essays worth engaging in conversation, as pieces to think about and to write with and against.

We have developed two new assignment sequences, "Exploring Identity, Exploring the Self" and "Deliberative Acts of Discovery," and we have revised the existing sequences, some to incorporate the new selections, others because, after teaching them again, we thought about them differently. We have also moved a number of the sequences to the e-Pages, where students can complete their assignments online. In addition to sequences focusing on academic writing, we have continued to offer sequences focusing on autobiographical writing and the personal essay. While there have always been assignments in *Ways of Reading* that ask students to use their experience as subject matter, these assignments invite students to look critically and historically at the autobiographical genre and insist that reading and thinking can *also* be represented as part of one's "personal" experience. Teaching these as examples of reading and writing projects has taught us that they have much to offer that students can study and imitate. We remain convinced that this kind of work helps students to think about sentences in useful ways. And we have continued to focus attention on prose models that challenge conventional forms and idioms, that complicate the usual ways of thinking about and representing knowledge and experience. There are several assignment sequences that ask students to write as though they too could participate in such revisionary work.

ACKNOWLEDGMENTS

With our colleagues, we have taught most of the selections in this book, including the new ones. Several of us worked together to prepare the assignment sequences; most of these, too, have been tested in class. As we have traveled around giving talks, we've met many people who have used *Ways of Reading*. We have been delighted to hear them speak about how it has served their teaching, and we have learned much from their advice and example. It is an unusual and exciting experience to see our course turned into a text, to see our work read, critiqued, revised, and expanded. We have many people to thank. The list that follows can't begin to name all those to whom we owe a debt. And it can't begin to express our gratitude.

We owe much to the friendship and wisdom of our colleagues at the University of Pittsburgh. There are old friends and colleagues with whom we have worked for a very long time: Don Bialostosky, Jean Ferguson Carr, Steve Carr, Nick Coles, Kathryn Flannery, Jean Grace, Paul Kameen, Geeta Kothari, Jennifer Lee, Beth Matway, Mariolina Salvatori, Jim Seitz, Phil Smith, Brenda Whitney, and Lois Williams. It is an honor and a pleasure to teach together with such colleagues; we have learned much from their example, their critique, and their suggestions. Stacey Waite, who made important contributions to the ninth edition, has joined us more formally and more officially on the tenth. You'll see her name on the title page. She is our new junior partner and will take over the project in time. You can see her hand in both the new selections and the new assignments and in the close revision of some older material, including the "Introduction." It has been a real pleasure to work with Stacey—a pleasure and an education. And we owe much to colleagues at other schools, especially to the graduate students at the University of Nebraska–Lincoln, who have been working with several of our assignments and one graduate student—Kristi Carter—who contributed a student paper to this tenth edition. Thanks to all who have followed our work with interest and offered their support and criticism. We are grateful for the notes, letters, and student papers.

We are fortunate to have a number of outstanding reviewers on the project: Sonja Andrus, University of Cincinnati Blue Ash College; Larry Beason, University of South Alabama; Wade Bentley, Weber State University; Simone Billings, Santa Clara University; Jeanne Bohannon, Georgia State University; David Calonne, Eastern Michigan University; Pamela Cantrell, University of Nevada, Las Vegas; Daniel Chaskes, University of Miami; Lois Lake Church, Quinnipiac University, University of Connecticut, Southern Connecticut State University, and Charter Oak State College; Tina Crafton, Rutgers University-Camden; Jeremiah Crotser, University at Buffalo; Kathy Czepiel, Quinnipiac University; Christy Friend, University of South Carolina; Lisa Giles, University of New England; Brenda Glascott, California State University, San Bernardino; Lawrence Gorman, East-West University; Marylou Gramm, University of Pittsburgh; Chris Grooms, Collin College; Carol V. Hamilton, University of Pittsburgh; Melissa Kaplan, Quinnipiac University; Adam Katz, Quinnipiac University; Erica Kaufman, Baruch College; Amy Kelly, Westminster College; Victoria Kingsley, University of Massachusetts Boston; John Levine, University of California, Berkeley; Jessica McCall, Black Hawk College; Melissa Nicolas, Drew University; Jenny Noyce, University of Oregon; Glenda Pritchett, Quinnipiac University; Lynn Reid, Fairleigh Dickinson University; Lori Robison, University of North Dakota; Lisa Roy-Davis, Collin College; Constance Sabo-Risley, San Antonio College; Joseph Scallorns, Virginia Tech; Margot Schilpp, Southern Connecticut State University and Quinnipiac University; Ian Sherman, Olympic College; Breena Solomon, University of Miami; Lauren Squires, University of North Carolina at Wilmington; Michael Stigman, Benedictine College; Kelly Sultzbach, University of Wisconsin-La Crosse; Ron Sweeney, University of the Fraser Valley; Nancy Thompson, Clark College; Josette Torres, Virginia Tech; Jeremy Voigt, Whatcom Community College.

Chuck Christensen, President Emeritus of Bedford/St. Martin's, and Joan Feinberg, Co-President of Macmillan Higher Education, helped to shape this project from its very beginning. They remain fine and thoughtful friends as well as fine and thoughtful editors. We thank Denise Wydra, Karen Henry, and Leasa

Burton for their continued guidance. John Sullivan joined the group for the fifth edition. He had taught from an earlier edition of *Ways of Reading* and had, for us, a wonderful sense of the book's approach to reading, writing, and teaching. John is organized, resourceful, generous, quick to offer suggestions and to take on extra work. He soon became as much a collaborator as an editor. It was a real pleasure to work with him. Deja Earley lent her keen insights as we located new selections for the text, and Regina Tavani oversaw development of the new manuscript. We owe a special thanks to Regina, who played a major role in helping to shape this new edition and in gathering materials for the e-Pages. Caryn Burtt and Linda Finigan handled permissions under the able guidance of Kalina Ingham and Martha Friedman. Brenna Cleeland assisted with many details. Bridget Leahy expertly guided the manuscript through production. Linda McLatchie was an excellent copyeditor, sensitive to the quirks of our prose and attentive to detail. Kimberly Hampton helped developed the book's e-Pages.

And, finally, we are grateful to Joyce, Vivian and Brie, and to Jesse, Dan, Kate, Matthew, and Ben, for their love and support.

RESOURCES FOR INSTRUCTORS AND STUDENTS

Instructor Resources

Ways of Reading doesn't stop with a book. Online, you'll find both free and affordable premium resources to help students get even more out of the book and your course. You'll also find convenient instructor resources and even a nationwide community of teachers. To learn more about or order any of the products below, contact your Bedford/St. Martin's sales representative, e-mail sales support (sales_support@bfwpub.com), or visit the Web site at **bedfordstmartins.com/waysofreading**.

We've updated ***Resources for Teaching Ways of Reading*** by including a new pedagogical essay by Hannah Gerrard. We continue to offer essays by graduate students; these essays give advice on how to work with the book. They stand as examples of the kinds of papers graduate students might write when they use *Ways of Reading* in conjunction with a teaching seminar. They stand best, however, as examples of graduate students speaking frankly to other graduate students about teaching and about *Ways of Reading*. In addition to the pedagogical essays, the instructor's manual includes entries on each selection and sequence, sample syllabi, additional sequences, and extensive resources for using *Ways of Reading* in the classroom, including a section of frequently asked questions. This manual is available in PDF that can be downloaded from the Bedford/St. Martin's Web site at **bedfordstmartins.com/waysofreading**. To obtain a print copy of the manual at no charge, contact your Bedford/St. Martin's sales representative.

Teaching Central offers the entire list of Bedford/St. Martin's print and online professional resources in one place. You'll find landmark reference works, sourcebooks on pedagogical issues, award-winning collections, and practical advice for the classroom — all free for instructors. Visit **bedfordstmartins.com/teachingcentral.**

Bits collects creative ideas for teaching a range of composition topics in an easily searchable blog format. A community of teachers — leading scholars, authors, and editors — discuss revision, research, grammar and style, technology, peer review, and much more. Take, use, adapt, and pass the ideas around. Then, come back to the site to comment or share your own suggestion. Visit **bedfordbits.com.**

Content cartridges for the most common course management systems—Angel, Blackboard, Canvas, Moodle, Desire2Learn, and Sakai—allow you to easily download digital materials from Bedford/St. Martin's for your course. Visit **bedfordstmartins.com/coursepacks** for more information.

Student Resources

Send students to free and open resources or upgrade to an expanding collection of innovative digital content.

Try *Re:Writing 2* for Fun
bedfordstmartins.com/rewriting

What's the fun of teaching writing if you can't try something new? The best collection of free writing resources on the Web, *Re:Writing 2* gives you and your students even more ways to think, watch, practice, and learn about writing concepts. Listen to Nancy Sommers on using a teacher's comments to revise. Try a logic puzzle. Consult our resources for writing centers. All free for the fun of trying it. Visit **bedfordstmartins.com/rewriting**.

VideoCentral is a growing collection of videos for the writing class that captures real-world, academic, and student writers talking about how and why they write. Writer and teacher Peter Berkow interviewed hundreds of people—from Michael Moore to Cynthia Selfe—to produce over 140 brief videos about topics such as revising and getting feedback. VideoCentral can be packaged with *Ways of Reading* at a significant discount. An activation code is required. To order VideoCentral packaged with the print book, use ISBN 978-1-457-67887-5.

ON THE COVER

The covers for the ten editions of *Ways of Reading* have all alluded to the history of the book. Our very first cover reproduced the marbled endpapers common in nineteenth-century book production. The cover to this edition comes from *Vector*, a work by the book artist Doug Beube. It considers the presence of the book in the twenty-first century, in a digital age.

According to Beube, his work explores the physical limits of this ancient device we call the book. And he does this by taking an old volume and, as a sculptor, by physically performing "quasi-software" functions upon it: cutting and pasting and exposing the text beneath the text.

Vector is made from four books by four different authors, one stacked on top of another, cantilevered and cut so that the end pages form a terraced slope, like the side of a pyramid or a Mayan ruin. The view on the cover is the view looking down on that slope. From this perspective, the text appears single, whole. But from the side, the view presents four authors in difficult balance.

You can find *Vector* at **dougbeube.com/artwork/2154852_Vector.html**.

Contents

---

e For readings that go beyond the printed page, see **bedfordstmartins.com/waysofreading**.

ANNE CARSON, SHORT TALKS **140**

"I will do anything to avoid boredom. It is the task of a lifetime. You can never know enough, never work enough, never use the infinitives and participles oddly enough, never impede the movements harshly enough, never leave the mind quickly enough."

[FROM *Short Talks*]

BRIAN DOYLE, JOYAS VOLADORAS **147**

"So much held in a heart in a lifetime. So much held in a heart in a day, an hour, a moment. We are utterly open with no one, in the end — not mother and father, not wife or husband, not lover, not child, not friend. We open windows to each other but we live alone in the house of the heart. Perhaps we must."

[FROM *The American Scholar*]

RALPH WALDO EMERSON, THE AMERICAN SCHOLAR

"The scholar is that man who must take up into himself all the ability of the time, all the contributions of the past, all the hopes of the future. He must be an university of knowledges. If there be one lesson more than another which should pierce his ear, it is, The World is nothing, the man is all; in yourself Is the law of all nature, and you know not yet how a globule of sap ascends; in yourself lumbers the whole of Reason; it is for you to know all, it is for you to dare all."

[*An Oration Delivered before the Phi Beta Kappa Society, at Cambridge, August 31, 1837*]

JOSHUA FOER, THE END OF REMEMBERING **160**

"As more and more of our lives move online, more and more is being captured and preserved in ways that are dramatically changing the relationship between our internal and external memories. We are moving toward a future, it seems, in which we will have all-encompassing external memories that record huge swaths of our daily activity."

[FROM *Moonwalking with Einstein*]

MICHEL FOUCAULT, PANOPTICISM **181**

"Our society is one not of spectacle, but of surveillance; under the surface of images, one invests bodies in depth; behind the great abstraction of exchange, there continues the meticulous, concrete training of useful forces; the circuits of communication are the supports of an accumulation and a centralization of knowledge; the play of signs defines the anchorages of power; it is not that the beautiful totality of the individual is amputated, repressed, altered by our social order, it is rather that the individual is

e bedfordstmartins.com/waysofreading

there were, all were agreed on this: the last was the biggest. It was this government! Where was the money to repair the road? Gone in their back pockets!"

[FROM *Among Muslims*]

"Any text is woven entirely with citations, references, echoes, cultural languages, which cut across it through and through in a vast stereophony. The citations that go to make up a text are anonymous, untraceable, and yet *already read*; they are quotations without inverted commas. The kernel, the soul—let us go further and say the substance, the bulk, the actual and valuable material of all human utterances—is plagiarism."

[FROM *The Ecstasy of Influence*]

"Can secular institutions of higher education be taught to use writing to foster a kind of critical optimism that is able to transform idle feelings of hope into viable plans for sustainable action? Can the first year writing course become a place where we engage productively with the dark realities of our time: violence, suicide, war, and terrorism, as well as fraudulence, complicity, and trauma? Can teachers of first year writing be moved beyond praising students for generating arguments without consequence, thought with no interest in action?"

[FROM *Writing at the End of the World*]

"Photographs attract false beliefs the way flypaper attracts flies. Why my skepticism? Because vision is privileged in our society and in our sensorium. We trust it; we place our confidence in it. Photography allows us to uncritically think. We *imagine* that photographs provide a magic path to truth."

[FROM *Believing Is Seeing*]

"A photograph, among other things, de-contextualizes — I'll use the fancy word — it de-contextualizes everything. You don't see above. You don't see below . . . You don't see to the left or to the right. You don't see before or after. You see this swatch of reality, two-dimensional reality, that's been torn out of the fabric of the world. And the only way we can know what we're looking at is to investigate."

[FROM *We've Forgotten that Photographers Are Connected to the Physical World*]

---

bedfordstmartins.com/waysofreading

WALKER PERCY, THE LOSS OF THE CREATURE **299**

"When a caste system becomes absolute, envy disappears. Yet the caste of layman-expert is not the fault of the expert. It is due altogether to the eager surrender of sovereignty by the layman so that he may take up the role not of the person but of the consumer."

[FROM *The Message in the Bottle*]

MARY LOUISE PRATT, ARTS OF THE CONTACT ZONE **317**

"I use this term [contact zone] to refer to social spaces where cultures meet, clash, and grapple with each other, often in contexts of highly asymmetrical relations of power, such as colonialism, slavery, or their aftermaths as they are lived out in many parts of the world today. Eventually I will use the term to reconsider the models of community that many of us rely on in teaching and theorizing and that are under challenge today."

[FROM *Profession 91*]

RICHARD RODRIGUEZ, THE ACHIEVEMENT OF DESIRE **338**

"What I am about to say to you has taken me more than twenty years to admit: *A primary reason for my success in the classroom was that I couldn't forget that schooling was changing me and separating me from the life I enjoyed before becoming a student.* That simple realization! For years I never spoke to anyone about it. Never mentioned a thing to my family or my teachers or classmates."

[FROM *Hunger of Memory*]

EDWARD SAID, STATES e

"Exile is a series of portraits without names, without contexts. Images that are largely unexplained, nameless, mute. I look at them without precise anecdotal knowledge, but their realistic exactness nevertheless makes a deeper impression than mere information. I cannot reach the actual people who were photographed, except through a European photographer who saw them for me."

[FROM *After the Last Sky*]

KATHRYN SCHULZ, EVIDENCE **362**

"This is the problem with the guesswork that underlies our cognitive system. When it works well (and, as we've seen, overall it works better than anything else around), it makes us fast, efficient thinkers capable of remarkable intellectual feats. But, as with so many systems, the strengths of inductive reasoning are also its weaknesses. For every way that induction

---

e **bedfordstmartins.com/waysofreading**

serves us admirably, it also creates a series of predictable biases in the way we think."

[FROM *Being Wrong*]

DAVID FOSTER WALLACE, AUTHORITY AND AMERICAN USAGE **388**

"One of the claim-clusters I'm going to spend a lot of both our time arguing for is that issues of English usage are fundamentally and inescapably political, and that putatively disinterested linguistic authorities like dictionaries are always the products of certain ideologies, and that as authorities they are accountable to the same basic standards of sanity and honesty and fairness as our political authorities."

[FROM *Consider the Lobster*]

JOHN EDGAR WIDEMAN, OUR TIME **422**

"The hardest habit to break, since it was a habit of a lifetime, would be listening to myself listening to him. That habit would destroy any chance of seeing my brother on his terms; and seeing him in his terms, learning his terms, seemed the whole point of learning his story. However numerous and comforting the similarities, we were different. The world had seized on the difference, allowed me room to thrive, while he'd been forced into a cage. Why did it work out that way? What was the nature of the difference? Why did it haunt me? Temporarily at least, to answer these questions, I had to root my fiction-writing self out of our exchanges. I had to teach myself to listen."

[FROM *Brothers and Keepers*]

Assignment Sequences **463**

WORKING WITH ASSIGNMENT SEQUENCES **465**
Working with a Sequence **466**

SEQUENCE ONE EXPLORING IDENTITY, EXPLORING THE SELF **469**

APPIAH *Racial Identities*
SAID *States*
BUTLER *Beside Oneself: On the Limits of Sexual Autonomy*
GRIFFIN *Our Secret*

ALTERNATIVE SELECTIONS

MILLER *The Dark Night of the Soul*
WIDEMAN *Our Time*
JAMIE *Shia Girls*

ASSIGNMENTS

1. *Narrative and Identity* APPIAH **470**
2. *Identity and Representation* SAID **471**
3. *The Concept of Human* BUTLER **471**

Additional Sequences included in the e-Pages

Additional Sequences included in *Resources for Teaching Ways of Reading*

Introduction: Ways of Reading

MAKING A MARK

Reading involves a fair measure of push and shove. You make your mark on a text, and it makes its mark on you. Reading is not simply a matter of hanging back and waiting for a piece, or its author, to tell you what the writing has to say. In fact, one of the difficult things about reading is that the pages before you will begin to speak only when the authors are silent and you begin to speak in their place, sometimes for them — doing their work, continuing their projects — and sometimes for yourself, following your own agenda.

This is an unusual way to talk about reading, we know. We have not mentioned finding information or locating an author's purpose or identifying main ideas, useful though these skills are, because the purpose of our book is to offer you occasions to imagine other ways of reading. We think of reading as a social interaction. We need only look to the complex social interactions we engage in every day to imagine the multiple possibilities for reading — sometimes peaceful and polite, sometimes contentious, sometimes hesitant and difficult. If you imagine your reading as a particular kind of social interaction, then you might be able to imagine, for example, a text you might feel shy around, perhaps because it is behaving in a way you find unusual or difficult. You might imagine a text that encourages you, like a friend might — or a text that provokes you like an older brother. Thinking about reading this way means, of course, that you have to do your part of the interaction. Engaging with reading in these ways is an essential part of engaging with reading *as a writer*.

We'd like you to imagine that when you read the works we've collected here, somebody is saying something to you, and we'd like you to imagine that you are in a position to speak back, to say something of your own in turn. In other words, we are not presenting our book as a miniature library (a place to find information), and we do not think of you, the reader, as a term-paper writer (a person looking for information to summarize or report).

When you read, you hear an author's voice as you move along; you believe a person with something to say is talking to you. You pay attention, even when you don't completely understand what is being said, and you attempt to relate what the author says to what you already know or expect to hear or learn, trusting that it will all make sense in the end. Even if you don't quite grasp everything you are reading at every moment (and you won't), and even if you don't remember everything you've read (no reader does—at least not in long, complex pieces), you begin to see the outlines of the author's project, the patterns and rhythms of that particular way of seeing and interpreting the world.

When you stop to talk or write about what you've read, the author is silent; you take over—it is your turn to write, to begin responding to what the author said. At that point, this author and his or her text become something you construct out of what you remember or what you notice as you go back through the text a second time, working from passages or examples, but filtering them through your own predisposition to see or read in particular ways.

In "The Achievement of Desire," one of the essays in this book, Richard Rodriguez tells the story of his education, of how he was drawn to imitate his teachers because of his desire to think and speak like them. His is not a simple story of hard work and success, however. In a sense, Rodriguez's education gave him what he wanted—status, knowledge, a way of understanding himself and his position in the world. At the same time, his education made it difficult to talk to his parents, to share their point of view; and to a degree, he felt himself becoming consumed by the powerful ways of seeing and understanding represented by his reading and his education. The essay can be seen as Rodriguez's attempt to weigh what he has gained against what he has lost.

If ten of us read his essay, each would begin with the same words on the page, but when we discuss or write about the essay, each will retell and interpret Rodriguez's story differently; we will emphasize different sections—some, for instance, might want to discuss the strange way Rodriguez learned to read, others might be taken by his difficult and changing relations to his teachers, and still others might want to think about Rodriguez's remarks about his mother and father.

Each of us will come to his or her own sense of what is significant, of what the point is, and the odds are good that what each of us makes of the essay will vary. We will all understand Rodriguez's story in our own ways, even though we read the same piece. At the same time, if we are working with Rodriguez's essay (and not putting it aside or ignoring its peculiar way of thinking about education), we will be working within a framework he has established, one that makes education stand, metaphorically, for a complicated interplay between permanence and change, imitation and freedom, loss and achievement.

In "The Achievement of Desire," Rodriguez tells of reading a book by Richard Hoggart, *The Uses of Literacy*. He was captivated by a section of this book in which

Hoggart defines a particular kind of student, the "scholarship boy." Here is what Rodriguez says:

> Then one day, leafing through Richard Hoggart's *The Uses of Literacy*, I found, in his description of the scholarship boy, myself. For the first time I realized that there were other students like me, and so I was able to frame the meaning of my academic success, its consequent price — the loss.

For Rodriguez, this phrase, "scholarship boy," became the focus of Hoggart's book. Other people, to be sure, would read that book and take different phrases or sections as the key to what Hoggart has to say. Some might argue that Rodriguez misread the book, that it is really about something else, about British culture, for example, or about the class system in England. The power and value of Rodriguez's reading, however, are represented by what he was able to *do* with what he read, not record information or summarize main ideas but, as he says, "frame the meaning of my academic success." Hoggart provided a frame, a way for Rodriguez to think and talk about his own history as a student. As he goes on in his essay, Rodriguez not only uses this frame to talk about his experience, but he resists it, argues with it. He casts his experience in Hoggart's terms, but then makes those terms work for him by seeing both what they can and what they cannot do. This combination of reading, thinking, and writing is what we mean by *active reading*, a way of reading we like to encourage in our students, a way of reading that invites students to think of themselves as strong readers, readers capable of creating their own unique and innovative readings even when they are not experts on the subject an author undertakes.

When we have taught "The Achievement of Desire" to our students, it has been almost impossible for them not to see themselves in Rodriguez's description of the scholarship boy (and this was true of students who were not minority students and not literally on scholarships). They, too, have found a way of framing (even inventing) their own lives as students — students whose histories involve both success and loss. When we have asked our students to write about this essay, however, some students have argued, and quite convincingly, that Rodriguez had to either abandon his family and culture or remain ignorant. Other students have argued equally convincingly that Rodriguez's anguish was destructive and self-serving, that he was trapped into seeing his situation in terms that he might have replaced with others. He did not necessarily have to turn his back on his family. Some have contended that Rodriguez's problems with his family had nothing to do with what he says about education, that he himself shows how imitation need not blindly lead a person away from his culture, and these student essays, too, have been convincing. And some students have imagined Rodriguez's piece as raising complex questions rather than inviting us to come to particular conclusion about education, culture, or family. Interacting with texts might mean, at times, making arguments or drawing conclusions about that text. But sometimes it can also mean recognizing the aspects of a text that might be posing unanswerable and complicated questions, questions that invite us to explore or inquire rather than to take a stance. When you begin to speak, what you have to say might not be a statement; it might be a question, an unsolvable problem, or a way of extending the work you see the author doing.

Reading, in other words, can be the occasion for you to put things together, to notice this idea or theme rather than that one, to follow a writer's announced or secret ends while simultaneously following your own, to articulate or acknowledge what you think the set of questions an author raises invites you to ask. When this happens, when you forge a reading of a story or an essay, you make your mark on it, casting it in your terms. But the story makes its mark on you as well, teaching you not only about a subject (Rodriguez's struggles with his teachers and his parents, for example) but also about a way of seeing and understanding a subject. The text provides the opportunity for you to see through someone else's powerful language, to imagine your own familiar settings through the images, metaphors, and ideas of others. Rodriguez's essay, in other words, can make its mark on readers, but they, too, if they are active readers, can make theirs on it. Just as you engage in various ways of reading while you read "The Achievement of Desire," Rodriguez, through his writing, also engages in ways of reading; he offers you his angle of looking; his writing invites you to see as he sees, to take up what it might mean to see the world from his viewpoint. An active reader tries, in her first reading, to understand the way of reading enacted by an author. Understanding the angle from which Rodriguez sees and reads the world helps an active reader respond more powerfully as a writer.

Readers learn to put things together by writing. This is not something you can do, at least not to any degree, while you are reading. It requires that you work on what you have read, and this work best takes shape when you sit down to write. We will have more to say about this kind of thinking in a later section of the introduction, but for now let us say that writing gives you a way of going to work on the text you have read. To write about a story or an essay, you go back to what you have read to find phrases or passages that define what for you are the key moments, those that help you interpret sections that seem difficult or troublesome or mysterious. If you are writing an essay of your own, the work that you are doing gives a purpose and a structure to that rereading.

READERS LEARN TO PUT THINGS TOGETHER BY WRITING.

Writing also, however, gives you a way of going back to work on the text of your own reading. It allows you to be self-critical and self-reflexive. You can revise not just to make your essay neat or tight or tidy but to see what kind of reader you have been, to examine the pattern and consequences in the choices you have made. Revision, in other words, gives you the chance to work on your essay, but it also gives you an opportunity to work on your reading — to qualify or extend or question your interpretation of, say, "The Achievement of Desire."

We can describe this process of "re-vision," or re-seeing, fairly simply. You should not expect to read "The Achievement of Desire" once and completely understand the essay or know what you want to say. You will work out what you have to say while you write. And once you have constructed a reading — once you have completed a draft of your essay, in other words — you can step back, see what you have done, and go back to work on it. Through this activity — writing and rewriting — we have seen our students become active and critical readers.

Not everything a reader reads is worth that kind of effort. The pieces we have chosen for this book all provide, we feel, powerful ways of seeing (or framing) our common experience. The selections cannot be quickly summarized. They are striking, surprising, sometimes troubling in how they challenge common ways of seeing the world. Some of them have captured and altered the way our culture sees and understands daily experience. The essays have changed the ways people think and write. In fact, every selection in the book is one that has given us, our students, and our colleagues that dramatic experience, almost like a discovery, when we suddenly saw things as we had never seen them before and, as a consequence, we had to work hard to understand what had happened and how our thinking had changed.

If we recall, for example, the first time we read Susan Griffin's "Our Secret" or John Edgar Wideman's "Our Time," we know that they have radically shaped our thinking. We carry these essays with us in our minds, mulling over them, working through them, hearing Griffin and Wideman in sentences we write or read. We introduce the essays in classes we teach whenever we can; we are surprised, reading them for the third or fourth time, to find things we didn't see before. It's not that we failed to "get" these essays the first time around. In fact, we're not sure we have captured them yet, at least not in any final sense, and we disagree in basic ways about what Griffin and Wideman are saying, about what questions are central to their inquiry, or about how these essays might best be used. Essays like these are not the sort that you can "get" like a loaf of bread at the store. We're each convinced that the essays are ours in that we know best what's going on in them, and yet we have also become theirs, creatures of these essays, because of the ways they have come to influence our seeing, talking, reading, and writing. This power of influence is something we welcome, yet it is also something we resist.

Our experience with these texts is a remarkable one and certainly hard to provide for others, but the challenges and surprises are reasons we read — we hope to be taken and changed in just these ways. Or, to be more accurate, it is why we read outside the daily requirements to keep up with the news or conduct our business. And it is why we bring reading into our writing courses.

WAYS OF READING

Before explaining how we organized this book, we would like to say more about the purpose and place of the kind of active, labor-intensive reading we've been referring to.

Readers face many kinds of experiences, and certain texts are written with specific situations in mind and invite specific ways of reading. Some texts, for instance, serve very practical purposes — they give directions or information. Others, like the short descriptive essays often used in English textbooks and anthologies, celebrate common and conventional ways of thinking and ask primarily to be admired. These texts seem self-contained; they announce their own meanings with little effort and ask little from the reader, making it clear how they want to be read and what they have to say. They ask only for a nod of the head or for the reader to take notes and give a sigh of admiration ("yes, that was very well said"). They are clear and direct. It is as though the authors could anticipate all the questions their essays might raise and solve all the problems a reader might imagine. There is not much work for a reader to do, in other words, except perhaps to take notes and, in the case of textbooks, to work step-by-step, trying to remember as much as possible. These readings mostly require us to behave ourselves, to accept what they offer and recall it later.

This is how assigned readings are often presented in university classrooms. Introductory textbooks (in biology or business, for instance) are good examples of books that ask to be read dutifully and passively. In these texts the writers are experts, and your job, as novice, is to digest what they have to say. And, perhaps appropriately at times, the task set before you is to summarize—so you can speak again to what the author said, so you can better remember what you read. Essay tests are an example of the writing tasks that often follow this kind of reading. You might, for instance, study the human nervous system through textbook readings and lectures and then be asked to write a summary of what you know from both sources. Or a teacher might ask you during a class discussion to paraphrase a paragraph from a textbook describing chemical cell communication to see if you understand what you've read.

Another typical classroom form of reading is reading for main ideas. With this kind of reading you are expected to figure out what most people (or most people within a certain specialized group of readers) would take as the main idea of a selection. There are good reasons to read for main ideas. For one, it is a way to learn how to imagine and anticipate the values and habits of a particular group—test-makers or, if you're studying business, Keynesian economists, perhaps. If you are studying business, to continue this example, you must learn to notice what Keynesian economists notice—for instance, when they analyze the problems of growing government debt—to share key terms, to know the theoretical positions they take, and to adopt for yourself their common examples and interpretations, their jargon, and their established findings.

There is certainly nothing wrong with reading for information or reading to learn what experts have to say about their fields of inquiry. These are not, however, the only ways to read, although they are the ones most often taught. Perhaps because we think of ourselves as writing teachers, we are concerned with presenting other ways of reading in the college and university curriculum.

A danger arises in assuming that reading is only a search for information or main ideas. There are ways of thinking through problems and working with written texts which are essential to our academic, professional, and personal lives, but that are not represented by summary and paraphrase or by note-taking and essay exams.

Student readers, for example, can take responsibility for determining the meaning of the text. They can work as though they were doing something other than finding ideas already there on the page, and they can be guided by their own impressions or questions as they read. We are not, now, talking about finding hidden meanings. If such things as hidden meanings can be said to exist, they are hidden by readers' habits and prejudices (by readers' assumptions that what they read should tell them what they already know) or by readers' timidity and passivity (by their unwillingness to take the responsibility to say what they notice or to pose their own questions).

Reading to locate meaning in the text places a premium on memory, yet an active reader is not necessarily a person with a good memory. This point may seem minor, but we have seen too many students haunted because they could not remember everything they read or retain a complete essay in their minds. A reader could set herself the task of remembering as much as she could from Walker Percy's "The Loss of the Creature," an essay filled with stories about tourists at the Grand Canyon and students in a biology class, but a reader could also do other things with that essay; a reader might figure out, for example, how students and tourists might be said to have a common problem seeing what they want to see. Students who read Percy's essay as a memory test end up worrying about bits and pieces (bits and pieces they could go back and find, if they had to) and turn their attention away from the more pressing problem of how to make sense of a difficult and often ambiguous essay.

A reader who needs to have access to something in the essay can use simple memory aids. A reader can go back and scan, for one thing, to find passages or examples that might be worth reconsidering. Or a reader can construct a personal index, making marks in the margin or underlining passages that seem interesting or mysterious or difficult. A mark is a way of saying, "This is something I might want to work on later." If you mark the selections in this book as you read them, you will give yourself a working record of what, at the first moment of reading, you felt might be worth a second reading.

If Percy's essay presents problems for a reader, they are problems of a different order from summary and recall. The essay is not the sort that tells you what it says. You would have difficulty finding one sentence that sums up or announces, in a loud and clear voice, what Percy is talking about. In fact, Percy's essay is challenging reading in part because it does not have a single easily identifiable main idea. A reader could infer that it has several points to make, none of which can be said easily, and some of which, perhaps, are contradictory. To search for information, or to ignore the rough edges in search of a single, paraphrasable idea, is to divert attention from the task at hand, which is not to remember what Percy says, but to speak about the essay and what it means to you, the reader. In this sense, the Percy essay is not the sum of its individual parts; it is, more accurately, what its readers make of it.

A reader could go to an expert on Percy to solve the problem of what to make of the essay—perhaps to a teacher, perhaps to the Internet or to a book in the library. And if the reader pays attention, he could remember what the expert said, or she could put down notes on paper (or in an e-file). But in doing either, the reader only rehearses the thoughts of others, abandoning the responsibility to make the essay meaningful, to become invested in the essay for one's own purposes. There are ways of reading, in other words, in which Percy's essay "The Loss of the Creature" is not what it means to the experts but what it means to you as a reader willing to take the chance to construct a reading. You can be the authority on Percy; you don't have to turn to others. The meaning of the essay, then, is something you develop as you go along, something for which you must take final responsibility. The meaning is forged from reading the essay, to be sure, but it is determined by what you *do* with the essay, by the connections you can make and your explanation of why those connections are important. This version of

Percy's essay will finally be yours; it will not be exactly what Percy said. (Only his words in the order he wrote them would say exactly what he said.) You will choose the path to take through his essay.

You'll notice (and we will discuss later) that we offer some "Questions for a Second Reading" once you've read through a piece one time. But what about that first reading, that first time you read a challenging and multidimensional piece of writing like the ones you find here? There are many ways to engage with a text as you read it for the first time. It's important to have a way to write on the text itself—not just to highlight sections you find interesting, troubling, or confusing (though you might do that, too), but to keep notes to yourself in the margins, perhaps writing questions that come up for you as you read, or writing down key words that will help you remember why you marked that particular place. Sometimes, with particularly difficult readings, we ask students to mark words, names, or phrases that they think would be useful hyperlinks—moments in the text where you wish you could click on the word or phrase in order to find out more. If you try this on your first read-through, you might learn something important; you might learn what you don't yet know about the text. Often times, being an engaged reader means paying attention both to what is familiar and what is unfamiliar about what you are reading.

If an essay or a story is not the sum of its parts but something you as a reader create by putting together those parts that seem to matter to you, then the way to begin, once you have read a selection in this collection, is by reviewing what you recall, by going back to those places that stick in your memory—or, perhaps, to those sections you marked with checks or notes in the margins. You can even return to those moments in which you *didn't* know exactly where the text was trying to lead you.

You begin by seeing what you can make of these memories and notes. You should realize that with essays as long and complex as those we've included in this book, you will never feel, after a single reading, as though you have command of everything you read. This is not a problem. After four or five readings (should you give any single essay that much attention), you may still feel that there are parts you missed or don't understand. This sense of incompleteness is part of the experience of reading. And it is part of the experience of an active reader. No reader could retain one of these essays in her mind, no matter how proficient her memory or how experienced she might be. No reader, at least no reader we would trust, would claim that he understood everything that Michel Foucault or Judith Butler or Edward Said had to say. What engaged and active readers know is that they have to begin, and they have to begin regardless of their doubts or hesitations. After your first reading of an essay you have a starting place, and you begin with your marked passages or examples or notes, with questions to answer, or with problems to solve. Active readings, in other words, put a premium on individual acts of attention and composition.

ENGAGED READERS, ENGAGING TEXTS

We chose pieces for this book that invite engaged readings. Our selections require more attention (or a different form of attention) than a written summary, a reduction to gist, or a recitation of main ideas. These are not "easy" reading. The challenges they present, however, do not make them inaccessible to college students. The essays are not specialized studies; they have interested, pleased, or piqued general and specialist audiences alike. To say that they are challenging is to say, then, that they leave some work for a reader to do. They are designed to teach a reader new ways to read (or to step outside habitual ways of reading), and they anticipate readers willing to take the time to learn. These readers need not be experts on the subject matter. Perhaps the most difficult problem for students is to believe that this is true.

You do not need experts to explain these stories and essays, although you could probably go to the library and find an expert guide to most of the selections we've included. Let's take, for example, John Berger's essay "Ways of Seeing." You could go to the library to find out how Berger is understood and regarded by experts, by literary critics or art historians, for example; you could learn how his work fits into an established body of work on art and representation. You could see what others have said about the writers he cites—Walter Benjamin, for example. You could see how others have read and made use of Berger. You could track one of his key terms, like "mystification."

Though it is often important to seek out other texts and to know what other people are saying or have said, it is often necessary and even desirable to begin on your own. Berger can also be read outside any official system of interpretation. He is talking, after all, about our daily experience. And when he addresses the reader, he addresses a person—not a five-paragraph formula writer. When he says, "The way we see things is affected by what we know and what we believe," *you* are part of that construction, part of the "we" he is invoking.

The primary question, then, is not what Berger's words might mean to an art historian or to those with credentials as professors or as cultural critics. The question is what you, the reader, can make of those words given your own experience, your goals, and the work you do with what he has written. In this sense, "Ways of Seeing" is not what it means to others (those who have already decided what it means) but what it means to you, and this meaning is something you compose when you write about the essay, even if the meaning you construct is tentative or uncertain.

I. A. Richards, a teacher, poet, and critic we admire, once said, "Read as though it made sense and perhaps it will." To take command of complex material like the selections in this book, you need not subordinate yourself to experts; you can assume the authority to provide such a reading on your own. This means you must allow yourself a certain tentativeness and recognize your limits. You should not assume that it is your job to solve all the problems these essays present. You can speak with authority while still acknowledging that complex issues *are* complex.

In "The American Scholar," Ralph Waldo Emerson says, "Meek young men grow up in libraries, believing it their duty to accept the views, which Cicero, which Locke, which Bacon, have given, forgetful that Cicero, Locke, and Bacon were only young men in libraries when they wrote these books." What Emerson offers here is not a fact but an attitude. There is creative reading, he says, as well as creative writing. It is up to you to treat authors as your equals, as people who will allow you to speak, too. At the same time, you must respect the difficulty and complexity of their texts and of the issues and questions they examine. Little is to be gained, in other words, by turning a complex essay into a message that would fit on a poster in a dorm room: "Be Yourself" or "Stand on Your Own Two Feet."

READING WITH AND AGAINST THE GRAIN

Reading, then, requires a difficult mix of authority and humility. On the one hand, a reader takes charge of a text; on the other, a reader gives generous attention to someone else's (a writer's) key terms and methods, commits his time to her examples, tries to think in her language, imagines that this strange work is important, compelling, at least for the moment. If, as we suggested earlier, reading is a kind of social interaction, this means you are equally a listener and a responder. It might help to think about what it really means to listen to another person, to try to understand their point of view before offering your own response.

Most of the questions in *Ways of Reading* will have you moving back and forth in these two modes, reading with and against the grain of a text, reproducing an author's methods, questioning his or her direction and authority. With Susan Bordo's essay "Beauty (Re)discovers the Male Body," for example, we have asked students to look at images from the contemporary media, to think about them in terms of her argument, and to write about them as she might—to see them and to understand them in her terms, through the lens of her essay. We have asked students to give themselves over to this essay, in other words—recognizing that this is not necessarily an easy thing to do. Notice what she would notice. Ask the questions she would ask. Try out her conclusions.

To read generously, to work inside someone else's system, to see your world in someone else's terms—we call this "reading with the grain." It is a way of working *with* a writer's ideas, in conjunction with someone else's text. As a way of reading, it can take different forms. In the reading and writing assignments that follow the selections in this book, you will sometimes be asked to summarize and paraphrase, to put others' ideas into your terms, to provide your account of what they are saying. This is a way of getting a tentative or provisional hold on a text, its examples and ideas; it allows you a place to begin to work. And sometimes you will be asked to extend a writer's project—to add your examples to someone else's argument, to read your experience through the frame of another's text, to try out the key terms and interpretive schemes in another writer's work. In the assignments that follow Bordo's essay, for example, students are asked both to reproduce her argument and to extend her terms to examples from their own experience.

We have also asked students to read against the grain, to read critically, to turn back, for example, *against* Bordo's project, to ask questions they believe might come as a surprise, to look for the limits of her vision, to provide alternate readings of her examples, to find examples that challenge her argument—to engage her, in other words, in dialogue. Susan Bordo, we say, is quite specific about her age and her experience, her point of view. You are placed at a different moment in time, your experience is different, your schooling and your exposure to images have prepared you differently. Your job, then, is not simply to reproduce Bordo's project in your writing and thinking, but to refine it, to extend it, to put it to the test.

Many of the essays in this book provide examples of writers working against the grain of common sense or everyday language. This is true of John Berger, for example, who redefines the "art museum" against the way it is usually understood. It is true of John Edgar Wideman, who reads against his own text while he writes it—asking questions that disturb the story as it emerges on the page. It is true of Judith Butler, Susan Griffin, and Kwame Anthony Appiah, whose writings show the signs of their efforts to work against the grain of the standard essay, of habitual ways of representing what it means to know something, to be somebody, to speak before others.

MANY OF THE ESSAYS IN THIS BOOK PROVIDE EXAMPLES OF WRITERS WORKING AGAINST THE GRAIN OF COMMON SENSE OR EVERYDAY LANGUAGE.

This, we've found, is the most difficult work for students to do, this working against the grain. For reasons good and bad, students typically define their skill by reproducing, rather than questioning or revising the work of their teachers (or the work of those their teachers ask them to read). It is important to read generously and carefully, and to learn to listen to the projects others have begun. But it is also important to know what you are doing—to understand where this work comes from, whose interests it serves, how and where it is kept together by will rather than desire, and what it might have to do with you. To fail to ask the fundamental questions—Where am I in this? How can I make my mark? Whose interests are represented? What can I learn by reading with or against the grain?—to fail to ask these questions is to mistake skill for understanding, and it is to misunderstand the goals of a liberal education. All of the essays in this book, we would argue, ask to be read, not simply reproduced; they ask to be read and to be read with a difference. Our goal is to make that difference possible.

Reading with and against the grain is one way to think about the work of reading. And even within this metaphor, there are more than two ways of reading. But we might also extend the work of the metaphor. Our students have explored this metaphor and have even come up with metaphors of their own for thinking about what reading is and what it means to do a reading. One student described reading as much like walking to the grocery store—one could take a direct route, focusing on the ultimate goal, perhaps making a list of items as he walked. One could also meander, not worrying about time or what items to purchase, but thinking instead about the sunset or the traffic patterns. Readers can be, in many ways, like walkers—sometimes focused and clear on their goals, sometimes allowing their minds to wander or notice something *other* than getting to the grocery store, sometimes ending up in places they didn't think they were going. Another student likened her reading to looking through a telescope in her astronomy course. For her, reading was like forming constellations, looking at a night sky for those sets of glimmers that might form something familiar, something she could name. A student who was studying civil engineering explained how reading, for him, seemed much like designing a bridge that connects two places. "It can look simple," he writes in an in-class writing activity. "When you drive over a bridge, you don't think about how many tiny details have gone into making the bridge stand. Reading is like that, too. Seems simple, but it's not." You might think of reading in a number of ways. The important part is that you broaden your understanding of what it means to read, that you challenge yourself to read in new ways so that you might then write in new ways as well.

WORKING WITH DIFFICULTY

When we chose the selections for this textbook, we chose them with the understanding that they are difficult to read. And we chose them knowing that students are not their primary audience, that the selections are not speaking directly to you. We chose them, in other words, knowing that we would be asking you to read something you were most likely not prepared to read. But this is what it means to be a student, and it is our goal to take our students seriously. Students have to do things they are not yet ready to do; this is how they learn. Students need to read materials that they are not yet ready to read. This is how they get started; this is where they begin. It is also the case that, in an academic setting, difficulty is not necessarily a problem. If something is hard to read, it is not necessarily the case that the writer is at fault. The work can be hard to read because the writer is thinking beyond the usual ways of thinking. It is hard because it *is* hard, in other words. The text is not saying the same old things in the same old ways.

We believe the best way to work on a difficult text is by *re*reading, and we provide exercises to direct this process ("Questions for a Second Reading"), but you can also work on the difficult text by writing — by taking possession of the work through sentences and paragraphs of your own, through summary, paraphrase, and quotation, by making another writer's work part of your work. The textbook is organized to provide ways for you to work on these difficult selections by writing and rereading. Each of the selections is followed by questions designed to help you get started.

To get a better sense of what we mean by "working with difficulty," it might be useful to look at an example. One of the selections in *Ways of Reading* is a chapter from a book titled *Pedagogy of the Oppressed*, by the Brazilian educator Paulo Freire. The chapter is titled "The 'Banking' Concept of Education," and the title summarizes the argument at its most simple level. The standard forms of education, Freire argues, define the teacher as the active agent and the student as the passive agent. The teacher has knowledge and makes deposits from this storehouse into the minds of students, who are expected to receive these deposits completely and without alteration — like moving money from a wallet to the bank vault. And this, he argues, is not a good thing.

One of the writing assignments attached to this selection asks students to think along with Freire and to use his argument to examine a situation from their own experience with schooling. Here is an essay (a very skillful essay) that we received from a freshman in the opening weeks of class. It is relatively short and to the point. It will be familiar. You should have no trouble following it, even if you haven't read the selection by Freire.

The "Banking" Concept of Education

As a high school senior, I took a sociology class that was a perfect example of the "banking" concept of education, as described by Freire. There were approximately thirty students enrolled in the class. Unless each of our brains was computerized for long-term memorization, I don't understand how we were expected to get anything out of the class.

Each class began with the copying of four to five pages of notes, which were already written on the blackboards when we entered the classroom. Fifteen to twenty minutes later, the teacher proceeded to pass out a worksheet, which was to be filled out using only the notes we previously copied as our reference. If a question was raised, her reply was, "It's in the notes."

With approximately ten minutes left in the period, we were instructed to pass our worksheets back one desk. Then, she read the answers to the worksheets and gave a grade according to how many questions we answered correctly.

During the semester, we didn't have any quizzes, and only one test, which consisted of matching and listing-type questions. All test information was taken directly from the daily worksheets, and on no occasion did she give an essay question. This is an example of a test question:

Name three forms of abuse that occur in the family.

1.

2.

3.

In order to pass the class, each piece of information printed on her handouts needed to be memorized. On one occasion, a fellow classmate summed up her technique of teaching perfectly by stating, "This is nothing but education by memorization!"

Anyone who cared at all about his grade in the class did quite well, according to his report card. Not much intelligence is required to memorize vocabulary terms. Needless to say, not too many of us learned much from the class, except that "education by memorization" and the "banking" concept of education, as Freire puts it, are definitely not an interesting or effective system of education.

The essay is confident and tidy and not wrong in its account of the "banking" concept of education. In five short paragraphs, the writer not only "got" Freire but also worked his high school sociology teacher and her teaching methods into the "banking" narrative. We asked the student (as we have asked many students since then): How did you do this? What was the secret? And he was quick to answer, "I read through the Freire essay, and I worked with what I understood and I ignored the rest." And it's true; he did. This is one way to get started. It's OK. You work with what you can.

The difficult sections of Freire's argument (the hard parts, the sections, and the passages our writer ignored) are related to a Marxist analysis of a *system* of education and its interests. Freire does not write just about individuals—a bad teacher and a smart student—although it is certainly easier (and in some ways more comforting) to think that schooling is simply a matter of individual moments and individual actors, good and bad. What is happening in our classrooms, Freire argues, is bigger than the intentions or actions of individuals. He says, for example, "Education as the exercise of domination stimulates the credulity of students, with the ideological intent (often not perceived by educators) of indoctrinating them to adapt to the world of oppression." He writes about how schools "regulate the way the world 'enters into' students." He calls for "problem-posing education": "Problem-posing education is revolutionary futurity." What is at stake, he says, is "humanity." What is required is "*conscientização*." He is concerned to promote education in service of "revolution": "A deepened consciousness of their situation leads people to apprehend that situation as an historical reality susceptible of transformation." There is more going on here, in other words, than can be represented simply by a teacher who is lazy or unimaginative.

The student's essay marks a skillful performance. He takes Freire's chapter and makes it consistent with what he knows to say. You hear that in this statement: "'education by memorization' and the 'banking' concept of education, as Freire puts it, are definitely not an interesting or effective system of education." Freire's language becomes consistent with his own (the "banking" concept can be filed away under "education by memorization"), and once this is achieved, the writer's need to do any real work with Freire's text becomes unnecessary—"needless to say." Working with difficult readings often requires a willingness to step outside of what you can conveniently control, and this process often begins with revision. As important as it was for this student to use his essay to get hold of Freire, to open a door or to get handhold, a place of purchase, a way to begin, it is equally important for a writer to take the next step—and the next step is to revise, particularly where revision is a way of reworking rather than just "fixing" what you have begun.

This was a student of ours, and after talking with him about the first draft, we suggested that he reread "The 'Banking' Concept of Education," this time paying particular attention to the difficult passages, the passages that were hard to understand, those that he had ignored the first time around. We suggested that his revised essay should bring some of those passages into the text. He did just this, and by changing the notion of what he was doing (by working *with* rather than *in spite of* difficulty), he wrote a very different essay. This was real revision, in other words, not just a matter of smoothing out the rough edges. The revision changed the way the writer read, and it changed the way the reader wrote. The revised essay was quite different (and not nearly so confident and skillful—and this was a good thing, a sign of learning). Here is a representative passage:

> We never really had to "think" in the class. In fact, we were never permitted to "think," we were merely expected to take in the information and

> store it like a computer. Freire calls this act a "violation of [men's] humanity" (p. 225). He states, "Any situation in which some individuals prevent others from engaging in the process of inquiry is one of violence" (p. 225). I believe what Freire is speaking of here is . . .

We'll keep his conclusion to ourselves, since the conclusion is not nearly so important as what has happened to the writer's understanding of what it means to work on a reading. In this revised paragraph, he brings in phrases from the text, and the phrases he brings in are not easy to handle; he has to struggle to put them to use or to make them make sense. The writer is trying to figure out the urgency in Freire's text. The story of the sociology class was one thing, but how do you get from there to a statement about a "violation of men's humanity"? The passage that is quoted is not just dumped in for color; it is there for the writer to work with, to try to deploy. And that is what comes next:

> He states, "Any situation in which some individuals prevent others from engaging in the process of inquiry is one of violence" (p. 225). I believe what Freire is speaking of here is . . .

The key moment in writing like this is the moment of translation: "I believe what Freire is speaking of here is . . ." This is where the writer must step forward to take responsibility for working inside the terms of Freire's project.

There is much to admire in this revision. It was early in the semester when writing is always risky, and it took courage and determination for a student to work with what he couldn't quite understand, couldn't sum up easily, couldn't command. You can see, even in this brief passage, that the writing has lost some of the confidence (or arrogance) of the first draft, and as the writer works to think with Freire about education as a system, the characters of the "student" and the "teacher" become different in this narrative. And this is good writing. It may not be as finished as it might need to be later in the semester, but it is writing where something is happening, where thought is taken seriously.

So, how do you work with a difficult text? You have to get started somewhere and sometime, and you will almost always find yourself writing before you have a sense that you have fully comprehended what you have read. You have to get started somewhere, and then you can go back to work again on what you have begun by rereading and rewriting. The textbook provides guidelines for rereading.

When you are looking for help with a particular selection, you can, for example, turn to the "Questions for a Second Reading." Read through *all* of them, whether they are assigned or not, since they provide several entry points, different ways in, many of them suggested to us by our students in class and in their essays. You might imagine that these questions and the writing assignments that follow (and you might read through these writing assignments, too) provide starting points. Each suggests a different path through the essay. No one can hold a long and complicated essay in mind all at once. Every reader needs a starting point, a way in. Having more than one possible starting point allows you to make choices.

Once you have an entry point, where you have entered and how you have entered will help to shape your sense of what is interesting or important in the text. In this sense, you (and not just the author) are organizing the essay or chapter. The text will present its shape in terms of sections or stages. You should look for these road signs — breaks in the text or phrases that indicate intellectual movement, like "on the other hand" or "in conclusion." You can be guided by these, to be sure, but you also give shape to what you read — and you do this most deliberately when you reread. This is where you find (and impose) patterns and connections that are not obvious and not already articulated but that make sense to you and give you a way to describe what you see in what you are reading. In our own teaching, we talk to our students about "scaffolds." The scaffold, we say, represents the way you are organizing the text, the way you are putting it together. A scaffold is made up of lines and passages from the text, the terms you've found that you want to work with, ideas that matter to you, your sense of the progress of the piece.

IN OUR OWN TEACHING, WE TALK TO OUR STUDENTS ABOUT "SCAFFOLDS." THE SCAFFOLD, WE SAY, REPRESENTS THE WAY YOU ARE ORGANIZING THE TEXT, THE WAY YOU ARE PUTTING IT TOGETHER.

The scaffold can also include the work of others. In groups or in class discussion, take notes on what other students say. This is good advice generally (you can always learn from your colleagues), but it is particularly useful in a class that features reading and writing. Your notes can document the ideas of others, to be sure, but most important, they can give you a sense of where other people are beginning, of where they have entered the text and what they are doing once they have started. You can infer the scaffold they have constructed to make sense of what they read, and this can give highlight and relief, even counterpoint, to your own. And use your teacher's comments and questions, including those on your first drafts, to get a sense of the shape of your work as a reader and a writer. This is not a hunt for ideas, for the right or proper or necessary thing to say about a text. It is a hunt for a method, for a way of making sense of a text without resorting only to summary.

READING AND WRITING: THE QUESTIONS AND ASSIGNMENTS

Active readers, we've said, remake what they have read to serve their own ends, putting things together, figuring out how ideas and examples relate, explaining as best they can material that is difficult or problematic, translating phrases like Richard Rodriguez's "scholarship boy" into their own terms. At these moments, it is hard to distinguish the act of reading from the act of writing. In fact, the connection between reading and writing can be seen as almost a literal one, since the best way you can show your reading of a rich and dense essay like "The Achievement of Desire" is by writing down your thoughts, placing one idea against another, commenting on what you've done, taking examples into account, looking back at where you began, perhaps changing your mind, and moving on.

Readers, however, seldom read a single essay in isolation, as though their only job were to arrive at some sense of what an essay has to say. Although we couldn't begin to provide examples of all the various uses of these ways of reading, it is often the case that readings provide information and direction for investigative projects, whether they are philosophical or scientific in nature. The reading and writing assignments that follow each selection in this book are designed to point you in certain directions, to give you ideas and projects to work with, and to challenge you to see one writer's ideas through another's.

You will find that the questions we have included in our reading and writing assignments often direct you to test what you think an author is saying by measuring it against your own experience. Paulo Freire, for example, in "The 'Banking' Concept of Education" talks about the experience of the student, and one way for you to develop or test your reading of his essay is to place what he says in the context of your own experience, searching for examples that are similar to his and examples that differ from his. If the writers in this book are urging you to give strong readings of your common experience, you have access to what they say because they are talking not only to you but about you. Freire has a method that he employs when he talks about the classroom—one that compares "banking" education with "problem-posing" education. You can try out his method and his terms on examples of your own, continuing his argument as though you were working with him on a common project. Or you can test his argument as though you want to see not only where and how it will work but also where and how it will not.

Readers, as we have said, seldom read an essay in isolation, as though, having once worked out a reading of Kwame Anthony Appiah's "Racial Identities," they could go on to something else, something unrelated. It is unusual for anyone, at least in an academic setting, to read in so random a fashion. Readers read most often because they have a project in hand—a question they are working on or a problem they are trying to solve. For example, if as a result of reading Appiah's essay you become interested in questions of race and identity, and you begin to notice things you would not have noticed before, then you can read other essays in the book through this frame. If you have a project in mind, that project will help determine how you read these other essays. Sections of an essay that might otherwise seem unimportant suddenly become important—Gloria Anzaldúa's unusual prose style, or John Wideman's account of his racial politics in Pittsburgh. Appiah may enable you to read Wideman's narrative differently. Wideman may spur you to rethink Appiah. In a sense, you have the chance to become an expert reader, a reader with a project in hand, one who has already done some reading, who has watched others at work, and who has begun to develop a method of analysis and a set of key terms. Imagining yourself operating alongside some of the major figures in contemporary thought can be great fun and heady work—particularly when you have the occasion to speak back to them.

You may find that you have to alter your sense of who a writer is and what a writer does as you work on your own writing. Writers are often told that they need to begin with a clear sense of what they want to do and what they want to say. The writing assignments we've written, we believe, give you a sense of what you want (or need) to do. We define a problem for you to work on, and the problem will frame the task for you. You will have to decide where you will go in the texts you have read to find materials to work with, the primary materials that will give you a place to begin as you work on your essay. It might be best, however, if you did not feel that you need to have a clear sense of what you want to say before you begin. You may begin to develop a sense of what you want to say while you are writing. It may also be the case that the subjects you will be writing about are too big for you to assume that you need to have all the answers or that it is up to you to have the final word or to solve the problems once and for all. When you work on your essays, you should cast yourself in the role of one who is exploring a question, examining what might be said, and speculating on possible rather than certain conclusions. Consider your responses provisional. Think of yourself as a writer intent on opening a subject up rather than closing one down.

THINK OF YOURSELF AS A WRITER INTENT ON OPENING A SUBJECT UP RATHER THAN CLOSING ONE DOWN.

Let us turn briefly now to the three categories of reading and writing assignments you will find in the book.

Questions for a Second Reading

Immediately following each selection are questions designed to guide your second reading. You may, as we've said, prefer to follow your own instincts as you search for the materials to build your understanding of the reading. These questions are meant to assist that process or develop those instincts. Most of the selections in the book are longer and more difficult than those you may be accustomed to reading. They are difficult enough that any reader would have to reread them and work to understand them; these questions are meant to suggest ways of beginning that work.

The second-reading questions characteristically ask you to consider the relations between ideas and examples in what you have read or to test specific statements in the essays against your own experience (so that you can get a sense of the author's habit of mind, his or her way of thinking about subjects that are available to you, too). Some turn your attention to what we take to be key terms or concepts, asking you to define these terms by observing how the writer uses them throughout the essay.

These questions have no simple answers; you will not find a correct answer hidden somewhere in the selection. In short, they are not the sorts of questions asked on SAT or ACT exams. They are real questions. They pose problems for interpretation or indicate sections where, to our minds, there is some interesting work for a reader to do. They are meant to reveal possible ways of reading the text, not to indicate that there is only one correct way, and that we have it.

You may find it useful to take notes as you read through each selection a second time, perhaps in a journal you can keep as a sourcebook for more formal written work. We will often also divide our students into groups, with each group working together with one of the second-reading questions in preparation for a report to the class. There are important advantages for you as a *writer* when you do this kind of close work with the text. Working through a second time, you get a better sense of the argument and of the *shape* of the argument; you get a sense of not only what the author is *saying* but what she is *doing*, and this prepares you to provide not only summary and paraphrase but also a sense of the author and her project. The work of rereading sends you back to the text; the second time through you can locate passages you might very well want to use in your own writing — passages that are particularly interesting to you, or illustrative, or even puzzling and obscure. These become the quotations you can use to bring the author's words into your essay, to bring them in as the object of scrutiny and discussion.

Assignments for Writing

This book actually offers three kinds of writing assignments: assignments that ask you to write about a single essay or story, assignments that ask you to read one selection through the frame of another, and longer sequences of assignments that define a project within which three or four of the selections serve as primary sources. All of these assignments serve a dual purpose. Like the second-reading questions, they suggest a way for you to reconsider the essays; they give you access from a different perspective. The assignments also encourage you to be an engaged reader and actively interpret what you have read. In one way or another, they all invite you to use a reading as a way of framing experience, as a source of terms and methods to enable you to interpret something else — some other text, events and objects around you, or your own memories and experience. The assignment sequences can be found at the end of the book and in *Resources for Teaching Ways of Reading*. The others ("Assignments for Writing" and "Making Connections") come immediately after each selection.

"Assignments for Writing" ask you to write about a single selection. Although some of these assignments call for you to paraphrase or reconstruct difficult passages, most ask you to interpret what you have read with a specific purpose in mind. For most of the essays, one question asks you to interpret a moment from your own experience through the frame of the essay — adapting its method, using its key terms, extending the range of its examples. Other assignments, however, ask you to turn an essay back on itself or to extend the conclusions of the essay by reconsidering the examples the writer has used to make his or her case.

When we talk with teachers and students using *Ways of Reading*, we are often asked about the wording of these assignments. The assignments are long. The wording is often unusual, unexpected. The assignments contain many questions, not simply one. The directions seem indirect, confusing. "Why?" we're asked. "How should we work with these?" When we write assignments, our goal is to point students toward a project, to provide a frame for their reading, a motive for writing, a way of asking certain kinds of questions. In that sense, the assignments should not be read as a set of directions to be followed literally. In fact, they are written to resist that reading, to forestall a writer's desire to simplify, to be efficient, to settle for the first clear line toward the finish. We want to provide a context to suggest how readers and writers might take time, be thoughtful. And we want the projects students work on to become their own. We hope to provoke varied responses, to leave the final decisions to the students. So the assignments try to be open and suggestive rather than narrow and direct. We ask lots of questions, but students don't need to answer them all (or any of them) once they begin to write. Our questions are meant to suggest ways of questioning, starting points. "What do you want?" Our own students ask this question. We want writers to make the most they can of what they read, including our questions and assignments.

So, what's the best way to work with an assignment? The writing assignments we have written will provide a context for writing, even a set of expectations, but the assignments do not provide a set of instructions. The first thing to do, then, is to ask yourself what, within this context, do you want to write about? What is on your mind? What is interesting or pressing for you? What direction can you take that will best allow you to stretch or to challenge yourself or to do something that will be new and interesting? We will often set aside class time to talk through an assignment and what possibilities it might suggest for each student's work. (We don't insist that everyone take the same track.) And we invite students to be in touch with us and with one another outside of class or online. Writers and scholars often rely on their friends and colleagues to help them get an angle, think about where to begin, understand what is new and interesting and what is old and dull. And, then, finally, the moment comes and you just sit down to the keyboard and start writing. There is no magic here, unfortunately. You write out what you can, and then you go back to what you have written to see what you are saying, and to see what comes next, and to think about how to shape it all into an essay to give to readers in the hope that they might call it "eloquent," "persuasive," "beautiful."

Making Connections

The connections questions will have you work with two or more readings at a time. These are not so much questions that ask you to compare or contrast the essays or stories as they are directions on how you might use one text as the context for interpreting another. Mary Louise Pratt, for example, in "Arts of the Contact Zone" looks at the work of a South American native, an Inca named Guaman Poma, writing in the seventeenth century to King Philip III of Spain. His work, she argues, can be read as a moment of contact, one in which different cultures and positions of power come together in a single text—in which a conquered person responds to the ways he is represented in the mind and the language of the conqueror. Pratt's reading of Guaman Poma's letter to King Philip, and the terms she uses to describe the way she reads it, provide a powerful context for a reader looking at essays by other writers, like Gloria Anzaldúa, for whom the "normal" or "standard" language of American culture is difficult, troubling, unsatisfactory, or incomplete. There are, then, assignments that ask you both to extend and to test Pratt's reading through your reading of alternative texts.

Reading one essay through the lens of another becomes a focused form of rereading. To write responses to these assignments, you will need to reread both of the assigned selections. The best way to begin is by taking a quick inventory of what you recall as points of connection. You could do this on your own, with a colleague, or in groups, but it is best to do it with pen and paper (or laptop) in hand. And before you reread, you should come to at least a provisional sense of what you want to do with the assignment. Then you can reread with a project in mind. Be sure to mark passages that you can work with later when you are writing. And look for passages that are interestingly different as well as those that complement each other.

The Assignment Sequences

The assignment sequences are more broad-ranging versions of the "Making Connections" assignments; in the sequences, several reading and writing assignments are linked and directed toward a single goal. They allow you to work on projects that require more time and incorporate more readings than would be possible in a single assignment. And they encourage you to develop your own point of view in concert with those of the professionals who wrote the essays and stories you are reading.

The assignments in a sequence build on one another, each relying on the ones before. A sequence will usually make use of four or five reading selections. The first is used to introduce an area of study or inquiry as well as to establish a frame of reference, a way of thinking about the subject. In the sequence titled "The Aims of Education," you begin with readings by Paulo Freire. The goal of the sequence is to provide a point for you to work from, one that you can open up to question. Subsequent assignments ask you to develop examples from your own schooling as you work through other accounts of education in, for example, Mary Louise Pratt's "Arts of the Contact Zone," Susan Griffin's "Our Secret," or Richard E. Miller's "The Dark Night of the Soul."

The sequences allow you to participate in an extended academic project, one in which you take a position, revise it, look at a new example, hear what someone else has to say, revise it again, and see what conclusions you can draw about your subject. These projects always take time — they go through stages and revisions as a writer develops a command over his material, pushing against habitual ways of thinking, learning to examine an issue from different angles, rejecting quick conclusions, seeing the power of understanding that comes from repeated effort, and feeling the pleasure writers take when they find their own place in significant conversations that connect to their lived experience.

THE SEQUENCES ALLOW YOU TO PARTICIPATE IN AN EXTENDED ACADEMIC PROJECT.

THE Readings

GLORIA Anzaldúa

Gloria Anzaldúa (1942–2004) grew up in southwest Texas, the physical and cultural borderland between the United States and Mexico, an area she called "*una herida abierta*," an open wound, "where the Third World grates against the first and bleeds." Defining herself as lesbian, feminist, Chicana—a representative of the new *mestiza*—she dramatically revised the usual narrative of American autobiography. "I am a border woman," she said. "I grew up between two cultures, the Mexican (with a heavy Indian influence) and the Anglo (as a member of a colonized people in our own territory). I have been straddling that *tejas*-Mexican border, and others, all my life." Cultural, physical, spiritual, sexual, linguistic—the borderlands defined by Anzaldúa extend beyond geography. "In fact," she said, "the Borderlands are present where two or more cultures edge each other, where people of different races occupy the same territory, where under, lower, middle, and upper classes touch, where the space between two individuals shrinks with intimacy." In a sense, her writing argues against the concept of an "authentic," unified, homogeneous culture, the pure "Mexican experience," a nostalgia that underlies much of the current interest in "ethnic" literature.

In the following selection from her book *Borderlands / La frontera: The New Mestiza* (1987), Anzaldúa mixes genres, moving between poetry and prose, weaving stories with sections that resemble the work of a cultural or political theorist. She tells us a story about her childhood, her culture, and her people that is at once both myth and history. Her prose, too, is mixed, shifting among Anglo-American English, Castilian Spanish, Tex-Mex, Northern Mexican dialect, and Nahuatl (Aztec), speaking to us in the particular mix that represents her linguistic heritage: "Presently this infant language, this bastard language, Chicano Spanish, is not approved by any society. But we Chicanos no longer feel that we need to beg entrance, that we need always to make the first overture—to translate to Anglos, Mexicans, and Latinos, apology blurting out of our mouths with every step. Today we ask to be met halfway. This book is our invitation to you." The book is an invitation, but not always an easy one. The chapter that follows make a variety of demands on the reader. The shifting styles, genres, and languages can be confusing or disturbing, but this is part of the effect of Anzaldúa's prose, part of the experience you are invited to share.

In a chapter from the book that is not included here, Anzaldúa gives this account of her writing:

> In looking at this book that I'm almost finished writing, I see a mosaic pattern (Aztec-like) emerging, a weaving pattern, thin here, thick there. I see a preoccupation with the deep structure, the underlying structure, with the gesso underpainting that is red earth, black earth. . . . This almost finished product seems an assemblage, a montage, a beaded work with several leitmotifs and with a central core, now appearing, now disappearing in a crazy dance. The whole thing has had a mind of its own, escaping me and insisting on putting together the pieces of its own puzzle with minimal direction from my will.

Beyond her prose, she sees the competing values of more traditionally organized narratives, "art typical of Western European cultures, [which] attempts to manage the energies of its own internal system. . . . It is dedicated to the validation of itself. Its task is to move humans by means of achieving mastery in content, technique, feeling. Western art is always whole and always 'in power.'"

Anzaldúa's prose puts you, as a reader, on the borderland; in a way, it re-creates the position of the *mestiza*. As you read, you will need to meet this prose halfway, generously, learning to read a text that announces its difference.

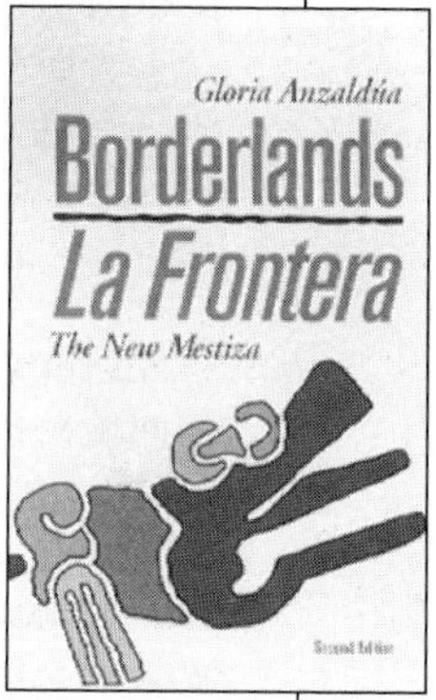

In addition to *Borderlands/La frontera*, Anzaldúa edited *Haciendo Caras: Making Face/Making Soul* (1990) and coedited an anthology, *This Bridge Called My Back: Writings by Radical Women of Color* (1983). She published a book for children, *Prietita and the Ghost Woman* (1996), which retells traditional Mexican folktales from a feminist perspective. A collection of *interviews, Interviews/Entrevistas*, was published in 2000, and a coedited anthology of multicultural feminist theory titled *This Bridge We Call Home: Radical Visions for Transformation* was published in 2002.

How to Tame a Wild Tongue

"We're going to have to control your tongue," the dentist says, pulling out all the metal from my mouth. Silver bits plop and tinkle into the basin. My mouth is a motherlode.

The dentist is cleaning out my roots. I get a whiff of the stench when I gasp. "I can't cap that tooth yet, you're still draining," he says.

"We're going to have to do something about your tongue," I hear the anger rising in his voice. My tongue keeps pushing out the wads of cotton, pushing back the drills, the long thin needles. "I've never seen anything as strong or as stubborn," he says. And I think, how do you tame a wild tongue, train it to be quiet, how do you bridle and saddle it? How do you make it lie down?

> Who is to say that robbing a people of
> its language is less violent than war?
>
> —RAY GWYN SMITH[1]

I remember being caught speaking Spanish at recess — that was good for three licks on the knuckles with a sharp ruler. I remember being sent to the corner of the classroom for "talking back" to the Anglo teacher when all I was trying to do was tell her how to pronounce my name. "If you want to be American, speak 'American.' If you don't like it, go back to Mexico where you belong."

"I want you to speak English. *Pa' hallar buen trabajo tienes que saber hablar el inglés bien. Qué vale toda tu educación si todavía hablas inglés con un* 'accent,'" my mother would say, mortified that I spoke English like a Mexican. At Pan American University, I and all Chicano students were required to take two speech classes. Their purpose: to get rid of our accents.

Attacks on one's form of expression with the intent to censor are a violation of the First Amendment. *El Anglo con cara de inocente nos arrancó la lengua.* Wild tongues can't be tamed, they can only be cut out.

OVERCOMING THE TRADITION OF SILENCE

> *Ahogadas, escupimos el oscuro.*
> *Peleando con nuestra propia sombra*
> *el silencio nos sepulta.*

En boca cerrada no entran moscas. "Flies don't enter a closed mouth" is a saying I kept hearing when I was a child. *Ser habladora* was to be a gossip and a liar, to talk too much. *Muchachitas bien criadas,* well-bred girls don't answer back. *Es una falta de respeto* to talk back to one's mother or father. I remember one of the sins I'd recite to the priest in the confession box the few times I went to confession: talking back to my mother, *hablar pa' 'tras, repelar. Hociocona, repelona, chismosa*, having a big mouth, questioning, carrying tales are all signs of being *mal criada*. In my culture they are all words that are derogatory if applied to women — I've never heard them applied to men.

The first time I heard two women, a Puerto Rican and a Cuban, say the word "*nosotras*," I was shocked. I had not known the word existed. Chicanas use *nosotros* whether we're male or female. We are robbed of our female being by the masculine plural. Language is a male discourse.

> And our tongues have become
> dry   the wilderness has
> dried out our tongues   and
> we have forgotten speech.
>
> — IRENA KLEPFISZ[2]

Even our own people, other Spanish speakers *nos quieren poner candados en la boca*. They would hold us back with their bag of *reglas de academia*.

OYÉ COMO LADRA: EL LENGUAJE DE LA FRONTERA

> *Quien tiene boca se equivoca.*
>
> — Mexican saying

"*Pocho*, cultural traitor, you're speaking the oppressor's language by speaking English, you're ruining the Spanish language," I have been accused by various Latinos and Latinas. Chicano Spanish is considered by the purist and by most Latinos deficient, a mutilation of Spanish.

WE SPEAK A PATOIS, A FORKED TONGUE, A VARIATION OF TWO LANGUAGES.

But Chicano Spanish is a border tongue which developed naturally. Change, evolución, *enriquecimiento de palabras nuevas por invención o adopción* have created variants of Chicano Spanish, *un nuevo lenguaje. Un lenguaje que corresponde a un modo de vivir*. Chicano Spanish is not incorrect, it is a living language.

For a people who are neither Spanish nor live in a country in which Spanish is the first language; for a people who live in a country in which English is the reigning tongue but who are not Anglo; for a people who cannot entirely identify with either standard (formal, Castilian) Spanish nor standard English, what recourse is left to them but to create their own language? A language which they can connect their identity to, one capable of communicating the realities and values true to themselves — a language with terms that are neither *español ni inglés*, but both. We speak a patois, a forked tongue, a variation of two languages.

Chicano Spanish sprang out of the Chicanos' need to identify ourselves as a distinct people. We needed a language with which we could communicate with ourselves, a secret language. For some of us, language is a homeland closer than the Southwest — for many Chicanos today live in the Midwest and the East. And because we are a complex, heterogeneous people, we speak many languages. Some of the languages we speak are

1. Standard English
2. Working-class and slang English
3. Standard Spanish
4. Standard Mexican Spanish
5. North Mexican Spanish dialect
6. Chicano Spanish (Texas, New Mexico, Arizona, and California have regional variations)
7. Tex-Mex
8. *Pachuco* (called *caló*)

My "home" tongues are the languages I speak with my sister and brothers, with my friends. They are the last five listed, with 6 and 7 being closest to my heart. From school, the media, and job situations, I've picked up standard and working-class English. From Mamagrande Locha and from reading Spanish and Mexican literature, I've picked up Standard Spanish and Standard Mexican Spanish. From *los recién llegados*, Mexican immigrants, and *braceros*, I learned the North Mexican dialect. With Mexicans I'll try to speak either Standard Mexican Spanish or the North Mexican dialect. From my parents and Chicanos living in the Valley, I picked up Chicano Texas Spanish, and I speak it with my mom, younger brother (who married a Mexican and who rarely mixes Spanish with English), aunts, and older relatives.

With Chicanas from *Nuevo México* or *Arizona* I will speak Chicano Spanish a little, but often they don't understand what I'm saying. With most California Chicanas I speak entirely in English (unless I forget). When I first moved to San Francisco, I'd rattle off something in Spanish, unintentionally embarrassing them. Often it is only with another Chicana *tejano* that I can talk freely.

Words distorted by English are known as anglicisms or *pochismos*. The pocho is an anglicized Mexican or American of Mexican origin who speaks Spanish with an accent characteristic of North Americans and who distorts and reconstructs the language according to the influence of English.[3] Tex-Mex, or Spanglish, comes most naturally to me. I may switch back and forth from English to Spanish in the same sentence or in the same word. With my sister and my brother Nune and with Chicano *tejano* contemporaries I speak in Tex-Mex.

From kids and people my own age I picked up *Pachuco*. *Pachuco* (the language of the zoot suiters) is a language of rebellion, both against Standard Spanish and Standard English. It is a secret language. Adults of the culture and outsiders cannot understand it. It is made up of slang words from both English and Spanish. *Ruca* means girl or woman, *vato* means guy or dude, *chale* means no, *simón* means yes, *churro* is sure, talk is *periquiar*, *pigionear* means petting, *que gacho* means how nerdy, *ponte águila* means watch out, death is called *la pelona*. Through lack of practice and not having others who can speak it, I've lost most of the *Pachuco* tongue.

CHICANO SPANISH

Chicanos, after 250 years of Spanish/Anglo colonization, have developed significant differences in the Spanish we speak. We collapse two adjacent vowels into a single syllable and sometimes shift the stress in certain words such as *maíz/maiz, cohete/cuete*. We leave out certain consonants when they appear between vowels: *lado/lao, mojado/mojao*. Chicanos from South Texas pronounce *f* as *j* as in *jue* (*fue*). Chicanos use "archaisms," words that are no longer in the Spanish language, words that have been evolved out. We say *semos, truje, haiga, ansina*, and *naiden*. We retain the "archaic" *j*, as in *jalar*, that derives from an earlier *h* (the French *halar* or the Germanic *halon* which was lost to standard Spanish in the sixteenth century), but which is still found in several regional dialects such as the one spoken in South Texas. (Due to geography, Chicanos from the Valley of South Texas were cut off linguistically from other Spanish speakers. We tend to use words that the Spaniards brought over from Medieval Spain. The majority of the Spanish colonizers in Mexico and the Southwest came from Extremadura — Hernán Cortés was one of them — and Andalucía. Andalucians pronounce *ll* like a *y*, and their *d*'s tend to be absorbed by adjacent vowels: *tirado* becomes *tirao*. They brought *el lenguaje popular, dialectos, y regionalismos*.)[4]

Chicanos and other Spanish speakers also shift *ll* to *y* and *z* to *s*.[5] We leave out initial syllables, saying *tar* for *estar*, *toy* for *estoy*, *hora* for *ahora* (*cubanos* and *puertorriqueños* also leave out initial letters of some words). We also leave out the final syllable such as *pa* for *para*. The intervocalic *y*, the *ll* as in *tortilla, ella, botella*, gets replaced by *tortia* or *toriya, ea, botea*. We add an additional syllable at the beginning of certain words: *atocar* for *tocar, agastar* for *gastar*. Sometimes we'll say *lavaste las vacijas*, other times *lavates* (substituting the *ates* verb endings for the *aste*).

We use anglicisms, words borrowed from English: *bola* from ball, *carpeta* from carpet, *máchina de lavar* (instead of *lavadora*) from washing machine. Tex-Mex argot, created by adding a Spanish sound at the beginning or end of an English word such as *cookiar* for cook, *watchar* for watch, *parkiar* for park, and *rapiar* for rape, is the result of the pressures on Spanish speakers to adapt to English.

We don't use the word *vosotros/as* or its accompanying verb form. We don't say *claro* (to mean yes), *imagínate*, or *me emociona*, unless we picked up Spanish from Latinas, out of a book, or in a classroom. Other Spanish-speaking groups are going through the same, or similar, development in their Spanish.

LINGUISTIC TERRORISM

Deslenguadas. Somos los del español deficiente. We are your linguistic nightmare, your linguistic aberration, your linguistic *mestisaje*, the subject of your *burla*. Because we speak with tongues of fire we are culturally crucified. Racially, culturally, and linguistically *somos huérfanos* — we speak an orphan tongue.

Chicanas who grew up speaking Chicano Spanish have internalized the belief that we speak poor Spanish. It is illegitimate, a bastard language. And because we internalize how our language has been used against us by the dominant culture, we use our language differences against each other.

Chicana feminists often skirt around each other with suspicion and hesitation. For the longest time I couldn't figure it out. Then it dawned on me. To be close to another Chicana is like looking into the mirror. We are afraid of what we'll see there. *Pena*. Shame. Low estimation of self. In childhood we are told that our language is wrong. Repeated attacks on our native tongue diminish our sense of self. The attacks continue throughout our lives.

Chicanas feel uncomfortable talking in Spanish to Latinas, afraid of their censure. Their language was not outlawed in their countries. They had a whole lifetime of being immersed in their native tongue; generations, centuries in which Spanish was a first language, taught in school, heard on radio and TV, and read in the newspaper.

If a person, Chicana or Latina, has a low estimation of my native tongue, she also has a low estimation of me. Often with *mexicanas y latinas* we'll speak English as a neutral language. Even among Chicanas we tend to speak English at parties or conferences. Yet, at the same time, we're afraid the other will think we're *agringadas* because we don't speak Chicano Spanish. We oppress each other trying to out-Chicano each other, vying to be the "real" Chicanas, to speak like Chicanos. There is no one Chicano language just as there is no one Chicano experience. A monolingual Chicana whose first language is English or Spanish is just as much a Chicana as one who speaks several variants of Spanish. A Chicana from Michigan or Chicago or Detroit is just as much a Chicana as one from the Southwest. Chicano Spanish is as diverse linguistically as it is regionally.

By the end of this [the twentieth] century, Spanish speakers will comprise the biggest minority group in the United States, a country where students in high schools and colleges are encouraged to take French classes because French is considered more "cultured." But for a language to remain alive it must be used.[6] By the end of this century English, and not Spanish, will be the mother tongue of most Chicanos and Latinos.

So, if you want to really hurt me, talk badly about my language. Ethnic identity is twin skin to linguistic identity — I am my language. Until I can take pride in my language, I cannot take pride in myself. Until I can accept as legitimate Chicano Texas Spanish, Tex-Mex, and all the other languages I speak, I cannot accept the legitimacy of myself. Until I am free to write bilingually and to switch codes without having always to translate, while I still have to speak English or Spanish when I would rather speak Spanglish, and as long as I have to accommodate the English speaker rather than having them accommodate me, my tongue will be illegitimate.

I will no longer be made to feel ashamed of existing. I will have my voice: Indian, Spanish, white. I will have my serpent's tongue — my woman's voice, my sexual voice, my poet's voice. I will overcome the tradition of silence.

My fingers
move sly against your palm
Like women everywhere, we speak in code. . . .
— MELANIE KAYE / KANTROWITZ[7]

"VISTAS," CORRIDOS, Y COMIDA: MY NATIVE TONGUE

In the 1960s, I read my first Chicano novel. It was *City of Night* by John Rechy, a gay Texan, son of a Scottish father and a Mexican mother. For days I walked around in stunned amazement that a Chicano could write and could get published. When I read *I Am Joaquín*[8] I was surprised to see a bilingual book by a Chicano in print. When I saw poetry written in Tex-Mex for the first time, a feeling of pure joy flashed through me. I felt like we really existed as a people. In 1971, when I started teaching High School English to Chicano students, I tried to supplement the required texts with works by Chicanos, only to be reprimanded and forbidden to do so by the principal. He claimed that I was supposed to teach "American" and English literature. At the risk of being fired, I swore my students to secrecy and slipped in Chicano short stories, poems, a play. In graduate school, while working toward a Ph.D., I had to "argue" with one adviser after the other, semester after semester, before I was allowed to make Chicano literature an area of focus.

Even before I read books by Chicanos or Mexicans, it was the Mexican movies I saw at the drive-in — the Thursday night special of $1.00 a carload — that gave me a sense of belonging. "*Vámonos a las vistas,*" my mother would call out and we'd all — grandmother, brothers, sister, and cousins — squeeze into the car. We'd wolf down cheese and bologna white bread sandwiches while watching Pedro Infante in melodramatic tearjerkers like *Nosotros los pobres*, the first "real" Mexican movie (that was not an imitation of European movies). I remember seeing *Cuando los hijos se van* and surmising that all Mexican movies played up the love a mother has for her children and what ungrateful sons and daughters suffer when they are not devoted to their mothers. I remember the singing-type "westerns" of Jorge Negrete and Miguel Aceves Mejía. When watching Mexican movies, I felt a sense of homecoming as well as alienation. People who were to amount to something didn't go to Mexican movies, or *bailes*, or tune their radios to *bolero*, *rancherita*, and *corrido* music.

The whole time I was growing up, there was *norteño* music sometimes called North Mexican border music, or Tex-Mex music, or Chicano music, or *cantina* (bar) music. I grew up listening to *conjuntos*, three- or four-piece bands made up of folk musicians playing guitar, *bajo sexto*, drums, and button accordion, which Chicanos had borrowed from the German immigrants who had come to Central Texas and Mexico to farm and build breweries. In the Rio Grande Valley, Steven Jordan and Little Joe Hernández were popular, and Flaco Jiménez was the accordion king. The rhythms of Tex-Mex music are those of the polka, also adapted from the Germans, who in turn had borrowed the polka from the Czechs and Bohemians.

I remember the hot, sultry evenings when *corridos* — songs of love and death on the Texas-Mexican borderlands — reverberated out of cheap amplifiers from the local *cantinas* and wafted in through my bedroom window.

Corridos first became widely used along the South Texas/Mexican border during the early conflict between Chicanos and Anglos. The *corridos* are usually about Mexican heroes who do valiant deeds against the Anglo oppressors. Pancho Villa's song, "*La cucaracha*," is the most famous one. *Corridos* of John F. Kennedy and his death are still very popular in the Valley. Older Chicanos remember Lydia Mendoza, one of the great border *corrido* singers who was called *la Gloria de Tejas*. Her "*El tango negro*," sung during the Great Depression, made her a singer of the people. The ever-present *corridos* narrated one hundred years of border history, bringing news of events as well as entertaining. These folk musicians and folk songs are our chief cultural mythmakers, and they made our hard lives seem bearable.

I grew up feeling ambivalent about our music. Country-western and rock-and-roll had more status. In the fifties and sixties, for the slightly educated and *agringado* Chicanos, there existed a sense of shame at being caught listening to our music. Yet I couldn't stop my feet from thumping to the music, could not stop humming the words, nor hide from myself the exhilaration I felt when I heard it.

There are more subtle ways that we internalize identification, especially in the forms of images and emotions. For me food and certain smells are tied to my identity, to my homeland. Woodsmoke curling up to an immense blue sky; woodsmoke perfuming my grandmother's clothes, her skin. The stench of cow manure and the yellow patches on the ground; the crack of a .22 rifle and the reek of cordite. Homemade white cheese sizzling in a pan, melting inside a folded *tortilla*. My sister Hilda's hot, spicy *menudo*, *chile colorado* making it deep red, pieces of *panza* and hominy floating on top. My brother Carito barbequing *fajitas* in the backyard. Even now and 3,000 miles away, I can see my mother spicing the ground beef, pork, and venison with *chile*. My mouth salivates at the thought of the hot steaming *tamales* I would be eating if I were home.

SI LE PREGUNTAS A MI MAMÁ, "¿QUÉ ERES?"

> Identity is the essential core of who
> we are as individuals, the conscious
> experience of the self inside.
>
> — GERSHEN KAUFMAN[9]

Nosotros los Chicanos straddle the borderlands. On one side of us, we are constantly exposed to the Spanish of the Mexicans, on the other side we hear the Anglos' incessant clamoring so that we forget our language. Among ourselves we don't say *nosotros los americanos, o nosotros los españoles, o nosotros los hispanos*. We say *nosotros los mexicanos* (by *mexicanos* we do not mean citizens of Mexico; we do not mean a national identity, but a racial one). We distinguish between *mexicanos del otro lado* and *mexicanos de este lado*. Deep in our hearts we believe that being Mexican has nothing to do with which country one lives in. Being Mexican is a state of soul — not one of mind, not one of citizenship. Neither eagle nor serpent, but both. And like the ocean, neither animal respects borders.

> *Dime con quien andas y te diré quien eres.*
> (Tell me who your friends are and I'll tell you who you are.)
> — Mexican saying

Si le preguntas a mi mamá, "¿Qué eres?" te dirá, "Soy mexicana." My brothers and sister say the same. I sometimes will answer "*soy mexicana*" and at others will say "*soy Chicana*" o "*soy tejana*." But I identified as "*Raza*" before I ever identified as "*mexicana*" or "Chicana."

As a culture, we call ourselves Spanish when referring to ourselves as a linguistic group and when copping out. It is then that we forget our predominant Indian genes. We are 70–80 percent Indian.[10] We call ourselves Hispanic[11] or Spanish-American or Latin American or Latin when linking ourselves to other Spanish-speaking peoples of the Western hemisphere and when copping out. We call ourselves Mexican-American[12] to signify we are neither Mexican nor American, but more the noun "American" than the adjective "Mexican" (and when copping out).

SI LE PREGUNTAS A MI MAMÁ, "¿QUÉ ERES?" TE DIRÁ, "SOY MEXICANA."

Chicanos and other people of color suffer economically for not acculturating. This voluntary (yet forced) alienation makes for psychological conflict, a kind of dual identity — we don't identify with the Anglo-American cultural values and we don't totally identify with the Mexican cultural values. We are a synergy of two cultures with various degrees of Mexicanness or Angloness. I have so internalized the borderland conflict that sometimes I feel like one cancels out the other and we are zero, nothing, no one. *A veces no soy nada ni nadie. Pero hasta cuando no lo soy, lo soy.*

When not copping out, when we know we are more than nothing, we call ourselves Mexican, referring to race and ancestry; *mestizo* when affirming both our Indian and Spanish (but we hardly ever own our Black) ancestry; Chicano when referring to a politically aware people born and/or raised in the United States; *Raza* when referring to Chicanos; *tejanos* when we are Chicanos from Texas.

Chicanos did not know we were a people until 1965 when Cesar Chavez and the farmworkers united and *I Am Joaquín* was published and *la Raza Unida* party was formed in Texas. With that recognition, we became a distinct people. Something momentous happened to the Chicano soul — we became aware of our reality and acquired a name and a language

(Chicano Spanish) that reflected that reality. Now that we had a name, some of the fragmented pieces began to fall together — who we were, what we were, how we had evolved. We began to get glimpses of what we might eventually become.

Yet the struggle of identities continues, the struggle of borders is our reality still. One day the inner struggle will cease and a true integration take place. In the meantime, *tenémos que hacer la lucha. ¿Quién está protegiendo los ranchos de mi gente? ¿Quién está tratando de cerrar la fisura entre la india y el blanco en nuestra sangre? El Chicano, si, el Chicano que anda como un ladrón en su propia casa.*

Los Chicanos, how patient we seem, how very patient. There is the quiet of the Indian about us.[13] We know how to survive. When other races have given up their tongue we've kept ours. We know what it is to live under the hammer blow of the dominant *norteamericano* culture. But more than we count the blows, we count the days the weeks the years the centuries the aeons until the white laws and commerce and customs will rot in the deserts they've created, lie bleached. *Humildes* yet proud, *quietos* yet wild, *nosotros los mexicanos-Chicanos* will walk by the crumbling ashes as we go about our business. Stubborn, persevering, impenetrable as stone, yet possessing a malleability that renders us unbreakable, we, the *mestizas* and *mestizos*, will remain.

NOTES

1 Ray Gwyn Smith, *Moorland Is Cold Country*, unpublished book.

2 Irena Klepfisz, "*Di rayze aheym* / The Journey Home," in *The Tribe of Dina: A Jewish Women's Anthology*, Melanie Kaye / Kantrowitz and Irena Klepfisz, eds. (Montpelier, VT: Sinister Wisdom Books, 1986), 49.

3 R. C. Ortega, *Dialectología Del Barrio*, trans. Hortencia S. Alwan (Los Angeles, CA: R. C. Ortega Publisher & Bookseller, 1977), 132.

4 Eduardo Hernandéz-Chávez, Andrew D. Cohen, and Anthony F. Beltramo, *El Lenguaje de los Chicanos: Regional and Social Characteristics of Language Used by Mexican Americans* (Arlington, VA: Center for Applied Linguistics, 1975), 39.

5 Hernandéz-Chávez, xvii.

6 Irena Klepfisz, "Secular Jewish Identity: Yidishkayt in America," in *The Tribe of Dina*, Kaye / Kantrowitz and Klepfisz, eds., 43.

7 Melanie Kaye / Kantrowitz, "Sign," in *We Speak in Code: Poems and Other Writings* (Pittsburgh, PA: Motheroot Publications, Inc., 1980), 85.

8 Rodolfo Gonzales, *I Am Joaquín/Yo Soy Joaquín* (New York, NY: Bantam Books, 1972). It was first published in 1967.

9 Gershen Kaufman, *Shame: The Power of Caring* (Cambridge, MA: Schenkman Books, Inc., 1980), 68.

10 John R. Chávez, *The Lost Land: The Chicano Images of the Southwest* (Albuquerque, NM: University of New Mexico Press, 1984), 88–90.

11 "Hispanic" is derived from *Hispanis* (*España*, a name given to the Iberian Peninsula in ancient times when it was a part of the Roman Empire) and is a term designated by the U.S. government to make it easier to handle us on paper.

12 The Treaty of Guadalupe Hidalgo created the Mexican-American in 1848.

13 Anglos, in order to alleviate their guilt for dispossessing the Chicano, stressed the Spanish part of us and perpetrated the myth of the Spanish Southwest. We have accepted the fiction that we are Hispanic, that is Spanish, in order to accommodate ourselves to the dominant culture and its abhorrence of Indians. Chávez, 88–91.

QUESTIONS FOR A SECOND READING

1. The most immediate challenge to many readers of this chapter will be the sections that are written in Spanish. Part of the point of a text that mixes languages is to give non-Spanish-speaking readers the feeling of being lost, excluded, left out. What is a reader to do with this prose? One could learn Spanish and come back to reread, but this is not a quick solution and, according to Anzaldúa, not even a completely satisfactory one, since some of her Spanish is drawn from communities of speakers not represented in textbooks and classes.

   So how do you read this text if you don't read Spanish? Do you ignore the words? sound them out? improvise? Anzaldúa gives translations of some words or phrases, but not all. Which ones does she translate? Why? Reread these chapters with the goal of explaining how you handled Anzaldúa's polyglot style.

2. This chapter is made up of shorter sections written in a variety of styles (some as prose poems, some with endnotes, some as stories). And while the sections are obviously ordered, the order is not a conventional argumentative one. The text is, as Anzaldúa says elsewhere in her book, "an assemblage, a montage, a beaded work, . . . a crazy dance":

   > In looking at this book that I'm almost finished writing, I see a mosaic pattern (Aztec-like) emerging, a weaving pattern, thin here, thick there. . . . This almost finished product seems an assemblage, a montage, a beaded work with several leitmotifs and with a central core, now appearing, now disappearing in a crazy dance. The whole thing has had a mind of its own, escaping me and insisting on putting together the pieces of its own puzzle with minimal direction from my will. It is a rebellious, willful entity, a precocious girl-child forced to grow up too quickly, rough, unyielding, with pieces of feather sticking out here and there, fur, twigs, clay. My child, but not for much longer. This female being is angry, sad, joyful, is Coatlicue, dove, horse, serpent, cactus. Though it is a flawed thing — clumsy, complex, groping, blind thing, for me it is alive, infused with spirit. I talk to it; it talks to me.

   This is not, in other words, a conventional text; it makes unexpected demands on a reader. As you reread, mark sections you could use to talk about how, through the text, Anzaldúa invents a reader and/or a way of reading. Who is Anzaldúa's ideal reader? What does he or she need to be able to do?

3. Although Anzaldúa's text is not a conventional one, it makes an argument and proposes terms and examples for its readers to negotiate. How might you summarize Anzaldúa's argument in this chapter? How does the chapter mark stages or parts of her argument? As you reread this selection, mark those passages where Anzaldúa seems to you to be creating a case or an argument. What are its key terms? its key examples? its conclusions?

ASSIGNMENTS FOR WRITING

1. Anzaldúa has described her text as a kind of crazy dance (see the second "Question for a Second Reading"); it is, she says, a text with a mind of its own, "putting together the pieces of its own puzzle with minimal direction from my will." Hers is a prose full of variety and seeming contradictions; it is a writing that could be said to represent the cultural "crossroads" which is her experience / sensibility.

    As an experiment whose goal is the development of an alternate (in Anzaldúa's terms, a mixed or *mestiza*) understanding, write an autobiographical text whose shape and motives could be described in her terms: a mosaic, woven, with numerous overlays; a montage, a beaded work, a crazy dance, drawing on the various ways of thinking, speaking, understanding that might be said to be part of your own mixed cultural position, your own mixed sensibility.

    To prepare for this essay, think about the different positions you could be said to occupy, the different voices that are part of your background or present, the competing ways of thinking that make up your points of view. Imagine that your goal is to present your world and your experience to those who are not necessarily prepared to be sympathetic or to understand. And, following Anzaldúa, you should work to construct a mixed text, not a single unified one. This will be hard, since you will be writing what might be called a "forbidden" text, one you have not been prepared to write.

2. In "*La Conciencia de la Mestiza* / Towards a New Consciousness," the last essay-like chapter in her book (the remaining chapters are made up of poems), Anzaldúa steps forward to define her role as writer and yours as reader. She says, among other things,

    > Many women and men of color do not want to have any dealings with white people. . . . Many feel that whites should help their own people rid themselves of race hatred and fear first. I, for one, choose to use some of my energy to serve as mediator. I think we need to allow whites to be our allies. Through our literature, art, *corridos*, and folktales we must share our history with them so when they set up committees to help Big Mountain Navajos or the Chicano farmworkers or los *Nicaragüenses* they won't turn people away because of their racial fears and ignorances. They will come to see that they are not helping us but following our lead.
    >
    > Individually, but also as a racial entity, we need to voice our needs. We need to say to white society: We need you to accept the fact that Chicanos are different, to acknowledge your rejection and negation of us. We need you to own the fact that you looked upon us as less than human, that you stole our lands, our personhood, our self-respect. We need you to make public restitution: to say that, to compensate

> for your own sense of defectiveness, you strive for power over us, you erase our history and our experience because it makes you feel guilty — you'd rather forget your brutish acts. To say you've split yourself from minority groups, that you disown us, that your dual consciousness splits off parts of yourself, transferring the "negative" parts onto us. . . . To say that you are afraid of us, that to put distance between us, you wear the mask of contempt. Admit that Mexico is your double, that she exists in the shadow of this country, that we are irrevocably tied to her. Gringo, accept the doppelganger in your psyche. By taking back your collective shadow the intracultural split will heal. And finally, tell us what you need from us.

This is only a part of the text — one of the ways it defines the roles of reader and writer — but it is one that asks to be taken account of, with its insistent list of what a white reader must do and say. (Of course not every reader is white, and not all white readers are the same. What Anzaldúa is defining here is a "white" way of reading.)

Write an essay in which you tell a story of reading, the story of your work with the chapter of *Borderlands/La frontera* reprinted here. Think about where you felt at home with the text and where you felt lost, where you knew what you were doing and where you needed help; think about the position (or positions) you have taken as a reader and how it measures up against the ways Anzaldúa has figured you in the text, the ways she has anticipated a response, imagined who you are and how you habitually think and read.

3. In "How to Tame a Wild Tongue," Anzaldúa says, "I will no longer be made to feel ashamed of existing. I will have my voice: Indian, Spanish, white. I will have my serpent's tongue — my woman's voice, my sexual voice, my poet's voice." Anzaldúa speaks about "having her voice," not a single, "authentic" voice, but one she names in these terms: Indian, Spanish, white; woman, lesbian, poet. What is "voice" as defined by this chapter? Where does it come from? What does it have to do with the act of writing or the writer?

   As you reread this chapter, mark those passages that you think best represent Anzaldúa's voices. Using these passages as examples, write an essay in which you discuss how these voices are different — both different from one another and different from a "standard" voice (as a "standard" voice is imagined by Anzaldúa). What do these voices represent? How do they figure in your reading? in her writing?

4. Anzaldúa's writing is difficult to categorize as an essay or a story or a poem; it has all of these within it. The writing may appear to have been just put together, but it is more likely that it was carefully crafted to represent the various voices Anzaldúa understands to be a part of her. She speaks directly about her voices — her woman's voice, her sexual voice, her poet's voice; her Indian, Spanish, and white voices on page 30 of "How to Tame a Wild Tongue."

Following Anzaldúa, write an argument of your own, one that requires you to use a variety of voices, in which you carefully present the various voices that you feel are a part of you or a part of the argument.

When you have completed this assignment, write a two-page essay in which you explain why the argument you made might be worth a reader's attention.

MAKING CONNECTIONS

1. In "Arts of the Contact Zone" (p. 317), Mary Louise Pratt talks about the "autoethnographic" text, "a text in which people undertake to describe themselves in ways that engage with representations others have made of them," and about "transculturation," the "processes whereby members of subordinated or marginal groups select and invent from materials transmitted by a dominant or metropolitan culture."

   Write an essay in which you present a reading of this chapter as an example of an autoethnographic and/or transcultural text. You should imagine that you are writing to someone who is not familiar with either Pratt's argument or Anzaldúa's book. Part of your work, then, is to present Anzaldúa's text to readers who don't have it in front of them. You have the example of Pratt's reading of Guaman Poma's *New Chronicle and Good Government*. And you have her discussion of the "literate arts of the contact zone." Think about how Anzaldúa's text might be similarly read, and about how her text does and doesn't fit Pratt's description. Your goal should be to add an example to Pratt's discussion and to qualify it, to give her discussion a new twist or spin now that you have had a chance to look at an additional example.

2. Writers often layer their essays with metaphors or, in Anzaldúa's case, with narratives that serve as kinds of metaphor. One way to identify moments of metaphor that layer a piece of writing is to notice when particular sentences or images seem to carry more than one meaning. For example, when Anzaldúa tells us what the dentist says ("We're going to have to do something about your tongue"), we might notice that the dentist's statement has more than one meaning, that what he literally says is meant to signal something else, something larger and more complex than this specific moment. Many of the writers in this collection make use of metaphor in their work, inviting readers to see multiple meanings in a single moment.

   Reread Anzaldúa, looking for those metaphorical moments, marking sentences that seem to point to something larger. Then, reread Brian Doyle's "Joyas Voladoras" (p. 147) or Susan Griffin's "Our Secret," (p. 233) looking for similar moments. Write an essay in which you guide your own reader through these authors' use of metaphor, choosing some specific examples from each essay. Consider the following questions: How do these passages point to something larger than themselves? How are you, as a reader, impacted by the use of the metaphor, and how does the metaphor serve to layer the essay—to complicated or illuminate its subject matter? Why do writers rely on metaphors?

3. Anzaldúa writes, "So, if you want to really hurt me, talk badly about my language. Ethnic identity is twin skin to linguistic identity—I am my language." (p. 30) In "How to Tame a Wild Tongue," Anzaldúa seems to suggest that our language(s) are essential to our identities, perhaps even essential to our humanity, or to what Judith Butler calls "a livable life." Both Butler and Anzaldúa seem concerned with, as Butler puts it, the ways "life itself becomes foreclosed when the right way is decided in advance, when we impose what is right for everyone and without finding a way to enter into community, and to discover there the 'right' in the midst of cultural translation." (p. 131) Butler wrote "Beside Oneself: On the Limits of Sexual Autonomy" about twenty years after Anzaldúa first published "How to Tame a Wild Tongue," and while Butler's pieces does not specifically address the linguistic particularities of Anzaldúa's piece, their work is certainly in conversation—raising some similar questions and offering some alternative ways of thinking about culture, identity, and language.

   Write an essay in which you enact some inquiry into a specific question (likely an unanswerable one) that you think is key for *both* Butler and Anzaldúa. You might begin with the question: what seems to be the central questions for each writer, and how do those central questions overlap? Once you've brainstormed a bit (perhaps even with classmates) about these central questions, choose one that is particularly interesting to you. In your essay, you'll want to both argue for the importance of asking this question in the first place *and* discuss the ways Butler and Anzaldúa offer you answers or approaches to this central question.

KWAME ANTHONY Appiah

Kwame Anthony Appiah (pronounced AP-eea, with the accent on the first syllable) was born in London; he grew up in Ghana, in the town of Asante; he took his MA and PhD degrees from Cambridge University in England; he is now a citizen of the United States. He has taught at Yale, Cornell, Duke, Harvard, and, most recently, Princeton, where he is the Laurence S. Rockefeller University Professor of Philosophy and a member of the University Center for Human Values. Appiah's father was Ghanaian and a leader in the struggle for Pan-Africanism and Ghanaian independence from Britain; his mother, originally Peggy Cripps, was British and the daughter of a leading figure in the Labour government. Appiah's work circulates widely and has won numerous awards. He was elected to the American Academy of Arts and Sciences and the American Philosophical Society and was inducted in 2008 into the American Academy of Arts and Letters.

Appiah's life illustrates the virtues of a "rooted cosmopolitanism," a term he offers to describe a desired way of living in the world, and it illustrates the difficulties we face in naming someone as black or white or African or American. In the preface to his book, *The Ethics of Identity* (2004), he says,

> What has proved especially vexatious, though, is the effort to take account of those social forms we now call identities: genders and sexual orientations, ethnicities and nationalities, professions and vocations. Identities make ethical claims because — and this is just a fact about the world we human beings have created — we make our lives as men and as women, as gay and as straight people, as Ghanaians and as Americans, as blacks and as whites. Immediately, conundrums start to assemble. Do identities represent a curb on autonomy, or do they provide its contours: What claims, if any, can identity groups as such justly make upon the state? These are concerns that have gained a certain measure of salience in recent political philosophy, but, as I hope to show, they are anything but newfangled. What's modern is that we conceptualize identity in particular ways. What's age-old is that when we are asked — and ask ourselves — who we are, we are being asked what we are as well. (p. xiv)

Appiah is an award-winning and prolific writer. His books include *Assertion and Conditionals* (1985); *For Truth in Semantics* (1986); *In My Father's*

House: Africa in the Philosophy of Culture (1992); *The Ethics of Identity* (2005); *Cosmopolitanism: Ethics in a World of Strangers* (2007); and *The Honor Code: How Moral Revolutions Happen* (2010). He is also the author of three mystery novels, *Avenging Angel* (1991), *Nobody Likes Letitia* (1994), and *Another Death in Venice* (1995); a textbook, *Thinking It Through: An Introduction to Contemporary Philosophy* (2003); and, with Henry Louis Gates Jr., the *Encarta Africana CD-ROM encyclopedia*. The selection that follows was taken from a book co-authored with Amy Gutmann, *Color Consciousness: The Political Morality of Race* (1996), winner of the 1997 Ralph J. Bunche award from the American Political Science Association. *Color Consciousness* is drawn from the lectures Appiah and Gutmann gave as the Tanner Lectures on Human Values at the University of California, San Diego. We've included one section from Appiah's half of the exchange, so at times you will hear him allude to things he said earlier in that chapter. The section we've provided can, however, easily stand alone and be read as a single, coherent essay.

As you read "Racial Identities," it will help to pay particular attention to *voice* — to the way the writer locates himself within available ways of speaking and thinking. Appiah writes as a philosopher. That is, he writes from within ideas, from within trains of thought. He is not necessarily endorsing these ways of thinking. They are not necessarily his thought processes, or ones he would endorse. He is trying them on, testing their consequences or limits, showing where they might lead.

You can't, in other words, quickly assume that an affirmative sentence expresses Appiah's own thoughts or beliefs. This is tricky. For example, listen to these sentences. Where might you locate Appiah?

> I have insisted that African-Americans do not have a single culture, in the sense of shared language, values, practices, and meanings. But many people who think of races as groups defined by shared cultures, conceive that sharing in a different way. They understand black people as sharing black culture by *definition*: jazz or hip-hop belongs to an African-American, whether she likes it or knows anything about it, because it is culturally marked as black. Jazz belongs to a black person who knows nothing about it more fully or naturally than it does to a white jazzman. (p. 52)

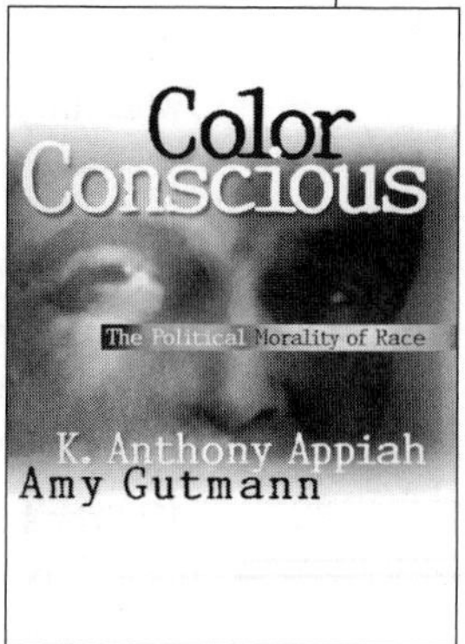

Appiah is not saying that he believes jazz belongs to a black person more fully or naturally than it does to a white person. He is saying that "many people" have a way of thinking about race and culture that will lead them to such statements or beliefs.

Learning to read along with a philosopher, with a writer who is thinking about ways of thinking, is challenging. As you read, keep an ear cocked for moments when Appiah gives voice to others, and be alert for those moments (and they are fewer) when he speaks for himself.

Racial Identities

"SPEAKING OF CIVILIZATIONS"

In 1911, responding to what was already clear evidence that race was not doing well as a biological concept, W.E.B. Du Bois, the African-American sociologist, historian, and activist, wrote in *The Crisis,* the magazine of the NAACP, which he edited:

> The leading scientists of the world have come forward . . . and laid down in categorical terms a series of propositions[1] which may be summarized as follows:
>
> 1. (a) It is not legitimate to argue from differences in physical characteristics to differences in mental characteristics . . .
>
> 2. The civilization of a . . . race at any particular moment of time offers no index to its innate or inherited capacities . . .[2]

And he concluded: "So far at least as intellectual and moral aptitudes are concerned we ought to speak of civilizations where we now speak of races."[3] I have argued before that Du Bois's proposal to "speak of civilizations" turns out not to replace a biological notion but simply to hide it from view.[4] I think there are various difficulties with the way that argument proceeded, and I should like to do better. So let me try to reconstruct a sociohistorical view that has more merit than I have previously conceded.

Among the most moving of Du Bois's statements of the meaning of "race" conceived in sociohistorical terms is the one in *Dusk of Dawn,* the "autobiography of a race concept," as he called it, which he published in 1940. Du Bois wrote:

> The actual ties of heritage between the individuals of this group, vary with the ancestors that they have in common with many others: Europeans and Semites, perhaps Mongolians, certainly American Indians. But the physical bond is least and the badge of color relatively unimportant save as a badge; the real essence of this kinship is its social heritage of slavery; the discrimination and insult; and this heritage binds together not simply the children of Africa, but extends through yellow Asia and into the South Seas. It is this unity that draws me to Africa.[5]

For reasons I shall be able to make clear only when I have given my account, Du Bois's own approach is somewhat misleading. So instead of proceeding with exegesis of Du Bois, I must turn next to the task of shaping a sociohistorical account of racial identity. Still, as it turns out, it is helpful to start from Du Bois's idea of the "badge of color."

RACIAL IDENTITY AND RACIAL IDENTIFICATION[6]

I have argued that Jefferson and Arnold thought that when they applied a racial label they were identifying people with a shared essence. I have argued, also, that they were wrong—and, I insist, not slightly but wildly wrong. Earlier in American history the label "African" was applied to many of those who would later be thought of as Negroes, by people who may have been under the impression that Africans had more in common culturally, socially, intellectually, and religiously than they actually did. Neither of these kinds of errors, however, stopped the labeling from having its effects. As slavery in North America became racialized in the colonial period, being identified as an African, or, later, as a Negro, carrying the "badge of color," had those predictable negative consequences, which Du Bois so memorably captured in the phrase "the social heritage of slavery; the discrimination and insult."

If we follow the badge of color from "African" to "Negro" to "colored race" to "black" to "Afro-American" (and this ignores such fascinating detours as the route by way of "Afro-Saxon") we are thus tracing the history not only of a signifier, a label, but also a history of its effects. At any time in this history there was, within the American colonies and the United States that succeeded them, a massive consensus, both among those labeled black and among those labeled white, as to who, in their own communities, fell under which labels. (As immigration from China and other parts of the "Far East" occurred, an Oriental label came to have equal stability.) There was, no doubt, some "passing"; but the very concept of passing implies that, if the relevant fact about the ancestry of these individuals had become known, most people would have taken them to be traveling under the wrong badge.

The major North American exception was in southern Louisiana, where a different system in which an intermediary Creole group, neither white nor black, had social recognition; but *Plessy v. Fergusson* reflected the extent to which the Louisiana Purchase effectively brought even that state gradually into the American mainstream of racial classification. For in that case Homer Adolph Plessy – a Creole gentleman who could certainly have passed in most places for white – discovered in 1896, after a long process of appeal, that the Supreme Court of the United States proposed to treat him as a Negro and therefore recognize the State of Louisiana's right to keep him and his white fellow citizens "separate but equal."

The result is that there are at least three sociocultural objects in America – blacks, whites and Orientals – whose membership at any time is relatively, and increasingly, determinate. These objects are historical in this sense: to identify all the members of these American races over time, you cannot seek a single criterion that applies equally always; you can find the starting point for the race – the subcontinental source of the population of individuals that defines its initial membership – and then apply at each historical moment the criteria of intertemporal continuity that apply at that moment to decide which individuals in the next generation count as belonging to the group. There is from the very beginning until the present, at the heart of the system, a simple rule that very few would dispute even today: where both parents are of a single race, the child is of the same race as the parents.

The criteria applicable at any time may leave vague boundaries. They certainly change, as the varying decisions about what proportion of African ancestry made one black or the current uncertainty as to how to assign the children of white-yellow "miscegenation" demonstrate. But they always definitely assign some people to the group and definitely rule out others; and for most of America's history the class of people about whom there was uncertainty (are the Florida Seminoles black or Indian?) was relatively small.[7]

Once the racial label is applied to people, ideas about what it refers to, ideas that may be much less consensual than the application of the label, come to have their social effects. But they have not only social effects but psychological ones as well; and they shape the ways people conceive of themselves and their projects. In particular, the labels can operate to shape what I want to call "identification": the process through which an individual intentionally shapes her projects — including her plans for her own life and her conception of the good — by reference to available labels, available identities.

Identification is central to what Ian Hacking has called "making up people."[8] Drawing on a number of examples, but centrally homosexuality and multiple personality syndrome, he defends what he calls a "dynamic nominalism," which argues that "numerous kinds of human beings and human acts come into being hand in hand with our invention of the categories labeling them."[9] I have just articulated a dynamic nominalism about a kind of person that is currently usually called "African-American."

Hacking reminds us of the philosophical truism, whose most influential formulation is in Elizabeth Anscombe's work on intention, that in intentional action people act "under descriptions"; that their actions are conceptually shaped. It follows, of course, that what people can do depends on what concepts they have available to them; and among the concepts that may shape one's action is the concept of a certain kind of person and the behavior appropriate to that kind.

Hacking offers as an example Sartre's brilliant evocation, in *Being and Nothingness,* of the Parisian *garçon de café:* "His movement is quick and forward, a little too precise, a little too rapid. He comes toward the patrons with a step a little too quick. He bends forward a little too eagerly, his eyes express an interest too solicitous for the order of the customer."[10] Hacking comments:

> Sartre's antihero chose to be a waiter. Evidently that was not a possible choice in other places, other times. There are servile people in most societies, and servants in many, but a waiter is something specific, and a *garçon de café* more specific. . . .

> As with almost every way in which it is possible to be a person, it is possible to be a *garçon de café* only at a certain time, in a certain place, in a certain social setting. The feudal serf putting food on my lady's table can no more choose to be a *garçon de café* than he can choose to be lord of the manor. But the impossibility is evidently of a different kind.[11]

The idea of the *garçon de café* lacks, so far as I can see, the sort of theoretical commitments that are trailed by the idea of the black and the white, the homosexual and the heterosexual. So it makes no sense to ask of someone who has a job as a *garçon de café* whether that is what he really is. The point is not that we do not have expectations of the *garçon de café:* that is why it is a recognizable identity. It is rather that those expectations are about the performance of the role; they depend on our assumption of intentional conformity to those expectations. As I spent some time arguing earlier, we *can* ask whether someone is really of a black race, because the constitution of this identity is generally theoretically committed: we expect people of a certain race to behave a certain way not simply because they are conforming to the script for that identity, performing that role, but because they have certain antecedent properties that are consequences of the label's properly applying to them. It is because ascription of racial identities — the process of applying the label to people, including ourselves — is based on more than intentional identification that there can be a gap between what a person ascriptively is and the racial identity he performs: it is this gap that makes passing possible.

Race is, in this way, like all the major forms of identification that are central to contemporary identity politics: female and male; gay, lesbian, and straight; black, white, yellow, red, and brown; Jewish-, Italian-, Japanese-, and Korean-American; even that most neglected of American identities, class. There is, in all of them, a set of theoretically committed criteria for ascription, not all of which are held by everybody, and which may not be consistent with one another even in the ascriptions of a single person; and there is then a process of identification in which the label shapes the intentional acts of (some of) those who fall under it.

It does not follow from the fact that identification shapes action, shapes life plans, that the identification itself must be thought of as voluntary. I don't recall ever choosing to identify as a male;[12] but being male has shaped many of my plans and actions. In fact, where my ascriptive identity is one on which almost all my fellow citizens agree, I am likely to have little sense of choice about whether the identity is mine; though I *can* choose how central my identification with it will be — choose, that is, how much I will organize my life around that identity. Thus if I am among those (like the unhappily labeled "straight-acting gay men," or most American Jews) who are able, if they choose, to escape

I DON'T RECALL EVER CHOOSING TO IDENTIFY AS A MALE, BUT BEING MALE HAS SHAPED MANY OF MY PLANS AND ACTIONS.

ascription, I may choose not to take up a gay or a Jewish identity; though this will require concealing facts about myself or my ancestry from others.

If, on the other hand, I fall into the class of those for whom the consensus on ascription is not clear — as among contemporary so-called biracials, or bisexuals, or those many white Americans of multiple identifiable ethnic heritages[13] — I may have a sense of identity options: but one way I may exercise them is by marking myself ethnically (as when someone chooses to wear an Irish pin) so that others will then be more likely to ascribe that identity to me.

DIFFERENCES AMONG DIFFERENCES

Collective identities differ, of course, in lots of ways; the body is central to race, gender, and sexuality but not so central to class and ethnicity. And, to repeat an important point, racial identification is simply harder to resist than ethnic identification. The reason is twofold. First, racial ascription is more socially salient: unless you are morphologically atypical for your racial group, strangers, friends, officials are always aware of it in public and private contexts, always notice it, almost never let it slip from view. Second — and again both in intimate settings and in public space — race is taken by so many more people to be the basis for treating people differentially. (In this respect, Jewish identity in America strikes me as being a long way along a line toward African-American identity: there are ways of speaking and acting and looking — and it matters very little whether they are "really" mostly cultural or mostly genetic — that are associated with being Jewish; and there are many people, white and black, Jewish and Gentile, for whom this identity is a central force in shaping their responses to others.)

This much about identification said, we can see that Du Bois's analytical problem was, in effect, that he believed that for racial labeling of this sort to have the obvious real effects that it did have — among them, crucially, his own identification with other black people and with Africa — there must be some real essence that held the race together. Our account of the history of the label reveals that this is a mistake: once we focus, as Du Bois almost saw, on the racial badge — the signifier rather than the signified, the word rather than the concept — we see both that the effects of the labeling are powerful and real and that false ideas, muddle and mistake and mischief, played a central role in determining both how the label was applied and to what purposes.

This, I believe, is why Du Bois so often found himself reduced, in his attempts to define race, to occult forces: if you look for a shared essence you won't get anything, so you'll come to believe you've missed it, because it is super-subtle, difficult to experience or identify: in short, mysterious. But if, as I say, you understand the sociohistorical process of construction of the race, you'll see that the label works despite the absence of an essence.

Perhaps, then, we can allow that what Du Bois was after was the idea of racial identity, which I shall roughly define as a label, R, associated with *ascriptions* by most people (where ascription involves descriptive criteria for applying the label); and *identifications* by those that fall under it (where identification implies a shaping role for the label in the intentional acts of the possessors, so that they sometimes act *as an* R), where there is a history of associating possessors of the label with an inherited racial essence (even if some who use the label no longer believe in racial essences).

In fact, we might argue that racial identities could persist even if nobody believed in racial essences, provided both ascription and identification continue.

There will be some who will object to my account that it does not give racism a central place in defining racial identity: it is obvious, I think, from the history I have explored, that racism has been central to the development of race theory. In that sense racism has been part of the story all along. But you might give an account of racial identity in which you counted nothing as a racial essence unless it implied a hierarchy among the races;[14] or unless the label played a role in racist practices. I have some sympathy with the former strategy; it would fit easily into my basic picture. To the latter strategy, however, I make the philosopher's objection that it confuses logical and causal priority: I have no doubt that racial theories grew up, in part, as rationalizations for mistreating blacks, Jews, Chinese, and various others. But I think it is useful to reserve the concept of racism, as opposed to ethnocentrism or simply inhumanity, for practices in which a race concept plays a central role. And I doubt you can explain racism without first explaining the race concept.

I *am* in sympathy, however, with an animating impulse behind such proposals, which is to make sure that here in America we do not have discussions of race in which racism disappears from view. As I pointed out, racial identification is hard to resist in part because racial ascription by others is so insistent; and its effects — especially, but by no means exclusively, the racist ones — are so hard to escape. It is obvious, I think, that the persistence of racism means that racial ascriptions have negative consequences for some and positive consequences for others — creating, in particular, the white-skin privilege that it is so easy for people who have it to forget; and it is clear, too, that for those who suffer from the negative consequences, racial identification is a predictable response, especially where the project it suggests is that the victims of racism should join together to resist it. I shall return later to some of the important moral consequences of present racism and the legacy of racisms of the past.

But before I do, I want to offer some grounds for preferring the account of racial identity I have proposed, which places racial essences at his heart, over some newer accounts that see racial identity as a species of cultural identity.

CULTURAL IDENTITY IN AN AGE OF MULTICULTURALISM

Most contemporary racial identification — whether it occurs in such obviously regressive forms as the white nationalism of the Aryan Nation or in an Afrocentrism about which, I believe, a more nuanced position is appropriate — most naturally expresses itself in forms that adhere to modified (and sometimes unreconstructed) versions of the old racial essences. But the legacy of the Holocaust and the old racist biology has led many to be wary of racial essences and to replace them with cultural essences. Before I turn to my final cautionary words about racial identifications, I want to explore, for a moment, the substitution of cultures for races that has occurred in the movement for multiculturalism.

In my dictionary I find as a definition for "culture" "the totality of socially transmitted behavior patterns, arts, beliefs, institutions, and all other products of human work and thought."[15] Like most dictionary definitions, this is, no doubt, a proposal on which one could improve. But it surely picks out a familiar constellation of ideas. That is, in fact, the sense in which anthropologists largely use the term nowadays. The culture of the Asante or the Zuni, for the anthropologist, includes every object they make — material culture — and everything they think and do.

The dictionary definition could have stopped there, leaving out the talk of "socially transmitted behavior patterns, arts, beliefs, institutions" because these *are* all products of human work and thought. They are mentioned because they are the residue of an older idea of culture than the anthropological one; something more like the idea we might now express with the word "civilization": the "socially transmitted behavior patterns" of ritual, etiquette, religion, games, arts; the values that they engender and reflect; and the institutions — family, school, church, state — that shape and are shaped by them.[16] The habit of shaking hands at meetings belongs to culture in the anthropologist's sense; the works of Sandro Botticelli and Martin Buber and Count Basie belong to culture also, but they belong to civilization as well.

There are tensions between the concepts of culture and of civilization. There is nothing, for example, that requires that an American culture should be a totality in any stronger sense than being the sum of all the things we make and do.

American civilization, on the other hand, would have to have a certain coherence. Some of what is done in America by Americans would not belong to American civilization because it was too individual (the particular bedtime rituals of a particular American family); some would not belong because it was not properly American, because (like a Hindi sentence, spoken in America) it does not properly cohere with the rest.

The second, connected, difference between culture and civilization is that the latter takes values to be more central to the enterprise, in two ways. First, civilization is centrally defined by moral and aesthetic values: and the coherence of a civilization is, primarily, the coherence of those values with each other and, then, of the group's behavior and institutions with its values. Second, civilizations are essentially to be evaluated: they can be better and worse, richer and poorer, more and less interesting. Anthropologists, on the whole, tend now to avoid the relative evaluation of cultures, adopting a sort of cultural relativism, whose coherence philosophers have tended to doubt. And they do not take values as more central to culture than, for example, beliefs, ideas, and practices.

The move from "civilization" to "culture" was the result of arguments. The move away from evaluation came first, once people recognized that much evaluation of other cultures by the Europeans and Americans who invented anthropology had been both ignorant and biased. Earlier criticisms of "lower" peoples turned out to involve crucial misunderstandings of their ideas; and it eventually seemed clear enough, too, that nothing more than differences of upbringing underlay the distaste of some Westerners for unfamiliar habits. It is a poor move from recognizing certain evaluations as mistaken to giving up evaluation altogether, and anthropologists who adopt cultural relativism often preach more than practice it. Still, this cultural relativism was a response to real errors. That it is the wrong response doesn't make the errors any less erroneous.

The arguments against "civilization" were in place well before the midcentury. More recently, anthropologists began to see that the idea of the coherence of a civilization got in the way of understanding important facts about other societies (and, in the end, about our own). For even in some of the "simplest" societies, there are different values and practices and beliefs and interests associated with different social groups (for example, women as opposed to men). To think of a civilization as coherent was to miss the fact that these different values and beliefs were not merely different but actually opposed. Worse, what had been presented as the coherent unified worldview of a tribal people often turned out, on later inspection, to be merely the ideology of a dominant group or interest.

But the very idea of a coherent structure of beliefs and values and practices depends on a model of culture that does not fit our times — as we can see if we explore, for a moment, the ideal type of a culture where it might seem to be appropriate.

A COMMON CULTURE

There is an ideal — and thus to a certain extent imaginary — type of small-scale, technologically uncomplicated, face-to-face society, where most interactions are with people whom you know, that we call "traditional." In such a society every adult who is not mentally disabled speaks the same language. All share a vocabulary and a grammar and an accent. While there will be some words in the language that are not known by everybody — the names of medicinal herbs, the language of some religious rituals — most are known to all normal adults. To share a language is to participate in a complex set of mutual expectations and understandings: but in such a society it is not only linguistic behavior that is coordinated through universally known expectations and understandings. People will share an understanding of many practices — marriages, funerals, other rites of passage — and will largely share their views about the general workings not only of the social but also of the natural world. Even those who are skeptical about particular elements of belief will nevertheless know what everyone is supposed to believe, and they will know it in enough detail to behave very often as if they believed it, too.

A similar point applies to many of the values of such societies. It may well be that some people, even some groups, do not share the values that are enunciated in public and taught to children. But, once more, the standard values are universally known, and even those who do not share them know what it would be to act in conformity with them and probably do so much of the time.

In such a traditional society we may speak of these shared beliefs, values, signs, and symbols as the common culture; not, to insist on a crucial point, in the sense that everyone in the group actually holds the beliefs and values but in the sense that everybody knows what they are and everybody knows that they are widely held in the society.

Now, the citizens of one of those large "imagined communities" of modernity we call "nations" need not have, in this sense, a common culture. There is no single shared body of ideas and practices in India, or, to take another example, in most contemporary African states. And there is not now and there has never been a common culture in the United States, either. The reason is simple: the United States has always been multilingual, and has always had minorities who did not speak or understand English. It has always had a plurality of religious traditions; beginning with American Indian religious and Puritans and Catholics and Jews and including now many varieties of Islam, Buddhism, Jainism, Taoism, Bahai, and so on. And many of these religious traditions have been quite unknown to one another. More than this, Americans have also always differed significantly even among those who do speak English, from North to South and East to West, and from country to city, in customs of greeting, notions of civility, and a whole host of other ways. The notion that what has held the United States together historically over its great geographical range is a common culture, like the common culture of my traditional society, is — to put it politely — not sociologically plausible.

THERE IS NOT NOW AND THERE HAS NEVER BEEN A COMMON CULTURE IN THE UNITED STATES.

The observation that there is no common American national culture will come as a surprise to many: observations about American culture, taken as a whole, are common. It is, for example, held to be individualist, litigious, racially obsessed. I think each of these claims is actually true, because what I mean when I say there is no common culture of the United States is not what is denied by someone who says that there is an American culture.

Such a person is describing large-scale tendencies within American life that are not necessarily participated in by all Americans. I do not mean to deny that these exist. But for such a tendency to be part of what I am calling the *common culture* they would have to derive from beliefs and values and practices (almost) universally shared and known to be so. And *that* they are not.

At the same time, it has also always been true that there was a dominant culture in these United States. It was Christian, it spoke English, and it identified with the high cultural traditions of Europe and, more particularly, of England. This dominant culture included much of the common culture of the dominant classes — the government and business and cultural elites — but it was familiar to many others who were subordinate to them. And it was not merely an effect but also an instrument of their domination.

The United States of America, then, has always been a society of many common cultures, which I will call, for convenience, sub-cultures, (noting, for the record, that this is not the way the word is used in sociology).

It would be natural, in the current climate, with its talk of multiculturalism, to assume that the primary subgroups to which these subcultures are attached will be ethnic and racial groups (with religious denominations conceived of as a species of ethnic group). It would be natural, too, to think that the characteristic difficulties of a multicultural society arise largely from the cultural differences between ethnic groups. I think this easy assimilation of ethnic and racial subgroups to subcultures is to be resisted.

First of all, it needs to be argued, and not simply assumed, that black Americans, say, taken as a group, *have* a common culture: values and beliefs and practices that they share and that they do not share with others. This is equally true for, say, Chinese-Americans; and it is a fortiori true of white Americans. What seems clear enough is that being an African-American or an Asian-American or white is an important social identity in the United States. Whether these are important social identities because these groups have shared common cultures is, on the other hand, quite doubtful, not least because it is doubtful whether they *have* common cultures at all.

The issue is important because an analysis of America's struggle with difference as a struggle among cultures suggests a mistaken analysis of how the problems of diversity arise. With differing cultures, we might expect misunderstandings arising out of ignorance of each others' values, practices, and beliefs; we might even expect conflicts because of differing values or beliefs. The paradigms of difficulty in a society of many cultures are misunderstandings of a word or a gesture; conflicts over who should take custody of the children after a divorce; whether to go the doctor or to the priest for healing.

Once we move from talking of cultures to identities whole new kinds of problems come into view. Racial and ethnic identities are, for example, essentially contrastive and relate centrally to social and political power; in this way they are like genders and sexualities.

Now, it is crucial to understanding gender and sexuality that women and men and gay and straight people grow up together in families, communities, denominations. Insofar as a common culture means common beliefs, values, and practices, gay people and straight people in most places have a common culture: and while there are societies in which the socialization of children is so structured by gender that women and men have seriously distinct cultures, this is not a feature of most "modern" societies. And it is perfectly possible for a black and a white American to grow up together in a shared adoptive family — with the same knowledge and values — and still grow into separate racial identities, in part because their experience outside the family, in public space, is bound to be racially differentiated.

I have insisted that we should distinguish between cultures and identities; but ethnic identities characteristically have cultural distinctions as one of their primary marks. That is why it is so easy to conflate them. Ethnic identities are created in family and community life. These — along with mass-mediated culture, the school, and the college — are, for most of us, the central sites of the social transmission of culture. Distinct practices, ideas, norms go with each ethnicity in part because people *want* to be ethnically distinct: because many people want the sense of solidarity that comes from being unlike others. With ethnicity in modern society, it is often the distinct identity that comes first, and the cultural distinction that is created and maintained because of it — not the other way around. The distinctive common cultures of ethnic and religious identities matter not simply because of their contents but also as markers of those identities.

I HAVE INSISTED THAT WE SHOULD DISTINGUISH BETWEEN CULTURES AND IDENTITIES. . . .

In the United States, not only ethnic but also racial boundaries are culturally marked. In *White Women, Race Matters: The Social Construction of Whiteness,*[17] Ruth Frankenberg records the anxiety of many white women who do not see themselves as white "ethnics" and worry, therefore, that they have no culture.[18] This is somewhat puzzling in people who live, as every normal human being does, in rich structures of knowledge, experience, value and meaning; through tastes and practices: it is perplexing, in short, in people with normal human lives. But the reason these women do not recognize that they have a culture is because none of these things that actually make up their cultural lives are marked as white, as belonging specially to them: and the things that *are* marked as white (racism, white privilege) are things they want to repudiate. Many African-Americans, on the other hand, have cultural lives in which the ways they eat, the churches they go to, the music they listen to, and the ways they speak *are* marked as black: their identities are marked by cultural differences.

I have insisted that African-Americans do not have a single culture, in the sense of shared language, values, practices, and meanings. But many people who think of races as groups defined by shared cultures, conceive that sharing in a different way. They understand black people as sharing black culture *by definition:* jazz or hip-hop belongs to an African-American, whether she likes it or knows anything about it, because it is culturally marked as black. Jazz belongs to a black person who knows nothing about it more fully or naturally than it does to a white jazzman.

WHAT MATTERS ABOUT CULTURE: ARNOLD AGAIN

This view is an instance of what my friend Skip Gates has called "cultural geneticism."[19] It has, in Bertrand Russell's wicked phrase, "the virtues of theft over honest toil." On this view, you earn rights to culture that is marked with the mark of your race — or your nation — simply by having a racial identity. For the old racialists, as we saw, your racial character was something that came with your essence; this new view recognizes that race does not bring culture, and generously offers, by the wave of a wand, to correct Nature's omission. It is as generous to whites as it is to blacks. Because Homer and Shakespeare are products of Western culture, they are awarded to white children who have never studied a word of them, never heard their names. And in this generous spirit the fact is forgotten that cultural geneticism deprives white people of jazz and black people of Shakespeare. This is a bad deal — as Du Bois would have insisted. "I sit with Shakespeare," the Bard of Great Barrington wrote, "and he winces not."

There is nothing in cultural geneticism of the ambition or the rigor of Matthew Arnold's conception, where culture is, as he says in *Culture and Anarchy,* "the disinterested and active use of reading, reflection and observation,"[20] and what is most valuable to us in culture, in the anthropological sense, is earned by intellectual labor, by self-cultivation. For Arnold, true culture is a process "which consists in becoming something rather than in having something, in an inward condition of the mind and spirit";[21] whose aim is a "perfection in which characters of beauty and intelligence are both present, which unites, 'the two noblest of things,' — as Swift, who of one of the two, at any rate, had himself all too little, most happily calls them in his *Battle of the Books,* — 'the two noblest of things, sweetness and light.'"[22]

Arnold's aim is not, in the proper sense, an elitist one: he believes that this cultivation is the proper aim of us all.

> This is the *social idea;* and the men of culture are the true apostles of equality. The great men of culture are those who have had a passion for diffusing, for making prevail, for carrying from one end of society to the other, the best knowledge, the best ideas of their time; who have laboured to divest knowledge of all that was harsh, uncouth, difficult, abstract, professional, exclusive; to humanise it, to make it efficient outside the clique of the cultivated and learned, yet still remaining the *best* knowledge and thought of the time, and a true source, therefore, of sweetness and light.[23]

If you have this view of culture, you will think of cultural geneticism as the doctrine of the ignorant or the lazy, or at least of those who pander to them. And it is a view of culture whose adoption would diminish any society that seriously adopted it.

Not only is the conflation of identities and cultures mistaken, the view of cultural possession that underlies that error is the view of the Philistine, who, in Arnold's translation of Epictetus, makes "a great fuss about exercise, a great fuss about eating, a great fuss about drinking, a great fuss about walking, a great fuss about riding. All these things ought to be done merely *by the way:* the formation of the spirit and character must be our real concern."[24]

IDENTITIES AND NORMS

I have been exploring these questions about culture in order to show how unsatisfactory an account of the significance of race that mistakes identity for culture can be. But if this is the wrong route from identity to moral and political concerns, is there a better way?

We need to go back to the analysis of racial identities. While the theories on which ascription is based need not themselves be normative, these identities come with normative as well as descriptive expectations; about which, once more, there may be both inconsistency in the thinking of individuals and fairly widespread disagreement among them. There is, for example, a very wide range of opinions among American Jews as to what their being Jewish commits them to; and while most Gentiles probably don't think about the matter very much, people often make remarks that suggest they admire the way in which, as they believe, Jews have "stuck together," an admiration that seems to presuppose the moral idea that it is, if not morally obligatory, then at least morally desirable, for those who share identities to take responsibility for each other. (Similar comments have been made increasingly often about Korean-Americans.)

We need, in short, to be clear that the relation between identities and moral life are complex. In the liberal tradition, to which I adhere, we see public morality as engaging each of us as individuals with our individuals "identities": and we have the notion, which comes (as Charles Taylor has rightly argued[25]) from the ethics of authenticity, that, other things being equal, people have the right to be acknowledged publicly as what they already really are. It is because someone is already authentically Jewish or gay that we deny them something in requiring them to hide this fact, to "pass," as we say, for something that they are not. Charles Taylor has suggested that we call the political issues raised by this fact the politics of recognition: a politics that asks us to acknowledge socially and politically the authentic identities of others.

IF WHAT MATTERS ABOUT ME IS MY INDIVIDUAL AND AUTHENTIC SELF, WHY IS SO MUCH CONTEMPORARY TALK OF IDENTITY ABOUT LARGE CATEGORIES — RACE, GENDER, ETHNICITY, NATIONALITY, SEXUALITY — THAT SEEM SO FAR FROM INDIVIDUAL?

As has often been pointed out, however, the way much discussion of recognition proceeds is strangely at odds with the individualist thrust of talk of authenticity and identity. If what matters about me is my individual and authentic self, why is so much contemporary talk of identity about large categories — race, gender, ethnicity, nationality, sexuality — that seem so far from individual? What is the relation between this collective language and the individualist thrust of the modern notion of the self? How has social life come to be so bound up with an idea of identity that has deep roots in romanticism with its celebration of the individual over against society?[26]

The connection between individual identity, on the one hand, and race and other collective identities, on the other, seems to be something like this: each person's individual identity is seen as having two major dimensions. There is a collective dimension, the intersection of her collective identities; and there is what I will call a personal dimension, consisting of other socially or morally important features of the person—intelligence, charm, wit, cupidity—that are not themselves the basis of forms of collective identity.

The distinction between these two dimensions of identity is, so to speak, a sociological rather than a logical distinction. In each dimension we are talking about properties that are important for social life. But only the collective identities count as social categories, kinds of person. There is a logical category but no social category of the witty, or the clever, or the charming, or the greedy: people who share these properties do not constitute a social group, in the relevant sense. The concept of authenticity is central to the connection between these two dimensions; and there is a problem in many current understandings of that relationship, a misunderstanding one can find, for example, in Charles Taylor's recent (brilliant) essay *Multiculturalism and the Politics of Recognition.*

AUTHENTICITY

Taylor captures the ideal of authenticity in a few elegant sentences: "There is a certain way of being that is *my* way. I am called upon to live my life in this way. . . . If I am not [true to myself], I miss the point of my life."[27] To elicit the problem, here, let me start with a point Taylor makes in passing about Herder: "I should note here that Herder applied his concept of originality at two levels, not only to the individual person among other persons, but also to the culture-bearing people among other peoples. Just like individuals, a Volk should be true to itself, that is, its own culture."[28] It seems to me that in this way of framing the issue less attention than necessary is paid to the connection between the originality of persons and of nations. After all, in many places nowadays, the individual identity, whose authenticity screams out for recognition, is likely to have an ethnic identity (which Herder would have seen as a national identity) as a component of its collective dimension. It is, among other things, my being, say, an African-American that shapes the authentic self that I seek to express.[29] And it is, in part, because I seek to express my self that I seek recognition of an African-American identity. This is the fact that makes problems: for recognition as an African-American means social acknowledgment of that collective identity, which requires not just recognizing its existence but actually demonstrating respect for it. If, in understanding myself as African-American, I see myself as resisting white norms, mainstream

American conventions, the racism (and, perhaps, the materialism or the individualism) of "white culture," why should I at the same time seek recognition from these white others?

There is, in other words, at least an irony in the way in which an ideal — you will recognize it if I call it the bohemian ideal — in which authenticity requires us to reject much that is conventional in our society is turned around and made the basis of a "politics of recognition."

Irony is not the bohemian's only problem. It seems to me that this notion of authenticity has built into it a series of errors of philosophical anthropology. It is, first of all, wrong in failing to see what Taylor so clearly recognizes, namely the way in which the self is, as he says, dialogically constituted. The rhetoric of authenticity proposes not only that I have a way of being that is all my own but that in developing it I must fight against the family, organized religion, society, the school, the state — all the forces of convention. This is wrong, however, not only because it is in dialogue with other people's understandings of who I am that I develop a conception of my own identity (Charles Taylor's point) but also because my identity is crucially constituted through concepts (and practices) made available to me by religion, society, school, and state, and mediated to varying degrees by the family (Hacking's point about "making up people"). Dialogue shapes the identity I develop as I grow up: but the very material out of which I form it is provided, in part, by my society, by what Taylor calls its language in "a broad sense."[30] I shall borrow and extend Taylor's term "monological" here to describe views of authenticity that make these connected errors.

I used the example of African-Americans just now, and it might seem that this complaint cannot be lodged against an American black nationalism: African-American identity, it might be said, is shaped by African-American society, culture, and religion. "It is dialogue with these black others that shapes the black self; it is from these black contexts that the concepts through which African-Americans shape themselves are derived. The white society, the white culture, over against which an African-American nationalism of the counterconventional kind poses itself, is therefore not part of what shapes the collective dimension of the individual identities of black people in the United States."

This claim is simply wrong. And what shows it is wrong is the fact that it is in part a recognition of a black identity by "white society" that is demanded by nationalism of this form. And "recognition" here means what Taylor means by it, not mere acknowledgment of one's existence. African-American identity, as I have argued, is centrally shaped by American society and institutions: it cannot be seen as constructed solely within African-American communities. African-American culture, if this means shared beliefs, values, practices, does not exist: what exists are African-American cultures, and though these are created and sustained in large measure by African-Americans, they cannot be understood without reference to the bearers of other American racial identities.

There is, I think, another error in the standard framing of authenticity as an ideal, and that is the philosophical realism (which is nowadays usually called "essentialism") that seems inherent in the way questions of authenticity are normally posed. Authenticity speaks of the real self buried in there, the self one has to dig out and express. It is only later, after romanticism, that the idea develops that one's self is something that one creates, makes up, so that every life should be an artwork whose creator is, in some sense, his or her own greatest creation. (This is, I suppose, an idea one of whose sources is Oscar Wilde; but it is surely very close to the self-cultivation that Arnold called "culture.")

Of course, neither the picture in which there is just an authentic nugget of selfhood, the core that is distinctively me, waiting to be dug out, nor the notion that I can simply make up any self I choose, should tempt us. We make up selves from a tool kit of options made available by our culture and society—in ways that I pointed out earlier. We do make choices, but we don't determine the options among which we choose.[31]

WE MAKE UP SELVES FROM A TOOL KIT OF OPTIONS MADE AVAILABLE BY OUR CULTURE AND SOCIETY . . . WE DO MAKE CHOICES, BUT WE DON'T DETERMINE THE OPTIONS AMONG WHICH WE CHOOSE.

If you agree with this, you will wonder how much of authenticity we should acknowledge in our political morality: and that will depend, I suppose, on whether an account of it can be developed that is neither essentialist nor monological.

It would be too large a claim that the identities that claim recognition in the multicultural chorus *must* be essentialist and monological. But it seems to me that one reasonable ground for suspicion of much contemporary multicultural talk is that the conceptions of collective identity they presuppose are indeed remarkably unsubtle in their understandings of the processes by which identities, both individual and collective, develop. The story I have told for African-American identity has a parallel for other collective identities: in all of them, I would argue, false theories play a central role in the application of the labels; in all of them the story is complex, involves "making up people," and cannot be explained by an appeal to an essence.

BEYOND IDENTITY

The large collective identities that call for recognition come with notions of how a proper person of that kind behaves: it is not that there is *one* way that blacks should behave, but that there are proper black modes of behavior. These notions provide loose norms or models, which play a role in shaping the life plans of those who make these collective identities central to their individual identities; of the identifications of those who fly under these banners.[32] Collective identities, in short, provide what we might call scripts: narratives that people can use in shaping their life plans and in telling their life stories. In our society (though not, perhaps, in the England of Addison and Steele) being witty does not in this way suggest the life script of "the wit." And that is why what I called the personal dimensions of identity work differently from the collective ones.

This is not just a point about modern Westerners: cross-culturally it matters to people that their lives have a certain narrative unity; they want to be able to tell a story of their lives that makes sense. The story—my story—should cohere in the way appropriate by the standards made available in my culture to a person of my identity. In telling that story, how I fit into the wider story of various collectivities is, for most of us, important. It is not just gender identities that give shape (through, for example, rites of passage into woman- or manhood) to one's life: ethnic and national identities too fit each individual story into a larger narrative. And some of the most "individualist" of individuals value such things. Hobbes spoke of the desire for glory as one of the dominating impulses of human beings, one that was bound to make trouble for social life. But glory can consist in fitting and being seen to fit into a collective history: and so, in the name of glory, one can end up doing the most social things of all.

CROSS-CULTURALLY IT MATTERS TO PEOPLE THAT THEIR LIVES HAVE A CERTAIN NARRATIVE UNITY; THEY WANT TO BE ABLE TO TELL A STORY OF THEIR LIVES THAT MAKES SENSE.

How does this general idea apply to our current situation in the multicultural West? We live in societies in which certain individuals have not been treated with equal dignity because they were, for example, women, homosexuals, blacks, Catholics. Because, as Taylor so persuasively argues, our identities are dialogically shaped, people who have these characteristics find them central—often, negatively central—to their identities. Nowadays there is a widespread agreement that the insults to their dignity and the limitations of their autonomy imposed in the name of these collective identities are seriously wrong. One form of healing of the self that those who have these identities participate in is learning to see these collective identities not as sources of limitation and insult but as a valuable part of what they centrally are. Because the ethics of authenticity requires us to express what we centrally are in our lives, they move next to the demand that they be recognized in social life as women, homosexuals, blacks, Catholics. Because there was no good reason to treat people of these sorts badly, and because the culture continues to provide degrading images of them nevertheless, they demand that we do cultural work to resist the stereotypes, to challenge the insults, to lift the restrictions.

These old restrictions suggested life scripts for the bearers of these identities, but they were negative ones. In order to construct a life with dignity, it seems natural to take the collective identity and construct positive life scripts instead.

An African-American after the Black Power movement takes the old script of self-hatred, the script in which he or she is a nigger, and works, in community with others, to construct a series of positive black life scripts. In these life scripts, being a Negro is recoded as being black: and this requires, among other things, refusing to assimilate to white norms of speech and behavior. And if one is to be black in a society that is racist then one has constantly to deal with assaults on one's dignity. In this context, insisting on the right to live a dignified life will not be enough. It will not even be enough to require that one be treated with equal dignity despite being black: for that will require a concession that being black counts naturally or to some degree against one's dignity. And so one will end up asking to be respected *as a black*.

I hope I seem sympathetic to this story. I *am* sympathetic. I see how the story goes. It may even be historically, strategically necessary for the story to go this way.[33] But I think we need to go on to the next necessary step, which is to ask whether the identities constructed in this way are ones we can all be happy with in the longer run. What demanding respect for people *as blacks* or *as gays* requires is that there be some scripts that go with being an African-American or having same-sex desires. There will be proper ways of being black and gay: there will be expectations to be met; demands will be made. It is at this point that someone who takes autonomy seriously will want to ask whether we have not replaced one kind of tyranny with another. If I had to choose between Uncle Tom and Black Power, I would, of course, choose the latter. But I would like not to have to choose. I would like other options. The politics of recognition requires that one's skin color, one's sexual body, should be politically acknowledged in ways that make it hard for those who want to treat their skin and their sexual body as personal dimensions of the self. And "personal" doesn't mean "secret" but "not too tightly scripted," "not too constrained by the demands and expectations of others."

IF I HAD TO CHOOSE BETWEEN UNCLE TOM AND BLACK POWER, I WOULD, OF COURSE, CHOOSE THE LATTER. BUT I WOULD LIKE NOT TO HAVE TO CHOOSE. I WOULD LIKE OTHER OPTIONS.

In short, so it seems to me, those who see potential for conflict between individual freedom and the politics of identity are right.

WHY DIFFERENCES BETWEEN GROUPS MATTER

But there is a different kind of worry about racial identities; one that has not to do with their being too tightly scripted but with a consequence of their very existence for social life. We can approach the problem by asking why differences between groups matter.

This is, I think, by no means obvious. If some minority groups — Korean-Americans, say — do especially well, most people feel, "More power to them." We worry, then, about the minorities that fail. And the main reason why people currently worry about minorities that fail is that group failure may be evidence of injustice to individuals. That is the respectable reason why there is so much interest in hypotheses, like those of Murray and Herrnstein, that suggest a different diagnosis. But let us suppose that we can get rid of what we might call Sowellian discrimination: discrimination, that is, as understood by Thomas Sowell, which is differential treatment based on false (or perhaps merely unwarranted) beliefs about the different average capacities of racial groups.[34]

Even without Sowellian discrimination socioeconomic disparities between groups threaten the fairness of our social arrangements. This issue can be kept clear only if we look at the matter from the point of view of an individual. Suppose I live in a society with two groups, blacks and whites. Suppose that, for whatever reason, the black group to which I obviously belong scores averagely low on a test that is genuinely predictive of job performance. Suppose the test is expensive. And suppose I would have, in fact, a high score on this test and that I would, in fact, perform well.[35] In these circumstances it may well be economically rational for an employer, knowing what group I belong to, simply not to give me the test, and thus not to hire me.[36] The employer has acted in a rational fashion; there is no Sowellian discrimination here. But most people will understand me if I say that I feel that this outcome is unfair. One way of putting the unfairness is to say, "What I can do and be with my talents is being held back because others, over whose failings I have no control, happen to have the characteristics they do."

Capitalism — like life — is full of such unfairness: luck — from lotteries to hurricanes — affects profit. And we can't get rid of all unfairness; for if we had perfect insurance, zero risk, there'd be no role for entrepreneurship, no markets, no capitalism. But we do think it proper to mitigate some risks. We think, for example, that we should do something about bad luck when it has large negative effects on individual people, or if it forces them below some socioeconomic baseline — we insure for car accidents, death, loss of home; the government helps those ruined by large-scale acts of God. We don't worry much about the chance production of small negative effects on individuals, even large numbers of individuals.

It is at least arguable that in our society the cost to competent, well-behaved individual blacks and Hispanics[37] of being constantly treated as if they have to measure up — the cost in stress, in anger, in lost opportunities — is pretty high.[38] It would be consistent with a general attitude of wanting to mitigate risks with large negative consequences for individuals to try to do something about it.[39]

This specific sort of unfairness — where a person is atypically competent in a group that is averagely less competent — is the result, among other things, of the fact that jobs are allocated by a profit-driven economy and the fact that I was born into a group in which I am atypical. The latter fact may or may not be the consequence of policies adopted by this society. Let's suppose it isn't: so society isn't, so to speak, causally responsible. According to some — for example, Thomas Sowell, again — that means it isn't morally responsible, either: you don't have to fix what you didn't break.

I'm not so sure. First, we can take collective responsibility, "as a society," for harms we didn't cause; as is recognized in the Americans with Disabilities Act. But second, the labor market is, after all, an institution: in a modern society it is kept in place by such arrangements as the laws of contract, the institution of money, laws creating and protecting private property, health and safety at work, and equal employment laws. Sowell may disapprove of some of these, but he can't disapprove of all of them; without all of them, there'd be no capitalism. So the outcome is the result not only of my bad luck but of its interaction with social arrangements, which could be different.

Thus once we grasp the unfairness of this situation, people might feel that something should be done about it. One possible thing would be to try to make sure there were no ethnic minorities significantly below norm in valuable skills. If the explanation for most significant differences between groups is not hereditary, this could be done, in part, by adopting policies that discouraged significant ethnic differentiation, which would gradually produce assimilation to a single cultural norm. Or it could be done by devoting resources most actively to the training of members of disadvantaged groups.

Another — more modest — move would be to pay special attention to finding talented members of minority groups who would not be found when employers were guided purely by profit.

A third — granted once more that the differences in question are not largely hereditary — would be to explore why there are such differences and to make known to people ways of giving themselves or their children whatever aptitudes will maximize their life chances, given their hereditary endowments.

Fourth, and finally, for those differences that were hereditary it would be possible to do research to seek to remedy the initial distribution by the genetic lottery — as we have done in making it possible for those without natural resistance to live in areas where malaria and yellow fever are endemic.

Each of these strategies would cost something, and the costs would be not only financial. Many people believe that the global homogenization of culture impoverishes the cultural fabric of our lives. It is a sentiment, indeed, we find in Arnold: "My brother Saxons have, as is well known, a terrible way with them of wanting to improve everything but themselves off the face of the earth; I have no passion for finding nothing but myself everywhere; I like variety to exist and to show itself to me, and I would not for the world have the lineaments of the Celtic genius lost."[40] The first strategy — of cultural assimilation — would undoubtedly escalate that process. And all these strategies would require more knowledge than we now have to apply in actual cases so as to guarantee their success. Anyone who shares my sense that there is an unfairness here to be met, an unfairness that has something to do with the idea that what matters is individual merit, should be interested in developing that kind of knowledge.

But I want to focus for a moment on a general effect of these four strategies. They would all produce a population less various in some of the respects that make a difference to major socioeconomic indicators. This would not mean that everybody would be the same as everybody else — but it could lead to a more recreational conception of racial identity. It would make African-American identity more like Irish-American identity is for most of those who care to keep the label. And that would allow us to resist one persistent feature of ethnoracial identities: that they risk becoming the obsessive focus, the be-all and end-all, of the lives of those who identify with them. They lead people to forget that their individual identities are complex and multifarious — that they have enthusiasms that do not flow from their race or ethnicity, interests and tastes that cross ethnoracial boundaries, that they have occupations or professions, are fans of clubs and groups. And they then lead them, in obliterating the identities they share with people outside their race or ethnicity, away from the possibility of identification with Others. Collective identities have a tendency, if I may coin a phrase, to "go imperial," dominating not only people of other identities, but the other identities, whose shape is exactly what makes each of us what we individually and distinctively are.

COLLECTIVE IDENTITIES HAVE A TENDENCY, IF I MAY COIN A PHRASE, TO "GO IMPERIAL" . . .

In policing this imperialism of identity — an imperialism as visible in racial identities as anywhere else — it is crucial to remember always that we are not simply black or white or yellow or brown, gay or straight or bisexual, Jewish, Christian, Moslem, Buddhist, or Confucian but that we are also brothers and sisters; parents and children; liberals, conservatives, and leftists; teachers and lawyers and auto-makers and gardeners; fans of the Padres and the Bruins; amateurs of grunge rock and lovers of Wagner; movie buffs; MTV-holics, mystery-readers; surfers and singers; poets and pet-lovers; students and teachers; friends and lovers. Racial identity can be the basis of resistance to racism; but even as we struggle against racism — and though we have made great progress, we have further still to go — let us not let our racial identities subject us to new tyrannies.

IN CONCLUSION

Much of what I have had to say in this essay will, no doubt, seem negative. It is true that I have defended an analytical notion of racial identity, but I have gone to worry about too hearty an endorsement of racial identification. Let me quote Matthew Arnold again, for the last time: "I thought, and I still think, that in this [Celtic] controversy, as in other controversies, it is most desirable both to believe and to profess that the work of construction is the fruitful and important work, and that we are demolishing only to prepare for it."[41] So here are my positive proposals: live with fractured identities; engage in identity play; find solidarity, yes, but recognize contingency, and, above all, practice irony.[42] In short I have only the proposals of a banal "postmodernism." And there is a regular response to these ideas from those who speak for the identities that now demand recognition, identities toward which so many people have struggled in dealing with the obstacles created by sexism, racism, homophobia. "It's all very well for you. You academics live a privileged life; you have steady jobs; solid incomes; status from your place in maintaining cultural capital. Trifle with your own identities, if you like; but leave mine alone."

To which I answer only: my job as an intellectual is to call it as I see it. I owe my fellow citizens respect, certainly, but not a feigned acquiescence. I have a duty to reflect on the probable consequences of what I say; and then, if I still think it worth saying, to accept responsibility for them. If I am wrong, I say, you do not need to plead that I should tolerate error for the sake of human liberation; you need only correct me. But if I am right, so it seems to me, there is a work of the imagination that we need to begin.

And so I look forward to taking up, along with others, the fruitful imaginative work of constructing collective identities for a democratic nation in a world of democratic nations; work that must go hand in hand with cultivating democracy here and encouraging it everywhere else. About the identities that will be useful in this project, let me say only this: the identities we need will have to recognize *both* the centrality of difference within human identity *and* the fundamental moral unity of humanity.

NOTES

1 This claim was prompted by G. Spiller, ed., *Papers in Inter-Racial Problems Communicated to the First Universal Races Congress Held at the University of London, July 26–29, 1911* (London: P. S. King and Son, 1911). Republished with an introduction by H. Aptheker (Secaucus, N.J.: Citadel Press, 1970).

2 W.E.B. Du Bois, "Races," in *Writings in Periodicals Edited by W.E.B. Du Bois, Vol. 1, 1911–1925,* compiled and edited by Herbert Aptheker (Milwood, N.Y.: Kraus-Thomson Organization Limited, 1983), p. 13.

3 Ibid., p. 14.

4 "The Uncompleted Argument: Du Bois and the Illusion of Race," reprinted from *Critical Inquiry* 12 (Autumn 1985). In *"Race," Writing and Difference,* ed. Henry Louis Gates, Jr. (Chicago: University of Chicago Press, 1986), pp. 21–37. Lucius Outlaw has remonstrated with me about this in the past; these rethinkings are prompted largely by discussion with him.

5 Du Bois, *Dusk of Dawn: An Essay toward an Autobiography of a Race Concept* (New York: Harcourt, Brace, 1940). Reprinted with introduction by Herbert Aptheker (Milwood, N.Y.: Kraus-Thomson Organization Limited, 1975), pp. 116–17.

6 I am conscious here of having been pushed to rethink my views by Stuart Hall's Du Bois lectures at Harvard in the spring of 1994, which began with a nuanced critique of my earlier work on Du Bois's views.

7 See Kevin Mulroy, *Freedom on the Border: The Seminole Maroons in Florida, the Indian Territory, Coahuila, and Texas* (Lubbock, Tex.: Texas Tech University Press, 1993).

8 Ian Hacking, "Making Up People" reprinted from *Reconstructing Individualism: Autonomy, Individuality and the Self in Western Thought,* ed. Thomas Heller, Morton Sousa, and David Wellbery (Stanford: Stanford University Press, 1986), in *Forms of Desire: Sexual Orientation and the Social Constructionist Controversy,* ed. Edward Stein (New York: Routledge, 1992), pp. 69–88 (page references are to this version).

9 Hacking, "Making Up People," p. 87.

10 Cited in ibid., p. 81.

11 Ibid., p. 82.

12 That I don't recall it doesn't *prove* that I didn't, of course.

13 See Mary C. Waters, *Ethnic Options: Choosing Identities in America* (Berkeley and Los Angeles: University of California Press, 1990).

[14] This is the proposal of a paper on metaphysical racism by Berel Lang at the New School for Social Research seminar "Race and Philosophy" in October 1994, from which I learned much.

[15] *American Heritage Dictionary III for DOS* (3d ed.) (Novato, Calif.: Word-star International Incorporated, 1993).

[16] The distinction between culture and civilization I am marking is not one that would have been thus marked in nineteenth-century ethnography or (as we would now say) social anthropology: culture and civilization were basically synonyms, and they were both primarily used in the singular. The distinctions I am making draw on what I take to be the contemporary resonances of these two words. If I had more time, I would explore the history of the culture concept the sort of way we have explored "race."

[17] Ruth Frankenberg, *White Women, Race Matters: The Social Construction of Whiteness* (Minneapolis: University of Minnesota Press, 1993).

[18] The discussion of this work is shaped by conversation with Larry Blum, Martha Minow, David Wilkins, and David Wong.

[19] Gates means the notion to cover thinking in terms of cultural patrimony quite generally, not just in the case of race. See Henry Louis Gates, Jr., *Loose Canons* (New York: Oxford University Press, 1993).

[20] Arnold, *Culture and Anarchy,* p. 119.

[21] Ibid., p. 33.

[22] Ibid., p.37.

[23] Ibid., p. 48. The phrase "sweetness and light" is from Jonathan Swift's *Battle of the Books* (1697). The contest between the ancients (represented there by the bee) and the moderns (represented by the spider) is won by the ancients, who provide, like the bee, both honey and wax—sweetness and light. Sweetness is, then, aesthetic, and light intellectual, perfection.

[24] Arnold, *Culture and Anarchy,* p. 36.

[25] Charles Taylor, *Multiculturalism and "The Politics of Recognition."* With commentary by Amy Gutmann, ed., K. Anthony Appiah, Jürgen Habermas, Steven C. Rockefeller, Michael Walzer, and Susan Wolf (Princeton: Princeton University Press, 1994).

[26] Taylor reminds us rightly of Trilling's profound contributions to our understanding of this history. I discuss Trilling's work in chap. 4 of *In My Father's House.*

[27] Taylor, *Multiculturalism,* p. 30.

[28] Ibid., p. 31.

[29] And, for Herder, this would be a paradigmatic national identity.

[30] The broad sense "cover[s] not only the words we speak, but also other modes of expression whereby we define ourselves, including the 'languages' of art, of gesture, of love, and the like" (p. 32).

[31] This is too simple, too, for reasons captured in Anthony Giddens's many discussions of "duality of structure."

[32] I say "make" here not because I think there is always conscious attention to the shaping of life plans or a substantial experience of choice but because I want to stress the antiessentialist point that there are choices that can be made.

[33] Compare what Sartre wrote in his "Orphée Noir," in *Anthologie de la Nouvelle Poésie Nègre et Malagache de Langue Francaise,* ed. L. S. Senghor, p. xiv. Sartre argued, in effect, that this move is a necessary step in a dialectical progression. In this passage he explicitly argues that what he calls an "antiracist racism" is a path to the "final unity . . . the abolition of differences of race."

[34] "Once the possibility of economic performance differences between groups is admitted, then differences in income, occupational 'representation,' and the like do not, in themselves, imply that decision-makers took race or ethnicity into account. However, in other cases, group membership may in fact be used as a proxy for economically meaningful variables, rather than reflecting either mistaken prejudices or even subjective affinities and animosities." Thomas Sowell, *Race and Culture,* p. 114.

[35] You need both these conditions, because a high score on a test that correlates well for some skill doesn't necessarily mean you will perform well. And, in fact, Sowell discusses the fact that the same IQ score predicts different levels of economic success for different ethnic groups; ibid., pp. 173, 182.

[36] Knowing this, I might offer to pay myself, if I had the money: but that makes the job worth less to me than to members of the other groups. So I lose out again.

[37] Let me explicitly point out that many of these people are not middle-class.

[38] I actually think that there is still rather more Sowellian discrimination than Sowell generally acknowledges; but that is another matter.

[39] It will seem to some that I've avoided an obvious argument here, which is that the inequalities in resources that result from differences in talents under capitalism need addressing. I agree. But the argument I am making here is meant to appeal to only extremely unradical individualist ideas; it's designed not to rely on arguing for egalitarian outcomes directly.

[40] Arnold, *On the Study of Celtic Literature,* p. 11.

[41] Ibid., p. ix.

[42] See, for example, Richard Rorty, *Contingency, Irony and Solidarity* (New York: Cambridge University Press, 1989), and my review of it: "Metaphys. Ed.," *Village Voice,* September 19, 1989, p. 55.

QUESTIONS FOR A SECOND READING

1. Appiah's essay is a reader-friendly one—that is, it goes out of its way to address, engage, anticipate, and assist its readers. This engagement is a *technical* feat; it is a strategy. It is the result of something Appiah *does* as a writer. His work suggests strategies that you, too, could adopt and use.

   Take note, for example, of the ways in which Appiah punctuates the text. Punctuation is often discussed in relation to the sentence. Writers use marks of punctuation (commas, dashes, colons, semicolons, parentheses) to organize sentences and to help readers locate themselves in relation to what they are reading. Writers also punctuate longer units of text, such as essays or chapters. Appiah's text provides an excellent model of this practice. You can notice immediately how he uses white space and subheadings to organize the essay into sections.

   There are also, however, many moments when Appiah speaks as a writer about the text he is writing (and that you are reading). He does this to remind you (and perhaps himself) where you have been and where you are going in relation to this long piece of writing. Here are some examples:

   > For reasons I shall be able to make clear only when I have given my account, Du Bois's own approach is somewhat misleading. So instead of proceeding with exegesis of Du Bois, I must turn next to the task of shaping a sociohistorical account of racial identity. (p. 42)

   > There will be some who will object to my account that it does not give racism a central place in defining racial identity. . . . (p. 47)

   > I shall return later to some of the important moral consequences of present racism and the legacy of racisms of the past. But before I do, I want to offer some grounds for preferring the account of racial identity I have proposed, which places racial essences at its heart, over some newer accounts that see racial identity as a species of cultural identity. (p. 47)

   > I have been exploring these questions about culture in order to show how unsatisfactory an account of the significance of race that mistakes identity for culture can be. But if this is the wrong route from identity to moral and political concerns, is there a better way? (p. 54)

   As you reread the text, take note of the places where Appiah is punctuating his essay—places where Appiah, as a writer, seems to have you, his reader, in mind.

2. Although this is a reader-friendly text, it is also a learned text. It contains casual references to writers and scholars whom you may not recognize:

W. E. B. Du Bois, Ian Hacking, Matthew Arnold, Charles Taylor, Thomas Sowell—to list just a few. Using the Internet as well as the library (so that you can put your hands on books and scholarly journals) and perhaps working in a group, create brief glosses on some of these writers and their work. Who are they? What are their concerns? And why might they be useful or interesting or important to Appiah?

3. We asked that you pay special attention to voice during your first reading of this essay. Remember that Appiah does not necessarily agree with all of the affirmative statements he makes—in many instances, he is instead exploring the potential consequences of a particular thought process or contention. In other instances, though, Appiah shifts back into his own voice and speaks for himself.

   Here, for example, is a moment when Appiah acknowledges the twist and turns of his methods. He has come to this position: "The notion that what has held the United States together historically over its great geographical range is a common culture . . . is—to put it politely—not sociologically plausible." He goes on:

   > The observation that there is no common American national culture will come as a surprise to many: observations about American culture, taken as a whole, are common. It is, for example, held to be individualist, litigious, racially obsessed. I think each of these claims is actually true, because what I mean when I say there is no common culture of the United States is not what is denied by someone who says that there is an American culture. (p. 50)

   As you reread, chart the moments when Appiah takes on (speaks from within) someone else's way of thinking and speaking. Also chart the moments when you feel he is finally speaking for himself. How do you know? When and where is Appiah most likely to come forward and to speak for himself?

4. In each section of his essay, Appiah works with key terms. He is the sort of philosopher who believes that in order to think better, we need to have a better command of our words, of the language we use to articulate what we know. Here are some clusters of terms from the essay: identity, identification, racial identity, racial identification, collective identities; culture, common culture, multiculturalism, civilization; narratives, scripts, life stories, authenticity; the politics of recognition, the politics of identity; freedom, tyranny, democracy.

   As you reread, take a particular term (or cluster of terms) that seems interesting, important, or compelling, and follow Appiah's use of this term (or cluster) through one of the subsections of the essay. Then, write a brief paragraph of translation. It could begin something like this: "In the section titled 'Cultural Identity in an Age of Multiculturalism,' Appiah talks about culture and civilization, and this is what I think he is trying to say. . . ." You might conclude: "This is important to him because. . . ."

5. As he prepares for the final section of his essay, Appiah offers a surprising list:

> In policing this imperialism of identity — an imperialism as visible in racial identities as anywhere else — it is crucial to remember always that we are not simply black or white or yellow or brown, gay or straight or bisexual, Jewish, Christian, Moslem, Buddhist, or Confucian but that we are also brothers and sisters; parents and children; liberals, conservatives and leftists; teachers and lawyers and automakers and gardeners; fans of the Padres and the Bruins; amateurs of grunge rock and lovers of Wagner; movie buffs; MTV-holics; mystery-readers; surfers and singers; poets and pet-lovers; students and teachers; friends and lovers. Racial identity can be the basis of resistance to racism; but even as we struggle against racism — and though we have made great progress, we have further still to go — let us not let our racial identities subject us to new tyrannies. (p. 62)

A list like that is a generous gesture. It invites additions; it invites *you* to join in. It is also a leveling gesture—Jewish or Christian, gay or straight, poets and pet-lovers, Padres and Bruins: all of these identity markers have equal status.

This long list is an invitation to, as Appiah advises, "engage in identity play." Retype the first part of the sentence, the words up to the "but" clause ("but that we are also. . . "), and then prepare your list. Your list should be a distinctive one that represents the range of identifications you might offer as working terms of identity. Think of the list as something you would present to the rest of the class.

When you are done with that sentence, take a minute to think about what your list represents—what it represents as an act, as a way of enacting as well as thinking about the "fruitful imaginative work of constructing collective identities for a democratic nation." (p. 63) Write out a short paragraph that you might offer as a response to Appiah's conclusion.

ASSIGNMENTS FOR WRITING

1. What might be the consequences of Appiah's argument? If, as a mental exercise (or because you are convinced), you follow Appiah's line of thought, what effects might this have on the ways you (or "we") think, act, speak, and write? What might change? How?

These questions offer a way to begin thinking about an essay. If you choose to write this essay, here is one approach to writing it.

Choose one or two of the essay's subsections and let them represent a line of argument. (Because the essay is long and complicated, it is difficult to work with in its entirety.) You'll need to bring this argument to your readers—smart people, but people who have not yet read "Racial Identities." To present Appiah's line of thinking, use a combination of summary, paraphrase, and block quotation. If you want to make reference to the shape of the entire essay, do so only in two or three sentences. Focus on the details in the subsection (or subsections) you have chosen as your point of focus.

Then, to make this project *your* project, and to make it an intellectual project (and not just a rehearsal of received opinion or an "I have a dream" speech), you will need to think carefully about something (an example, most likely) that you can bring to the discussion, something you can bring into conversation with the examples provided by Appiah. Think about this. The choice is important. For ideas, look to your reading (or viewing or listening), to your immediate experience, to the current institutional, political, or cultural scenes where you are or have been a player—look to situations that you know well.

Your account of Appiah's thinking will certainly be important to what you write, but equally important will be the example you provide. Your example will allow you to focus your attention to racial thinking as it is (or has been) most crucially and most interestingly present to you and to your generation or cohorts, to the people for whom you feel authorized to speak.

2. Consider this passage from "Racial Identities":

> Collective identities, in short, provide what we might call scripts: narratives that people can use in shaping their life plans and in telling their life stories. In our society (though not, perhaps, in the England of Addison and Steele) being witty does not in this way suggest the life script of "the wit." And that is why what I called the personal dimensions of identity work differently from the collective ones.
>
> This is not just a point about modern Westerners: cross-culturally it matters to people that their lives have a certain narrative unity; they want to be able to tell a story of their lives that makes sense. The story — my story — should cohere in the way appropriate by the standards made available in my culture to a person of my identity. In telling that story, how I fit into the wider story of various collectivities is, for most of us, important. (pp. 57–58)

Your project in this assignment is to consider the terms, the stages, the conclusions, and the consequences of Appiah's argument in his essay "Racial Identities." If, as a mental exercise (or because you are convinced), you accept Appiah's notion that "Collective identities, in short, provide what we might call scripts: narratives that people can use in shaping their life plans and in telling their life stories," (pp. 57–58) how might you tell a story that places yourself in relation to the available scripts, to the life stories available to a person like you—a person of your culture (or collectivity), a person of your age, now, in the second decade of the twenty-first century?

You are not required to write in the genre of the memoir (as though you were writing a chapter of your autobiography), but many find that doing so is an inviting way to begin. What a reader wants is a view of you and your world, not in the pen-pal sense of what you look like or what you prefer in music, but with the goal of understanding something more general, something about people like you, something about what it is that shapes and defines a person or an identity in this place and at this point in time. In Appiah's terms, your writing will negotiate the competing demands of a life and a "script," of the personal and the collective, of individual freedom and the politics of identity.

We are trying to avoid the word "essay" in describing this project, since that word carries certain generic restrictions. Our advice is for you to begin not with a generalization but with some specific scene or scenes. Begin with a story (or stories) rather than with an argument. If people are speaking, you may choose to let them speak as characters speak in fiction. You may write in the first person if you find it helpful to do so.

3. In the final section of his essay, "In Conclusion," Appiah says, "So here are my positive proposals: live with fractured identities; engage in identity play; find solidarity, yes, but recognize contingency, and, above all, practice irony." (p. 62)

   What might it mean to live a life in these terms? Write an essay in which you present Appiah's conclusion to readers (smart readers, interesting readers) who have not yet read Appiah's essay. Where do these positive proposals come from? What is at stake in putting them into play? Why does Appiah express them with such urgency?

   Write an essay in which you present Appiah's conclusion but where you also extend those conclusions to consider the contexts within which you hear and receive these proposals. Who else is telling you how to live your life? What advice is being provided to you? Where and by whom? What examples of appropriate conduct are offered to you by the culture — in books or movies, in magazines, or online? What forms of advice do you listen to or seek out? What uses or contexts can you imagine for words or phrases like "fractured identities," "identity play," "contingency," and "irony"?

   Appiah says, "If I am wrong, . . . you need only correct me. But if I am right, so it seems to me, there is a work of the imagination that we need to begin." (p. 63) With some particular examples in mind, what might you say in turn?

MAKING CONNECTIONS

1. Both John Edgar Wideman's "Our Time," (p. 422) and Kwame Anthony Appiah's "Racial Identities," call attention to the difficulties of representing and understanding the experience of those whom we call "African Americans" — the difficulty of telling their story, of getting it right, of recovering experience from the representations of others.

   Write an essay in which you represent these two texts as examples of writers working on a problem that has a particular urgency for all Americans, not just black Americans. How might you name this problem? What do you find compelling in each of these approaches to the problem? And what might this problem have to do with you — as a writer, a thinker, a person, and a citizen?

2. Both Kwame Anthony Appiah's "Racial Identities," and David Foster Wallace's "Authority and American Usage" (p. 388) have distinctive styles, voices, and methods. A character emerges in each essay, a figure representing one version of a well-schooled, learned and articulate adult, an intellectual—someone who reads widely, who thinks closely, freshly, and methodically about big questions, someone with ideas and with style, someone who is defined in relation to sources, to books, and other writers, and someone who takes pains to engage his readers. This is an intellectual, then, who has a desire to reach others, to address them, to bring them into his point of view.

   Write an essay in which you discuss the figure of the intellectual represented in these two essays. You'll need to work closely with a few key and representative moments in the texts. Your essay should assess this figure in relation to your own education—better yet, in relation to the kind of figure you intend to cut as a well-schooled adult, as an intellectual, as a person with ideas and knowledge and something to say.

3. In her essay "Evidence," (p. 362), Kathryn Schulz says:

   > Descartes was right to fear that this way of thinking ["believing things based on paltry evidence"] would cause us to make mistakes; it does. Since he was interested in knowing the truth, and knowing that he knew it, he tried to develop a model for thinking that could curtail the possibility of error. . . . In fact, curtailing error was the goal of most models of optimal human cognition proposed by most thinkers throughout most of history, and it is the goal behind our own broadly shared image of the ideal thinker. Some of these models, like Descartes', sought to curtail error through radical doubt. Others sought to curtail it through formal logic—using valued premises to derive necessarily valid conclusions. Others, including our shared one of the ideal thinker, seek to curtail it through a kind of general due diligence: careful attention to evidence and counter-evidence, coupled with a prudent avoidance of preconceived notions. (p. 364)

   "Due diligence," "a model for thinking," and the "ideal thinker." Over time, writing has been one of the ways human beings have tried to find forms and methods to represent (and preserve and transmit) models for thinking. You've received these models through instruction. Topic sentence, example, conclusion—these comprise a model for thinking. And every time you have been assigned something to read (and every time you have chosen something to read), you were presented with a "model for thinking," a model in practice.

   For this assignment, turn to Appiah's prose in "Racial Identities" as a case in point. How would you characterize his approach to belief and evidence? Schulz brings many examples into her essay. What might she do with Appiah? Where and how might his work fit into her argument?

You can speak generally, to be sure, but you should also work with two or three close examples, sections of the text that you can present to a reader by means of paraphrase and block quotation. Here you can see Appiah in action, modeling a way of thinking. How would you characterize this? How would you compare his style with Schulz's? Who, to you, comes closest to the "ideal thinker"?

ALISON Bechdel

Acclaimed writer and cartoonist Alison Bechdel was born in Lock Haven, Pennsylvania, in 1960. Bechdel rose to fame as the creator of the long-running comic strip *Dykes to Watch Out For*. The strip, which ran for twenty-five years, gained so much recognition that it was translated into five languages and appeared in over fifty publications around the world. In 2006, Bechdel published her first book, *Fun Home: A Family Tragicomic*. The book became an award-winning bestseller, a rare accomplishment for a book best described as a graphic memoir. Bechdel's work is both intimately biographical and intensely political. Through her cartoons, she takes on some complicated and contested subjects including family, sexuality, gender, and the difficult terrain of writing autobiographically in the first place. Bechdel's cartoons have appeared in numerous national venues—among them, *Slate, Entertainment Weekly, McSweeney's,* and the *New York Times Book Review*. She also guest edited the 2011 edition of the annual *Best American Comics* anthology.

The selection included here is from Alison Bechdel's most recent book, *Are You My Mother? A Comic Drama* (2012). Named a *New York Times* Notable Book of the Year and listed among *TIME*'s ten best nonfiction books of the year, *Are You My Mother?* explores Bechdel's complex relationship with her mother. The book also raises some deeply layered questions about why and how we become the individual selves we become. Ultimately, much of Bechdel's work is a chronicle of self and selves as she tries to capture, in her drawings, the rich possibility of each moment she offers her readers.

The book's title is taken from P. D. Eastman's popular children's book of the same name. In an interview with poet Sophie Mayer, Bechdel said, "Most people don't delve. Maybe because they're embarrassed. But it's what I want to talk about. I realized that my primary goal in life is to change." Bechdel is interested in psychoanalysis, in the composing process, and in the trajectory of one life as it intersects with others. "The Ordinary Devoted Mother," presented on the following pages, is the first chapter of *Are You My Mother?* The book opens with an epigraph from Virginia Woolf that reads: "For nothing was simply one thing."

1 The Ordinary Devoted Mother

WHILE ENGAGED IN SOME SORT OF HOME-IMPROVEMENT PROJECT, I INADVERTENTLY BLOCK MY EXIT FROM A DANK CELLAR.
SLAM!
clunk
I START TO PANIC.
THE ONLY WAY OUT IS TO SQUEEZE THROUGH THE SMALL, SPIDERY WINDOW.
!

I WALK ALONG THE BROOK, LOOKING FOR A PLACE TO CROSS.
THE STEPPING STONES ARE UNDERWATER.
THE POOL IS DEEP AND MURKY. IT'S WARM OUT. I'M NOT WEARING ANYTHING I NEED TO WORRY ABOUT GETTING WET.
I HAVE SOME CONCERN ABOUT THE DIRTY WATER...
..BUT THIS ONLY SLIGHTLY DIMINISHES A SUBLIME FEELING OF SURRENDER.

MOM...
THIS STORY BEGINS WHEN I BEGAN TO TELL ANOTHER STORY.
HANH HNNH
I HAD THE DREAM ABOUT THE BROOK RIGHT BEFORE I TOLD MY MOTHER I WAS WRITING A MEMOIR ABOUT MY FATHER.
...I HAVE SOMETHING TO TELL YOU.
MOM, I WANT TO TELL YOU SOME-THING.

THE EMOTION OF THE DREAM STUCK WITH ME FOR DAYS. I HAD GOTTEN MYSELF OUT OF A DEAD PLACE AND PLUNGED WITH BLIND TRUST INTO A VITAL, SENSUOUS ONE.
OKAY. THEN SHE'LL SAY, "WHAT?"
4
AND I'LL SAY...
WHAT? WHAT WILL YOU SAY, ALISON?
YOU SMARMY, SELF-INDULGENT, SOLIPSISTIC PIECE OF *SHIT.*
OKAY.
I'LL SAY, "I'M WRITING A BOOK ABOUT DAD."
AND SHE'LL SAY, **"WHAAAAT?!!"**
I'D HAD SOME PRACTICE IN TELLING MY MOTHER DIFFICULT THINGS.

I FELT KIND OF LIKE I DID TWENTY YEARS EARLIER, WHEN I WAS PREPARING TO TELL HER I WAS A LESBIAN.
WHY AM I TELLING HER AT ALL?
AND KIND OF LIKE I DID FIVE YEARS BEFORE THAT, WHEN I WAS WORKING UP THE COURAGE TO TELL HER I'D GOTTEN MY FIRST PERIOD. THAT HAD TAKEN ME SIX MONTHS.
OKAY, SO SHE MIGHT FREAK OUT AT FIRST, BUT THEN SHE'LL SAY, "WHY?"
THIS STORY--A MEMOIR ABOUT MY MOTHER--COULD BEGIN WITH EITHER OF THOSE SCENES.
UHH...IT'S JUST SOMETHING I NEED TO DO.
... AND SHE'LL SAY, "WHY?"
I WANT TO GIVE HIM A PROPER FUNERAL. I WANT TO TELL THE TRUTH.
BUT AS I CONSIDER MOVING THE BEGINNING FURTHER BACK IN TIME, BEFORE THE COMING OUT, BEFORE THE FIRST PERIOD...
Scranton
"THE TRUTH?!"
...I SEE THAT PERHAPS THE REAL PROBLEM WITH THIS MEMOIR ABOUT MY MOTHER IS THAT IT HAS NO BEGINNING.
YEAH. HIS BISEXUALITY, THE SUICIDE. YOU DON'T MIND, DO YOU?

SORT OF LIKE HOW I'D UNDERSTOOD HUMAN REPRODUCTION AS A CHILD. I WAS AN EGG INSIDE MY MOTHER WHEN SHE WAS STILL AN EGG INSIDE HER MOTHER, AND SO FORTH AND SO ON.
A DIZZYING, INFINITE REGRESS.
I DON'T WANT TO HURT YOU BUT I HAVE TO DO THIS.
ROAD WORK
THERE'S A CERTAIN RELIEF IN KNOWING THAT I AM A TERMINUS.
EVEN IF I'D EVER HAD THE SLIGHTEST URGE TO REPRODUCE, IT'S TOO LATE NOW. I'M RUNNING OUT OF EGGS.
MY CLOCKWORKLIKE MENSTRUAL CYCLE SKIPPED ITS FIRST BEAT THE VERY WEEK, IN MY FORTY-FIFTH YEAR, THAT I SAT DOWN TO BEGIN WRITING ABOUT MY MOTHER.
NO SHOULDER
I HOPE THAT IN TIME YOU'LL COME TO UNDERSTAND...
OF COURSE, THE POINT AT WHICH I BEGAN TO WRITE THE STORY IS NOT THE SAME AS THE POINT AT WHICH THE STORY BEGINS.
OH, THAT'S GOOD. SANCTIMONIOUS AND PATRONIZING.
YOU CAN'T LIVE AND WRITE AT THE SAME TIME.
?

JESUS!
AKT 849
YOU CRAZY FUCK!
!?

IT HAD BEEN A STROEHMANN SUNBEAM BREAD TRUCK THAT KILLED MY FATHER...
...THAT MY FATHER LIKELY JUMPED IN FRONT OF.
STROEHMANN
Sunbeam
BREAD
AFTER SUCH A CURIOUSLY LITERAL AND FIGURATIVE BRUSH WITH DEATH, TELLING MY MOTHER ABOUT THE BOOK LOOMED RATHER SMALLER.
AND A FEW DAYS LATER, RETURNING WITH HER FROM A STRING OF ERRANDS, I DID IT.
YOU MEAN, THIS IS SOMETHING YOU HAVE TO DO?
WELL, YEAH.
I CAN'T HELP YOU. YOU'RE ON YOUR OWN.

ON THE WHOLE, IT WENT AS WELL AS I COULD HAVE HOPED. MOM'S BOYFRIEND, BOB, CAME OVER FOR DINNER THAT NIGHT.
SHE SAYS IT'S SOMETHING SHE HAS TO DO.
AND YOU'RE OKAY WITH IT?
I FEEL RECKLESS. TELL EVERYONE.
I'M GONNA GO DO MY PUZZLE.
BOB IS A RETIRED PSYCHIATRIST. HE HAD SOME INSIGHT INTO MY BROOK DREAM.
WATER IS USUALLY ABOUT CREATIVITY. THAT SEEMS AUSPICIOUS FOR YOUR PROJECT.
I JUST HOPE IT WON'T BE ALL ANGRY, ALL ABOUT HOW AWFUL YOUR FATHER WAS.
THIS IS ONE OF MY DIFFICULTIES NOW...
...MY FEAR THAT MOM WILL FIND THIS MEMOIR ABOUT HER "ANGRY." ANOTHER DIFFICULTY IS THE FACT THAT THE STORY OF MY MOTHER AND ME IS UNFOLDING EVEN AS I WRITE IT.
DID YOU SEE DANIEL MENDELSOHN'S ARTICLE ON MEMOIR IN *THE NEW YORKER*?
UH...NO.
IT'S GOOD. ISN'T HE THE ONE WHO BEAT YOU FOR THAT PRIZE?
UH... YEAH.
JANUARY

YET ANOTHER DIFFICULTY IS THE FACT THAT MY MOTHER CONSIDERS MEMOIR A SUSPECT GENRE. THIS ADDS A CONFUSING OBSERVER EFFECT TO THE WHOLE PROCESS.
WHAT'S IT ABOUT?
OH, YOU KNOW. INACCURACY, EXHIBITIONISM, NARCISSISM, THOSE FAKE MEMOIRS.
INDEED, MY FOREMOST DIFFICULTY IS THE EXTENT TO WHICH I HAVE INTERNALIZED MY MOTHER'S CRITICAL FACULTIES.
AS OF THIS MOMENT, I'VE BEEN STRUGGLING FOR FOUR YEARS WITH THE WRITING OF THIS BOOK, THIS MEMOIR ABOUT MY MOTHER.
DID I TELL YOU I'M ORDERING THAT CHLORINE-RESISTANT SWIMSUIT?
I TALK TO MY MOTHER ALMOST EVERY DAY. THAT IS, I CALL, SHE TALKS, I LISTEN. THAT'S OUR PATTERN.
IT COSTS A HUNDRED DOLLARS, BUT I GO THROUGH SEVERAL SPEEDOS A YEAR.
I MUST CONFESS THAT I HAVE TAKEN TO TRANSCRIBING WHAT SHE SAYS. I DON'T THINK SHE KNOWS I'M DOING IT, WHICH MAKES IT A BIT UNETHICAL.
1/29/2010, 4:15pm
article in New Yorker on memoir
Isn't daniel mendelsohn the one who be
A new chlorine-resistant swimsuit, for $1
Maybe I'll decide to spring for it. I go th
not sure about size. Sizes don't mean anything any more?
somebody bought that house down the street when it was up for auction, and t
flipped it. They covered up the original painted brick and slapped on vinyl siding
They ruined it. You know how it was when I moved up here. A woman wanted t
up vinyl siding and the arch. review board said no, but the town overruled them
THE ARCHITECTURAL REVIEW BOARD SAID SHE COULDN'T PUT UP VINYL SIDING, BUT THE TOWN OVERRULED THEM BECAUSE SHE'S A POOR WIDOW.

BUT I WANT TO CAPTURE HER VOICE, HER PRECISE WORDING, HER DEADPAN HUMOR. I DON'T THINK I COULD POSSIBLY RE-CREATE IT ON MY OWN.
WELL, I'M A POOR WIDOW, TOO, AND I DON'T WANT TO LOOK AT VINYL SIDING!
I'M TRYING SO HARD TO GET DOWN WHAT SHE'S SAYING THAT I'M NOT REALLY LISTENING PROPERLY.
UH HUH...
I WOULD HAVE MORE SCRUPLES ABOUT THIS, I LIKE TO THINK, IF I DIDN'T SUSPECT THAT SHE WAS NOT SO MUCH TALKING TO ME AS DRAFTING HER OWN DAILY JOURNAL ENTRY OUT LOUD.
MY MOTHER HAS ALWAYS KEPT A JOURNAL. SHE INSISTS THIS IS JUST A RECORD OF THINGS SHE'S DONE. OF EXTERNAL, AS OPPOSED TO INTERNAL, EXPERIENCE.
I SHARE THIS COMPULSION FOR KEEPING TRACK OF LIFE.
MY MOTHER LOGS HER DAILY ACTIVITIES IN HER JOURNAL. AND EVERY DAY SHE READS ANOTHER JOURNAL--THE *NEW YORK TIMES*.
IF YOU'RE GOING OUT, CAN YOU GET ME A COPY OF TO-DAY'S PAPER?

NOT ONLINE. THE NEWSPRINT, THE THING ITSELF.
THE TRUCK DIDN'T GET HERE BECAUSE OF THE BLIZZARD, SO NO ONE HAS IT.
YOU WANT ME TO MAIL TODAY'S *NEW YORK TIMES* FROM VERMONT TO PENNSYLVANIA?
I KNOW! IT'S MY OCD. BUT I HATE MISSING ANY NEWS. AND THE PUZZLE.
I OFTEN THINK OF THIS PASSAGE FROM VIRGINIA WOOLF'S DIARY: "WHAT A DISGRACEFUL LAPSE! NOTHING ADDED TO MY DISQUISITION, & LIFE ALLOWED TO WASTE LIKE A TAP LEFT RUNNING. ELEVEN DAYS UNRECORDED."
I STARTED MY OWN DIARY AS A CHILD. AND WHEN A SPELL OF OBSESSIVE-COMPULSIVE DISORDER MADE MY ENTRIES TOO TIME-CONSUMING, MY MOTHER SAT ON MY BED AND TOOK DICTATION.
MOTHER WENT TO SCHOOL TO SUBSTITUTE TEACH. MARY-JO BROUGHT IN A LOVE TEST THAT WE DID ON THE BUS.
GETTING HER UNDIVIDED ATTENTION WAS A RARE TREAT. IT FELT MIRACULOUS, ACTUALLY--LIKE PERSUADING A HUMMINGBIRD TO PERCH ON YOUR FINGER.
I DIDN'T GET MUCH DONE. I WENT TO MY PIANO LESSON. I GOT BACH'S MINUET.
SHE WAS LISTENING TO ME. WHAT-EVER I SAID, SHE WROTE DOWN.
I FOUND THIS CALMING. COMPOSING.

MY MOTHER COMPOSED ME AS I NOW COMPOSE HER.
SHE LIKES TO USE SCRUB-BING BUBBLES, BUT I TOLD HER TO USE THE COMET.
FLICKATICKA
TACKATICKA
TIC
THE RUNNING TAP OF HER LIFE FLOWS THROUGH MY FINGERS.
SOMETIMES THERE WILL BE A LULL AND MY MOTHER WILL ASK ME THIS QUESTION:
HOW ARE YOU DOING?
MY CONSIDERABLE VERBAL APTITUDE OFTEN FAILS ME COMPLETELY WHEN I'M TALKING TO MY MOTHER.
When she cleans the bathro
to use the comet.
She asks how I'm doing.
THROUGHOUT MY TWENTIES AND THIRTIES, SHE NEVER ASKED ME ABOUT MY LIFE.
EVEN NOW, WHEN SHE POSES THE QUESTION POINT-BLANK, I KNOW HER ATTENTION FOR MY ANSWER IS LIMITED.
UHH...
THE PRESSURE TO BE CONCISE, ENTERTAIN-ING, AND APPOSITE IN THIS SMALL WINDOW IS FIERCE. MORE OFTEN THAN NOT, I PASS WITH A "FINE. NOTHING NEW TO REPORT."
I...

BUT I KNOW I CAN'T BLAME HER FOR DOMINATING OUR CONVERSATIONS IF I REFUSE TO PARTICIPATE. SO SOMETIMES, LIKE TODAY, I DIVULGE SOMETHING.
I HAVE TO REWRITE MY BOOK.
WHAT?!
I HAVE TO START OVER. I...I FEEL LIKE I'M WRITING AROUND SOMETHING.
HA!
SHE'S LAUGHING IN WHAT SEEMS LIKE AN UNDERSTANDING WAY. SHE DOESN'T ASK ME WHAT IT IS THAT I'M WRITING AROUND.
YOU HAVE TOO MANY STRANDS!
SHE KNOWS THIS BOOK IS ABOUT MY RELATIONSHIP WITH HER, AND SHE SEEMS TO FEEL ABOUT IT ROUGHLY THE WAY SHE FELT ABOUT THE BOOK ON MY FATHER--RESIGNED.
WELL, I READ IT IN THE WRONG ORDER. I COULDN'T FIGURE OUT THE PAGINATION. I'LL HAVE TO LOOK AT IT AGAIN.
I HAD RECENTLY SENT HER WHAT I THOUGHT WAS THE FIRST CHAPTER. WE DISCUSSED IT, FOR ABOUT THREE MINUTES, DURING MY CHRISTMAS VISIT.

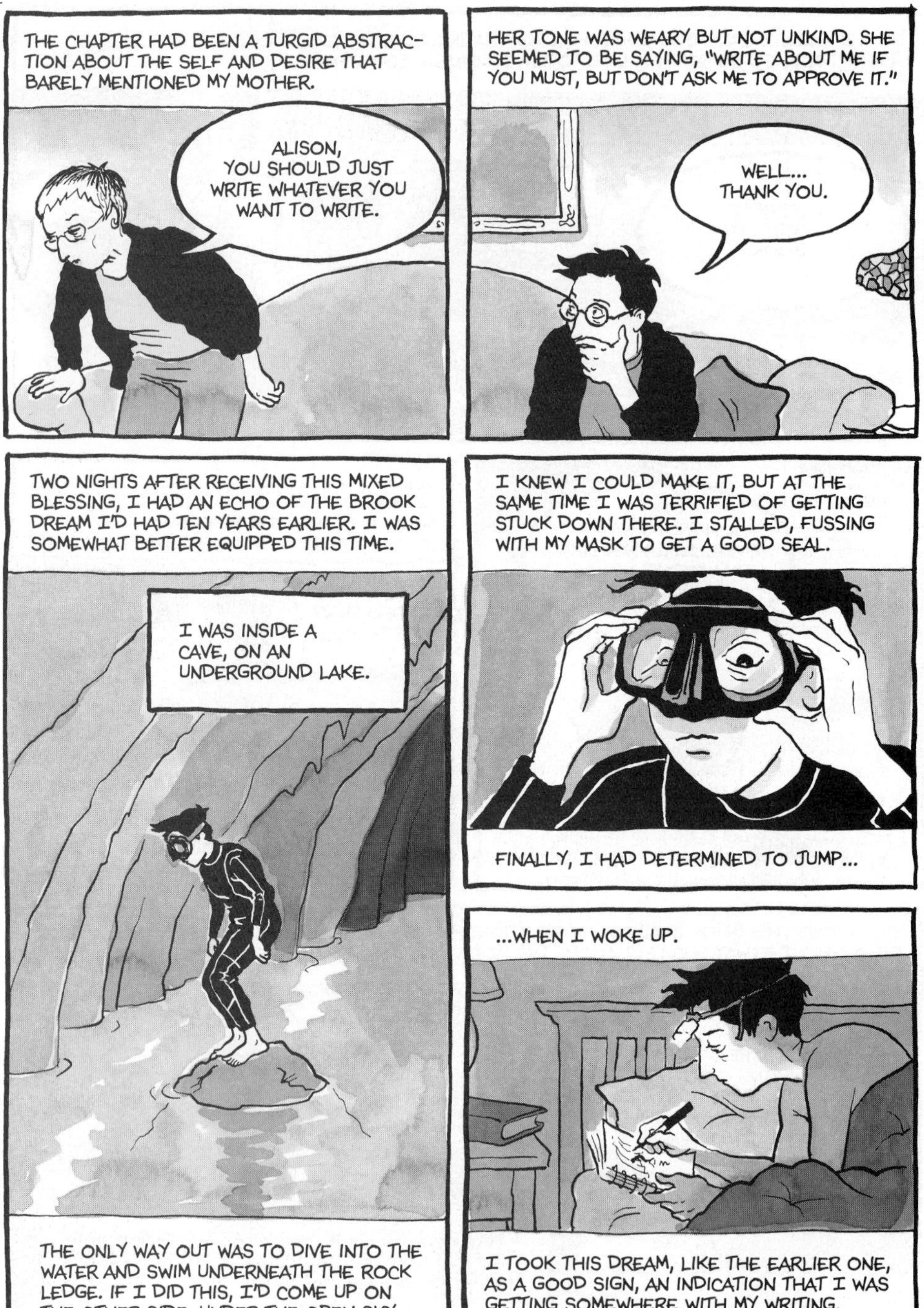
THE CHAPTER HAD BEEN A TURGID ABSTRACTION ABOUT THE SELF AND DESIRE THAT BARELY MENTIONED MY MOTHER.
ALISON, YOU SHOULD JUST WRITE WHATEVER YOU WANT TO WRITE.
HER TONE WAS WEARY BUT NOT UNKIND. SHE SEEMED TO BE SAYING, "WRITE ABOUT ME IF YOU MUST, BUT DON'T ASK ME TO APPROVE IT."
WELL... THANK YOU.
TWO NIGHTS AFTER RECEIVING THIS MIXED BLESSING, I HAD AN ECHO OF THE BROOK DREAM I'D HAD TEN YEARS EARLIER. I WAS SOMEWHAT BETTER EQUIPPED THIS TIME.
I WAS INSIDE A CAVE, ON AN UNDERGROUND LAKE.
THE ONLY WAY OUT WAS TO DIVE INTO THE WATER AND SWIM UNDERNEATH THE ROCK LEDGE. IF I DID THIS, I'D COME UP ON THE OTHER SIDE, UNDER THE OPEN SKY.
I KNEW I COULD MAKE IT, BUT AT THE SAME TIME I WAS TERRIFIED OF GETTING STUCK DOWN THERE. I STALLED, FUSSING WITH MY MASK TO GET A GOOD SEAL.
FINALLY, I HAD DETERMINED TO JUMP...
...WHEN I WOKE UP.
I TOOK THIS DREAM, LIKE THE EARLIER ONE, AS A GOOD SIGN, AN INDICATION THAT I WAS GETTING SOMEWHERE WITH MY WRITING.

BUT WITHIN A FEW DAYS, IT BECAME CLEAR THAT "GETTING SOMEWHERE" MEANT STARTING OVER. THIS FELT ODDLY ENCOURAGING.
Thursday, January 28
week 4 of 2010
173 days
7
8AM Write
IT HAD BEEN FIVE MONTHS SINCE THIS BOOK WAS DUE, AND SIX SINCE MY LAST PERIOD.
LIKE MY MOTHER, I KEEP A LOG OF THE EVENTS OF DAILY, EXTERNAL LIFE. BUT UNLIKE HER, I ALSO RECORD A GREAT DEAL OF INFORMATION ABOUT MY INTERNAL LIFE.
ALTHOUGH I'M OFTEN CONFUSED ABOUT PRECISELY WHERE THE DEMARCATION LIES.
VIRGINIA WOOLF SEEMS TO HAVE CONSIDERED HER OWN DIARY TO BE MORE OF AN EXTERNAL RECORD, AN ACCOUNT OF "LIFE" RATHER THAN "THE SOUL."
Monday 19 February
How it would interest me if this diary were ever to become a real diary: something in which I could see changes, trace moods developing; but then I should have to speak of the soul, & did I not banish the soul when I began? What happens is, as usual, that I'm going to write about the soul, & life breaks in. Talking of diaries sets me thinking of old Kate, in the dining room at 4 Rosary Gardens; & how she opened the cabinet (wh. I remember) & there in a row on a shelf were her diaries from Jan 1 1877.13 Some were brown; others red; all the same to a t. And I made her read an entry; one of many thousand days, like pebbles
WOOLF'S DISMISSAL OF "THE SOUL" REMINDS ME A BIT OF MY MOTHER'S INSISTENCE THAT HER OWN JOURNAL IS LITTLE MORE THAN A COMPLETED TO-DO LIST, THAT SHE NEVER RE-READS IT...
To the Lighthouse
Virginia Woolf
...THAT IN FACT SHE'S THROWN WHOLE CHUNKS OF IT AWAY.
MOMENTS of BEING
AUTOBIOGRAPHICAL WRITING
VIRGINIA WOOLF
Anne Olivier Bell
THE DIARY of VIRGINIA WOOLF
VOLUME TWO
1920-1924
2002

I'M SURE THESE THINGS ARE TRUE.
BUT THE WAY SHE SAYS THEM FEELS LIKE AN IMPLIED CRITICISM. AS IF SHE'S COMPARING HER OWN SELFLESSNESS TO MY SELF-ABSORPTION.
BUT OF COURSE THAT'S JUST EVIDENCE OF MY SELF-ABSORPTION. MY MOTHER IS PROBABLY NOT THINKING ANYTHING LIKE THIS.
MOMENTS of BEING
IN FACT, MY DESIRE TO THINK THAT SHE'S THINKING OF ME AT ALL IS A BIT PATHETIC.
SHE LOOMS MUCH LARGER IN MY PSYCHE THAN I LOOM IN HERS. WOOLF SAYS THAT HER OWN MOTHER, WHO DIED WHEN VIRGINIA WAS THIRTEEN, OBSESSED HER UNTIL SHE WAS FORTY-FOUR.
when I was thirteen, until I was forty-four. Then one day walking round Tavistock Square I made up, as I sometimes make up my books, *To the Lighthouse*; in a great, apparently involuntary, rush.
LET'S LEAVE ASIDE THE ANNOYING RAPIDITY WITH WHICH SHE DISPATCHED THIS MASTERPIECE. THE POINT IS, WHAT HAPPENED AFTERWARD.
when it was written, I ceased to be obsessed by my mother. I no longer hear her voice; I do not see her.
I suppose that I did for myself what psycho-analysts do for their patients. I expressed some very long felt and deeply felt emotion. And in expressing it I explained it and then laid it to rest. But what is
I'VE BEEN IN THERAPY FOR NEARLY MY ENTIRE ADULT LIFE AND HAVE NOT LAID MY DEEPLY FELT EMOTIONS ABOUT MY MOTHER TO REST.
MY LIFE IS A MESS. I'VE BEEN IN A REALLY SOLID RELATIONSHIP FOR EIGHT YEARS...
BUT I KEEP GETTING ATTRACTED TO OTHER PEOPLE.
I STARTED SEEING MY CURRENT THERAPIST, CAROL, TEN YEARS AGO.
I'M WRITING THIS MEMOIR ABOUT MY DAD'S SUICIDE AND FOR EVERY SENTENCE I PUT DOWN, I DELETE TWO.

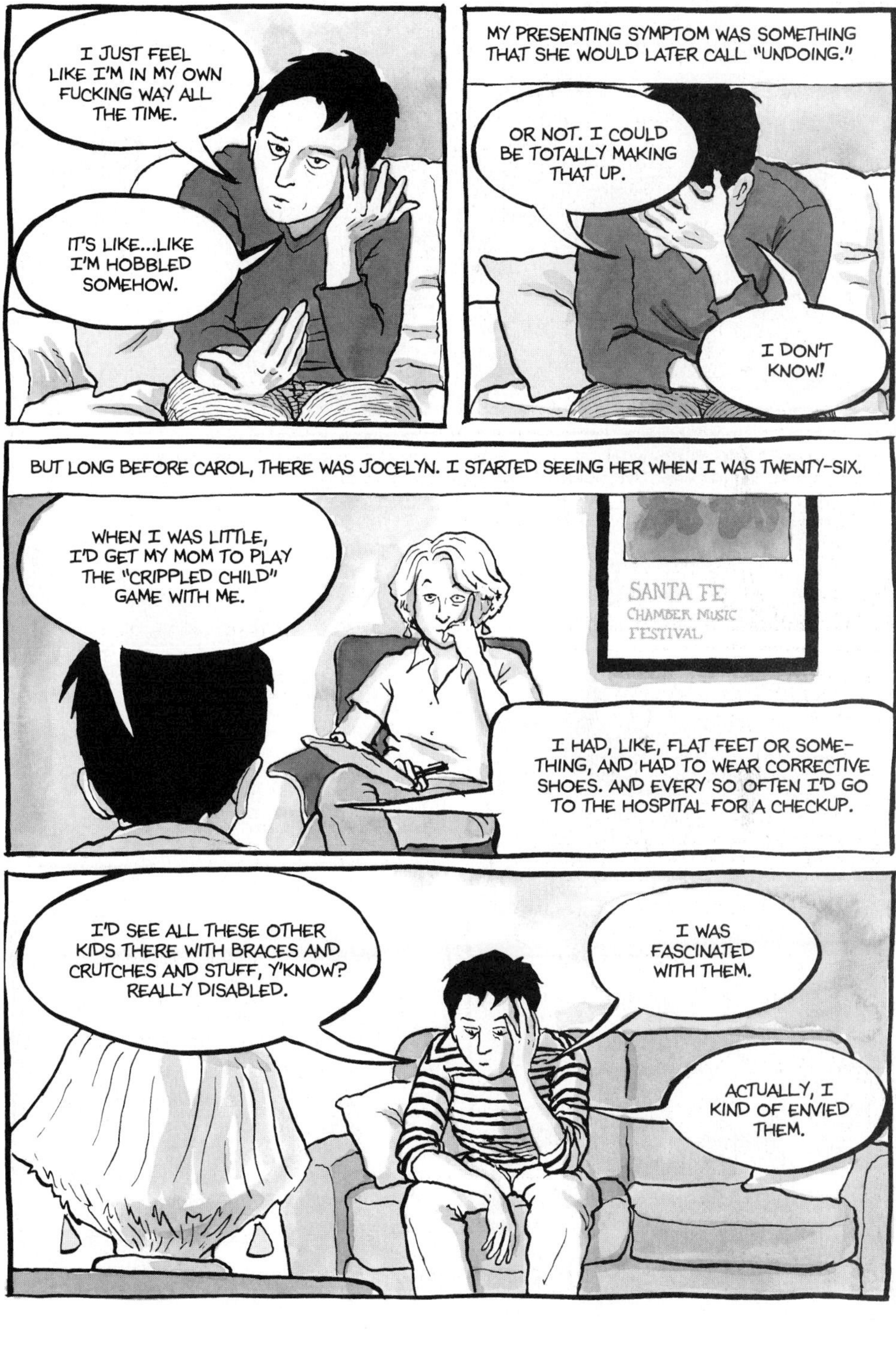
I JUST FEEL LIKE I'M IN MY OWN FUCKING WAY ALL THE TIME.
IT'S LIKE...LIKE I'M HOBBLED SOMEHOW.
MY PRESENTING SYMPTOM WAS SOMETHING THAT SHE WOULD LATER CALL "UNDOING."
OR NOT. I COULD BE TOTALLY MAKING THAT UP.
I DON'T KNOW!
BUT LONG BEFORE CAROL, THERE WAS JOCELYN. I STARTED SEEING HER WHEN I WAS TWENTY-SIX.
WHEN I WAS LITTLE, I'D GET MY MOM TO PLAY THE "CRIPPLED CHILD" GAME WITH ME.
SANTA FE
CHAMBER MUSIC
FESTIVAL
I HAD, LIKE, FLAT FEET OR SOMETHING, AND HAD TO WEAR CORRECTIVE SHOES. AND EVERY SO OFTEN I'D GO TO THE HOSPITAL FOR A CHECKUP.
I'D SEE ALL THESE OTHER KIDS THERE WITH BRACES AND CRUTCHES AND STUFF, Y'KNOW? REALLY DISABLED.
I WAS FASCINATED WITH THEM.
ACTUALLY, I KIND OF ENVIED THEM.

I'D PRETEND I WAS A "CRIPPLED" CHILD, AND MOM WOULD PLAY ALONG WITH IT.
YOU'LL NEED THESE CRUTCHES.
IT WAS SO FUN. WHEREVER I WENT WITH THE FANTASY, SHE WAS RIGHT THERE.
FOR MY FIRST TWO YEARS WITH CAROL, I JUST SAT ON THE COUCH. BUT THEN I BEGAN LYING DOWN ON IT. IN THE TIME I'VE BEEN SEEING HER, SHE HAS BECOME A PSYCHOANALYST.
WHY AM I LYING HERE?
ANALYSIS AND THERAPY ARE DIFFERENT IN MANY WAYS, BUT THE SEATING ARRANGEMENT IS A BIG ONE.
I SHOULD BE WORKING.
IN THIS POSITION THE PATIENT CAN'T SEE THE ANALYST. AND LYING DOWN, IN THEORY, ALLOWS MORE READY ACCESS TO THE UNCONSCIOUS.
I'M NEVER GONNA GET THIS FUCKING BOOK DONE.

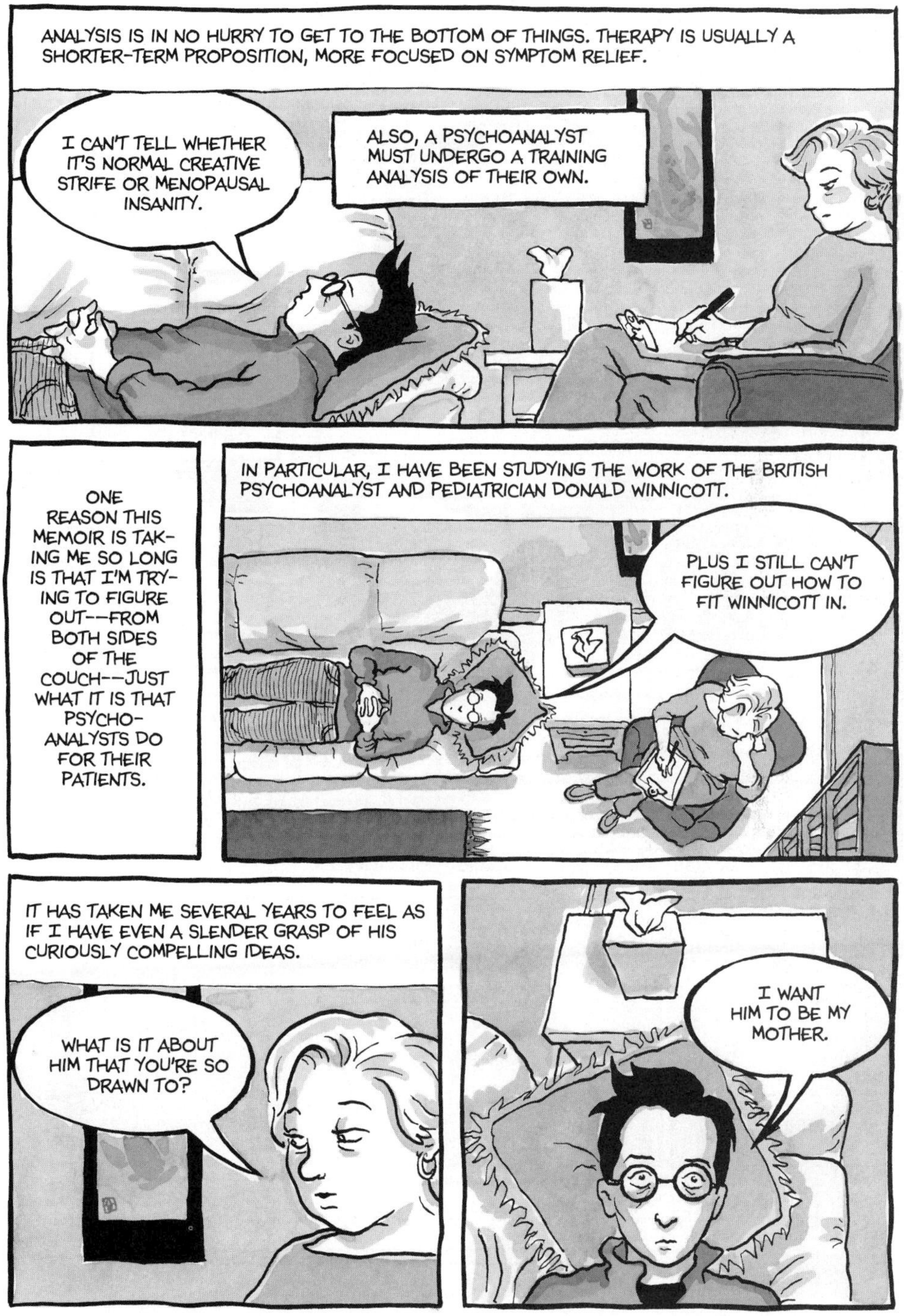
ANALYSIS IS IN NO HURRY TO GET TO THE BOTTOM OF THINGS. THERAPY IS USUALLY A SHORTER-TERM PROPOSITION, MORE FOCUSED ON SYMPTOM RELIEF.
I CAN'T TELL WHETHER IT'S NORMAL CREATIVE STRIFE OR MENOPAUSAL INSANITY.
ALSO, A PSYCHOANALYST MUST UNDERGO A TRAINING ANALYSIS OF THEIR OWN.
ONE REASON THIS MEMOIR IS TAKING ME SO LONG IS THAT I'M TRYING TO FIGURE OUT--FROM BOTH SIDES OF THE COUCH--JUST WHAT IT IS THAT PSYCHOANALYSTS DO FOR THEIR PATIENTS.
IN PARTICULAR, I HAVE BEEN STUDYING THE WORK OF THE BRITISH PSYCHOANALYST AND PEDIATRICIAN DONALD WINNICOTT.
PLUS I STILL CAN'T FIGURE OUT HOW TO FIT WINNICOTT IN.
IT HAS TAKEN ME SEVERAL YEARS TO FEEL AS IF I HAVE EVEN A SLENDER GRASP OF HIS CURIOUSLY COMPELLING IDEAS.
WHAT IS IT ABOUT HIM THAT YOU'RE SO DRAWN TO?
I WANT HIM TO BE MY MOTHER.

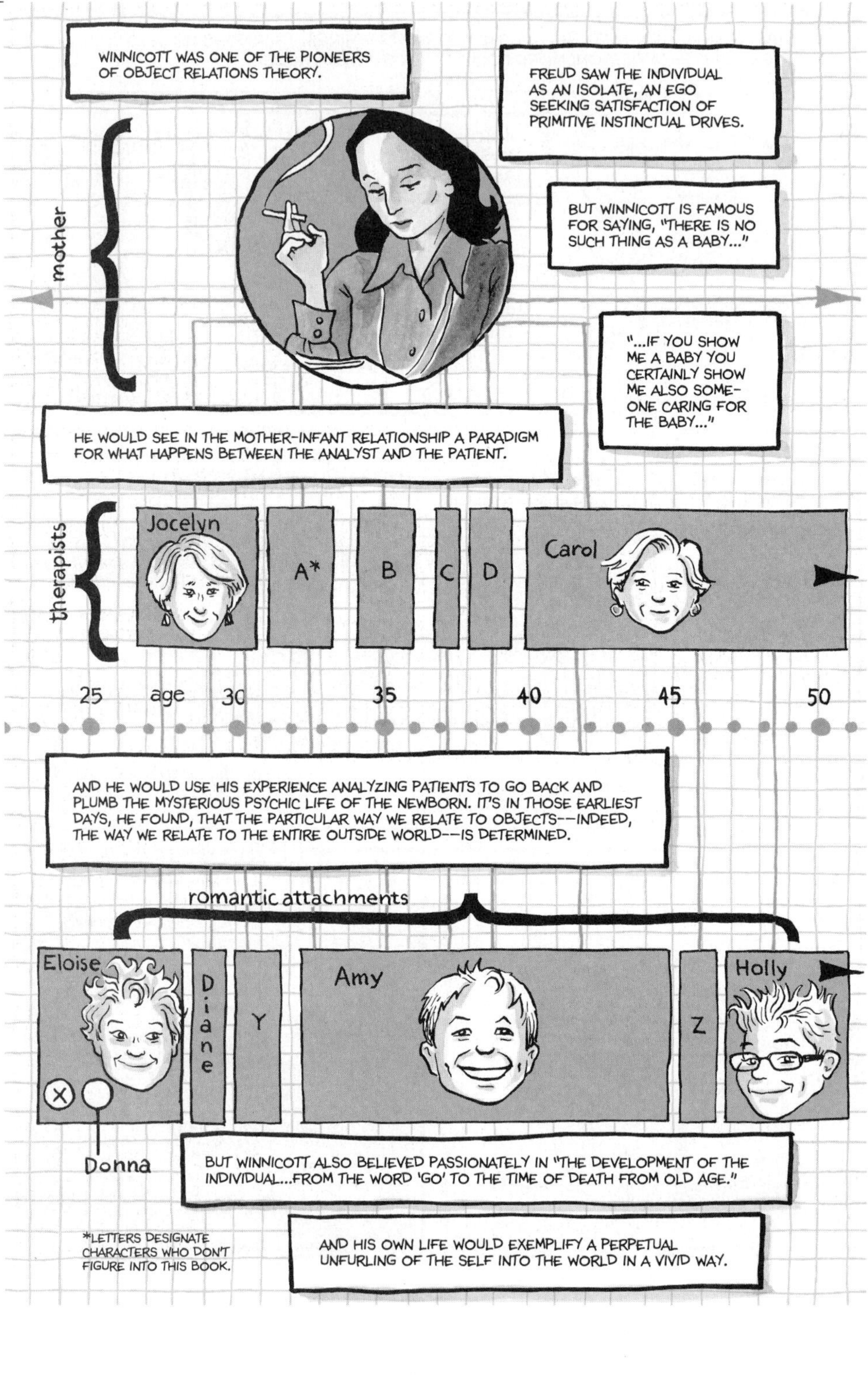
WINNICOTT WAS ONE OF THE PIONEERS OF OBJECT RELATIONS THEORY.
FREUD SAW THE INDIVIDUAL AS AN ISOLATE, AN EGO SEEKING SATISFACTION OF PRIMITIVE INSTINCTUAL DRIVES.
BUT WINNICOTT IS FAMOUS FOR SAYING, "THERE IS NO SUCH THING AS A BABY..."
mother
"...IF YOU SHOW ME A BABY YOU CERTAINLY SHOW ME ALSO SOMEONE CARING FOR THE BABY..."
HE WOULD SEE IN THE MOTHER-INFANT RELATIONSHIP A PARADIGM FOR WHAT HAPPENS BETWEEN THE ANALYST AND THE PATIENT.
therapists
Jocelyn
A*
B
C
D
Carol
25
age
30
35
40
45
50
AND HE WOULD USE HIS EXPERIENCE ANALYZING PATIENTS TO GO BACK AND PLUMB THE MYSTERIOUS PSYCHIC LIFE OF THE NEWBORN. IT'S IN THOSE EARLIEST DAYS, HE FOUND, THAT THE PARTICULAR WAY WE RELATE TO OBJECTS--INDEED, THE WAY WE RELATE TO THE ENTIRE OUTSIDE WORLD--IS DETERMINED.
romantic attachments
Eloise
Diane
Y
Amy
Z
Holly
Donna
BUT WINNICOTT ALSO BELIEVED PASSIONATELY IN "THE DEVELOPMENT OF THE INDIVIDUAL...FROM THE WORD 'GO' TO THE TIME OF DEATH FROM OLD AGE."
*LETTERS DESIGNATE CHARACTERS WHO DON'T FIGURE INTO THIS BOOK.
AND HIS OWN LIFE WOULD EXEMPLIFY A PERPETUAL UNFURLING OF THE SELF INTO THE WORLD IN A VIVID WAY.

WHY DO YOU WANT HIM TO BE YOUR MOTHER?
I DUNNO.
BUT I KNOW THAT IF HE HAD BEEN MY MOTHER, I WOULDN'T BE SUFFERING OVER THIS BOOK.
I'D BE DOING SOMETHING USEFUL.
THE THING IS, I CAN'T WRITE THIS BOOK UNTIL I GET HER OUT OF MY HEAD.
BUT THE ONLY WAY TO GET HER OUT OF MY HEAD IS BY WRITING THE BOOK!
IT'S A PARADOX.
MY MOTHER'S EDITORIAL VOICE--PRECISIAN, DISPASSIONATE, ELEGANT, ADVERBLESS--IS LODGED DEEP IN MY TEMPORAL LOBES.
OR A DILEMMA OR SOMETHING.
I DON'T KNOW.
I DON'T KNOW ANYTHING.
HOW I ENVY THE INVOLUNTARY TORRENT OF WORDS AND IMAGES THAT CAME TO VIRGINIA WOOLF THAT DAY IN TAVISTOCK SQUARE.

IT WAS SOMETIME BETWEEN OCTOBER 1924 AND THE FOLLOWING SPRING.
WOOLF NEVER UNDERWENT PSYCHOANALYSIS. HER BROTHER ADRIAN DID, THOUGH.
VIRGINIA WROTE RATHER SNIDELY TO HER SISTER, "I GATHER THAT HIS TRAGEDY--AS THE DR. CALLS IT--IS ALL OUR DOING. HE WAS SUPPRESSED AS A CHILD."
WOOLF WOULDN'T REALLY READ FREUD FOR ANOTHER TEN YEARS OR SO...
...THOUGH THE HOGARTH PRESS, WHICH SHE FOUNDED WITH HER HUSBAND, LEONARD, HAD JUST PUBLISHED HIS COLLECTED PAPERS.
THESE HAD BEEN TRANSLATED BY JAMES AND ALIX STRACHEY, THE BROTHER AND SISTER-IN-LAW OF VIRGINIA'S CLOSE FRIEND LYTTON.

GENERAL
JAMES STRACHEY HAD BEEN ANALYZED BY FREUD AND WAS A PRACTICING PSYCHOANALYST IN NEIGHBORING GORDON SQUARE.
IN FACT, HERE COMES ONE OF HIS PATIENTS NOW. A YOUNG DOCTOR OF CHILDREN'S MEDICINE.
DONALD WOODS WINNICOTT WORKS AT TWO HOSPITALS AND HAS AN OFFICE IN HARLEY STREET.
BUT TODAY, LET'S SAY HE'S COMING FROM THE QUEEN'S HOSPITAL FOR CHILDREN. HE'D PROBABLY HAVE TAKEN THE UNDERGROUND FROM BETHNAL GREEN.
NO, THERE WAS NO BETHNAL GREEN STOP IN 1925. LET'S SAY HE WALKS TO LIVERPOOL STREET STATION AND CATCHES THE TUBE TO KING'S CROSS.
CRESCENT
KING'S CROSS ST PANCRAS
EUSTON
ANGEL
EUSTON SQUARE
RUSSELL SQUARE
OLD STREET
WARREN ST
GOODGE ST
ALDERSGATE
BRITISH MUSEUM
CHANCERY LANE
POST OFFICE
LIVERPOOL STREET
HOLBORN
ALDWYCH
MANSION HOUSE
BANK
ALDGATE
LEICESTER SQUARE
COVENT GARDEN
BLACKFRIARS
TEMPLE
CHARING CROSS
CANNON STREET
MONUMENT
TRAFALGAR
WATERLOO

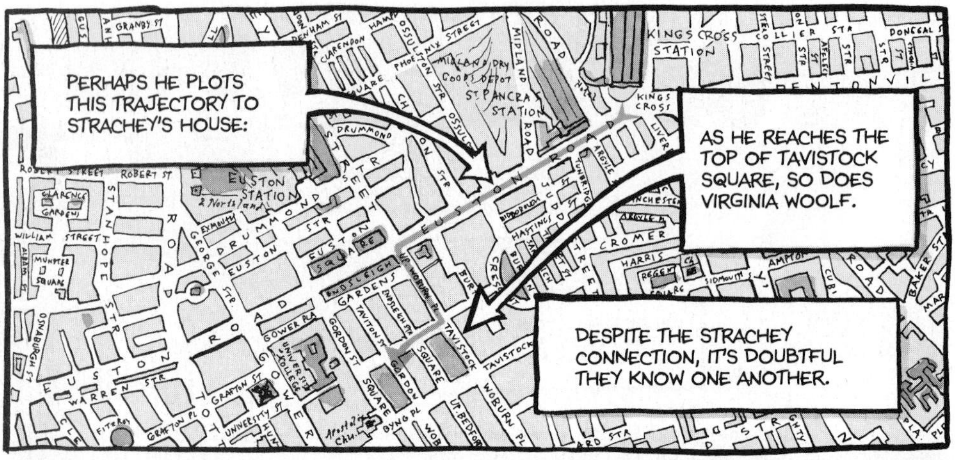
PERHAPS HE PLOTS THIS TRAJECTORY TO STRACHEY'S HOUSE:
AS HE REACHES THE TOP OF TAVISTOCK SQUARE, SO DOES VIRGINIA WOOLF.
DESPITE THE STRACHEY CONNECTION, IT'S DOUBTFUL THEY KNOW ONE ANOTHER.

DONALD IS TWENTY-NINE, THE SON OF A MERCHANT, IN AWE OF HIS ANALYST'S CULTIVATED BLOOMSBURY WORLD.
WOOLF IS AT THE CENTER OF THAT WORLD, MIDDLE-AGED AND BECOMING FAMOUS.
WINNICOTT WILL EVENTUALLY BE PUBLISHED BY THE HOGARTH PRESS, BUT NOT UNTIL SOME TIME AFTER VIRGINIA'S DEATH.

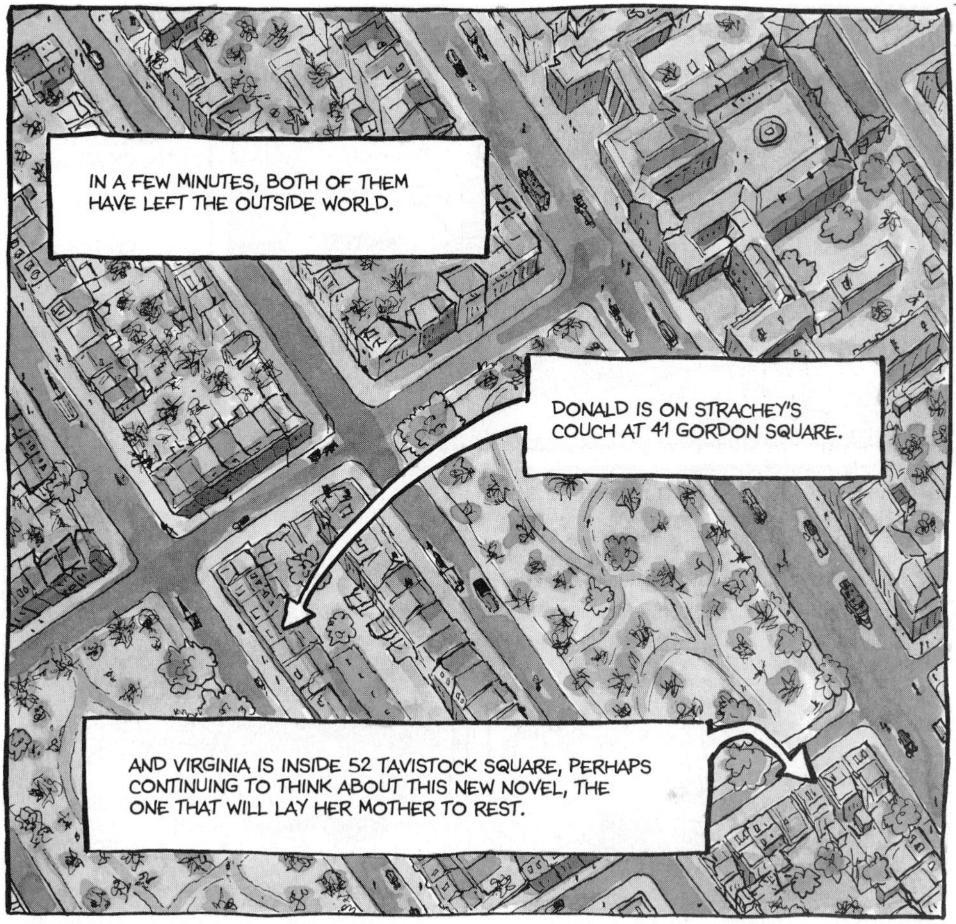
IN A FEW MINUTES, BOTH OF THEM HAVE LEFT THE OUTSIDE WORLD.
DONALD IS ON STRACHEY'S COUCH AT 41 GORDON SQUARE.
AND VIRGINIA IS INSIDE 52 TAVISTOCK SQUARE, PERHAPS CONTINUING TO THINK ABOUT THIS NEW NOVEL, THE ONE THAT WILL LAY HER MOTHER TO REST.

DONALD IS VERY POSSIBLY THINKING ABOUT HIS MOTHER, TOO. SHE HAS EITHER JUST DIED, OR WILL DIE BEFORE 1925 IS OUT. I CAN'T FIND THE EXACT DATE.
MY MOTHER WAS DISGUISED IN A BEARSKIN. THEN HER PENIS POPPED OUT AND CASTRATED ME.
THIS WAS AN ACTUAL DREAM OF WINNICOTT'S. ALTHOUGH I AM ENJOYING THIS LITTLE FORAY INTO FICTION, I FEEL THE NECESSITY OF "CLINGING AS TIGHT TO FACTS AS I CAN," AS WOOLF WROTE IN HER 1923 DIARY ABOUT HER PROGRESS ON *MRS. DALLOWAY.*

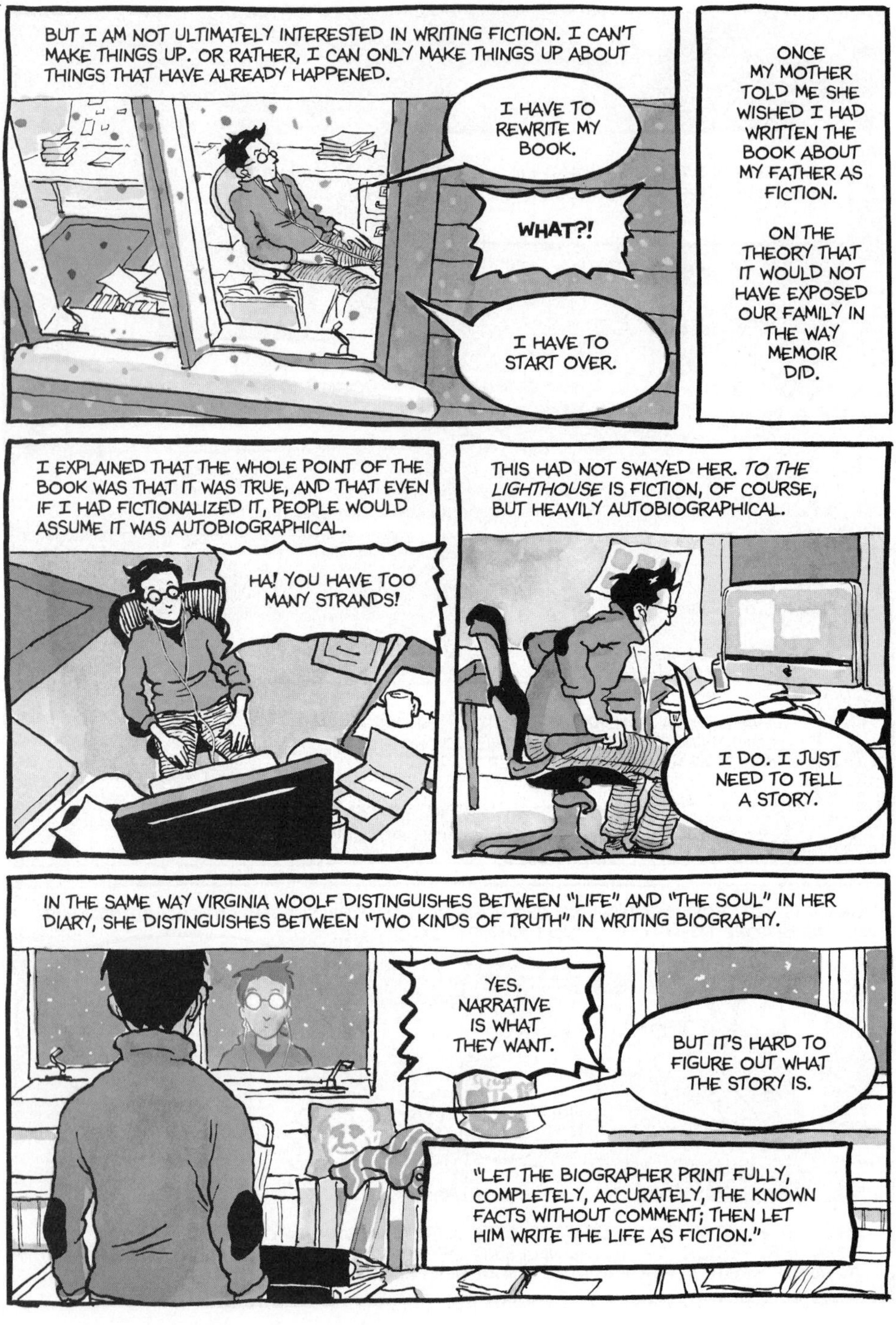
BUT I AM NOT ULTIMATELY INTERESTED IN WRITING FICTION. I CAN'T MAKE THINGS UP. OR RATHER, I CAN ONLY MAKE THINGS UP ABOUT THINGS THAT HAVE ALREADY HAPPENED.
I HAVE TO REWRITE MY BOOK.
WHAT?!
I HAVE TO START OVER.
ONCE MY MOTHER TOLD ME SHE WISHED I HAD WRITTEN THE BOOK ABOUT MY FATHER AS FICTION.
ON THE THEORY THAT IT WOULD NOT HAVE EXPOSED OUR FAMILY IN THE WAY MEMOIR DID.
I EXPLAINED THAT THE WHOLE POINT OF THE BOOK WAS THAT IT WAS TRUE, AND THAT EVEN IF I HAD FICTIONALIZED IT, PEOPLE WOULD ASSUME IT WAS AUTOBIOGRAPHICAL.
HA! YOU HAVE TOO MANY STRANDS!
THIS HAD NOT SWAYED HER. *TO THE LIGHTHOUSE* IS FICTION, OF COURSE, BUT HEAVILY AUTOBIOGRAPHICAL.
I DO. I JUST NEED TO TELL A STORY.
IN THE SAME WAY VIRGINIA WOOLF DISTINGUISHES BETWEEN "LIFE" AND "THE SOUL" IN HER DIARY, SHE DISTINGUISHES BETWEEN "TWO KINDS OF TRUTH" IN WRITING BIOGRAPHY.
YES. NARRATIVE IS WHAT THEY WANT.
BUT IT'S HARD TO FIGURE OUT WHAT THE STORY IS.
"LET THE BIOGRAPHER PRINT FULLY, COMPLETELY, ACCURATELY, THE KNOWN FACTS WITHOUT COMMENT; THEN LET HIM WRITE THE LIFE AS FICTION."

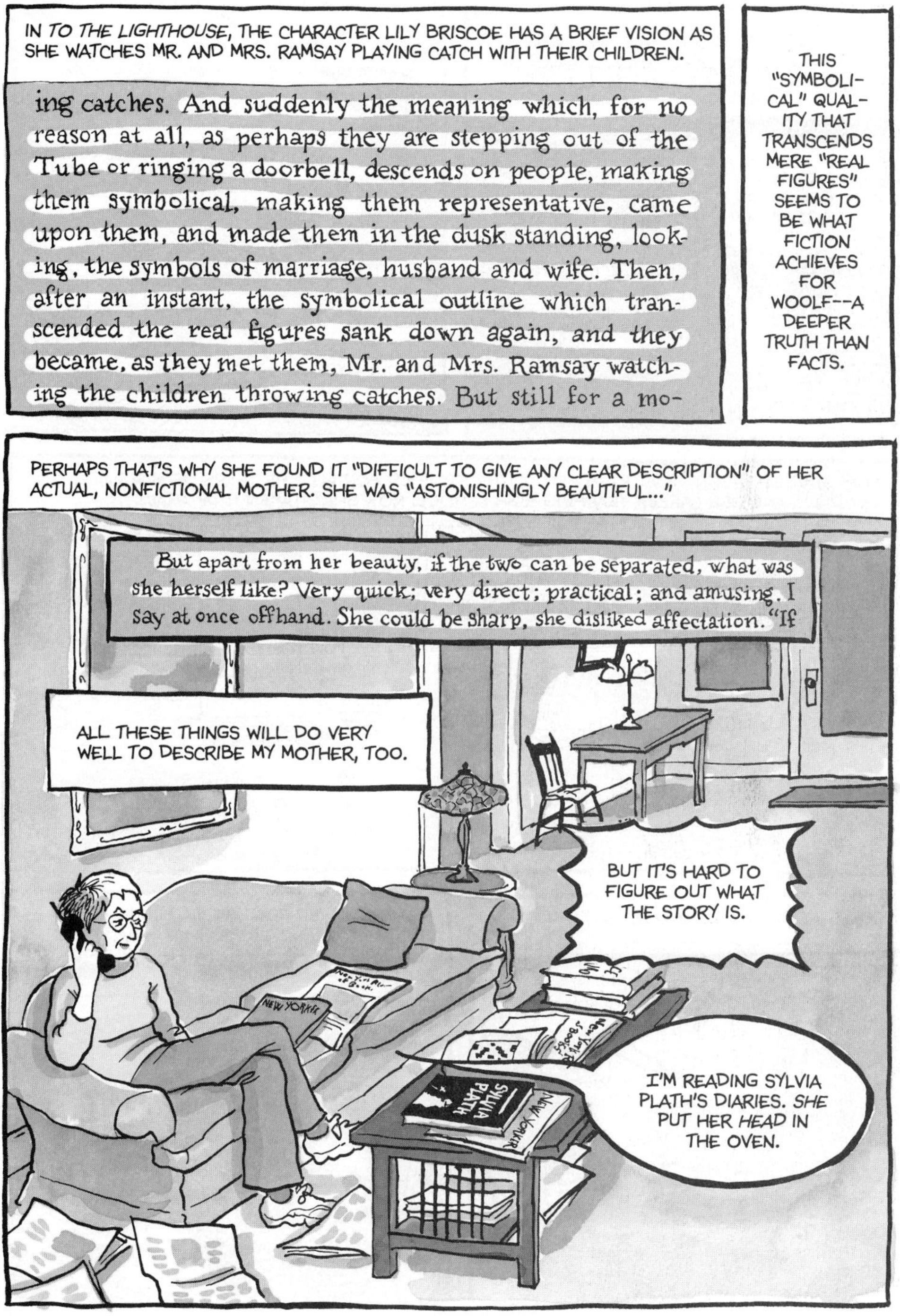
IN *TO THE LIGHTHOUSE*, THE CHARACTER LILY BRISCOE HAS A BRIEF VISION AS SHE WATCHES MR. AND MRS. RAMSAY PLAYING CATCH WITH THEIR CHILDREN.
ing catches. And suddenly the meaning which, for no reason at all, as perhaps they are stepping out of the Tube or ringing a doorbell, descends on people, making them symbolical, making them representative, came upon them, and made them in the dusk standing, looking, the symbols of marriage, husband and wife. Then, after an instant, the symbolical outline which transcended the real figures sank down again, and they became, as they met them, Mr. and Mrs. Ramsay watching the children throwing catches. But still for a mo-
THIS "SYMBOLICAL" QUALITY THAT TRANSCENDS MERE "REAL FIGURES" SEEMS TO BE WHAT FICTION ACHIEVES FOR WOOLF--A DEEPER TRUTH THAN FACTS.
PERHAPS THAT'S WHY SHE FOUND IT "DIFFICULT TO GIVE ANY CLEAR DESCRIPTION" OF HER ACTUAL, NONFICTIONAL MOTHER. SHE WAS "ASTONISHINGLY BEAUTIFUL..."
But apart from her beauty, if the two can be separated, what was she herself like? Very quick; very direct; practical; and amusing. I say at once offhand. She could be sharp, she disliked affectation. "If
ALL THESE THINGS WILL DO VERY WELL TO DESCRIBE MY MOTHER, TOO.
BUT IT'S HARD TO FIGURE OUT WHAT THE STORY IS.
I'M READING SYLVIA PLATH'S DIARIES. *SHE* PUT HER *HEAD* IN THE OVEN.
NEW YORK
SYLVIA PLATH
NEW YORKER

MOM MEANS THIS KINDLY, COMMISERATINGLY. "OH, THE WRITER'S LIFE." STILL, I THINK OF MY OWN OVEN AND AM GLAD IT'S ELECTRIC.
OH! I FOUND MY LOST POEM!
GREAT! I WAS GONNA TELL YOU HOW TO SEARCH THE COMPUTER.
I FIGURED IT OUT MYSELF!
MOM STARTED WRITING POETRY IN HER YOUTH, STOPPED FOR ALL THE YEARS OF MARRIAGE, CHILDREN, AND HER CAREER TEACHING HIGH SCHOOL. NOW SHE'S TAKEN IT UP AGAIN.
OH, THE JEHOVAH'S WITNESS LADY IS AT THE DOOR. I HAVE TO GO.
UH...OKAY.
SHE INSISTS THAT SHE'S NOT A POET.
BYE.
I HAVE NEVER READ SYLVIA PLATH. MY MOTHER HAS NEVER READ VIRGINIA WOOLF. IN GENERAL, WE HAVE STAYED OUT OF ONE ANOTHER'S WAY LIKE THIS.

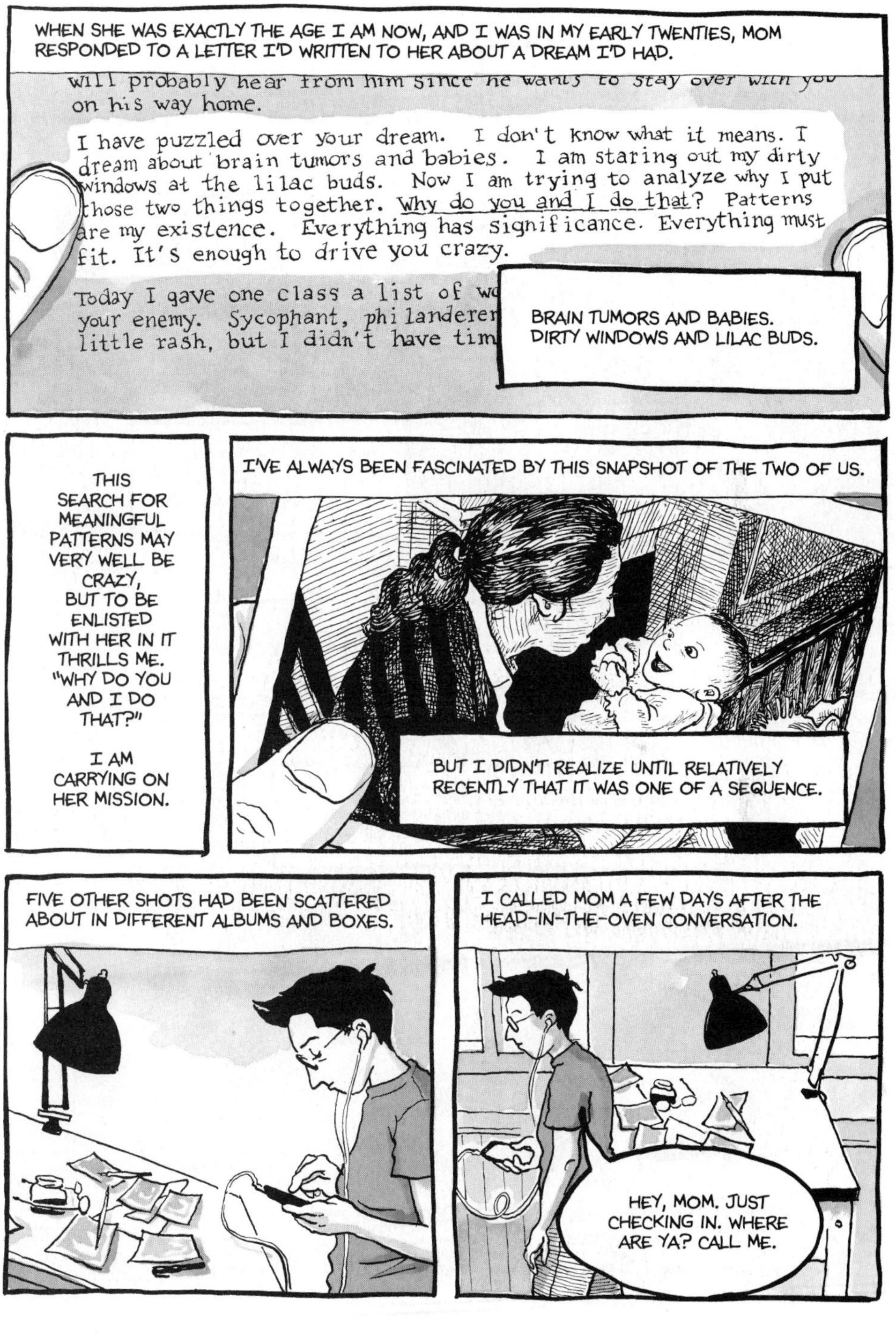
WHEN SHE WAS EXACTLY THE AGE I AM NOW, AND I WAS IN MY EARLY TWENTIES, MOM RESPONDED TO A LETTER I'D WRITTEN TO HER ABOUT A DREAM I'D HAD.
will probably hear from him since he wants to stay over with you on his way home.
I have puzzled over your dream. I don't know what it means. I dream about brain tumors and babies. I am staring out my dirty windows at the lilac buds. Now I am trying to analyze why I put those two things together. Why do you and I do that? Patterns are my existence. Everything has significance. Everything must fit. It's enough to drive you crazy.
Today I gave one class a list of w
your enemy. Sycophant, philanderer
little rash, but I didn't have tim
BRAIN TUMORS AND BABIES. DIRTY WINDOWS AND LILAC BUDS.
THIS SEARCH FOR MEANINGFUL PATTERNS MAY VERY WELL BE CRAZY, BUT TO BE ENLISTED WITH HER IN IT THRILLS ME. "WHY DO YOU AND I DO THAT?"
I AM CARRYING ON HER MISSION.
I'VE ALWAYS BEEN FASCINATED BY THIS SNAPSHOT OF THE TWO OF US.
BUT I DIDN'T REALIZE UNTIL RELATIVELY RECENTLY THAT IT WAS ONE OF A SEQUENCE.
FIVE OTHER SHOTS HAD BEEN SCATTERED ABOUT IN DIFFERENT ALBUMS AND BOXES.
I CALLED MOM A FEW DAYS AFTER THE HEAD-IN-THE-OVEN CONVERSATION.
HEY, MOM. JUST CHECKING IN. WHERE ARE YA? CALL ME.

I DON'T HAVE THE NEGATIVES, SO THERE'S NO WAY TO KNOW THEIR CHRONOLOGICAL ORDER. BUT I'VE ARRANGED THEM ACCORDING TO MY OWN NARRATIVE.
MOM IS MAKING FACES AND PRESUMABLY SOUNDS AT ME. IN EACH SHOT, I REFLECT HER EXPRESSION AND THE SHAPE OF HER MOUTH WITH UNCANNY PRECISION.
BUT "THERE IS NOTHING MYSTICAL ABOUT THIS," SAYS DONALD WINNICOTT, IN *THE ORDINARY DEVOTED MOTHER.*
agrees, that *ordinarily* the woman enters into a phase, a phase from which she *ordinarily* recovers in the weeks and months after the baby's birth, in which to a large extent she is the baby and the baby is her. There is nothing mystical about
FOR A LONG TIME I RESISTED INCLUDING MY PRESENT-DAY INTERACTIONS WITH MOM IN THIS BOOK PRECISELY BECAUSE THEY'RE SO "ORDINARY."
DRRINNG!
MOM!
HI. I WAS AT THE GYM. HAD TO GET MY LAPS IN.
Gerber®
POPS UP
SAFETY BUTTON
JAN · 61 ·
HELIX
Christmas '60
Alison 3 mo.

I COULDN'T BELIEVE LADY GAGA ON THE GRAMMYS LAST NIGHT. PUH-LEASE. I LIKE PUNK. I LIKE WEIRD!
BUT SHE CAN'T DRESS LIKE THAT WITH THOSE THIGHS. IF I HAD ANOTHER LIFE TO LIVE, I'D COSTUME ROCK DIVAS.
THEN I STARTED SEEING HOW THE TRANSCENDENT WOULD ALMOST ALWAYS CREEP INTO THE EVERYDAY.
JAN
I DIDN'T GET MUCH SLEEP LAST NIGHT. I KEPT HAVING THESE DREAMS ABOUT DAD.
I GUESS IT'S FROM READING SYLVIA PLATH'S JOURNALS. SHE AND TED HUGHES ARE ALWAYS FIGHTING.
'60
IN MY ARRANGEMENT OF THESE PHOTOS, THE RAPPORT BETWEEN MOM AND ME BUILDS UNTIL I SHRIEK WITH JOY.
THEN THE MOMENT IS SHATTERED AS I NOTICE THE MAN WITH THE CAMERA.
SHE'S SUCH A SPOILED BRAT.
AT THREE MONTHS, I HAD SEEN ENOUGH OF MY FATHER'S RAGES TO BE WARY OF HIM.
Alison 3 mos.
Locust Lane
GERMANY
PURAPLAS
HI-POLYM

THE PHOTOS WERE TAKEN RIGHT ABOUT THE TIME MOM REALIZED THAT SHE WAS PREGNANT AGAIN.
SHE'S A SNOB, TOO. A SNOB AND A BRAT.
I THOUGHT YOU LIKED HER.
THERE ARE THREE MAIN REASONS, WINNICOTT SAYS, WHY A MOTHER MIGHT NOT BE ABLE TO "GIVE HERSELF OVER TO THIS PREOCCUPATION WITH THE CARE OF HER INFANT."
SHE'S ALWAYS ASKING HER THERAPIST FOR PERMISSION TO HATE HER MOTHER.
ONE, SHE DIES. TWO, SHE "STARTS UP A NEW PREGNANCY BEFORE THE TIME THAT SHE HAD THOUGHT OUT AS APPROPRIATE." THREE...
THE ORDINARY DEVOTED MOTHER
ing. Or a mother becomes depressed and she can feel herself depriving her child of what the child needs, but she cannot help the onset of a mood swing, which may quite easily be reactive to something that has impinged in her private life. Here she is causing trouble, but no one would blame her.
In other words there are all manner of reasons why some children do get let down before they are able to avoid being wounded or maimed in personality by the fact.
Here I must go back to the idea of blame. It is necessary for us to be able to look at human growth and development, with all its complexities that are internal or personal to the child, and we must be able to say; here the ordinary devoted mother factor failed, without blaming anyone. For my part I have no interest whatever in apportioning blame. Mothers
"AM I ALLOWED TO HATE MY MOTHER?"
"NO!"
OH, SERENA'S GRANDDAUGHTER JUST GOT HER PERIOD. SHE'S ONLY TWELVE. THAT'S SO SAD. TWELVE IS TOO YOUNG.
UHH...I THINK TWELVE IS KINDA NORMAL.

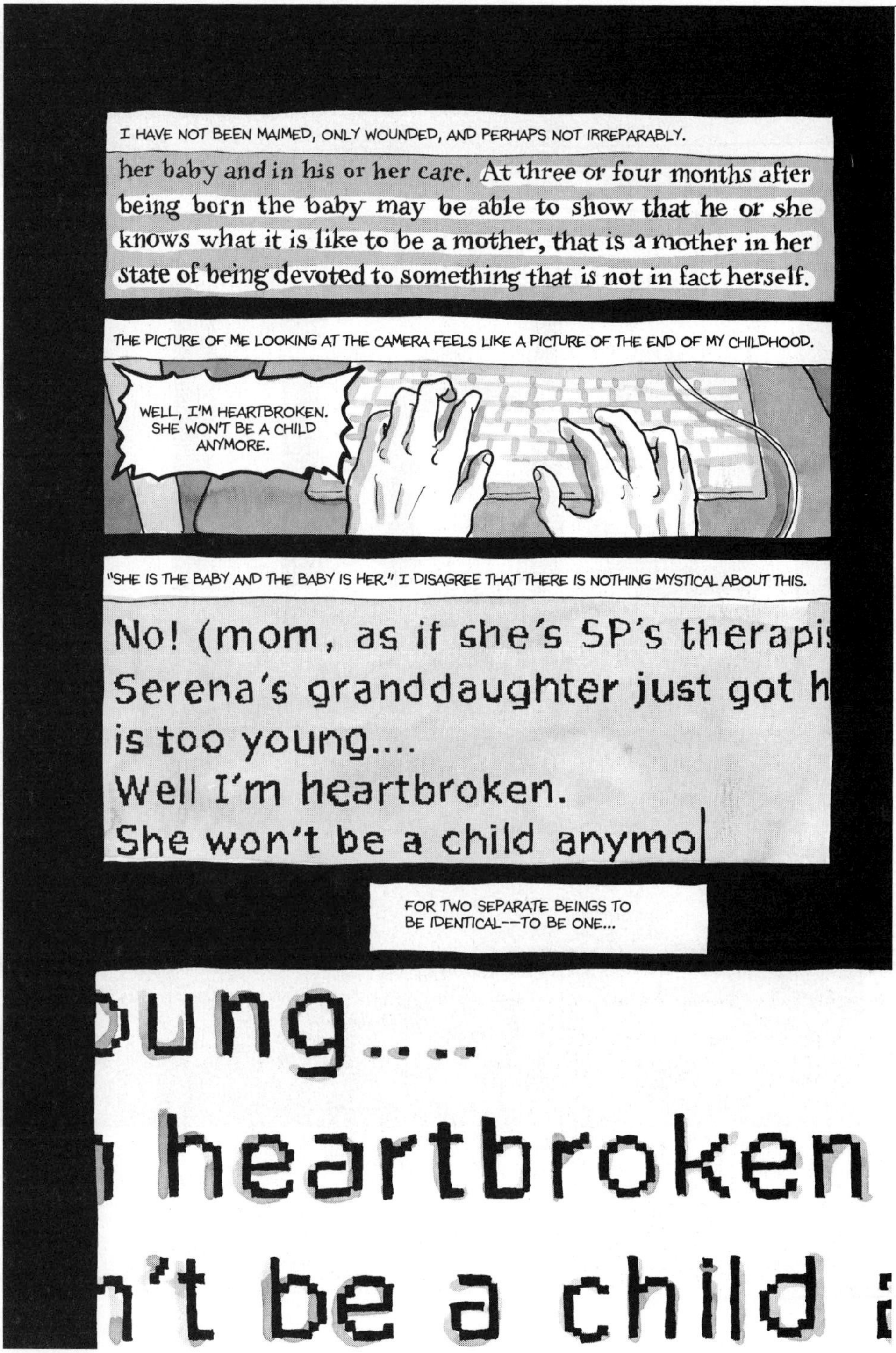
I HAVE NOT BEEN MAIMED, ONLY WOUNDED, AND PERHAPS NOT IRREPARABLY.
her baby and in his or her care. At three or four months after being born the baby may be able to show that he or she knows what it is like to be a mother, that is a mother in her state of being devoted to something that is not in fact herself.
THE PICTURE OF ME LOOKING AT THE CAMERA FEELS LIKE A PICTURE OF THE END OF MY CHILDHOOD.
WELL, I'M HEARTBROKEN. SHE WON'T BE A CHILD ANYMORE.
"SHE IS THE BABY AND THE BABY IS HER." I DISAGREE THAT THERE IS NOTHING MYSTICAL ABOUT THIS.
No! (mom, as if she's SP's therapis
Serena's granddaughter just got h
is too young....
Well I'm heartbroken.
She won't be a child anymo
FOR TWO SEPARATE BEINGS TO BE IDENTICAL--TO BE ONE...
oung....
heartbroken
n't be a child

...THIS SEEMS TO ME AS MYSTICAL, AS TRANSCENDENT OF THE LAWS OF EVERYDAY REALITY, AS IT GETS.
child

QUESTIONS FOR A SECOND READING

1. You might think of Bechdel's work as taking place in a series of frames, with each individual drawing existing in its own particular frame. Reread several pages of Bechdel's work and choose a single frame that seems layered and interesting to you. What do you notice about the frame Bechdel has created? What is the relationship between the words and images? How does the single frame exist as its own independent story? What is unique about reading a frame as opposed to reading, for example, a sentence or paragraph?

2. What do you imagine the composing process of this kind of work to be like? What does a graphic writer like Bechdel have to think about or consider that writers of only text might not consider? Try to create (even if you are not a particularly strong visual artist) a frame, or a few frames, of your own. What do you notice about the process? What is illuminated for you about the connections or distinctions between graphic composition and purely textual composition?

3. In the opening passages we've offered to this reading, Bechdel suggests that "delving" is important to her. In what ways do you see this work as an act of delving? What is it delving into? You might start by reading widely about the word "delve." What is its definition and history? Your library will likely have access to the online *Oxford English Dictionary*, which is a good resource for such a task. Once you feel like you have a sense of the word's nuances and meanings, how would you put the term in conversation with Bechdel's work and her project?

4. In the first "Question for a Second Reading," we invited you to think about a single frame of Bechdel's piece. But you might also consider a set of frames in succession. Choose several frames that speak to each other in a way that builds a complex narrative. What does this set of frames ask of you as a reader? How does the work of a graphic writer, like Bechdel, teach a particular way of reading? What can this set of frames tell you about what it means to read this kind of piece?

ASSIGNMENTS FOR WRITING

1. Bechdel writes, "Of course the point at which I began to write the story is not the same as the point at which the story begins." (p. 79) We might read this statement as a commentary on the work of composing autobiography or memoir. She remarks later, "Another difficulty is the fact that the story of my mother and me is unfolding even as I write it." (p. 82)

   Consider Bechdel's comments about writing this book and about herself. What does she seem to be suggesting about the difficulties of writing autobiographical work? How would it be different if her work were composed of only words, or if it were a more conventional memoir of mother and daughter? How does her chosen form of graphic memoir enable and limit what she is able to do in writing about herself and her family?

Think of an autobiographical narrative you are familiar with, perhaps in literature or film. You might want to think of a story that involves a mother and daughter, like Bechdel's does. Write an essay in which you discuss the differences between this familiar narrative and Bechdel's work. In your discussion, you'll want to provide particular sets of frames or clusters from Bechdel's work and specific moments in the narrative with which you are familiar as examples. What is the relationship between the two autobiographical approaches? What does Bechdel's graphic work do that the other narrative does not do? What can you say about Bechdel's approach from looking at it alongside this other example?

2. Writing and reading are major themes in Bechdel's work. There's the story of Bechdel writing the very work we are reading. There is her journaling, her mother's journaling, and Bechdel's references to writers like Virginia Woolf and Sylvia Plath. So one way of reading "The Ordinary Devoted Mother" is to understand the piece as being about reading and writing—and perhaps also about the life of the mind.

   If you think of the piece as being about the work of reading and writing, what does Bechdel seem to suggest about what writing does, where it comes from, and what it is for? What is Bechdel's philosophy on reading and writing as far as you can tell? What does her work tell you about the process of its own making? Write an essay in which you offer Bechdel's theory of composition, making an argument for how Bechdel understands the creative process of writing.

3. Compose a piece of graphic memoir. Your piece need not be as long as Bechdel's, but you should think of yourself as imitating Bechdel, taking on her ways of composing. You can come up with your cartoon frames by either drawing them or, if you know how, constructing them digitally in whatever ways you can.

   Once you've composed seven to ten frames, write an afterword in which you explore what you discovered in the process of trying to compose like Bechdel does. What was it like? How did the process reveal something to you about your own methods of composing? What did you learn from trying Bechdel's approach?

MAKING CONNECTIONS

1. Although Bechdel is exclusively a cartoonist, you might consider her alongside some of the other authors in this book who pair their textual writing

with images. Errol Morris ("Seeing is Believing"), Edward Said ("States"), and Susan Bordo ("Beauty (Re)discovers the Male Body") (all located in e-Pages) each make use of images as they compose their individual writing projects. Although these writers' texts differ from the other ones in many ways, all of them try to engage both visual and textual pathways in order to enact their various lines of inquiry.

Write an essay in which you try to describe the multiple ways in which these authors utilize images. How do photographs of bodies or places affect you in comparison to Bechdel's drawings? How does each of these writers work with images, and what are the purposes of those images? What would it be like if Bechdel offered actual photographs of her family instead of cartoons? How might such a change affect our reading of the piece? Conversely, what if Bordo's images were satirical cartoons or comic strips? Another way to think about this topic is to pose the question: do images convey a kind of argument in the way writing does? If they do convey an argument, how might you describe that process to other readers?

2. Bechdel's work seems particularly focused on the relationship between parents and children (whether those children are small or grown). Imagine Bechdel's work in conversation with Susan Griffin's essay "Our Secret." (p. 233) How do both authors imagine the relationship between parenting and the selves we become? Which particular passages from both selections suggest this relationship to you?

   Do Griffin and Bechdel appear to agree on how adult-child relationships work? How might you complicate or enrich each author's understanding of the ways parents shape the lives of their children? You may, in this question, draw from your own experiences as someone's child to help you think through these questions.

3. Both Alison Bechdel and Judith Butler are writers whose work is often studied in courses focused on gender and sexuality, as both authors are particularly interested in these aspects of identity. Return again to Butler's notion of being "beside oneself" in her essay of the same name (p. 114). Write your own essay in which you examine Bechdel's work through the lens of Butler's terminology. Is Bechdel "beside herself" as Butler defines it? How might reading Bechdel's work through Butler's terminology help us see another dimension of Bechdel's project?

---

e See the e-Pages at bedfordstmartins.com/waysofreading.

JUDITH Butler

Judith Butler is the Maxine Elliot Professor in the departments of rhetoric and comparative literature at the University of California at Berkeley. She is also the Hannah Arendt Professor of Philosophy at the European Graduate School in Saas-Fee, Switzerland, where she teaches an intensive summer seminar. She was an undergraduate at Bennington College and then Yale University; she received her PhD in philosophy from Yale in 1984. Her first training as a philosopher, she said, was at the synagogue in her hometown, Cleveland.

Butler is a prolific and controversial writer; her topics are gender, sexuality, and, most recently, war. Her books include *Subjects of Desire: Hegelian Reflections in Twentieth-Century France* (1987); *Gender Trouble: Feminism and the Subversion of Identity* (1990); *Bodies That Matter: On the Discursive Limits of "Sex"* (1993); *The Psychic Life of Power: Theories of Subjection* (1997); *Excitable Speech: A Politics of the Performative* (1997); *Antigone's Claim: Kinship between Life and Death* (2000); *Hegemony, Contingency, Universality* (2000, with Ernesto Laclau and Slavoj Žižek); *Precarious Life: Powers of Violence and Mourning* (2004); *Undoing Gender*, a collection of essays, including the selection that follows (2004); *Giving an Account of Oneself* (2005); and *Frames of War: When Is Life Grievable?* (2009).

Butler's second book, *Gender Trouble*, was extraordinarily successful—that is, it was widely read around the world, translated into several languages, taught in graduate and undergraduate seminars, and referenced in thousands of books and essays. It is, perhaps, one of the most important books of its time; it remains profoundly influential. The argument calls into question the commonplace and controlling assumption that human beings are divided into two clear-cut groups, men and women. Butler challenges this binary, demonstrating that much that is taken for granted about gender is problematic, even illogical. Whatever the individual body, gender identity is more complicated, more diverse, more flexible than assumed by a simple binary, male and female. Gender identity, she argues, is "performative"; it is not the natural result of who we are biologically; it is a product, rather, of how we think, act, imagine, and desire, and these performances are subject to change.

> There is no gender identity behind the expressions of gender; . . . identity is performatively constituted by the very "expressions" that are said to be its results. (*Gender Trouble*, p. 25)

This was the compelling and difficult conclusion: although gender identity is shaped by cultural norms and conventions, and although bodies and biology matter, gender identity is mutable, available to change. It is open to revision, resistance, subversion, and improvisation — sometimes willed, sometimes not. This thought was terrifying for some and liberating for others.

Butler is known for the difficulty of her prose. In fact, the difficulty could be said to be exemplary. In 1998, she was announced as the "winner" of a Bad Writing Contest sponsored by the journal *Philosophy and Literature*, where her prose was singled out for its "anxiety-inducing obscurity." The incident garnered substantial attention in the academic and popular press and became an important point of reference as the nation tried to sort out its relation to the academy, to intellectuals, and to their attempts to bring critical theory to bear on matters of daily life and common concern. In her response to the award, Butler pointed out that the "winners" tended to be people who were writing against common-sense understandings of gender, race, class, and nation. She argued that prose is easy to read when it says what we already know and believe, but that it is harder to read (and to write) a prose that is struggling against the usual ways of thinking and speaking.

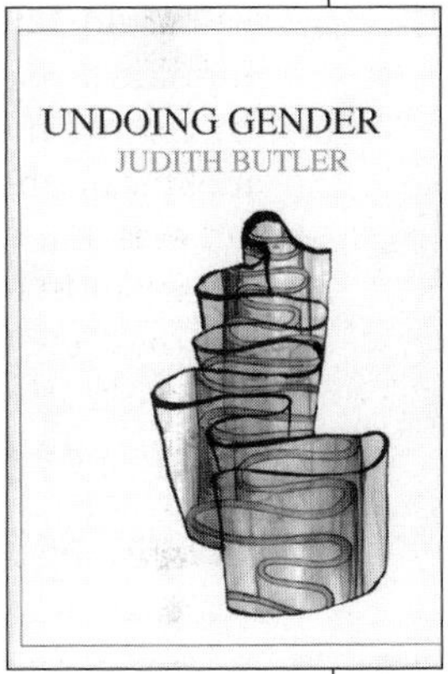

> There is a lot in ordinary language and in received grammar that constrains our thinking. . . . I'm not sure we're going to be able to struggle effectively against those constraints or work within them in a productive way unless we see the ways in which grammar is both producing and constraining our sense of what the world is. (*Excitable Speech: The Politics of the Performative,* pp. 732–33)

Anxiety, perhaps, is the necessary effect of such a project, an alternative to complacency. And so, she concluded in a *New York Times* op-ed article, the controversy was not so much about her prose as about what was appropriate in the classroom and in academic life. "We have an intellectual disagreement about what kind of world we want to live in, and what intellectual resources we must preserve as we make our way toward the politically new."

The other side of the argument is easier to grasp and easier to represent — that such prose is self-indulgent, divisive, posturing, disrespectful of its audience. One thing is certain, however. Butler is widely read and widely cited and is one of the most important, controversial, and influential theorists of our time. Her writing has changed the ways we think, speak, and write about sexuality, gender, and desire. The selection that follows thinks about gender identity in relation to the question of what "constitutes the human," who is granted this recognition and who is not. Butler raises this as a philosophical question, but she is also very interested in the political, in the actual human beings whose lives bear the consequence of being understood as impossible, illegible, and thereby alien, located outside the common understandings of what it means to be a person.

To watch a video of Butler elaborating on the role behavior plays in creating gender, visit the e-Pages at bedfordstmartins.com/waysofreading. Questions and assignments follow the piece.

Beside Oneself: On the Limits of Sexual Autonomy

What makes for a livable world is no idle question. It is not merely a question for philosophers. It is posed in various idioms all the time by people in various walks of life. If that makes them all philosophers, then that is a conclusion I am happy to embrace. It becomes a question for ethics, I think, not only when we ask the personal question, what makes my own life bearable, but when we ask, from a position of power, and from the point of view of distributive justice, what makes, or ought to make, the lives of others bearable? Somewhere in the answer we find ourselves not only committed to a certain view of what life is, and what it should be, but also of what constitutes the human, the distinctively human life, and what does not. There is always a risk of anthropocentrism here if one assumes that the distinctively human life is valuable — or most valuable — or is the only way to think the problem of value. But perhaps to counter that tendency it is necessary to ask both the question of life and the question of the human, and not to let them fully collapse into one another.

WE ARE CONSTITUTED POLITICALLY IN PART BY VIRTUE OF THE SOCIAL VULNERABILITY OF OUR BODIES; WE ARE CONSTITUTED AS FIELDS OF DESIRE AND PHYSICAL VULNERABILITY, AT ONCE PUBLICLY ASSERTIVE AND VULNERABLE.

I would like to start, and to end, with the question of the human, of who counts as the human, and the related question of whose lives count as lives, and with a question that has preoccupied many of us for years: what makes for a grievable life? I believe that whatever differences exist within the international gay and lesbian community, and there are many, we all have some notion of what it is to have lost somebody. And if we've lost, then it seems to follow that we have had, that we have desired and loved, and struggled to find the conditions for our desire. We have all lost someone in recent decades from AIDS, but there are other losses that inflict us, other diseases; moreover, we are, as a community, subjected to violence, even if some of us individually have not been. And this means that we are constituted politically in part by virtue of the social vulnerability of our bodies; we are constituted as fields of desire and physical vulnerability, at once publicly assertive and vulnerable.

I am not sure I know when mourning is successful, or when one has fully mourned another human being. I'm certain, though, that it does not mean that one has forgotten the person, or that something else comes along to take his or her place. I don't think it works that way. I think instead that one mourns when one accepts the fact that the loss one undergoes will be one that changes you, changes you possibly forever, and that mourning has to do with agreeing to undergo a transformation the full result of which you cannot know in advance. So there is losing, and there is the transformative effect of loss, and this latter cannot be charted or planned. I don't think, for instance, you can invoke a Protestant ethic when it comes to loss. You can't say, "Oh, I'll go through loss this way, and that will be the result, and I'll apply myself to the task, and I'll endeavor to achieve the resolution of grief that is before me." I think one is hit by waves, and that one starts out the day with an aim, a project, a plan, and one finds oneself foiled. One finds oneself fallen. One is exhausted but does not know why. Something is larger than one's own deliberate plan or project, larger than one's own knowing. Something takes hold, but is this something coming from the self, from the outside, or from some region where the difference between the two is indeterminable? What is it that claims us at such moments, such that we are not the masters of ourselves? To what are we tied? And by what are we seized?

It may seem that one is undergoing something temporary, but it could be that in this experience something about who we are is revealed, something that delineates the ties we have to others, that shows us that those ties constitute a sense of self, compose who we are, and that when we lose them, we lose our composure in some fundamental sense: we do not know who we are or what to do. Many people think that grief is privatizing, that it returns us to a solitary situation, but I think it exposes the constitutive sociality of the self, a basis for thinking a political community of a complex order.

It is not just that I might be said to "have" these relations, or that I might sit back and view them at a distance, enumerating them, explaining what this friendship means, what that lover meant or means to me. On the contrary, grief displays the way in which we are in the thrall of our relations with others that we cannot always recount or explain, that often interrupts the self-conscious account of ourselves we might try to provide in ways that challenge the very notion of ourselves as autonomous and in control. I might try to tell a story about what I am feeling, but it would have to be a story in which the very "I" who seeks to tell the story is stopped in the midst of the telling. The very "I" is called into question by its relation to the one to whom I address myself. This relation to the Other does not precisely ruin my story or reduce me to speechlessness, but it does, invariably, clutter my speech with signs of its undoing.

Let's face it. We're undone by each other. And if we're not, we're missing something. If this seems so clearly the case with grief, it is only because it was already the case with desire. One does not always stay intact. It may be that one wants to, or does, but it may also be that despite one's best efforts, one is undone, in the face of the other, by the touch, by the scent, by the feel, by the prospect of the touch, by the memory of the feel. And so when we speak about *my* sexuality or *my* gender, as we do (and as we must) we mean something complicated by it. Neither of these is precisely a possession, but both are to be understood as *modes of being dispossessed,* ways of being for another or, indeed, by virtue of another. It does not suffice to say that I am promoting a relational view of the self over an autonomous one, or trying to redescribe autonomy in terms of relationality. The term "relationality" sutures the rupture in the relation we seek to describe, a rupture that is constitutive of identity itself. This means that we will have to approach the problem of conceptualizing dispossession with circumspection. One way of doing this is through the notion of ecstasy.

We tend to narrate the history of the broader movement for sexual freedom in such a way that ecstasy figures in the 60s and 70s and persists midway through the 80s. But maybe ecstasy is more historically persistent than that, maybe it is with us all along. To be ec-static means, literally, to be outside oneself, and this can have several meanings: to be transported beyond oneself by a passion, but also to be *beside oneself* with rage or grief. I think that if I can still speak to a "we," and include myself within its terms, I am speaking to those of us who are living in certain ways *beside ourselves*, whether it is in sexual passion, or emotional grief, or political rage. In a sense, the predicament is to understand what kind of community is composed of those who are beside themselves.

We have an interesting political predicament, since most of the time when we hear about "rights," we understand them as pertaining to individuals, or when we argue for protection against discrimination, we argue as a group or a class. And in that language and in that context, we have to present ourselves as bounded beings, distinct, recognizable, delineated, subjects before the law, a community defined by sameness. Indeed, we had better be able to use that language to secure legal protections and entitlements. But perhaps we make a mistake if we take the definitions of who we are, legally, to be adequate descriptions of what we are about. Although this language might well establish our legitimacy within a legal framework ensconced in liberal versions of human ontology, it fails to do justice to passion and grief and rage, all of which tear us from ourselves, bind us to others, transport us, undo us, and implicate us in lives that are not are own, sometimes fatally, irreversibly.

It is not easy to understand how a political community is wrought from such ties. One speaks, and one speaks for another, to another, and yet there is no way to collapse the distinction between the other and myself. When we say "we" we do nothing more than designate this as very problematic. We do not solve it. And perhaps it is, and ought to be, insoluble. We ask that the state, for instance, keep its laws off our bodies, and we call for principles of bodily self-defense and bodily integrity to be accepted as political goods. Yet, it is through the body that gender and sexuality become exposed to others, implicated in social processes, inscribed by cultural norms, and apprehended in their social meanings. In a sense, to be a body is to be given over to others even as a body is, emphatically, "one's own," that over which we must claim rights of autonomy. This is as true for the claims made by lesbians, gays, and bisexuals in favor of sexual freedom as it is for transsexual and transgender claims to self-determination; as it is for intersex claims to be free of coerced medical, surgical, and psychiatric interventions; as it is for all claims to be free from racist attacks, physical and verbal; and as it is for feminism's claim to reproductive freedom. It is difficult, if not impossible, to make these claims without recourse to autonomy and, specifically, a sense of bodily autonomy. Bodily autonomy, however, is a lively paradox. I am not suggesting, though, that we cease to make these claims. We have to, we must. And I'm not saying that we have to make these claims reluctantly or strategically. They are part of the normative aspiration of any movement that seeks to maximize the protection and the freedoms of sexual and gender minorities, of women, defined with the broadest possible compass, of racial and ethnic minorities, especially as they cut across all the other categories. But is there another normative aspiration that we must also seek to articulate and to defend? Is there a way in which the place of the body in all of these struggles opens up a different conception of politics?

The body implies mortality, vulnerability, agency: the skin and the flesh expose us to the gaze of others but also to touch and to violence. The body can be the agency and instrument of all these as well, or the site where "doing" and "being done to" become equivocal. Although we struggle for rights over our own bodies, the very bodies for which we struggle are not quite ever only our own. The body has its invariably public dimension; constituted as a social phenomenon in the public sphere, my body is and is not mine. Given over from the start to the world of others, bearing their imprint, formed within the crucible of social life, the body is only later, and with some uncertainty, that to which I lay claim as my own. Indeed, if I seek to deny the fact that my body relates me — against my will and from the start — to others I do not choose to have in proximity to myself (the subway or the tube are excellent examples of this dimension of sociality), and if I build a notion of "autonomy" on the basis of the denial of this sphere or a primary and unwilled physical proximity with others, then do I precisely deny the social and political conditions of my embodiment in the name of autonomy? If I am struggling *for* autonomy, do I not need to be struggling for something else as well, a conception of myself as invariably in community, impressed upon by others, impressing them as well, and in ways that are not always clearly delineable, in forms that are not fully predictable?

Is there a way that we might struggle for autonomy in many spheres but also consider the demands that are imposed upon us by living in a world of beings who are, by definition, physically dependent on one another, physically vulnerable to one another? Is this not another way of imagining community in such a way that it becomes incumbent upon us to consider very carefully when and where we engage violence, for violence is, always, an exploitation of that primary tie, that primary way in which we are, as bodies, outside ourselves, for one another?

If we might then return to the problem of grief, to the moments in which one undergoes something outside of one's control and finds that one is beside oneself, not at one with oneself, we can say grief contains within it the possibility of apprehending the fundamental sociality of embodied life, the ways in which we are from the start, and by virtue of being a bodily being, already given over, beyond ourselves, implicated in lives that are not our own. Can this situation, one that is so dramatic for sexual minorities, one that establishes a very specific political perspective for anyone who works in the field of sexual and gender politics, supply a perspective with which to begin to apprehend the contemporary global situation?

Mourning, fear, anxiety, rage. In the United States after September 11, 2001, we have been everywhere surrounded with violence, of having perpetrated it, having suffered it, living in fear of it, planning more of it. Violence is surely a touch of the worst order, a way in which the human vulnerability to other humans is exposed in its most terrifying way, a way in which we are given over, without control, to the will of another, the way in which life itself can be expunged by the willful action of another. To the extent that we commit violence, we are acting upon another, putting others at risk, causing damage to others. In a way, we all live with this particular vulnerability, a vulnerability to the other that is part of bodily life, but this vulnerability becomes highly exacerbated under certain social and political conditions. Although the dominant mode in the United States has been to shore up sovereignty and security to minimize or, indeed, foreclose this vulnerability, it can serve another function and another ideal. The fact that our lives are dependent on others can become the basis of claims for nonmilitaristic political solutions, one which we cannot will away, one which we must attend to, even abide by, as we begin to think about what politics might be implied by staying with the thought of corporeal vulnerability itself.

Is there something to be gained from grieving, from tarrying with grief, remaining exposed to its apparent tolerability and not endeavoring to seek a resolution for grief through violence? Is there something to be gained in the political domain by maintaining grief as part of the framework by which we think our international ties? If we stay with the sense of loss, are we left feeling only passive and powerless, as some fear? Or are we, rather, returned to a sense of human vulnerability, to our collective responsibility for the physical lives of one another? The attempt to foreclose that vulnerability, to banish it, to make ourselves secure at the expense [of] every other human consideration, is surely also to eradicate one of the most important resources from which we must take our bearings and find our way.

To grieve, and to make grief itself into a resource for politics, is not to be resigned to a simple passivity or powerlessness. It is, rather, to allow oneself to extrapolate from this experience of vulnerability to the vulnerability that others suffer through military incursions, occupations, suddenly declared wars, and police brutality. That our very survival can be determined by those we do not know and over whom there is no final control means that life is precarious, and that politics must consider what forms of social and political organization seek best to sustain precarious lives across the globe.

There is a more general conception of the human at work here, one in which we are, from the start, given over to the other, one in which we are, from the start, even prior to individuation itself, and by virtue of our embodiment, given over to an other: this makes us vulnerable to violence, but also to another range of touch, a range that includes the eradication of our being at the one end, and the physical support for our lives, at the other.

We cannot endeavor to "rectify" this situation. And we cannot recover the source of this vulnerability, for it precedes the formation of "I." This condition of being laid bare from the start, dependent on those we do not know, is one with which we cannot precisely argue. We come into the world unknowing and dependent, and, to a certain degree, we remain that way. We can try, from the point of view of autonomy, to argue with this situation, but we are perhaps foolish, if not dangerous, when we do. Of course, we can say that for some this primary scene is extraordinary, loving, and receptive, a warm tissue of relations that support and nurture life in its infancy. For others, this is, however, a scene of abandonment or violence or starvation; they are bodies given over to nothing, or to brutality, or to no sustenance. No matter what the valence of that scene is, however, the fact remains that infancy constitutes a necessary dependency, one that we never fully leave behind. Bodies still must be apprehended as given over. Part of understanding the oppression of lives is precisely to understand that there is no way to argue away this condition of a primary vulnerability, of being given over to the touch of the other, even if, or precisely when, there is no other there, and no support for our lives. To counter oppression requires that one understand that lives are supported and maintained differentially, that there are radically different ways in which human physical vulnerability is distributed across the globe. Certain lives will be highly protected, and the abrogation of their claims to sanctity will be sufficient to mobilize the forces of war. And other lives will not find such fast and furious support and will not even qualify as "grievable."

What are the cultural contours of the notion of the human at work here? And how do the contours that we accept as the cultural frame for the human limit the extent to which we can avow loss as loss? This is surely a question that lesbian, gay, and bi-studies has asked in relation to violence against sexual minorities, and that transgendered people have asked as they have been singled out for harassment and sometimes murder, and that intersexed people have asked, whose formative years have so often been marked by an unwanted violence against their bodies in the name of a normative notion of human morphology. This is no doubt as well the basis of a profound affinity between movements centered on gender and sexuality with efforts to counter the normative human morphologies and capacities that condemn or efface those who are physically challenged. It must, as well, also be part of the affinity with antiracist struggles, given the racial differential that undergirds the culturally viable notions of the human — ones that we see acted out in dramatic and terrifying ways in the global arena at the present time.

So what is the relation between violence and what is "unreal," between violence and unreality that attends to those who become the victims of violence, and where does the notion of the ungrievable life come in? On the level of discourse, certain lives are not considered lives at all, they cannot be humanized; they fit no dominant frame for the human, and their dehumanization occurs first, at this level. This level then gives rise to a physical violence that in some sense delivers the message of dehumanization, which is already at work in the culture.

So it is not just that a discourse exists in which there is no frame and no story and no name for such a life, or that violence might be said to realize or apply this discourse. Violence against those who are already not quite lives, who are living in a state of suspension between life and death, leaves a mark that is no mark. If there is a discourse, it is a silent and melancholic writing in which there have been no lives, and no losses, there has been no common physical condition, no vulnerability that serves as the basis for an apprehension of our commonality, and there has been no sundering of that commonality. None of this takes place on the order of the event. None of this takes place. How many lives have been lost from AIDS in Africa in the last few years? Where are the media representations of this loss, the discursive elaborations of what these losses mean for communities there?

I began this chapter with a suggestion that perhaps the interrelated movements and modes of inquiry that collect here might need to consider autonomy as one dimension of their normative aspirations, one value to realize when we ask ourselves, in what direction ought we to proceed, and what kinds of values ought we to be realizing? I suggested as well that the way in which the body figures in gender and sexuality studies, and in the struggles for a less oppressive social world for the otherwise gendered and for sexual minorities of all kinds, is precisely to underscore the value of being beside oneself, of being a porous boundary, given over to others, finding oneself in a trajectory of desire in which one is taken out of oneself, and resituated irreversibly in a field of others in which one is not the presumptive center. The particular sociality that belongs to bodily life, to sexual life, and to becoming gendered (which is always, to a certain extent, becoming gendered *for others*) establishes a field of ethical enmeshment with others and a sense of disorientation for the first-person, that is, the perspective of the ego. As bodies, we are always for something more than, and other than, ourselves. To articulate this as an entitlement is not always easy, but perhaps not impossible. It suggests, for instance, that "association" is not a luxury, but one of the very conditions and prerogatives of freedom. Indeed, the kinds of associations we maintain importantly take many forms. It will not do to extol the marriage norm as the new ideal for this movement, as the Human Rights Campaign has erroneously done.[1] No doubt, marriage and same-sex domestic partnerships should certainly be available as options, but to install either as a model for sexual legitimacy is precisely to constrain the sociality of the body in acceptable ways. In light

AS BODIES, WE ARE ALWAYS FOR SOMETHING MORE THAN, AND OTHER THAN, OURSELVES.

of seriously damaging judicial decisions against second parent adoptions in recent years, it is crucial to expand our notions of kinship beyond the heterosexual frame. It would be a mistake, however, to reduce kinship to family, or to assume that all sustaining community and friendship ties are extrapolations of kin relations.

I make the argument [elsewhere] . . . that kinship ties that bind persons to one another may well be no more or less than the intensification of community ties, may or may not be based on enduring or exclusive sexual relations, may well consist of ex-lovers, nonlovers, friends, and community members. The relations of kinship cross the boundaries between community and family and sometimes redefine the meaning of friendship as well. When these modes of intimate association produce sustaining webs of relationships, they constitute a "breakdown" of traditional kinship that displaces the presumption that biological and sexual relations structure kinship centrally. In addition, the incest taboo that governs kinship ties, producing a necessary exogamy, does not necessarily operate among friends in the same way or, for that matter, in networks of communities. Within these frames, sexuality is no longer exclusively regulated by the rules of kinship at the same time that the durable tie can be situated outside of the conjugal frame. Sexuality becomes open to a number of social articulations that do not always imply binding relations or conjugal ties. That not all of our relations last or are meant to, however, does not mean that we are immune to grief. On the contrary, sexuality outside the field of monogamy well may open us to a different sense of community, intensifying the question of where one finds enduring ties, and so become the condition for an attunement to losses that exceed a discretely private realm.

Nevertheless, those who live outside the conjugal frame or maintain modes of social organization for sexuality that are neither monogamous nor quasi-marital are more and more considered unreal, and their lows and losses less than "true" loves and "true" losses. The derealization of this domain of human intimacy and sociality works by denying reality and truth to the relations at issue.

The question of who and what is considered real and true is apparently a question of knowledge. But it is also, as Michel Foucault makes plain, a question of power. Having or bearing "truth" and "reality" is an enormously powerful prerogative within the social world, one way that power dissimulates as ontology. According to Foucault, one of the first tasks of a radical critique is to discern the relation "between mechanisms of coercion and elements of knowledge."[2] Here we are confronted with the limits of what is knowable, limits that exercise a certain force, but are not grounded in any necessity, limits that can only be read or interrogated by risking a certain security through departing from an established ontology: "[N]othing can exist as an element of knowledge if, on the one hand, it . . . does not conform to a set of rules and constraints characteristic, for example, of a given type of scientific discourse in a given period, and if, on the other hand, it does not possess the effects of coercion or simply the incentives peculiar to what is scientifically validated or simply rational or simply generally accepted, etc."[3] Knowledge and power are not finally separable but work together to establish a set of subtle and explicit criteria for thinking the world: "It is therefore not a matter of describing what knowledge is and what power is and how one would repress the other or how the other would abuse the one, but rather, a nexus of knowledge-power has to be described so that we can grasp what constitutes the acceptability of a system. . . ."[4]

What this means is that one looks *both* for the conditions by which the object field is constituted, and for *the limits* of those conditions. The limits are to be found where the reproducibility of the conditions is not secure, the site where conditions are contingent, transformable. In Foucault's terms, "schematically speaking, we have perpetual mobility, essential fragility or rather the complex interplay between what replicates the same process and what transforms it."[5] To intervene in the name of transformation means precisely to disrupt what has become settled knowledge and knowable reality, and to use, as it were, one's unreality to make an otherwise impossible or illegible claim. I think that when the unreal lays claim to reality, or enters into its domain, something other than a simple assimilation into prevailing norms can and does take place. The norms themselves can become rattled, display their instability, and become open to resignification.

In recent years, the new gender politics has offered numerous challenges from transgendered and transsexual peoples to established feminist and lesbian/gay frameworks, and the intersex movement has rendered more complex the concerns and demands of sexual rights advocates. If some on the Left thought that these concerns were not properly or substantively political, they have been under pressure to rethink the political sphere in terms of its gendered and sexual presuppositions. The suggestion that butch, femme, and transgendered lives are not essential referents for a refashioning of political life, and for a more just and equitable society, fails to acknowledge the violence that the otherwise gendered suffer in the public world and fails as well to recognize that embodiment denotes a contested set of norms governing who will count as a viable subject within the sphere of politics. Indeed, if we consider that human bodies are not experienced without recourse to some ideality, some frame for experience itself, and that this is as true for the experience of one's own body as it is for experiencing another, and if we accept that that ideality and frame are socially articulated, we can see how it is that embodiment is not thinkable without a relation to a norm, or a set of norms. The struggle to rework the norms by which bodies are experienced is thus crucial not only to disability politics, but to the intersex and transgendered movements as they contest forcibly imposed ideals of what bodies ought to be like. The embodied relation to the norm exercises a transformative potential. To posit possibilities beyond the norm or, indeed, a different future for the norm itself, is part of the work of fantasy when we understand fantasy as taking the body as a point of departure for an articulation that is not always constrained by the body as it is. If we accept that altering these norms that decide normative human morphology gives differential "reality" to different kinds of humans as a result, then we are compelled to affirm that transgendered lives have a potential and actual impact on political life at its most fundamental level, that is, who counts as a human, and what norms govern the appearance of "real" humanness.

Moreover, fantasy is part of the articulation of the possible; it moves us beyond what is merely actual and present into a realm of possibility, the not yet actualized or the not actualizable. The struggle to survive is not really separable from the cultural life of fantasy, and the foreclosure of fantasy — through censorship, degradation, or other means — is one strategy for providing for the social death of persons. Fantasy is not the opposite of reality; it is what reality forecloses, and, as a result, it defines the limits of reality, constituting it as its constitutive outside. The critical promise of fantasy, when and where it exists, is to challenge the contingent limits of what will and will not be called reality. Fantasy is what allows us to imagine ourselves and others otherwise; it establishes the possible in excess of the real; it points elsewhere, and when it is embodied, it brings the elsewhere home.

How do drag, butch, femme, transgender, transsexual persons enter into the political field? They make us not only question what is real, and what "must" be, but they also show us how the norms that govern contemporary notions of reality can be questioned and how new modes of reality can become instituted. These practices of instituting new modes of reality take place in part through the scene of embodiment, where the body is not understood as a static and accomplished fact, but as an aging process, a mode of becoming that, in becoming otherwise, exceeds the norm, reworks the norm, and makes us see how realities to which we thought we were confined are not written in stone. Some people have asked me what is the use of increasing possibilities for gender. I tend to answer: Possibility is not a luxury; it is as crucial as bread. I think we should not underestimate what the thought of the possible does for those for whom the very issue of survival is most urgent. If the answer to the question, is life possible, is yes, that is surely something significant. It cannot, however, be taken for granted as the answer. That is a question whose answer is sometimes "no," or one that has no ready answer, or one that bespeaks an ongoing agony. For many who can and do answer the question in the affirmative, that answer is hard won, if won at all, an accomplishment that is fundamentally conditioned by reality being structured or restructured in such a way that the affirmation becomes possible.

One of the central tasks of lesbian and gay international rights is to assert in clear and public terms the reality of homosexuality, not as an inner truth, not as a sexual practice, but as one of the defining features of the social world in its very intelligibility. In other words, it is one thing to assert the reality of lesbian and gay lives as a reality, and to insist that these are lives worthy of protection in their specificity and commonality; but it is quite another to insist that the very public assertion of gayness calls into question what counts as reality and what counts as a human life. Indeed, the task of international lesbian and gay politics is no less than a remaking of reality, a reconstituting of the human, and a brokering of the question, what is and is not livable? So what is the injustice opposed by such work? I would put it this way: to be called unreal and to have that call, as it were, institutionalized as a form of differential treatment, is to become the other against whom (or against which) the human is made. It is the inhuman, the beyond the human, the less than human, the border that secures the human in its ostensible reality. To be called a copy, to be called unreal, is one way in which one can be oppressed, but consider that it is more fundamental than that. To be oppressed means that you already exist as a subject of some kind, you are there as the visible and oppressed other for the master subject, as a possible or potential subject, but to be unreal is something else again. To be oppressed you must first become intelligible. To find that you are fundamentally unintelligible (indeed, that the laws of culture and of language find you to be an impossibility) is to find that you have not yet achieved access to the human, to find yourself speaking only and always *as if you were* human, but with the sense that you are not, to find that your language is hollow, that no recognition is forthcoming because the norms by which recognition takes place are not in your favor.

We might think that the question of how one does one's gender is a merely cultural question, or an indulgence on the part of those who insist on exercising bourgeois freedom in excessive dimensions. To say, however, that gender is performative is not simply to insist on a right to produce a pleasurable and subversive spectacle but to allegorize the spectacular and consequential ways in which reality is both reproduced and contested. This has consequences for how gender presentations are criminalized and pathologized, how subjects who cross gender risk internment and imprisonment, why violence against transgendered subjects is not recognized as violence, and why this violence is sometimes inflicted by the very states that should be offering such subjects protection from violence.

What if new forms of gender are possible? How does this affect the ways that we live and the concrete needs of the human community? And how are we to distinguish between forms of gender possibility that are valuable and those that are not? I would say that it is not a question merely of producing a new future for genders that do not yet exist. The genders I have in mind have been in existence for a long time, but they have not been admitted into the terms that govern reality. So it is a question of developing within law, psychiatry, social, and literary theory a new legitimating lexicon for the gender complexity that we have been living for a long time. Because the norms governing reality have not admitted these forms to be real, we will, of necessity, call them "new."

What place does the thinking of the possible have within political theorizing? Is the problem that we have no norm to distinguish among kinds of possibility, or does that only appear to be a problem if we fail to comprehend "possibility" itself as a norm? Possibility is an aspiration, something we might hope will be equitably distributed, something that might be socially secured, something that cannot be taken for granted, especially if it is apprehended phenomenologically. The point is not to prescribe new gender norms, as if one were under an obligation to supply a measure, gauge, or norm for the adjudication of competing gender presentations. The normative aspiration at work here has to do with the ability to live and breathe and move and would no doubt belong somewhere in what is called a philosophy of freedom. The thought of a possible life is only an indulgence for those who already know themselves to be possible. For those who are still looking to become possible, possibility is a necessity.

It was Spinoza who claimed that every human being seeks to persist in his own being, and he made this principle of self-persistence, the *conatus,* into the basis of his ethics and, indeed, his politics. When Hegel made the claim that desire is always a desire for recognition, he was, in a way, extrapolating upon this Spinozistic point, telling us, effectively, that to persist in one's own being is only possible on the condition that we are engaged in receiving and offering recognition. If we are not recognizable, if there are no norms of recognition by which we are recognizable, then it is not possible to persist in one's own being, and we are not possible beings; we have been foreclosed from possibility. We think of norms of recognition perhaps as residing already in a cultural world into which we are born, but these norms change, and with the changes in these norms come changes in what does and does not count as recognizably human. To twist the Hegelian argument in a Foucaultian direction: norms of recognition function to produce and to deproduce the notion of the human. This is made true in a specific way when we consider how international norms work in the context of lesbian and gay human rights, especially as they insist that certain kinds of violences are impermissible, that certain lives are vulnerable and worthy of protection, that certain deaths are grievable and worthy of public recognition.

To say that the desire to persist in one's own being depends on norms of recognition is to say that the basis of one's autonomy, one's persistence as an "I" through time, depends fundamentally on a social norm that exceeds that "I," that positions that "I" ec-statically, outside of itself in a world of complex and historically changing norms. In effect, our lives, our very persistence, depend upon such norms or, at least, on the possibility that we will be able to negotiate within them, derive our agency from the field of their operation. In our very ability to persist, we are dependent on what is outside of us, on a broader sociality, and this dependency is the basis of our endurance and survivability. When we assert our "right," as we do and we must, we are not carving out a place for our autonomy — if by autonomy we mean a state of individuation, taken as self-persisting prior to and apart from any relations of dependency on the world of others. We do not negotiate with norms or with Others subsequent to our coming into the world. We come into the world on the condition that the social world is already there, laying the groundwork for us. This implies that I cannot persist without norms of recognition that support my persistence: the sense of possibility pertaining to me must first be imagined from somewhere else before I can begin to imagine myself. My reflexivity is not only socially mediated, but socially constituted. I cannot be who I am without drawing upon the sociality of norms that precede and exceed me. In this sense, I am outside myself from the outset, and must be, in order to survive, and in order to enter into the realm of the possible.

To assert sexual rights, then, takes on a specific meaning against this background. It means, for instance, that when we struggle for rights, we are not simply struggling for rights that attach to my person, but we are struggling *to be conceived as persons*. And there is a difference between the former and the latter. If we are struggling for rights that attach, or should attach, to my personhood, then we assume that personhood as already constituted. But if we are struggling not only to be conceived as persons, but to create a social transformation of the very meaning of personhood, then the assertion of rights becomes a way of intervening into the social and political process by which the human is articulated. International human rights is always in the process of subjecting the human to redefinition and renegotiation. It mobilizes the human in the service of rights, but also rewrites the human and rearticulates the human when it comes up against the cultural limits of its working conception of the human, as it does and must.

I CANNOT BE WHO I AM WITHOUT DRAWING UPON THE SOCIALITY OF NORMS THAT PRECEDE AND EXCEED ME.

Lesbian and gay human rights takes sexuality, in some sense, to be its issue. Sexuality is not simply an attribute one has or a disposition or patterned set of inclinations. It is a mode of being disposed toward others, including in the mode of fantasy, and sometimes only in the mode of fantasy. If we are outside of ourselves as sexual beings, given over from the start, crafted in part through primary relations of dependency and attachment, then it would seem that our being beside ourselves, outside ourselves, is there as a function of sexuality itself, where sexuality is not this or that dimension of our existence, not the key or bedrock of our existence, but, rather, as coextensive with existence, as Merleau-Ponty once aptly suggested.[6]

I have tried here to argue that our very sense of personhood is linked to the desire for recognition, and that desire places us outside ourselves, in a realm of social norms that we do not fully choose, but that provides the horizon and the resource for any sense of choice that we have. *This means that the ec-static character of our existence is essential to the possibility of persisting as human.* In this sense, we can see how sexual rights brings together two related domains of ec-stasy, two connected ways of being outside of ourselves. As sexual, we are dependent on a world of others, vulnerable to need, violence, betrayal, compulsion, fantasy; we project desire, and we have it projected onto us. To be part of a sexual minority means, most emphatically, that we are also dependent on the protection of public and private spaces, on legal sanctions that protect us from violence, on safeguards of various institutional kinds against unwanted aggression imposed upon us, and the violent actions they sometimes instigate. In this sense, our very lives, and the persistence of our desire, depend on there being norms of recognition that produce and sustain our viability as human. Thus, when we speak about sexual rights, we are not merely talking about rights that pertain to our individual desires but to the norms on which our very individuality depends. That means that the discourse of rights avows our dependency, the mode of our being in the hands of others, a mode of being with and for others without which we cannot be.

I served for a few years on the board of the International Gay and Lesbian Human Rights Commission, a group that is located in San Francisco. It is part of a broad international coalition of groups and individuals who struggle to establish both equality and justice for sexual minorities, including transgender and intersexed individuals as well as persons with HIV or AIDS.[7] What astonished me time and again was how often the organization was asked to respond to immediate acts of violence against sexual minorities, especially when that violence was not redressed in any way by local police or government in various places in the globe. I had to reflect on what sort of anxiety is prompted by the public appearance of someone who is openly gay, or presumed to be gay, someone whose gender does not conform to norms, someone whose sexuality defies public prohibitions, someone whose body does not conform with certain morphological ideals. What motivates those who are driven to kill someone for being gay, to threaten to kill someone for being intersexed, or would be driven to kill because of the public appearance of someone who is transgendered?

The desire to kill someone, or killing someone, for not conforming to the gender norm by which a person is "supposed" to live suggests that life itself requires a set of sheltering norms, and that to be outside it, to live outside it, is to court death. The person who threatens violence proceeds from the anxious and rigid belief that a sense of world and a sense of self will be radically undermined if such a being, uncategorizable, is permitted to live within the social world. The negation, through violence, of that body is a vain and violent effort to restore order, to renew the social world on the basis of intelligible gender, and to refuse the challenge to rethink that world as something other than natural or necessary. This is not far removed from the threat of death, or the murder itself, of transsexuals in various countries, and of gay men who read as "feminine" or gay women who read as "masculine." These crimes are not always immediately recognized as criminal acts. Sometimes they are denounced by governments and international agencies; sometimes they are not included as legible or real crimes against humanity by those very institutions.

If we oppose this violence, then we oppose it in the name of what? What is the alternative to this violence, and for what transformation of the social world do I call? This violence emerges from a profound desire to keep the order of binary gender natural or necessary, to make of it a structure, either natural or cultural, or both, that no human can oppose, and still remain human. If a person opposes norms of binary gender not just by having a critical point of view about them, but by incorporating norms critically, and that stylized opposition is legible, then it seems that violence emerges precisely as the demand to undo that legibility, to question its possibility, to render it unreal and impossible in the face of its appearance to the contrary. This is, then, no simple difference in points of view. To counter that embodied opposition by violence is to say, effectively, that this body, this challenge to an accepted version of the world is and shall be unthinkable. The effort to enforce the boundaries of what will be regarded as real requires stalling what is contingent, frail, open to fundamental transformation in the gendered order of things.

An ethical query emerges in light of such an analysis: how might we encounter the difference that calls our grids of intelligibility into question without trying to foreclose the challenge that the difference delivers? What might it mean to learn to live in the anxiety of that challenge, to feel the surety of one's epistemological and ontological anchor go, but to be willing, in the name of the human, to allow the human to become something other than what it is traditionally assumed to be? This means that we must learn to live and to embrace the destruction and rearticulation of the human in the name of a more capacious and, finally, less violent world, not knowing in advance what precise form our humanness does and will take. It means we must be open to its permutations, in the name of nonviolence. As Adriana Cavarero points out, paraphrasing Arendt, the question we pose to the Other is simple and unanswerable: "who are you?"[8] The violent response is the one that does not ask, and does not seek to know. It wants to shore up what it knows, to expunge what threatens it with not-knowing, what forces it to reconsider the presuppositions of its world, their contingency, their malleability. The nonviolent response lives with its unknowingness about the Other in the face of the Other, since sustaining the bond that the question opens is finally more valuable than knowing in advance what holds us in common, as if we already have all the resources we need to know what defines the human, what its future life might be.

THAT WE CANNOT PREDICT OR CONTROL WHAT PERMUTATIONS OF THE HUMAN MIGHT ARISE DOES NOT MEAN THAT WE MUST VALUE ALL POSSIBLE PERMUTATIONS OF THE HUMAN.

That we cannot predict or control what permutations of the human might arise does not mean that we must value all possible permutations of the human; it does not mean that we cannot struggle for the realization of certain values, democratic and nonviolent, international and antiracist. The point is only that to struggle for those values is precisely to avow that one's own position is not sufficient to elaborate the spectrum of the human, that one must enter into a collective work in which one's own status as a subject must, for democratic reasons, become disoriented, exposed to what it does not know.

The point is not to apply social norms to lived social instances, to order and define them (as Foucault has criticized), nor is it to find justificatory mechanisms for the grounding of social norms that are extrasocial (even as they operate under the name of the social). There are times when both of these activities do and must take place: we level judgments against criminals for illegal acts, and so subject them to a normalizing procedure; we consider our grounds for action in collective contexts and try to find modes of deliberation and reflection about which we can agree. But neither of these is all we do with norms. Through recourse to norms, the sphere of the humanly intelligible is circumscribed, and this circumscription is consequential for any ethics and any conception of social transformation. We might try to claim that we must *first* know the fundamentals of the human in order to preserve and promote human life as we know it. But what if the very categories of the human have excluded those who should be described and sheltered within its terms? What if those who ought to belong to the human do not operate within the modes of reasoning and justifying validity claims that have been proffered by western forms of rationalism? Have we ever yet known the human? And what might it take to approach that knowing? Should we be wary of knowing it too soon or of any final or definitive knowing? If we take the field of the human for granted, then we fail to think critically and ethically about the consequential ways that the human is being produced, reproduced, and deproduced. This latter inquiry does not exhaust the field of ethics, but I cannot imagine a responsible ethics or theory of social transformation operating without it.

The necessity of keeping our notion of the human open to a future articulation is essential to the project of international human rights discourse and politics. We see this time and again when the very notion of the human is presupposed; the human is defined in advance, in terms that are distinctively western, very often American, and, therefore, partial and parochial. When we start with the human as a foundation, then the human at issue in human rights is already known, already defined. And yet, the human is supposed to be the ground for a set of rights and obligations that are global in reach. How we move from the local to the international (conceived globally in such a way that it does not recirculate the presumption that all humans belong to established nation-states) is a major question for international politics, but it takes a specific form for international lesbian, gay, bi-, trans-, and intersex struggles as well as for feminism. An anti-imperialist or, minimally, nonimperialist conception of international human rights must call into question what is meant by the human and learn from the various ways and means by which it is defined across cultural venues. This means that local conceptions of what is human or, indeed, of what the basic conditions and needs of human life are, must be subjected to reinterpretation, since there are historical and cultural circumstances in which the human is defined differently. Its basic needs and, hence, basic entitlements are made known through various media, through various kinds of practices, spoken and performed.

A reductive relativism would say that we cannot speak of the human or of international human rights, since there are only and always local and provisional understandings of these terms, and that the generalizations themselves do violence to the specificity of the meanings in question. This is not my view. I'm not ready to rest there. Indeed, I think we are compelled to speak of the human, and of the international, and to find out in particular how human rights do and do not work, for example, in favor of women, of what women are, and what they are not. But to speak in this way, and to call for social transformations in the name of women, we must also be part of a critical democratic project. Moreover, the category of women has been used differentially and with exclusionary aims, and not all women have been included within its terms; women have not been fully incorporated into the human. Both categories are still in process, underway, unfulfilled, thus we do not yet know and cannot ever definitively know in what the human finally consists. This means that we must follow a double path in politics: we must use this language to assert an entitlement to conditions of life in ways that affirm the constitutive role of sexuality and gender in political life, and we must also subject our very categories to critical scrutiny. We must find out the limits of their inclusivity and translatability, the presuppositions they include, the ways in which they must be expanded, destroyed, or reworked both to encompass and open up what it is to be human and gendered. When the United Nations conference at Beijing met a few years ago, there was a discourse on "women's human rights" (or when we hear of the International Gay and Lesbian Human Rights Commission), which strikes many people as a paradox. Women's human rights? Lesbian and gay human rights? But think about what this coupling actually does. It performs the human as contingent, a category that has in the past, and continues in the present, to define a variable and restricted population, which may or may not include lesbians and gays, may or may not include women, which has several racial and ethnic differentials at work in its operation. It says that such groups have their own set of human rights, that what human may mean when we think about the humanness of women is perhaps different from what human has meant when it has functioned as presumptively male. It also says that these terms are defined, variably, in relation to one another. And we could certainly make a similar argument about race. Which populations have qualified as the human and which have not? What is the history of this category? Where are we in its history at this time?

I would suggest that in this last process, we can only rearticulate or resignify the basic categories of ontology, of being human, of being gendered, of being recognizably sexual, to the extent that we submit ourselves to a process of cultural translation. The point is not to assimilate foreign or unfamiliar notions of gender or humanness into our own as if it is simply a matter of incorporating alienness into an established lexicon. Cultural translation is also a process of yielding our most fundamental categories, that is, seeing how and why they break up, require resignification when they encounter the limits of an available episteme: what is unknown or not yet known. It is crucial to recognize that the notion of the human will only be built over time in and by the process of cultural translation, where it is not a translation between two languages that stay enclosed, distinct, unified. But rather, *translation will compel each language to change in order to apprehend the other,* and this apprehension, at the limit of what is familiar, parochial, and already known, will be the occasion for both an ethical and social transformation. It will constitute a loss, a disorientation, but one in which the human stands a chance of coming into being anew.

When we ask what makes a life livable, we are asking about certain normative conditions that must be fulfilled for life to become life. And so there are at least two senses of life, the one that refers to the minimum biological form of living, and another that intervenes at the start, which establishes minimum conditions for a livable life with regard to human life.[9] And this does not imply that we can disregard the merely living in favor of the livable life, but that we must ask, as we asked about gender violence, what humans require in order to maintain and reproduce the conditions of their own livability. And what are our politics such that we are, in whatever way is possible, both conceptualizing the possibility of the livable life, and arranging for its institutional support? There will always be disagreement about what this means, and those who claim that a single political direction is necessitated by virtue of this commitment will be mistaken. But this is only because to live is to live a life politically, in relation to power, in relation to others, in the act of assuming responsibility for a collective future. To assume responsibility for a future, however, is not to know its direction fully in advance, since the future, especially the future with and for others, requires a certain openness and unknowingness; it implies becoming part of a process the outcome of which no one subject can surely predict. It also implies that a certain agonism and contestation over the course of direction will and must be in play. Contestation must be in play for politics to become democratic. Democracy does not speak in unison; its tunes are dissonant, and necessarily so. It is not a predictable process; it must be undergone, like a passion must be undergone. It may also be that life itself becomes foreclosed when the right way is decided in advance, when we impose what is right for everyone and without finding a way to enter into community, and to discover there the "right" in the midst of cultural translation. It may be that what is right and what is good consist in staying open to the tensions that beset the most fundamental categories we require, in knowing unknowingness at the core of what we know, and what we need, and in recognizing the sign of life in what we undergo without certainty about what will come.

NOTES

1 The Human Rights Campaign is the main lobbying organization for lesbian and gay rights in the United States. Situated in Washington, D.C., it has maintained that gay marriage is the number one priority of lesbian and gay politics in the U.S. See www.hrc.org. [All notes are Butler's.]

2 Michel Foucault, "What is Critique?" in *The Politics of Truth,* 50. This essay is reprinted with an essay by me entitled "Critique as Virtue" in David Ingram, *The Political.*

3 "What is Critique?" 52.

4 Ibid., 52–53.

5 Ibid., 58.

[6] Maurice Merleau-Ponty, *The Phenomenology of Perception.*
[7] See www.iglhrc.org for more information on the mission and accomplishments of this organization.
[8] See Adriana Cavarero, *Relating Narratives,* 20–29 and 87–92.
[9] See Giorgio Agamben, *Homo Sacer: Sovereign Power and Bare Life,* 1–12.

BIBLIOGRAPHY

Agamben, Giorgio. *Homo Sacer: Sovereign Power and Bare Life.* Translated by Daniel Heller-Roazen. Stanford: Stanford University Press, 1998.
Cavarero, Adriana. *Relating Narratives: Storytelling and Selfhood.* Translated by Paul A. Kottman. London: Routledge, 2000.
Foucault, Michel. "What is Critique?" *The Politics of Truth,* edited by Sylvere Lotringer and Lysa Hochroth. New York: Semiotext(e), 1997.
Ingram, David. *The Political.* San Francisco: Wiley-Blackwell, 2002.
Merleau-Ponty, Maurice. "The Body in its Sexual Being." *The Phenomenology of Perception.* Translated by Colin Smith. New York: Routledge, 1967.

QUESTIONS FOR A SECOND READING

1. Butler's "Beside Oneself: On the Limits of Sexual Autonomy" is a philosophical essay, and one of the difficulties it presents to a reader is its emphasis on conceptual language. The sentences most often refer to concepts or ideas rather than to people, places, or events in the concrete, tangible, or observable world. It refers to the *human* or to the *body,* but without telling the stories of particular humans or particular bodies. And this can be frustrating. Without something concrete, without some situation or context in which the conceptual can take shape, these conceptual terms can lose their force or meaning. (If there is a story here, it is the story of a struggle to understand and to articulate a response to the essay's opening question: What makes for a livable world?)

   As you reread Butler, pay attention to the conceptual terms that recur. Words like *ethics, power, life, grief, agency,* and *possibility* punctuate this essay, and it is through these key terms that Butler attempts to describe and theorize the world we live in. Pick one of these terms (or one of your own choosing) and pay particular attention to the ways it is used. How is it defined in its initial context? Beyond its dictionary definition, what does this particular term come to mean for Butler? For you as a reader? And how is its meaning elaborated or consolidated or complicated by its uses later in the text?

2. At one point Butler says, "I might try to tell a story about what I am feeling, but it would have to be a story in which the very 'I' who seeks to tell the story is stopped in the midst of the telling. The very 'I' is called into question by its relation to the one to whom I address myself" (p. 115).

   As you reread, pay attention to personal pronouns, such as "I," "we," "one," "you," "our," "my," and "your." In an essay about how we are "constituted," the struggle to claim identity in relation to others is played out in the arena of the sentence. Choose a paragraph where the play of personal pronouns is particularly odd or rich, and be prepared to describe what Butler is doing. And be prepared to think out loud (or to think on the page) about the relationship between what the writer is doing (the deed of writing) and what the paragraph says.

3. Judith Butler writes in the field of Queer Theory. Queer theorists are concerned with queer lives, queer writing, and the study of gender and sexuality. In "Beside Oneself: On the Limits of Sexual Autonomy," Butler raises questions about the visibility, intelligibility, and recognition of gays and lesbians and also about the lives of those who may not conform to any fixed or binary gender norms. She writes:

    > To find that you are fundamentally unintelligible (indeed, that the laws of culture and of language find you to be an impossibility) is to find that you have not yet achieved access to the human, to find yourself speaking only and always *as if you were* human, but with the sense that you are not, to find that your language is hollow, that no recognition is forthcoming because the norms by which recognition takes place are not in your favor. (p. 124)

    This is a long sentence, and a complicated one. Butler knows this; she knows that it will be difficult for a reader, so she provides what help she can with the parenthetical phrase and the italics. It is useful, as Butler's reader, to practice reading and rereading her sentences, to unfold them slowly, word by word. What does it mean to be "unintelligible"? Why might being unintelligible also mean not having "access to the human" or having a "hollow" language? What examples can you think of that might help someone to better understand Butler's claim about gender and sexuality? And finally, what seems to be at stake in making this claim?

    As an exercise in reading and in understanding, write a paraphrase, a translation of this sentence (or a Butler sentence of your own choosing). And in the sentence or sentences of your paraphrase, imitate Butler's rhythm and style.

4. The opening lines of Butler's essay might be understood as an invitation to participate with her in one of the traditions of philosophy. She writes:

    > What makes for a livable world is no idle question. It is not merely a question for philosophers. It is posed in various idioms all the time by people in various walks of life. If that makes them all philosophers, then that is a conclusion I am happy to embrace. (p. 114)

    Stylistically, Butler makes use of questions as a way of enacting philosophical inquiry. As you reread, pay attention to Butler's questions and, through these, to the method and the rhythm of philosophical inquiry. How would you describe the use, placement, and pacing of her questions? How does one question seem to lead to another? Where do they come from? How do they work together to make an argument?

ASSIGNMENTS FOR WRITING

1. The opening lines of Butler's essay might be understood as an invitation to participate with her in one of the traditions of philosophy. She writes:

> What makes for a livable world is no idle question. It is not merely a question for philosophers. It is posed in various idioms all the time by people in various walks of life. If that makes them all philosophers, then that is a conclusion I am happy to embrace. It becomes a question for ethics, I think, not only when we ask the personal question, what makes my own life bearable, but when we ask, from a position of power, and from the point of view of distributive justice, what makes, or ought to make, the lives of others bearable? Somewhere in the answer we find ourselves not only committed to a certain view of what life is, and what it should be, but also of what constitutes the human, the distinctively human life, and what does not. (p. 114)

Write an essay that takes up this invitation — and that takes it up in specific reference to what Butler has offered in "Beside Oneself: On the Limits of Sexual Autonomy." You will need, then, to take some time to represent her essay — both what it says and what it does. The "Questions for a Second Reading" should be helpful in preparing for this. Imagine an audience of smart people, people who may even know something about Butler but who have not read this essay. You have read it, and you want to give them a sense of how and why you find it interesting and important. But you'll also need to take time to address her questions in your own terms: What makes for a livable world? What constitutes the human? Don't slight this part of your essay. Give yourself as many pages as you gave Butler. You should, however, make it clear that you are writing in response to what you have read. You'll want to indicate, both directly and indirectly, how your thoughts are shaped by, indebted to, or in response to hers.

2. Consider the following passage from Butler's "Beside Oneself: On the Limits of Sexual Autonomy":

> To be ec-static means, literally, to be outside oneself, and this can have several meanings: to be transported beyond oneself by a passion, but also to be *beside oneself* with rage or grief. I think that if I can still speak to a "we," and include myself within its terms, I am speaking to those of us who are living in certain ways *beside ourselves*, whether it is in sexual passion, or emotional grief, or political rage. In a sense, the predicament is to understand what kind of community is composed of those who are beside themselves. (p. 116)

To be *beside oneself* is an idiomatic phrase — which suggests that the meaning of the phrase cannot be determined literally but rather has some figurative connotation. In this sense, for someone not familiar with the idiom, the phrase might even be misleading or misunderstood. Butler takes this idiomatic phrase to its theoretical and social conclusions, thinking carefully about what exactly the figurative expression means to say, what it wants us to say, how it has been used, and how it might be made to serve as a fresh tool for thinking. This is a bold project, and one that takes both a critical eye and creative thought.

We might think of all idiomatic expressions as carrying important social, political, and emotional meanings that, while they might not always be visible on the surface or in everyday conversation, propose a way of thinking: *Blood is thicker than water. I was out of my mind. He is out of touch. She has gone out on a limb. It is all water under the bridge.* For this assignment, write an essay that takes up a particular idiomatic phrase as a tool for thinking through an issue that is important to you. Choose carefully — both the issue and the idiom. There should be an urgency in your writing, as there is in Butler's. And, to locate your essay as a reading of Butler, the urgency should be similarly thoughtful and modulated. You are offering your essay as a response to hers, as a similar exercise in thinking.

MAKING CONNECTIONS

1. At a key point in her essay, Butler refers to the work of Michel Foucault:

> The question of who and what is considered real and true is apparently a question of knowledge. But it is also, as Michel Foucault makes plain, a question of power. Having or bearing "truth" and "reality" is an enormously powerful prerogative within the social world, one way that power dissimulates as ontology. According to Foucault, one of the first tasks of a radical critique is to discern the relation "between mechanisms of coercion and elements of knowledge." (p. 121)

And she goes on for some length to work with passages from Foucault, although not from his book *Discipline and Punish*. One of its chapters, "Panopticism," is a selection in *Ways of Reading*. Take some time to reread Butler's essay, paying particular attention to her use of Foucault. Where and why is Foucault helpful to her? In what ways is she providing a new argument or a counterargument? And take time to reread "Panopticism." What passages might be useful in extending or challenging Butler's argument in "Beside Oneself"? Using these two sources, write an essay in which you talk about Butler and Foucault and their engagement with what might be called "radical critique," an effort (in the terms offered above) to "discern the relation 'between mechanisms of coercion and elements of knowledge.'"

Note: The assignment limits you to these two sources, the two selections in the textbook. Butler and Foucault have written much, and their work circulates widely. You are most likely not in a position to speak about everything they have written or about all that has been written about them. We wanted to define a starting point that was manageable. Still, if you wanted to do more research, you might begin by reading the Foucault essay that Butler cites, "What Is Critique?"; you might go to the library to look through books by Butler and Foucault, choosing one or two that seem to offer themselves as next steps; or you could go to essays written by scholars who, like you, are trying to think about the two together.

e 2. In his essay "States," Edward Said theorizes about the notion of exile in relation to Palestinian identity, offering a study of exile and dislocation through his analysis of photographs taken by Jean Mohr. Consider the following passage:

> We turn ourselves into objects not for sale, but for scrutiny. People ask us, as if looking into an exhibit case, "What is it you Palestinians want?" — as if we can put our demands into a single neat phrase. All of us speak of *awdah*, "return," but do we mean that literally, or do we mean "we must restore ourselves to ourselves"? (para. 31)

When Said talks about being looked at as though in an exhibit case, we might understand him as being concerned with the problem of dehumanization. After all, to be in an exhibit case is to be captured, trapped, or even dead. We might understand Butler as also wrestling with the problem of dehumanization; she writes: "I would like to start, and to end, with the question of the human, of who counts as the human, and the related question of whose lives count as lives, and with a question that has preoccupied many of us for years: what makes for a grievable life?"

Write an essay in which you consider the ways Said and Butler might be said to be speaking with each other. How might the condition of exile be like the condition of being *beside oneself*? What kind of connections — whether you see them as productive or problematic, or both at once — can be made between the ways Said talks about nation, identity, and home, and the ways Butler talks about gender and sexuality? What passages from each seem to have the other in mind? How does each struggle with reference, with pronouns like "we" and "our"?

e 3. Richard Miller, in "The Dark Night of the Soul," asks a simple and disturbing question. Institutions of higher education teach, and have taught, the "literate arts," reading and writing, always with the assumption that they improve our lives and make us better as human beings. But do they? Miller asks, "Is there any way to justify or explain a life spent working with — and teaching others to work with—texts?"

Miller's essay is divided into sections; most sections consider a particular text: Krakauer's *Into the Wild*, Descartes's *Meditations*, Mary Karr's *The Liar's*

---

e See the e-Pages at bedfordstmartins.com/waysofreading.

Club. Reread Miller in order to get a sense of his argument, style, and method, and then write a section that could be added to "The Dark Night of the Soul" with Butler's "Beside Oneself" as its subject. You could talk about your reading of the text—and what it has to offer. You could talk about its use, as represented in this textbook, in your class, or in the writing of your colleagues. You might also talk about where you might insert your entry into the essay "The Dark Night of the Soul."

ANNE Carson

Anne Carson (b. 1950) grew up in small towns in Ontario, Canada. She was raised in an Irish Catholic family with parents who had active reading lives: her father, a banker, was an avid reader of history books, and her mother read the many books that arrived in the *Reader's Digest* collections. As a teenager, Carson became determined to study ancient Greek and found a teacher to help her during the lunch period. She attended the University of Toronto, where she studied Latin and Greek, and earned a BA in 1974 and a master's degree in classics in 1975. Carson has taught at McGill University in Montreal, Princeton, Emory University, the University of Michigan, and New York University. She is a poet, an essayist, a novelist, a translator, a librettist, and a literary critic. She is one of the most versatile, dynamic, and respected writers of our time.

In addition to *Short Talks* (1992), from which the following selection is taken, she has published a number of critically acclaimed and often genre-bending works, including *Eros the Bittersweet* (1986); *Plainwater* (1995); *Autobiography of Red* (1998); *Men in the Off Hours* (2001); *The Beauty of the Husband* (2002), which won the T. S. Eliot Poetry Prize, making Carson the first woman to have been given this honor; and a collection of essays entitled *Decreation: Poetry, Essays, Opera* (2005). Carson has also translated several collections of classic Greek poetry, including *If Not, Winter: Fragments of Sappho* (2002), *An Oresteia: Agamemnon by Aiskhylos; Elektra by Sophokles; Orestes by Euripides* (2009), and *Antigonick* (2012). Carson has been the recipient of a significant number of prizes and awards — among them a Guggenheim Fellowship, a Lannan Award, a Pushcart Prize, the Griffin Poetry Prize, and a 2000 MacArthur "Genius" Award.

The entries in Carson's *Short Talks* have been called prose poems, miniature lectures, flash fiction, meditations, even essays. And, as with much of Carson's work, *Short Talks* seems to resist classification as any particular *kind* of literature. Carson has said the pieces emerged out of "a bunch of drawings which [she] put titles on, and then the titles got longer and longer until the drawings disappeared." Carson is a particularly erudite writer, drawing from various fields of knowledge and enacting innovative and often playful experiments with language and thought. In a 2006 interview in *The Guardian*, Carson said: "I don't know that we really think any thoughts; we think connections between thoughts. That's where the mind moves, that's what's new, and the thoughts themselves have probably been there in my head or lots of other people's heads for a long time. But the jumps between them are entirely at that moment." This nontraditional way of thinking *about* thinking itself seems one of the qualities that drives Carson's work.

Short Talks

INTRODUCTION

Early one morning words were missing. Before that, words were not. Facts were, faces were. In a good story, Aristotle tells us, everything that happens is pushed by something else. Three old women were bending in the fields. What use is it to question us? they said. Well it shortly became clear that they knew everything there is to know about the snowy fields and the blue-green shoots and the plant called "audacity," which poets mistake for violets. I began to copy out everything that was said. The marks construct an instant of nature gradually, without the boredom of a story. I emphasize this. I will do anything to avoid boredom. It is the task of a lifetime. You can never know enough, never work enough, never use the infinitives and participles oddly enough, never impede the movement harshly enough, never leave the mind quickly enough.

ON *HOMO SAPIENS*

With small cuts Cro-Magnon man recorded the moon's phases on the handles of his tools, thinking about her as he worked. Animals. Horizon. Face in a pan of water. In every story I tell comes a point where I can see no further. I hate that point. It is why they call storytellers blind — a taunt.

ON GERTRUDE STEIN ABOUT 9:30

How curious. I had no idea! Today has ended.

ON TROUT

In haiku there are various sorts of expressions about trout — "autumn trout" and "descending trout" and "rusty trout" are some I have heard. Descending trout and rusty trout are trout that have laid their eggs. Worn out, completely exhausted, they are going down to the sea. Of course there were occasionally trout that spent the winter in deep pools. These were called "remaining trout."

ON PARMENIDES

We pride ourselves on being civilized people. Yet what if the names for things were utterly different? Italy, for example. I have a friend named Andreas, an Italian. He has lived in Argentina as well as England, and also

Costa Rica for some time. Everywhere he lives, he invites people over for supper. It is a lot of work. Artichoke pasta. Peaches. His deep smile never fades. What if the proper name for Italy turns out to be Brzoy—will Andreas continue to travel the world like the wandering moon with her borrowed light? I fear we failed to understand what he was saying or his reasons. What if every time he said *cities,* he meant *delusion,* for example.

ON MAJOR AND MINOR

Major things are wind, evil, a good fighting horse, prepositions, inexhaustible love, the way people choose their king. Minor things include dirt, the names of schools of philosophy, mood and not having a mood, the correct time. There are more major things than minor things overall, yet there are more minor things than I have written here, but it is disheartening to list them. When I think of you reading this, I do not want you to be taken captive, separated by a wire mesh lined with glass from your life itself, like some Elektra.

ON THE RULES OF PERSPECTIVE

A bad trick. Mistake. Dishonesty. These are the views of Braque. Why? Braque rejected perspective. Why? Someone who spends his life drawing profiles will end up believing that man has one eye, Braque felt. Braque wanted to take full possession of objects. He said as much in published interviews. Watching the small shiny planes of the landscape recede out of his grasp filled Braque with loss so he smashed them. *Nature morte,* said Braque.

ON *LE BONHEUR D'ETRE BIEN AIMÉE*

Day after day I think of you as soon as I wake up. Someone has put cries of birds on the air like jewels.

ON RECTIFICATION

Kafka liked to have his watch an hour and a half fast. Felice kept setting it right. Nonetheless for five years they almost married. He made a list of arguments for and against marriage, including inability to bear the assault of his own life (for) and the sight of the nightshirts laid out on his parents' beds at 10:30 (against). Hemorrhage saved him. When advised not to speak by doctors in the sanatorium, he left glass sentences all over the floor. Felice, says one of them, had too much nakedness left in her.

ON WALKING BACKWARDS

My mother forbad us to walk backwards. That is how the dead walk, she would say. Where did she get this idea? Perhaps from a bad translation. The dead, after all, do not walk backwards but they do walk behind us.

They have no lungs and cannot call out but would love for us to turn around. They are victims of love, many of them.

ON THE MONA LISA

Every day he poured his question into her, as you pour water from one vessel into another, and it poured back. Don't tell me he was painting his mother, lust, et cetera. There is a moment when the water is not in one vessel nor in the other — what a thirst it was, and he supposed that when the canvas became completely empty he would stop. But women are strong. She knew vessels, she knew water, she knew mortal thirst.

ON WATERPROOFING

Franz Kafka was Jewish. He had a sister, Ottla, Jewish. Ottla married a jurist, Josef David, not Jewish. When the Nuremberg Laws were introduced to Bohemia-Moravia in 1942, quiet Ottla suggested to Josef David that they divorce. He at first refused. She spoke about sleep shapes and property and their two daughters and a rational approach. She did not mention, because she did not yet know the word, Auschwitz, where she would die in October 1943. After putting the apartment in order she packed a rucksack and was given a good shoeshine by Josef David. He applied a coat of grease. Now they are waterproof, he said.

ON SYLVIA PLATH

Did you see her mother on television? She said plain, burned things. She said I thought it an excellent poem but it hurt me. She did not say jungle fear. She did not say jungle hatred wild jungle weeping chop it back chop it. She said self-government she said end of the road. She did not say humming in the middle of the air what you came for chop.

ON READING

Some fathers hate to read but love to take the family on trips. Some children hate trips but love to read. Funny how often these find themselves passengers in the same automobile. I glimpsed the stupendous clear-cut shoulders of the Rockies from between paragraphs of *Madame Bovary*. Cloud shadows roved languidly across her huge rock throat, traced her fir flanks. Since those days, I do not look at hair on female flesh without thinking, Deciduous?

ON SUNDAY DINNER WITH FATHER

Are you going to put that chair back where it belongs or just leave it there looking like a uterus? (Our balcony is a breezy June balcony.) Are you going to let your face distorted by warring desires pour down on us all through the meal or tidy yourself so we can at least enjoy our dessert?

(We weight down the corners of everything on the table with little solid-silver laws.) Are you going to nick your throat open on those woodpecker scalps as you do every Sunday night or just sit quietly while Laetitia plays her clarinet for us? (My father, who smokes a brand of cigar called Dimanche Eternel, uses them as ashtrays.)

ON HEDONISM

Beauty makes me hopeless. I don't care why anymore I just want to get away. When I look at the city of Paris I long to wrap my legs around it. When I watch you dancing there is a heartless immensity like a sailor in a dead-calm sea. Desires as round as peaches bloom in me all night, I no longer gather what falls.

ON SHELTER

You can write on a wall with a fish heart, it's because of the phosphorus. They eat it. There are shacks like that down along the river. I am writing this to be as wrong as possible to you. Replace the door when you leave, it says. Now you tell me how wrong that is, how long it glows. Tell me.

QUESTIONS FOR A SECOND READING

1. As you reread "Short Talks," you may not be familiar with all the names or texts that serve as quick points of reference: from Aristotle to Gertrude Stein to Sylvia Plath to *Madame Bovary*. Choose one reference that seems interesting or compelling to you and, in groups or on your own, go to the library (as well as the Internet) to gather materials and to take notes. (We ask you to use the library so that you can learn your way around it, but also so that you can put your hands on books. It makes a difference.) Here are some questions to ask: Who is this person? What is this text? How does it (or he or she) serve as a point of reference in "Short Talks"? What is Carson doing here?

   In preparation for class discussion, write a gloss, an explanatory paragraph outlining your responses to these questions that can be of use to other students in your class.

2. "Short Talks" provides references to writers and artists. It is also often voiced as a personal narrative, a familiar example of someone telling you something about their thoughts and experiences. As you reread, pull out the threads of this personal narrative. Who is speaking? about what? to what ends? with what urgency? How would you characterize the speaker in this text?

3. The form of Carson's "Short Talks" presents challenges, but it also presents opportunities. As you reread, think about this text as a type of experimental essay. How does it draw on the conventions of the essay? How does it defy

or revise those conventions? How would you describe its formal features in relation to what you understand to be conventional essay form? How does "Short Talks" satisfy or challenge a reader's expectations?

Be prepared to discuss these questions in class—and come with other questions of your own. Also prepare a Carson-like text—four paragraphs, each with a subheading, that seem like "Short Talks" in style and intent.

ASSIGNMENTS FOR WRITING

1. In the "Introduction" in "Short Talks," Carson says:

> You can never know enough, never work enough, never use the infinitives and participles oddly enough, never impede the movement harshly enough, never leave the mind quickly enough. (p. 140)

This passage may or may not be a way of announcing the essay's subject or topic. As you reread "Short Talks," read it with the goal of taking a position on what this essay is "about." What is it "about"? And what might be the connections between its subject and its style or method, these short units of prose, each with a subheading?

Write an essay in which you present your understanding of "Short Talks," what it does and what it has to say. You can take as your audience your colleagues in class, or you could be addressing readers like you who will be coming to "Short Talks" for the first time. Be sure to work closely from examples, examples drawn both from the text and from your experience as a reader of this text.

2. The form of Carson's "Short Talks" presents challenges, but it also presents opportunities. This assignment takes the third of the "Questions for a Second Reading" and converts it into a more ambitious writing assignment. Let's begin with what we said before:

> As you reread, think about this text as a type of experimental essay. How does it draw on the conventions of the essay? How does it defy or revise those conventions? How would you describe its formal features in relation to what you understand to be conventional essay form? How does "Short Talks" satisfy or challenge a reader's expectations?

Prepare an essay that is Carson-like. It should be, at minimum, as long as hers. It should be similar in style and intent. Her work is your model and inspiration, and yet this project is also yours. A reader should be able to see where and how your work is in conversation with hers; a reader should also be able to see what you bring to the table. Be sure that your essay has an "Introduction," something to orient a reader to what follows. (Introductions often are either written last or seriously revised once the project is complete.)

MAKING CONNECTIONS

1. Like "Short Talks," Brian Doyle's piece "Joyas Voladoras" (p. 147) blurs the boundaries of genre. Doyle's piece both is and is not an essay. It is perhaps experimental, pushing the boundaries of form, much like Carson's piece. Both Carson and Doyle raise interesting questions about what prose can do, and about what it might be good for.

   Reread "Joyas Voladoras" alongside "Short Talks," noting as you read the distinctive features of each writer's style. It is up to you to identify and name those features. It will be useful, as well, to note the stylistic overlaps and other commonalities between the two texts.

   Write an essay in which you consider the genre of the essay—its form and style, its limits and possibilities—through your examination of these two pieces. You'll need to work closely with examples, both from the text and from your experience as a reader of these texts.

2. Consider the following sentence from Susan Griffin's "Our Secret": "The V-1 rocket is a winged plane powered by a duct motor with a pulsating flow of fuel." Or this sentence from Anne Carson's "Short Talks": "Kafka liked to have his watch an hour and a half fast." Or this sentence from Walker Percy's "The Loss of the Creature": "Garcia López de Cárdenas discovered the Grand Canyon and was amazed at the sight." Or this statement from Brian Doyle's "Joyas Voladoras": "The biggest heart in the world is inside the blue whale."

   All of the statements above might be considered "facts" or called "factual information." Each writer is making a declarative statement that makes a claim about what is so. Using the quotations above, or perhaps using other quotations from other selections in *Ways of Reading*, write an essay in which you consider each writer's use of declarative statements or "facts." What, in your understanding, is a fact? How do the writers you have chosen to examine challenge or support your notion of facts? What are their facts for? What, in other words, are some of the ways these writers use facts—for what purposes or to what ends?

BRIAN Doyle

Brian Doyle (b. 1956) lives in Portland, Oregon, where he is the editor of the University of Portland's *Portland Magazine.* Doyle's essays have appeared in such nationally renowned journals as *Harper's Magazine, Atlantic Monthly, The American Scholar*, and *Orion*. He won an *American Scholar* best essay award in 2000.

Doyle has published more than ten books, including *Two Voices* (1996), written with his father and winner of both the Catholic Press Association Book Award and a Christopher Award; *Credo: Essays on Grace, Altar Boys, Bees, Kneeling, Saints, the Mass, Priests, Strong Women, Epiphanies, a Wake, and the Haunting Thin Energetic Dusty Figure* (1999); *Saints Passionate and Peculiar* (2002); *Leaping: Revelations and Epiphanies* (2003); *Spirited Men: Story, Soul and Substance* (2004), a collection of essays about musicians and writers from William Blake to Van Morrison; and *Epiphanies and Elegies: Very Short Stories* (2007). His book *The Wet Engine: Exploring the Mad Wild Miracle of the Heart* (2005) is a long essay and meditation inspired by the experience of having a son, Liam, who was born with three rather than four chambers in his heart. More recently, Doyle published *Mink River* (2010), his fiction debut, as well as *Grace Notes* (2011), a collection of essays about his spiritual journey as a Catholic. In honor of his work, Doyle was the recipient of the 2008 American Academy of Arts and Letters Award in Literature.

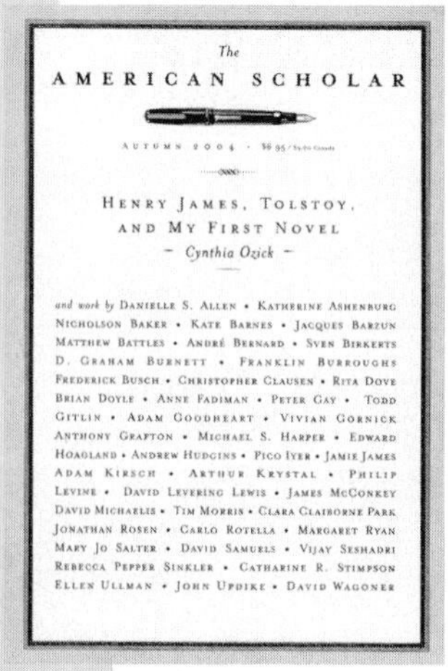

Doyle has said that he sees writing as a form of meditation and contemplation, and his essays display deep examination and keen observation. He has said of himself as a writer: "I am a small man who writes small essays about small matters." The essay that follows, "Joyas Voladoras," opens with something small, a hummingbird's heart. But, as is the case for most of Doyle's work, the essay turns the reader's attention to things much larger. "Joyas Voladoras" was originally published in *The American Scholar* (Autumn 2004); it was selected for *Best American Essays, 2005*.

Joyas Voladoras

Consider the hummingbird for a long moment. A hummingbird's heart beats ten times a second. A hummingbird's heart is the size of a pencil eraser. A hummingbird's heart is a lot of the hummingbird. *Joyas Voladoras,* flying jewels, the first white explorers in the Americas called them, and the white men had never seen such creatures, for hummingbirds came into the world only in the Americas, nowhere else in the universe, more than three hundred species of them whirring and zooming and nectaring in hummer time zones nine times removed from ours, their hearts hammering faster than we could clearly hear if we pressed our elephantine ears to their infinitesimal chests.

Each one visits a thousand flowers a day. They can dive at sixty miles an hour. They can fly backwards. They can fly more than five hundred miles without pausing to rest. But when they rest they come close to death: on frigid nights, or when they are starving, they retreat into torpor, their metabolic rate slowing to a fifteenth of their normal sleep rate, their hearts sludging nearly to a halt, barely beating, and if they are not soon warmed, if they do not soon find that which is sweet, their hearts grow cold, and they cease to be. Consider for a moment those hummingbirds who did not open their eyes again today, this very day, in the Americas: bearded helmet-crests and booted racket-tails, violet-tailed sylphs and violet-capped wood-nymphs, crimson topazes and purple-crowned fairies, red-tailed comets and amethyst woodstars, rainbow-bearded thornbills and glittering-bellied emeralds, velvet-purple coronets and golden-bellied star-frontlets, fiery-tailed awlbills and Andean hillstars, spatuletails and pufflegs, each the most amazing thing you have never seen, each thunderous wild heart the size of an infant's fingernail, each mad heart silent, a brilliant music stilled.

Hummingbirds, like all flying birds but more so, have incredible enormous immense ferocious metabolisms. To drive those metabolisms they have race-car hearts that eat oxygen at an eye-popping rate. Their hearts are built of thinner, leaner fibers than ours. Their arteries are stiffer and more taut. They have more mitochondria in their heart muscles — anything to gulp more oxygen. Their hearts are stripped to the skin for the war against gravity and inertia, the mad search for food, the insane idea of flight. The price of their ambition is a life closer to death; they suffer heart attacks and aneurysms and ruptures more than any other living creature. It's expensive to fly. You burn out. You fry the machine. You melt the engine.

Every creature on earth has approximately two billion heartbeats to spend in a lifetime. You can spend them slowly, like a tortoise, and live to be two hundred years old, or you can spend them fast, like a hummingbird, and live to be two years old.

The biggest heart in the world is inside the blue whale. It weighs more than seven tons. It's as big as a room. It *is* a room, with four chambers. A child could walk around in it, head high, bending only to step through the valves. The valves are as big as the swinging doors in a saloon. This house of a heart drives a creature a hundred feet long. When this creature is born it is twenty feet long and weighs four tons. It is waaaaay bigger than your car. It drinks a hundred gallons of milk from its mama every day and gains two hundred pounds a day and when it is seven or eight years old it endures an unimaginable puberty and then it essentially disappears from human ken, for next to nothing is known of the mating habits, travel patterns, diet, social life, language, social structure, diseases, spirituality, wars, stories, despairs, and arts of the blue whale. There are perhaps ten thousand blue whales in the world, living in every ocean on earth, and of the largest mammal who ever lived we know nearly nothing. But we know this: the animals with the largest hearts in the world generally travel in pairs, and their penetrating moaning cries, their piercing yearning tongue, can be heard underwater for miles and miles.

Mammals and birds have hearts with four chambers. Reptiles and turtles have hearts with three chambers. Fish have hearts with two chambers. Insects and mollusks have hearts with one chamber. Worms have hearts with one chamber, although they may have as many as eleven single-chambered hearts. Unicellular bacteria have no hearts at all; but even they have fluid eternally in motion, washing from one side of the cell to the other, swirling and whirling. No living being is without interior liquid motion. We all churn inside.

So much held in a heart in a lifetime. So much held in a heart in a day, an hour, a moment. We are utterly open with no one, in the end — not mother and father, not wife or husband, not lover, not child, not friend. We open windows to each but we live alone in the house of the heart. Perhaps we must. Perhaps we could not bear to be so naked, for fear of a constantly harrowed heart. When young we think there will come one person who will savor and sustain us always; when we are older we know this is the dream of a child, that all hearts finally are bruised and scarred, scored and torn, repaired by time and will, patched by force of character, yet fragile and rickety forevermore, no matter how ferocious the defense and how many bricks you bring to the wall. You can brick up your heart as stout and tight and hard and cold and impregnable as you possibly can and down it comes in an instant, felled by a woman's second glance, a child's apple breath, the shatter of glass in the road, the words *I have something to tell you,* a cat with a broken spine dragging itself into the forest to die, the brush of your mother's papery ancient hand in the thicket of your hair, the memory of your father's voice early in the morning echoing from the kitchen where he is making pancakes for his children.

QUESTIONS FOR A SECOND READING

1. One of the fascinating aspects of Doyle's short essay is the way he is able to move from talking about hummingbirds, blue whales, and hearts to sentences that are about something else — or at least seem to be pointing to something else, pointing *away* from hummingbirds, blue whales, and hearts and pointing *toward*—well, what?

   Reread Doyle's essay with particular attention to moments you see this pointing *away* from the subject. Perhaps you might underline any sentences that seem to want us to think about more than the literal subject at hand. Once you've identified these moments in the essay, consider the following questions: How can you tell that Doyle is moving your attention away from the literal content of the essay? What signals seem to indicate that movement? And finally, can you see anything that Doyle does to prepare you for these moments — what gestures, grammatical constructions, phrases seem to let us know that his piece is going to be about something more than hummingbirds?

2. On the surface, some moments in Doyle's essay may seem as though he is merely supplying his reader with facts about hummingbirds, blue whales, and hearts. But given the rest of the essay, for Doyle, offering his reader facts seems to be about something more than providing information. As you reread Doyle's essay, think carefully about what the "facts" in his essay are doing. Are they providing information? What kind? What else can these "facts" be said to be doing in the essay? If Doyle is not meaning to write a report on the size of hearts, then why does he give all of this information about hearts? What are these sentences for?

3. From its opening sentence, Doyle's essay "Joyas Voladoras" is addressed directly to you: "Consider the hummingbird for a long moment." And, at the end, Doyle writes as though he can speak for you, using "we" freely and with a confident eloquence: "When young we think there will come one person who will savor and sustain us always; when we are older we know this is the dream of a child." Does this work? Do you, in fact, inhabit these sentences in the ways the writer seems to assume you will?

   As you reread, pay attention to the ways you are addressed in this essay, the ways you are invited (or pulled) into the text. How does Doyle do this? Why does he do this? Could the essay have been written otherwise? (Could you rewrite a paragraph to show a different style of address?) Does it work for you?

4. As you reread, pay attention to sentences and paragraphs and the spaces in between. Choose a characteristic sentence, a characteristic paragraph, and a characteristic moment of transition. Be prepared to describe what each is doing and how each works—how it works for the reader, how it works for the writer. And, as an exercise, write a Doyle-like sentence of your own, one with the shape and rhythm of the sentence you have chosen.

ASSIGNMENTS FOR WRITING

1. The form of Doyle's "Joyas Voladoras" could be said to present challenges, but it could also be said to present pleasure and opportunity. As you reread, think about this text as a type of experimental essay. How does it draw on the conventions of the essay? How does it defy or revise those conventions? How would you describe its formal features in relation to what you understand to be conventional essay form? How does "Joyas Voladoras" engage a reader? How does it satisfy or challenge a reader's expectations?

   Prepare an essay that is Doyle-like. It should be, at minimum, as long as his. It should be similar in style and intent. His work is your model and inspiration, and yet this project is also yours. A reader should be able to see where and how your work is in conversation with his; a reader should also be able to see what you bring to the table. And, when you are done, write a brief "Introduction" or "Afterword," something to orient your reader to what follows or something to provide your reader with a context at the end.

2. We suspect that at some point in your educational history, someone has asked you to "find the main idea" of an essay. Often when students are asked to do this kind of work, there is one central argument or one significant point. Your job is to find it and bring it home. "Joyas Voladoras" is an essay without such a structure, without a conventional "thesis statement," without a conventional introduction and conclusion.

   It can be read, of course, as though it presented a conventional challenge. As you reread the essay, and in preparation for writing an essay of your own, ask yourself, "What is this essay about?" How do these six paragraphs come to a single conclusion? What is this conclusion? (And why is Doyle so hesitant to write it out?) Write this essay, making good use of examples from the text. You will be demonstrating your ability, as a reader, to find meaning in what you read. Let this serve as "Part One."

   In "Part Two," write briefly, and perhaps in a different, more reflective style, about what you have done and about what is lost in "Joyas Voladoras" (or in the experience of its reader) when such a reading is imposed upon the essay.

(Note: What is a "more reflective style"? Doyle provides an example. A reflective style can also simply rely on sentences that are tentative, questioning, exploratory, sentences that look at things from various angles—"not only this but, perhaps, also that.")

MAKING CONNECTIONS

1. Consider the following sentence from Anne Carson's "Short Talks": "Kafka liked to have his watch an hour and a half fast." Or this statement from Susan Griffin's "Our Secret": "The life plan of the body is encoded in the DNA molecule, a substance that has the ability to hold information and to replicate itself." Or this sentence from Walker Percy's "The Loss of the Creature": "Garcia López de Cárdenas discovered the Grand Canyon and was amazed at the sight." Or this statement from Brian Doyle's "Joyas Voladoras": "The biggest heart in the world is inside the blue whale."

   All of the above statements might be considered "facts" or called "factual information." Each writer is making a declarative statement that makes a claim about what is so. Using the quotations above, or perhaps using other quotations from other selections in *Ways of Reading*, write an essay in which you consider each writer's use of declarative statements or "facts." What, in your understanding, is a fact? How do the writers you have chosen to examine challenge or support your notion of facts? What are their facts for? What, in other words, are some of the ways these writers use facts—for what purposes or to what ends?

2. Reread Halberstam's "Animating Revolt and Revolting Animation," (p. 271) paying particular attention to where Halberstam offers a critique of the ways human beings often see or read animal behavior. In her discussion of *March of the Penguins*, she asserts that the voice-over "remains resolutely human and refuses to ever see the 'penguin logics' that structure their frigid quest."

   What does Halberstam mean here, and other places in the essay, about the ways humans interpret or make use of animal behavior? What exactly is Halberstam's argument?

   Once you give your reader a sense of that argument, we invite you to write an essay in which you test that argument out on Doyle's "Joyas Voladoras." As you read Doyle's lyric essay, consider these questions: Would Halberstam say that Doyle, in the way he makes use of the hummingbirds, refuses to see "hummingbird logics" or "blue whale logics"? In what ways is Doyle's essay implicated in Halberstam's argument? Or, in what ways does Doyle escape Halberstam's critique? How is Doyle's essay different from, or similar to, the voice-over in *March of the Penguins*?

ENGAGING WITH STUDENT WRITING

Below we have gathered two essays by students, both of which grapple with the difficult and complicated work of writing an essay that imitates Doyle (a task offered to you in Question 1 under "Assignments for Writing," p. 150). Whether you intend to compose your own Doyle-like essay or not, the writers in these essays offer their readers a chance to recognize and reflect upon the kinds of moves Doyle makes as a writer. You can learn a lot about an essay by trying to imitate it. And you can learn a lot about writing from watching these two writers engage with Doyle's project as they take on the ways of composing and knowing that Doyle seems to enact in "Joyas Voladoras."

Hidden

By Robert Giraud

Consider the chameleon for a couple of minutes. Chameleons are known best for their amazing ability to blend in with their surroundings. They change the color of their skin to match whatever is around them. Chameleons do this not because they want to, but because it is their means of protection against predators. They are naturally a light brown color, which is already an advantage in their native lands such as Madagascar, the Middle East, Africa, and southern Europe. Chameleons only change color if there is significant danger present. If a predator can't see its prey, it will have a hard time killing it.

Some species of chameleons change color for more than just protection from predators. They also change color based on the temperature. They will turn to a dark color in the morning to take in more heat and turn to a light gray color when it is hot to attract less heat. These chameleons sometimes become even half dark and half light gray as they try to balance their body temperature. Other species change color to intimidate a predator or to show anger; they generally turn a darker color. Chameleons even change color for mating purposes. The males will turn a light color to show off for the females. The chameleon is brown, as I stare at it now. But slowly, almost majestically, it changes to the light green of the foliage behind it. I am curious as to why, though. I neither see nor hear anything but the wind. Sure enough, a hawk swoops down but seems to have lost what it was looking for.

Leopards also use camouflage, but for the opposite reason. They blend into their surroundings to make it easier to catch prey. Most leopards are spotted so that they can blend into the jungles of Africa. Some leopards, however, are completely black. These leopards are more commonly known as black panthers. They hunt at night or in the shadows when they are nearly impossible to see. They stalk a wide variety of animals, from dung beetles to very large antelopes and everything in between. They have no problem attacking humans if they have trouble finding other prey, or if they are weak or injured. There have been instances where leopards have been seen taking down crocodiles that are on land. Camouflage can only go so far for the leopard. Sadly, some leopards, such as the snow leopard, are becoming endangered because poachers are killing them for the pelts and illegal trade on the black market. Leopards use camouflage to be the hunter, not to avoid being hunted. I am observing a panther as I write this. I only know it is a panther because I am wearing night vision goggles, as it is pitch black outside. I notice a young antelope sleeping off in the distance. The panther seems to have spotted the antelope before I did, as it is lurking swiftly through the trees. I know what is coming next. The antelope never saw it coming.

Leaf butterflies may possess the best camouflage on the face of the earth. Predators, such as birds, rarely find and prey on these creatures because they are so well hidden. Leaf butterflies, as you might expect, look like dead leaves. They even have fake leaf veins. Leaf butterflies use their camouflage solely for the purpose of protection. They literally have no other means of defense. If a bird is smart enough to spot out a leaf butterfly, it will swoop down and eat it. There would be nothing that the leaf butterfly could do to defend itself. That is why their camouflage has to be so well designed. Otherwise, they would be extinct in a matter of years.

Many animals, no matter what biome they live in, no matter what the temperature is, no matter if they are predator or prey, have camouflage. Camouflage is essential to wildlife. It is used as protection. It is used to make stalking prey easier. It is used in mating rituals. It is used every day in nature. Without camouflage, many creatures would be extinct. The leaf butterfly would be eaten in seconds, because it would make for an easy target. The leopard would have no way of sneaking up on its prey and would have a tremendously difficult time finding enough food to survive. Not only is camouflage essential to wildlife, it is vital to the continuance of many different species of animals.

Here I am, wearing a plain white t-shirt and a pair of denim blue jeans. Walking through the hallways at school, blending into the crowd. I try not to give anyone a reason to criticize me. I just walk with the crowd, going with the flow, wherever it takes me. I am seemingly unnoticed; no one stops to say "Hi" or "How is your day?" I do not step on toes and I don't pick sides. I blend in to go unnoticed. Bullies pass me in the hallway and don't pick on me. By blending in I have stayed safe, but I also feel alone. Maybe it would be good to go against the grain, to stand out above others. But then I risk judgment; I risk being bullied for being different. I turn on the TV when I get home and hear the terrible news. A man had hidden in the shadows of a dark alley, wearing all black. The homeless man never saw it coming. My face turns red. I'm angry. I yell at the TV and throw the remote. I'm angry that the man would commit such a heinous crime. And for what? The homeless man had nothing of value to give to the man. It was just completely senseless. I storm out of the house, cursing as I fade into the night.

Robert Giraud's essay, "Hidden," adopts many of Brian Doyle's writerly moves. It would be an interesting exercise to move back and forth between Doyle's and Giraud's essays, noting for yourself moments where they echo one another, or perhaps moments where the essays seem different from one another. Giraud's ending is powerful: "I stormed out of the house. Cursing as I faded into the night." One of the remarkable aspects of Giraud's ending is the multiple ways we might interpret that final sentence where the author himself disappears through camouflage. At first, a reader might even feel familiar with Giraud's idea of camouflage as connected to ways in which humans adapt to their environments, but as his essay progresses the metaphor seems to get more and more complex. It might be interesting to have a discussion about whether this deepening of complexity happens in the planning of the essay or in the writing and revising. Often, writers have to write in order to uncover what they might be able to say.

Beyond Any Imagination

By Haley Gray-Dekraai

Visualize 1,400,000,000,000,000,000 tons of water. Picture that weighing heavily upon you, as you swim farther and farther into the freezing cold depths below. Gaze around you at your surroundings. Notice the 250,000 other species swimming around you; you are not alone. As you swim in this icy water you can taste the saltiness that surrounds you. Seaweed and plants along the coral reef brush up against you as you try to swim through this dark blue water. It gets lighter and lighter as you start heading for the surface until it's almost a crystal blue color. The plants start to fade away and you can see the rays of the sun start to shine through the water. You break the surface with your hands and take that first breath that you've been holding in so long.

The ocean covers 71 percent of the earth's surface. It contains 96.5 percent of the total water on earth. It is constantly moving, rising and falling, going in and out between obstacles in its path and never stopping. Long ago many people were afraid of this giant body of water. It can tear boats apart and drag you down under and never let you go. People were afraid of the unknown. Some thought that if you went past the equator there would be boiling water there and giant sea monsters that would eat you and your boat in one bite. We still to this day haven't even explored half of the ocean and the life within it. This giant body of water holds over 1.7 million plants and animals inside of it and there is said to be five million more to discover. Think about it for a moment and what this all means. There is a whole different world when it comes to living in the ocean. Everywhere you explore, you would run into another species. You might even discover a place where no one has ever been and not even know it. You just might even run into a creature that has never been documented before and swim right past it, but this is the ocean. Anything is possible.

Water in general is a mysterious thing. It can weigh almost nothing in your hands, but out in the ocean having a wave hit you can knock you over or push you down into the water. It can carry you along with its current or even let you float atop it like you weigh nothing. Water can make a 46,328 ton ship like the *Titanic* float on its surface. Water has no feelings; it does its own thing. So if your ship were to hit an iceberg it would show you no mercy. You are on your own. The ship is starting to suck you down. As you're under water you may notice the coral reefs and see that they are like an underwater city all by themselves. Corals and algae make up the framework that rises up off the ocean floor and attract many diverse inhabitants. They are very fragile and as the temperature starts to rise, the water gets warmer and the coral reefs may start to die. You can also notice the deep gouges from boats that have run over some of the coral that are very visible as you pass them by. All of this happens in the ocean and is just sitting out there for us to discover.

When it rains or snows, mists or hails, or a hurricane or typhoon comes your way, all of these very different types of weather have one thing in common, water. Water is how these storms are created and formed, how it causes damage and produces its effects, even how we know it's there and can feel the moisture upon our delicate skin. Most people know that when the air is warm outside it will turn the water from the ocean, lakes and ponds into vapor that rises into the air. That water vapor forms clouds, which contain small drops of water or ice crystals. As the clouds rise higher in the sky the air there becomes much colder, causing the water vapor in the clouds to become too heavy and to start to fall down, which we know as rain or snow. But making rain is no easy task; it takes approximately one million droplets of water to make a single raindrop. What's even more impressive is how hail is formed. Hail forms from updrafts within thunderstorms as it pushes the rain high into the clouds where very cold air freezes it. Once frozen it starts to fall but gets caught in another strong updraft where it gathers more moisture on its way back up, making it larger. The longer this process occurs, the larger the ice becomes, causing more damage upon impact. (The largest hail stone's circumference was that of a soccer ball and was discovered right here in Nebraska.)

In Nebraska, every day we look at the Weather Channel to determine what the weather is going to be like for the following day, since the weather is very unpredictable here. We need to be able to know how to dress and to see if we need to bring other essential items with us for that day, such as an umbrella in case it rains. All you can do is wish for beautiful days on the day you have plans outdoors, but even wishing doesn't always work. It's all up to Mother Nature and what she has in store for that particular day, and for you to just mercifully follow along with her plans and to adjust to it.

Weather works in all sorts of mysterious ways. It can rain and help the plants and crops grow or it can merely disappear and leave you with nothing but wilted flowers and a brown-looking yard. Elephants rely on the weather as well, in hopes of having it rain and fill their murky watering holes with luscious cold water. If the weather doesn't respond to their needs they must then pack up and go out in search for another water source. They usually try and drink alone but in certain situations will drink with others. They are pretty smart creatures. They like clean water and so they will dig until they have found water that has been filtered by the sand. They take about 10 liters of water in through their trunks and then spray it into their mouths. Elephants will consume about 100 to 300 liters of water per day depending on the temperature outside.

Even though elephants weigh about seven thousand to thirteen thousand pounds, they are very good swimmers. Their giant body actually helps them swim because it acts like a flotation device. Long ago it was said that they would swim to new land masses or other islands and settle there, hoping to find more food and water. They would swim these many hundreds of miles in hope of finding a better life for themselves, not even knowing if it would be more desirable for them where ever they might end up. Some elephants will swim up to 300 miles to travel to another island just to get some food and then swim back. As they are swimming in the coldness of the sea their heads will stay submerged until they have reached their destination. Their long muscular trunks are like a built-in snorkel for them and they use it to take in that oxygen they so desperately need while they are under water. Their four large legs kick at the water to keep them moving forward and closer to where they're trying to go. They are very determined creatures and don't tire easily.

As you approach the largest land mammal on this earth, you might experience a little sense of fear knowing that it could crush you in a split second. But as you grow near to this amazing creature and look deep into its black button like eyes, you can see the image of the ocean splashing around in it. You can see all the mystery and wonder it holds. You can see everything it is feeling or has felt in its life time. You can feel its strong trunk wrap around you and place you upon its gray wrinkled back. It shows you just what it's capable of doing with its trunk that can measure up to five to six feet long and can weigh up to four hundred pounds. There are two extended ridges on the end of the African elephant's trunk which they use like we use our fingers. It bends its head down and uses its trunk to dig in search for cleaner water to take a nice long drink. You notice the gentleness of the elephant and how it can grab a branch of dark berries, so as to not to lose any, and hold them up for you, so you too can taste the sweet juicy flavor inside of them. You can feel the uneven powerful steps the elephant takes as it walks and notice its muscles tensing up as it rips up small trees in its path. It lets you down as it nears a watering hole and uses its trunk to suck up water, and you watch as it curls its trunk back and aim towards the back of its body; where it can't reach, it shoots a powerful spray of water onto itself in order to take a bath. Other elephants nearby are putting mud all over themselves to kill parasites, prevent sunburns and keep the bugs away. When there isn't any water nearby they might even do the same thing, but it's called dusting and they put dust all over themselves to help keep them cool.

On a hot sunny summer day people will stand over a cold sparkling swimming pool. The little waves are flowing in a couple different directions from the wind. The water is so clear you can see all the way to the floor of the pool. You jump. You can feel the coldness engulfing you as you break the surface with your feet and start heading towards the bottom of the pool. You can feel the water hitting every inch of your skin and soaking your hair as you go under all the way.

People can swim a 200-meter individual medley in one minute and 56.88 seconds like Michael Phelps or swim across the Atlantic ocean like Benoit Lecomte did in 1998. People have swum across the English Channel many times after a woman first demonstrated that it could be done. Almost anyone can learn how to swim and most people enjoy swimming.

We are a very unique species. Always trying to move forward and coming up with new ideas and things no one has ever done before. We are much like water, constantly moving and never giving up. We express emotion when we are sad and upset through our tears that fall down our face, and we show we have worked hard through the perspiration that we shed. Water is all around us and is within us; we are made up of about seventy five percent of water.

For animals, water is sought out to meet basic needs, such as to satisfy their thirst and cool their bodies. However, because people as a species are more intelligent, they have come to associate more meaning with water than just how essential it is for us to drink. In religious beliefs water is used in holy and sacred ways. They find someone like a priest who has blessed some water and will take it with them and feel protected or even safer with it. People will go to great lengths to seek out water with these and other special properties. Stories have been written about searches for a fountain of youth, and [some] even spend fortunes on it if they think they will be getting a little portion of water from there.

We drink it, we bath in it, we swim in it, we cook with it and we wash our hands in it. We are essentially the protectors and destroyers of our water. We can try and preserve it and make sure to keep it clean and useable for us to drink or we can merely not take notice and not worry if we're polluting our water for our use and for future generations. We are the only species with the power and responsibility to make sure the earth's water stays clean, safe and available. Throughout history, cultures and communities have devised methods for improving the quality, safety, availability, convenience, and efficiency of the delivery of water, cold and hot, to us for our many uses. For many of us, we have come to take our access of good water for granted. In general, we want and expect consistency from day to day, including the immediate availability of water for whatever need or task that comes up in our routine schedules. We don't worry about how the water comes to us; we just expect it to be there and ready to use.

Haley Gray-Dekraai begins her essay, "Beyond Any Imagination," by plummeting her readers into the depths of the ocean. She turns her audience into fish, moving them around the water so that they might see the ocean from inside of it. When Gray-Dekraai worked on this essay, she engaged in numerous discussions in her class writing workshop about how to make the "facts" included in the essay feel as powerful as Doyle's "facts" seem to feel. The class had a lively discussion about what makes a declarative statement of fact seem meaningful beyond its transmission of information. It can often be useful for a writer to think about which of his or her details seem most significant and how syntax and diction contribute to conveying that significance. At one time or another, most writers have been told to "include more detail" or "use their senses to describe more detail." These are certainly important writing skills, but the truth is that details themselves do not make meaning. Put another way, not all details are created equal. You might try looking at Gray-Dekraai's essay alongside Giraud's and Doyle's. Which facts seem most profound? What makes them feel that way?

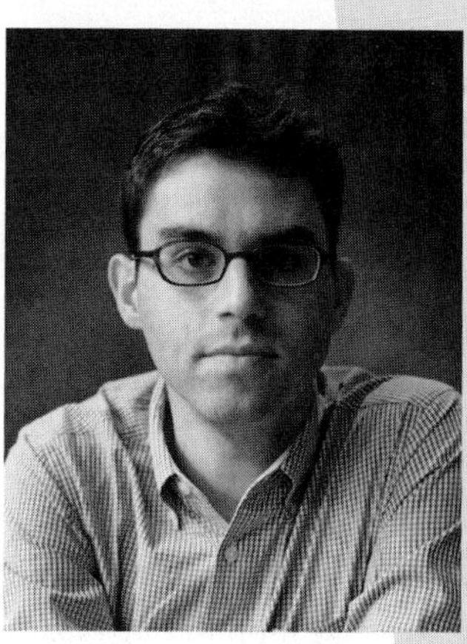

JOSHUA Foer

Joshua Foer (b. 1982 in Washington, D.C.) is a journalist and science writer. He graduated from Yale University in 2004 with a degree in evolutionary biology and later became the 2006 United States Memory Champion. Foer set out on a journalism project to study "mental athletes" — individuals who can memorize lists of thousands of numbers in minutes. He decided to join them, to try his hand at enriching his ability to remember and memorize. The result is his book, *Moonwalking with Einstein: The Art and Science of Remembering Everything* (2011), which has been celebrated by critics and will eventually become a film produced by Columbia Pictures. Of his book, Michiko Kakutani writes in the *New York Times*:

> How did Mr. Foer come to join the ranks of these competitive mnemonists? How did he go from being a guy with an average memory — who regularly forgot his friends' phone numbers and where he left his car keys (or, for that matter, his car) — to being one of those extraterrestrials able to memorize a deck of cards in 1 minute 40 seconds? The chronicle of his metamorphosis forms the spine of this engaging book.

Moonwalking with Einstein is an international bestseller and has been translated into more than thirty-one languages. The chapter we have chosen from Foer's book, titled "The End of Remembering," reveals some of the science, philosophy, and art that shape the ways we think about and understand memory. Foer raises provocative questions in this piece about the capacity of the human mind, the influence of technologies upon that mind, and the place of memory in the twenty-first century.

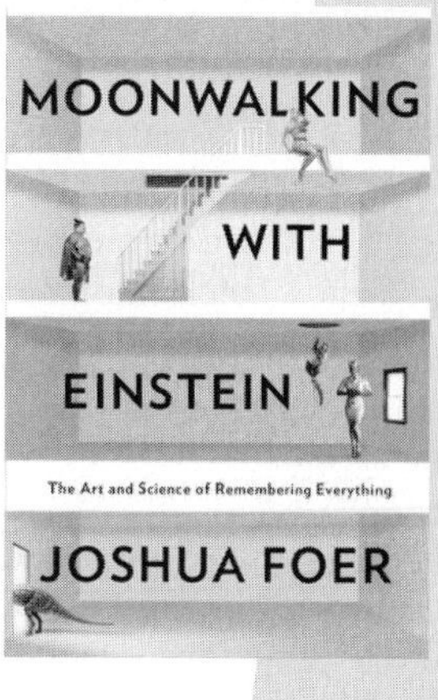

Joshua Foer has become a powerful force even in larger popular culture, appearing on shows like *The Colbert Report* and *The Dr. Oz Show*. The chapter we have chosen follows a chapter in the book where Foer discusses poetry as an oral tradition. Here, he poses these questions before moving to "The End of Remembering." He asks, "How did memory, once so essential, end up so marginalized? Why did these techniques disappear? How, I wondered, did our culture end up forgetting how to remember?"

The End of Remembering

Once upon a time, there was nothing to do with thoughts except remember them. There was no alphabet to transcribe them in, no paper to set them down upon. Anything that had to be preserved had to be preserved in memory. Any story that would be retold, any idea that would be transmitted, any piece of information that would be conveyed, first had to be remembered.

Today it often seems we remember very little. When I wake up, the first thing I do is check my day planner, which remembers my schedule so that I don't have to. When I climb into my car, I enter my destination into a GPS device, whose spatial memory supplants my own. When I sit down to work, I hit the play button on a digital voice recorder or open up a notebook that holds the contents of my interviews. I have photographs to store the images I want to remember, books to store knowledge, and now, thanks to Google, I rarely have to remember anything more than the right set of search terms to access humankind's collective memory. Growing up, in the days when you still had to punch seven buttons, or turn a clunky rotary dial, to make a telephone call, I could recall the numbers of all my close friends and family. Today, I'm not sure if I know more than four phone numbers by heart. And that's probably more than most. According to a survey conducted in 2007 by a neuropsychologist at Trinity College Dublin, fully a third of Brits under the age of thirty can't remember even their own home land line number without pulling it up on their handsets. The same survey found that 30 percent of adults can't remember the birthdays of more than three immediate family members. Our gadgets have eliminated the need to remember such things anymore.

TODAY, I'M NOT SURE IF I KNOW MORE THAN FOUR PHONE NUMBERS BY HEART.

Forgotten phone numbers and birthdays represent minor erosions of our everyday memory, but they are part of a much larger story of how we've supplanted our own natural memory with a vast superstructure of technological crutches — from the alphabet to the BlackBerry. These technologies of storing information outside our minds have helped make our modern world possible, but they've also changed how we think and how we use our brains.

In Plato's *Phaedrus*, Socrates describes how the Egyptian god Theuth, inventor of writing, came to Thamus, the king of Egypt, and offered to bestow his wonderful invention upon the Egyptian people. "Here is a branch of learning that will . . . improve their memories," Theuth said to the Egyptian king. "My discovery provides a recipe for both memory and wisdom." But Thamus was reluctant to accept the gift. "If men learn this, it will implant forgetfulness in their souls," he told the god. "They will cease to exercise their memory and become forgetful; they will rely on that which is written, calling things to remembrance no longer from within themselves, but by means of external marks. What you have discovered is a recipe not for memory, but for reminding. And it is no true wisdom that you offer your disciples, but only its semblance, for by telling them of many things without teaching them anything, you will make them seem to know much, while for the most part they will know nothing. And as men filled not with wisdom but with the conceit of wisdom, they will be a burden to their fellow-men."

Socrates goes on to disparage the idea of passing on his own knowledge through writing, saying it would be "singularly simple-minded to believe that written words can do anything more than remind one of what one already knows." Writing, for Socrates, could never be anything more than a cue for memory — a way of calling to mind information already in one's head. Socrates feared that writing would lead the culture down a treacherous path toward intellectual and moral decay, because even while the quantity of knowledge available to people might increase, they themselves would come to resemble empty vessels. I wonder if Socrates would have appreciated the flagrant irony: It's only because his pupils Plato and Xenophon put his disdain for the written word into written words that we have any knowledge of it today.

Socrates lived in the fifth century B.C., at a time when writing was ascendant in Greece, and his own views were already becoming antiquated. Why was he so put off by the idea of putting pen to paper? Securing memories on the page would seem to be an immensely superior way of retaining knowledge compared to trying to hold it in the brain. The brain is always making mistakes, forgetting, misremembering. Writing is how we overcome those essential biological constraints. It allows our memories to be pulled out of the fallible wetware of the brain and secured on the less fallible page, where they can be made permanent and (one sometimes hopes) disseminated far, wide, and across time. Writing allows ideas to be passed across generations, without fear of the kind of natural mutation that is necessarily a part of oral traditions.

THE BRAIN IS ALWAYS MAKING MISTAKES, FORGETTING, MISREMEMBERING. WRITING IS HOW WE OVERCOME THOSE ESSENTIAL BIOLOGICAL CONSTRAINTS.

To understand why memory was so important in the world of Socrates, we have to understand something about the evolution of writing, and how different early books were in both form and function. We have to go back to an age before printing, before indexes and tables of contents, before the codex parceled texts into pages and bound them at the edge, before punctuation marks, before lowercase letters, even before there were spaces between words.

Today we write things down precisely so we don't have to hold them in our memories. But through at least the late Middle Ages, books served not as replacements for memory, but rather as memory aids. As Thomas Aquinas put it, "Things are written down in material books to help the memory." One read in order to remember, and books were the best available tools for impressing information into the mind. In fact, manuscripts were often copied for no reason other than to help their copier memorize them.

In the time of Socrates, Greek texts were written on long, continuous scrolls — some stretching up to sixty feet — pasted together from sheets of pressed papyrus reeds imported from the Nile Delta. These texts were cumbersome to read, and even more cumbersome to write. It would be tough to invent a less user-friendly way of accessing information. In fact, it wasn't until about 200 B.C. that the most basic punctuation marks were invented by Aristophanes of Byzantium, the director of the Library of Alexandria, and all they consisted of was a single dot at either the bottom, middle, or top of the line letting readers know how long to pause between sentences. Instead, words ran together in an unending stream of capital letters known as *scriptio continua*, broken up by neither spaces nor punctuation. Words that started on one line would spill over onto the next without even a hyphen.

> ASYOUCANSEEITSNOTVERYEASYTOREADTE
> XTWRITTENWITHOUTSPACESORPUNCTUATI
> ONOFANYKINDOREVENHELPFULLYPOSITIO
> NEDLINEBREAKSANDYETTHISWASEXACTLY
> THEFORMOFINSCRIPTIONUSEDINANCIENT
> GREECE

Unlike the letters in this book, which form words that carry semantic meaning, letters written in *scriptio continua* functioned more like musical notes. They signified the sounds that were meant to come out of one's mouth. Reconstituting those sounds into discrete packets of words that could be understood first required hearing them. And just as it is difficult for all but the most gifted musicians to read musical notes without actually singing them, so too was it difficult to read texts written in *scriptio continua* without speaking them aloud. In fact, we know that well into the Middle Ages, reading was an activity almost always carried out aloud, a kind of performance, and one most often given before an audience. "Lend ears" is a phrase often repeated in medieval texts. When St. Augustine, in the fourth century A.D., observed his teacher St. Ambrose reading to himself without moving his tongue or murmuring, he thought the unusual behavior so note-worthy as to record it in his *Confessions*. It was probably not until about the ninth century, around the same time that spacing became common and the catalog of punctuation marks grew richer, that the page provided enough information for silent reading to become common.

The difficulties associated with reading such texts meant that there was a very different relationship between reading and memory than the one we know today. Since sight-reading *scriptio continua* was difficult, reciting a text aloud with fluency required a reader to have a degree of familiarity with it. He — and it was mostly he's — had to prepare with it, punctuate it in his mind, memorize it — in part, if not in full — because turning a string of sounds into meaning was not something you could do easily on the fly. The text had to be learned before it could be performed. After all, the way one punctuated a text written in *scriptio continua* could make all the difference in the world. As the historian Jocelyn Penny Small pointed out, GODISNOWHERE comes out a lot differently when rendered as GOD IS NOW HERE versus GOD IS NOWHERE.

What's more, a scroll written in *scriptio continua* had to be read top to bottom if anything was to be taken from it. A scroll has just a single point of entry, the first word. Because it has to be unwound to be read, and because there are no punctuation marks or paragraphs to break up the text — to say nothing of page numbers, a table of contents, chapter divisions, and an index — it is impossible to find a specific piece of information without scanning the whole thing, head to toe. It is not a text that can be easily consulted — until it is memorized. This is a key point. Ancient texts couldn't be readily scanned. You couldn't pull a scroll off the shelf and quickly find a specific excerpt unless you had some baseline familiarity with the entire text. The scroll existed not to hold its contents externally, but rather to help its reader navigate its contents internally.

One of the last places where this tradition of recitation still survives is in the reading of the Torah, an ancient handwritten scroll that can take upward of a year to inscribe. The Torah is written without vowels or punctuation (though it does have spaces, an innovation that came to Hebrew before Greek), which means it's extremely difficult to sightread. Though Jews are specifically commanded not to recite the Torah from memory, there's no way to read a section of the Torah *without* having invested a lot of time familiarizing yourself with it, as any once-bar-mitzvahed boy can tell you. I can personally vouch for this. On the day I became a man, I was really just a parrot in a yarmulke.

Though years of language use condition us not to notice, *scriptio continua* has more in common with the way we actually speak than the artificial word divisions on this page. Spoken sentences flow together seamlessly as one long, blurry drawn-out sound. We don't speak with spaces. Where one word ends and another begins is a relatively arbitrary linguistic convention. If you look at a sonographic chart visualizing the sound waves of someone speaking English, it's practically impossible to tell where the spaces are, which is one of the reasons why it's proven so difficult to train computers to recognize speech. Without sophisticated artificial intelligence capable of figuring out context, a computer has no way of telling the difference between "The stuffy nose may dim liquor" and "The stuff he knows made him lick her."

WHERE ONE WORD ENDS AND ANOTHER BEGINS IS A RELATIVELY ARBITRARY LINGUISTIC CONVENTION.

For a period, Latin scribes actually did try separating words with dots, but in the second century A.D., there was a reversion — a giant and very curious step backward, it would seem — to the old continuous script used by the Greeks. Spaces weren't seen again in Western writing for another nine hundred years. From our vantage point today, separating words seems like a no-brainer. But the fact that it was tried and rejected says a lot about how people used to read. So, too, does the fact that the ancient Greek word most commonly used to signify "to read" was *ánagignósko*, which means to "know again," or "to recollect." Reading as an act of remembering: From our modern vantage point, could there be a more unfamiliar relationship between reader and text?

Today, when we live amid a deluge of printed words — would you believe that ten billion volumes were printed last year? — it's hard to imagine what it must have been like to read in the age before Gutenberg, when a book was a rare and costly handwritten object that could take a scribe months of labor to produce. Even as late as the fifteenth century, there might be just several dozen copies of any given text in existence, and those copies were quite probably chained to a desk or lectern in some university library, which, if it contained a hundred other books, would have been considered particularly well stocked. If you were a medieval scholar reading a book, you knew that there was a reasonable likelihood you'd never see that particular text again, and so a high premium was placed on remembering what you read. You couldn't just pull a book off the shelf to consult it for a quote or an idea. For one thing, modern bookshelves with their rows of outward-facing spines hadn't even been invented yet. That didn't happen until sometime around the sixteenth century. For another thing, books still tended to be heavy, hardly portable objects. It was only in the thirteenth century that bookmaking technology advanced to the point that the Bible could be compiled in a single volume rather than a collection of independent books, and yet it still weighed more than ten pounds. And even if you did happen to have a text you needed close at hand, the chances of finding what you were looking for without reading the whole thing start to finish were slim. Indexes were not yet common, nor were page numbers or tables of contents.

But these gaps were gradually filled. And as the book itself changed, so too did the crucial role of memory in reading. By about the year 400, the parchment codex, with its leaves of pages bound at the spine like a modern hardcover, had all but completely replaced scrolls as the preferred way to read. No longer did a reader have to unfurl a long document to find a passage. A reader could just turn to the appropriate page.

The first concordance of the Bible, a grand index that consumed the labors of five hundred Parisian monks, was compiled in the thirteenth century, around the same time that chapter divisions were introduced. For the first time, a reader could refer to the Bible without having previously memorized it. One could find a passage without knowing it by heart or reading the text all the way through. Soon after the concordance, other books with alphabetical indexes, page numbers, and tables of contents began to appear, and as they did, they again helped change the essence of what a book was.

The problem of the book before the index and table of contents is that for all the material contained in a scroll or between the covers of a book, it was impossible to navigate. What makes the brain such an incredible tool is not just the sheer volume of information it contains but the ease and efficiency with which it can find that information. It uses the greatest random-access indexing system ever invented — one that computer scientists haven't come even close to replicating. Whereas an index in the back of a book provides a single address — a page number — for each important subject, each subject in the brain has hundreds if not thousands of addresses. Our internal memories are associational, nonlinear. You don't need to know where a particular memory is stored in order to find it. It simply turns up — or doesn't — when you need it. Because of the dense network that interconnects our memories, we can skip around from memory to memory and idea to idea very rapidly. From Barry White to the color white to milk to the Milky Way is a long voyage conceptually, but a short jaunt neurologically.

FROM BARRY WHITE TO THE COLOR WHITE TO MILK TO THE MILKY WAY IS A LONG VOYAGE CONCEPTUALLY, BUT A SHORT JAUNT NEUROLOGICALLY.

Indexes were a major advance because they allowed books to be accessed in the nonlinear way we access our internal memories. They helped turn the book into something like a modern CD, where you can skip directly to the track you want, as compared to unindexed books, which, like cassette tapes, force you to troll laboriously through large swaths of material in order to find the bit you're looking for. Along with page numbers and tables of contents, the index changed what a book was, and what it could do for scholars. The historian Ivan Illich has argued that this represented an invention of such magnitude that "it seems reasonable to speak of the pre- and post-index Middle Ages." As books became easier and easier to consult, the imperative to hold their contents in memory became less and less relevant, and the very notion of what it meant to be erudite began to evolve from possessing information internally to knowing where to find information in the labyrinthine world of external memory.

To our memory-bound predecessors, the goal of training one's memory was not to become a "living book," but rather a "living concordance," a walking index of everything one had read, and all the information one had acquired. It was about more than merely possessing an internal library of facts, quotes, and ideas; it was about building an organizational scheme for accessing them. Consider, for example, Peter of Ravenna, a leading fifteenth-century Italian jurist (also, one gets the impression, one of the fifteenth century's leading self-promoters) who authored one of the era's most successful books on memory training. Titled *Phoenix*, it was translated into several languages and reprinted all across Europe. It was just the most famous of a handful of memory treatises created from the thirteenth century onward that helped make memory techniques that had long been the exclusive purview of scholars and monks available to a wider audience of doctors, lawyers, tradesmen, and everyday folks who just wanted to remember stuff. One finds books from the period on every variety of mnemonic subject, including how to use the art of memory in gambling, how to use it to keep track of debts, how to memorize the contents of ships, how to remember the names of acquaintances, and how to memorize playing cards. Peter, for his part, bragged of having memorized twenty thousand legal points, a thousand texts by Ovid, two hundred of Cicero's speeches and sayings, three hundred sayings of philosophers, seven thousand texts from Scripture, as well as a host of other classical works.

For leisure, he would reread books cached away in his many memory palaces. "When I left my country to visit as a pilgrim the cities of Italy, I can truly say I carried everything I owned with me," he wrote. To store all those images, Peter started with a hundred thousand loci, but he was always picking up new memory palaces on his travels across Europe. He constructed a mental library of sources and quotations on every important subject, classified alphabetically. He boasts, for example, that filed away in his brain under the letter A were sources on the subjects "*de alimentis, de alienatione, de absentia, de arbitris, de appellationibus, et de similibus quae jure nostro habentur incipientibus in dicta littera A*"—"about provisions, about foreign property, about absence, about judges, about appeals, and about similar matters in our law which begin with the letter A." Each piece of knowledge was assigned a specific address. When he wished to expound on a given topic, he simply reached into the proper chamber of the proper memory palace and pulled out the proper source.

When the point of reading is, as it was for Peter of Ravenna, remembering, you approach a text very differently than most of us do today. Now we put a premium on reading quickly and widely, and that breeds a kind of superficiality in our reading, and in what we seek to get out of books. You can't read a page a minute, the rate at which you're probably reading this book, and expect to remember what you've read for any considerable length of time. If something is going to be made memorable, it has to be dwelled upon, repeated.

In his essay "The First Steps Toward a History of Reading," Robert Darnton describes a switch from "intensive" to "extensive" reading that occurred as books began to proliferate. Until relatively recently, people read "intensively," says Darnton. "They had only a few books—the Bible, an almanac, a devotional work or two—and they read them over and over again, usually aloud and in groups, so that a narrow range of traditional literature became deeply impressed on their consciousness."

But after the printing press appeared around 1440, things began gradually to change. In the first century after Gutenberg, the number of books in existence increased fourteenfold. It became possible, for the first time, for people without great wealth to have a small library in their own homes, and a trove of easily consulted external memories close at hand.

Today, we read books "extensively," without much in the way of sustained focus, and, with rare exceptions, we read each book only once. We value quantity of reading over quality of reading. We have no choice, if we want to keep up with the broader culture. Even in the most highly specialized fields, it can be a Sisyphean task to try to stay on top of the ever-growing mountain of words loosed upon the world each day.

Few of us make any serious effort to remember what we read. When I read a book, what do I hope will stay with me a year later? If it's a work of nonfiction, the thesis, maybe, if the book has one. A few savory details, perhaps. If it's fiction, the broadest outline of the plot, something about the main characters (at least their names), and an overall critical judgment about the book. Even these are likely to fade. Looking up at my shelves, at the books that have drained so many of my waking hours, is always a dispiriting experience. *One Hundred Years of Solitude*: I remember magical realism and that I enjoyed it. But that's about it. I don't even recall when I read it. About *Wuthering Heights* I remember exactly two things: that I read it in a high school English class and that there was a character named Heathcliff. I couldn't say whether I liked the book or not.

I don't think I'm an exceptionally bad reader. I suspect that many people, maybe even most, are like me. We read and read and read, and we forget and forget and forget. So why do we bother? Michel de Montaigne expressed the dilemma of extensive reading in the sixteenth century: "I leaf through books, I do not study them," he wrote. "What I retain of them is something I no longer recognize as anyone else's. It is only the material from which my judgment has profited, and the thoughts and ideas with which it has become imbued; the author, the place, the words, and other circumstances, I immediately forget." He goes on to explain how "to compensate a little for the treachery and weakness of my memory," he adopted the habit of writing in the back of every book a short critical judgment, so as to have at least some general idea of what the tome was about and what he thought of it.

You might think that the advent of printing, and the ability to more easily offload memories from brains onto paper, would have immediately rendered the old memory techniques irrelevant. But that's not what happened. At least not right away. In fact, paradoxically, at exactly the moment when a neat rendering of history would suggest that the art of memory should have been on its way to obsolescence, it underwent its greatest renaissance.

Ever since Simonides, the art of memory had been about creating architectural spaces in the imagination. But in the sixteenth century, an Italian philosopher and alchemist named Giulio Camillo — known as "Divine Camillo" to his many admirers and "the Quack" to his many detractors — had the clever idea of making concrete what had for the previous two thousand years always been an ethereal idea. It occurred to him that the system would work a whole lot better if someone transformed the metaphor of the memory palace into a real wooden building. He imagined creating a "Theater of Memory" that would serve as a universal library containing all the knowledge of mankind. It may sound like the premise of a

Borges story, but it was a very real project, with very real backers, and it made Camillo into one of the most famous men in all of Europe. King Francis I of France made Camillo promise that the secrets of his theater would never be revealed to anyone but him, and invested five hundred ducats toward its completion.

Camillo's wooden memory palace was shaped like a Roman amphitheater, but instead of the spectator sitting in the seats looking down on the stage, he stood in the center and looked up at a round, seven-tiered edifice. All around the theater were paintings of Kabbalistic and mythological figures as well as endless rows of drawers and boxes filled with cards, on which were printed everything that was known, and — it was claimed — everything that was knowable, including quotations from all the great authors, categorized according to subject. All you had to do was meditate on an emblematic image and the entirety of knowledge stored in that section of the theater would be called immediately to mind, allowing you to "be able to discourse on any subject no less fluently than Cicero." Camillo promised that "by means of the doctrine of loci and images, we can hold in the mind and master all human concepts and all the things that are in the entire world."

That was a grand claim, and with hindsight, sure, it sounds like hocus-pocus. But Camillo was convinced that there existed a set of magical symbols that could organically represent the entire cosmos. Just as the image of the she-male represented the concept of e-mailing in that first memory palace I built to house Ed's to-do list, Camillo believed there were images that could encapsulate vast and powerful concepts about the universe, and simply by memorizing those images, one would be able understand the hidden connections underlying everything.

A scale wooden model of Camillo's theater was exhibited in Venice and Paris, and hundreds — perhaps thousands — of cards were drafted to fill the theater's boxes and drawers. The artists Titian and Salviati were enlisted to paint the theater's symbolic imagery. However, that seems to be about as far as things got. The theater was never actually completed, and all that remains of the grand scheme is a short, post-humously published manifesto, *The Idea of the Theater*, dictated on his deathbed over the course of a week. Written in the future tense without any images or diagrams, it is, to put it mildly, a confusing book.

Though history had largely forgotten the man who promised the ultimate technology for remembering — "divine" lost out to "quack" in almost every assessment — Camillo's reputation was resurrected in the twentieth century thanks to the efforts of the historian Frances Yates, who helped reconstruct the theater's blueprints in her book *The Art of Memory*, and the Italian literature professor Lina Bolzoni, who has helped explain how Camillo's theater was more than just the work of a nut job, but actually the apotheosis of an entire era's ideas about memory.

The Renaissance, with its fresh translations of ancient Greek texts, brought about a renewed fascination with Plato's old idea that there is a transcendental ideal reality of which our own world is but a pale shadow.

In Camillo's Neoplatonic vision of the universe, images in the mind were a way of accessing that ideal realm, and the art of memory was a secret key to unlocking the occult structure of the universe. Memory was transformed from a tool of rhetoric, as it had been for the ancients, or an instrument of pious meditation, as it had been for the medieval scholastic philosophers, into a purely mystical art.

Even more than Camillo, the greatest practitioner of this dark, mystical form of mnemonics was the Dominican friar Giordano Bruno. In his book *On the Shadow of Ideas*, published in 1582, Bruno promised that his art "will help not only the memory but also all the powers of the soul." Memory training, for Bruno, was the key to spiritual enlightenment.

Bruno had literally come up with a new twist on the old art of memory. Drawing inspiration from the palindromically named thirteenth-century Catalan philosopher and mystic Ramon Llull, Bruno invented a device that would allow him to turn any word into a unique image. Bruno imagined a series of concentric wheels, each of which had 150 two-letter pairs around its perimeter, corresponding to all of the combinations that could be formed by the thirty letters of the alphabet (the twenty-three letters of classical Latin, plus seven Greek and Hebrew letters that didn't have an equivalent in the Latin alphabet) and the five vowels: AA, AE, AI, AO, AU, BA, BE, BO, etc. On the innermost wheel, the 150 two-letter combinations were each paired with a different mythological or occult figure. On the perimeter of the second wheel were 150 actions and predicaments — "sailing," "on the carpet," "broken" — corresponding to another set of letter pairs. The third wheel consisted of 150 adjectives, the fourth wheel had 150 objects, and the fifth wheel had 150 "circumstances," such as "dressed in pearls" or "riding a sea monster." By properly aligning the wheels, any word up to five syllables long could be translated into a unique, vivid image. For example, the word *crocitus*, Latin for "croaking of a raven," becomes an image of the Roman diety "Pilumnus advancing rapidly on the back of a donkey with a bandage on his arm and a parrot on his head." Bruno was convinced that his opaque and divinely loopy invention was a major step forward for the arts of memory, analogous in scale, he proclaimed, to the technological leap from carving letters in trees to the printing press.

Bruno's scheme, tinged with magic and the occult, deeply troubled the church. His unorthodox ideas, which included such heresies as a belief in Copernican heliocentrism and a conviction that Mary wasn't really a virgin, ultimately landed him in the unforgiving arms of the Inquisition. In 1600, he was burned at the stake in the Campo dei Fiori in Rome and his ashes dispersed in the Tiber River. Today, a statue of Bruno stands in the plaza where he was immolated, a beacon to free-thinkers and mental athletes the world over.

Once the Enlightenment had finally put to bed the Renaissance's obsession with occult memory theaters and Llullian wheels, the art of memory passed into a new but no less harebrained era — the age of the "get smart quick" scheme — which to this day it hasn't yet escaped. Over a hundred treatises on mnemonics were published in the nineteenth century, with titles like "American Mnemotechny" and "How to Remember." They bear a conspicuous resemblance to the memory improvement books that can be found in the self-help aisle at bookstores today. The most popular of these nineteenth-century mnemonic handbooks was written by Professor Alphonse Loisette, an American "memory doctor" who, despite his prolific remembering, "had somehow forgotten that he was born Marcus Dwight Larrowe and that he had no degree," as one article notes. The fact that I was able to find 136 used copies of Loisette's 1886 book *Physiological Memory: The Instantaneous Art of Never Forgetting* selling for as little as $1.25 on the Internet is evidence of its once immense popularity.

Loisette's book is essentially a collection of mnemonic systems for remembering sundry trivia, like the order of American presidents, the counties of Ireland, the Morse telegraphic alphabet, the British territorial regiments, and the names and uses of the nine pairs of cranial nerves. Loisette claimed his system was wholly unrelated to classical mnemonics, for which he professed disdain, and that he had discovered, entirely by himself, the "laws of natural memory."

Loisette charged as much as twenty-five dollars (more than five hundred dollars in today's money) to impart this knowledge to his pupils in seminars held all across the country, including classes at just about every prestigious university on the eastern seaboard. Inductees into the "Loisette System" were made to sign a contract binding them to secrecy, with a penalty of five hundred dollars (over ten thousand dollars in today's money) should they divulge the professor's methods. There was, it seems, good money to be made peddling secrets of memory improvement to a credulous American audience. According to the doctor's own numbers, he earned today's equivalent of almost a half million dollars over a single fourteen-week stretch in the winter of 1887.

In 1887, Samuel L. Clemens, better known as Mark Twain, first crossed paths with Loisette and enrolled in a memory course lasting several weeks. Twain used to say that his "memory was never loaded with anything but blank cartridges," and had long had an interest in memory improvement. He came out of the course a deep believer in Loisette's system. In fact, he was so taken with Loisette that he independently published a broadside claiming that ten thousand dollars an hour would be a bargain for the invaluable tricks the doctor was imparting. He would later regret this testimonial, but not until after it found its way onto virtually every piece of printed matter Loisette produced.

In 1888, G. S. Fellows, out of "that keen sense of justice and innate love of liberty, characteristic of every true American" published a book called *"Loisette" Exposed* that set out to clarify that "Professor" "Loisette" — yes, both appellations bore their own set of scare quotes — was both a "humbug and a fraud." The 224-page book revealed that his methods were either ripped off and repackaged from older sources or else obscenely oversold. Surely Loisette's humbuggery and fraudulence ought to have been self-evident to someone as versed in the ways of the world as Mark Twain, but Twain was a profligate fad chaser, and always interested in the next big thing. (His personal investment of $300,000 — $7 million today — in the Paige typesetter, an early competitor of the Linotype, was only the most ruinous of several ambitious projects he poured his money into.)

Twain himself was continually experimenting with new memory techniques to aid him on the lecture circuit. At one point early in his career, he wrote the first letter of topics he planned to drop into his speech on each of his ten fingernails, but that never really worked, since audiences began to suspect him of having some sort of vain interest in his hands. During the summer of 1883, while he was writing *Huckleberry Finn*, Twain procrastinated by developing a game to teach his children the English monarchs. It worked by mapping out the lengths of their reigns using pegs along a road near his home. Twain was essentially turning his backyard into a memory palace. In 1885, he patented "Mark Twain's Memory Builder: A Game for Acquiring and Retaining All Sorts of Facts and Dates." Twain's notebooks are filled with pages dedicated to his spatial memory game.

Twain imagined national clubs organized around his mnemonic game, regular newspaper columns, a book, and international competitions with prizes. He became convinced that the entire corpus of historical and scientific facts that any American student needed to know could be taught through his ingenious invention. "Poets, statesmen, artists, heroes, battles, plagues, cataclysms, revolutions . . . the invention of the logarithm, the microscope, the steam-engine, the telegraph — anything and everything all over the world — we dumped it all in among the English pegs," he wrote in his 1899 essay "How to Make History Dates Stick." Unfortunately, like the Paige typesetter, the game turned out to be a financial bust, and Twain was eventually forced to abandon it. He wrote to his friend the novelist William Dean Howells, "If you haven't ever tried to invent an indoor historical game, don't."

Like so many before him, Twain had gotten swept up in the promise of vanquishing forgetfulness. He had drunk of the same wacky elixir that had intoxicated Camillo and Bruno and Peter of Ravenna, and his story should probably be read as a cautionary tale to anyone embarking on a course of memory training. Perhaps, in retrospect, the resemblances between Dr. Loisette and today's memory gurus should have sent me running for the hills. And yet they didn't.

Twain lived in an age when the technologies for storing and retrieving external memories — paper, books, the recently invented photograph and phonograph — were still primitive compared to what we have today. He could not have foreseen how the proliferation of digital information at the beginning of the twenty-first century would hasten the pace at which our culture has become capable of externalizing its memories. With our blogs and tweets, digital cameras, and unlimited-gigabyte e-mail archives, participation in the online culture now means creating a trail of always present, ever searchable, unforgetting external memories that only grows as one ages. As more and more of our lives move online, more and more is being captured and preserved in ways that are dramatically changing the relationship between our internal and external memories. We are moving toward a future, it seems, in which we will have all-encompassing external memories that record huge swaths of our daily activity.

I was convinced of this by a seventy-three-year-old computer scientist at Microsoft named Gordon Bell. Bell sees himself as the vanguard of a new movement that takes the externalization of memory to its logical extreme: a final escape from the biology of remembering.

"Each day that passes I forget more and remember less," writes Bell in his book *Total Recall: How the E-Memory Revolution Will Change Everything*. "What if you could overcome this fate? What if you never had to forget anything, but had complete control over what you remembered—and when?"

For the last decade, Bell has kept a digital "surrogate memory" to supplement the one in his brain. It ensures that a record is kept of anything and everything that might be forgotten. A miniature digital camera, called a SenseCam, dangles around his neck and records every sight that passes before his eyes. A digital recorder captures every sound he hears. Every phone call placed through his landline gets taped and every piece of paper Bell reads is immediately scanned into his computer. Bell, who is completely bald, often smiling, and wears rectangular glasses and a black turtleneck, calls this process of obsessive archiving "lifelogging."

All this obsessive recording may seem strange, but thanks to the plummeting price of digital storage, the increasing ubiquity of digital sensors, and better artificial intelligence to sort through the mess of data we're constantly collecting, it's becoming easier and easier to capture and remember ever more information from the world around us. We may never walk around with cameras dangling from our necks, but Bell's vision of a future in which computers remember everything that happens to us is not nearly as absurd as it might at first sound.

Bell made his name and fortune as an early computing pioneer at the Digital Equipment Corporation in the 1960s and '70s. (He's been called the "Frank Lloyd Wright of computers.") He's an engineer by nature, which means he sees problems and tries to build solutions. With the SenseCam, he is trying to fix an elemental human problem: that we forget our lives almost as fast as we live them. But why should any memory fade when there are technological solutions that can preserve it?

WITH THE SENSECAM, HE IS TRYING TO FIX AN ELEMENTAL HUMAN PROBLEM: THAT WE FORGET OUR LIVES ALMOST AS FAST AS WE LIVE THEM.

In 1998, with the help of his assistant Vicki Rozyki, Bell began backfilling his lifelog by systematically scanning every document in the dozens of banker boxes he'd amassed since the 1950s. All of his old photos, engineering notebooks, and papers were digitized. Even the logos on his T-shirts couldn't escape the scanner bed. Bell, who had always been a meticulous preservationist, figures he's probably scanned and thrown away three quarters of all the stuff he's ever owned. Today his lifelog takes up 170 gigabytes, and is growing at the rate of about a gigabyte each month. It includes over 100,000 e-mails, 65,000 photos, 100,000 documents, and 2,000 phone calls. It fits comfortably on a hundred-dollar hard drive.

Bell can pull off some sensational stunts with his "surrogate memory." With his custom search engine, he can, in an instant, figure out where he was and whom he was with at any moment in time, and then, in theory, check to see what that person said. And because he's got a photographic record of everywhere he's ever been and everything he's ever seen, he has no excuse for ever losing anything. His digital memory never forgets.

Photographs, videos, and digital recordings are, like books, prosthetics for our memories—chapters in the long journey that began when the Egyptian god Theuth came to King Thamus and offered him the gift of writing as a "recipe for both memory and wisdom." Lifelogging is the logical next step. Maybe even the logical final step, a kind of *reductio ad absurdum* of a cultural transformation that has been slowly unfolding for millennia.

I wanted to meet Bell and see his external memory at work. His project would seem to offer the ultimate counterargument to all the effort I was investing in training my internal memory. If we're bound to have computers that never forget, why bother having brains that remember?

When I visited his immaculate Microsoft Research office overlooking the San Francisco Bay, Bell wanted to show me how he uses his external memory to help find things that have gone missing in his internal memory. Because memories are associative, finding the odd misplaced fact is often an act of triangulation. "The other day, I was trying to find a house I had looked at online," Bell told me, leaning back in his chair. "All I could remember about it is that I was talking to the realtor on the phone at the time." He pulled up a time line of his life on his computer, found the phone conversation on it, and then immediately pulled up all the Web sites he was looking at while he was on the phone. "I call them information barbs," says Bell. "All you need is to remember a hook." The more barbs there are stored in one's digital memory, the easier it is to find what you're looking for.

Bell has a wealth of external memories at his fingertips. By far the biggest problem Bell faces is how to avoid the fate of Funes and S and keep from drowning in a sea of meaningless trivia. So much of remembering happens at the moment of encoding, because we only tend to remember what we pay attention to. But Bell's lifelog pays attention to everything. "Don't ever filter, and never throw anything away" is his motto.

"Do you ever feel burdened by the sheer volume of memories you're collecting?" I asked him.

He scoffed at the notion. "No way. I feel this is tremendously freeing."

The SenseCam is not a beautiful machine. It's a black box, about the size of a pack of cigarettes, that dangles around Bell's neck. Inconspicuous it's not. But then again, the first computers took up entire rooms and the earliest cell phones were the size of cinder blocks. It doesn't take much imagination to see how future versions of the SenseCam could be embedded in a pair of eyeglasses, or inconspicuously sewn into clothing, or even somehow tucked under the surface of the skin or embedded in a retina.

For now, Bell's internal and external memories don't mesh seamlessly. In order for him to access one of his stored external memories, he still has to find it on his computer and "re-input" it into his brain through his eyes and ears. His lifelog may be an extension of him, but it's not yet a part of him. But is it so far-fetched to believe that at some point in the not-too-distant future the chasm between what Bell's computer knows and what his mind knows may disappear entirely? Eventually, our brains may be connected directly and seamlessly to our lifelogs, so that our external memories will function and feel as if they are entirely internal. And of course, they will also be connected to the greatest external memory repository of all, the Internet. A surrogate memory that recalls everything and can be accessed as naturally as the memories stored in our neurons: It would be the decisive weapon in the war against forgetting.

This may sound like science fiction, but already cochlear implants can convert sound waves directly into electrical impulses and channel them into the brain stem, allowing previously deaf people to hear. In fact, they've already been installed in more than 200,000 human heads. And primitive cognitive implants that create a direct interface between the brain and computers have already allowed paraplegics and patients with ALS (Lou Gehrig's disease) to control a computer cursor, a prosthetic limb, even a digital voice simply through the force of thought. These neuroprosthetics, which are still highly experimental and have been implanted in only a handful of patients, essentially wiretap the brain, and allow direct communication between man and machine. The next step is a brain-computer interface that lets the mind exchange data directly with a digital memory bank, a project that a few cutting-edge researchers are already working on, and which is bound to become a major area of research in the decades ahead.

You don't have to be a reactionary, a fundamentalist, or a Luddite to wonder whether plugging brains into computers and seamlessly merging internal and external memory would ultimately be such a terrific idea. Today bioethicists work up sweats over such hot-potato topics as genetic engineering and neurotropic "cognitive steroids," but these kinds of enhancements are just tweaking the dials compared with what it would mean to fully marry our internal and external memories. A smarter, taller, stronger, disease-resistant person who lives to 150 is still, in the end, just a person. But if we could give someone a perfect memory and a mind that taps directly into the entire collective knowledge of humanity, well, that's when we might need to consider expanding our vocabulary.

But perhaps instead of thinking of these memories as externalized or off-loaded — as categorically different from memories that reside in the brain — we should view them as *extensions* of our internal memories. After all, even internal memories are accessible only by degrees.

There are events and facts I know I know, but I don't know how to find. Even if I can't immediately recall where I celebrated my seventh birthday or the name of my second cousin's wife, those facts are nevertheless lurking somewhere in my brain, waiting for the right cue to pop back into consciousness, in just the same way that all the facts in Wikipedia are lurking just a mouse click away.

We Westerners tend to think of the "self," the elusive essence of who we are, as if it were some starkly delimited entity. Even if modern cognitive neuroscience has rejected the old Cartesian idea of a homuncular soul that resides in the pineal gland and controls the human body, most of us still believe there is a distinct "me" somewhere up there driving the bus. In fact, what we think of as "me" is almost certainly something far more diffuse and hazier than it's comfortable to contemplate. At the least, most people assume that their self could not possibly extend beyond the boundaries of their epidermis into books, computers, a lifelog. But why should that be the case? Our memories, the essence of our selfhood, are actually bound up in a whole lot more than the neurons in our brain. At least as far back as Socrates's diatribe against writing, our memories have always extended beyond our brains and into other storage containers. Bell's lifelogging project simply brings that truth into focus.

QUESTIONS FOR A SECOND READING

1. Foer writes, "I don't think I am an exceptionally bad reader. I suspect that many people, maybe even most, are like me. We read and read and read, and we forget and forget and forget. So why do we bother?" (p. 167) What, as far as you can tell, does Foer seem to think about his own question? How would *you* answer this question? Why *do* we bother reading?

2. Foer offers us an interesting historical narrative about the relationship between memory and writing, and about how the technologies of writing and reading have changed the ways people learn and think. He writes, "As books became easier and easier to consult, the imperative to hold their contents in memory became less and less relevant, and the very notion of what it meant to be erudite began to evolve from possessing information internally to knowing where to find information in the labyrinthine world of external memory." (p. 165) Spend some time with this passage. What do you think Foer is trying to say here? What does it lead you to think about? As you reread, what other passages would you want to put into conversation with this passage on books? How does this passage connect to what you see as Foer's larger project in this piece?

3. Some might make the argument that computers profoundly impact our ability to remember things in the same way the technology of writing has. Who

needs to remember who Galileo is, for example, if one can Google him in seconds? As you reread this essay, look to see what else Foer has to say about memory's past, present, and future. What questions does he seem to want to raise about memory?

ASSIGNMENTS FOR WRITING

1. Foer tells us that "[e]ver since Simonides, the art of memory had been about creating architectural spaces in the imagination." (p. 167) He names "the memory palace" as the metaphor through which memory could be understood. Foer even describes how this memory palace was made "into a real wooden building." Write an essay in which you explore the possibilities and limits the metaphor offers.

   What does this metaphor help us understand about memory? What questions come up for you as you think through the metaphor? Why might Simonides and others think to use this particular metaphor to think about memory? Why *this* metaphor and not another?

   You might also go to Joshua Foer's Web site (joshuafoer.com) and watch his TED Talk to help you think through these questions about the metaphor of the memory palace.

2. An online search for Joshua Foer's lecture "The OK Plateau" will lead you to a video in which Foer argues that the "OK Plateau" is a state of mind in which humans consider themselves "good enough." In this lecture, Foer advocates for moving beyond this state of mind and becoming an expert. He says, "Experts step outside their comfort zone and study themselves failing . . . They crave and thrive on immediate and constant feedback."

   Find this lecture online and write an essay in which you explore the idea of "expertise" as it connects to both Foer's lecture and the chapter you've read here. What, for Joshua Foer, constitutes an "expert"? What are the possibilities and limits in thinking of experts and expertise in the ways Foer articulates? In what subject or topic is Joshua Foer (or other mental athletes who compete in memory decathlons) an expert? Do you believe he is an expert according to *your* definition of that term?

MAKING CONNECTIONS

1. Joshua Foer not only posits some claims about memory but also raises some questions about reading as he connects reading itself with the concept of remembering. For example, he writes, "If something is going to be made memorable, it has to be dwelled upon, repeated." (p. 166) Here, and many other places in this excerpt, he explores how we read and even asks questions about why we read.

Choose, and prepare to write about, a few passages where reading seems to be a way of questioning the role and future of memory. Then, return to the introduction to *Ways of Reading* (p. 1) and gather some of the most significant claims we seem to make about reading.

What is the relationship between the ideas Foer expresses about reading and the ideas expressed in the introduction to this book? How might you put these two texts in direct conversation with one another? What are the connections between them? And what do you have to add to the questions about reading that both texts seem to raise?

2. In his essay, "The 'Banking' Concept of Education," (p. 216) Paulo Freire describes the "banking concept" in the following way: "Education thus becomes an act of depositing, in which the students are the depositories and the teacher is the depositor. Instead of communicating, the teacher issues communiqués and makes deposits which the students patiently receive, memorize, and repeat." (p. 216) Spend some time rereading Freire and thinking about what the word "memorize" means in the context of his argument. What does Freire understand as memorization? What might Freire's understanding have to do with Foer's understanding of memory, if anything?

   Using passages from both selections, formulate an argument about how Freire's and Foer's notions of memory and memorization might illuminate one another. What might Foer say to Freire and vice versa? If you want to be ambitious about this writing project, you might do some research on each author and the context for these particular pieces of writing. When, and in what cultural context, were these pieces written? How does each author's specific historical context help you understand the possibilities (or limits) of putting the two texts in conversation with one another?

3. Foer details the innovation of computer scientist Gordon Bell, who wears his "SenseCam" around his neck. The device acts as a "surrogate memory." Foer says of Bell, "With the SenseCam, he is trying to fix an elemental human problem: that we forget our lives almost as fast as we live them." (p. 172)

   One could read Foer's arguments about memory as philosophically linked to Susan Griffin's understanding of memory in "Our Secret." (p. 233) One could even say that Griffin's essay illuminates the political aspects of memory and the attendant dangers of forgetting. Griffin ends her essay, "And so in the daylight you try to erase what you have encountered and to forget those tracks that are laid even as if someplace in your body, even as part of yourself." (p. 264)

   Write an essay in which you discuss the ways Foer and Griffin might illuminate one another's idea about memory and forgetting. You might choose to begin with Griffin's conclusion. What does it have to do with Foer's chapter? Find other passages from Griffin that seem deeply connected to memory. How do those passages fit into the picture Foer paints of memory?

MICHEL Foucault

Michel Foucault (1926–1984) stands at the beginning of the twenty-first century as one of the world's leading intellectuals. He was trained as a philosopher, but much of his work, like that presented in *Discipline and Punish: The Birth of the Prison* (1975), traces the presence of certain ideas across European history. So he could also be thought of as a historian, but a historian whose goal is to revise the usual understanding of history — not as a progressive sequence but as a series of repetitions governed by powerful ideas, terms, and figures. Foucault was also a public intellectual, involved in such prominent issues as prison reform. He wrote frequently for French newspapers and reviews. His death from AIDS was front-page news in *Le Monde*, the French equivalent of the *New York Times*. He taught at several French universities and in 1970 was appointed to a professorship at the Collège de France, the highest position in the French system. He traveled widely, visiting and lecturing at universities throughout the world.

Foucault's work is central to much current work in the humanities and the social sciences. In fact, it is hard to imagine any area of the academy that has not been influenced by his writing. There is a certain irony in all this, since Foucault argued persuasively that we need to give up thinking about knowledge as individually produced; we have to stop thinking the way we do about the "author" or the "genius," about individuality or creativity; we have to stop thinking as though there were truths that stand beyond the interests of a given moment. It is both dangerous and wrong, he argued, to assume that knowledge is disinterested. Edward Said had this to say of Foucault:

> His great critical contribution was to dissolve the anthropological models of identity and subjecthood underlying research in the humanistic and social sciences. Instead of seeing everything in culture and society as ultimately emanating from either a sort of unchanging Cartesian ego or a heroic solitary artist, Foucault proposed the much juster notion that all work, like social life itself, is collective. The principal task therefore is to circumvent or break down the ideological biases that prevent us from saying that what enables a doctor to practice medicine or a historian to write history is not mainly a set of individual gifts, but an ability to follow rules that are taken for granted as an unconscious a priori by all professionals. More than anyone before him, Foucault

> specified rules for those rules, and even more impressively, he showed how over long periods of time the rules became epistemological enforcers of what (as well as of how) people thought, lived, and spoke.

These rules, these unconscious enforcers, are visible in "discourse"—ways of thinking and speaking and acting that we take for granted as naturally or inevitably there but that are constructed over time and preserved by those who act without question, without stepping outside the discourse and thinking critically. But, says Foucault, there is no place "outside" the discourse, no free, clear space. There is always only another discursive position. A person in thinking, living, and speaking expresses not merely himself or herself but the thoughts and roles and phrases governed by the available ways of thinking and speaking. The key questions to ask, then, according to Foucault, are not Who said this? or Is it original? or Is it true? or Is it authentic? but Who talks this way? or What unspoken rules govern this way of speaking? or Where is this discourse used? Who gets to use it? when? and to what end?

The following selection is the third chapter of *Discipline and Punish: The Birth of the Prison* (translated from the French by Alan Sheridan). In this book, Foucault is concerned with the relationships between knowledge and power, arguing that knowledge is not pure and abstract but is implicated in networks of power relations. Or, as he puts it elsewhere, people govern themselves "through the production of truth." This includes the "truths" that determine how we imagine and manage the boundaries between the "normal" and the transgressive, the lawful and the delinquent. In a characteristic move, Foucault reverses our intuitive sense of how things are. He argues, for example, that it is not the case that prisons serve the courts and a system of justice but that the courts are the products, the servants of "the prison," the prison as an idea, as the central figure in a way of thinking about transgression, order, and the body, a way of thinking that is persistent and general, present, for example, through all efforts to produce the normal or "disciplined individual": "in the central position that [the prison] occupies, it is not alone, but linked to a whole series of 'carceral' mechanisms which seem distinct enough—since they are intended to alleviate pain, to cure, to comfort—but which all tend, like the prison, to exercise a power of normalization." Knowledge stands in an antagonistic role in *Discipline and Punish*; it is part of a problem, not a route to a solution.

You will find "Panopticism" difficult reading. All readers find Foucault's prose tough going. It helps to realize that it is necessarily difficult. Foucault, remember, is trying to work outside of, or in spite of, the usual ways of thinking and writing. He is trying not to reproduce the standard discourse but to point to what it cannot or will not say. He is trying to make gestures beyond what is ordinarily, normally said. So his prose struggles with its own situation. Again, as Edward Said says, "What [Foucault] was interested in . . . was 'the more' that can be discovered lurking in signs and discourses but that is irreducible to language and speech; 'it is this "more,"' he said, 'that we must reveal and describe.' Such a concern appears to be both devious and obscure, yet it accounts for a lot that is especially unsettling in Foucault's writing. There is no

such thing as being at home in his writing, neither for reader nor for writer." While readers find Foucault difficult, he is widely read and widely cited. His books include *The Birth of the Clinic: An Archaeology of Medical Perception* (1963), *The Order of Things: An Archaeology of the Human Sciences* (1966), *The Archaeology of Knowledge* (1969), *Madness and Civilization* (1971), and the three-volume *History of Sexuality* (1976, 1979, 1984).

Panopticism

The following, according to an order published at the end of the seventeenth century, were the measures to be taken when the plague appeared in a town.[1]

First, a strict spatial partitioning: the closing of the town and its outlying districts, a prohibition to leave the town on pain of death, the killing of all stray animals; the division of the town into distinct quarters, each governed by an intendant. Each street is placed under the authority of a syndic, who keeps it under surveillance; if he leaves the street, he will be condemned to death. On the appointed day, everyone is ordered to stay indoors: it is forbidden to leave on pain of death. The syndic himself comes to lock the door of each house from the outside; he takes the key with him and hands it over to the intendant of the quarter; the intendant keeps it until the end of the quarantine. Each family will have made its own provisions; but, for bread and wine, small wooden canals are set up between the street and the interior of the houses, thus allowing each person to receive his ration without communicating with the suppliers and other residents; meat, fish, and herbs will be hoisted up into the houses with pulleys and baskets. If it is absolutely necessary to leave the house, it will be done in turn, avoiding any meeting. Only the intendants, syndics, and guards will move about the streets and also, between the infected houses, from one corpse to another, the "crows," who can be left to die: these are "people of little substance who carry the sick, bury the dead, clean, and do many vile and abject offices." It is a segmented, immobile, frozen space. Each individual is fixed in his place. And, if he moves, he does so at the risk of his life, contagion, or punishment.

Inspection functions ceaselessly. The gaze is alert everywhere: "A considerable body of militia, commanded by good officers and men of substance," guards at the gates, at the town hall, and in every quarter to ensure the prompt obedience of the people and the most absolute authority of the magistrates, "as also to observe all disorder, theft and extortion." At each of the town gates there will be an observation post; at the end of each street sentinels. Every day, the intendant visits the quarter in his charge, inquires whether the syndics have carried out their tasks, whether the inhabitants have anything to complain of; they "observe their actions." Every day, too, the syndic goes into the street for which he is responsible; stops before each house: gets all the inhabitants to appear at the windows (those who live overlooking the courtyard will be allocated a window looking onto the street at which no one but they may show themselves); he calls each of them by name; informs himself as to the state of each and every one of them — "in which respect the inhabitants will be compelled to speak the truth under pain of death"; if someone does not appear at the window, the syndic must ask why: "In this way he will find out easily enough whether dead or sick are being concealed." Everyone locked up in his cage, everyone at his window, answering to his name and showing himself when asked — it is the great review of the living and the dead.

EVERYONE LOCKED UP IN HIS CAGE, EVERYONE AT HIS WINDOW, ANSWERING TO HIS NAME AND SHOWING HIMSELF WHEN ASKED — IT IS THE GREAT REVIEW OF THE LIVING AND THE DEAD.

This surveillance is based on a system of permanent registration: reports from the syndics to the intendants, from the intendants to the magistrates or mayor. At the beginning of the "lock up," the role of each of the inhabitants present in the town is laid down, one by one; this document bears "the name, age, sex of everyone, notwithstanding his condition": a copy is sent to the intendant of the quarter, another to the office of the town hall, another to enable the syndic to make his daily roll call. Everything that may be observed during the course of the visits — deaths, illnesses, complaints, irregularities — is noted down and transmitted to the intendants and magistrates. The magistrates have complete control over medical treatment; they have appointed a physician in charge; no other practitioner may treat, no apothecary prepare medicine, no confessor visit a sick person without having received from him a written note "to prevent anyone from concealing and dealing with those sick of the contagion, unknown to the magistrates." The registration of the pathological must be constantly centralized. The relation of each individual to his disease and to his death passes through the representatives of power, the registration they make of it, the decisions they take on it.

Five or six days after the beginning of the quarantine, the process of purifying the houses one by one is begun. All the inhabitants are made to leave; in each room "the furniture and goods" are raised from the ground or suspended from the air; perfume is poured around the room; after carefully sealing the windows, doors, and even the keyholes with wax, the perfume is set alight. Finally, the entire house is closed while the perfume is consumed; those who have carried out the work are searched, as they were on entry, "in the presence of the residents of the house, to see that they did not have something on their persons as they left that they did not have on entering." Four hours later, the residents are allowed to reenter their homes.

This enclosed, segmented space, observed at every point, in which the individuals are inserted in a fixed place, in which the slightest movements are supervised, in which all events are recorded, in which an uninterrupted work of writing links the center and periphery, in which power is exercised without division, according to a continuous hierarchical figure, in which each individual is constantly located, examined, and distributed among the living beings, the sick, and the dead — all this constitutes a compact model of the disciplinary mechanism. The plague is met by order;

its function is to sort out every possible confusion: that of the disease, which is transmitted when bodies are mixed together; that of the evil, which is increased when fear and death overcome prohibitions. It lays down for each individual his place, his body, his disease, and his death, his well-being, by means of an omnipresent and omniscient power that subdivides itself in a regular, uninterrupted way even to the ultimate determination of the individual, of what characterizes him, of what belongs to him, of what happens to him. Against the plague, which is a mixture, discipline brings into play its power, which is one of analysis. A whole literary fiction of the festival grew up around the plague: suspended laws, lifted prohibitions, the frenzy of passing time, bodies mingling together without respect, individuals unmasked, abandoning their statutory identity and the figure under which they had been recognized, allowing a quite different truth to appear. But there was also a political dream of the plague, which was exactly its reverse: not the collective festival, but strict divisions; not laws transgressed, but the penetration of regulation into even the smallest details of everyday life through the mediation of the complete hierarchy that assured the capillary functioning of power; not masks that were put on and taken off, but the assignment to each individual of his "true" name, his "true" place, his "true" body, his "true" disease. The plague as a form, at once real and imaginary, of disorder had as its medical and political correlative discipline. Behind the disciplinary mechanisms can be read the haunting memory of "contagions," of the plague, of rebellions, crimes, vagabondage, desertions, people who appear and disappear, live and die in disorder.

If it is true that the leper gave rise to rituals of exclusion, which to a certain extent provided the model for and general form of the great Confinement, then the plague gave rise to disciplinary projects. Rather than the massive, binary division between one set of people and another, it called for multiple separations, individualizing distributions, an organization in depth of surveillance and control, an intensification and a ramification of power. The leper was caught up in a practice of rejection, of exile-enclosure; he was left to his doom in a mass among which it was useless to differentiate; those sick of the plague were caught up in a meticulous tactical partitioning in which individual differentiations were the constricting effects of a power that multiplied, articulated, and subdivided itself; the great confinement on the one hand; the correct training on the other. The leper and his separation; the plague and its segmentations. The first is marked; the second analyzed and distributed. The exile of the leper and the arrest of the plague do not bring with them the same political dream. The first is that of a pure community, the second that of a disciplined society. Two ways of exercising power over men, of controlling their relations, of separating out their dangerous mixtures. The plague-stricken town, traversed throughout with hierarchy, surveillance, observation, writing; the town immobilized by the functioning of an extensive power that bears in a distinct way over all individual bodies — this is the utopia of the perfectly governed city. The plague (envisaged as a possibility at least) is the trial in the course of which one may define ideally the exercise of disciplinary power. In order to make rights and laws function according to pure theory, the jurists place themselves in imagination in the state of nature; in order to see perfect disciplines functioning, rulers dreamed of the state of plague. Underlying disciplinary projects the image of the plague stands for all forms of confusion and disorder; just as the image of the leper, cut off from all human contact, underlies projects of exclusion.

They are different projects, then, but not incompatible ones. We see them coming slowly together, and it is the peculiarity of the nineteenth century that it applied to the space of exclusion of which the leper was the symbolic inhabitant (beggars, vagabonds, madmen, and the disorderly formed the real population) the technique of power proper to disciplinary partitioning. Treat "lepers" as "plague victims," project the subtle segmentations of discipline onto the confused space of internment, combine it with the methods of analytical distribution proper to power, individualize the excluded, but use procedures of individualization to mark exclusion—this is what was operated regularly by disciplinary power from the beginning of the nineteenth century in the psychiatric asylum, the penitentiary, the reformatory, the approved school, and to some extent, the hospital. Generally speaking, all the authorities exercising individual control function according to a double mode; that of binary division and branding (mad/sane; dangerous/harmless; normal/abnormal); and that of coercive assignment, of differential distribution (who he is; where he must be; how he is to be characterized; how he is to be recognized; how a constant surveillance is to be exercised over him in an individual way, etc.). On the one hand, the lepers are treated as plague victims; the tactics of individualizing disciplines are imposed on the excluded; and, on the other hand, the universality of disciplinary controls makes it possible to brand the "leper" and to bring into play against him the dualistic mechanisms of exclusion. The constant division between the normal and the abnormal, to which every individual is subjected, brings us back to our own time, by applying the binary branding and exile of the leper to quite different objects; the existence of a whole set of techniques and institutions for measuring, supervising, and correcting the abnormal brings into play the disciplinary mechanisms to which the fear of the plague gave rise. All the mechanisms of power which, even today, are disposed around the abnormal individual, to brand him and to alter him, are composed of those two forms from which they distantly derive.

Bentham's *Panopticon* is the architectural figure of this composition. We know the principle on which it was based: at the periphery, an annular building; at the center, a tower; this tower is pierced with wide windows that open onto the inner side of the ring; the peripheric building is divided into cells, each of which extends the whole width of the building; they have two windows, one on the inside, corresponding to the windows of the tower; the other, on the outside, allows the light to cross the cell from one end to the other. All that is needed, then, is to place a supervisor in a central tower and to shut up in each cell a madman, a patient, a con-

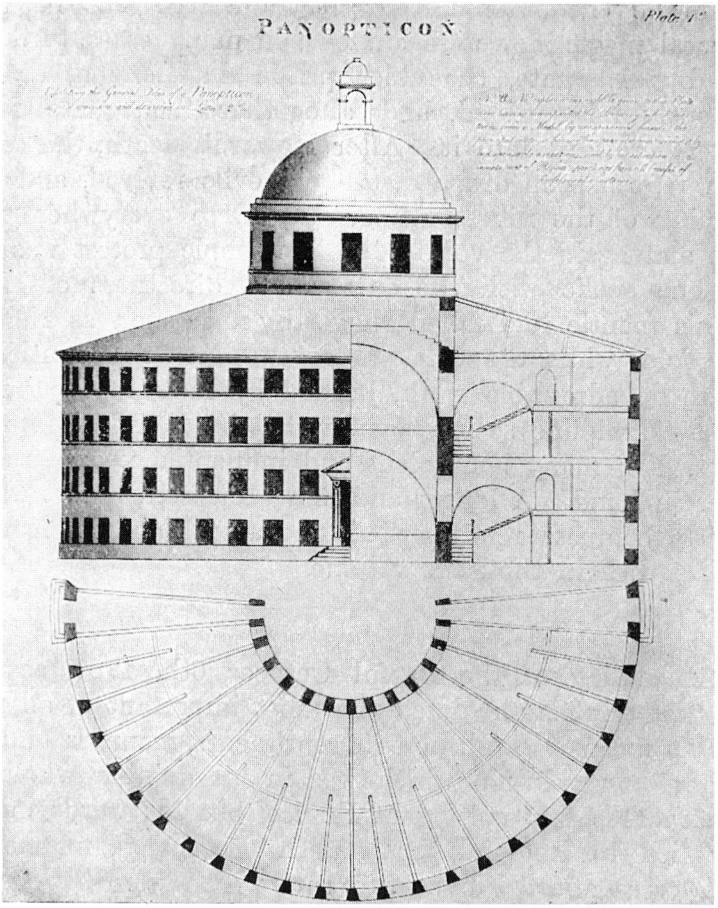

Plan of the Panopticon by J. Bentham (*The Works of Jeremy Bentham*, ed. Bowring, vol. IV, 1843, 172–73).

demned man, a worker, or a schoolboy. By the effect of backlighting, one can observe from the tower, standing out precisely against the light, the small captive shadows in the cells of the periphery. They are like so many cages, so many small theaters, in which each actor is alone, perfectly individualized and constantly visible. The panoptic mechanism arranges spatial unities that make it possible to see constantly and to recognize immediately. In short, it reverses the principle of the dungeon; or rather of its three functions — to enclose, to deprive of light, and to hide — it preserves only the first and eliminates the other two. Full lighting and the eye of a supervisor capture better than darkness, which is ultimately protected. Visibility is a trap.

To begin with, this made it possible — as a negative effect — to avoid those compact, swarming, howling masses that were to be found in places of confinement, those painted by Goya or described by Howard. Each individual, in his place, is securely confined to a cell from which he is seen from the front by the supervisor; but the side walls prevent him from coming into contact with his companions. He is seen, but he does not see; he is the object of information, never a subject in communication. The arrangement of his room, opposite the central tower, imposes on him an axial visibility; but the divisions of the ring, those separated cells, imply a lateral invisibility. And this invisibility is a guarantee of order. If the inmates are convicts, there is no danger of a plot, an attempt at collective escape, the planning of new crimes for the future, bad reciprocal influences; if they are patients, there is no danger of contagion; if they are madmen, there is no risk of their committing violence upon one another;

Handwriting model. *Collections historiques de l'I.N.R.D.P.*

if they are schoolchildren, there is no copying, no noise, no chatter, no waste of time; if they are workers, there are no disorders, no theft, no coalitions, none of those distractions that slow down the rate of work, make it less perfect, or cause accidents. The crowd, a compact mass, a locus of multiple exchanges, individualities merging together, a collective effect, is abolished and replaced by a collection of separated individualities. From the point of view of the guardian, it is replaced by a multiplicity that can be numbered and supervised; from the point of view of the inmates, by a sequestered and observed solitude (Bentham 60–64).

Hence the major effect of the Panopticon: to induce in the inmate a state of conscious and permanent visibility that assures the automatic functioning of power. So to arrange things that the surveillance is permanent in its effects even if it is discontinuous in its action; that the perfection of power should tend to render its actual exercise unnecessary; that this architectural apparatus should be a machine for creating and sustaining a power relation independent of the person who exercises it; in short, that the inmates should be caught up in a power situation of which they are themselves the bearers. To achieve this, it is at once too much and too little that the prisoner should be constantly observed by an inspector: too little, for what matters is that he knows himself to be observed; too much, because he has no need in fact of being so. In view of this, Bentham laid down the principle that power should be visible and unverifiable. Visible: the inmate will constantly have before his eyes the tall outline of the central tower from which he is spied upon. Unverifiable: the inmate must never know whether he is being looked at at any one moment; but he must be sure that he may always be so. In order to make the presence or absence of the inspector unverifiable, so that the prisoners, in their cells, cannot even see a shadow, Bentham envisaged not only venetian blinds on the windows of the central observation hall, but, on the inside, partitions that intersected the hall at right angles and, in order to pass from one quarter to the other, not doors but zigzag openings; for the slightest noise, a gleam of light, a brightness in a half-opened door would betray the presence of the guardian.[2] The Panopticon is a machine for dissociating the see/being seen dyad: in the peripheric ring, one is totally seen, without ever seeing; in the central tower, one sees everything without ever being seen.[3]

It is an important mechanism, for it automatizes and disindividualizes power. Power has its principle not so much in a person as in a certain concerted distribution of bodies, surfaces, lights, gazes; in an arrangement whose internal mechanisms produce the relation in which individuals are caught up. The ceremonies, the rituals, the marks by which the sovereign's surplus power was manifested are useless. There is a machinery that assures dissymmetry, disequilibrium, difference. Consequently, it does not matter who exercises power. Any individual, taken almost at random, can operate the machine: in the absence of the director, his family, his friends, his visitors, even his servants (Bentham 45). Similarly, it does not matter what motive animates him: the curiosity of the indiscreet, the malice of a

Interior of the penitentiary at Stateville, United States, twentieth century.

child, the thirst for knowledge of a philosopher who wishes to visit this museum of human nature, or the perversity of those who take pleasure in spying and punishing. The more numerous those anonymous and temporary observers are, the greater the risk for the inmate of being surprised and the greater his anxious awareness of being observed. The Panopticon is a marvelous machine which, whatever use one may wish to put it to, produces homogeneous effects of power.

A real subjection is born mechanically from a fictitious relation. So it is not necessary to use force to constrain the convict to good behavior, the madman to calm, the worker to work, the schoolboy to application, the patient to the observation of the regulations. Bentham was surprised that panoptic institutions could be so light: there were no more bars, no more

Lecture on the evils of alcoholism in the auditorium of Fresnes prison.

chains, no more heavy locks; all that was needed was that the separations should be clear and the openings well arranged. The heaviness of the old "houses of security," with their fortresslike architecture, could be replaced by the simple, economic geometry of a "house of certainty." The efficiency of power, its constraining force have, in a sense, passed over to the other side — to the side of its surface of application. He who is subjected to a field of visibility, and who knows it, assumes responsibility for the constraints of power; he makes them play spontaneously upon himself; he inscribes in himself the power relation in which he simultaneously plays both roles; he becomes the principle of his own subjection. By this very fact, the external power may throw off its physical

HE WHO IS SUBJECTED TO A FIELD OF VISIBILITY, AND WHO KNOWS IT, ASSUMES RESPONSIBILITY FOR THE CONSTRAINTS OF POWER.

weight; it tends to the noncorporal; and, the more it approaches this limit, the more constant, profound, and permanent are its effects: it is a perpetual victory that avoids any physical confrontation and which is always decided in advance.

Bentham does not say whether he was inspired, in his project, by Le Vaux's menagerie at Versailles: the first menagerie in which the different elements are not, as they traditionally were, distributed in a park (Loisel 104–7). At the center was an octagonal pavilion which, on the first floor, consisted of only a single room, the king's *salon*; on every side large windows looked out onto seven cages (the eighth side was reserved for the entrance), containing different species of animals. By Bentham's time, this menagerie had disappeared. But one finds in the program of the Panopticon a similar concern with individualizing observation, with characterization and classification, with the analytical arrangement of space. The Panopticon is a royal menagerie; the animal is replaced by man, individual distribution by specific grouping, and the king by the machinery of a furtive power. With this exception, the Panopticon also does the work of a naturalist. It makes it possible to draw up differences: among patients, to observe the symptoms of each individual, without the proximity of beds, the circulation of miasmas, the effects of contagion confusing the clinical tables; among schoolchildren, it makes it possible to observe performances (without there being any imitation or copying), to map aptitudes, to assess characters, to draw up rigorous classifications, and in relation to normal development, to distinguish "laziness and stubbornness" from "incurable imbecility"; among workers, it makes it possible to note the aptitudes of each worker, compare the time he takes to perform a task, and if they are paid by the day, to calculate their wages (Bentham 60–64).

So much for the question of observation. But the Panopticon was also a laboratory; it could be used as a machine to carry out experiments, to alter behavior, to train or correct individuals. To experiment with medicines and monitor their effects. To try out different punishments on prisoners, according to their crimes and character, and to seek the most effective ones. To teach different techniques simultaneously to the workers, to decide which is the best. To try out pedagogical experiments — and in particular to take up once again the well-debated problem of secluded education, by using orphans. One would see what would happen when, in their sixteenth or eighteenth year, they were presented with other boys or girls; one could verify whether, as Helvetius thought, anyone could learn anything; one would follow "the genealogy of every observable idea"; one could bring up different children according to different systems of thought, making certain children believe that two and two do not make four or that the moon is a cheese, then put them together when they are twenty or twenty-five years old; one would then have discussions that would be worth a great deal more than the sermons or lectures on which so much money is spent; one would have at least an opportunity of making discoveries in the domain of metaphysics. The Panopticon is a privileged place for experiments on men, and for analyzing with complete certainty the transformations that may be obtained from them. The Panopticon may even provide an apparatus for supervising its own mechanisms. In this central tower, the director may spy on all the employees that he has under his orders: nurses, doctors, foremen, teachers, warders; he will be able to judge them continuously, alter their behavior, impose upon them the methods he thinks best; and it will even be possible to observe the director himself. An inspector arriving unexpectedly at the center of the Panopticon will be able to judge at a glance, without anything being concealed from him, how the entire establishment is functioning. And, in any case, enclosed as he is in the middle of this architectural mechanism, is not the director's own fate entirely bound up with it? The incompetent physician who has allowed contagion to spread, the incompetent prison governor or workshop manager will be the first victims of an epidemic or a revolt. "'By every tie I could devise,' said the master of the Panopticon, 'my own fate had been bound up by me with theirs'" (Bentham 177). The Panopticon functions as a kind of laboratory of power. Thanks to its mechanisms of observation, it gains in efficiency and in the ability to penetrate into men's behavior; knowledge follows the advances of power, discovering new objects of knowledge over all the surfaces on which power is exercised.

The plague-stricken town, the panoptic establishment — the differences are important. They mark, at a distance of a century and a half, the transformations of the disciplinary program. In the first case, there is an exceptional situation: against an extraordinary evil, power is mobilized; it makes itself everywhere present and visible; it invents new mechanisms; it separates, it immobilizes, it partitions; it constructs for a time what is both a counter-city and the perfect society; it imposes an ideal functioning, but one that is reduced, in the final analysis, like the evil that it combats, to a simple dualism of life and death: that which moves brings death, and one kills that which moves. The Panopticon, on the other hand, must be understood as a generalizable model of functioning; a way of defining power relations in terms of the everyday life of men. No doubt Bentham presents it as a particular institution, closed in upon itself. Utopias, perfectly closed in upon themselves, are common enough. As opposed to the ruined prisons, littered with mechanisms of torture, to be seen in Piranese's engravings, the Panopticon presents a cruel, ingenious cage. The fact that it should have given rise, even in our own time, to so many variations, projected or realized, is evidence of the imaginary intensity that it has possessed for almost two hundred years. But the Panopticon must not be understood as a dream building: it is the diagram of a mechanism of power reduced to its ideal form; its functioning, abstracted from any obstacle, resistance, or friction, must be represented as a pure architectural and optical system: it is in fact a figure of political technology that may and must be detached from any specific use.

It is polyvalent in its applications; it serves to reform prisoners, but also to treat patients, to instruct schoolchildren, to confine the insane, to supervise workers, to put beggars and idlers to work. It is a type of location of bodies in space, of distribution of individuals in relation to one another, of hierarchical organization, of disposition of centers and channels of power, of definition of the instruments and modes of intervention of power, which can be implemented in hospitals, workshops, schools, prisons. Whenever one is dealing with a multiplicity of individuals on whom a task or a particular form of behavior must be imposed, the panoptic schema may be used. It is — necessary modifications apart — applicable "to all establishments whatsoever, in which, within a space not too large to be covered or commanded by buildings, a number of persons are meant to be kept under inspection" (Bentham 40; although Bentham takes the penitentiary house as his prime example, it is because it has many different functions to fulfill — safe custody, confinement, solitude, forced labor, and instruction).

In each of its applications, it makes it possible to perfect the exercise of power. It does this in several ways: because it can reduce the number of those who exercise it, while increasing the number of those on whom it is exercised. Because it is possible to intervene at any moment and because the constant pressure acts even before the offenses, mistakes, or crimes have been committed. Because, in these conditions, its strength is that it never intervenes, it is exercised spontaneously and without noise, it constitutes a mechanism whose effects follow from one another. Because, without any physical instrument other than architecture and geometry, it acts directly on individuals; it gives "power of mind over mind." The panoptic schema makes any apparatus of power more intense: it assures its economy (in material, in personnel, in time); it assures its efficacity by its preventative character, its continuous functioning, and its automatic mechanisms. It is a way of obtaining from power "in hitherto unexampled quantity," "a great and new instrument of government . . . ; its great excellence consists in the great strength it is capable of giving to *any* institution it may be thought proper to apply it to" (Bentham 66).

It's a case of "it's easy once you've thought of it" in the political sphere. It can in fact be integrated into any function (education, medical treatment, production, punishment); it can increase the effect of this function, by being linked closely with it; it can constitute a mixed mechanism in which relations of power (and of knowledge) may be precisely adjusted, in the smallest detail, to the processes that are to be supervised; it can establish a direct proportion between "surplus power" and "surplus production." In short, it arranges things in such a way that the exercise of power is not added on from the outside, like a rigid, heavy constraint, to the functions it invests, but is so subtly present in them as to increase their efficiency by itself increasing its own points of contact. The panoptic mechanism is not simply a hinge, a point of exchange between a mechanism of power and a function; it is a way of making power relations function in a function, and of making a function function through these power relations. Bentham's preface to *Panopticon* opens with a list of the benefits to be obtained from his "inspection-house": *"Morals reformed — health preserved — industry invigorated — instruction diffused — public burthens lightened* — Economy seated, as it were, upon a rock — the gordian knot of the Poor-Laws not cut, but untied – all by a simple idea in architecture!" (Bentham 39).

Furthermore, the arrangement of this machine is such that its enclosed nature does not preclude a permanent presence from the outside: we have seen that anyone may come and exercise in the central tower the functions of surveillance, and that, this being the case, he can gain a clear idea of the way in which the surveillance is practiced. In fact, any panoptic institution, even if it is as rigorously closed as a penitentiary, may without difficulty be subjected to such irregular and constant inspections: and not only by the appointed inspectors, but also by the public; any member of society will have the right to come and see with his own eyes how the schools, hospitals, factories, prisons function. There is no risk, therefore, that the increase of power created by the panoptic machine may degenerate into tyranny; the disciplinary mechanism will be democratically controlled, since it will be constantly accessible "to the great tribunal committee of the world."[4] This Panopticon, subtly arranged so that an observer may observe, at a glance, so many different individuals, also enables everyone to come and observe any of the observers. The seeing machine was once a sort of dark room into which individuals spied; it has become a transparent building in which the exercise of power may be supervised by society as a whole.

The panoptic schema, without disappearing as such or losing any of its properties, was destined to spread throughout the social body; its vocation was to become a generalized function. The plague-stricken town provided an exceptional disciplinary model: perfect, but absolutely violent; to the disease that brought death, power opposed its perpetual threat of death; life inside it was reduced to its simplest expression; it was, against the power of death, the meticulous exercise of the right of the sword. The Panopticon, on the other hand, has a role of amplification; although it arranges power, although it is intended to make it more economic and more effective, it does so not for power itself, nor for the immediate salvation of a threatened society: its aim is to strengthen the social forces – to increase production, to develop the economy, spread education, raise the level of public morality; to increase and multiply.

How is power to be strengthened in such a way that, far from impeding progress, far from weighing upon it with its rules and regulations, it actually facilitates such progress? What intensificator of power will be able at the same time to be a multiplicator of production? How will power, by increasing its forces, be able to increase those of society instead of confiscating them or impeding them? The Panopticon's solution to this problem is that the productive increase of power can be assured only if, on the one hand, it can be exercised continuously in the very foundations of society, in the subtlest possible way, and if, on the other hand, it functions outside these sudden, violent, discontinuous forms that are bound up with the exercise of sovereignty. The body of the king, with its strange material and physical presence, with the force that he himself deploys or transmits to some few others, is at the opposite extreme of this new physics of power represented by panopticism; the domain of panopticism is, on the contrary, that whole lower region, that region of irregular bodies, with their details, their multiple movements, their heterogeneous forces, their spatial relations; what are required are mechanisms that analyze distributions, gaps, series, combinations, and which use instruments that render visible, record, differentiate, and compare: a physics of a relational and multiple power, which has its maximum intensity not in the person of the king, but in the bodies that can be individualized by these relations. At the theoretical level, Bentham defines another way of analyzing the social body and the power relations that traverse it; in terms of practice, he defines a procedure of subordination of bodies and forces that must increase the utility of power while practicing the economy of the prince. Panopticism is the general principle of a new "political anatomy" whose object and end are not the relations of sovereignty but the relations of discipline.

The celebrated, transparent, circular cage, with its high tower, powerful and knowing, may have been for Bentham a project of a perfect disciplinary institution; but he also set out to show how one may "unlock" the disciplines and get them to function in a diffused, multiple, polyvalent way throughout the whole social body. These disciplines, which the classical age had elaborated in specific, relatively enclosed places — barracks, schools, workshops — and whose total implementation had been imagined only at the limited and temporary scale of a plague-stricken town, Bentham dreamed of transforming into a network of mechanisms that would be everywhere and always alert, running through society without interruption in space or in time. The panoptic arrangement provides the formula for this generalization. It programs, at the level of an elementary and easily transferable mechanism, the basic functioning of a society penetrated through and through with disciplinary mechanisms.

There are two images, then, of discipline. At one extreme, the discipline-blockade, the enclosed institution, established on the edges of society, turned inwards towards negative functions: arresting evil, breaking communications, suspending time. At the other extreme, with panopticism, is the discipline-mechanism: a functional mechanism that must improve the exercise of power by making it lighter, more rapid, more effective, a design of subtle coercion for a society to come. The movement from one project to the other, from a schema of exceptional discipline to one of a generalized surveillance, rests on a historical transformation: the gradual extension of the mechanisms of discipline throughout the seventeenth and eighteenth centuries, their spread throughout the whole social body, the formation of what might be called in general the disciplinary society.

A whole disciplinary generalization — the Benthamite physics of power represents an acknowledgment of this — had operated throughout the classical age. The spread of disciplinary institutions, whose network was beginning to cover an ever larger surface and occupying above all a less and less marginal position, testifies to this: what was an islet, a privileged place, a circumstantial measure, or a singular model, became a general formula; the regulations characteristic of the Protestant and pious armies of William of Orange or of Gustavus Adolphus were transformed into regulations for all the armies of Europe; the model colleges of the Jesuits, or the schools of Batencour or Demia, following the example set by Sturm, provided the outlines for the general forms of educational discipline; the ordering of the naval and military hospitals provided the model for the entire reorganization of hospitals in the eighteenth century.

But this extension of the disciplinary institutions was no doubt only the most visible aspect of various, more profound processes.

1. *The functional inversion of the disciplines.* At first, they were expected to neutralize dangers, to fix useless or disturbed populations, to avoid the inconveniences of over-large assemblies; now they were being asked to play a positive role, for they were becoming able to do so, to increase the possible utility of individuals. Military discipline is no longer a mere means of preventing looting, desertion, or failure to obey orders among the troops; it has become a basic technique to enable the army to exist, not as an assembled crowd, but as a unity that derives from this very unity an increase in its forces; discipline increases the skill of each individual, coordinates these skills, accelerates movements, increases fire power, broadens the fronts of attack without reducing their vigor, increases the capacity for resistance, etc. The discipline of the workshop, while remaining a way of enforcing respect for the regulations and authorities, of preventing thefts or losses, tends to increase aptitudes, speeds, output, and therefore profits; it still exerts a moral influence over behavior, but more and more it treats actions in terms of their results, introduces bodies into a machinery, forces into an economy. When, in the seventeenth century, the provincial schools or the Christian elementary schools were founded, the justifications given for them were above all negative: those poor who were unable to bring up their children left them "in ignorance of their obligations: given the difficulties they have in earning a living, and themselves having been badly brought up, they are unable to communicate a sound upbringing that they themselves never had"; this involves three major inconveniences: ignorance of God, idleness (with its consequent drunkenness, impurity, larceny, brigandage), and the formation of those gangs of beggars, always ready to stir up public disorder and "virtually to exhaust the funds of the Hôtel-Dieu" (Demia 60–61). Now, at the beginning of the Revolution, the end laid down for primary education was to be, among other things, to "fortify," to "develop the body," to prepare the child "for a future in some mechanical work," to give him "an observant eye, a sure hand and prompt habits" (Talleyrand's Report to the Constituent Assembly, 10 September 1791, quoted by Léon 106). The disciplines function increasingly as techniques for making useful individuals. Hence their emergence from a marginal position on the confines of society, and detachment from the forms of exclusion or expiation, confinement, or retreat. Hence the slow loosening of their kinship with religious regularities and enclosures. Hence also their

rooting in the most important, most central, and most productive sectors of society. They become attached to some of the great essential functions: factory production, the transmission of knowledge, the diffusion of aptitudes and skills, the war-machine. Hence, too, the double tendency one sees developing throughout the eighteenth century to increase the number of disciplinary institutions and to discipline the existing apparatuses.

2. *The swarming of disciplinary mechanisms*. While, on the one hand, the disciplinary establishments increase, their mechanisms have a certain tendency to become "deinstitutionalized," to emerge from the closed fortresses in which they once functioned and to circulate in a "free" state; the massive, compact disciplines are broken down into flexible methods of control, which may be transferred and adapted. Sometimes the closed apparatuses add to their internal and specific function a role of external surveillance, developing around themselves a whole margin of lateral controls. Thus the Christian School must not simply train docile children; it must also make it possible to supervise the parents, to gain information as to their way of life, their resources, their piety, their morals. The school tends to constitute minute social observatories that penetrate even to the adults and exercise regular supervision over them: the bad behavior of the child, or his absence, is a legitimate pretext, according to Demia, for one to go and question the neighbors, especially if there is any reason to believe that the family will not tell the truth; one can then go and question the parents themselves, to find out whether they know their catechism and the prayers, whether they are determined to root out the vices of their children, how many beds there are in the house and what the sleeping arrangements are; the visit may end with the giving of alms, the present of a religious picture, or the provision of additional beds (Demia 39–40). Similarly, the hospital is increasingly conceived of as a base for the medical observation of the population outside; after the burning down of the Hôtel-Dieu in 1772, there were several demands that the large buildings, so heavy and so disordered, should be replaced by a series of smaller hospitals; their function would be to take in the sick of the quarter, but also to gather information, to be alert to any endemic or epidemic phenomena, to open dispensaries, to give advice to the inhabitants, and to keep the authorities informed of the sanitary state of the region.[5]

ONE ALSO SEES THE SPREAD OF DISCIPLINARY PROCEDURES, NOT IN THE FORM OF ENCLOSED INSTITUTIONS, BUT AS CENTERS OF OBSERVATION DISSEMINATED THROUGHOUT SOCIETY.

One also sees the spread of disciplinary procedures, not in the form of enclosed institutions, but as centers of observation disseminated throughout society. Religious groups and charity organizations had long played this role of "disciplining" the population. From the Counter-Reformation to the philanthropy of the July monarchy, initiatives of this type continued to increase; their aims were religious (conversion and moralization), economic (aid and encouragement to work), or political (the struggle against discontent or agitation). One has only to cite by way of example the regulations for the charity associations in the Paris parishes. The territory to be covered was divided into quarters and cantons and the members of the associations divided themselves up along the same lines. These members had to visit their respective areas regularly. "They will strive to eradicate places of ill-repute, tobacco shops, life-classes, gaming houses, public scandals, blasphemy, impiety, and any other disorders that may come to their knowledge." They will also have to make individual visits to the poor; and the information to be obtained is laid down in regulations: the stability of the lodging, knowledge of prayers, attendance at the sacraments, knowledge of a trade, morality (and "whether they have not fallen into poverty through their own fault"); lastly, "one must learn by skillful questioning in what way they behave at home. Whether there is peace between them and their neighbors, whether they are careful to bring up their children in the fear of God . . . , whether they do not have their older children of different sexes sleeping together and with them, whether they do not allow licentiousness and cajolery in their families, especially in their older daughters. If one has any doubts as to whether they are married, one must ask to see their marriage certificate."[6]

3. *The state-control of the mechanisms of the discipline*. In England, it was private religious groups that carried out, for a long time, the functions of social discipline (cf. Radzinovitz 203–14); in France, although a part of this role remained in the hands of parish guilds or charity associations, another — and no doubt the most important part — was very soon taken over by the police apparatus.

The organization of a centralized police had long been regarded, even by contemporaries, as the most direct expression of royal absolutism; the sovereign had wished to have "his own magistrate to whom he might directly entrust his orders, his commissions, intentions, and who was entrusted with the execution of orders and orders under the King's private seal" (a note by Duval, first secretary at the police magistrature, quoted in Funck-Brentano, I). In effect, in taking over a number of preexisting functions — the search for criminals, urban surveillance, economic and political supervision — the police magistratures and the magistrature-general that presided over them in Paris transposed them into a single, strict, administrative machine: "All the radiations of force and information that spread from the circumference culminate in the magistrate-general. . . . It is he who operates all the wheels that together produce order and harmony. The effects of his administration cannot be better compared than to the movement of the celestial bodies" (Des Essarts 344, 528).

But, although the police as an institution were certainly organized in the form of a state apparatus, and although this was certainly linked directly to the center of political sovereignty, the type of power that it exercises, the mechanisms it operates, and the elements to which it applies them are specific. It is an apparatus that must be coextensive with the entire social body and not only by the extreme limits that it embraces, but by the minuteness of the details it is concerned with. Police power must bear "over everything": it is not, however, the totality of the state nor of the kingdom as visible and invisible body of the monarch; it is the dust of events, actions, behavior, opinions — "everything that happens";[7] the police are concerned with "those things of every moment," those "unimportant things," of which Catherine II spoke in her Great Instruction (Supplement to the *Instruction for the Drawing Up of a New Code*, 1769, article 535). With the police, one is in the indefinite world of a supervision that seeks ideally to reach the most elementary particle, the most passing phenomenon of the social body: "The ministry of the magistrates and police officers is of the greatest importance; the objects that it embraces are in a sense definite, one may perceive them only by a sufficiently detailed examination" (Delamare, unnumbered preface): the infinitely small of political power.

And, in order to be exercised, this power had to be given the instrument of permanent, exhaustive, omnipresent surveillance, capable of making all visible, as long as it could itself remain invisible. It had to be like a faceless gaze that transformed the whole social body into a field of perception: thousands of eyes posted everywhere, mobile attentions ever on the alert, a long, hierarchized network which, according to Le Maire, comprised for Paris the forty-eight *commissaires*, the twenty *inspecteurs*, then the "observers," who were paid regularly, the *"basses mouches,"* or secret agents, who were paid by the day, then the informers, paid according to the job done, and finally the prostitutes. And this unceasing observation had to be accumulated in a series of reports and registers; throughout the eighteenth century, an immense police text increasingly covered society by means of a complex documentary organization (on the police registers in the eighteenth century, cf. Chassaigne). And, unlike the methods of judicial or administrative writing, what was registered in this way were forms of behavior, attitudes, possibilities, suspicions — a permanent account of individuals' behavior.

Now, it should be noted that, although this police supervision was entirely "in the hands of the king," it did not function in a single direction. It was in fact a double-entry system: it had to correspond, by manipulating the machinery of justice, to the immediate wishes of the king, but it was also capable of responding to solicitations from below; the celebrated *lettres de cachet*, or orders under the king's private seal, which were long the symbol of arbitrary royal rule and which brought detention into disrepute on political grounds, were in fact demanded by families, masters, local notables, neighbors, parish priests; and their function was to punish by confinement a whole infrapenality, that of disorder, agitation, disobedience, bad conduct; those things that Ledoux wanted to exclude from his architecturally perfect city and which he called "offenses of nonsurveillance." In short, the eighteenth-century police added a disciplinary function to its role as the auxiliary of justice in the pursuit of criminals and as an instrument for the political supervision of plots, opposition movements, or revolts. It was a complex function since it linked the absolute power of the monarch to the lowest levels of power disseminated in society; since, between these different, enclosed institutions of discipline (workshops, armies, schools), it extended an intermediary network, acting where they could not intervene, disciplining the nondisciplinary spaces; but it filled in the gaps, linked them together, guaranteed with its armed force an interstitial discipline and a metadiscipline. "By means of a wise police, the sovereign accustoms the people to order and obedience" (Vattel 162).

The organization of the police apparatus in the eighteenth century sanctioned a generalization of the disciplines that became coextensive with the state itself. Although it was linked in the most explicit way with everything in the royal power that exceeded the exercise of regular justice, it is understandable why the police offered such slight resistance to the rearrangement of the judicial power; and why it has not ceased to impose its prerogatives upon it, with ever-increasing weight, right up to the present day; this is no doubt because it is the secular arm of the judiciary; but it is also because, to a far greater degree than the judicial institution, it is identified, by reason of its extent and mechanisms, with a society of the disciplinary type. Yet it would be wrong to believe that the disciplinary functions were confiscated and absorbed once and for all by a state apparatus.

"Discipline" may be identified neither with an institution nor with an apparatus; it is a type of power, a modality for its exercise, comprising a whole set of instruments, techniques, procedures, levels of application, targets; it is a "physics" or an "anatomy" of power, a technology. And it may be taken over either by "specialized" institutions (the penitentiaries or "houses of correction" of the nineteenth century), or by institutions that use it as an essential instrument for a particular end (schools, hospitals), or by preexisting authorities that find in it a means of reinforcing or reorganizing their internal mechanisms of power (one day we should show how intrafamilial relations, essentially in the parents-children cell, have become "disciplined," absorbing since the classical age external schemata, first educational and military, then medical, psychiatric, psychological, which have made the family the privileged locus of emergence for the disciplinary question of the normal and the abnormal), or by apparatuses that have made discipline their principle of internal functioning (the disciplinarization of the administrative apparatus from the Napoleonic period), or finally by state apparatuses whose major, if not exclusive, function is to assure that discipline reigns over society as a whole (the police).

On the whole, therefore, one can speak of the formation of a disciplinary society in this movement that stretches from the enclosed disciplines, a sort of social "quarantine," to an indefinitely generalizable mechanism of "panopticism." Not because the disciplinary modality of power has replaced all the others; but because it has infiltrated the others, sometimes undermining them, but serving as an intermediary between them, linking them together, extending them, and above all making it possible to bring the effects of power to the most minute and distant elements. It assures an infinitesimal distribution of the power relations.

A few years after Bentham, Julius gave this society its birth certificate (Julius 384–86). Speaking of the panoptic principle, he said that there was much more there than architectural ingenuity: it was an event in the "history of the human mind." In appearance, it is merely the solution of a technical problem; but, through it, a whole type of society emerges. Antiquity had been a civilization of spectacle. "To render accessible to a multitude of men the inspection of a small number of objects": this was the problem to which the architecture of temples, theaters, and circuses responded. With spectacle, there was a predominance of public life, the intensity of festivals, sensual proximity. In these rituals in which blood flowed, society found new vigor and formed for a moment a single great body. The modern age poses the opposite problem: "To procure for a small number, or even for a single individual, the instantaneous view of a great multitude." In a society in which the principal elements are no longer the community and public life, but, on the one hand, private individuals and, on the other, the state, relations can be regulated only in a form that is the exact reverse of the spectacle: "It was to the modern age, to the ever-growing influence of the state, to its ever more profound intervention in all the details and all the relations of social life, that was reserved the task of increasing and perfecting its guarantees, by using and directing towards that great aim the building and distribution of buildings intended to observe a great multitude of men at the same time."

Julius saw as a fulfilled historical process that which Bentham had described as a technical program. Our society is one not of spectacle, but of surveillance; under the surface of images, one invests bodies in depth; behind the great abstraction of exchange, there continues the meticulous, concrete training of useful forces; the circuits of communication are the supports of an accumulation and a centralization of knowledge; the play of signs defines the anchorages of power; it is not that the beautiful totality of the individual is amputated, repressed, altered by our social order, it is rather that the individual is carefully fabricated in it, according to a whole technique of forces and bodies. We are much less Greeks than we believe. We are neither in the amphitheater, nor on the stage, but in the panoptic machine, invested by its effects of power, which we bring to ourselves since we are part of its mechanism. The importance, in historical mythology, of the Napoleonic character probably derives from the fact that it is at the point of junction of the monarchical, ritual exercise of sovereignty and the hierarchical, permanent exercise of indefinite discipline. He is the individual who looms over everything with a single gaze which no detail, however minute, can escape: "You may consider that no part of the Empire is without surveillance, no crime, no offense, no contravention that remains unpunished, and that the eye of the genius who can enlighten all embraces the whole of this vast machine, without, however, the slightest detail escaping his attention" (Treilhard 14). At the moment of its full blossoming, the disciplinary society still assumes with the Emperor the old aspect of the power of spectacle. As a monarch who is at one and the same time a usurper of the ancient throne and the organizer of the new state, he combined into a single symbolic, ultimate figure the whole of the long process by which the pomp of sovereignty, the necessarily spectacular manifestations of power, were extinguished one by one in the daily exercise of surveillance, in a panopticism in which the vigilance of intersecting gazes was soon to render useless both the eagle and the sun.

The formation of the disciplinary society is connected with a number of broad historical processes — economic, juridico-political, and lastly, scientific — of which it forms part.

1. Generally speaking, it might be said that the disciplines are techniques for assuring the ordering of human multiplicities. It is true that there is nothing exceptional or even characteristic in this: every system of power is presented with the same problem. But the peculiarity of the disciplines is that they try to define in relation to the multiplicities a tactics of power that fulfills three criteria: firstly, to obtain the exercise of power at the lowest possible cost (economically, by the low expenditure it involves; politically, by its discretion, its low exteriorization, its relative invisibility, the little resistance it arouses); secondly, to bring the effects of this social power to their maximum intensity and to extend them as far as possible, without either failure or interval; thirdly, to link this "economic" growth of power with the output of the apparatuses (educational, military, industrial, or medical) within which it is exercised; in short, to increase both the docility and the utility of all the elements of the system. This triple objective of the disciplines corresponds to a well-known historical conjuncture. One aspect of this conjuncture was the large demographic thrust of the eighteenth century; an increase in the floating population (one of the primary objects of discipline is to fix; it is an antinomadic technique); a change of quantitative scale in the groups to be supervised or manipulated (from the beginning of the seventeenth century to the eve of the French Revolution, the school population had been increasing rapidly, as had no doubt the hospital population; by the end of the eighteenth century, the peacetime army exceeded 200,000 men). The other aspect of the conjuncture was the growth in the apparatus of production, which was becoming more and more extended and complex; it was also becoming more costly and its profitability had to be increased. The development of the disciplinary methods corresponded to these two processes, or rather, no doubt, to the new need to adjust their correlation. Neither the residual forms of feudal power nor the structures of the administrative monarchy, nor the local mechanisms of supervision, nor the unstable, tangled mass they all formed together could carry out this role: they were hindered from doing so by the irregular and inadequate extension of their network, by their often conflicting functioning, but above all by the "costly" nature of the power that was exercised in them. It was costly in several senses: because directly it cost a great deal to the Treasury; because the system of corrupt offices and farmed-out taxes weighed indirectly, but very heavily, on the population; because the resistance it encountered forced it into a cycle of perpetual reinforcement; because it proceeded essentially by levying (levying on money or products by royal, seigniorial, ecclesiastical taxation; levying on men or time by *corvées* of press-ganging, by locking up or banishing vagabonds). The development of the disciplines marks

the appearance of elementary techniques belonging to a quite different economy: mechanisms of power which, instead of proceeding by deduction, are integrated into the productive efficiency of the apparatuses from within, into the growth of this efficiency and into the use of what it produces. For the old principle of "levying-violence," which governed the economy of power, the disciplines substitute the principle of "mildness-production-profit." These are the techniques that make it possible to adjust the multiplicity of men and the multiplication of the apparatuses of production (and this means not only "production" in the strict sense, but also the production of knowledge and skills in the school, the production of health in the hospitals, the production of destructive force in the army).

In this task of adjustment, discipline had to solve a number of problems for which the old economy of power was not sufficiently equipped. It could reduce the inefficiency of mass phenomena: reduce what, in a multiplicity, makes it much less manageable than a unity; reduce what is opposed to the use of each of its elements and of their sum; reduce everything that may counter the advantages of number. That is why discipline fixes; it arrests or regulates movements; it clears up confusion; it dissipates compact groupings of individuals wandering about the country in unpredictable ways; it establishes calculated distributions. It must also master all the forces that are formed from the very constitution of an organized multiplicity; it must neutralize the effects of counterpower that spring from them and which form a resistance to the power that wishes to dominate it: agitations, revolts, spontaneous organizations, coalitions — anything that may establish horizontal conjunctions. Hence the fact that the disciplines use procedures of partitioning and verticality, that they introduce, between the different elements at the same level, as solid separations as possible, that they define compact hierarchical networks, in short, that they oppose to the intrinsic, adverse force of multiplicity the technique of the continuous, individualizing pyramid. They must also increase the particular utility of each element of the multiplicity, but by means that are the most rapid and the least costly, that is to say, by using the multiplicity itself as an instrument of this growth. Hence, in order to extract from bodies the maximum time and force, the use of those overall methods known as timetables, collective training, exercises, total and detailed surveillance. Furthermore, the disciplines must increase the effect of utility proper to the multiplicities, so that each is made more useful than the simple sum of its elements: it is in order to increase the utilizable effects of the multiple that the disciplines define tactics of distribution, reciprocal adjustment of bodies, gestures, and rhythms, differentiation of capacities, reciprocal coordination in relation to apparatuses or tasks. Lastly, the disciplines have to bring into play the power relations, not above but inside the very texture of the multiplicity, as discreetly as possible, as well articulated on the other functions of these multiplicities and also in the least expensive way possible: to this correspond anonymous instruments of power, coextensive with the multiplicity that they regiment, such as hierarchical surveillance, continuous registration, perpetual assessment, and classification.

In short, to substitute for a power that is manifested through the brilliance of those who exercise it, a power that insidiously objectifies those on whom it is applied; to form a body of knowledge about these individuals, rather than to deploy the ostentatious signs of sovereignty. In a word, the disciplines are the ensemble of minute technical inventions that made it possible to increase the useful size of multiplicities by decreasing the inconveniences of the power which, in order to make them useful, must control them. A multiplicity, whether in a workshop or a nation, an army or a school, reaches the threshold of a discipline when the relation of the one to the other becomes favorable.

If the economic take-off of the West began with the techniques that made possible the accumulation of capital, it might perhaps be said that the methods for administering the accumulation of men made possible a political take-off in relation to the traditional, ritual, costly, violent forms of power, which soon fell into disuse and were superseded by a subtle, calculated technology of subjection. In fact, the two processes — the accumulation of men and the accumulation of capital — cannot be separated; it would not have been possible to solve the problem of the accumulation of men without the growth of an apparatus of production capable of both sustaining them and using them; conversely, the techniques that made the cumulative multiplicity of men useful accelerated the accumulation of capital. At a less general level, the technological mutations of the apparatus of production, the division of labor and the elaboration of the disciplinary techniques sustained an ensemble of very close relations (cf. Marx, *Capital*, vol. I, chapter XIII and the very interesting analysis in Guerry and Deleule). Each makes the other possible and necessary; each provides a model for the other. The disciplinary pyramid constituted the small cell of power within which the separation, coordination, and supervision of tasks was imposed and made efficient; and analytical partitioning of time, gestures, and bodily forces constituted an operational schema that could easily be transferred from the groups to be subjected to the mechanisms of production; the massive projection of military methods onto industrial organization was an example of this modeling of the division of labor following the model laid down by the schemata of power. But, on the other hand, the technical analysis of the process of production, its "mechanical" breaking-down, were projected onto the labor force whose task it was to implement it: the constitution of those disciplinary machines in which the individual forces that they bring together are composed into a whole and therefore increased is the effect of this projection. Let us say that discipline is the unitary technique by which the body is reduced as a "political" force at the least cost and maximized as a useful force. The growth of a capitalist economy gave rise to the specific modality of disciplinary power, whose general formulas, techniques of submitting forces and bodies, in short, "political anatomy," could be operated in the most diverse political regimes, apparatuses, or institutions.

2. The panoptic modality of power — at the elementary, technical, merely physical level at which it is situated — is not under the immediate

dependence or a direct extension of the great juridico-political structures of a society; it is nonetheless not absolutely independent. Historically, the process by which the bourgeoisie became in the course of the eighteenth century the politically dominant class was masked by the establishment of an explicit, coded, and formally egalitarian juridical framework, made possible by the organization of a parliamentary, representative regime. But the development and generalization of disciplinary mechanisms constituted the other, dark side of these processes. The general juridical form that guaranteed a system of rights that were egalitarian in principle was supported by these tiny, everyday, physical mechanisms, by all those systems of micropower that are essentially nonegalitarian and asymmetrical that we call the disciplines. And although, in a formal way, the representative regime makes it possible, directly or indirectly, with or without relays, for the will of all to form the fundamental authority of sovereignty, the disciplines provide, at the base, a guarantee of the submission of forces and bodies. The real, corporal disciplines constituted the foundation of the formal, juridical liberties. The contract may have been regarded as the ideal foundation of law and political power; panopticism constituted the technique, universally widespread, of coercion. It continued to work in depth on the juridical structures of society, in order to make the effective mechanisms of power function in opposition to the formal framework that it had acquired. The "Enlightenment," which discovered the liberties, also invented the disciplines.

In appearance, the disciplines constitute nothing more than an infra-law. They seem to extend the general forms defined by law to the infinitesimal level of individual lives; or they appear as methods of training that enable individuals to become integrated into these general demands. They seem to constitute the same type of law on a different scale, thereby making it more meticulous and more indulgent. The disciplines should be regarded as a sort of counterlaw. They have the precise role of introducing insuperable asymmetries and excluding reciprocities. First, because discipline creates between individuals a "private" link, which is a relation of constraints entirely different from contractual obligation; the acceptance of a discipline may be underwritten by contract; the way in which it is imposed, the mechanisms it brings into play, the nonreversible subordination of one group of people by another, the "surplus" power that is always fixed on the same side, the inequality of position of the different "partners" in relation to the common regulation, all these distinguish the disciplinary link from the contractual link, and make it possible to distort the contractual link systematically from the moment it has as its content a mechanism of discipline. We know, for example, how many real procedures undermine the legal fiction of the work contract: workshop discipline is not the least important. Moreover, whereas the juridical systems

THE DEVELOPMENT AND GENERALIZATION OF DISCIPLINARY MECHANISMS CONSTITUTED THE OTHER, DARK SIDE OF THESE PROCESSES.

define juridical subjects according to universal norms, the disciplines characterize, classify, specialize; they distribute along a scale, around a norm, hierarchize individuals in relation to one another and, if necessary, disqualify and invalidate. In any case, in the space and during the time in which they exercise their control and bring into play the asymmetries of their power, they effect a suspension of the law that is never total, but is never annulled either. Regular and institutional as it may be, the discipline, in its mechanism, is a "counterlaw." And, although the universal juridicism of modern society seems to fix limits on the exercise of power, its universally widespread panopticism enables it to operate, on the underside of the law, a machinery that is both immense and minute, which supports, reinforces, multiplies the asymmetry of power and undermines the limits that are traced around the law. The minute disciplines, the panopticisms of every day may well be below the level of emergence of the great apparatuses and the great political struggles. But, in the genealogy of modern society, they have been, with the class domination that traverses it, the political counterpart of the juridical norms according to which power was redistributed. Hence, no doubt, the importance that has been given for so long to the small techniques of discipline, to those apparently insignificant tricks that it has invented, and even to those "sciences" that give it a respectable face; hence the fear of abandoning them if one cannot find any substitute; hence the affirmation that they are at the very foundation of society, and an element in its equilibrium, whereas they are a series of mechanisms for unbalancing power relations definitively and everywhere; hence the persistence in regarding them as the humble, but concrete form of every morality, whereas they are a set of physico-political techniques.

To return to the problem of legal punishments, the prison with all the corrective technology at its disposal is to be resituated at the point where the codified power to punish turns into a disciplinary power to observe; at the point where the universal punishments of the law are applied selectively to certain individuals and always the same ones; at the point where the redefinition of the juridical subject by the penalty becomes a useful training of the criminal; at the point where the law is inverted and passes outside itself, and where the counterlaw becomes the effective and institutionalized content of the juridical forms. What generalizes the power to punish, then, is not the universal consciousness of the law in each juridical subject; it is the regular extension, the infinitely minute web of panoptic techniques.

3. Taken one by one, most of these techniques have a long history behind them. But what was new, in the eighteenth century, was that, by being combined and generalized, they attained a level at which the formation of knowledge and the increase of power regularly reinforce one another in a circular process. At this point, the disciplines crossed the "technological" threshold. First the hospital, then the school, then, later, the workshop were not simply "reordered" by the disciplines; they became, thanks to them, apparatuses such that any mechanism of

objectification could be used in them as an instrument of subjection, and any growth of power could give rise in them to possible branches of knowledge; it was this link, proper to the technological systems, that made possible within the disciplinary element the formation of clinical medicine, psychiatry, child psychology, educational psychology, the rationalization of labor. It is a double process, then: an epistemological "thaw" through a refinement of power relations; a multiplication of the effects of power through the formation and accumulation of new forms of knowledge.

The extension of the disciplinary methods is inscribed in a broad historical process: the development at about the same time of many other technologies — agronomical, industrial, economic. But it must be recognized that, compared with the mining industries, the emerging chemical industries or methods of national accountancy, compared with the blast furnaces or the steam engine, panopticism has received little attention. It is regarded as not much more than a bizarre little utopia, a perverse dream — rather as though Bentham had been the Fourier of a police society, and the Phalanstery had taken on the form of the Panopticon. And yet this represented the abstract formula of a very real technology, that of individuals. There were many reasons why it received little praise; the most obvious is that the discourses to which it gave rise rarely acquired, except in the academic classifications, the status of sciences; but the real reason is no doubt that the power that it operates and which it augments is a direct, physical power that men exercise upon one another. An inglorious culmination had an origin that could be only grudgingly acknowledged. But it would be unjust to compare the disciplinary techniques with such inventions as the steam engine or Amici's microscope. They are much less; and yet, in a way, they are much more. If a historical equivalent or at least a point of comparison had to be found for them, it would be rather in the "inquisitorial" technique.

The eighteenth century invented the techniques of discipline and the examination, rather as the Middle Ages invented the judicial investigation. But it did so by quite different means. The investigation procedure, an old fiscal and administrative technique, had developed above all with the reorganization of the Church and the increase of the princely states in the twelfth and thirteenth centuries. At this time it permeated to a very large degree the jurisprudence first of the ecclesiastical courts, then of the lay courts. The investigation as an authoritarian search for a truth observed or attested was thus opposed to the old procedures of the oath, the ordeal, the judicial duel, the judgment of God, or even of the transaction between private individuals. The investigation was the sovereign power arrogating to itself the right to establish the truth by a number of regulated techniques. Now, although the investigation has since then been an integral part of Western justice (even up to our own day), one must not forget either its political origin, its link with the birth of the states and of monarchical sovereignty, or its later extension and its role in the formation of knowledge. In fact, the investigation has been the no doubt crude, but fundamental, element in the constitution of the empirical sciences; it has been the juridico-political matrix of this experimental knowledge, which, as we know, was very rapidly released at the end of the Middle Ages. It is perhaps true to say that, in Greece, mathematics were born from techniques of measurement; the sciences of nature, in any case, were born, to some extent, at the end of the Middle Ages, from the practices of investigation. The great empirical knowledge that covered the things of the world and transcribed them into the ordering of an indefinite discourse that observes, describes, and establishes the "facts" (at a time when the Western world was beginning the economic and political conquest of this same world) had its operating model no doubt in the Inquisition — that immense invention that our recent mildness has placed in the dark recesses of our memory. But what this politico-juridical, administrative, and criminal, religious and lay, investigation was to the sciences of nature, disciplinary analysis has been to the sciences of man. These sciences, which have so delighted our "humanity" for over a century, have their technical matrix in the petty, malicious minutiae of the disciplines and their investigations. These investigations are perhaps to psychology, psychiatry, pedagogy, criminology, and so many other strange sciences, what the terrible power of investigation was to the calm knowledge of the animals, the plants, or the earth. Another power, another knowledge. On the threshold of the classical age, Bacon, lawyer and statesman, tried to develop a methodology of investigation for the empirical sciences. What Great Observer will produce the methodology of examination for the human sciences? Unless, of course, such a thing is not possible. For, although it is true that, in becoming a technique for the empirical sciences, the investigation has detached itself from the inquisitorial procedure, in which it was historically rooted, the examination has remained extremely close to the disciplinary power that shaped it. It has always been and still is an intrinsic element of the disciplines. Of course it seems to have undergone a speculative purification by integrating itself with such sciences as psychology and psychiatry. And, in effect, its appearance in the form of tests, interviews, interrogations, and consultations is apparently in order to rectify the mechanisms of discipline: educational psychology is supposed to correct the rigors of the school, just as the medical or psychiatric interview is supposed to rectify the effects of the discipline of work. But we must not be misled; these techniques merely refer individuals from one disciplinary authority to another, and they reproduce, in a concentrated or formalized form, the schema of power-knowledge proper to each discipline (on this subject, cf. Tort). The great investigation that gave rise to the sciences of nature has become detached from its politico-juridical model; the examination, on the other hand, is still caught up in disciplinary technology.

In the Middle Ages, the procedure of investigation gradually superseded the old accusatory justice, by a process initiated from above; the disciplinary technique, on the other hand, insidiously and as if from below, has invaded a penal justice that is still, in principle, inquisitorial. All the great movements of extension that characterize modern penality—the problematization of the criminal behind his crime, the concern with a punishment that is a correction, a therapy, a normalization, the division of the act of judgment between various authorities that are supposed to measure, assess, diagnose, cure, transform individuals—all this betrays the penetration of the disciplinary examination into the judicial inquisition.

What is now imposed on penal justice as its point of application, its "useful" object, will no longer be the body of the guilty man set up against the body of the king; nor will it be the juridical subject of an ideal contract; it will be the disciplinary individual. The extreme point of penal justice under the Ancien Régime was the infinite segmentation of the body of the regicide: a manifestation of the strongest power over the body of the greatest criminal, whose total destruction made the crime explode into its truth. The ideal point of penality today would be an indefinite discipline: an interrogation without end, an investigation that would be extended without limit to a meticulous and ever more analytical observation, a judgment that would at the same time be the constitution of a file that was never closed, the calculated leniency of a penalty that would be interlaced with the ruthless curiosity of an examination, a procedure that would be at the same time the permanent measure of a gap in relation to an inaccessible norm and the asymptotic movement that strives to meet in infinity. The public execution was the logical culmination of a procedure governed by the Inquisition. The practice of placing individuals under "observation" is a natural extension of a justice imbued with disciplinary methods and examination procedures. Is it surprising that the cellular prison, with its regular chronologies, forced labor, its authorities of surveillance and registration, its experts in normality, who continue and multiply the functions of the judge, should have become the modern instrument of penalty? Is it surprising that prisons resemble factories, schools, barracks, hospitals, which all resemble prisons?

NOTES

[1] Archives militaires de Vincennes, A 1,516 91 sc. Pièce. This regulation is broadly similar to a whole series of others that date from the same period and earlier. [All notes are Foucault's.]

[2] In the *Postscript to the Panopticon*, 1791, Bentham adds dark inspection galleries painted in black around the inspector's lodge, each making it possible to observe two stories of cells.

[3] In his first version of the *Panopticon*, Bentham had also imagined an acoustic surveillance, operated by means of pipes leading from the cells to the central tower. In the *Postscript* he abandoned the idea, perhaps because he could not introduce into it the principle of dissymmetry and prevent the prisoners from hearing the inspector as well as the inspector hearing them. Julius tried to develop a system of dissymmetrical listening (Julius 18).

[4] Imagining this continuous flow of visitors entering the central tower by an underground passage and then observing the circular landscape of the Panopticon, was Bentham aware of the Panoramas that Barker was constructing at exactly the same period (the first seems to have dated from 1787) and in which the visitors, occupying the central place, saw unfolding around them a landscape, a city, or a battle? The visitors occupied exactly the place of the sovereign gaze.

[5] In the second half of the eighteenth century, it was often suggested that the army should be used for the surveillance and general partitioning of the population. The army, as yet to undergo discipline in the seventeenth century, was regarded as a force capable of instilling it. Cf., for example, Servan, *Le Soldat citoyen*, 1780.

[6] Arsenal, MS. 2565. Under this number, one also finds regulations for charity associations of the seventeenth and eighteenth centuries.

[7] Le Maire in a memorandum written at the request of Sartine, in answer to sixteen questions posed by Joseph II on the Parisian police. This memorandum was published by Gazier in 1879.

BIBLIOGRAPHY

Archives militaires de Vincennes, A 1,516 91 sc.
Bentham, J., *Works*, ed. Bowring, IV, 1843.
Chassaigne, M., *La Lieutenance générale de police*, 1906.
Delamare, N., *Traité de police*, 1705.
Demia, C., *Règlement pour les écoles de la ville de Lyon*, 1716.
Des Essarts, T. N., *Dictionnaire universel de police*, 1787.
Funck-Brentano, F., *Catalogue des manuscrits de la bibliothèque de l'Arsenal*, IX.
Guerry, F., and Deleule, D., *Le Corps productif*, 1973.
Julius, N. H., *Leçons sur les prisons*, I, 1831 (Fr. trans.).
Léon, A., *La Révolution française et l'éducation technique*, 1968.
Loisel, G., *Histoire des ménageries*, II, 1912.
Marx, Karl, *Capital*, vol. I, ed. 1970.
Radzinovitz, L., *The English Criminal Law*, II, 1956.
Servan, J., *Le Soldat citoyen*, 1780.
Tort, Michel, *Q.I.*, 1974.
Treilhard, J. B., *Motifs du code d'instruction criminelle*, 1808.
Vattel, E. de, *Le Droit des gens*, 1768.

QUESTIONS FOR A SECOND READING

1. Foucault's text begins with an account of a system enacted in the seventeenth century to control the spread of plague. After describing this system of surveillance, he compares it to the "rituals of exclusion" used to control lepers. He says, "The exile of the leper and the arrest of the plague do not bring with them the same political dream." At many points he sets up similar pairings, all in an attempt to understand the relations of power and knowledge in modern public life.

   As you reread, mark the various points at which Foucault works out the differences between a prior and the current "political dream" of order. What techniques or instruments belong to each? What moments in history are defined by each? How and where are they visible in public life?

2. Toward the end of the chapter Foucault says, "The extension of the disciplinary methods is inscribed in a broad historical process." Foucault writes a difficult kind of history (at one point he calls it a genealogy), since it does not make use of the usual form of historical narrative—with characters, plots, scenes, and action. As you reread, take notes that will allow you to trace time, place, and sequence (and, if you can, agents and agency) in Foucault's account of the formation of the disciplinary society based on technologies of surveillance. Why do you think he avoids a narrative mode of presentation?

3. As you reread Foucault's text, bring forward the stages in his presentation (or the development of his argument). Mark those moments that you consider

key or central to the working out of his argument concerning the panopticon. What sentences of his would you use to represent key moments in the text? The text at times turns to numbered sections. How, for example, do they function? Describe the beginning, middle, and end of the essay. Describe the skeleton or understructure of the chapter. What are its various stages or steps? How do they relate to one another?

ASSIGNMENTS FOR WRITING

1. About three-quarters of the way into this chapter, Foucault says,

> Our society is one not of spectacle, but of surveillance; under the surface of images, one invests bodies in depth; behind the great abstraction of exchange, there continues the meticulous, concrete training of useful forces; the circuits of communication are the supports of an accumulation and a centralization of knowledge; the play of signs defines the anchorages of power; it is not that the beautiful totality of the individual is amputated, repressed, altered by our social order, it is rather that the individual is carefully fabricated in it, according to a whole technique of forces and bodies. (p. 200)

This prose is eloquent and insists on its importance to our moment and our society; it is also very hard to read or to paraphrase. Who is doing what to whom? How do we think about the individual's being carefully fabricated in the social order?

Take this chapter as a problem to solve. What is it about? What are its key arguments? its examples and conclusions? Write an essay that summarizes "Panopticism." Imagine that you are writing for readers who have read the chapter (although they won't have the pages in front of them). You will need to take time to present and discuss examples from the text. Your job is to help your readers figure out what it says. You get the chance to take the lead and be the teacher. You should feel free to acknowledge that you don't understand certain sections even as you write about them.

So, how do you write about something you don't completely understand? Here's a suggestion: when you have completed your summary, read it over and treat it as a draft. Ask questions like these: What have I left out? What was I tempted to ignore or finesse? Go back to those sections of the chapter that you ignored and bring them into your essay. Revise by adding discussions of some of the very sections you don't understand. You can write about what you think Foucault *might* be saying—you can, that is, be cautious and tentative; you can admit that the text is what it is, hard to read. You don't have to master this text. You do, however, need to see what you can make of it.

2. About a third of the way through his text, Foucault asserts, "The Panopticon is a marvelous machine which, whatever use one may wish to put it to, produces

homogeneous effects of power." Write an essay in which you explain the machinery of the panopticon as a mechanism of power. Paraphrase Foucault and, where it seems appropriate, use his words. Present Foucault's account as you understand it. As part of your essay, and in order to explain what he is getting at, include two examples — one of his, perhaps, and then one of your own.

3. Perhaps the most surprising thing about Foucault's argument in "Panopticism" is the way it equates prisons with schools, hospitals, and workplaces, sites we are accustomed to imagining as very different from a prison. Foucault argues against our commonly accepted understanding of such things.

At the end of the chapter Foucault asks two questions. These are rhetorical questions, strategically placed at the end. Presumably we are prepared to feel their force and to think of possible answers.

> Is it surprising that the cellular prison, with its regular chronologies, forced labor, its authorities of surveillance and registration, its experts in normality, who continue and multiply the functions of the judge, should have become the modern instrument of penalty? Is it surprising that prisons resemble factories, schools, barracks, hospitals, which all resemble prisons? (p. 208)

For this assignment, take the invitation of Foucault's conclusion. No, you want to respond, it is not surprising that "experts in normality, who continue and multiply the functions of the judge, should have become the modern instrument of penalty." No, it is not surprising that "prisons resemble factories, schools, barracks, hospitals, which all resemble prisons." Why isn't it surprising? Or, why isn't it surprising if you are thinking along with Foucault?

Write an essay in which you explore one of these possible resemblances. You may, if you choose, cite Foucault. You can certainly pick up some of his key terms or examples and put them into play. You should imagine, however, that it is your turn. With your work on Foucault behind you, you are writing to a general audience about "experts in normality" and the key sites of surveillance and control.

MAKING CONNECTIONS

1. Both John Berger in "Ways of Seeing" and Michel Foucault in "Panopticism" discuss what Foucault calls "power relations." Berger claims that "the entire art of the past has now become a political issue," and he makes a case for the evolution of a "new language of images" which could "confer a new kind of power" if people were to understand history in art. Foucault argues that the Panopticon signals an "inspired" change in power relations. "It is," he says,

> an important mechanism, for it automatizes and disindividualizes power. Power has its principle not so much in a person as in a certain

See the e-Pages at bedfordstmartins.com/waysofreading.

> concerted distribution of bodies, surfaces, lights, gazes; in an arrangement whose internal mechanisms produce the relation in which individuals are caught up. (p. 187)

Both Berger and Foucault create arguments about power, its methods and goals. As you read through their essays, mark passages you might use to explain how each author thinks about power—where it comes from, who has it, how it works, where you look for it, how you know when you see it, what it does, where it goes. You should reread the essays as a pair, as part of a single project in which you are looking to explain theories of power.

Write an essay in which you present and explain "Ways of Seeing" and "Panopticism" as examples of Berger's and Foucault's theories of power. Both Berger and Foucault are arguing against usual understandings of power and knowledge and history. In this sense, their projects are similar. You should be sure, however, to look for differences as well as similarities.

2. At the end of "Panopticism," Foucault asks two questions. These are rhetorical questions, strategically placed at the end. Presumably we are prepared to feel their force and to think of possible answers.

> Is it surprising that the cellular prison, with its regular chronologies, forced labor, its authorities of surveillance and registration, its experts in normality, who continue and multiply the functions of the judge, should have become the modern instrument of penalty? Is it surprising that prisons resemble factories, schools, barracks, hospitals, which all resemble prisons? (p. 208)

Is Foucault making the same argument as Paulo Freire, in "The 'Banking' Concept of Education" (p. 216)? Reread the Freire essay with Foucault's general argument in mind and thinking through the particular image (and institution) of the panopticon. How might you summarize these two arguments and their take on schooling? Freire, who speaks of a revolution in education, imagines a future in which students might be "free." Free in what sense? Does he have an answer to Foucault's concerns? Or does Foucault have an argument that might trump Freire's optimism?

You should assume an audience interested in education. It will not be the case, however, that they have read these two essays. You will need, then, to be careful in providing summary, paraphrase, and quotation. You will need to provide the background to an argument that you (and your readers) can identify as *yours*.

3. At a key point in her essay "Beside Oneself: On the Limits of Sexual Autonomy" (p. 114), Judith Butler refers to the work of Michel Foucault:

> The question of who and what is considered real and true is apparently a question of knowledge. But it is also, as Michel Foucault makes plain, a question of power. Having or bearing "truth" and "reality" is an enormously powerful prerogative within the social world, one way that power dissimulates as ontology. According to

> Foucault, one of the first tasks of a radical critique is to discern the relation "between mechanisms of coercion and elements of knowledge." (p. 121)

And she goes on for some length to work with passages from Foucault, although not from his book *Discipline and Punish*.

Take some time to reread Butler's essay, paying particular attention to her use of Foucault. Where and why is Foucault helpful to her? In what ways is she providing a new argument or a counterargument? And take time to reread "Panopticism." What passages might be useful in extending or challenging Butler's argument in "Beside Oneself"? Using these two sources, write an essay in which you talk about Butler and Foucault and their engagement with what might be called "radical critique," an effort (in the terms offered above) to "discern the relation 'between mechanisms of coercion and elements of knowledge.'"

Note: The assignment limits you to these two sources, the two selections in the textbook. Butler and Foucault have written much, and their work circulates widely. You are most likely not in a position to speak about everything they have written or about all that has been written about them. We wanted to define a starting point that was manageable. Still, if you want to do more research, you might begin by reading the Foucault essay that Butler cites, "What Is Critique?"; you might go to the library to look through books by Butler and Foucault, choosing one or two that seem to offer themselves as next steps; or you could go to essays written by scholars who, as you are, are trying to think about the two together.

4. One way to think about Foucault's text is to see Foucault as developing a theory of discipline, raising questions about the way discipline works—as a metaphor, as institutional regulation, and perhaps also as societal norms. Foucault tells us: "One also sees the spread of disciplinary procedures, not in the form of enclosed institutions, but as centers of observation disseminated throughout society." (p. 196) One might also say that Susan Griffin's "Our Secret" (p. 233) is also about this idea of discipline.

   Reread "Our Secret," marking in the margins any passages that seem connected to Foucault's theory of discipline. Choose three particular passages from Griffin that strike you as good examples through which to explore Foucault's theory. Write an essay that further theorizes discipline by involving Griffin's passages in the conversation. What does Griffin have to offer to this theory? How are Griffin and Foucault doing the same kind of work? Where, if anywhere, might they diverge?

PAULO Freire

Paulo Freire (pronounce it "Fr-air-ah" unless you can make a Portuguese "r") was one of the most influential radical educators of our world. A native of Recife, Brazil, he spent most of his early career working in poverty-stricken areas of his homeland, developing methods for teaching illiterate adults to read and write and (as he would say) to think critically and, thereby, to take power over their own lives. Because he has created a classroom where teachers and students have equal power and equal dignity, his work has stood as a model for educators around the world. It led also to sixteen years of exile after the military coup in Brazil in 1964. During that time he taught in Europe and in the United States and worked for the Allende government in Chile, training the teachers whose job it would be to bring modern agricultural methods to the peasants.

Freire (1921–1997) worked with the adult education programs of UNESCO, the Chilean Institute of Agrarian Reform, and the World Council of Churches. He was professor of educational philosophy at the Catholic University of São Paulo. He is the author of *Education for Critical Consciousness, The Politics of Education, Pedagogy of the Oppressed, Revised Edition* (from which the following essay is drawn), and *Learning to Question: A Pedagogy of Liberation* (with Antonio Faundez). *Pedagogy of Indignation*, the first English translations of Freire's late-life reflections on personal development, was published in 2004.

For Freire, education is not an objective process, if by objective we mean "neutral" or "without bias or prejudice." Because teachers could be said to have something that their students lack, it is impossible to have a "neutral" classroom; and when teachers present a subject to their students, they also present a point of view on that subject. The choice, according to Freire, is fairly simple: teachers either work "for the liberation of the people — their humanization — or for their domestication, their domination." The practice of teaching, however, is anything but simple. According to Freire, a teacher's most crucial skill is his or her ability to assist students' struggle to gain control over the conditions of their lives, and this means helping them not only to know but "to know that they know."

Freire edited, along with Henry A. Giroux, a series of books on education and teaching. In *Literacy: Reading the Word and the World*, a book for the series, Freire describes the interrelationship between reading the written word and understanding the world that surrounds us.

> My parents introduced me to reading the word at a certain moment in this rich experience of understanding my immediate world. Deciphering the word flowed naturally from reading my particular world; it was not something superimposed on it. I learned to read and write on the grounds of the backyard of my house, in the shade of the mango trees, with words from my world rather than from the wider world of my parents. The earth was my blackboard, the sticks my chalk.

For Freire, reading the written word involves understanding a text in its very particular social and historical context. Thus reading always involves "critical perception, interpretation, and *rewriting* of what is read."

The "Banking" Concept of Education

A careful analysis of the teacher-student relationship at any level, inside or outside the school, reveals its fundamentally *narrative* character. This relationship involves a narrating Subject (the teacher) and patient, listening objects (the students). The contents, whether values or empirical dimensions of reality, tend in the process of being narrated to become lifeless and petrified. Education is suffering from narration sickness.

The teacher talks about reality as if it were motionless, static, compartmentalized, and predictable. Or else he expounds on a topic completely alien to the existential experience of the students. His task is to "fill" the students with the contents of his narration — contents which are detached from reality, disconnected from the totality that engendered them and could give them significance. Words are emptied of their concreteness and become a hollow, alienated, and alienating verbosity.

The outstanding characteristic of this narrative education, then, is the sonority of words, not their transforming power. "Four times four is sixteen; the capital of Pará is Belém." The student records, memorizes, and repeats these phrases without perceiving what four times four really means, or realizing the true significance of "capital" in the affirmation "the capital of Pará is Belém," that is, what Belém means for Pará and what Pará means for Brazil.

EDUCATION THUS BECOMES AN ACT OF DEPOSITING, IN WHICH THE STUDENTS ARE THE DEPOSITORIES AND THE TEACHER IS THE DEPOSITOR.

Narration (with the teacher as narrator) leads the students to memorize mechanically the narrated content. Worse yet, it turns them into "containers," into "receptacles" to be "filled" by the teacher. The more completely she fills the receptacles, the better a teacher she is. The more meekly the receptacles permit themselves to be filled, the better students they are.

Education thus becomes an act of depositing, in which the students are the depositories and the teacher is the depositor. Instead of communicating, the teacher issues communiqués and makes deposits which the students patiently receive, memorize, and repeat. This is the "banking" concept of education, in which the scope of action allowed to the students extends only as far as receiving, filing, and storing the deposits. They do, it is true, have the opportunity to become collectors or cataloguers of the things they store. But in the last analysis, it is the people themselves who are filed away through the lack of creativity, transformation, and knowledge in this (at best) misguided system. For apart from inquiry, apart from the praxis, individuals cannot be truly human. Knowledge emerges only through invention and re-invention, through the restless, impatient, continuing, hopeful inquiry human beings pursue in the world, with the world, and with each other.

In the banking concept of education, knowledge is a gift bestowed by those who consider themselves knowledgeable upon those whom they consider to know nothing. Projecting an absolute ignorance onto others, a characteristic of the ideology of oppression, negates education and knowledge as processes of inquiry. The teacher presents himself to his students as their necessary opposite; by considering their ignorance absolute, he justifies his own existence. The students, alienated like the slave in the Hegelian dialectic, accept their ignorance as justifying the teacher's existence — but, unlike the slave, they never discover that they educate the teacher.

The *raison d'être* of libertarian education, on the other hand, lies in its drive towards reconciliation. Education must begin with the solution of the teacher-student contradiction, by reconciling the poles of the contradiction so that both are simultaneously teachers *and* students.

This solution is not (nor can it be) found in the banking concept. On the contrary, banking education maintains and even stimulates the contradiction through the following attitudes and practices, which mirror oppressive society as a whole:

a. the teacher teaches and the students are taught;
b. the teacher knows everything and the students know nothing;
c. the teacher thinks and the students are thought about;
d. the teacher talks and the students listen — meekly;
e. the teacher disciplines and the students are disciplined;
f. the teacher chooses and enforces his choice, and the students comply;
g. the teacher acts and the students have the illusion of acting through the action of the teacher;
h. the teacher chooses the program content, and the students (who were not consulted) adapt to it;
i. the teacher confuses the authority of knowledge with his or her own professional authority, which she and he sets in opposition to the freedom of the students;
j. the teacher is the Subject of the learning process, while the pupils are mere objects.

It is not surprising that the banking concept of education regards men as adaptable, manageable beings. The more students work at storing the deposits entrusted to them, the less they develop the critical consciousness which would result from their intervention in the world as transformers of that world. The more completely they accept the passive role imposed on them, the more they tend simply to adapt to the world as it is and to the fragmented view of reality deposited in them.

The capability of banking education to minimize or annul the students' creative power and to stimulate their credulity serves the interests of the oppressors, who care neither to have the world revealed nor to see it transformed. The oppressors use their "humanitarianism" to preserve a profitable situation. Thus they react almost instinctively against any experiment in education which stimulates the critical faculties and is not content with a partial view of reality but always seeks out the ties which link one point to another and one problem to another.

Indeed, the interests of the oppressors lie in "changing the consciousness of the oppressed, not the situation which oppresses them";[1] for the more the oppressed can be led to adapt to that situation, the more easily they can be dominated. To achieve this end, the oppressors use the banking concept of education in conjunction with a paternalistic social action apparatus, within which the oppressed receive the euphemistic title of "welfare recipients." They are treated as individual cases, as marginal persons who deviate from the general configuration of a "good, organized, and just" society. The oppressed are regarded as the pathology of the healthy society, which must therefore adjust these "incompetent and lazy" folk to its own patterns by changing their mentality. These marginals need to be "integrated," "incorporated" into the healthy society that they have "forsaken."

The truth is, however, that the oppressed are not "marginals," are not people living "outside" society. They have always been "inside" — inside the structure which made them "beings for others." The solution is not to "integrate" them into the structure of oppression, but to transform that structure so that they can become "beings for themselves." Such transformation, of course, would undermine the oppressors' purposes; hence their utilization of the banking concept of education to avoid the threat of student *conscientização*.[2]

The banking approach to adult education, for example, will never propose to students that they critically consider reality. It will deal instead with such vital questions as whether Roger gave green grass to the goat, and insist upon the importance of learning that, on the contrary, Roger gave green grass to the rabbit. The "humanism" of the banking approach masks the effort to turn women and men into automatons — the very negation of their ontological vocation to be more fully human.

Those who use the banking approach, knowingly or unknowingly (for there are innumerable well-intentioned bank-clerk teachers who do not realize that they are serving only to dehumanize), fail to perceive that the deposits themselves contain contradictions about reality. But, sooner or later, these contradictions may lead formerly passive students to turn against their domestication and the attempt to domesticate reality. They may discover through existential experience that their present way of life is irreconcilable with their vocation to become fully human. They may perceive through their relations with reality that reality is really a *process*, undergoing constant transformation. If men and women are searchers and their ontological vocation is humanization, sooner or later they may perceive the contradiction in which banking education seeks to maintain them, and then engage themselves in the struggle for their liberation.

But the humanist, revolutionary educator cannot wait for this possibility to materialize. From the outset, her efforts must coincide with those of the students to engage in critical thinking and the quest for mutual humanization. His efforts must be imbued with a profound trust in people and their creative power. To achieve this, they must be partners of the students in their relations with them.

The banking concept does not admit to such partnership — and necessarily so. To resolve the teacher-student contradiction, to exchange the role of depositor, prescriber, domesticator, for the role of student among students would be to undermine the power of oppression and serve the cause of liberation.

Implicit in the banking concept is the assumption of a dichotomy between human beings and the world: a person is merely *in* the world, not *with* the world or with others; the individual is spectator, not re-creator. In this view, the person is not a conscious being (*corpo consciente*); he or she is rather the possessor of *a* consciousness: an empty "mind" passively open to the reception of deposits of reality from the world outside. For example, my desk, my books, my coffee cup, all the objects before me — as bits of the world which surrounds me — would be "inside" me, exactly as I am inside my study right now. This view makes no distinction between being accessible to consciousness and entering consciousness. The distinction, however, is essential: the objects which surround me are simply accessible to my consciousness, not located within it. I am aware of them, but they are not inside me.

It follows logically from the banking notion of consciousness that the educator's role is to regulate the way the world "enters into" the students. The teacher's task is to organize a process which already occurs spontaneously, to "fill" the students by making deposits of information which he or she considers to constitute true knowledge.[3] And since people "receive" the world as passive entities, education should make them more passive still, and adapt them to the world. The educated individual is the adapted person, because she or he is better "fit" for the world. Translated into practice, this concept is well suited to the purposes of the oppressors, whose tranquility rests on how well people fit the world the oppressors have created, and how little they question it.

The more completely the majority adapt to the purposes which the dominant minority prescribe for them (thereby depriving them of the right to their own purposes), the more easily the minority can continue to prescribe. The theory and practice of banking education serve this end quite efficiently. Verbalistic lessons, reading requirements,[4] the methods for evaluating "knowledge," the distance between the teacher and the taught, the criteria for promotion: everything in this ready-to-wear approach serves to obviate thinking.

The bank-clerk educator does not realize that there is no true security in his hypertrophied role, that one must seek to live *with* others in solidarity. One cannot impose oneself, nor even merely co-exist with one's students. Solidarity requires true communication, and the concept by which such an educator is guided fears and proscribes communication.

Yet only through communication can human life hold meaning. The teacher's thinking is authenticated only by the authenticity of the students' thinking. The teacher cannot think for her students, nor can she impose her thoughts on them. Authentic thinking, thinking that is concerned about *reality*, does not take place in ivory tower isolation, but only in communication. If it is true that thought has meaning only when generated by action upon the world, the subordination of students to teachers becomes impossible.

Because banking education begins with a false understanding of men and women as objects, it cannot promote the development of what Fromm calls "biophily," but instead produces its opposite: "necrophily."

> While life is characterized by growth in a structured, functional manner, the necrophilous person loves all that does not grow, all that is mechanical. The necrophilous person is driven by the desire to transform the organic into the inorganic, to approach life mechanically, as if all living persons were things.... Memory, rather than experience; having, rather than being, is what counts. The necrophilous person can relate to an object — a flower or a person — only if he possesses it; hence a threat to his possession is a threat to himself; if he loses possession he loses contact with the world.... He loves control, and in the act of controlling he kills life.[5]

Oppression — overwhelming control — is necrophilic; it is nourished by love of death, not life. The banking concept of education, which serves the interests of oppression, is also necrophilic. Based on a mechanistic, static, naturalistic, spatialized view of consciousness, it transforms students into receiving objects. It attempts to control thinking and action, leads women and men to adjust to the world, and inhibits their creative power.

When their efforts to act responsibly are frustrated, when they find themselves unable to use their faculties, people suffer. "This suffering due to impotence is rooted in the very fact that the human equilibrium has been disturbed."[6] But the inability to act which causes people's anguish also causes them to reject their impotence, by attempting

> to restore [their] capacity to act. But can [they], and how? One way is to submit to and identify with a person or group having power. By this symbolic participation in another person's life, [men have] the illusion of acting, when in reality [they] only submit to and become part of those who act.[7]

Populist manifestations perhaps best exemplify this type of behavior by the oppressed, who, by identifying with charismatic leaders, come to feel that they themselves are active and effective. The rebellion they express as they emerge in the historical process is motivated by that desire to act effectively. The dominant elites consider the remedy to be more domination and repression, carried out in the name of freedom, order, and social peace (that is, the peace of the elites). Thus they can condemn — logically, from their point of view — "the violence of a strike by workers and [can] call upon the state in the same breath to use violence in putting down the strike."[8]

Education as the exercise of domination stimulates the credulity of students, with the ideological intent (often not perceived by educators) of indoctrinating them to adapt to the world of oppression. This accusation is not made in the naïve hope that the dominant elites will thereby simply abandon the practice. Its objective is to call the attention of true humanists to the fact that they cannot use banking educational methods in the pursuit of liberation, for they would only negate that very pursuit. Nor may a revolutionary society inherit these methods from an oppressor society. The revolutionary society which practices banking education is either misguided or mistrusting of people. In either event, it is threatened by the specter of reaction.

Unfortunately, those who espouse the cause of liberation are themselves surrounded and influenced by the climate which generates the banking concept, and often do not perceive its true significance or its dehumanizing power. Paradoxically, then, they utilize this same instrument of alienation in what they consider an effort to liberate. Indeed, some "revolutionaries" brand as "innocents," "dreamers," or even "reactionaries" those who would challenge this educational practice. But one does not liberate people by alienating them. Authentic liberation — the process of humanization — is not another deposit to be made in men. Liberation is a praxis: the action and reflection of men and women upon their world in order to transform it. Those truly committed to the cause of liberation can accept neither the mechanistic concept of consciousness as an empty vessel to be filled, nor the use of banking methods of domination (propaganda, slogans — deposits) in the name of liberation.

Those truly committed to liberation must reject the banking concept in its entirety, adopting instead a concept of women and men as conscious beings, and consciousness as consciousness intent upon the world. They must abandon the educational goal of deposit-making and replace it with the posing of the problems of human beings in their relations with the world. "Problem-posing" education, responding to the essence of consciousness — *intentionality* — rejects communiqués and embodies communications. It epitomizes the special characteristic of consciousness: being *conscious of*, not only as intent on objects but as turned in upon itself in a Jasperian "split" — consciousness as consciousness *of* consciousness.

Liberating education consists in acts of cognition, not transferrals of information. It is a learning situation in which the cognizable object (far from being the end of the cognitive act) intermediates the cognitive actors — teacher on the one hand and students on the other. Accordingly, the practice of problem-posing education entails at the outset that the teacher-student contradiction be resolved. Dialogical relations — indispensable to the capacity of cognitive actors to cooperate in perceiving the same cognizable object — are otherwise impossible.

Indeed, problem-posing education, which breaks with the vertical patterns characteristic of banking education, can fulfill its function as the practice of freedom only if it can overcome the above contradiction. Through dialogue, the teacher-of-the-students and the students-of-the-teacher cease to exist and a new term emerges: teacher-student with students-teachers. The teacher is no longer merely the-one-who-teaches, but one who is himself taught in dialogue with the students, who in turn while being taught also teach. They become jointly responsible for a process in which all grow. In this process, arguments based on "authority" are no longer valid; in order to function, authority must be *on the side of* freedom, not *against* it. Here, no one teaches another, nor is anyone self-taught. People teach each other, mediated by the world, by the cognizable objects which in banking education are "owned" by the teacher.

The banking concept (with its tendency to dichotomize everything) distinguishes two stages in the action of the educator. During the first, he cognizes a cognizable object while he prepares his lessons in his study or his laboratory; during the second, he expounds to his students about that object. The students are not called upon to know, but to memorize the contents narrated by the teacher. Nor do the students practice any act of cognition, since the object towards which that act should be directed is the property of the teacher rather than a medium evoking the critical reflection of both teacher and students. Hence in the name of the "preservation of culture and knowledge" we have a system which achieves neither true knowledge nor true culture.

The problem-posing method does not dichotomize the activity of the teacher-student: she is not "cognitive" at one point and "narrative" at another. She is always "cognitive," whether preparing a project or engaging in dialogue with the students. He does not regard cognizable objects as his private property, but as the object of reflection by himself and the students. In this way, the problem-posing educator constantly re-forms his reflections in the reflection of the students. The students — no longer docile listeners — are now critical co-investigators in dialogue with the teacher. The teacher presents the material to the students for their consideration, and re-considers her earlier considerations as the students express their own. The role of the problem-posing educator is to create, together with the students, the conditions under which knowledge at the level of the *doxa* is superseded by true knowledge, at the level of the *logos*.

Whereas banking education anesthetizes and inhibits creative power, problem-posing education involves a constant unveiling of reality. The former attempts to maintain the *submersion* of consciousness; the latter strives for the *emergence* of consciousness and *critical intervention* in reality.

Students, as they are increasingly posed with problems relating to themselves in the world and with the world, will feel increasingly challenged and obliged to respond to that challenge. Because they apprehend the challenge as interrelated to other problems within a total context, not as a theoretical question, the resulting comprehension tends to be increasingly critical and thus constantly less alienated. Their response to the challenge evokes new challenges, followed by new understandings; and gradually the students come to regard themselves as committed.

Education as the practice of freedom — as opposed to education as the practice of domination — denies that man is abstract, isolated, independent, and unattached to the world; it also denies that the world exists as a reality apart from people. Authentic reflection considers neither abstract man nor the world without people, but people in their relations with the world. In these relations consciousness and world are simultaneous: consciousness neither precedes the world nor follows it.

> La conscience et le monde sont donnés d'un même coup: extérieur par essence à la conscience, le monde est, par essence relatif à elle.[9]

In one of our culture circles in Chile, the group was discussing (based on a codification) the anthropological concept of culture. In the midst of the discussion, a peasant who by banking standards was completely ignorant said: "Now I see that without man there is no world." When the educator responded: "Let's say, for the sake of argument, that all the men on earth were to die, but that the earth itself remained, together with trees, birds, animals, rivers, seas, the stars . . . wouldn't all this be a world?" "Oh no," the peasant replied emphatically. "There would be no one to say: 'This is a world.'"

AUTHENTIC REFLECTION CONSIDERS NEITHER ABSTRACT MAN NOR THE WORLD WITHOUT PEOPLE, BUT PEOPLE IN THEIR RELATIONS WITH THE WORLD.

The peasant wished to express the idea that there would be lacking the consciousness of the world which necessarily implies the world of consciousness. *I* cannot exist without a *not-I*. In turn, the *not-I* depends on that existence. The world which brings consciousness into existence becomes the world *of* that consciousness. Hence, the previously cited affirmation of Sartre: *"La conscience et le monde sont donnés d'un même coup."*

As women and men, simultaneously reflecting on themselves and on the world, increase the scope of their perception, they begin to direct their observations towards previously inconspicuous phenomena:

> In perception properly so-called, as an explicit awareness [*Gewahren*], I am turned towards the object, to the paper, for instance. I apprehend it as being this here and now. The apprehension is a singling out, every object having a background in experience. Around and about the paper lie books, pencils, inkwell, and so forth, and these in a certain sense are also "perceived," perceptually there, in the "field of intuition"; but while I was turned towards the paper there was no turning in their direction, nor any apprehending of them, not even in a secondary sense. They appeared and yet were not singled out, were not posited on their own account. Every perception of a thing has such a zone of background intuitions or background awareness, if "intuiting" already includes the state of being turned towards, and this also is a "conscious experience," or more briefly

> a "consciousness of" all indeed that in point of fact lies in the co-perceived objective background.[10]

That which had existed objectively but had not been perceived in its deeper implications (if indeed it was perceived at all) begins to "stand out," assuming the character of a problem and therefore of challenge. Thus, men and women begin to single out elements from their "background awarenesses" and to reflect upon them. These elements are now objects of their consideration, and, as such, objects of their action and cognition.

In problem-posing education, people develop their power to perceive critically *the way they exist* in the world *with which* and *in which* they find themselves; they come to see the world not as a static reality, but as a reality in process, in transformation. Although the dialectical relations of women and men with the world exist independently of how these relations are perceived (or whether or not they are perceived at all), it is also true that the form of action they adopt is to a large extent a function of how they perceive themselves in the world. Hence, the teacher-student and the students-teachers reflect simultaneously on themselves and the world without dichotomizing this reflection from action, and thus establish an authentic form of thought and action.

Once again, the two educational concepts and practices under analysis come into conflict. Banking education (for obvious reasons) attempts, by mythicizing reality, to conceal certain facts which explain the way human beings exist in the world; problem-posing education sets itself the task of demythologizing. Banking education resists dialogue; problem-posing education regards dialogue as indispensable to the act of cognition which unveils reality. Banking education treats students as objects of assistance; problem-posing education makes them critical thinkers. Banking education inhibits creativity and domesticates (although it cannot completely destroy) the *intentionality* of consciousness by isolating consciousness from the world, thereby denying people their ontological and historical vocation of becoming more fully human. Problem-posing education bases itself on creativity and stimulates true reflection and action upon reality; thereby responding to the vocation of persons as beings who are authentic only when engaged in inquiry and creative transformation. In sum: banking theory and practice, as immobilizing and fixating forces, fail to acknowledge men and women as historical beings; problem-posing theory and practice take the people's historicity as their starting point.

Problem-posing education affirms men and women as beings in the process of *becoming* — as unfinished, uncompleted beings in and with a likewise unfinished reality. Indeed, in contrast to other animals who are unfinished, but not historical, people know themselves to be unfinished; they are aware of their incompletion. In this incompletion and this awareness lie the very roots of education as an exclusively human manifestation. The unfinished character of human beings and the transformational character of reality necessitate that education be an ongoing activity.

Education is thus constantly remade in the praxis. In order to *be*, it must *become*. Its "duration" (in the Bergsonian meaning of the word) is found in the interplay of the opposites *permanence* and *change*. The banking method emphasizes permanence and becomes reactionary; problem-posing education — which accepts neither a "well-behaved" present nor a predetermined future — roots itself in the dynamic present and becomes revolutionary.

Problem-posing education is revolutionary futurity. Hence, it is prophetic (and, as such, hopeful). Hence, it corresponds to the historical nature of humankind. Hence, it affirms women and men as beings who transcend themselves, who move forward and look ahead, for whom immobility represents a fatal threat, for whom looking at the past must only be a means of understanding more clearly what and who they are so that they can more wisely build the future. Hence, it identifies with the movement which engages people as beings aware of their incompletion — an historical movement which has its point of departure, its Subjects and its objective.

The point of departure of the movement lies in the people themselves. But since people do not exist apart from the world, apart from reality, the movement must begin with the human-world relationship. Accordingly, the point of departure must always be with men and women in the "here and now," which constitutes the situation within which they are submerged, from which they emerge, and in which they intervene. Only by starting from this situation — which determines their perception of it — can they begin to move. To do this authentically they must perceive their state not as fated and unalterable, but merely as limiting — and therefore challenging.

Whereas the banking method directly or indirectly reinforces men's fatalistic perception of their situation, the problem-posing method presents this very situation to them as a problem. As the situation becomes the object of their cognition, the naïve or magical perception which produced their fatalism gives way to perception which is able to perceive itself even as it perceives reality, and can thus be critically objective about that reality.

A deepened consciousness of their situation leads people to apprehend that situation as an historical reality susceptible of transformation. Resignation gives way to the drive for transformation and inquiry, over which men feel themselves to be in control. If people, as historical beings necessarily engaged with other people in a movement of inquiry, did not control that movement, it would be (and is) a violation of their humanity. Any situation in which some individuals prevent others from engaging in the process of inquiry is one of violence. The means used are not important; to alienate human beings from their own decision making is to change them into objects.

This movement of inquiry must be directed towards humanization — the people's historical vocation. The pursuit of full humanity, however, cannot be carried out in isolation or individualism, but only in fellowship and solidarity; therefore it cannot unfold in the antagonistic relations between oppressors and oppressed. No one can be authentically human while he prevents others from being so. Attempting *to be more* human, individualistically, leads to *having more*, egotistically, a form of dehumanization. Not that it is not fundamental *to have* in order *to be* human. Precisely because it *is* necessary, some men's *having* must not be allowed to constitute an obstacle to others' *having*, must not consolidate the power of the former to crush the latter.

Problem-posing education, as a humanist and liberating praxis, posits as fundamental that the people subjected to domination must fight for their emancipation. To that end, it enables teachers and students to become Subjects of the educational process by overcoming authoritarianism and an alienating intellectualism; it also enables people to overcome their false perception of reality. The world — no longer something to be described with deceptive words — becomes the object of that transforming action by men and women which results in their humanization.

Problem-posing education does not and cannot serve the interests of the oppressor. No oppressive order could permit the oppressed to begin to question: Why? While only a revolutionary society can carry out this education in systematic terms, the revolutionary leaders need not take full power before they can employ the method. In the revolutionary process, the leaders cannot utilize the banking method as an interim measure, justified on grounds of expediency, with the intention of *later* behaving in a genuinely revolutionary fashion. They must be revolutionary — that is to say, dialogical — from the outset.

NOTES

[1] Simone de Beauvoir, *La pensée de droite, aujourd'hui* (Paris); ST, *El pensamiento político de la derecha* (Buenos Aires, 1963), p. 34. [All notes are Freire's, unless indicated by Eds.]

[2] According to Freire's translator, "The term *conscientização* refers to learning to perceive social, political, and economic contradictions, and to take action against the oppressive elements of reality" [Eds.].

[3] This concept corresponds to what Sartre calls the "digestive" or "nutritive" concept of education, in which knowledge is "fed" by the teacher to the students to "fill them out." See Jean-Paul Sartre, "Une idée fundamentale de la phénomenologie de Husserl: L'intentionalité," *Situations* I (Paris, 1947).

[4] For example, some professors specify in their reading lists that a book should be read from pages 10 to 15 — and do this to "help" their students!

[5] Erich Fromm, *The Heart of Man* (New York, 1966), p. 41.

[6] Ibid., p. 31.

[7] Ibid.

[8] Reinhold Niebuhr, *Moral Man and Immoral Society* (New York, 1960), p. 130.

[9] Sartre, op. cit., p. 32. [The passage is obscure but could be read as "Consciousness and the world are given at one and the same time: the exterior world as it enters consciousness is relative to our ways of seeing and understanding that world." — Eds.]

[10] Edmund Husserl, *Ideas — General Introduction to Pure Phenomenology* (London, 1969), pp. 105–6.

QUESTIONS FOR A SECOND READING

1. While Freire speaks powerfully about the politics of the classroom, he provides few examples of actual classroom situations. As you go back through the essay, try to ground (or to test) what he says with examples of your own. What would take place in a "problem-posing" class in English, history, psychology, or math? What is an "authentic form of thought and action"? How might you describe what Freire refers to as "reflection"? What, really, might teachers be expected to learn from their students? What example can you give of a time when you were "conscious of consciousness" and it made a difference to you with your schoolwork?

   You might also look for moments when Freire does provide examples of his own. On page 219, for example, Freire makes the distinction between a student's role as "spectator" and as "re-creator" by referring to his own relationship to the objects on his desk. How might you explain this distinction? Or, how might you use the example of his books and coffee cup to explain the distinction he makes between "being accessible to consciousness" and "entering consciousness"?

2. Freire uses two terms drawn from Marxist literature: *praxis* and *alienation*. From the way these words are used in the essay, how would you define them? and how might they be applied to the study of education?

3. A writer can be thought of as a teacher and a reader as a student. If you think of Freire as your teacher in this essay, does he enact his own principles? Does he speak to you as though he were making deposits in a bank? Or is there a way in which the essay allows for dialogue? Look for sections in the essay you could use to talk about the role Freire casts you in as a reader.

Questions

ASSIGNMENTS FOR WRITING

1. Surely all of us, anyone who has made it through twelve years of formal education, can think of a class, or an occasion outside of class, to serve as a quick example of what Freire calls the "banking" concept of education, where students were turned into "containers" to be "filled" by their teachers. If Freire is to be useful to you, however, he must do more than enable you to call up quick examples. He should allow you to say more than that a teacher once treated you like a container or that a teacher once gave you your freedom.

   Write an essay that focuses on a rich and illustrative incident from your own educational experience and read it (that is, interpret it) as Freire would. You will need to provide careful detail: things that were said and done, perhaps the exact wording of an assignment, a textbook, or a teacher's comments. And you will need to turn to the language of Freire's argument, to take key phrases and passages and see how they might be used to investigate your case.

To do this, you will need to read your account as not simply the story of you and your teacher, since Freire is writing not about individual personalities (an innocent student and a mean teacher, a rude teacher, or a thoughtless teacher) but about the roles we are cast in, whether we choose to be or not, by our culture and its institutions. The key question, then, is not who you were or who your teacher was but what roles you played and how those roles can lead you to better understand the larger narrative or drama of Education (an organized attempt to "regulate the way the world 'enters into' the students").

Freire would not want you to work passively or mechanically, however, as though you were following orders. He would want you to make your own mark on the work he has begun. Use your example, in other words, as a way of testing and examining what Freire says, *particularly those passages that you find difficult or obscure.*

2. Problem-posing education, according to Freire, "sets itself the task of demythologizing"; it "stimulates true reflection and action"; it allows students to be "engaged in inquiry and creative transformation." These are grand and powerful phrases, and it is interesting to consider what they might mean if applied to the work of a course in reading and writing.

   If the object for study were Freire's essay "The 'Banking' Concept of Education," what would Freire (or a teacher determined to adapt his practices) ask students to *do* with the essay? What writing assignment might he set for his students? Prepare that assignment, or a set of questions or guidelines or instructions (or whatever) that Freire might prepare for his class.

   Once you've prepared the writing assignment, write the essay that you think would best fulfill it. And once you've completed the essay, go on, finally, to write the teacher's comments on it — to write what you think Freire, or a teacher following his example, might write on a piece of student work.

MAKING CONNECTIONS

1. Freire says,

> Students, as they are increasingly posed with problems relating to themselves in the world and with the world, will feel increasingly challenged and obliged to respond to that challenge. Because they apprehend the challenge as interrelated to other problems within a total context, not as a theoretical question, the resulting comprehension tends to be increasingly critical and thus constantly less alienated. (p. 222)

Students learn to respond, Freire says, through dialogue with their teachers. Freire could be said to serve as your first teacher here. He has raised the issue for you and given you some language you can use to frame questions and to imagine the possibilities of response.

Using one of the essays in this book as a starting point, pose a problem that challenges you and makes you feel obliged to respond, a problem that, in Freire's terms, relates to you "in the world and with the world." This is a chance for you, in other words, to pose a Freirian question and then to write a Freirian essay, all as an exercise in the practice of freedom.

When you are done, you might reread what you have written to see how it resembles or differs from what you are used to writing. What are the indications that you are working with greater freedom? If you find evidence of alienation or "domination," to what would you attribute it, and what, then, might you do to overcome it?

2. Freire writes about the distribution of power and authority in the classroom and argues that education too often alienates individuals from their own historical situation. Richard Rodriguez, in "The Achievement of Desire" (p. 338), writes about his education as a process of difficult but necessary alienation from his home, his childhood, and his family. And he writes about power — about the power that he gained and lost as he became increasingly successful as a student.

   But Freire and Rodriguez write about education as a central event in the shaping of an adult life. It is interesting to imagine what they might have to say to each other. Write a dialogue between the two in which they discuss what Rodriguez has written in "The Achievement of Desire." What would they say to each other? What questions would they ask? How would they respond to each other in the give-and-take of conversation?

   Note: This should be a dialogue, not a debate. Your speakers are trying to learn something about each other and about education. They are not trying to win points or convince a jury.

3. Freire writes, "The truth is, however, that the oppressed are not 'marginals,' are not people living 'outside' society. They have always been 'inside' — inside the structure which made them 'beings for others.' The solution is not to 'integrate' them into the structure of oppression, but to transform that structure so they can become 'beings for themselves.'" (p. 218) A reader might say that both Judith Halberstam and Judith Butler are concerned with how those who are considered "outside society" are positioned, understood, and regulated by social forces (part of that "structure of oppression" Freire mentions).

   Reread Halberstam's "Animating Revolt and Revolting Animation" (p. 271) or Butler's "Beside Oneself: On the Limits of Sexual Autonomy" (p. 114), noting those places in the text where either of these authors might provide you with language to help explain or account for Freire's above claim. How can Butler or Halberstam help you further understand the terms Freire uses — terms like "beings for themselves" or "structure of oppression"?

Write an essay in which you illuminate the possible meanings of Freire's passage by engaging with specific passages or terms from Butler or Halberstam. You might also draw examples from your own life or from the lives of others in order to help your reader understand the complex relationship between the two texts you focus on in your essay.

SUSAN

Griffin

Susan Griffin (b. 1943) is a well-known and respected feminist writer, poet, essayist, lecturer, teacher, playwright, and filmmaker. She has published more than twenty books, including an Emmy Award–winning play, *Voices*, with a preface by Adrienne Rich (1975); three books of poetry, *Like the Iris of an Eye* (1976), *Unremembered Country* (1987), and *Bending Home: Selected and New Poems* (1998); and four books of nonfiction that have become key feminist texts, *Women and Nature: The Roaring inside Her* (1978), *Rape: The Power of Consciousness* (1979), *Pornography and Silence: Culture's Revenge against Nature* (1981), and *A Chorus of Stones: The Private Life of War* (1992). Her most recent books are *What Her Body Thought: A Journey into the Shadows* (1999), on her battle with illness; *The Book of the Courtesans: A Catalog of Their Virtues* (2002), which includes biographies of courtesans throughout history; *Wrestling with the Angel of Democracy: On Being an American Citizen* (2008), an examination of democratic ideals; and, with Karin Lofthus Carrington, *Transforming Terror: Remembering the Soul of the World* (2013), a meditation on the ways in which human interdependence and compassion can overcome violence.

We've included here an abridged version of "Our Secret," which is taken from a chapter from Susan Griffin's moving and powerful book *A Chorus of Stones*, winner of the Bay Area Book Reviewers Association Award and a finalist for the Pulitzer Prize in nonfiction. The book explores the connections between present and past, public life and private life, an individual life and the lives of others. Griffin writes, for example, "I do not see my life as separate from history. In my mind my family secrets mingle with the secrets of statesmen and bombers." In one section of the book she writes of her mother's alcoholism and her father's response to it. In another she writes of her paternal grandmother, who was banished from the family for reasons never spoken. Next to these she thinks about Heinrich Himmler, head of the Nazi secret police, or Hugh Trenchard of the British Royal Air Force, who introduced the saturation bombing of cities and civilians to modern warfare, or Wernher von Braun and the development of rockets and rocketry. "As I held these [figures and scenes] in my mind," she writes, "a certain energy was generated between them. There were two subjects but one theme: denying and bearing witness."

A Chorus of Stones combines the skills of a careful researcher working with the documentary records of war, the imaginative powers of a novelist entering the lives and experiences of those long dead, and a poet's attention to language. It is a remarkable piece of writing, producing in its form and style the very experience of surprise and connectedness that Griffin presents as the product of her research. "It's not a historian's history," she once told an interviewer. "What's in it is true, but I think of it as a book that verges on myth and legend, because those are the ways we find the deepest meanings and significance of events."

Griffin's history is not a historian's history; her sociology is not a sociologist's; her psychology is not written in conventional forms or registers. She is actively engaged in the key research projects of our time, providing new knowledge and new ways of thinking and seeing, but she works outside the usual forms and boundaries of the academic disciplines. There are other ways of thinking about this, she seems to say. There are other ways to do this work. Her book on rape, for example, ends with a collage of women's voices, excerpts from public documents, and bits and pieces from the academy.

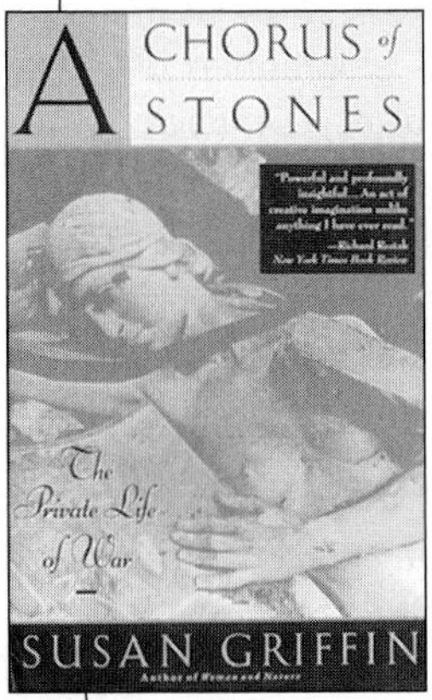

"Our Secret" has its own peculiar structure and features — the sections in italics, for example. As a piece of writing, it proceeds with a design that is not concerned to move quickly or efficiently from introduction to conclusion. It is, rather, a kind of collage or collection of stories, sketches, anecdotes, fragments. While the sections in the essay are presented as fragments, the essay is not, however, deeply confusing or disorienting. The pleasure of the text, in fact, is moving from here to there, feeling a thread of connection at one point, being surprised by a new direction at another. The writing is careful, thoughtful, controlled, even if this is not the kind of essay that announces its thesis and then collects examples for support. It takes a different attitude toward examples — and toward the kind of thinking one might bring to bear in gathering them and thinking them through. As Griffin says, "the telling and hearing of a story is not a simple act." It is not simple and, as her writing teaches us, it is not straightforward. As you read this essay, think of it as a lesson in reading, writing, and thinking. Think of it as a lesson in working differently. And you might ask why it is that this kind of writing is seldom taught in school.

Our Secret

The nucleus of the cell derives its name from the Latin nux, *meaning nut. Like the stone in a cherry, it is found in the center of the cell, and like this stone, keeps its precious kernel in a shell.*

She is across the room from me. I am in a chair facing her. We sit together in the late darkness of a summer night. As she speaks the space between us grows larger. She has entered her past. She is speaking of her childhood. Her father. The war. Did I know her father fought in the Battle of the Bulge? What was it for him, this great and terrible battle? She cannot say. He never spoke of it at home. They knew so little, her mother, her brothers, herself. Outside, the sea has disappeared. One finds the water now only by the city lights that cease to shine at its edges. California. She moved here with her family when her father became the commander of a military base. There were nuclear missiles standing just blocks from where she lived. But her father never spoke about them. Only after many years away from home did she learn what these weapons were.

The first guided missile is developed in Germany, during World War II. It is known as the Vergeltungswaffe, *or the Vengeance weapon. Later, it will be called the V-1 rocket.*

She is speaking of another life, another way of living. I give her the name Laura here. She speaks of the time after the war, when the cold war was just beginning. The way we are talking now, Laura tells me, was not possible in her family. I nod in recognition. Certain questions were never answered. She learned what not to ask. She begins to tell me a story. Once when she was six years old she went out with her father on a long trip. It was not even a year since the war ended. They were living in Germany.

They drove for miles and miles. Finally they turned into a small road at the edge of a village and drove through a wide gate in a high wall. The survivors were all gone. But there were other signs of this event beyond and yet still within her comprehension. Shoes in great piles. Bones. Women's hair, clothes, stains, a terrible odor. She began to cry a child's frightened tears and then to scream. She had no words for what she saw. Her father admonished her to be still. Only years later, and in a classroom, did she find out the name of this place and what had happened here.

The shell surrounding the nucleus is not hard and rigid; it is a porous membrane. These pores allow only some substances to pass through them, mediating the movement of materials in and out of the nucleus.

Often I have looked back into my past with a new insight only to find that some old, hardly recollected feeling fits into a larger pattern of meaning. Time can be measured in many ways. We see time as moving forward and hope that by our efforts this motion is toward improvement. When the atomic bomb exploded, many who survived the blast say time stopped with the flash of light and was held suspended until the ash began to descend. Now, in my mind, I can feel myself moving backward in time. I am as if on a train. And the train pushes into history. This history seems to exist somewhere, waiting, a foreign country behind a border and, perhaps, also inside me. From the windows of my train, I can see what those outside do not see. They do not see each other, or the whole landscape through which the track is laid. This is a straight track, but still there are bends to fit the shape of the earth. There are even circles. And returns.

The missile is guided by a programmed mechanism. There is no electronic device that can be jammed. Once it is fired it cannot stop.

It is 1945 and a film is released in Germany. This film has been made for other nations to see. On the screen a train pulls into a station. The train is full of children. A man in a uniform greets the children warmly as they step off the train. Then the camera cuts to boys and girls who are swimming. The boys and girls race to see who can reach the other side of the pool first. Then a woman goes to a post office. A man goes to a bank. Men and women sit drinking coffee at a cafe. The film is called *The Führer Presents the Jews with a City*. It has been made at Terezin concentration camp.

Through the pores of the nuclear membrane a steady stream of ribonucleic acid, RNA, the basic material from which the cell is made, flows out.

It is wartime and a woman is writing a letter. *Everyone is on the brink of starvation*, she says. In the right-hand corner of the page she has written *Nordhausen, Germany 1944*. She is writing to Hans. *Do you remember*, she asks, the day this war was declared? The beauty of the place. The beauty of the sea. *And I bathed in it that day, for the last time.*

In the same year, someone else is also writing a letter. In the right-hand corner he has put his name followed by a title. *Heinrich Himmler. Reichsführer, SS. Make no mention of the special treatment of the Jews*, he says, use only the words Transportation of the Jews toward the Russian East.

A few months later this man will deliver a speech to a secret meeting of leaders in the district of Posen. *Now you know all about it, and you will keep quiet*, he will tell them. Now we share a secret and *we should take our secret to our graves.*

The missile flies from three to four thousand feet above the earth and this makes it difficult to attack from the ground.

The woman who writes of starvation is a painter in her seventy-seventh year. She has lost one grandchild to this war. And a son to the war before. Both boys were named Peter. Among the drawings she makes which have already become famous: a terrified mother grasps a child, *Death Seizes Children*; an old man curls over the bent body of an old woman, *Parents*; a thin face emerges white from charcoal, *Beggars*.

A small but critical part of the RNA flowing out of the pores holds most of the knowledge issued by the nucleus. These threads of RNA act as messengers.

Encountering such images, one is grateful to be spared. But is one ever really free of the fate of others? I was born in 1943, in the midst of this war. And I sense now that my life is still bound up with the lives of those who lived and died in this time. Even with Heinrich Himmler. All the details of his existence, his birth, childhood, adult years, death, still resonate here on earth.

The V-1 rocket is a winged plane powered by a duct motor with a pulsating flow of fuel.

It is April 1943, Heinrich Himmler, Reichsführer SS, has gained control of the production of rockets for the Third Reich. The SS Totenkampf stand guard with machine guns trained at the entrance to a long tunnel, two miles deep, fourteen yards wide and ten yards high, sequestered in the Harz Mountains near Nordhausen. Once an old mining shaft, this tunnel serves now as a secret factory for the manufacture of V-1 and V-2 missiles. The guards aim their machine guns at the factory workers who are inmates of concentration camp Dora.

I SENSE NOW THAT MY LIFE IS STILL BOUND UP WITH THE LIVES OF THOSE WHO LIVED AND DIED IN THIS TIME. EVEN WITH HEINRICH HIMMLER.

Most of the RNA flowing out of the cell is destined for the construction of a substance needed to compensate for the continual wearing away of the cell.

It is 1925. Heinrich Himmler, who is now twenty-five years old, has been hired as a secretary by the chief of the Nazi Party in Landshut. He sits behind a small desk in a room overcrowded with party records, correspondence, and newspaper files. On the wall facing him he can see a portrait of Adolf Hitler. He hopes one day to meet the Führer. In anticipation of that day, while he believes no one watches, he practices speaking to this portrait.

It is 1922. Heinrich visits friends who have a three-year-old child. Before going to bed this child is allowed to run about naked. And this disturbs Heinrich. He writes in his diary, *One should teach a child a sense of shame.*

It is the summer of 1910. Heinrich begins his first diary. He is ten years old. He has just completed elementary school. His father tells him his childhood is over now. In the fall he will enter Wilhelms Gymnasium. There the grades he earns will determine his prospects for the future. From now on he must learn to take himself seriously.

Eight out of ten of the guided missiles will land within eight miles of their targets.

His father Gebhard is a schoolmaster. He knows the requirements. He provides the boy with pen and ink. Gebhard was once a tutor for Prince Heinrich of Wittelsbach. He has named his son Heinrich after this prince. He is grateful that the prince consented to be Heinrich's godparent. Heinrich is to write in his diary every day. Gebhard writes the first entry in his son's diary, to show the boy how it is to be done.

July 13, Departed at 11:50 and arrive safely on the bus in L. We have a very pretty house. In the afternoon we drink coffee at the coffee house.

I open the cover of the journal I began to keep just as I started my work on this book. I want to see what is on the first page. *It is here I begin a new life*, I wrote. Suffering many losses at once, I was alone and lonely. Yet suddenly I felt a new responsibility for myself. *The very act of keeping a journal*, I sensed, would help me into this life that would now be my own.

Inside the nucleus is the nucleolus where the synthesis of RNA takes place. Each nucleolus is filled with a small jungle of fern-like structures all of whose fronds and stalks move and rotate in perfect synchrony.

It is 1910. The twenty-second of July. Gebhard adds the words *first swim* to his son's brief entry, *thirteenth wedding anniversary of my dear parents.* 1911. Over several entries Heinrich lists each of thirty-seven times he takes a swim, in chronological order. *11:37 A.M. Departed for Lindau.* He does not write of his feelings. *August 8, Walk in the park.* Or dreams. *August 10, Bad weather.*

In the last few years I have been searching, though for what precisely I cannot say. Something still hidden which lies in the direction of Heinrich Himmler's life. I have been to Berlin and Munich on this search, and I have walked over the gravel at Dachau. Now as I sit here I read once again the fragments from Heinrich's boyhood diary that exist in English. I have begun to think of these words as ciphers. Repeat them to myself, hoping to find a door into the mind of this man, even as his character first forms so that I might learn how it is he becomes himself.

The task is not easy. The earliest entries in this diary betray so little. Like the words of a schoolboy commanded to write what the teacher requires of him, they are wooden and stiff. The stamp of his father's character is so heavy on this language that I catch not even a breath of a self here. It is easy to see how this would be true. One simply has to imagine Gebhard standing behind Heinrich and tapping his foot.

His father must have loomed large to him. Did Gebhard lay his hand on Heinrich's shoulder? The weight of that hand would not be comforting. It would be a warning. A reminder. Heinrich must straighten up now and be still. Yet perhaps he turns his head. Maybe there is a sound outside. A bird. Or his brother Gebhard's voice. But from the dark form behind him he hears a name pronounced. This is his name, *Heinrich*. The sound rolls sharply off his father's tongue. He turns his head back. He does not know what to write. He wants to turn to this form and beseech him, but this man who is his father is more silent than stone. And now when Heinrich can feel impatience all around him, he wants to ask, *What should I write?* The edge of his father's voice has gotten sharper. *Why can't you remember?* Just write what happened yesterday. And make sure you get the date right. *Don't you remember?* We took a walk in the park together and we ran into the duchess. Be certain you spell her name correctly. And look here, you must get the title right. That is extremely important. Cross it out. Do it again. *The title.*

The boy is relieved. His mind has not been working. His thoughts were like paralyzed limbs, immobile. Now he is in motion again. He writes the sentences as they are dictated to him. *The park.* He crosses out the name. He writes it again. Spelling it right. *The duchess.* And his father makes one more correction. The boy has not put down the correct time for their walk in the park.

And who is the man standing behind? In a photograph I have before me of the aging Professor and Frau Himmler, as they pose before a wall carefully composed with paintings and family portraits, Frau Himmler adorned with a demure lace collar, both she and the professor smiling kindly from behind steel-rimmed glasses, the professor somewhat rounded with age, in a dark three-piece suit and polka-dot tie, looks so ordinary.

The missile carries a warhead weighing 1,870 pounds. It has three different fuses to insure detonation.

Ordinary. What an astonishing array of images hide behind this word. The ordinary is of course never ordinary. I think of it now as a kind of mask, not an animated mask that expresses the essence of an inner truth, but a mask that falls like dead weight over the human face, making flesh a stationary object. One has difficulty penetrating the heavy mask that Gebhard and his family wore, difficulty piercing through to the creatures behind.

It must not have been an easy task to create this mask. One detects the dimensions of the struggle in the advice of German child-rearing experts from this and the last century. *Crush the will,* they write. *Establish dominance. Permit no disobedience. Suppress everything in the child.*

I have seen illustrations from the books of one of these experts, perhaps the most famous of these pedagogues, Dr. Daniel Gottlieb Moritz Schreber. At first glance these pictures recall images of torture. But they are instead pictures of children whose posture or behavior is being corrected. A brace up the spine, a belt tied to a waist and the hair at the back of the neck so the child will be discouraged from slumping, a metal plate at the edge of a desk keeping the child from curling over her work, a child tied to a bed to prevent poor sleeping posture or masturbation. And there are other methods recommended in the text. An enema to be given before bedtime. The child immersed in ice-cold water up to the hips, before sleep.

The nightmare images of the German child-rearing practices that one discovers in this book call to mind the catastrophic events of recent German history. I first encountered this pedagogy in the writing of Alice Miller. At one time a psychoanalyst, she was haunted by the question, *What could make a person conceive the plan of gassing millions of human beings to death?* In her work, she traces the origins of this violence to childhood.

Of course there cannot be one answer to such a monumental riddle, nor does any event in history have a single cause. Rather a field exists, like a field of gravity that is created by the movements of many bodies. Each life is influenced and it in turn becomes an influence. Whatever is a cause is also an effect. Childhood experience is just one element in the determining field.

As a man who made history, Heinrich Himmler shaped many childhoods, including, in the most subtle of ways, my own. And an earlier history, a history of governments, of wars, of social customs, an idea of gender, the history of a religion leading to the idea of original sin, shaped Heinrich Himmler's childhood as certainly as any philosophy of child raising. One can take for instance any formative condition of his private life, the fact that he was a frail child, for example, favored by his mother, who could not meet masculine standards, and show that this circumstance derived its real meaning from a larger social system that gave inordinate significance to masculinity.

Yet to enter history through childhood experience shifts one's perspective not away from history but instead to an earlier time just before history has finally shaped us. Is there a child who existed before the conventional history that we tell of ourselves, one who, though invisible to us, still shapes events, even through this absence? How does our sense of history change when we consider childhood, and perhaps more important, why is it that until now we have chosen to ignore this point of origination, the birthplace and womb of ourselves, in our consideration of public events?

In the silence that reverberates around this question, an image is born in my mind. I can see a child's body, small, curled into itself, knees bent toward the chest, head bending softly into pillows and blankets, in a posture thought unhealthy by Dr. Schreber, hand raised to the face, delicate mouth making a circle around the thumb. There is comfort as well as sadness in this image. It is a kind of a self-portrait, drawn both from memory and from a feeling that is still inside me. As I dwell for a moment with this image I can imagine Heinrich in this posture, silent, curled, fetal, giving comfort to himself.

But now, alongside this earlier image, another is born. It is as if these two images were twins, always traveling in the world of thought together. One does not come to mind without the other. In this second portrait, which is also made of feeling and memory, a child's hands are tied into mittens. And by a string extending from one of the mittens, her hand is tied to the bars of her crib. She is not supposed to be putting her finger in her mouth. And she is crying out in rage while she yanks her hand violently trying to free herself of her bonds.

To most of existence there is an inner and an outer world. Skin, bark, surface of the ocean open to reveal other realities. What is inside shapes and sustains what appears. So it is too with human consciousness. And yet the mind rarely has a simple connection to the inner life. At a certain age we begin to define ourselves, to choose an image of who we are. I am this and not that, we say, attempting thus to erase whatever is within us that does not fit our idea of who we should be. In time we forget our earliest selves and replace that memory with the image we have constructed at the bidding of others.

One can see this process occur in the language of Heinrich's diaries. If in the earliest entries, except for the wooden style of a boy who obeys authority, Heinrich's character is hardly apparent, over time this stilted style becomes his own. As one reads on, one no longer thinks of a boy who is forced to the task, but of a prudish and rigid young man.

In Heinrich's boyhood diaries no one has been able to find any record of rage or of events that inspire such rage. Yet one cannot assume from this evidence that such did not exist. His father would have permitted neither anger nor even the memory of it to enter these pages. That there must be no visible trace of resentment toward the parent was the pedagogy of the age. Dr. Schreber believed that children should learn to be grateful. The pain and humiliation children endure are meant to benefit them. The parent is only trying to save the child's soul.

Now, for different reasons, I too find myself on the track of a child's soul. The dimensions of Heinrich Himmler's life have put me on this track. I am trying to grasp the inner state of his being. For a time the soul ceased to exist in the modern mind. One thought of a human being as a kind of machine, or as a cog in the greater mechanism of society, operating within another machine, the earth, which itself operates within the greater mechanical design of the universe.

When I was in Berlin, I spoke to a rabbi who had, it seemed to me, lost his faith. When I asked him if he still believed in God, he simply shook his head and widened his eyes as if to say, *How is this possible?* He had been telling me about his congregation: older people, many of Polish origin, survivors of the holocaust who were not able to leave Germany after the war because they were too ill to travel. He was poised in this painful place by choice. He had come to lead this congregation only temporarily but, once feeling the condition of his people, decided to stay. Still, despite his answer, and as much as the holocaust made a terrible argument for the death of the spirit, talking in that small study with this man, I could feel from him the light of something surviving.

The religious tradition that shaped Heinrich's childhood argues that the soul is not part of flesh but is instead a prisoner of the body. But suppose the soul is meant to live in and through the body and to know itself in the heart of earthly existence?

Then the soul is an integral part of the child's whole being, and its growth is thus part of the child's growth. It is, for example, like a seed planted underground in the soil, naturally moving toward the light. And it comes into its fullest manifestation thus only when seen, especially when self meeting self returns a gaze.

What then occurs if the soul in its small beginnings is forced to take on a secret life? A boy learns, for instance, to hide his thoughts from his father simply by failing to record them in his journals. He harbors his secrets in fear and guilt, confessing them to no one until in time the voice of his father chastising him becomes his own. A small war is waged in his mind. Daily implosions take place under his skin, by which in increments something in him seems to disappear. Gradually his father's voice subsumes the vitality of all his desires and even his rage, so that now what he wants most passionately is his own obedience, and his rage is aimed at his own failures. As over time his secrets fade from memory, he ceases to tell them, even to himself, so that finally a day arrives when he believes the image he has made of himself in his diaries is true.

The child, Dr. Schreber advised, *should be permeated by the impossibility of locking something in his heart.* The doctor who gave this advice had a son who was hospitalized for disabling schizophrenia. Another of his children committed suicide. But this was not taken as a warning against his approach. His methods of educating children were so much a part of the canon of everyday life in Germany that they were introduced into the state school system.

That this philosophy was taught in school gives me an interior view of the catastrophe to follow. It adds a certain dimension to my image of these events to know that a nation of citizens learned that no part of themselves could be safe from the scrutiny of authority, nothing locked in the heart, and at the same time to discover that the head of the secret police of this nation was the son of a schoolmaster. It was this man, after all, Heinrich Himmler, Reichsführer SS, who was later to say, speaking of the mass arrests of Jews, *Protective custody is an act of care.*

The polite manner of young Heinrich's diaries reminds me of life in my grandmother's home. Not the grandmother I lost and later found, but the one who, for many years, raised me. She was my mother's mother. The family would assemble in the living room together, sitting with a certain reserve, afraid to soil the surfaces. What was it that by accident might have been made visible?

All our family photographs were posed. We stood together in groups of three or four and squinted into the sun. My grandmother directed us to smile. I have carried one of these photographs with me for years without acknowledging to myself that in it my mother has the look she always had when she drank too much. In another photograph, taken near the time of my parents' divorce, I can see that my father is almost crying, though I could not see this earlier. I must have felt obliged to see only what my grandmother wanted us to see. Tranquil, domestic scenes.

In the matrix of the mitochondria all the processes of transformation join together in a central vortex.

We were not comfortable with ourselves as a family. There was a great shared suffering and yet we never wept together, except for my mother, who would alternately weep and then rage when she was drunk. Together, under my grandmother's tutelage, we kept up appearances. Her effort was ceaseless.

When at the age of six I went to live with her, my grandmother worked to reshape me. I learned what she thought was correct grammar. The manners she had studied in books of etiquette were passed on to me, not by casual example but through anxious memorization and drill. Napkin to be lifted by the corner and swept onto the lap. Hand to be clasped firmly but not too firmly.

We were not to the manner born. On one side my great-grandfather was a farmer, and on the other a butcher newly emigrated from Ireland, who still spoke with a brogue. Both great-grandfathers drank too much, the one in public houses, the other more quietly at home. The great-grandfather who farmed was my grandmother's father. He was not wealthy but he aspired to gentility. My grandmother inherited both his aspiration and his failure.

We considered ourselves finer than the neighbors to our left with their chaotic household. But when certain visitors came, we were as if driven by an inward, secret panic that who we really were might be discovered. Inadvertently, by some careless gesture, we might reveal to these visitors who were our betters that we did not belong with them, that we were not real. Though of course we never spoke of this, to anyone, not even ourselves.

Gebhard Himmler's family was newly risen from poverty. Just as in my family, the Himmlers' gentility was a thinly laid surface, maintained no doubt only with great effort. Gebhard's father had come from a family of peasants and small artisans. Such a living etched from the soil, and by one's hands, is tenuous and hard. As is frequently the case with young men born to poverty, Johann became a soldier. And, like many young soldiers, he got himself into trouble more than once for brawling and general mischief. On one occasion he was reproved for what was called *immoral behavior with a low woman.* But nothing of this history survived in his son's version of him. By the time Gebhard was born, Johann was fifty-six years old and had reformed his ways. Having joined the royal police force of Bavaria, over the years he rose to the rank of sergeant. He was a respectable man, with a respectable position.

Perhaps Gebhard never learned of his father's less than respectable past. He was only three years old when Johann died. If he had the slightest notion, he did not breathe a word to his own children. Johann became the icon of the Himmler family, the heroic soldier who single-handedly brought his family from the obscurity of poverty into the warm light of the favored. Yet obscure histories have a way of casting a shadow over the present. Those who are born to propriety have a sense of entitlement, and this affords them some ease as they execute the correct mannerisms of their class. More recent members of the elect are less certain of themselves; around the edges of newly minted refinement one discerns a certain fearfulness, expressed perhaps as uncertainty, or as its opposite, rigidity.

One can sense that rigidity in Gebhard's face as a younger man. In a photograph of the Himmler family, Gebhard, who towers in the background, seems severe. He has the face of one who looks for mistakes. He is vigilant. Heinrich's mother looks very small next to him, almost as if she is cowering. She has that look I have seen many times on my father's face, which one can only describe as ameliorating. Heinrich is very small. He stands closest to the camera, shimmering in a white dress. His face is pretty, even delicate.

HE HAS THE FACE OF ONE WHO LOOKS FOR MISTAKES. HE IS VIGILANT.

I am looking now at the etching called *Poverty*, made in 1897. Near the center, calling my attention, a woman holds her head in her hands. She stares through her hands into the face of a sleeping infant. Though the infant and the sheet and pillow around are filled with light, one recognizes that the child is dying. In a darker corner, two worried figures huddle, a father and another child. Room, mother, father, child exist in lines, a multitude of lines, and each line is filled with a rare intelligence.

Just as the physicist's scrutiny changes the object of perception, so does art transmute experience. One cannot look upon what Käthe Kollwitz has drawn without feeling. The lines around the child are bleak with unreason. Never have I seen so clearly that what we call poverty is simply a raw exposure to the terror and fragility of life. But there is more in this image. There is meaning in the frame. One can feel the artist's eyes. Her gaze is in one place soft, in another intense. Like the light around the infant, her attention interrupts the shadow that falls across the room.

The artist's choice of subject and the way she saw it were both radical departures, not only from certain acceptable assumptions in the world of art, but also from established social ideas because the poor were thought of as less than human. The death of a child to a poor parent was supposed to be a less painful event. In her depiction, the artist told a different story.

Heinrich is entering a new school now, and so his father makes a list of all his future classmates. Beside the name of each child he writes the child's father's name, what this father does for a living, and his social position. Heinrich must be careful, Gebhard tells him, to choose whom he befriends. In his diaries the boy seldom mentions his friends by name. Instead he writes that he played, for instance, with the landlord's child.

There is so much for Heinrich to learn. Gebhard must teach him the right way to bow. The proper forms of greeting. The history of his family; the history of his nation. Its heroes. His grandfather's illustrious military past. There is an order in the world and Heinrich has a place in this order which he must be trained to fill. His life is strictly scheduled. At this hour a walk in the woods so that he can appreciate nature. After that a game of chess to develop his mind. And after that piano, so that he will be cultured.

If a part of himself has vanished, that part of the self that feels and wants, and from which hence a coherent life might be shaped, Heinrich is not at sea yet. He has no time to drift or feel lost. Each moment has been spoken for, every move prescribed. He has only to carry out his father's plans for him.

But everything in his life is not as it should be. He is not popular among his classmates. Should it surprise us to learn that he has a penchant for listening to the secrets of his companions, and that afterward he repeats these secrets to his father, the schoolmaster? There is perhaps a secret he would like to learn and one he would like to tell, but this has long since been forgotten. Whatever he learns now he must tell his father. He must not keep anything from him. He must keep his father's good will at all costs. For, without his father, he does not exist.

And there is another reason Heinrich is not accepted by his classmates. He is frail. As an infant, stricken by influenza, he came close to perishing and his body still retains the mark of that illness. He is not strong. He is not good at the games the other boys play. At school he tries over and over to raise himself on the crossbars, unsuccessfully. He covets the popularity of his stronger, more masculine brother, Gebhard. But he cannot keep up with his brother. One day, when they go out for a simple bicycle ride together, Heinrich falls into the mud and returns with his clothes torn.

It is 1914. A war begins. There are parades. Young men marching in uniform. Tearful ceremonies at the railway station. Songs. Decorations. Heinrich is enthusiastic. The war has given him a sense of purpose in life. Like other boys, he plays at soldiering. He follows the war closely, writing in his diary of the progress of armies, *This time with 40 Army Corps and Russia and France against Germany.* The entries he makes do not seem so listless now; they have a new vigor. As the war continues, a new ambition gradually takes the shape of determination. Is this the way he will finally prove himself? Heinrich wants to be a soldier. And above all he wants a uniform.

It is 1915. In her journal Käthe Kollwitz records a disturbing sight. The night before at the opera she found herself sitting next to a young soldier. He was blinded. He sat *without stirring, his hands on his knees, his head erect.* She could not stop looking at him, and the memory of him, she writes now, *cuts her to the quick.*

It is 1916. As Heinrich comes of age he implores his father to help him find a regiment. He has many heated opinions about the war. But his thoughts are like the thoughts and feelings of many adolescents; what he expresses has no steady line of reason. His opinions are filled with contradictions, and he lacks that awareness of self which can turn ambivalence into an inner dialogue. Yet, beneath this amorphous bravado, there is a pattern. As if he were trying on different attitudes, Heinrich swings from harshness to compassion. In one place he writes, *The Russian prisoners multiply like vermin.* (Should I write here that this is a word he will one day use for Jews?) But later he is sympathetic to the same prisoners because they are so far away from home. Writing once of *the silly old women and petty bourgeois . . . who so dislike war,* in another entry, he remembers the young men he has seen depart on trains and he asks, *How many are alive today?*

Is the direction of any life inevitable? Or are there crossroads, points at which the direction might be changed? I am looking again at the Himmler family. Heinrich's infant face resembles the face of his mother. His face is soft. And his mother? In the photograph she is a fading presence. She occupied the same position as did most women in German families, secondary and obedient to the undisputed power of her husband. She has a slight smile which for some reason reminds me of the smile of a child I saw in a photograph from an album made by the SS. This child's image was captured as she stood on the platform at Auschwitz. In the photograph she emanates a certain frailty. Her smile is a very feminine smile. Asking, or perhaps pleading, *Don't hurt me.*

Is it possible that Heinrich, looking into that child's face, might have seen himself there? What is it in a life that makes one able to see oneself in others? Such affinities do not stop with obvious resemblance. There is a sense in which we all enter the lives of others.

It is 1917, and a boy who will be named Heinz is born to Catholic parents living in Vienna. Heinz's father bears a certain resemblance to Heinrich's father. He is a civil servant and, also like Gebhard, he is pedantic and correct in all he does. Heinrich will never meet this boy. And yet their paths will cross.

Early in the same year as Heinz's birth, Heinrich's father has finally succeeded in getting him into a regiment. As the war continues for one more year, Heinrich comes close to achieving his dream. He will be a soldier. He is sent to officer's training. Yet he is not entirely happy. *The food is bad*, he writes to his mother, *and there is not enough of it. It is cold. There are bedbugs. The room is barren.* Can she send him food? A blanket? Why doesn't she write him more often? Has she forgotten him? They are calling up troops. Suppose he should be called to the front and die?

But something turns in him. Does he sit on the edge of a neat, narrow military bunk bed as he writes in his diary that he does not want to be like a boy who whines to his mother? Now, he writes a different letter: *I am once more a soldier body and soul.* He loves his uniform; the oath he has learned to write; the first inspection he passes. He signs his letters now, *Miles Heinrich.* Soldier Heinrich.

I am looking at another photograph. It is of two boys. They are both in military uniform. Gebhard, Heinrich's older brother, is thicker and taller. Next to him Heinrich is still diminutive. But his face has become harder, and his smile, though faint like his mother's smile, has gained a new quality, harsh and stiff like the little collar he wears.

Most men can remember a time in their lives when they were not so different from girls, and they also remember when that time ended. In ancient Greece a young boy lived with his mother, practicing a feminine life in her household, until the day he was taken from her into the camp of men. From this day forward the life that had been soft and graceful became rigorous and hard, as the older boy was prepared for the life of a soldier.

My grandfather on my mother's side was a contemporary of Heinrich Himmler. He was the youngest boy in the family and an especially pretty child. Like Heinrich and all small boys in this period, he was dressed in a lace gown. His hair was long and curled about his face. Like Heinrich, he was his mother's favorite. She wanted to keep him in his finery. He was so beautiful in it, and he was her last child. My great-grandmother Sarah had a dreamy, artistic nature, and in his early years my grandfather took after her. But all of this made him seem girlish. And his father and older brothers teased him mercilessly. Life improved for him only when he graduated to long pants. With them he lost his dreamy nature too.

The soul is often imagined to be feminine. All those qualities thought of as soulful, a dreaminess or artistic sensibility, are supposed to come more naturally to women. Ephemeral, half seen, half present, nearly ghostly, with only the vaguest relation to the practical world of physical law, the soul appears to us as lost. The hero, with his more masculine virtues, must go in search of her. But there is another, older story of the soul. In this story she is firmly planted on the earth. She is incarnate and visible everywhere. Neither is she faint of heart, nor fading in her resolve. It is she, in fact, who goes bravely in search of desire.

1918. Suddenly the war is over. Germany has lost. Heinrich has failed to win his commission. He has not fought in a single battle. Prince Heinrich, his namesake, has died. The prince will be decorated for heroism, after his death. Heinrich returns home, not an officer or even a soldier any longer. He returns to school, completing his studies at the gymnasium and then the university. But he is adrift. Purposeless. And like the world he belongs to, dissatisfied. Neither man nor boy, he does not know what he wants.

Until now he could rely on a strict regimen provided by his father. Nothing was left uncertain or undefined for long in his father's house. The thoroughness of Gebhard's hold over his family comes alive for me through this procedure: every package, letter, or money order to pass through the door was by Gebhard's command to be duly recorded. And I begin to grasp a sense of Gebhard's priorities when I read that Heinrich, on one of his leaves home during the war, assisted his mother in this task. The shadow of his father's habits will stretch out over history. They will fall over an office in Berlin through which the SS, and the entire network of concentration camps, are administered. Every single piece of paper issued with regard to this office will pass over Heinrich's desk, and to each page he will add his own initials. Schedules for trains. Orders for building supplies. Adjustments in salaries. No detail will escape his surmise or fail to be recorded.

But at this moment in his life Heinrich is facing a void. I remember a similar void, when a long and intimate relationship ended. What I felt then was fear. And at times panic. In a journal I kept after this separation, I wrote, *Direct knowledge of the illusory nature of panic. The feeling that I had let everything go out of control.* I could turn in only one direction: inward. Each day I abated my fears for a time by observing myself. But what exists in that direction for Heinrich? He has not been allowed to inhabit that terrain. His inner life has been sealed off both from his father and himself.

I am not certain what I am working for, he writes, and then, not able to let this uncertainty remain, he adds, *I work because it is my duty.* He spends long hours in his room, seldom leaving the house at all. He is at sea. Still somewhat the adolescent, unformed, not knowing what face he should put on when going out into the world, in his journal he confesses that he still lacks that *naturally superior kind of manner that he would dearly like to possess.*

Is it any wonder then that he is so eager to rejoin the army? The army gave purpose and order to his life. He wants his uniform again. In his uniform he knows who he is. But his frailty haunts him. Over and over he shows up at recruiting stations throughout Bavaria only to be turned away each time, with the single word, *Untauglich*. Unfit. At night the echo of this word keeps him awake.

When he tries to recover his pride, he suffers another failure of a similar kind. A student of agriculture at the university, now he dreams of becoming a farmer. He believes he can take strength and vitality from the soil. After all his own applications are rejected, his father finds him a position in the countryside. He rides toward his new life on his motorcycle and is pelted by torrents of rain. Though he is cold and hungry, he is also exuberant. He has defeated his own weakness. But after only a few weeks his body fails him again. He returns home ill with typhus and must face the void once more.

What Germany needs now is a man of iron. How easy it is to hear the irony of these words Heinrich records in his journal. But at this moment in history, he is hearing another kind of echo. There are so many others who agree with him. The treaty of Versailles is taken as a humiliation. An unforgivable weakness, it is argued, has been allowed to invade the nation.

1920. 1922. 1923. Heinrich is twenty, twenty-two, twenty-three. He is growing up with the century. And he starts to adopt certain opinions popular at this time. As I imagine myself in his frame of mind, facing a void, cast into unknown waters, these opinions appear like rescue ships on the horizon, a promise of *terra firma*, the known.

It is for instance fashionable to argue that the emergence of female equality has drained the nation of its strength. At social gatherings Heinrich likes to discuss the differences between men and women. That twilight area between the certainties of gender, homosexuality, horrifies him. A man should be a man and a woman a woman. Sexually explicit illustrations in a book by Oscar Wilde horrify him. Uncomfortable with the opposite sex, so much so that one of his female friends believes he hates women, he has strong feelings about how men and women ought to relate. *A real man,* he sets down in his diary, *should love a woman as a child who must be admonished perhaps even punished, when she is foolish, though she must also be protected and looked after because she is so weak.*

As I try to enter Heinrich's experience, the feeling I sense behind these words is of immense comfort. I know who I am. My role in life, what I am to feel, what I am to be, has been made clear. I am a man. I am the strong protector. And what's more, I am needed. There is one who is weak. One who is weaker than I am. And I am the one who must protect her.

And yet behind the apparent calm of my present mood, there is an uneasiness. Who is this one that I protect? Does she tell me the truth about herself? I am beginning to suspect that she hides herself from me. There is something secretive in her nature. She is an unknown, even dangerous, territory.

The year is 1924. And Heinrich is still fascinated with secrets. He discovers that his brother's fiancée has committed one or maybe even two indiscretions. At his urging, Gebhard breaks off the engagement. But

Heinrich is still not satisfied. He writes a friend who lives near his brother's former fiancée, *Do you know of any other shameful stories?* After this, he hires a private detective to look into her past.

Is it any coincidence that in the same year he writes in his diary that he has met a *great man, genuine and pure?* This man, he notes, may be the new leader Germany is seeking. He finds he shares a certain drift of thought with this man. He is discovering who he is now, partly by affinity and partly by negation. In his picture of himself, a profile begins to emerge cast in light and shadow. He knows now who he is and who he is not. He is not Jewish.

And increasingly he becomes obsessed with who he is not. In this pursuit, his curiosity is fed by best-selling books, posters, films, journals; he is part of a larger social movement, and this no doubt gives him comfort, and one cannot, in studying the landscape of his mind as set against the landscape of the social body, discover where he ends and the milieu of this time begins. He is perhaps like a particle in a wave, a wave which has only the most elusive relationship with the physical world, existing as an afterimage in the mind.

I can imagine him sitting at a small desk in his bedroom, still in his father's home. Is it the same desk where he was required to record some desultory sentences in his diary every day? He is bent over a book. It is evening. The light is on, shining on the pages of the book. Which book among the books he has listed in his journal does he read now? Is it *Das Liebesnest* (*The Lovenest*), telling the story of a liaison between a Jewish man and a gentile woman? *Rasse*? Explaining the concept of racial superiority? Or is it *Juden Schuldbuch* (*The Book of Jewish Guilt*). Or *Die Sünde wider das Blut* (*The Sin Against the Blood*).

One can follow somewhat his train of thought here and there where he makes comments on what he reads in his journal. When he reads *Tscheka*, for instance, a history of the secret police in Russia, he says he is disappointed. *Everyone knows*, he writes, that the Jews control the secret police in Russia. But nowhere in the pages of this book does he find a mention of this "fact."

His mind has begun to take a definite shape, even a predictable pattern. Everywhere he casts his eyes he will discover a certain word. Wherever his thoughts wander he brings them back to this word. *Jew. Jude. Jew.* With this word he is on firm ground again. In the sound of the word, a box is closed, a box with all the necessary documents, with all the papers in order.

My grandfather was an anti-Semite. He had a long list of enemies that he liked to recite. Blacks were among them. And Catholics. And the English. He was Protestant and Irish. Because of his drinking he retired early (though we never discussed the cause). In my childhood I often found him sitting alone in the living room that was darkened by closed venetian blinds which kept all our colors from fading. Lonely myself, I would try to speak with him. His repertoire was small. When I was younger he would tell me stories of his childhood, and I loved those stories. He talked about the dog named Blackie that was his then. A ceramic statue of a small black dog resembling him stood near the fireplace. He loved this dog in a way that was almost painful to hear. But he could never enter that intricate world of expressed emotion in which the shadings of one's life as it is felt and experienced become articulated. This way of speaking was left to the women of our family. As I grew older and he could no longer tell me the story of his dog, he would talk to me about politics. It was then that, with a passion he revealed nowhere else, he would recite to me his long list filled with everyone he hated.

I did not like to listen to my grandfather speak this way. His face would get red, and his voice took on a grating tone that seemed to abrade not only the ears but some other slower, calmer velocity within the body of the room. His eyes, no longer looking at me, blazed with a kind of blindness. There was no reaching him at these moments. He was beyond any kind of touch or remembering. Even so, reciting the long list of those he hated, he came temporarily alive. Then, once out of this frame of mind, he lapsed into a kind of fog which we called, in the family, his retirement.

THERE WAS NO REACHING HIM AT THESE MOMENTS. HE WAS BEYOND ANY KIND OF TOUCH OR REMEMBERING.

There was another part of my grandfather's mind that also disturbed me. But this passion was veiled. I stood at the borders of it occasionally catching glimpses. He had a stack of magazines by the chair he always occupied. They were devoted to the subject of crime, and the crimes were always grisly, involving photographs of women or girls uncovered in ditches, hacked to pieces or otherwise mutilated. I was never supposed to look in these magazines, but I did. What I saw there could not be reconciled with the other experience I had of my grandfather, fond of me, gentle, almost anachronistically protective.

Heinrich Himmler was also fascinated with crime. Along with books about Jews, he read avidly on the subjects of police work, espionage, torture. Despite his high ideals regarding chastity, he was drawn to torrid, even pornographic fiction, including *Ein Sadist im Priesterrock* (*A Sadist in Priestly Attire*) which he read quickly, noting in his journal that it was a book *about the corruption of women and girls . . . in Paris.*

Entering the odd and often inconsistent maze of his opinions, I feel a certain queasiness. I cannot find a balance point. I search in vain for some center, that place which is in us all, and is perhaps even beyond nationality, or even gender, the felt core of existence, which seems to be at the same time the most real. In Heinrich's morass of thought there are no connecting threads, no integrated whole. I find only the opinions themselves, standing in an odd relation to gravity, as if hastily formed, a rickety, perilous structure.

I am looking at a photograph. It was taken in 1925. Or perhaps 1926. A group of men pose before a doorway in Landshut. Over this doorway is a wreathed swastika. Nearly all the men are in uniform. Some wear shiny black boots. Heinrich is among them. He is the slightest, very thin. Heinrich Himmler. He is near the front. At the far left there is the blurred figure of a man who has been caught in motion as he rushes to join the other men. Of course I know his feeling. The desire to partake, and even to be part of memory.

Photographs are strange creations. They are depictions of a moment that is always passing; after the shutter closes, the subject moves out of the frame and begins to change outwardly or inwardly. One ages. One shifts to a different state of consciousness. Subtle changes can take place in an instant, perhaps one does not even feel them — but they are perceptible to the camera.

The idea we have of reality as a fixed quantity is an illusion. Everything moves. And the process of knowing oneself is in constant motion too, because the self is always changing. Nowhere is this so evident as in the process of art which takes one at once into the self and into *terra incognita*, the land of the unknown. *I am groping in the dark*, the artist Käthe Kollwitz writes in her journal. Here, I imagine she is not so much uttering a cry of despair as making a simple statement. A sense of emptiness always precedes creation.

Now, as I imagine Himmler, dressed in his neat uniform, seated behind his desk at party headquarters, I can feel the void he feared begin to recede. In every way his life has taken on definition. He has a purpose and a schedule. Even the place left by the cessation of his father's lessons has now been filled. He is surrounded by men whose ideas he begins to adopt. From Alfred Rosenberg he learns about the history of Aryan blood, a line Rosenberg traces back to thousands of years before Christ. From Walther Darré he learns that the countryside is a source of Nordic strength. (And that Jews gravitate toward cities.)

Yet I do not find the calmness of a man who has found himself in the descriptions I have encountered of Heinrich Himmler. Rather, he is filled with an anxious ambivalence. If there was once someone in him who felt strongly one way or the other, this one has long ago vanished. In a room filled with other leaders, he seems to fade into the woodwork, his manner obsequious, his effect inconsequential. He cannot make a decision alone. He is known to seek the advice of other men for even the smallest decisions. In the years to come it will be whispered that he is being led by his own assistant, Reinhard Heydrich. He has made only one decision on his own with a consistent resolve. Following Hitler with unwavering loyalty, he is known as *der treue Heinrich*, true Heinrich. He describes himself as an instrument of the Führer's will.

But still he has something of his own. Something hidden. And this will make him powerful. He is a gatherer of secrets. As he supervises the sale of advertising space for the Nazi newspaper, *Völkischer Beobachter*, he instructs the members of his staff to gather information, not only on the party enemies, the socialists and the communists, but on Nazi Party members themselves. In his small office he sits surrounded by voluminous files that are filled with secrets. From this he will build his secret police. By 1925, with an order from Adolf Hitler, the Schutzstaffel, or SS, has become an official institution.

His life is moving now. Yet in this motion one has the feeling not of a flow, as in the flow of water in a cell, nor as the flow of rivers toward an ocean, but of an engine, a locomotive moving at high speed, or even a missile, traveling above the ground. History has an uncanny way of creating its own metaphors. In 1930, months after Himmler is elected to the Reichstag, Wernher von Braun begins his experiments with liquid fuel missiles that will one day soon lead to the development of the V-2 rocket.

The successful journey of a missile depends upon the study of ballistics. Gravitational fields vary at different heights. The relationship of a projectile to the earth's surface will determine its trajectory. The missile may give the illusion of liberation from the earth, or even abandon. Young men dreaming of space often invest the missile with these qualities. Yet, paradoxically, one is more free of the consideration of gravity while traveling the surface of the earth on foot. There is no necessity for mathematical calculation for each step, nor does one need to apply Newton's laws to take a walk. But the missile has in a sense been forced away from its own presence; the wisdom that is part of its own weight has been transgressed. It finds itself thus careening in a space devoid of memory, always on the verge of falling, but not falling and hence like one who is constantly afraid of illusion, gripped by an anxiety that cannot be resolved even by a fate that threatens catastrophe.

The catastrophes which came to pass after Heinrich Himmler's astonishing ascent to power did not occur in his own life, but came to rest in the lives of others, distant from him, and out of the context of his daily world. It is 1931. Heinz, the boy born in Vienna to Catholic parents, has just turned sixteen, and he is beginning to learn something about himself. All around him his school friends are falling in love with girls. But when he searches inside himself, he finds no such feelings. He is pulled in a different direction. He finds that he is still drawn to another boy. He does not yet know, or even guess, that these feelings will one day place him in the territory of a target.

It is 1933. Heinrich Himmler, Reichsführer SS, has become President of the Bavarian police. In this capacity he begins a campaign against *subversive elements*. Opposition journalists, Jewish business owners, Social Democrats, Communists — names culled from a list compiled on index cards by Himmler's deputy, Reinhard Heydrich — are rounded up and arrested. When the prisons become too crowded, Himmler builds temporary camps. Then, on March 22, the Reichsführer opens the first official and permanent concentration camp at Dachau.

It is 1934. Himmler's power and prestige in the Reich are growing. Yet someone stands in his way. Within the hierarchy of the state police forces,

Ernst Röhm, Commandant of the SA, stands over him. But Himmler has made an alliance with Hermann Göring, who as President Minister of Prussia controls the Prussian police, known as the Gestapo. Through a telephone-tapping technique Göring has uncovered evidence of a seditious plot planned by Röhm against the Führer, and he brings this evidence to Himmler. The Führer, having his own reasons to proceed against Röhm, a notorious homosexual and a socialist, empowers the SS and the Gestapo to form an execution committee. This committee will assassinate Röhm, along with the other leaders of the SA. And in the same year, Göring transfers control of the Gestapo to the SS.

But something else less easy to conquer stands in the way of his dreams for himself. It is his own body. I can see him now as he struggles. He is on a playing field in Berlin. And he has broken out in a sweat. He has been trying once again to earn the Reich's sports badge, an honor whose requirements he himself established but cannot seem to fulfill. For three years he has exercised and practiced. On one day he will lift the required weights or run the required laps, but at every trial he fails to throw the discus far enough. His attempt is always a few centimeters short.

And once he is Reichsführer, he will set certain other standards for superiority that, no matter how heroic his efforts, he will never be able to meet. A sign of the *Übermensch*, he says, is blondness, but he himself is dark. He says he is careful to weed out any applicant for the SS who shows traces of a mongolian ancestry, but he himself has the narrow eyes he takes as a sign of such a descent. *I have refused to accept any man whose size was below six feet because I know only men of a certain size have the necessary quality of blood*, he declares, standing just five foot seven behind the podium.

It is the same year, and Heinz, who is certain now that he is a homosexual, has decided to end the silence which he feels to be a burden to him. From the earliest years of his childhood he has trusted his mother with all of his secrets. Now he will tell her another secret, the secret of whom he loves. *My dear child*, she tells him, *it is your life and you must live it.*

It is 1936. Though he does not know it, Himmler is moving into the sphere of Heinz's life now. He has organized a special section of the Gestapo to deal with homosexuality and abortion. On October 11, he declares in a public speech, *Germany's forebears knew what to do with homosexuals. They drowned them in bogs.* This was not punishment, he argues, but *the extermination of unnatural existence.*

As I read these words from Himmler's speech, they call to mind an image from a more recent past, an event I nearly witnessed. On my return from Berlin and after my search for my grandmother, I spent a few days in Maine, close to the city of Bangor. This is a quiet town, not much used to violence. But just days before I arrived a young man had been murdered there. He was a homosexual. He wore an earring in one ear. While he walked home one evening with another man, three boys stopped him on the street. They threw him to the ground and began to kick him. He had trouble catching his breath. He was asthmatic. They picked him up and carried him to a railing of a nearby bridge. He told them he could not swim. Yet still, they threw him over the railing of the bridge into the stream, and he drowned. I saw a picture of him printed in the newspaper. That kind of beauty only very graceful children possess shined through his adult features. It was said that he had come to New England to live with his lover. But the love had failed, and before he died he was piecing his life back together.

When Himmler heard that one of his heroes, Frederick the Great, was a homosexual, he refused to believe his ears. I remember the year when my sister announced to my family that she was a lesbian. I can still recall the chill of fear that went up my spine at the sound of the word "queer." We came of age in the fifties; this was a decade of conformity, awash with mood both public and private, bearing on the life of the body and the body politic. Day after day my grandfather would sit in front of the television set watching as Joseph McCarthy interrogated witnesses about their loyalty to the flag. At the same time, a strict definition of what a woman or a man is had returned to capture the shared imagination. In school I was taught sewing and cooking, and I learned to carry my books in front of my chest to strengthen the muscles which held up my breasts.

I was not happy to hear that my sister was a homosexual. Moved from one member of my family to another, I did not feel secure in the love of others. As the child of divorce I was already different. *Where are your mother and father? Why don't you live with them?* I dreaded these questions. Now my sister, whom I adored and in many ways had patterned myself after, had become an outcast, moved even further out of the circle than I.

It is March 1938. Germany has invaded Austria. Himmler has put on a field-gray uniform for the occasion. Two hand grenades dangle from his Sam Browne belt. Accompanied by a special command unit of twenty-eight men armed with tommy guns and light machine guns, he proceeds to Vienna. Here he will set up Gestapo headquarters in the Hotel Metropole before he returns to Berlin.

It is a Friday, in March of 1939. Heinz, who is twenty-two years old now, and a university student, has received a summons. He is to appear for questioning at the Hotel Metropole. Telling his mother it can't be anything serious, he leaves. He enters a room and stands before a desk. The man behind the desk does not raise his head to nod. He continues to write. When he puts his pen down and looks up at the young man, he tells him, *You are a queer, homosexual, admit it.* Heinz tries to deny this. But the man behind the desk pulls out a photograph. He sees two faces here he knows. His own face and the face of his lover. He begins to weep.

I have come to believe that every life bears in some way on every other. The motion of cause and effect is like the motion of a wave in water, continuous, within and not without the matrix of being, so that all consequences, whether we know them or not, are intimately embedded in our experience. But the missile, as it hurls toward its target, has lost its context. It has been driven farther than the eye can see. How can one speak of direction any longer? Nothing in the space the missile passes through can seem familiar. In the process of flight, alienated by terror, this motion has become estranged from life, has fallen out of the natural rhythm of events.

I am imagining Himmler as he sits behind his desk in January of 1940. The procedures of introduction into the concentration camps have all been outlined or authorized by Himmler himself. He supervises every detail of these operations. Following his father's penchant for order, he makes many very explicit rules, and requires that reports be filed continually. Train schedules, orders for food supplies, descriptions of punishments all pass over his desk. He sits behind a massive door of carved wood, in his office, paneled in light, unvarnished oak, behind a desk that is normally empty, and clean, except for the bust of Hitler he displays at one end, and a little drummer boy at the other, between which he reads, considers and initials countless pieces of paper.

One should teach a child a sense of shame. These words of Himmler's journals come back to me as I imagine Heinz now standing naked in the snow. The weather is below zero. After a while he is taken to a cold shower, and then issued an ill-fitting uniform. Now he is ordered to stand with the other prisoners once more out in the cold while the commandant reads the rules. All the prisoners in these barracks are homosexuals. There are pink triangles sewn to their uniforms. They must sleep with the light on, they are told, and with their hands outside their blankets. This is a rule made especially for homosexual men. Any man caught with his hands under his blankets will be taken outside into the icy night where several bowls of water will be poured over him, and where he will be made to stand for an hour.

Except for the fact that this punishment usually led to death from cold and exposure, this practice reminds me of Dr. Schreber's procedure for curing children of masturbation. Just a few nights ago I woke up with this thought: *Was Dr. Schreber afraid of children?* Or the child he once was? Fear is often just beneath the tyrant's fury, a fear that must grow with the trajectory of his flight from himself. At Dachau I went inside a barrack. It was a standard design, similar in many camps. The plan of the camps too was standard, and resembled, so I was told by a German friend, the camp sites designed for the Hitler Youth. This seemed to me significant, not as a clue in an analysis, but more like a gesture that colors and changes a speaker's words.

It is 1941. And Heinrich Himmler pays a visit to the Russian front. He has been put in charge of organizing the *Einsatzgruppen*, moving groups of men who carry out the killing of civilians and partisans. He watches as a deep pit is dug by the captured men and women. Then, suddenly, a young man catches his eye. He is struck by some quality the man possesses. He takes a liking to him. He has the commandant of the *Einsatzgruppen* bring the young man to him. *Who was your father?* he asks. *Your mother? Your grandparents? Do you have at least one grandparent who was not Jewish?* He is trying to save the young man. But he answers no to all the questions. So Himmler, strictly following the letter of the law, watches as the young man is put to death.

The captured men, women, and children are ordered to remove their clothing then. Naked, they stand before the pit they have dug. Some scream. Some attempt escape. The young men in uniform place their rifles against their shoulders and fire into the naked bodies. They do not fall silently. There are cries. There are open wounds. There are faces blown apart. Stomachs opened up. The dying groan. Weep. Flutter. Open their mouths.

There is no photograph of the particular moment when Heinrich Himmler stares into the face of death. What does he look like? Is he pale? He is stricken, the accounts tell us, and more than he thought he would be. He has imagined something quieter, more efficient, like the even rows of numbers, the alphabetical lists of names he likes to put in his files. Something he might be able to understand and contain. But one cannot contain death so easily.

Death with Girl in Her Lap. One of many studies the artist did of death. A girl is drawn, her body dead or almost dead, in that suspended state where the breath is almost gone. There is no movement. No will. The lines the artist has drawn are simple. She has not rendered the natural form of head, arm, buttock, thigh exactly. But all these lines hold the feeling of a body in them. And as my eyes rest on this image, I can feel my own fear of death, and also, the largeness of grief, how grief will not let you remain insulated from your own feelings, or from life itself. It is as if I knew this girl. And death, too, appears to know her, cradling the fragile body with tenderness; she seems to understand the sorrow of dying. Perhaps this figure has taken into herself all the deaths she has witnessed. And in this way, she has become merciful.

Because Himmler finds it so difficult to witness these deaths, the commandant makes an appeal to him. If it is hard for you, he says, think what it must be for these young men who must carry out these executions, day after day. Shaken by what he has seen and heard, Himmler returns to Berlin resolved to ease the pain of these men. He will consult an engineer and set him to work immediately on new designs. Before the year has ended, he presents the *Einsatzgruppen* with a mobile killing truck. Now the young men will not have to witness death day after day. A hose from the exhaust pipe funnels fumes into a chamber built on the bed of a covered truck, which has a red cross painted on its side so its passengers will not be alarmed as they enter it.

To a certain kind of mind, what is hidden away ceases to exist.

Himmler does not like to watch the suffering of his prisoners. In this sense he does not witness the consequences of his own commands. But the mind is like a landscape in which nothing really ever disappears. What seems to have vanished has only transmuted to another form. Not wishing to witness what he has set in motion, still, in a silent part of himself, he must imagine what takes place. So, just as the child is made to live out the unclaimed imagination of the parent, others under Himmler's power were made to bear witness for him. Homosexuals were forced to witness and sometimes take part in the punishment of other homosexuals, Poles of other Poles, Jews of Jews. And as far as possible, the hands of the men of the SS were protected from the touch of death. Other prisoners were required to bury the bodies, or burn them in the ovens.

Hélène was turned in by a Jewish man who was trying, no doubt, to save his own life, and she was put under arrest by another Jewish man, an inmate of the same camp to which she was taken. She was grateful that she herself had not been forced to do harm. But something haunted her. A death that came to stand in place of her own death. As we walked through the streets of Paris she told me this story.

By the time of her arrest she was married and had a young son. Her husband was taken from their apartment during one of the mass arrests that began in July of 1942. Hélène was out at the time with her son. For some time she wandered the streets of Paris. She would sleep at night at the homes of various friends and acquaintances, leaving in the early morning so that she would not arouse suspicion among the neighbors. This was the hardest time, she told me, because there was so little food, even less than she was to have at Drancy. She had no ration card or any way of earning money. Her whole existence was illegal. She had to be as if invisible. She collected scraps from the street. It was on the street that she told me this story, as we walked from the fourth arrondissement to the fifth, crossing the bridge near Notre Dame, making our way toward the Boulevard St. Michel.

Her husband was a citizen of a neutral country and for this reason legally destined for another camp. From this camp he would not be deported. Instead he was taken to the French concentration camp at Drancy. After his arrest, hoping to help him, Hélène managed to take his papers to the Swiss Consulate. But the papers remained there. After her own arrest she was taken with her son to Drancy, where she was reunited with her husband. He told her that her efforts were useless. But still again and again she found ways to smuggle out letters to friends asking them to take her husband's papers from the Swiss Consulate to the camp at Drancy. One of these letters was to save their lives.

After a few months, preparations began to send Hélène and her family to Auschwitz. Along with many other women, she was taken to have her hair cut short, though those consigned to that task decided she should keep her long, blond hair. Still, she was herded along with the others to the train station and packed into the cars. Then, just two hours before the train was scheduled to leave, Hélène, her son, and her husband were pulled from the train. Her husband's papers had been brought by the Swiss consul to the camp. The Commandant, by assuming Hélène shared the same nationality with her husband, had made a fortuitous mistake.

But the train had to have a specific number of passengers before it could leave. In Hélène's place the guards brought a young man. She would never forget his face, she told me, or his name. Later she tried to find out whether he had lived or died but could learn nothing.

IN HÉLÈNE'S PLACE THE GUARDS BROUGHT A YOUNG MAN. SHE WOULD NEVER FORGET HIS FACE, SHE TOLD ME, OR HIS NAME. LATER SHE TRIED TO FIND OUT WHETHER HE HAD LIVED OR DIED BUT COULD LEARN NOTHING.

Himmler did not partake in the actual preparations for what he called "the final solution." Nor did he attend the Wannsee Conference where the decision to annihilate millions of human beings was made. He sent his assistant Heydrich. Yet Heydrich, who was there, did not count himself entirely present. He could say that each decision he made was at the bequest of Heinrich Himmler. In this way an odd system of insulation was created. These crimes, these murders of millions, were all carried out in absentia, as if by no one in particular.

This ghostlike quality, the strange absence of a knowing conscience, as if the living creature had abandoned the shell, was spread throughout the entire chain of command. So a French bureaucrat writing a letter in 1942 speaks in detail of the mass arrests that he himself supervised as if he had no other part in these murders except as a kind of spiritless cog in a vast machine whose force compelled him from without. *The German authorities have set aside especially for that purpose enough trains to transport 30,000 Jews,* he writes. *It is therefore necessary that the arrests made should correspond to the capacity of the trains.*

It is August 23, 1943. The first inmates of concentration camp Dora have arrived. Is there some reason why an unusually high percentage of prisoners ordered to work in this camp are homosexuals? They are set to work immediately, working with few tools, often with bare hands, to convert long tunnels carved into the Harz Mountains into a factory for the manufacture of missiles. They work for eighteen hours each day. Six of these hours are set aside for formal procedures, roll calls, official rituals of the camp. For six hours they must try to sleep in the tunnels, on the damp earth, in the same area where the machines, pickaxes, explosions, and drills are making a continually deafening noise, twenty-four hours of every day. They are fed very little. They see the daylight only once a week, at the Sunday roll call. The tunnels themselves are illuminated with faint light bulbs. The production of missiles has been moved here because the factories at Peenemünde were bombed. Because the secret work at Peenemünde had been revealed to the Allies by an informer, after the bombing the Reichsführer SS proposed that the factories should be installed in a concentration camp. Here, he argued, security could be more easily enforced; only the guards had any freedom, and they were subject to the harsh discipline of the SS. The labor itself could be hidden under the soil of the Harz Mountains.

Memory can be like a long, half-lit tunnel, a tunnel where one is likely to encounter phantoms of a self, long concealed, no longer nourished with the force of consciousness, existing in a tortured state between life and death. In his account of his years at Peenemünde, Wernher von Braun never mentions concentration camp Dora. Yet he was seen there more than once by inmates who remembered him. As the designing engineer, he had to supervise many details of production. Conditions at camp Dora could not have escaped his attention. Dora did not have its own crematorium. And so many men and women died in the course of a day that the bodies waiting to be picked up by trucks and taken to the ovens of Buchenwald were piled high next to the entrance to the tunnels.

Perhaps von Braun told himself that what went on in those tunnels had nothing to do with him. He had not wished for these events, had not wanted them. The orders came from someone who had power over him. In the course of this writing I remembered a childhood incident that made me disown myself in the same way. My best friend, who was my neighbor, had a mean streak and because of this had a kind of power over the rest of us who played with her. For a year I left my grandmother's house to live with my mother again. On my return I had been replaced by another little girl, and the two of them excluded me. But finally my chance arrived. My friend had a quarrel with her new friend and enlisted me in an act of revenge. Together we cornered her at the back of a yard, pushing her into the garbage cans, yelling nasty words at her, throwing things at her.

My friend led the attack, inventing the strategies and the words which were hurled. With part of myself I knew what it was to be the object of this kind of assault. But I also knew this was the way to regain my place with my friend. Later I disowned my acts, as if I had not committed them. Because I was under the sway of my friend's power, I told myself that what I did was really her doing. And in this way became unreal to myself. It was as if my voice threatening her, my own anger, and my voice calling names, had never existed.

I was told this story by a woman who survived the holocaust. The war had not yet begun. Nor the exiles. Nor the mass arrests. But history was on the point of these events, tipping over, ready to fall into the relentless path of consequences. She was then just a child, playing games in the street. And one day she found herself part of a circle of other children. They had surrounded a little boy and were calling him names because he was Jewish. He was her friend. But she thought if she left this circle, or came to his defense, she herself would lose her standing among the others. Then, suddenly, in an angry voice her mother called her in from the street. As soon as the door shut behind her, her mother began to shout, words incomprehensible to her, and slapped her across the face. *Your father*, her mother finally said, after crying, and in a quieter voice, *was Jewish*. Her father had been dead for three years. Soon after this day her mother too would die. As the danger grew worse her gentile relatives would not harbor her any longer, and she joined the fate of those who tried to live in the margins, as if invisible, as if mere shadows, terrified of a direct glance, of recognition, existing at the unsteady boundary of consciousness.

In disowning the effects we have on others, we disown ourselves. My father watched the suffering of my childhood and did nothing. He was aware of my mother's alcoholism and the state of her mind when she drank. He knew my grandmother to be tyrannical. We could speak together of these things almost dispassionately, as if both of us were disinterested witnesses to a fascinating social drama. But after a day's visit with him, spent at the park, or riding horses, or at the movies, he would send me back into that world of suffering we had discussed so dispassionately.

His disinterest in my condition was not heartless. It reflected the distance he kept from his own experience. One could sense his suffering but he never expressed it directly. He was absent to a part of himself. He was closer to tears than many men, but he never shed those tears. If I cried he would fall into a frightened silence. And because of this, though I spent a great deal of time with him, he was always in a certain sense an absent father. Unknowingly I responded in kind, for years, feeling a vaguely defined anger that would neither let me love nor hate him.

My father learned his disinterest under the guise of masculinity. Boys don't cry. There are whole disciplines, institutions, rubrics in our culture which serve as categories of denial.

Science is such a category. The torture and death that Heinrich Himmler found disturbing to witness became acceptable to him when it fell under this rubric. He liked to watch the scientific experiments in the concentration camps. And then there is the rubric of military order. I am looking at a photograph. It was taken in 1941 in the Ukraine. The men of an *einsatzgruppen* are assembled in a group pose. In front of them their rifles rest in ceremonial order, composed into tripods. They stand straight and tall. They are clean-shaven and their uniforms are immaculate, in *apple-pie order*, as we would say in America.

It is not surprising that cleanliness in a profession that sheds blood would become a compulsion. Blood would evidence guilt and fear to a mind trying to escape the consequence of its decisions. It is late in the night when Laura tells me one more story. Her father is about to be sent to Europe, where he will fight in the Battle of the Bulge and become a general. For weeks her mother has prepared a party. The guests begin to arrive in formal dress and sparkling uniforms. The white-gloved junior officers stand to open the doors. Her mother, regal in satin and jewels, starts to descend the staircase. Laura sits on the top stair watching, dressed in her pajamas. Then suddenly a pool of blood appears at her mother's feet, her mother falls to the floor, and almost as quickly, without a word uttered, a junior officer sweeps up the stairs, removes her mother into a waiting car, while another one cleans up the blood. No one tells Laura that her mother has had a miscarriage, and the party continues as if no event had taken place, no small or large death, as if no death were about to take place, nor any blood be spilled.

But the nature of the material world frustrates our efforts to remain free of the suffering of others. The mobile killing van that Himmler summoned into being had some defects. Gas from the exhaust pipes leaked into the cabin where the drivers sat and made them ill. When they went to remove the bodies from the van they were covered with blood and excrement, and their faces bore expressions of anguish. Himmler's engineers fixed the leak, increased the flow of gas so the deaths would be quicker, and built in a drain to collect the bodily fluids that are part of death.

There are times when no engineers can contain death. Over this same landscape through which the mobile killing vans traveled, an invisible cloud would one day spread, and from it would descend a toxic substance that would work its way into the soil and the water, the plants and the bodies of animals, and into human cells, not only in this landscape of the Ukraine, but in the fjords of Norway, the fields of Italy and France, and even here, in the far reaches of California, bringing a death that recalled, more than forty years later, those earlier hidden deaths.

You can see pictures of them. Whole families, whole communities. The fabric on their backs almost worn through. Bodies as if ebbing away before your eyes. Poised on an edge. The cold visible around the thin joints of arms and knees. A bed made in a doorway. Moving then, over time, deeper and deeper into the shadows. Off the streets. Into back rooms, and then to the attics or the cellars. Windows blackened. Given less and less to eat. Moving into smaller and smaller spaces. Sequestered away like forbidden thoughts, or secrets.

Could he have seen in these images of those he had forced into hiding and suffering, into agony and death, an image of the outer reaches of his own consciousness? It is only now that I can begin to see he has become part of them. Those whose fate he sealed. Heinrich Himmler. A part of Jewish history. Remembered by those who fell into the net of his unclaimed life.

Claimed as a facet of the wound, part of the tissue of the scar. A mark on the body of our minds, both those of us who know this history and those who do not.

For there is a sense in which we are all witnesses. Hunger, desperation, pain, loneliness, these are all visible in the streets about us. The way of life we live, a life we have never really chosen, forces us to walk past what we see. And out at the edge, beyond what we see or hear, we can feel a greater suffering, cries from a present or past starvation, a present or past torture, cries of those we have never met, coming to us in our dreams, and even if these cries do not survive in our waking knowledge, still, they live on in the part of ourselves we have ceased to know.

I think now of the missile again and how it came into being. Scientific inventions do not spring whole like Athena from the head of Zeus from the analytic implications of scientific discoveries. Technological advance takes shape slowly in the womb of society and is influenced and fed by our shared imagination. What we create thus mirrors the recesses of our own minds, and perhaps also hidden capacities. Television mimics the ability to see in the mind's eye. And the rocket? Perhaps the night flight of the soul, that ability celebrated in witches to send our thoughts as if through the air to those distant from us, to send images of ourselves, and even our secret feelings, out into an atmosphere beyond ourselves, to see worlds far flung from and strange to us becomes manifest in a sinister fashion in the missile.

Self-portrait in charcoal. Since the earliest rendering she made of her own image, much time has passed. The viewer here has moved closer. Now the artist's head fills the frame. She is much older in years and her features have taken on that androgyny which she thought necessary to the work of an artist. Her hair is white on the paper where the charcoal has not touched it. She is in profile and facing a definite direction. Her eyes look in that direction. But they do not focus on anyone or anything. The portrait is soft, the charcoal rubbed almost gently over the surface, here light, here dark. Her posture is one not so much of resolution as resignation. The portrait was drawn just after the First World War, the war in which her son Peter died. I have seen these eyes in the faces of those who grieve, eyes that are looking but not focused, seeing perhaps what is no longer visible.

After the war, German scientists who developed the V-1 and V-2 rocket immigrate to the United States where they continue to work on rocketry. Using the Vengeance weapon as a prototype, they develop the first ICBM missiles.

On the twenty-third of May 1945, as the war in Europe comes to an end, Heinrich Himmler is taken prisoner by the Allied command. He has removed the military insignia from his clothing, and he wears a patch over one eye. Disguised in this manner, and carrying the identity papers of a man he had condemned to death, he attempts to cross over the border at

Bremervörde. No one at the checkpoint suspects him of being the Reichsführer SS. But once under the scrutiny of the guards, all his courage fails him. Like a trembling schoolboy, he blurts out the truth. Now he will be taken to a center for interrogation, stripped of his clothing and searched. He will refuse to wear the uniform of the enemy, so he will be given a blanket to wrap over his underclothing. Taken to a second center for interrogation, he will be forced to remove this blanket and his underclothes. The interrogators, wishing to make certain he has no poison hidden anywhere, no means by which to end his life and hence avoid giving testimony, will surround his naked body. They will ask him to open his mouth. But just as one of them sees a black capsule wedged between his teeth, he will jerk his head away and swallow. All attempts to save his life will fail. He will not survive to tell his own story. His secrets will die with him.

There were many who lived through those years who did not wish to speak of what they saw or did. None of the German rocket engineers bore witness to what they saw at concentration camp Dora. Common rank and file members of the Nazi Party, those without whose efforts or silent support the machinery could not have gone on, fell almost as a mass into silence. In Berlin and Munich I spoke to many men and women, in my generation or younger, who were the children of soldiers, or party members, or SS men, or generals, or simply believers. Their parents would not speak to them of what had happened. The atmosphere in both cities was as if a pall had been placed over memory. And thus the shared mind of this nation has no roots, no continuous link with what keeps life in a pattern of meaning.

Lately I have come to believe that an as yet undiscovered human need and even a property of matter is the desire for revelation. The truth within us has a way of coming out despite all conscious efforts to conceal it. I have heard stories from those in the generation after the war, all speaking of the same struggle to ferret truth from the silence of their parents so that they themselves could begin to live. One born the year the war ended was never told a word about concentration camps, at home or in school. She began to wake in the early morning hours with nightmares which mirrored down to fine and accurate detail the conditions of the camps. Another woman searching casually through some trunks in the attic of her home found a series of pamphlets, virulently and cruelly anti-Semitic, which had been written by her grandfather, a high Nazi official. Still another pieced together the truth of her father's life, a member of the Gestapo, a man she remembered as playful by contrast to her stern mother. He died in the war. Only over time could she put certain pieces together. How he had had a man working under him beaten. And then, how he had beaten her.

Many of those who survived the holocaust could not bear the memories of what happened to them and, trying to bury the past, they too fell into silence. Others continue to speak as they are able. The manner of speech varies. At an artist's retreat in the Santa Cruz Mountains I met a woman who survived Bergen Belsen and Auschwitz. She inscribes the number eight in many of her paintings. And the number two. This is the story she is telling with those numbers. It was raining the night she arrived with her mother, six brothers and sisters at Auschwitz. It fell very hard, she told me. We were walking in the early evening up a hill brown in the California fall. The path was strewn with yellow leaves illuminated by the sun in its descent. They had endured the long trip from Hungary to Poland, without food or water. They were very tired. Now the sky seemed very black but the platform, lit up with stadium lights, was blinding after the darkness of the train. She would never, she told me, forget the shouting. It is as if she still cannot get the sound out of her ears. The Gestapo gave one shrill order after another, in a language she did not yet understand. They were herded in confusion, blows coming down on them randomly from the guards, past a tall man in a cape. This was Dr. Mengele. He made a single gesture toward all her family and continued it toward her but in a different direction. For days, weeks, months after she had learned what their fate had been she kept walking in the direction of their parting and beyond toward the vanishing point of her vision of them.

There were seven from her family who died there that night. The eighth to die was her father. He was sent to a different camp and died on the day of liberation. Only two lived, she and one brother. The story of one life cannot be told separately from the story of other lives. Who are we? The question is not simple. What we call the self is part of a larger matrix of relationship and society. Had we been born to a different family, in a different time, to a different world, we would not be the same. All the lives that surround us are in us.

In the last decade the Soviet Union improves its antiballistic missiles to make them maneuverable and capable of hovering in midair. The United States continues to develop and test the MX missile, with advanced inertial guidance, capable of delivering ten prearmed electronically guided warheads, each with maneuverability, possessing the power and accuracy to penetrate hardened silos. And the Soviet Union begins to design a series of smaller one-warhead mobile missiles, the SS-25, to be driven around by truck, and the SS-X-24, to be drawn on railroad tracks. And the United States develops a new warhead for the Trident missile carrying fourteen smaller warheads that can be released in a barrage along a track or a road.

A train is making its way through Germany. All along its route those who are in the cars can look out and see those who are outside the cars. And those who are outside can see those who are inside. Sometimes words are exchanged. Sometimes there is a plea for water. And sometimes, at the risk of life, water is given. Sometimes names are called out, or curses are spoken, under the breath. And sometimes there is only silence.

Who are those on the inside and where are they going? There are rumors. It is best not to ask. There are potatoes to buy with the last of the rations. There is a pot boiling on the stove. And, at any rate, the train has gone; the people have vanished. You did not know them. You will not see them again. Except perhaps in your dreams. But what do those images mean? Images of strangers. Agony that is not yours. A face that does not belong to you. And so in the daylight you try to erase what you have encountered and to forget those tracks that are laid even as if someplace in your body, even as part of yourself.

QUESTIONS FOR A SECOND READING

1. One of the challenges a reader faces with Griffin's text is knowing what to make of it. It's a long piece, but the reading is not difficult. The sections are short and straightforward. While the essay is made up of fragments, the arrangement is not deeply confusing or disorienting. Still, the piece has no single controlling idea; it does not move from thesis to conclusion. One way of reading the essay is to see what one can make of it, what it might add up to. In this sense, the work of reading is to find one idea, passage, image, or metaphor — something in the text — and use this to organize the essay.

   As you prepare to work back through the text, think about the point of reference you could use to organize your reading. Is the essay "about" Himmler? secrets? fascism? art? Germany? the United States? families and child-rearing? gay and lesbian sexuality? Can one of the brief sections be taken as a key to the text? What about the italicized sections — how are they to be used?

   You should not assume that one of these is the right way to read. Assume, rather, that one way of working with the text is to organize it around a single point of reference, something you could say that Griffin "put there" for you to notice and to use.

   Or you might want to do this in your name rather than Griffin's. That is, you might, as you reread, chart the connections *you* make, connections that you feel belong to you (to your past, your interests, your way of reading), and think about where and how you are drawn into the text (and with what you take to be Griffin's interests and desires). You might want to be prepared to talk about why you sum things up the way you do.

2. Although this is not the kind of prose you would expect to find in a textbook for a history course, and although the project is not what we usually think of as a "research" project, Griffin is a careful researcher. The project is serious and deliberate; it is "about" history, both family history and world history. Griffin knows what she is doing. So what *is* Griffin's project? As you reread, look to those sections where Griffin seems to be speaking to her readers about her work — about how she reads and how she writes, about how she gathers her materials and how she studies them. What is she doing? What is at stake in adopting such methods? How and why might you teach someone to do this work?

ASSIGNMENTS FOR WRITING

1. Griffin's text gathers together related fragments and works on them, but does so without yoking examples to a single, predetermined argument or thesis. In this sense, it is a kind of anti-essay. One of the difficulties readers of this text face is in its retelling. If someone says to you, "Well, what was it about?" the answer is not easy or obvious. The text is so far-reaching, so carefully composed of interrelated stories and reflections, and so suggestive in its implications and in the connections it enables that it is difficult to summarize without violence, without seriously reducing the text.

   But, imagine that somebody asks, "Well, what was it about?" Write an essay in which you present your reading of "Our Secret." You want to give your reader a sense of what the text is like (or what it is like to read the text), and you want to make clear that the account you are giving is your reading, your way of working it through. You might, in fact, want to suggest what you leave out or put to the side. (The first second-reading question might help you prepare for this.)

2. Griffin argues that we—all of us, especially all of us who read her essay—are part of a complex web of connections. At one point she says,

   > Who are we? The question is not simple. What we call the self is part of a larger matrix of relationship and society. Had we been born to a different family, in a different time, to a different world, we would not be the same. All the lives that surround us are in us. (p. 263)

   At another point she asks, "Is there any one of us who can count ourselves outside the circle circumscribed by our common past?" She speaks of a "field,"

   > like a field of gravity that is created by the movements of many bodies. Each life is influenced and it in turn becomes an influence. Whatever is a cause is also an effect. Childhood experience is just one element in the determining field. (p. 238)

   One way of thinking about this concept of the self (and of interrelatedness), at least under Griffin's guidance, is to work on the connections that she implies and asserts. As you reread the selection, look for powerful and surprising juxtapositions, fragments that stand together in interesting and suggestive ways. Think about the arguments represented by the blank space between those sections. (And look for Griffin's written statements about "relatedness.") Look for connections that seem important to the text (and to you) and representative of Griffin's thinking (and yours). Then, write an essay in which you use these examples to think through your understanding of Griffin's claims for this "larger matrix," the "determining field," or our "common past."

3. It is useful to think of Griffin's prose as experimental. She is trying to do something that she can't do in the "usual" essay form. She wants to make a different kind of argument or engage her reader in a different manner. And

so she mixes personal and academic writing. She assembles fragments and puts seemingly unrelated material into surprising and suggestive relationships. She breaks the "plane" of the page with italicized intersections. She organizes her material, but not in the usual mode of thesis-example-conclusion. The arrangement is not nearly so linear. At one point, when she seems to be prepared to argue that German child-rearing practices produced the Holocaust, she quickly says:

> Of course there cannot be one answer to such a monumental riddle, nor does any event in history have a single cause. Rather a field exists, like a field of gravity that is created by the movements of many bodies. Each life is influenced and it in turn becomes an influence. Whatever is a cause is also an effect. Childhood experience is just one element in the determining field. (p. 238)

Her prose serves to create a "field," one where many bodies are set in relationship.

It is useful, then, to think about Griffin's prose as the enactment of a method, as a way of doing a certain kind of intellectual work. One way to study this, to feel its effects, is to imitate it, to take it as a model. For this assignment, write a Griffin-like essay, one similar in its methods of organization and argument. You will need to think about the stories you might tell, about the stories and texts you might gather (stories and texts not your own). As you write, you will want to think carefully about arrangement and about commentary (about where, that is, you will speak to your reader *as* the writer of the piece). You should not feel bound to Griffin's subject matter, but you should feel that you are working in her spirit.

MAKING CONNECTIONS

1. Is it surprising that prisons resemble factories, schools, barracks, hospitals, which all resemble prisons? (p. 208)

   — MICHEL FOUCAULT
   Panopticism

   The child, Dr. Schreber advised, *should be permeated by the impossibility of locking something in his heart.* . . .

   That this philosophy was taught in school gives me an interior view of the catastrophe to follow. It adds a certain dimension to my image of these events to know that a nation of citizens learned that no part of themselves could be safe from the scrutiny of authority, nothing locked in the heart, and at the same time to discover that the head of the secret police of this nation was the son of a schoolmaster. It was this man, after all, Heinrich Himmler, Reichsführer SS, who was later to say, speaking of the mass arrests of Jews, *Protective custody is an act of care.* (p. 240)

   — SUSAN GRIFFIN
   Our Secret

JUDITH

Halberstam

Judith Halberstam, also known as Jack Halberstam, is Professor of English, American Studies, and Ethnicity and Gender Studies at the University of Southern California. She specializes in cultural studies, queer theory, and visual culture. Much of Halberstam's work draws on film, works of art, and images and ideas that circulate in popular culture. Halberstam completed her undergraduate education at the University of California, Berkeley, and earned her PhD from the University of Minnesota.

Halberstam's published books include *Skin Shows: Gothic Horror and the Technology of Monsters* (1995), a study of popular gothic cultures from *Frankenstein* to contemporary horror film; *Female Masculinity* (1998), which focuses on the ways masculinity is enacted by non-males who are subverting normative gender expression; and *In a Queer Time and Place: Transgender Bodies, Subcultural Lives* (2005), a philosophical meditation on temporality and queer culture that pays particular attention to Brandon Teena, who was murdered in 1993 in a horrific hate crime. One might say that Halberstam's work takes up questions of gender ambiguity, providing her readers with what we might call "queer moments"—moments where conventional understandings of gender and sexuality break down. Halberstam's most recent books are *Gaga Feminism: Sex, Gender, and the End of Normal* (2012) and *The Queer Art of Failure* (2011), an excerpt of which appears in the pages that follow.

Many readers will recognize the references in the titles and descriptions of Halberstam's book projects. For instance, many of us know Lady Gaga as a pop singer and icon of our time; many readers might have read *Frankenstein* or seen the film; additionally, some readers might be familiar with the name Brandon Teena, either from news stories or from the 1999 film *Boys Don't Cry,* which is said to be based on Brandon Teena's life.

The recognizability of Halberstam's references is an important aspect of her work. She invites her readers to see differently something they may have seen before, something that seems familiar. So while, for example, a reader may have seen any number of performances, videos, or representations of Lady Gaga, Halberstam invites us to revise, or to see again, those seemingly familiar images. Her book *The Queer Art of Failure* asks readers to revisit and rethink some relatively popular films — such as *March of the Penguins, Chicken*

Run, and *Finding Nemo* — in order to critique common notions of success and failure, which, for Halberstam, are tied to normative constructions of sexuality and family.

In the introduction to *The Queer Art of Failure*, Halberstam describes her project in the book as one that "dismantles the logics of success and failure with which we currently live" (2). She offers us examples of several arenas in which success and failure are part of how we understand ourselves. We find models of success in education, in sports, in gender, in the idea that our lives have trajectories of norms that we must succeed at following. Halberstam suggests that perhaps failure is more desired, more productive than we thought, and she invites us, in an age of GPS technology and digital maps at our fingertips, to "get lost," to rewrite the narratives of our failure. *The Queer Art of Failure*, from which we take the chapter "Animating Revolt and Revolting Animation," asks a very provocative question: "We are all used to having our dreams crushed, our hopes smashed, our illusions shattered, but what comes after hope?" (1).

Animating Revolt and Revolting Animation

> The chickens are revolting!
> — Mr. Tweedy in *Chicken Run*

Animated films for children revel in the domain of failure. To captivate the child audience, an animated film cannot deal only in the realms of success and triumph and perfection. Childhood, as many queers in particular recall, is a long lesson in humility, awkwardness, limitation, and what Kathryn Bond Stockton has called "growing sideways." Stockton proposes that childhood is an essentially queer experience in a society that acknowledges through its extensive training programs for children that heterosexuality is not born but made. If we were all already normative and heterosexual to begin with in our desires, orientations, and modes of being, then presumably we would not need such strict parental guidance to deliver us all to our common destinies of marriage, child rearing, and hetero-reproduction. If you believe that children need training, you assume and allow for the fact that they are always already anarchic and rebellious, out of order and out of time. Animated films nowadays succeed, I think, to the extent to which they are able to address the disorderly child, the child who sees his or her family and parents as the problem, the child who knows there is a bigger world out there beyond the family, if only he or she could reach it. Animated films are for children who believe that "things" (toys, nonhuman animals, rocks, sponges) are as lively as humans and who can glimpse other worlds underlying and overwriting this one. Of course this notion of other worlds has long been a conceit of children's literature; the Narnia stories, for example, enchant the child reader by offering access to a new world through the back of the wardrobe. While much children's literature simply offers a new world too closely matched to the old one it left behind, recent animated films actually revel in innovation and make ample use of the wonderfully childish territory of revolt.

In the opening sequence in the classic claymation feature *Chicken Run* (2000, directed by Peter Lord and Nick Park), Mr. Tweedy, a bumbling farmer, informs his much more efficient wife that the chickens are "organized." Mrs. Tweedy dismisses his outrageous notion and tells him to focus more on profits, explaining to him that they are not getting enough out of their chickens and need to move on from egg harvesting to the chicken potpie industry. As Mrs. Tweedy ponders new modes of production, Mr. Tweedy keeps an eye on the chicken coop, scanning for signs of activity and escape. The scene is now set for a battle between production and labor, human and animal, management and employees, containment and

1. *Chicken Run*, directed by Peter Lord and Nick Park, 2000.
"The chickens are organized!"

escape. *Chicken Run* and other animated feature films draw much of their dramatic intensity from the struggle between human and nonhuman creatures. Most animated features are allegorical in form and adhere to a fairly formulaic narrative scheme. But as even this short scene indicates, the allegory and the formula do not simply line up with the conventional generic schemes of Hollywood cinema. Rather animation pits two groups against each other in settings that closely resemble what used to be called "class struggle," and they offer numerous scenarios of revolt and alternatives to the grim, mechanical, industrial cycles of production and consumption. In this first clip Mr. Tweedy's intuitive sense that the chickens on his farm "are organized" competes with Mrs. Tweedy's assertion that the only thing more stupid than chickens is Mr. Tweedy himself. His paranoid suspicions lose out to her exploitive zeal until the moment when the two finally agree that "the chickens are revolting."

What are we to make of this Marxist allegory in the form of a children's film, this animal farm narrative of resistance, revolt, and utopia pitted against new waves of industrialization and featuring claymation birds in the role of the revolutionary subject? How do neo-anarchistic narrative forms find their way into children's entertainment, and what do adult viewers make of them? More important, what does animation have to do with revolution? And how do revolutionary themes in animated film connect to queer notions of self?

I want to offer a thesis about a new genre of animated feature films that use CGI technology instead of standard linear animation techniques and that surprisingly foreground the themes of revolution and transformation. I call this genre "Pixarvolt" in order to link the technology to the thematic focus. In the new animation films certain topics that would never appear in adult-themed films are central to the success and emotional impact of these narratives. Furthermore, and perhaps even more surprisingly, the Pixarvolt films make subtle as well as overt connections between communitarian revolt and queer embodiment and thereby articulate, in ways that theory and popular narrative have not, the sometimes counterintuitive links between queerness and socialist struggle. While many Marxist scholars have characterized and dismissed queer politics as "body politics" or as simply superficial, these films recognize that alternative forms of embodiment and desire are central to the struggle against corporate domination. The queer is not represented as a singularity but as part of an assemblage of resistant technologies that include collectivity, imagination, and a kind of situationist commitment to surprise and shock.

Let's begin by asking some questions about the process of animation, its generic potential, and the ways the Pixarvolts imagine the human and the nonhuman and rethink embodiment and social relations. Beginning with *Toy Story* in 1995 (directed by John Lasseter), animation entered a new era. As is well known, *Toy Story*, the first Pixar film, was the first animation to be wholly generated by a computer; it changed animation from a two-dimensional set of images to a three-dimensional space within which point-of-view shots and perspective were rendered with startling liveness. Telling an archetypal story about a world of toys who awaken when the children are away, *Toy Story* managed to engage child audiences with the fantasy of live toys and adults with the nostalgic narrative of a cowboy, Woody, whose primacy in the toy kingdom is being challenged by a new model, the futuristic space doll Buzz Lightyear. While kids delighted in the spectacle of a toy box teeming with life, reminiscent of "Nutcracker Suite," adults were treated to a smart drama about toys that exploit their own *toyness* and other toys that do not realize they are not humans. The whole complex narrative about past and present, adult and child, live and machinic is a metacommentary on the set of narrative possibilities that this new wave of animation enables and exploits. It also seemed to establish the parameters of the new genre of CGI: *Toy Story* marks the genre as irrevocably male (the boy child and his relation to the prosthetic and phallic capabilities of his male toys), centered on the domestic (the playroom) and unchangeably Oedipal (always father-son dynamics as the motor or, in a few cases, a mother-daughter rivalry, as in Coraline). But the new wave of animated features is also deeply interested in social hierarchies (parent-child but also owner-owned), quite curious about the relations between an outside and an inside world (the real world and the world of the bedroom), and powered by a vigorous desire for revolution, transformation, and rebellion (toy versus child, toy versus toy, child versus adult, child versus child). Finally, like many of the films that followed, *Toy Story* betrays a high level of self-consciousness about its own relation to innovation, transformation, and tradition.

2. Toy Story, directed by John Lasseter, 1995.
"The first CGI Feature Film for Pixar."

Most of the CGI films that followed *Toy Story* map their dramatic territory in remarkably similar ways, and most retain certain key features (such as the Oedipal theme) while changing the mise-en-scène — from bedroom to seabed or barnyard, from toys to chickens or rats or fish or penguins, from the cycle of toy production to other industrial settings. Most remain entranced by the plot of captivity followed by dramatic escape and culminating in a utopian dream of freedom. A cynical critic might find this narrative to be a blueprint for the normative rites of passage in the human life cycle, showing the child viewer the journey from childhood captivity to adolescent escape and adult freedom. A more radical reading allows the narrative to be utopian, to tell of the real change that children may still believe is possible and desirable. The queer reading also refuses to allow the radical thematics of animated film to be dismissed as "childish" by questioning the temporal order that assigns dreams of transformation to pre-adulthood and that claims the accommodation of dysfunctional presents as part and parcel of normative adulthood.

How does *Chicken Run,* a film about "revolting chickens," imagine a utopian alternative? In a meeting in the chicken coop the lead chicken, Ginger, proposes to her sisterhood that there must be more to life than sitting around and producing eggs for the Tweedys or not producing eggs and ending up on the chopping block. She then outlines a utopian future in a green meadow (an image of which appears on an orange crate in the coop), where there are no farmers and no production schedule and no one is in charge. The future that Ginger outlines for her claymation friends relies very much on the utopian concept of escape as exodus, conjured variously by Paolo Virno in A *Grammar of the Multitude* and by Hardt and Negri in *Multitude,* but here escape is not the war camp model that most people project onto *Chicken Run*'s narrative. The film is indeed quoting *The Great Escape, Colditz, Stalag 17,* and other films whose setting is the Second World War, but war is not the mise-en-scène; rather, remarkably, the transition from feudalism to industrial capitalism frames a life-and-death story about rising up, flying the coop, and creating the conditions for escape from the materials already available. *Chicken Run* is different from *Toy Story* in that the Oedipal falls away as a point of reference in favor of a Gramscian structure of counterhegemony engineered by organic (chicken) intellectuals. In this film an anarchist's utopia is actually realized as a stateless place without a farmer, an unfenced territory with no owners, a diverse (sort of, they are mostly female) collective motivated by survival, pleasure, and the control of one's own labor. The chickens dream up and inhabit this utopian field, which we glimpse briefly at the film's conclusion, and they find their way there by eschewing a "natural" solution to their imprisonment (flying out of the coop using their wings) and engineering an ideological one (they must all pull together to power the plane they build). *Chicken Run* also rejects the individualistic solution offered by Rocky the Rooster (voiced by Mel Gibson) in favor of group logics. As for the queer element, well, they are chickens, and so, at least in *Chicken Run,* utopia is a green field full of female birds with just the occasional rooster strutting around. The revolution in this instance is feminist and animated.

PENGUIN LOVE

Building new worlds by accessing new forms of sociality through animals turns around the usual equation in literature that makes the animal an allegorical stand-in in a moral fable about human folly (*Animal Farm* by Orwell, for example). Most often we project human worlds onto the supposedly blank slate of animality, and then we create the animals we need in order to locate our own human behaviors in "nature" or "the wild" or "civilization." As the *Chicken Run* example shows, however, animated animals allow us to explore ideas about humanness, alterity, and alternative imaginaries in relation to new forms of representation.

But what is the status of the "animal" in animation? Animation, animal sociality, and biodiversity can be considered in relation to the notion of transbiology developed by Sarah Franklin and Donna Haraway. For Haraway, and for Franklin, the transbiological refers to the new conceptions of the self, the body, nature, and the human within waves of new technological advancement, such as cloning and cell regeneration. Franklin uses the history of Dolly the cloned sheep to explore the ways kinship, genealogy, and reproduction are remade, resituated by the birth and death of the cloned subject. She elaborates a transbiological field by building on Haraway's theorization of the cyborg in her infamous "Cyborg Manifesto," and she returns to earlier work by Haraway that concerned itself with biogenetic extensions of the body and of the experience of embodiment. Franklin explains, "I want to suggest that in the same way that the cyborg was useful to learn to see an altered landscape of the biological, the technical, and the informatic, similarly Haraway's 'kinding' semiotics of trans can help identify features of the postgenomic turn in the biosciences and biomedicine toward the idioms of immortalization, regeneration, and totipotency. However, by reversing Haraway's introduction of *trans-* as the exception or rogue element (as in the *transuranic* elements) I suggest that *transbiology* — a biology that is not only born and bred, or born and made, but *made and born* — is indeed today more the norm than the exception" (2006:171). The transbiological conjures hybrid entities or in-between states of being that represent subtle or even glaring shifts in our understanding of the body and of bodily transformation. The female cyborg, the transgenic mouse, the cloned sheep that Franklin researches, in which reproduction is "reassembled and rearranged," the Tamagotchi toys studied by Sherrie Turkle, and the new forms of animation I consider here, all question and shift the location, the terms, and the meanings of the artificial boundaries between humans, animals, machines, states of life and death, animation and reanimation, living, evolving, becoming, and transforming. They also refuse the idea of human exceptionalism and place the human firmly within a universe of multiple modes of being.

ANIMATED ANIMALS ALLOW US TO EXPLORE IDEAS ABOUT HUMANNESS.

Human exceptionalism comes in many forms. It might manifest as a simple belief in the uniqueness and centrality of humanness within a world shared with other kinds of life, but it might also show itself through gross and crude forms of anthropomorphism; in this case the human projects all of his or her uninspired and unexamined conceptions about life and living onto animals, who may actually foster far more creative or at least more surprising modes of living and sharing space. For example, in one of the most popular of the "Modern Love" columns — a popular weekly column in the *New York Times* dedicated to charting and narrating the strange fictions of contemporary desire and romance — titled "What Shamu Taught Me about a Happy Marriage," Amy Sutherland describes how she adapted animal training techniques that she learned at Sea World for use at home on her husband.[1] While the column purports to offer a location for the diverse musings of postmodern lovers on the peculiarities of modern love, it is actually a primer for adult heterosexuality. Occasionally a gay man or a lesbian will write about his or her normative liaison, its ups and downs, and will plea for the right to become "mature" through marriage, but mostly the column is dedicated to detailing, in mundane and banal intricacy, the roller-coaster ride of bourgeois heterosexuality and its supposed infinite variety and elasticity. The typical "Modern Love" essay will begin with a complaint, usually and predictably a female complaint about male implacability, but as we approach the end of the piece resolution will fall from the sky in the manner of a divine vision, and the disgruntled partner will quickly see that the very thing that she found irritating about her partner is also the very thing that makes him, well, him! That is, unique, flawed, human, and lovable.

Sutherland's essay is true to form. After complaints about her beloved husband's execrable domestic habits, she settles on a series of training techniques by placing him within a male taxonomy: "The exotic animal known as Scott is a loner, but an alpha male. So hierarchy matters, but being in a group doesn't so much. He has the balance of a gymnast, but moves slowly, especially when getting dressed. Skiing comes naturally, but being on time does not. He's an omnivore, and what a trainer would call food-driven." The resolution of the problem of Scott depends upon the hilarious scenario within which Sutherland brings her animal training techniques home and puts them to work on her recalcitrant mate. Using methods that are effective on exotic animals, she manages her husband with techniques ranging from a reward system for good behavior to a studied indifference to bad behavior. Amazingly the techniques work, and, what's more, she learns along the way that not only is she training her husband, but her husband, being not only adaptable and malleable but also intelligent and capable of learning, has started to use animal training techniques on her. Modern marriage, the essay concludes, in line with the "modern love" ideology, is an exercise in simultaneous evolution, each mate adjusting slightly to the quirks and foibles of the other, never blaming the structure, trying not to turn on each other, and ultimately triumphing by staying together no matter what the cost.

Amusing as Sutherland's essay may be, it is also a stunning example of how, as Laura Kipnis puts it in *Against Love,* we maneuver around "the large, festering contradictions at the epicenter of love in our time" (2004: 13). Kipnis argues that we tend to blame each other or ourselves for the failures of the social structures we inhabit, rather than critiquing the structures (like marriage) themselves. Indeed so committed are we to these cumbersome structures and so lazy are we about coming up with alternatives to them that we bolster our sense of the rightness of

WE TEND TO BLAME EACH OTHER OR OURSELVES FOR THE FAILURES OF THE SOCIAL STRUCTURES WE INHABIT, RATHER THAN CRITIQUING THE STRUCTURES (LIKE MARRIAGE) THEMSELVES.

hetero-normative coupledom by drawing on animal narratives in order to place ourselves back in some primal and "natural" world. Sutherland, for example, happily casts herself and Scott as exotic animals in a world of exotic animals and their trainers; of course the very idea of the exotic, as we know from all kinds of postcolonial theories of tourism and orientalism, depends upon an increasingly outdated notion of the domestic, the familiar, and the known, all of which come into being by positing a relation to the foreign, the alien, and the indecipherable. Not only does Sutherland domesticate the fabulous variation of the animals she is studying by making common cause with them, but she also exoticizes the all too banal setting of her own domestic dramas, and in the process she reimposes the boundary between human and nonhuman. Her humorous adaptation of animal husbandry into husband training might require a footnote now, given the death in 2010 of a Sea World trainer who was dragged into deep waters and drowned by the whale she had been training and working with for years. While Sutherland lavished her regard on the metaphor of gentle mutual training techniques, the death of the trainer reminds us of the violence that inheres in all attempts to alter the behavior of another being.

The essay as a whole contributes to the ongoing manic project of the renaturalization of heterosexuality and the stabilization of relations between men and women. And yet Sutherland's piece, humor and all, for all of its commitments to the human, remains in creative debt to the intellectually imaginative work of Donna Haraway in *Primate Visions.* Haraway reversed the relations of looking between primatologists and the animals they studied and argued that, first, the primates look back, and second, the stories we tell are much more about humans than about animals. She wrote, "Especially western people produce stories about primates while simultaneously telling stories about the relations of nature and culture, animal and human, body and mind, origin and future" (1990: 5). Similarly people who write the "Modern Love" column, these vernacular anthropologists of romance, produce stories about animals in order to locate heterosexuality in its supposedly natural setting. In Sutherland's essay the casting of women and men in the roles of trainers and animals also refers indirectly to Haraway's reconceptualization of the relationship between humans and dogs in her *Companion Species Manifesto: Dogs, People and Significant Otherness* (2003). While the earlier cyborg manifesto productively questioned the centrality of the notion of a soft and bodily, antitechnological "womanhood" to an idealized construction of the human, the later manifesto decentralizes the human altogether in its account of the relationship between dogs and humans — and refuses to accept the common wisdom about the dog-human relationship. For Haraway, the dog is not a representation of something about the human but an equal player in the drama of evolution and a site of "significant otherness." The problem with Haraway's vivid and original rewriting of the evolutionary process from the perspective of the dog is that it seems to reinvest in the idea of nature per se and leaves certain myths about evolution itself intact.

In fact Haraway herself seems to be invested in the "modern love" paradigm of seeing animals as either extensions of humans or their moral superiors. As Heidi J. Nast comments in a polemical call for "critical pet studies," a new disposition toward "pet love" has largely gone unnoticed in social theory and "where pet lives are addressed directly, most studies shun a critical international perspective, instead charting the cultural histories of pet-human relationships or, like Haraway, showing how true pet love might invoke a superior ethical stance" (2006: 896). Nast proposes that we examine the investments we are making in pets and in a pet industry in the twenty-first century and calls for a "scholarly geographical elaboration" of who owns pets, where they live, what kinds of affective and financial investments they have made in pet love, and who lies outside the orbit of pet love. She writes, "Those with no affinity for pets or those who are afraid of them are today deemed social or psychological misfits and cranks, while those who love them are situated as morally and even spiritually superior, such judgments having become hegemonic in the last two decades" (896). Like adults who choose not to reproduce, people with no interest in pets occupy a very specific spot in contemporary sexual hierarchies. In her anatomy of pet love Nast asks, "Why, for example, are women and queers such central purveyors of the language and institutions of pet love? And why are the most commodified forms of pet love and the most organized pets-rights movements emanating primarily out of elite (and in the U.S., Canada and Europe) 'white' contexts?" (898). Her account of pet love registers the need for new graphs and pyramids of sexual oppression and privilege, new models to replace the ones Gayle Rubin produced nearly two decades ago in "Thinking Sex" to complicate the relations between heterosexual privilege and gay oppression. In a postindustrial landscape where the size of white families has plummeted, where the nuclear family itself has become something of an anachronism, and where a majority of women live outside of conventional marriages, the elevation of pets to the status of love objects certainly demands attention. In a recent song by the radical rapper Common, he asks, "Why white folks focus on dogs and yoga? / While people on the low end tryin to ball and get over?" Why indeed? It's all for modern love.

While the relationship between sexuality and reproduction has never been much more than a theological fantasy, new technologies of reproduction and new rationales for nonreproductive behavior call for new languages of desire, embodiment, and the social relations between reproductive and nonreproductive bodies. At the very moment of its impending redundancy, some newly popular animal documentaries seek to map reproductive heterosexuality onto space; they particularly seek to "discover" it in nature by telling tales about awesomely creative animal societies. But a powerfully queer counterdiscourse in areas as diverse as evolutionary biology, avant-garde art productions, animated feature films, and horror

THE ELEVATION OF PETS TO THE STATUS OF LOVE OBJECTS CERTAINLY DEMANDS ATTENTION.

films unwrites resistant strains of heterosexuality and recasts them in an improbably but persistently queer universe.

So let's turn to a popular text about the spectacular strangeness of animals to see how documentary-style features tend to humanize animal life. While animal documentaries use voice-overs and invisible cameras to try to provide a God's-eye view of "nature" and to explain every type of animal behavior in ways that reduce animals to human-like creatures, we might think of animation as a way of maintaining the animality of animal social worlds. I will return to the question of animation later in the chapter, but here I want to discuss *The March of the Penguins* (2005) as an egregious form of anthropomorphism on the one hand and the source of alternative forms of family, parenting, and sociality on the other.

In his absorbing documentary about the astonishing life cycle of Antarctica's emperor penguins, Luc Jacquet framed the spectacle of the penguins' long and brutal journey to their ancestral breeding grounds as a story about love, survival, resilience, determination, and the hetero-reproductive family unit. Emperor penguins, for those who missed the film (or the Christian Right's perverse readings of it), are the only remaining inhabitants of a particularly brutal Antarctic landscape that was once covered in verdant forests but is now a bleak and icy wilderness. Due to global warming, however, the ice is melting, and the survival of the penguins depends on a long trek that they must make once a year, in March, from the ocean to a plateau seventy miles inland, where the ice is thick and fast enough to support them through their breeding cycle. The journey out to the breeding grounds is awkward for the penguins, which swim much faster than they waddle, and yet the trek is only the first leg of a punishing shuttle they will make in the next few months, back and forth between the inland nesting area and the ocean, where they feed. This may not sound like a riveting narrative, but the film was a huge success around the world.

The film's success depends upon several factors: first, it plays to a basic human curiosity about how and why the penguins undertake such a brutal circuit; second, it provides intimate footage of these animals that seems almost magical given the unforgiving landscape and that has a titillating effect given the access the director provides to these creatures; and third, it cements the visual and the natural with a sticky and sentimental voice-over (provided by Morgan Freeman in the version released in the U.S.) about the transcendence of love and the power of family that supposedly motivate the penguins to pursue reproduction in such inhospitable conditions. Despite the astonishing footage, the glorious beauty of the setting and of the birds themselves, *The March of the Penguins* ultimately trains its attention on only a fraction of the story of penguin communities because its gaze remains so obstinately trained upon the comforting spectacle of "the couple," "the family unit," "love," "loss," heterosexual reproduction, and the emotional architecture that supposedly welds all these moving parts together. However, the focus on heterosexual reproduction is misleading and mistaken, and ultimately it blots out a far more compelling story about cooperation, collectivity, and nonheterosexual, nonreproductive behaviors.

Several skeptical critics remarked that, amazing as the story might be, this was not evidence of romantic love among penguins, and "love" was targeted as the most telling symptom of the film's annoying anthropomorphism.[2] But heterosexual reproduction, the most insistent framing device in the film, is never questioned either by the filmmakers or the critics. Indeed Christian fundamentalists promoted the film as a moving text about monogamy, sacrifice, and child rearing. And this despite the fact that the penguins are monogamous for only one year, and that they promptly abandon all responsibility for their offspring once the small penguins have survived the first few months of arctic life. While conventional animal documentaries like *The March of the Penguins* continue to insist on the heterosexuality of nature, the evolutionary biologist Joan Roughgarden insists that we examine nature anew for evidence of the odd and nonreproductive and nonheterosexual and non-gender-stable phenomena that characterize most animal life. Roughgarden's wonderful study of evolutionary diversity, *Evolution's Rainbow* (2004), explains that most biologists observe "nature" through a narrow and biased lens of socionormativity and therefore misinterpret all kinds of biodiversity. And so, although transsexual fish, hermaphroditic hyenas, nonmonogamous birds, and homosexual lizards all play a role in the survival and evolution of the species, their function has been mostly misunderstood and folded into rigid and unimaginative hetero-familial schemes of reproductive zeal and the survival of the fittest. Roughgarden explains that human observers misread (capitalist) competition into (nonmonetary) cooperative animal societies and activities; they also misunderstand the relations between strength and dominance and overestimate the primacy of reproductive dynamics.

In an essay in the *New York Times* magazine published in 2010 humorously titled "The Love That Dare Not Squawk Its Name," Jon Mooallem asks, "Can animals be gay?"[3] Using the example of mating pairs of albatrosses who were assumed to be paired up in male-female configurations but actually were mostly female-female bonded pairs, Mooallem interviews some biologists about the phenomenon. Noting that the biologists Marlene Zuk and Lindsay C. Young assiduously avoid using anthropomorphizing language about the birds they study, Mooallem reports that when Young did slip up and call the colony of albatrosses "the largest proportion of—I don't know what the correct term is: 'homosexual animals'?—in the world," the media response was massive. Young found herself in the middle of a national debate about whether homosexuality among animals proved the rightness and naturalness of gay and lesbian proclivities among humans! Predictably North American Christians were outraged that this is the research their "tax dollars" were funding. Other media found the story irresistible; on Comedy Central, for example, Stephen Colbert warned that "albatresbians were threatening American family values with a Sappho-avian agenda"!

The more interesting story in this essay, however — more interesting than the discussion of what to call same-sex animal couples, that is — concerns the blind spots of animal researchers themselves. Mooallem rightly notes that researchers constantly provide alibis and excuses for the same-sex sexual behavior they observe, but he also discovers that most researchers do not actually know the sex of the animal they are observing, and so they infer sex based on behavior and relational sets. This has led to all kinds of misreporting on heterosexual courtship because the sex of the creatures in question is not actually scrutinized, and mixed-sex couples, as with the albatrosses and certainly with penguins, very often end up being same-sex couples. In the case of the albatrosses, researchers thought they were finding evidence of a "super-normal clutch" when they found two eggs in a nest rather than one; it never occurred to them that the two birds incubating the eggs were both female and each had an egg. The narrative of male superfertility was more comforting and appealing. Thus intuitive evidence that contradicts the contorted narratives that scientists put together is ignored because heterosexuality is the "human" lens through which all animal behavior is studied.

How should we think about so-called homosexual behavior among animals? Well, as the *New York Times* essay suggests by way of Joan Roughgarden, anything that falls outside of heterosexual behavior is not necessarily homosexual, and anything that conforms to human understandings of heterosexual behavior may not be heterosexual. In fact Roughgarden prefers to think about animals as creatures who may "multitask" with their private parts: some of what we call sexual contact between animals may be basic communication, some of the behavior may be adaptive, some survival-oriented, some reproductive, much of it improvised.

Which brings us back to the penguins and their long march into the snowy, icy, and devastating landscape of Antarctica. It is easy, especially given the voice-over, to see the penguin world as made up of little heroic families striving to complete their natural and pregiven need to reproduce. The voice-over provides a beautiful but nonsensical narrative that remains resolutely human and refuses to ever see the "penguin logics" that structure their frigid quest. When the penguins mass on the ice to find partners, we are asked to see a school prom with rejected and spurned partners on the edges of the dance floor and true romance and soul mates in its center. When the mating rituals begin, we are told of elegant and balletic dances, though we see awkward, difficult, and undignified couplings. When the female penguin finally produces the valuable egg and must now pass the egg from her feet to the male's feet in order to free herself to go and feed, the voice-over reaches hysteria

WHEN THE PENGUINS MASS ON THE ICE TO FIND PARTNERS, WE ARE ASKED TO SEE A SCHOOL PROM WITH REJECTED AND SPURNED PARTNERS ON THE EDGES OF THE DANCE FLOOR AND TRUE ROMANCE AND SOUL MATES IN ITS CENTER.

pitch and sees sorrow and heartbreak in every unsuccessful transfer. We are never told how many penguins are successful in passing their egg, how many might decide not to be successful in order to save themselves the effort of a hard winter, how much of the transfer ritual might be accidental, and so on. The narrative ascribes stigma and envy to nonreproductive penguins, sacrifice and a Protestant work ethic to the reproducers, and sees a capitalist hetero-reproductive family rather than the larger group.

Ultimately the voice-over and the Christian attribution of "intelligent design" to the penguins' activity must ignore many inconvenient facts. The penguins are not monogamous; they mate for one year and then move on. The partners find each other after returning from feeding by recognizing each other's call, not by some innate and mysterious coupling instinct. Perhaps most important, the nonreproductive penguins are not merely extras in the drama of hetero-reproduction; in fact the homo or nonrepro queer penguins are totally necessary to the temporary reproductive unit. They provide warmth in the huddle and probably extra food, and they do not leave for warmer climes but accept a part in the penguin collective in order to enable reproduction and to survive. Survival in this penguin world has little to do with fitness and everything to do with collective will. And once the reproductive cycle draws to a close, what happens then? The parent penguins do protect their young in terms of warmth, but the parents do nothing to stave off attacks by aerial predators; there the young penguins are on their own. And once the baby penguins reach the age when they too can take to the water, the parent penguins slip gratefully into another element with not even a backward glance to see if the next generation follows. The young penguins now have five years of freedom, five glorious, nonreproductive, family-free years before they too must undertake the long march. The long march of the penguins is proof neither of heterosexuality in nature nor of the reproductive imperative not of intelligent design. It is a resolutely animal narrative about cooperation, affiliation, and the anachronism of the homo-hetero divide. The indifference in the film to all nonreproductive behaviors obscures the more complex narratives of penguin life: we learn in the first five minutes of the film that female penguins far outnumber their male counterparts, and yet repercussions of this gender ratio are never explored; we see with our own eyes that only a few of the penguins continue to carry eggs through the winter, but the film provides no narrative at all for the birds who don't carry eggs; we can presume that all kinds of odd and adaptive behaviors take place in order to enhance the penguins' chances for survival (for example, the adoption of orphaned penguins), but the film tells us nothing about this. In fact while the visual narrative reveals a wild world of nonhuman kinship and affiliation, the voice-over relegates this world to the realm of the unimaginable and unnatural.

The March of the Penguins has created a whole genre of penguin animation, beginning with Warner Brothers' *Happy Feet* in 2006, soon followed by Sony Pictures' *Surf's Up* and Bob Saget's animated spoof *The*

Farce of the Penguins for Thinkfilms. The primary appeal of the penguins, based on the success of *Happy Feet* anyway, seems to be the heart-rending narratives of family and survival that contemporary viewers are projecting onto the austere images of these odd birds. On account of the voice-over, however, we could say that *The March of the Penguins* is already animated, already an animated feature film, and in fact in the French and German versions the penguins are given individual voices rather than narrated by a "voice of god" trick. Here the animation works not to emphasize the difference between humans and nonhumans, as it does in so many Pixar features, but instead makes the penguins into virtual puppets for the drama of human, modern love that cinema is so eager to tell.

QUEER CREATURES, MONSTROUS ANIMATION

May the best monster win!
— Sully in *Monsters, Inc.*

Pixarvolt films often link the animals to new forms of being and offer us different ways of thinking about being, relation, reproduction, and ideology. The animation lab grows odd human-like creatures and reimagines the human not as animal but as animation — as a set of selves that must appeal to human modes of identification not through simple visual tricks of recognition but through voice cues and facial expressions and actions.

3. *Monsters, Inc.,* directed by Pete Doctor and David Silverman, 2001. "May the best monster win!"

Gromit, in *Wallace and Gromit,* for example, has no mouth and does not speak, yet he conveys infinite reservoirs of resourcefulness and intelligence in his eyes and in the smallest movements of his eyes within his face (which A.O. Scott in the *New York Times* compares to the face of Garbo). Dory, *in Finding Nemo,* has no memory but represents a kind of eccentric form of knowing which allows her to swim circles around the rather tame and conservative Marlin. How do modes of identification with animated creatures work? Does the child viewer actually feel a kinship with the ahistorical Dory and the speechless Gromit and with the repetition that characterizes all of the narratives? Why do spectators (conservative parents, for instance) endorse these queer and monstrous narratives despite their radical messages, and how does the whimsical nature of the animated world allow for the smuggling of radical narratives into otherwise clichéd interactions about friendship, loyalty, and family values?

THE ANIMATION LAB GROWS ODD HUMAN-LIKE CREATURES AND REIMAGINES THE HUMAN NOT AS ANIMAL BUT AS ANIMATION.

As we saw with *Toy Story,* the Pixarvolt films often proceed by way of fairly conventional narratives about individual struggle against the automated process of innovation, and they often pit an individual, independent, and original character against the conformist sensibilities of the masses. But this summary is somewhat misleading, because more often than not the individual character actually serves as a gateway to intricate stories of collective action, anticapitalist critique, group bonding, and alternative imaginings of community, space, embodiment, and responsibility. Often the animal or creature that stands apart from the community is not a heroic individual but a symbol of selfishness who must be taught how to think collectively. For example, in *Over the Hedge* (2006, directed by Tim Johnson) by DreamWorks the film stages a dramatic standoff between some woodland creatures and their new junk-food-consuming, pollution-spewing, SUV-driving, trash-producing, water-wasting, anti-environmentalist human neighbors. When the creatures awake from their winter hibernation they discover that while they were sleeping, a soulless suburban development stole their woodland space and the humans have erected a huge partition, a hedge, to fence them out. At first it seems as if the narrative will be motored by our interest in a plucky raccoon called RJ, but ultimately RJ must join forces with the other creatures — squirrels, porcupines, skunks, turtles, and bears — in a cross-species alliance to destroy the colonizers, tear down the partition, and upend the suburbanites' depiction of them as "vermin." Similarly in *Finding Nemo* the most valuable lesson that Nemo learns is not to "be himself" or "follow his dreams," but, more like Ginger in *Chicken Run,* he learns to think with others and to work for a more collective futurity. *In Monsters, Inc.* (directed by Pete Doctor and David Silverman, 2001) monsters hired to scare children find an affinity with them that wins out over a corporate alliance with the adults who run the scream factory.

Fairy tales have always occupied the ambiguous territory between childhood and adulthood, home and away, harm and safety. They also tend to be as populated by monsters as by "normal" or even ideal people; in fact the relations between monsters and princesses, dragons and knights, scary creatures and human saviors open doors to alternative worlds and allow children to confront archetypal fears, engage in prepubescent fantasy, and indulge infantile desires about being scared, eaten, chased, and demolished. *Monsters, Inc.* makes monstrosity into a commodity and imagines what happens when the child victim of monstrous bogeymen speaks back to her demons and in the process both scares them and creates bonds of affection, affiliation, identification, and desire between her and the monsters. This bond between child and monster, as we know from looking at other texts, is unusual because it allows for the crossing of the divide between the fantasy world and the human world, but also because it imagines a girl child as the vehicle for the transgression of boundaries. The human-monster bond is queer in its reorganization of family and affinity and in the way it interrupts and disrupts more conventional romantic bonds in the film.

THE HUMAN-MONSTER BOND IS QUEER IN ITS REORGANIZATION OF FAMILY AND AFFINITY AND IN THE WAY IT INTERRUPTS AND DISRUPTS MORE CONVENTIONAL ROMANTIC BONDS IN THE FILM.

The antihumanist discourse in Pixarvolts is confirmed by the black-and-white depiction of actual humans in these films. We see the humans only through the eyes of the animated creatures, and in *Over the Hedge, Finding Nemo,* and *Chicken Run* they look empty, lifeless, and inert—in fact, unanimated. The Pixarvolt genre makes animation itself into a feature of kinetic political action rather than just an elaborate form of puppetry. The human and nonhuman are featured as animated and unanimated but also as constructed and unreconstructed. In a telling moment

4. *Over the Hedge*, directed by Tim Johnson, 2006. "Collective thinking."

5. *Robots,* directed by Chris Wedge, 2005. "Making babies!"

in *Robots* (2005, directed by Chris Wedge), for example, a male robot announces to the world that he will soon be a father. What follows is a fascinating origin story that locates construction at the heart of the animated self. When he gets home, his wife informs him that he has "missed the delivery," and the camera pans to an unopened box of baby robot parts. The mother and father then begin to assemble their child using both the new parts and some salvaged parts (a grandfather's eyes, for example). The labor of producing the baby is queer in that it is shared and improvised, of culture rather than nature, an act of construction rather than reproduction. In a final hilarious note of punctuation, the mother robot asks the father robot what he thinks the "spare part" that came with the kit might be. The father responds, "We did want a boy, didn't we?" and proceeds to hammer the phallus into place. Like some parody of social construction, this children's film imagines embodiment as an assemblage of parts and sees some as optional, some as interchangeable; indeed later in the film the little boy robot wears some of his sister's clothes.

An animated self allows for the deconstruction of ideas of a timeless and natural humanity. The idea of the human does tend to return in some form or another over the course of the animated film, usually as a desire for uniqueness, or an unalienated relation to work and to others, or as a fantasy of liberty, but the notion of a robotic and engineered self takes the animated feature well into the genealogical territory of Harawayesque cyborgs. In *Robots* the cyborgean metaphor is extended into a fabulous political allegory of recycling and transformation. When a big corporation, powered by a nefarious Oedipal triangle of a dominant mother, a wicked son, and an ineffectual father (a common triangle in both fairy tales and animated features), tries to phase out some robots in order to introduce new models, Rodney Coppertop goes to the big city to argue that older models are salvageable and transformable. While Rodney is also part of an Oedipal triangle (good mother, courageous son, expiring father), he becomes powerful, like Nemo, only when he abandons the family and makes common cause with a larger collectivity. This notion of the assembled self and its relation to an ever-shifting and improvised multitude ultimately rests upon and recirculates an antihumanist understanding of sociality.

Not all animated films manage to resist the lure of humanism, and so not all animated films fit comfortably into what I am calling the Pixarvolt genre. What separates the Pixarvolt from the merely pixilated? One answer turns upon the difference between collective revolutionary selves and a more conventional notion of a fully realized individuality. The non-Pixarvolt animated features prefer family to collectivity, human individuality to social bonding, extraordinary individuals to diverse communities. For example, *The Incredibles* builds its story around the supposedly heroic drama of male midlife crisis and invests in an Ayn Randian or scientologist notion of the special people who must resist social pressures to suppress their superpowers in order to fit in with the drab masses. *Happy Feet* similarly casts its lot with individualism and makes a heroic figure out of the dancing penguin who cannot fit in his community . . . at first. Eventually of course the community expands to incorporate him, but sadly they learn valuable lessons along the way about the importance of every single one of the rather uniform penguins learning to "be themselves." Of course if the penguins really were being themselves, that is, penguins, they would not be singing Earth, Wind & Fire songs in black-face, as they do in the movie, and searching for soul mates; they would be making odd squawking noises and settling down for one year with one mate and then moving on.

OF COURSE IF THE PENGUINS REALLY WERE BEING THEMSELVES, THAT IS, PENGUINS, THEY WOULD NOT BE SINGING EARTH, WIND & FIRE SONGS IN BLACK-FACE, AS THEY DO IN THE MOVIE, AND SEARCHING FOR SOUL MATES; THEY WOULD BE MAKING ODD SQUAWKING NOISES AND SETTLING DOWN FOR ONE YEAR WITH ONE MATE AND THEN MOVING ON.

In *Over the Hedge, Robots, Finding Nemo,* and other Pixarvolts desire for difference is not connected to a neoliberal "Be yourself" mentality or to special individualism for "incredible" people; rather the Pixarvolt films connect individualism to selfishness, to untrammeled consumption, and they oppose it with a collective mentality. Two thematics can transform a potential Pixarvolt film into a tame and conventional cartoon: an overemphasis on nuclear *family* and a normative investment in coupled *romance*. The Pixarvolt films, unlike their unrevolting conventional animation counterparts, seem to know that their main audience is children, and they seem to also know that children do not invest in the same things that adults invest in: children are not coupled, they are not romantic, they do not have a religious morality, they are not afraid of death or failure, they are collective creatures, they are in a constant state of rebellion against their parents, and they are not the masters of their domain. Children stumble, bumble, fail, fall, hurt; they are mired in difference, not in control of their bodies, not in charge of their lives, and they live according to schedules not of their own making. The Pixarvolt films offer an animated world of triumph for the little guys, a revolution against the business world of the father and the domestic sphere of the mother—in fact very often the mother is simply dead and the father is enfeebled (as in *Robots, Monsters, Inc., Finding Nemo,* and *Over the Hedge*). Gender in these films is shifty and ambiguous (transsexual fish in *Finding Nemo,* other-species-identified pig in *Babe*); sexualities are amorphous and polymorphous (the homoerotics of SpongeBob's and Patrick's relationship and of Wallace's and Gromit's domesticity); class is clearly marked in terms of labor and species diversity; bodily ability is quite often at issue (Nemo's small fin, Shrek's giganticism); and only race falls all too often in familiar and stereotyped patterns of characterization (the overly sexual "African American" skunk in *Over the Hedge,* the "African American" donkey in Shrek). I believe that despite the inability of these films to reimagine race, the Pixarvolt features have animated a new space for the imagining of alternatives.

As Sianne Ngai comments in an excellent chapter on race and "animatedness" in her book *Ugly Feelings,* "animatedness" is an ambivalent mode of representation, especially when it comes to race, because it reveals the ideological conditions of "speech" and ventriloquism but it also threatens to reassert grotesque stereotypes by fixing on caricature and excess in its attempts to make its nonhuman subjects come alive. Ngai grapples with the contradictions in the TV animated series *The PJ's,* a "formation" production featuring Eddie Murphy and focusing on a black, non-middle-class community. In her meticulous analysis of the show's genesis, genealogy, and reception, Ngai describes the array of responses the puppets provoked, many of them negative and many focused on the ugliness of the puppetry and the racial caricatures that the critics felt the show revived. Ngai responds to the charge of the ugliness of the images by arguing that the show actually "introduced a new possibility for racial representation in the medium of television: one that ambitiously sought to reclaim the grotesque and/or ugly, as a powerful aesthetic of exaggeration, crudeness, and distortion" (2005: 105). She examines *The PJ's* scathing social critique and its intertextual web of references to black popular culture in relation to its technology, the stop-motion process, which, she claims, exploits the relationship between rigidity and elasticity both literally and figuratively: "*The PJ's* reminds us that there can be ways of inhabiting a social role that actually distort its boundaries, changing the status of 'role' from that which purely confines or constricts to the site at which new possibilities for human agency might be explored" (117). Obviously *Happy Feet* does not exploit the tension between rigidity and elasticity in the same ways that *The PJ's* does in Ngai's reading of the show.

The Pixarvolt films show how important it is to recognize the weirdness of bodies, sexualities, and genders in other animal life worlds, not to mention other animated universes. The fish in *Finding Nemo* and the

6. *Bee Movie*, directed by Steve Hickner and Simon J. Smith, 2007.
"Drones and queens"

chickens in *Chicken Run* actually manage to produce new meanings of male and female; in the former, Marlin is a parent but not a father, for example, and in the latter, Ginger is a romantic but not willing to sacrifice politics for romance. The all-female society of chickens allows for unforeseen feminist implications to this utopian fantasy. *Chicken Run,* however, is one of the few animated films to exploit its animal world symbolics. Other features about ants and bees, also all-female worlds, fall short when using these social insect worlds to tell human stories.

Take the Pixar production *Bee Movie* (2007, directed by Steve Hickner and Simon J. Smith), starring Jerry Seinfeld. The film certainly lives up to our expectations of finding narratives about collective resistance to capitalist exploitation. Even as liberal a critic as Roger Ebert noticed that *Bee Movie* contains some rather odd Marxist elements. He writes in his review of the film, "What Barry [the bee voiced by Seinfeld] mostly discovers from human society is, gasp!, that humans rob the bees of all their honey and eat it. He and Adam, his best pal, even visit a bee farm, which looks like forced labor of the worst sort. Their instant analysis of the human-bee economic relationship is pure Marxism, if only they knew it." And indeed it is: Barry is not satisfied with working in the hive doing the same thing everyday, and so he decides to become a pollinator instead of a worker bee. But when he explores the outside world he finds out that all the labor in his hive is for naught, given that the honey the bees are making is being harvested, packaged, and sold by humans. Taking a very non-Marxist approach to remedying this exploitive situation, Barry sues humankind and along the way romances and befriends a human. Now while the romance between Barry and the human could have produced a fascinating trans-biological scenario of interspecies sex, instead it just becomes a vehicle for the heterosexualization of the homoerotic hive.

While it unintentionally skirts communist critiques of work, profit, and the alienation of the labor force, *Bee Movie* forcefully and deliberately replaces the queerly gendered nature of the hive with a masculinist plot about macho pollinators, dogged male workers, and domestic female home keepers. But as Natalie Angier points out in the science section of the *New York Times:*

> By bowdlerizing the basic complexion of a great insect society, Mr. Seinfeld's "Bee Movie" follows in the well-pheromoned path of Woody Allen as a whiny worker ant in *Antz* and Dave Foley playing a klutzy forager ant in *A Bug's Life*. Maybe it's silly to fault cartoons for biological inaccuracies when the insects are already talking like Chris Rock and wearing Phyllis Diller hats. But isn't it bad enough that in Hollywood's animated family fare about rats, clownfish, penguins, lions, hyenas and other relatively large animals, the overwhelming majority of characters are male, despite nature's preferred sex ratio of roughly 50-50? Must even obligately female creatures like worker bees and soldier ants be given sex change surgery, too? Besides, there's no need to go with the faux: the life of an authentic male social insect is thrilling, poignant and cartoonish enough.[4]

She goes on to detail the absurd life cycle of the male drone, noting that only .05 percent of the hive is male:

> The male honeybee's form bespeaks his sole function. He has large eyes to help find queens and extra antenna segments to help smell queens, but he is otherwise ill equipped to survive. On reaching adulthood, he must linger in the hive for a few days until his exoskeleton dries and his wing muscles mature, all the while begging food from his sisters and thus living up to his tainted name, drone. . . . After a male deposits sperm in the queen, his little "endophallus" snaps off, and he falls to the ground. In her single nuptial flight, the queen will collect and store in her body the sperm offerings of some 20 doomed males, more than enough to fertilize a long life's worth of eggs.

Angier concludes dramatically, "A successful male is a dead male, a failure staggers home and begs to be fed and to try again tomorrow." Sounding more like a Valerie Solanas handbook for social change than a popular science meditation on insect life, Angier's essay captures the essentially strange variations of gender, sex, labor, and pleasure in other animal life worlds, variations that often appear in Pixarvolt animation but are skirted in other, less revolting films like *Bee Movie.*

I want to conclude this chapter by turning back to the queerness of the bees and the potential queerness of all allegorical narratives of animal sociality and by advocating for "creative anthropomorphism" over and against endless narratives of human exceptionalism that deploy ordinary and banal forms of anthropomorphism when much more creative versions would lead us in unexpected directions. Hardt's and Negri's notion of the swarm in *Multitude* (2005), like Linebaugh's and Rediker's model of the hydra in *Many-Headed Hydra* (2001), imagines oppositional groups in terms of real or fantasized beasts that rise up to subvert the singularity of the human with the multiplicity of the unruly mob. In practicing creative anthropomorphism we invent the models of resistance we need and lack in reference to other lifeworlds, animal and monstrous. Bees, as many political commentators over the years have noted, signify a model for collective behavior (Preston 2005), the social animal par excellence. A common proverb posits, *Ulla apis, nulla apis,* "One bee is no bee," marking the essentially "political" and "collective" identity of the bee. Bees have long been used to signify political community; they have been represented as examples of the benevolence of state power (Vergil), the power of the monarchy (Shakespeare), the effectiveness of a Protestant work ethic, the orderliness of government, and more (Preston 2005). But bees have also represented the menacing power of the mob, the buzzing beast of anarchism, the mindless conformity of fascism, the organized and soulless labor structures proposed by communism, and the potential ruthlessness of matriarchal power (the ejection of the male drones by the female worker bees). Most recently the bees have served as an analogy for the kinds of movements that oppose global capitalism. Using the analogy of bees or ants, Hardt and Negri combine organic with inorganic to come up with a "networked swarm" of resistance that the system of a "sovereign state of security" contends with. The swarm presents as a mass rather than a unitary enemy and offers no obvious target; thinking as a single superorganism, the swarm is elusive, ephemeral, in flight. Like ants, the bee, a social animal, offers a highly sophisticated, multifunctional model of political life. In movies, too, the bees have been cast as friend and foe, and in some fabulations the bee is Africanized and aggressive (*Deadly Swarm,* directed by Paul Andresen 2003), communist and swarming (*The Swarm,* 1978, directed by Irwin Allen), intelligent and deadly (*The Bees,* 1978, directed by Alfredo Zacharias); bees as ecoterrorists attack humans and swarm in the UN building in New York until defused by a human-made virus that makes them homosexual, female, and dangerous (*Queen Bee,* 1955, directed by Ranald Macdougall and starring Joan Crawford). In *Invasion of the Bee Girls* (1973, directed by Denis Sanders) apian women kill men after sex. Above all, the bee is female and queer and given to the production not of babies but of an addictive nectar, honey. The transbiological element here has to do with the alternative meanings of gender when biology is not in the service of reproduction and patriarchy.

The dream of an alternative way of being is often confused with utopian thinking and then dismissed as naïve, simplistic, or a blatant misunderstanding of the nature of power in modernity. And yet the possibility of other forms of being, other forms of knowing, a world with different sites for justice and injustice, a mode of being where the emphasis falls less on money and work and competition and more on cooperation, trade, and sharing animates all kinds of knowledge projects and should not be dismissed as irrelevant or naïve. In *Monsters, Inc.,* for example,

THE DREAM OF AN ALTERNATIVE WAY OF BEING IS OFTEN CONFUSED WITH UTOPIAN THINKING AND THEN DISMISSED AS NAÏVE, SIMPLISTIC, OR A BLATANT MISUNDERSTANDING OF THE NATURE OF POWER IN MODERNITY.

fear generates revenue for corporate barons, and the screams of children actually power the city of Monstropolis. The film offers a kind of prophetic vision of post-9/11 life in the U.S., where the production of monsters allows the governing elites to scare a population into quietude while generating profits for their own dastardly schemes. This direct link between fear and profit is more pointed in this children's feature than in most adult films produced in the era of postmodern anxiety. Again, a cynical reading of the world of animation will always return to the notion that difficult topics are raised and contained in children's films precisely so that they do not have to be discussed elsewhere and also so that the politics of rebellion can be cast as immature, pre-Oedipal, childish, foolish, fantastical, and rooted in a commitment to failure. But a more dynamic and radical engagement with animation understands that the rebellion is ongoing and that the new technologies of children's fantasy do much more than produce revolting animation. They also offer us the real and compelling possibility of animating revolt.

NOTES

[1] Amy Sutherland, "What Shamu Taught Me about a Happy Marriage," *New York Times*, 25 June 2006, Style section.

[2] See, for example, Roger Ebert, "March of the Penguins," *Chicago Sun-Times*, 8 July 2005; Stephen Holden, "The Lives and Loves (Perhaps) of Emperor Penguins," *New York Times*, 24 June 2005. Holden writes, "Although 'March of the Penguins' stops mercifully short of trying to make us identify with the hardships overcome by a single penguin family, it conveys an intimate sense of the life of the emperor penguin. But love? I don't think so."

[3] Jon Mooallem, "The Love That Dare Not Squawk Its Name: Can Animals Be Gay," *New York Times*, 31 March 2010, Magazine section.

[4] Natalie Angier, "In Hollywood Hives, the Males Rule," *New York Times*, 13 November 2007, Science section.

QUESTIONS FOR A SECOND READING

1. Although Halberstam makes references to films, words, and ideas that are likely familiar to you, other words or names may seem strikingly unfamiliar, even strange. In the spirit of failure, choose a term, a reference, or a name from the reading that you did not understand or that was unfamiliar. Then, using a digital search, find out as much as you possibly can about that term or reference.

   As you read about the term, think about why you have not heard it before. Why might this term or reference have been out of your line of sight or experience? How does knowing more about it help inform your reading of Halberstam? In other words, what can this term or reference illuminate about the reading that you might not have seen before knowing more?

2. Choose one of the films Halberstam mentions in this chapter. Make a list of all the ideas Halberstam has about this particular film. This might be a film you have never seen, or one you have seen before. Watch the film. You might even find a group of classmates who are interested in watching the film with you.

As you watch the film, keep the list you made in mind. What can Halberstam help you to notice about the film? How do you see her ideas play out in parts of the film she does not discuss? Are there any moments in the film that seem to trouble or complicate her arguments? After looking at the film more closely, what do you have to say to Halberstam?

3. Halberstam is writing in a discipline called "Queer Theory." You might not have heard that term before or be familiar with this particular discipline, though many colleges and universities have courses with this title. As you reread Halberstam, pay attention to the word "queer" when she uses it.

   From reading the chapter, what can you tell about this word? How does Halberstam use it, or what do you think she means when she says it? Keep in mind that she might not always mean the same thing each time. How does her understanding of the word invite you to revisit your own understanding or prior experience of the word?

4. Halberstam asks the following: "Why do spectators (conservative parents, for instance) endorse these queer and monstrous narratives despite their radical messages, and how does the whimsical nature of the animated world allow for the smuggling of radical narratives into otherwise clichéd interactions about friendship, loyalty, and family values?" (p. 285)

   How would you answer this question? What answer does she provide? What do you think Halberstam means by "radical narratives"? Why "queer"? Why "monstrous"? And what might these narratives have to do with clichés?

ASSIGNMENTS FOR WRITING

1. Part of the intellectual work Halberstam is doing in this piece is taking a film we might recognize as familiar (films like *Finding Nemo* or *March of the Penguins*) and inviting us to see something new about that familiar film. Think about an animated film you've seen recently. Watch this film again with Halberstam's writing in mind. Then, write an essay in which you consider the film's potential for what Halberstam calls "animating revolt."

   To begin your essay, you may have to explain to your reader what Halberstam means by "animating revolt," which is one half of her title for this piece of writing. To write an essay that takes up Halberstam's method of looking, you'll want to ask yourself: What would Halberstam notice about this film? What passages from her essay would guide someone to read this film in a particular way? How does the film illuminate, complicate, or extend Halberstam's central questions?

2. Halberstam covers quite a lot of ground in this short piece, and her arguments are grounded in ideas and assumptions about many subjects, not just the films she discusses. One might say that her essay is about science, or

children, or family, or animals. Write an essay discussing one of these other subjects you find in the essay. If "Animating Revolt and Revolting Animation" is also about one of these subjects (for example, children), then what does the essay assume or say about children? Why might it be important to notice this other aspect of Halberstam's work? What can it tell us about her central questions or arguments? You might begin by gathering a set of three or four passages from Halberstam's work where she mentions this other subject you want to discuss.

3. Halberstam seems interested in what she calls "multiple modes of being" and, as she says, "the possibility of other forms of being, other forms of knowing." (p. 292) Now that you've studied this piece of writing, what might these phrases mean as Halberstam employs them? What is the difference between being and knowing? How does Halberstam understand the relationship between being and knowing?

   Look for passages in Halberstam's piece where she seems to give you some language through which to explain the difference between being and knowing. Then, write an essay in which you use those passages to explain Halberstam's understanding of these terms. Once you feel you've given your own reader a good sense of Halberstam's terms, consider the question: why does the distinction between these terms matter for Halberstam — and how, or why, might they matter to you (or to all of us)?

MAKING CONNECTIONS

1. In "Evidence," (p. 362) Kathryn Schulz tell us that:

   > . . . if we want to improve our relationship to evidence, we must take a more active role in how we think — must, in a sense, take the reins of our own minds. To do this, we must query and speak and investigate and open our eyes. Specifically, and crucially, we must learn to actively combat our inductive biases: to deliberately seek out evidence that challenges our beliefs, and to take seriously such evidence when we come across it. (p. 377)

   Schulz suggests here that looking for evidence and ideas that go against what we already believe to be true is to "take the reins of our own minds." One might see Judith Halberstam's work on animation as seeking out evidence that goes against dominant or accepted truths.

   Write an essay in which you explore Halberstam's work through the lens of Schulz's claims about improving "our relationship to evidence." What is Halberstam's relationship to evidence? How does she "combat our inductive biases"? If you think of yourself as taking on Schulz's view of evidence, and seeking out evidence that challenges your own beliefs, how might Halberstam's work be a way for you to do that? What, in Halberstam's writing, challenges your beliefs about the culture in which you live? If you take

Schulz's project seriously, what might be productive about the perhaps contrarian evidence Halberstam offers? How do both authors invite you to reread culture—or to reconsider the methods you use when you do so?

2. Halberstam offers a critique of the ways human beings often see or read animal behavior. In her discussion of *March of the Penguins*, she asserts that the voiceover "remains resolutely human and refuses to ever see the 'penguin logics' that structure their frigid quest."

   Reread this section of her piece. What does Halberstam mean here, and other places in the essay, when she discusses the ways humans interpret or make use of animal behavior? Write an essay in which you explain Halberstam's argument. Once you give your reader a sense of that argument, we invite you to test that argument out on Brian Doyle's "Joyas Voladoras." (p. 147) As you read Doyle's lyric essay, consider these questions: Would Halberstam say that Doyle, in the way he makes use of the hummingbirds, refuses to see "hummingbird logics" or "blue whale logics"? In what ways is Doyle's essay implicated in Halberstam's argument? Or, in what ways does Doyle escape Halberstam's critique? How is Doyle's essay different from, or similar to, the voiceover in *March of the Penguins*?

3. In "Beside Oneself: On the Limits of Sexual Autonomy," (p. 114) Judith Butler discusses the idea of entering "into the realm of the possible." What does it mean to be in the "realm of the possible" and how can this term helps us read Halberstam's essay? How can Butler's essay prepare or teach someone to read Halberstam's essay? What philosophies do these writers seem to share? How can you tell?

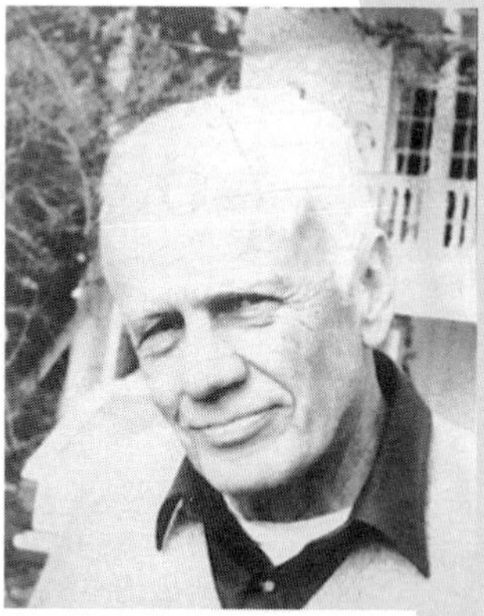

WALKER
Percy

Walker Percy, in his midforties, after a life of relative obscurity as, he said, a "failed physician," wrote his first novel, *The Moviegoer*. It won the National Book Award for fiction in 1962, and Percy emerged as one of this country's leading novelists. Little in his background would have predicted such a career.

After graduating from Columbia University's medical school in 1941, Percy (1916–1990) worked at Bellevue Hospital in New York City. He soon contracted tuberculosis from performing autopsies and was sent to a sanitorium to recover, where, as he said, "I was in bed so much, alone so much, that I had nothing to do but read and think. I began to question everything I had once believed." He returned to medicine briefly but suffered a relapse and during his long recovery began "to make reading a full-time occupation." He left medicine, but not until 1954, almost a decade later, did he publish his first essay, "Symbol as Need."

The essays that followed, including "The Loss of the Creature," all dealt with the relationships between language and understanding or belief. In the later essays, Percy seemed to turn away from academic forms of argument and to depend more and more on stories or anecdotes from daily life — to write, in fact, as a storyteller and to be wary of abstraction or explanation. Robert Coles has said that Percy's failure to find a form that would reach a larger audience may have led him to try his hand at a novel. You will notice in the essay that follows that Percy delights in piling example upon example; he never seems to settle down to a topic sentence, or any sentence for that matter, that sums everything up and makes the examples superfluous.

In addition to *The Moviegoer*, Percy wrote five other novels, including *Lancelot* (1977) and *The Thanatos Syndrome* (1987). He published two books of essays, *The Message in the Bottle: How Queer Man Is, How Queer Language Is, and What One Has to Do with the Other* (1975, from which "The Loss of the Creature" is taken), and *Lost in the Cosmos: The Last Self-Help Book* (1983). Percy died at his home in Covington, Louisiana, on May 10, 1990, leaving a considerable amount of unpublished work, some of which was gathered into a posthumous collection, *Signposts in a Strange Land* (1991). *The Correspondence of Shelby Foote and Walker Percy* was published in 1996.

The Loss of the Creature

I

Every explorer names his island Formosa, beautiful. To him it is beautiful because, being first, he has access to it and can see it for what it is. But to no one else is it ever as beautiful — except the rare man who manages to recover it, who knows that it has to be recovered.

Garcia López de Cárdenas discovered the Grand Canyon and was amazed at the sight. It can be imagined: One crosses miles of desert, breaks through the mesquite, and there it is at one's feet. Later the government set the place aside as a national park, hoping to pass along to millions the experience of Cárdenas. Does not one see the same sight from the Bright Angel Lodge that Cárdenas saw?

The assumption is that the Grand Canyon is a remarkably interesting and beautiful place and that if it had a certain value *P* for Cárdenas, the same value *P* may be transmitted to any number of sightseers — just as Banting's discovery of insulin can be transmitted to any number of diabetics. A counterinfluence is at work, however, and it would be nearer the truth to say that if the place is seen by a million sightseers, a single sightseer does not receive value *P* but a millionth part of value *P*.

THE THING IS NO LONGER THE THING AS IT CONFRONTED THE SPANIARD; IT IS RATHER THAT WHICH HAS ALREADY BEEN FORMULATED — BY PICTURE POSTCARD, GEOGRAPHY BOOK, TOURIST FOLDERS, AND THE WORDS *GRAND CANYON.*

It is assumed that since the Grand Canyon has the fixed interest value *P*, tours can be organized for any number of people. A man in Boston decides to spend his vacation at the Grand Canyon. He visits his travel bureau, looks at the folder, signs up for a two-week tour. He and his family take the tour, see the Grand Canyon, and return to Boston. May we say that this man has seen the Grand Canyon? Possibly he has. But it is more likely that what he has done is the one sure way not to see the canyon.

Why is it almost impossible to gaze directly at the Grand Canyon under these circumstances and see it for what it is — as one picks up a strange object from one's back yard and gazes directly at it? It is almost impossible because the Grand Canyon, the thing as it is, has been appropriated by the symbolic complex which has already been formed in the sightseer's mind. Seeing the canyon under approved circumstances is seeing the symbolic complex head on. The thing is no longer the thing as it confronted the Spaniard; it is rather that which has already been formulated — by picture postcard, geography book, tourist folders, and the words *Grand Canyon*. As a result of this preformulation, the source of the sightseer's pleasure undergoes a shift. Where the wonder and delight of the Spaniard arose from his penetration of the thing itself, from a progressive discovery of depths, patterns, colors, shadows, etc., now the sightseer measures his satisfaction *by the degree to which the canyon conforms to the preformed complex*. If it does so, if it looks just like the postcard, he is pleased; he might even say, "Why it is every bit as beautiful as a picture postcard!" He feels he has not been cheated. But if it does not conform, if the colors are somber, he will not be able to see it directly; he will only be conscious of the disparity between what it is and what it is supposed to be. He will say later that he was unlucky in not being there at the right time. The highest point, the term of the sightseer's satisfaction, is not the sovereign discovery of the thing before him; it is rather the measuring up of the thing to the criterion of the preformed symbolic complex.

Seeing the canyon is made even more difficult by what the sightseer does when the moment arrives, when sovereign knower confronts the thing to be known. Instead of looking at it, he photographs it. There is no confrontation at all. At the end of forty years of preformulation and with the Grand Canyon yawning at his feet, what does he do? He waives his right of seeing and knowing and records symbols for the next forty years. For him there is no present; there is only the past of what has been formulated and seen and the future of what has been formulated and not seen. The present is surrendered to the past and the future.

The sightseer may be aware that something is wrong. He may simply be bored; or he may be conscious of the difficulty: that the great thing yawning at his feet somehow eludes him. The harder he looks at it, the less he can see. It eludes everybody. The tourist cannot see it; the bellboy at the Bright Angel Lodge cannot see it: for him it is only one side of the space he lives in, like one wall of a room; to the ranger it is a tissue of everyday signs relevant to his own prospects — the blue haze down there means that he will probably get rained on during the donkey ride.

How can the sightseer recover the Grand Canyon? He can recover it in any number of ways, all sharing in common the stratagem of avoiding the approved confrontation of the tour and the Park Service.

It may be recovered by leaving the beaten track. The tourist leaves the tour, camps in the back country. He arises before dawn and approaches the South Rim through a wild terrain where there are no trails and no railed-in lookout points. In other words, he sees the canyon by avoiding all the facilities for seeing the canyon. If the benevolent Park Service hears about this fellow and thinks he has a good idea and places the following notice in the Bright Angel Lodge: *Consult ranger for information on getting off the beaten track* — the end result will only be the closing of another access to the canyon.

It may be recovered by a dialectical movement which brings one back to the beaten track but at a level above it. For example, after a lifetime of avoiding the beaten track and guided tours, a man may deliberately seek out the most beaten track of all, the most commonplace tour imaginable:

he may visit the canyon by a Greyhound tour in the company of a party from Terre Haute — just as a man who has lived in New York all his life may visit the Statue of Liberty. (Such dialectical savorings of the familiar as the familiar are, of course, a favorite stratagem of *The New Yorker* magazine.) The thing is recovered from familiarity by means of an exercise in familiarity. Our complex friend stands behind his fellow tourists at the Bright Angel Lodge and sees the canyon through them and their predicament, their picture taking and busy disregard. In a sense, he exploits his fellow tourists; he stands on their shoulders to see the canyon.

Such a man is far more advanced in the dialectic than the sightseer who is trying to get off the beaten track — getting up at dawn and approaching the canyon through the mesquite. This stratagem is, in fact, for our complex man the weariest, most beaten track of all.

It may be recovered as a consequence of a breakdown of the symbolic machinery by which the experts present the experience to the consumer. A family visits the canyon in the usual way. But shortly after their arrival, the park is closed by an outbreak of typhus in the south. They have the canyon to themselves. What do they mean when they tell the home folks of their good luck: "We had the whole place to ourselves"? How does one see the thing better when the others are absent? Is looking like sucking: the more lookers, the less there is to see? They could hardly answer, but by saying this they testify to a state of affairs which is considerably more complex than the simple statement of the schoolbook about the Spaniard and the millions who followed him. It is a state in which there is a complex distribution of sovereignty, of zoning.

It may be recovered in a time of national disaster. The Bright Angel Lodge is converted into a rest home, a function that has nothing to do with the canyon a few yards away. A wounded man is brought in. He regains consciousness; there outside his window is the canyon.

The most extreme case of access by privilege conferred by disaster is the Huxleyan novel of the adventures of the surviving remnant after the great wars of the twentieth century. An expedition from Australia lands in Southern California and heads east. They stumble across the Bright Angel Lodge, now fallen into ruins. The trails are grown over, the guard rails fallen away, the dime telescope at Battleship Point rusted. But there is the canyon, exposed at last. Exposed by what? By the decay of those facilities which were designed to help the sightseer.

This dialectic of sightseeing cannot be taken into account by planners, for the object of the dialectic is nothing other than the subversion of the efforts of the planners.

The dialectic is not known to objective theorists, psychologists, and the like. Yet it is quite well known in the fantasy-consciousness of the popular arts. The devices by which the museum exhibit, the Grand Canyon, the ordinary thing, is recovered have long since been stumbled upon. A movie shows a man visiting the Grand Canyon. But the movie maker knows something the planner does not know. He knows that one cannot take the sight frontally. The canyon must be approached by the stratagems we have mentioned: the Inside Track, the Familiar Revisited, the Accidental Encounter. Who is the stranger at the Bright Angel Lodge? Is he the ordinary tourist from Terre Haute that he makes himself out to be? He is not. He has another objective in mind, to revenge his wronged brother, counterespionage, etc. By virtue of the fact that he has other fish to fry, he may take a stroll along the rim after supper and then we can see the canyon through him. The movie accomplishes its purpose by concealing it. Overtly the characters (the American family marooned by typhus) and we the onlookers experience pity for the sufferers, and the family experience anxiety for themselves; covertly and in truth they are the happiest of people and we are happy through them, for we have the canyon to ourselves. The movie cashes in on the recovery of sovereignty through disaster. Not only is the canyon now accessible to the remnant: the members of the remnant are now accessible to each other, a whole new ensemble of relations becomes possible — friendship, love, hatred, clandestine sexual adventures. In a movie when a man sits next to a woman on a bus, it is necessary either that the bus break down or that the woman lose her memory. (The question occurs to one: Do you imagine there are sightseers who see sights just as they are supposed to? a family who live in Terre Haute, who decide to take the canyon tour, who go there, see it, enjoy it immensely, and go home content? a family who are entirely innocent of all the barriers, zones, losses of sovereignty I have been talking about? Wouldn't most people be sorry if Battleship Point fell into the canyon, carrying all one's fellow passengers to their death, leaving one alone on the South Rim? I cannot answer this. Perhaps there are such people. Certainly a great many American families would swear they had no such problems, that they came, saw, and went away happy. Yet it is just these families who would be happiest if they had gotten the Inside Track and been among the surviving remnant.)

It is now apparent that as between the many measures which may be taken to overcome the opacity, the boredom, of the direct confrontation of the thing or creature in its citadel of symbolic investiture, some are less authentic than others. That is to say, some stratagems obviously serve other purposes than that of providing access to being — for example, various unconscious motivations which it is not necessary to go into here.

Let us take an example in which the recovery of being is ambiguous, where it may under the same circumstances contain both authentic and unauthentic components. An American couple, we will say, drives down into Mexico. They see the usual sights and have a fair time of it. Yet they are never without the sense of missing something. Although Taxco and Cuernavaca are interesting and picturesque as advertised, they fall short of "it." What do the couple have in mind by "it"? What do they really hope for? What sort of experience could they have in Mexico so that upon their return, they would feel that "it" had happened? We have a clue: Their hope has something to do with their own role as tourists in a foreign country and the way in which they conceive this role. It has something to do with other American tourists. Certainly they feel that they are very far from "it" when, after traveling five thousand miles, they arrive at the plaza in Guanajuato only to find themselves surrounded by a dozen other couples from the Midwest.

Already we may distinguish authentic and unauthentic elements. First, we see the problem the couple faces and we understand their efforts to surmount it. The problem is to find an "unspoiled" place. "Unspoiled" does not mean only that a place is left physically intact; it means also that it is not encrusted by renown and by the familiar (as in Taxco), that it has not been discovered by others. We understand that the couple really want to get at the place and enjoy it. Yet at the same time we wonder if there is not something wrong in their dislike of their compatriots. Does access to the place require the exclusion of others?

Let us see what happens.

The couple decide to drive from Guanajuato to Mexico City. On the way they get lost. After hours on a rocky mountain road, they find themselves in a tiny valley not even marked on the map. There they discover an Indian village. Some sort of religious festival is going on. It is apparently a corn dance in supplication of the rain god.

The couple know at once that this is "it." They are entranced. They spend several days in the village, observing the Indians and being themselves observed with friendly curiosity.

Now may we not say that the sightseers have at last come face to face with an authentic sight, a sight which is charming, quaint, picturesque, unspoiled, and that they see the sight and come away rewarded? Possibly this may occur. Yet it is more likely that what happens is a far cry indeed from an immediate encounter with being, that the experience, while masquerading as such, is in truth a rather desperate impersonation. I use the word *desperate* advisedly to signify an actual loss of hope.

The clue to the spuriousness of their enjoyment of the village and the festival is a certain restiveness in the sightseers themselves. It is given expression by their repeated exclamations that "this is too good to be true," and by their anxiety that it may not prove to be so perfect, and finally by their downright relief at leaving the valley and having the experience in the bag, so to speak — that is, safely embalmed in memory and movie film.

What is the source of their anxiety during the visit? Does it not mean that the couple are looking at the place with a certain standard of performance in mind? Are they like Fabre, who gazed at the world about him with wonder, letting it be what it is; or are they not like the overanxious mother who sees her child as one performing, now doing badly, now doing well? The village is their child and their love for it is an anxious love because they are afraid that at any moment it might fail them.

We have another clue in their subsequent remark to an ethnologist friend. "How we wished you had been there with us! What a perfect goldmine of folkways! Every minute we would say to each other, if only you were here! You must return with us." This surely testifies to a generosity of spirit, a willingness to share their experience with others, not at all like their feelings toward their fellow Iowans on the plaza at Guanajuato!

I am afraid this is not the case at all. It is true that they longed for their ethnologist friend, but it was for an entirely different reason. They wanted him, not to share their experience, but to certify their experience as genuine.

"This is it" and "Now we are really living" do not necessarily refer to the sovereign encounter of the person with the sight that enlivens the mind and gladdens the heart. It means that now at last we are having the acceptable experience. The present experience is always measured by a prototype, the "it" of their dreams. "Now I am really living" means that now I am filling the role of sightseer and the sight is living up to the prototype of sights. This quaint and picturesque village is measured by a Platonic ideal of the Quaint and the Picturesque.

Hence their anxiety during the encounter. For at any minute something could go wrong. A fellow Iowan might emerge from a 'dobe hut; the chief might show them his Sears catalog. (If the failures are "wrong" enough, as these are, they might still be turned to account as rueful conversation pieces. "There we were expecting the chief to bring us a churinga and he shows up with a Sears catalog!") They have snatched victory from disaster, but their experience always runs the danger of failure.

They need the ethnologist to certify their experience as genuine. This is borne out by their behavior when the three of them return for the next corn dance. During the dance, the couple do not watch the goings-on; instead they watch the ethnologist! Their highest hope is that their friend should find the dance interesting. And if he should show signs of true absorption, an interest in the goings-on so powerful that he becomes oblivious of his friends — then their cup is full. "Didn't we tell you?" they say at last. What they want from him is not ethnological explanations; all they want is his approval.

What has taken place is a radical loss of sovereignty over that which is as much theirs as it is the ethnologist's. The fault does not lie with the ethnologist. He has no wish to stake a claim to the village; in fact, he desires the opposite: he will bore his friends to death by telling them about the village and the meaning of the folkways. A degree of sovereignty has been surrendered by the couple. It is the nature of the loss, moreover, that they are not aware of the loss, beyond a certain uneasiness. (Even if they read this and admitted it, it would be very difficult for them to bridge the gap in their confrontation of the world. Their consciousness of the corn dance cannot escape their consciousness of their consciousness, so that with the onset of the first direct enjoyment, their higher consciousness pounces and certifies: "Now you are doing it! Now you are really living!" and, in certifying the experience, sets it at nought.)

Their basic placement in the world is such that they recognize a priority of title of the expert over his particular department of being. The whole horizon of being is staked out by "them," the experts. The highest satisfaction of the sightseer (not merely the tourist but any layman seer of sights) is that his sight should be certified as genuine. The worst of this impoverishment is that there is no sense of impoverishment. The surrender of title is so complete that it never even occurs to one to reassert title. A poor man may envy the rich man, but the sightseer does not envy the expert. When a caste system becomes absolute, envy disappears. Yet the caste of layman-expert is not the fault of the expert. It is due altogether to the eager surrender of sovereignty by the layman so that he may take up the role not of the person but of the consumer.

I do not refer only to the special relation of layman to theorist. I refer to the general situation in which sovereignty is surrendered to a class of privileged knowers, whether these be theorists or artists. A reader may surrender sovereignty over that which has been written about, just as a consumer may surrender sovereignty over a thing which has been theorized about. The consumer is content to receive an experience just as it has been presented to him by theorists and planners. The reader may also be content to judge life by whether it has or has not been formulated by those who know and write about life. A young man goes to France. He too has a fair time of it, sees the sights, enjoys the food. On his last day, in fact as he sits in a restaurant in Le Havre waiting for his boat, something happens. A group of French students in the restaurant get into an impassioned argument over a recent play. A riot takes place. Madame la concierge joins in, swinging her mop at the rioters. Our young American is transported. This is "it." And he had almost left France without seeing "it"!

WHEN A CASTE SYSTEM BECOMES ABSOLUTE, ENVY DISAPPEARS. YET THE CASTE OF LAYMAN-EXPERT IS NOT THE FAULT OF THE EXPERT. IT IS DUE ALTOGETHER TO THE EAGER SURRENDER OF SOVEREIGNTY BY THE LAYMAN.

But the young man's delight is ambiguous. On the one hand, it is a pleasure for him to encounter the same Gallic temperament he had heard about from Puccini and Rolland. But on the other hand, the source of his pleasure testifies to a certain alienation. For the young man is actually barred from a direct encounter with anything French excepting only that which has been set forth, authenticated by Puccini and Rolland — those who know. If he had encountered the restaurant scene without reading Hemingway, without knowing that the performance was so typically, charmingly French, he would not have been delighted. He would only have been anxious at seeing things get so out of hand. The source of his delight is the sanction of those who know.

This loss of sovereignty is not a marginal process, as might appear from my example of estranged sightseers. It is a generalized surrender of the horizon to those experts within whose competence a particular segment of the horizon is thought to lie. Kwakiutls are surrendered to Franz Boas; decaying Southern mansions are surrendered to Faulkner and Tennessee Williams. So that, although it is by no means the intention of the expert to expropriate sovereignty — in fact he would not even know what sovereignty meant in this context — the danger of theory and consumption is a seduction and deprivation of the consumer.

In the New Mexico desert, natives occasionally come across strange-looking artifacts which have fallen from the skies and which are stenciled: *Return to U.S. Experimental Project, Alamogordo. Reward.* The finder returns the object and is rewarded. He knows nothing of the nature of the object he has found and does not care to know. The sole role of the native, the highest role he can play, is that of finder and returner of the mysterious equipment.

The same is true of the laymen's relation to *natural* objects in a modern technical society. No matter what the object or event is, whether it is a star, a swallow, a Kwakiutl, a "psychological phenomenon," the layman who confronts it does not confront it as a sovereign person, as Crusoe confronts a seashell he finds on the beach. The highest role he can conceive himself as playing is to be able to recognize the title of the object, to return it to the appropriate expert and have it certified as a genuine find. He does not even permit himself to see the thing — as Gerard Hopkins could see a rock or a cloud or a field. If anyone asks him why he doesn't look, he may reply that he didn't take that subject in college (or he hasn't read Faulkner).

This loss of sovereignty extends even to oneself. There is the neurotic who asks nothing more of his doctor than that his symptoms should prove interesting. When all else fails, the poor fellow has nothing to offer but his own neurosis. But even this is sufficient if only the doctor will show interest when he says, "Last night I had a curious sort of dream; perhaps it will be significant to one who knows about such things. It seems I was standing in a sort of alley — " (I have nothing else to offer you but my own unhappiness. Please say that it, at least, measures up, that it is a *proper* sort of unhappiness.)

II

A young Falkland Islander walking along a beach and spying a dead dogfish and going to work on it with his jackknife has, in a fashion wholly unprovided in modern educational theory, a great advantage over the Scarsdale high-school pupil who finds the dogfish on his laboratory desk. Similarly the citizen of Huxley's *Brave New World* who stumbles across a volume of Shakespeare in some vine-grown ruins and squats on a potsherd to read it is in a fairer way of getting at a sonnet than the Harvard sophomore taking English Poetry II.

The educator whose business it is to teach students biology or poetry is unaware of a whole ensemble of relations which exist between the student and the dogfish and between the student and the Shakespeare sonnet. To put it bluntly: A student who has the desire to get at a dogfish or a Shakespeare sonnet may have the greatest difficulty in salvaging the creature itself from the educational package in which it is presented. The great difficulty is that he is not aware that there is a difficulty; surely, he thinks, in such a fine classroom, with such a fine textbook, the sonnet must come across! What's wrong with me?

The sonnet and the dogfish are obscured by two different processes. The sonnet is obscured by the symbolic package which is formulated not by the sonnet itself but by the *media* through which the sonnet is transmitted, the media which the educators believe for some reason to be transparent. The new textbook, the type, the smell of the page, the classroom, the aluminum windows and the winter sky, the personality of Miss Hawkins — these media which are supposed to transmit the sonnet may only succeed in transmitting themselves. It is only the hardiest and cleverest of students who can salvage the sonnet from this many-tissued package. It is only the rarest student who knows that the sonnet must be salvaged from the package. (The educator is well aware that something is wrong, that there is a fatal gap between the student's learning and the student's life: the student reads the poem, appears to understand it, and gives all the answers. But what does he recall if he should happen to read a Shakespeare sonnet twenty years later? Does he recall the poem or does he recall the smell of the page and the smell of Miss Hawkins?)

One might object, pointing out that Huxley's citizen reading his sonnet in the ruins and the Falkland Islander looking at his dogfish on the beach also receive them in a certain package. Yes, but the difference lies in the fundamental placement of the student in the world, a placement which makes it possible to extract the thing from the package. The pupil at Scarsdale High sees himself placed as a consumer receiving an experience-package; but the Falkland Islander exploring his dogfish is a person exercising the sovereign right of a person in his lordship and mastery of creation. He too could use an instructor and a book and a technique, but he would use them as his subordinates, just as he uses his jackknife. The biology student does not use his scalpel as an instrument, he uses it as a magic wand! Since it is a "scientific instrument," it should do "scientific things."

IT IS ONLY THE HARDIEST AND CLEVEREST OF STUDENTS WHO CAN SALVAGE THE SONNET FROM THIS MANY-TISSUED PACKAGE.

The dogfish is concealed in the same symbolic package as the sonnet. But the dogfish suffers an additional loss. As a consequence of this double deprivation, the Sarah Lawrence student who scores A in zoology is apt to know very little about a dogfish. She is twice removed from the dogfish, once by the symbolic complex by which the dogfish is concealed, once again by the spoliation of the dogfish by theory which renders it invisible. Through no fault of zoology instructors, it is nevertheless a fact that the zoology laboratory at Sarah Lawrence College is one of the few places in the world where it is all but impossible to see a dogfish.

The dogfish, the tree, the seashell, the American Negro, the dream, are rendered invisible by a shift of reality from concrete thing to theory which Whitehead has called the fallacy of misplaced concreteness. It is the mistaking of an idea, a principle, an abstraction, for the real. As a consequence of the shift, the "specimen" is seen as less real than the theory of the specimen. As Kierkegaard said, once a person is seen as a specimen of a race or a species, at that very moment he ceases to be an individual. Then there are no more individuals but only specimens.

To illustrate: A student enters a laboratory which, in the pragmatic view, offers the student the optimum conditions under which an educational experience may be had. In the existential view, however — that view of the student in which he is regarded not as a receptacle of experience but as a knowing being whose peculiar property it is to see himself as being in a certain situation — the modern laboratory could not have been more effectively designed to conceal the dogfish forever.

The student comes to his desk. On it, neatly arranged by his instructor, he finds his laboratory manual, a dissecting board, instruments, and a mimeographed list:

Exercise 22: Materials
1 dissecting board
1 scalpel
1 forceps
1 probe
1 bottle india ink and syringe
1 specimen of *Squalus acanthias*

The clue of the situation in which the student finds himself is to be found in the last item: 1 specimen of *Squalus acanthias*.

The phrase *specimen of* expresses in the most succinct way imaginable the radical character of the loss of being which has occurred under his very nose. To refer to the dogfish, the unique concrete existent before him, as a "specimen of *Squalus acanthias*" reveals by its grammar the spoliation of the dogfish by the theoretical method. This phrase, *specimen of*, example of, instance of, indicates the ontological status of the individual creature in the eyes of the theorist. The dogfish itself is seen as a rather shabby expression of an ideal reality, the species *Squalus acanthias*. The result is the radical devaluation of the individual dogfish. (The *reductio ad absurdum* of Whitehead's shift is Toynbee's employment of it in his historical method. If a gram of NaCl is referred to by the chemist as a "sample of" NaCl, one may think of it as such and not much is missed by the oversight of the act of being of this particular pinch of salt, but when the Jews and the Jewish religion are understood as — in Toynbee's favorite phrase — a "classical example of" such and such a kind of *Voelkerwanderung*, we begin to suspect that something is being left out.)

If we look into the ways in which the student can recover the dogfish (or the sonnet), we will see that they have in common the stratagem of avoiding the educator's direct presentation of the object as a lesson to be learned and restoring access to sonnet and dogfish as beings to be known, reasserting the sovereignty of knower over known.

In truth, the biography of scientists and poets is usually the story of the discovery of the indirect approach, the circumvention of the educator's presentation — the young man who was sent to the *Technikum* and on his way fell into the habit of loitering in book stores and reading poetry;

or the young man dutifully attending law school who on the way became curious about the comings and goings of ants. One remembers the scene in *The Heart Is a Lonely Hunter* where the girl hides in the bushes to hear the Capehart in the big house play Beethoven. Perhaps she was the lucky one after all. Think of the unhappy souls inside, who see the record, worry about scratches, and most of all worry about whether they are *getting it*, whether they are bona fide music lovers. What is the best way to hear Beethoven: sitting in a proper silence around the Capehart or eavesdropping from an azalea bush?

However it may come about, we notice two traits of the second situation: (1) an openness of the thing before one — instead of being an exercise to be learned according to an approved mode, it is a garden of delights which beckons to one; (2) a sovereignty of the knower — instead of being a consumer of a prepared experience, I am a sovereign wayfarer, a wanderer in the neighborhood of being who stumbles into the garden.

One can think of two sorts of circumstances through which the thing may be restored to the person. (There is always, of course, the direct recovery: A student may simply be strong enough, brave enough, clever enough to take the dogfish and the sonnet by storm, to wrest control of it from the educators and the educational package.) First by ordeal: The Bomb falls; when the young man recovers consciousness in the shambles of the biology laboratory, there not ten inches from his nose lies the dogfish. Now all at once he can see it directly and without let, just as the exile or the prisoner or the sick man sees the sparrow at his window in all its inexhaustibility; just as the commuter who has had a heart attack sees his own hand for the first time. In these cases, the simulacrum of everydayness and of consumption has been destroyed by disaster; in the case of the bomb, literally destroyed. Secondly, by apprenticeship to a great man: one day a great biologist walks into the laboratory; he stops in front of our student's desk; he leans over, picks up the dogfish, and, ignoring instruments and procedure, probes with a broken fingernail into the little carcass. "Now here is a curious business," he says, ignoring also the proper jargon of the specialty. "Look here how this little duct reverses its direction and drops into the pelvis. Now if you would look into a coelacanth, you would see that it —" And all at once the student can see. The technician and the sophomore who loves his textbooks are always offended by the genuine research man because the latter is usually a little vague and always humble before the thing; he doesn't have much use for the equipment or the jargon. Whereas the technician is never vague and never humble before the thing; he holds the thing disposed of by the principle, the formula, the textbook outline; and he thinks a great deal of equipment and jargon.

But since neither of these methods of recovering the dogfish is pedagogically feasible — perhaps the great man even less so than the Bomb — I wish to propose the following educational technique which should prove equally effective for Harvard and Shreveport High School. I propose that English poetry and biology should be taught as usual, but that at irregular intervals, poetry students should find dogfishes on their desks and biology students should find Shakespeare sonnets on their dissection boards. I am serious in declaring that a Sarah Lawrence English major who began poking about in a dogfish with a bobby pin would learn more in thirty minutes than a biology major in a whole semester; and that the latter upon reading on her dissecting board

> That time of year Thou may'st in me behold
> When yellow leaves, or none, or few, do hang
> Upon those boughs which shake against the cold —
> Bare ruin'd choirs where late the sweet birds sang

might catch fire at the beauty of it.

The situation of the tourist at the Grand Canyon and the biology student are special cases of a predicament in which everyone finds himself in a modern technical society — a society, that is, in which there is a division between expert and layman, planner and consumer, in which experts and planners take special measures to teach and edify the consumer. The measures taken are measures appropriate to the consumer: the expert and the planner *know* and *plan*, but the consumer *needs* and *experiences*.

There is a double deprivation. First, the thing is lost through its packaging. The very means by which the thing is presented for consumption, the very techniques by which the thing is made available as an item of need-satisfaction, these very means operate to remove the thing from the sovereignty of the knower. A loss of title occurs. The measures which the museum curator takes to present the thing to the public are self-liquidating. The upshot of the curator's efforts are not that everyone can see the exhibit but that no one can see it. The curator protests: Why are they so indifferent? Why do they even deface the exhibit? Don't they know it is theirs? But it is not theirs. It is his, the curator's. By the most exclusive sort of zoning, the museum exhibit, the park oak tree, is part of an ensemble, a package, which is almost impenetrable to them. The archaeologist who puts his find in a museum so that everyone can see it accomplishes the reverse of his expectations. The result of his action is that no one can see it now but the archaeologist. He would have done better to keep it in his pocket and show it now and then to strangers.

The tourist who carves his initials in a public place, which is theoretically "his" in the first place, has good reasons for doing so, reasons which the exhibitor and planner know nothing about. He does so because in his role of consumer of an experience (a "recreational experience" to satisfy a "recreational need") he knows that he is disinherited. He is deprived of his title over being. He knows very well that he is in a very special sort of zone in which his only rights are the rights of a consumer. He moves like a ghost through schoolroom, city streets, trains, parks, movies. He carves his initials as a last desperate measure to escape his ghostly role of consumer. He is saying in effect: I am not a ghost after all; I am a sovereign person. And he establishes title the only way remaining to him, by staking his claim over one square inch of wood or stone.

Does this mean that we should get rid of museums? No, but it means that the sightseer should be prepared to enter into a struggle to recover a sight from a museum.

The second loss is the spoliation of the thing, the tree, the rock, the swallow, by the layman's misunderstanding of scientific theory. He believes that the thing is *disposed of* by theory, that it stands in the Platonic relation of being a *specimen* of such and such an underlying principle. In the transmission of scientific theory from theorist to layman, the expectation of the theorist is reversed. Instead of the marvels of the universe being made available to the public, the universe is disposed of by theory. The loss of sovereignty takes this form: as a result of the science of botany, trees are not made available to every man. On the contrary. The tree loses its proper density and mystery as a concrete existent and, as merely another *specimen* of a species, becomes itself nugatory.

Does this mean that there is no use taking biology at Harvard and Shreveport High? No, but it means that the student should know what a fight he has on his hands to rescue the specimen from the educational package. The educator is only partly to blame. For there is nothing the educator can do to provide for this need of the student. Everything the educator does only succeeds in becoming, for the student, part of the educational package. The highest role of the educator is the maieutic role of Socrates: to help the student come to himself not as a consumer of experience but as a sovereign individual.

The thing is twice lost to the consumer. First, sovereignty is lost: it is theirs, not his. Second, it is radically devalued by theory. This is a loss which has been brought about by science but through no fault of the scientist and through no fault of scientific theory. The loss has come about as a consequence of the seduction of the layman by science. The layman will be seduced as long as he regards beings as consumer items to be experienced rather than prizes to be won, and as long as he waives his sovereign rights as a person and accepts his role of consumer as the highest estate to which the layman can aspire.

As Mounier said, the person is not something one can study and provide for; he is something one struggles for. But unless he also struggles for himself, unless he knows that there is a struggle, he is going to be just what the planners think he is.

QUESTIONS FOR A SECOND READING

1. Percy's essay proceeds by adding example to example, one after another. If all the examples were meant to illustrate the same thing, the same general point or idea, then one would most likely have been enough. The rest would have been redundant. It makes sense, then, to assume that each

example gives a different view of what Percy is saying, that each modifies the others, or qualifies them, or adds a piece that was otherwise lacking. It's as though Percy needed one more to get it right or to figure out what was missing along the way. As you read back through the essay, pay particular attention to the *differences* between the examples (between the various tourists going to the Grand Canyon, or between the tourists at the Grand Canyon and the tourists in Mexico). Also note the logic or system that leads from one to the next. What progress of thought is represented by the movement from one example to another, or from tourists to students?

2. The essay is filled with talk about "loss"—the loss of sovereignty, the loss of the creature—but it is resolutely ambiguous about what it is that we have lost. As you work your way back through, note the passages that describe what we are missing and why we should care. Are we to believe, for example, that Cárdenas actually had it (whatever "it" is)—that he had no preconceived notions when he saw the Grand Canyon? Mightn't he have said, "I claim this for my queen" or "There I see the glory of God" or "This wilderness is not fit for man"? To whom, or in the name of what, is this loss that Percy chronicles such a matter of concern? If this is not just Percy's peculiar prejudice, if we are asked to share his concerns, whose interests or what interests are represented here?

3. The essay is made up of stories or anecdotes, all of them fanciful. Percy did not, in other words, turn to first-person accounts of visitors to the Grand Canyon or to statements by actual students or teachers. Why not, do you suppose? What does this choice say about his "method"—about what it can and can't do? As you reread the essay, look for sections you could use to talk about the power and limits of Percy's method.

ASSIGNMENTS FOR WRITING

1. Percy tells several stories—some of them quite good stories—but it is often hard to know just what he is getting at, just what point he is trying to make. If he's making an argument, it's not the sort of argument that is easy to summarize. And if the stories (or anecdotes) are meant to serve as examples, they are not the sort of examples that lead directly to a single, general conclusion or that serve to clarify a point or support an obvious thesis. In fact, at the very moment when you expect Percy to come forward and pull things together, he offers yet another story, as though another example, rather than any general statement, would get you closer to what he is saying.

   There are, at the same time, terms and phrases to suggest that this is an essay with a point to make. Percy talks, for example, about "the loss of sovereignty," "symbolic packages," "consumers of experience," and "dialectic," and it seems that these terms and phrases are meant to name or comment on key scenes, situations, or characters in the examples.

For this assignment, tell a story of your own, one that is suggested by the stories Percy tells — perhaps a story about a time you went looking for something or at something, or about a time when you did or did not find a dogfish in your Shakespeare class. You should imagine that you are carrying out a project that Walker Percy has begun, a project that has you looking back at your own experience through the lens of "The Loss of the Creature," noticing what Percy would notice and following the paths that he would find interesting. Try to bring the terms that Percy uses — like "sovereign," "consumer," "expert," and "dialectic" — to bear on the story you have to tell. Feel free to imitate Percy's style and method in your essay.

2. Percy charts several routes to the Grand Canyon: you can take the packaged tour, you can get off the beaten track, you can wait for a disaster, you can follow the "dialectical movement which brings one back to the beaten track but at a level above it." This last path (or stratagem), he says, is for the complex traveler.

> Our complex friend stands behind his fellow tourists at the Bright Angel Lodge and sees the canyon through them and their predicament, their picture taking and busy disregard. In a sense, he exploits his fellow tourists; he stands on their shoulders to see the canyon. (p. 300)

The complex traveler sees the Grand Canyon through the example of the common tourists with "their predicament, their picture taking and busy disregard." He "stands on their shoulders" to see the canyon. This distinction between complex and common approaches is an important one in the essay. It is interesting to imagine how the distinction could be put to work to define ways of reading.

Suppose that you read "The Loss of the Creature" as a common reader. What would you see? What would you identify as key sections of the text? What would you miss? What would you say about what you see?

If you think of yourself, now, as a complex reader, modeled after any of Percy's more complex tourists or students, what would you see? What would you identify as key sections of the text? What would you miss? What would you say about what you see?

For this assignment, write an essay with three sections. You may number them, if you choose. The first section should represent the work of a common reader with "The Loss of the Creature," and the second should represent the work of a complex reader. The third section should look back and comment on the previous two. In particular, you might address these questions: Why might a person prefer one reading over the other? What is to be gained or lost with both?

MAKING CONNECTIONS

1. Errol Morris's photographic essay "Will the Real Hooded Man Please Stand Up?" shares many of Percy's concerns. In fact, it is easy to imagine Morris using "The Loss of the Creature" as a title for his own essay. Percy is broadly concerned with all experience, with how we do (or don't) encounter what is there before us. Morris's primary concern is with how we encounter photographic images specifically. He says:

> Photographs attract false beliefs the way flypaper attracts flies. Why my skepticism? Because vision is privileged in our society and in our sensorium. We trust it; we place our confidence in it. Photography allows us to uncritically think. We imagine that photographs provide a magic path to truth.
>
> What's more, photographs allow us to think we know more than we really do. We can imagine a context that isn't really there.

Morris and Percy ask similar questions, and they write with similar urgency. Let's take their projects' similarities as a starting point. What are they? Make a brief list. Then, as you reread the essays, think primarily about the differences. Both are concerned with loss. What, for each, has been lost? What are the reasons? What are the consequences? What options are available for restoration?

Write an essay in which you use Percy's or Morris's point of view as a starting point. Then, consider the other's understanding of loss, its origins, and its consequences.

2.

> But the difference lies in the fundamental placement of the student in the world. . . . (Walker Percy, p. 306)
>
> What I am about to say to you has taken me more than twenty years to admit: *A primary reason for my success in the classroom was that I couldn't forget that schooling was changing me and separating me from the life I enjoyed before becoming a student.* (Richard Rodriguez, p. 339)

Both Percy and Richard Rodriguez, in "The Achievement of Desire" (p. 338), write about students and how they are "placed" in the world by teachers and by the way schools characteristically represent knowledge, the novice, and the expert. And both tell stories to make their points, stories of characteristic students in characteristic situations. Write an essay in which you tell a story of your own, one meant to serve as a corrective or a supplement to the stories Percy and Rodriguez tell. You will want both to tell your story and to use it as a way of returning to and commenting on Percy and Rodriguez and the arguments they make. Your authority can rest on the fact that you are a student and as a consequence have ways of understanding that position that they do not.

e See the e-Pages at bedfordstmartins.com/waysofreading.

3. Percy develops a metaphor of tourists observing the Grand Canyon to make arguments about the ways in which a preconceived "symbolic complex" prevents tourists from actually seeing the sites they've come to see — in this case, the Grand Canyon itself. The tourists, Percy argues, instead see whatever it is they expect to see. Reread "The Loss of the Creature" alongside "Shia Girls" and identify moments and language in Percy's essay that you could use to explore the preconceived symbolic complexes that you bring to reading "Shia Girls." Mark the passages in "Shia Girls" where you think you're behaving like Percy's tourists or like his student trying to study the dogfish. What is getting between you and those passages?

   Write an essay in which you reflect on your reading of specific passages in Jamie's essay, using Percy's ideas and language to identify your preconceived notions or beliefs or impressions — the symbolic complexes — that could be said to influence, shape, or even prevent your understanding of Jamie's passages.

See the e-Pages at bedfordstmartins.com/waysofreading.

MARY LOUISE Pratt

Mary Louise Pratt (b. 1948) grew up in Listowel, Ontario, a small Canadian farm town. She got her BA at the University of Toronto and her PhD from Stanford University, where for nearly thirty years she was a professor in the departments of comparative literature and Spanish and Portuguese. At Stanford, she was one of the cofounders of the new freshman culture program, a controversial series of required courses that replaced the old Western civilization core courses. The course she is particularly associated with is called "Europe and the Americas"; it brings together European representations of the Americas with indigenous American texts. As you might guess from the essay that follows, the program at Stanford expanded the range of countries, languages, cultures, and texts that are seen as a necessary introduction to the world; it also, however, revised the very idea of culture that many of us take for granted—particularly the idea that culture, at its best, expresses common values in a common language. Among other awards and honors, Pratt is the recipient of a Guggenheim Fellowship and a Fellowship at the Center for Advanced Study in the Behavioral Sciences, Stanford University. She is Silver Professor in the Department of Spanish and Portuguese at New York University. She served as president of the Modern Language Association for 2003.

Pratt is the author of *Toward a Speech Act Theory of Literary Discourse* (1977) and coauthor of *Women, Culture, and Politics in Latin America* (1990), the textbook *Linguistics for Students of Literature* (1980), *Amor Brujo: The Images and Culture of Love in the Andes* (1990), and *Imperial Eyes: Studies in Travel Writing and Transculturation* (1992). The essay that follows was revised to serve as the introduction to *Imperial Eyes*, which examines European travel writing in the eighteenth and nineteenth centuries, when Europe was "discovering" Africa and the Americas. It argues that travel writing produced "the rest of the world" for European readers. It didn't "report" on Africa or South America; it produced an "Africa" or an "America" for European consumption. Travel writing produced places that could be thought of as barren, empty, undeveloped, inconceivable, needful of European influence and control, ready to serve European industrial, intellectual, and commercial interests. The reports of travelers or, later, scientists and anthropologists are part of a more general process by which the emerging industrial nations took possession of new territory.

The European understanding of Peru, for example, came through European accounts, not from attempts to understand or elicit responses from Andeans, Peruvian natives. Such a response was delivered when an Andean, Guaman Poma, wrote to King Philip III of Spain, but his letter was unreadable. Pratt is interested in just those moments of contact between peoples and cultures. She is interested in how King Philip read (or failed to read) a letter from Peru, but also in how someone like Guaman Poma prepared himself to write to the king of Spain. To fix these moments, she makes use of a phrase she coined, the "contact zone," which, she says,

> I use to refer to the space of colonial encounters, the space in which peoples geographically and historically separated come into contact with each other and establish ongoing relations, usually involving conditions of coercion, radical inequality, and intractable conflict. . . . By using the term "contact," I aim to foreground the interactive, improvisational dimensions of colonial encounters so easily ignored or suppressed by diffusionist accounts of conquest and domination. A "contact" perspective emphasizes how subjects are constituted in and by their relations to each other. It treats the relations among colonizers and colonized, or travelers and "travelees," not in terms of separateness or apartheid, but in terms of copresence, interaction, interlocking understandings and practices.

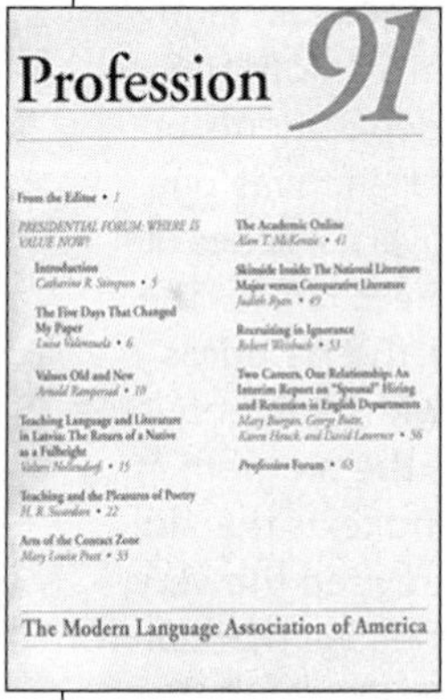

"Arts of the Contact Zone" was first written as a lecture. It was delivered as a keynote address at the second Modern Language Association Literacy Conference, held in Pittsburgh, Pennsylvania, in 1990.

Arts of the Contact Zone

Whenever the subject of literacy comes up, what often pops first into my mind is a conversation I overheard eight years ago between my son Sam and his best friend, Willie, aged six and seven, respectively: "Why don't you trade me Many Trails for Carl Yats . . . Yesits . . . Ya-strum-scrum." "That's not how you say it, dummy, it's Carl Yes . . . Yes . . . oh, I don't know." Sam and Willie had just discovered baseball cards. Many Trails was their decoding, with the help of first-grade English phonics, of the name Manny Trillo. The name they were quite rightly stumped on was Carl Yastrzemski. That was the first time I remembered seeing them put their incipient literacy to their own use, and I was of course thrilled.

Sam and Willie learned a lot about phonics that year by trying to decipher surnames on baseball cards, and a lot about cities, states, heights, weights, places of birth, stages of life. In the years that followed, I watched Sam apply his arithmetic skills to working out batting averages and subtracting retirement years from rookie years; I watched him develop senses of patterning and order by arranging and rearranging his cards for hours on end, and aesthetic judgment by comparing different photos, different series, layouts, and color schemes. American geography and history took shape in his mind through baseball cards. Much of his social life revolved around trading them, and he learned about exchange, fairness, trust, the importance of processes as opposed to results, what it means to get cheated, taken advantage of, even robbed. Baseball cards were the medium of his economic life too. Nowhere better to learn the power and arbitrariness of money, the absolute divorce between use value and exchange value, notions of long- and short-term investment, the possibility of personal values that are independent of market values.

Baseball cards meant baseball card shows, where there was much to be learned about adult worlds as well. And baseball cards opened the door to baseball books, shelves and shelves of encyclopedias, magazines, histories, biographies, novels, books of jokes, anecdotes, cartoons, even poems. Sam learned the history of American racism and the struggle against it through baseball; he saw the Depression and two world wars from behind home plate. He learned the meaning of commodified labor, what it means for one's body and talents to be owned and dispensed by another. He knows something about Japan, Taiwan, Cuba, and Central America and how men and boys do things there. Through the history and experience of baseball stadiums he thought about architecture, light, wind, topography, meteorology, the dynamics of public space. He learned the meaning of expertise, of knowing about something well enough that you can start a conversation with a stranger and feel sure of holding your own. Even with an adult — especially with an adult. Throughout his preadolescent years, baseball history was Sam's luminous point of contact with grown-ups, his lifeline to caring. And, of course, all this time he was also playing baseball, struggling his way through the stages of the local Little League system, lucky enough to be a pretty good player, loving the game and coming to know deeply his strengths and weaknesses.

Literacy began for Sam with the newly pronounceable names on the picture cards and brought him what has been easily the broadest, most varied, most enduring, and most integrated experience of his thirteen-year life. Like many parents, I was delighted to see schooling give Sam the tools with which to find and open all these doors. At the same time I found it unforgivable that schooling itself gave him nothing remotely as meaningful to do, let alone anything that would actually take him beyond the referential, masculinist ethos of baseball and its lore.

However, I was not invited here to speak as a parent, nor as an expert on literacy. I was asked to speak as an MLA [Modern Language Association] member working in the elite academy. In that capacity my contribution is undoubtedly supposed to be abstract, irrelevant, and anchored outside the real world. I wouldn't dream of disappointing anyone. I propose immediately to head back several centuries to a text that has a few points in common with baseball cards and raises thoughts about what Tony Sarmiento, in his comments to the conference, called new visions of literacy. In 1908 a Peruvianist named Richard Pietschmann was exploring in the Danish Royal Archive in Copenhagen and came across a manuscript. It was dated in the city of Cuzco in Peru, in the year 1613, some forty years after the final fall of the Inca empire to the Spanish and signed with an unmistakably Andean indigenous name: Felipe Guaman Poma de Ayala. Written in a mixture of Quechua and ungrammatical, expressive Spanish, the manuscript was a letter addressed by an unknown but apparently literate Andean to King Philip III of Spain. What stunned Pietschmann was that the letter was twelve hundred pages long. There were almost eight hundred pages of written text and four hundred of captioned line drawings. It was titled *The First New Chronicle and Good Government.* No one knew (or knows) how the manuscript got to the library in Copenhagen or how long it had been there. No one, it appeared, had ever bothered to read it or figured out how. Quechua was not thought of as a written language in 1908, nor Andean culture as a literate culture.

THE LETTER GOT THERE, ONLY 350 YEARS TOO LATE, A MIRACLE AND A TERRIBLE TRAGEDY.

Pietschmann prepared a paper on his find, which he presented in London in 1912, a year after the rediscovery of Machu Picchu by Hiram Bingham. Reception, by an international congress of Americanists, was apparently confused. It took twenty-five years for a facsimile edition of the work to appear in Paris. It was not till the late 1970s, as positivist reading habits gave way to interpretive studies and colonial elitisms to post-colonial pluralisms, that Western scholars found ways of reading Guaman Poma's *New Chronicle and Good Government* as the extraordinary intercultural tour de force that it was. The letter got there, only 350 years too late, a miracle and a terrible tragedy.

I propose to say a few more words about this erstwhile unreadable text, in order to lay out some thoughts about writing and literacy in what I like to call the *contact zones*. I use this term to refer to social spaces where cultures meet, clash, and grapple with each other, often in contexts of highly asymmetrical relations of power, such as colonialism, slavery, or their aftermaths as they are lived out in many parts of the world today. Eventually I will use the term to reconsider the models of community that many of us rely on in teaching and theorizing and that are under challenge today. But first a little more about Guaman Poma's giant letter to Philip III.

Insofar as anything is known about him at all, Guaman Poma exemplified the sociocultural complexities produced by conquest and empire. He was an indigenous Andean who claimed noble Inca descent and who had adopted (at least in some sense) Christianity. He may have worked in the Spanish colonial administration as an interpreter, scribe, or assistant to a Spanish tax collector — as a mediator, in short. He says he learned to write from his half brother, a mestizo whose Spanish father had given him access to religious education.

Guaman Poma's letter to the king is written in two languages (Spanish and Quechua) and two parts. The first is called the *Nueva corónica*, "New Chronicle." The title is important. The chronicle of course was the main writing apparatus through which the Spanish presented their American conquests to themselves. It constituted one of the main official discourses. In writing a "new chronicle," Guaman Poma took over the official Spanish genre for his own ends. Those ends were, roughly, to construct a new picture of the world, a picture of a Christian world with Andean rather than European peoples at the center of it — Cuzco, not Jerusalem. In the *New Chronicle* Guaman Poma begins by rewriting the Christian history of the world from Adam and Eve (Fig. 1), incorporating the Amerindians into it as offspring of one of the sons of Noah. He identifies five ages of Christian history that he links in parallel with the five ages of canonical Andean history — separate but equal trajectories that diverge with Noah and reintersect not with Columbus but with Saint Bartholomew, claimed to have preceded Columbus in the Americas. In a couple of hundred pages, Guaman Poma constructs a veritable encyclopedia of Inca and pre-Inca history, customs, laws, social forms, public offices, and dynastic leaders. The depictions resemble European manners and customs description, but also reproduce the meticulous detail with which knowledge in Inca society was stored on *quipus* and in the oral memories of elders.

Guaman Poma's *New Chronicle* is an instance of what I have proposed to call an *autoethnographic* text, by which I mean a text in which people undertake to describe themselves in ways that engage with representations others have made of them. Thus if ethnographic texts are those in which European metropolitan subjects represent to themselves their others (usually their conquered others), autoethnographic texts are representations that the so-defined others construct *in response to* or in dialogue with those

Where two cultures meet

Figure 1. Adam and Eve.

texts. Autoethnographic texts are not, then, what are usually thought of as autochthonous forms of expression or self-representation (as the Andean *quipus* were). Rather they involve a selective collaboration with and appropriation of idioms of the metropolis or the conqueror. These are merged or infiltrated to varying degrees with indigenous idioms to create self-representations intended to intervene in metropolitan modes of understanding. Autoethnographic works are often addressed to both metropolitan audiences and the speaker's own community. Their reception is thus highly indeterminate. Such texts often constitute a marginalized group's point of entry into the dominant circuits of print culture. It is interesting to think, for example, of American slave autobiography in its autoethnographic dimensions, which in some respects distinguish it from Euramerican autobiographical tradition. The concept might help explain why some of the earliest published writing by Chicanas took the form of folkloric manners and customs sketches written in English and published in English-language newspapers or folklore magazines (see Treviño). Autoethnographic representation often involves concrete collaborations between people, as between literate ex-slaves and abolitionist intellectuals, or between Guaman

Poma and the Inca elders who were his informants. Often, as in Guaman Poma, it involves more than one language. In recent decades autoethnography, critique, and resistance have reconnected with writing in a contemporary creation of the contact zone, the *testimonio.*

Guaman Poma's *New Chronicle* ends with a revisionist account of the Spanish conquest, which, he argues, should have been a peaceful encounter of equals with the potential for benefiting both, but for the mindless greed of the Spanish. He parodies Spanish history. Following contact with the Incas, he writes, "In all Castille, there was a great commotion. All day and at night in their dreams the Spaniards were saying, 'Yndias, yndias, oro, plata, oro, plata del Piru'" ("Indies, Indies, gold, silver, gold, silver from Peru") (Fig. 2). The Spanish, he writes, brought nothing of value to share with the Andeans, nothing "but armor and guns con la codicia de oro, plata, oro y plata, yndias, a las Yndias, Piru" ("with the lust for gold, silver, gold and silver, Indies, the Indies, Peru") (p. 372). I quote these words as an example of a conquered subject using the conqueror's language to construct a parodic, oppositional representation of the conqueror's own speech. Guaman Poma mirrors back to the Spanish (in their language,

Figure 2. Conquista. Meeting of Spaniard and Inca. The Inca says in Quechua, "You eat this gold?" Spaniard replies in Spanish, "We eat this gold."

which is alien to him) an image of themselves that they often suppress and will therefore surely recognize. Such are the dynamics of language, writing, and representation in contact zones.

The second half of the epistle continues the critique. It is titled *Buen gobierno y justicia,* "Good Government and Justice," and combines a description of colonial society in the Andean region with a passionate denunciation of Spanish exploitation and abuse. (These, at the time he was writing, were decimating the population of the Andes at a genocidal rate. In fact, the potential loss of the labor force became a main cause for reform of the system.) Guaman Poma's most implacable hostility is invoked by the clergy, followed by the dreaded *corregidores,* or colonial overseers (Fig. 3). He also praises good works, Christian habits, and just men where he finds them, and offers at length his views as to what constitutes "good government and justice." The Indies, he argues, should be administered through a collaboration of Inca and Spanish elites. The epistle ends with an imaginary question-and-answer session in which, in a reversal of hierarchy, the king is depicted asking Guaman Poma questions about how to reform the empire — a dialogue imagined across the many lines that

Figure 3. Corregidor de minas. Catalog of Spanish abuses of indigenous labor force.

divide the Andean scribe from the imperial monarch, and in which the subordinated subject single-handedly gives himself authority in the colonizer's language and verbal repertoire. In a way, it worked — this extraordinary text did get written — but in a way it did not, for the letter never reached its addressee.

To grasp the import of Guaman Poma's project, one needs to keep in mind that the Incas had no system of writing. Their huge empire is said to be the only known instance of a full-blown bureaucratic state society built and administered without writing. Guaman Poma constructs his text by appropriating and adapting pieces of the representational repertoire of the invaders. He does not simply imitate or reproduce it; he selects and adapts it along Andean lines to express (bilingually, mind you) Andean interests and aspirations. Ethnographers have used the term *transculturation* to describe processes whereby members of subordinated or marginal groups select and invent from materials transmitted by a dominant or metropolitan culture. The term, originally coined by Cuban sociologist Fernando Ortiz in the 1940s, aimed to replace overly reductive concepts of acculturation and assimilation used to characterize culture under conquest. While subordinate peoples do not usually control what emanates from the dominant culture, they do determine to varying extents what gets absorbed into their own and what it gets used for. Transculturation, like autoethnography, is a phenomenon of the contact zone.

TRANSCULTURATION, LIKE AUTOETHNOGRAPHY, IS A PHENOMENON OF THE CONTACT ZONE.

As scholars have realized only relatively recently, the transcultural character of Guaman Poma's text is intricately apparent in its visual as well as its written component. The genre of the four hundred line drawings is European — there seems to have been no tradition of representational drawing among the Incas — but in their execution they deploy specifically Andean systems of spatial symbolism that express Andean values and aspirations.[1]

In Figure 1, for instance, Adam is depicted on the left-hand side below the sun, while Eve is on the right-hand side below the moon, and slightly lower than Adam. The two are divided by the diagonal of Adam's digging stick. In Andean spatial symbolism, the diagonal descending from the sun marks the basic line of power and authority dividing upper from lower, male from female, dominant from subordinate. In Figure 2, the Inca appears in the same position as Adam, with the Spaniard opposite, and the two at the same height. In Figure 3, depicting Spanish abuses of power, the symbolic pattern is reversed. The Spaniard is in a high position indicating dominance, but on the "wrong" (right-hand) side. The diagonals of his lance and that of the servant doing the flogging mark out a line of illegitimate, though real, power. The Andean figures continue to occupy the left-hand side of the picture, but clearly as victims. Guaman Poma wrote that the Spanish conquest had produced *"un mundo al revés,"* "a world in reverse."

In sum, Guaman Poma's text is truly a product of the contact zone. If one thinks of cultures, or literatures, as discrete, coherently structured, monolingual edifices, Guaman Poma's text, and indeed any autoethnographic work, appears anomalous or chaotic — as it apparently did to the European scholars Pietschmann spoke to in 1912. If one does not think of cultures this way, then Guaman Poma's text is simply heterogeneous, as the Andean region was itself and remains today. Such a text is heterogeneous on the reception end as well as the production end: it will read very differently to people in different positions in the contact zone. Because it deploys European and Andean systems of meaning making, the letter necessarily means differently to bilingual Spanish-Quechua speakers and to monolingual speakers in either language; the drawings mean differently to monocultural readers, Spanish or Andean, and to bicultural readers responding to the Andean symbolic structures embodied in European genres.

In the Andes in the early 1600s there existed a literate public with considerable intercultural competence and degrees of bilingualism. Unfortunately, such a community did not exist in the Spanish court with which Guaman Poma was trying to make contact. It is interesting to note that in the same year Guaman Poma sent off his letter, a text by another Peruvian was adopted in official circles in Spain as the canonical Christian mediation between the Spanish conquest and Inca history. It was another huge encyclopedic work, titled the *Royal Commentaries of the Incas,* written, tellingly, by a mestizo, Inca Garcilaso de la Vega. Like the mestizo half brother who taught Guaman Poma to read and write, Inca Garcilaso was the son of an Inca princess and a Spanish official, and had lived in Spain since he was seventeen. Though he too spoke Quechua, his book is written in eloquent, standard Spanish, without illustrations. While Guaman Poma's life's work sat somewhere unread, the *Royal Commentaries* was edited and reedited in Spain and the New World, a mediation that coded the Andean past and present in ways thought unthreatening to colonial hierarchy.[2] The textual hierarchy persists; the *Royal Commentaries* today remains a staple item on PhD reading lists in Spanish, while the *New Chronicle and Good Government,* despite the ready availability of several fine editions, is not. However, though Guaman Poma's text did not reach its destination, the transcultural currents of expression it exemplifies continued to evolve in the Andes, as they still do, less in writing than in storytelling, ritual, song, dance-drama, painting and sculpture, dress, textile art, forms of governance, religious belief, and many other vernacular art forms. All express the effects of long-term contact and intractable, unequal conflict.

Autoethnography, transculturation, critique, collaboration, bilingualism, mediation, parody, denunciation, imaginary dialogue, vernacular expression — these are some of the literate arts of the contact zone. Miscomprehension, incomprehension, dead letters, unread masterpieces, absolute heterogeneity of meaning — these are some of the perils of writing in the contact zone. They all live among us today in the transnationalized metropolis of the United States and are becoming more widely visible, more pressing, and, like Guaman Poma's text, more decipherable to those who once would have ignored them in defense of a stable, centered sense of knowledge and reality.

CONTACT AND COMMUNITY

The idea of the contact zone is intended in part to contrast with ideas of community that underlie much of the thinking about language, communication, and culture that gets done in the academy. A couple of years ago, thinking about the linguistic theories I knew, I tried to make sense of a utopian quality that often seemed to characterize social analyses of language by the academy. Languages were seen as living in "speech communities," and these tended to be theorized as discrete, self-defined, coherent entities, held together by a homogeneous competence or grammar shared identically and equally among all the members. This abstract idea of the speech community seemed to reflect, among other things, the utopian way modern nations conceive of themselves as what Benedict Anderson calls "imagined communities."[3] In a book of that title, Anderson observes that with the possible exception of what he calls "primordial villages," human communities exist as *imagined* entities in which people "will never know most of their fellow-members, meet them or even hear of them, yet in the mind of each lives the image of their communion." "Communities are distinguished," he goes on to say, "not by their falsity/genuineness, but by *the style in which they are imagined*" (15; emphasis mine). Anderson proposes three features that characterize the style in which the modern nation is imagined. First, it is imagined as *limited*, by "finite, if elastic, boundaries"; second, it is imagined as *sovereign*; and, third, it is imagined as *fraternal*, "a deep, horizontal comradeship" for which millions of people are prepared "not so much to kill as willingly to die" (15). As the image suggests, the nation-community is embodied metonymically in the finite, sovereign, fraternal figure of the citizen-soldier.

Anderson argues that European bourgeoisies were distinguished by their ability to "achieve solidarity on an essentially imagined basis" (74) on a scale far greater than that of elites of other times and places. Writing and literacy play a central role in this argument. Anderson maintains, as have others, that the main instrument that made bourgeois nation-building projects possible was print capitalism. The commercial circulation of books in the various European vernaculars, he argues, was what first created the invisible networks that would eventually constitute the literate elites and those they ruled as nations. (Estimates are that 180 million books were put into circulation in Europe between the years 1500 and 1600 alone.)

Now obviously this style of imagining of modern nations, as Anderson describes it, is strongly utopian, embodying values like equality, fraternity, liberty, which the societies often profess but systematically fail to realize. The prototype of the modern nation as imagined community was, it seemed to me, mirrored in ways people thought about language and the speech community. Many commentators have pointed out how modern views of language as code and competence assume a unified and homogeneous social world in which language exists as a shared patrimony — as a device, precisely, for imagining community. An image of a universally shared literacy is also part of the picture. The prototypical manifestation of language is generally taken to be the speech of individual adult native speakers face-to-face (as in Saussure's famous diagram) in monolingual, even monodialectal situations — in short, the most homogeneous case linguistically and socially. The same goes for written communication. Now one could certainly imagine a theory that assumed different things — that argued, for instance, that the most revealing speech situation for understanding language was one involving a gathering of people each of whom spoke two languages and understood a third and held only one language in common with any of the others. It depends on what workings of language you want to see or want to see first, on what you choose to define as normative.

In keeping with autonomous, fraternal models of community, analyses of language use commonly assume that principles of cooperation and shared understanding are normally in effect. Descriptions of interactions between people in conversation, classrooms, medical and bureaucratic settings, readily take it for granted that the situation is governed by a single set of rules or norms shared by all participants. The analysis focuses then on how those rules produce or fail to produce an orderly, coherent exchange. Models involving games and moves are often used to describe interactions. Despite whatever conflicts or systematic social differences might be in play, it is assumed that all participants are engaged in the same game and that the game is the same for all players. Often it is. But of course it often is not, as, for example, when speakers are from different classes or cultures, or one party is exercising authority and another is submitting to it or questioning it. Last year one of my children moved to a new elementary school that had more open classrooms and more flexible curricula than the conventional school he started out in. A few days into the term, we asked him what it was like at the new school. "Well," he said, "they're a lot nicer, and they have a lot less rules. But know *why* they're nicer?" "Why?" I asked. "So you'll obey all the rules they don't have," he replied. This is a very coherent analysis with considerable elegance and explanatory power, but probably not the one his teacher would have given.

When linguistic (or literate) interaction is described in terms of orderliness, games, moves, or scripts, usually only legitimate moves are actually named as part of the system, where legitimacy is defined from the point of view of the party in authority — regardless of what other parties might see themselves as doing. Teacher-pupil language, for example, tends to be described almost entirely from the point of view of the teacher and teaching, not from the point of view of pupils and pupiling (the word doesn't even exist, though the thing certainly does). If a classroom is analyzed as a social world unified and homogenized with respect to the teacher, whatever students do other than what the teacher specifies is invisible or anomalous to the analysis. This can be true in practice as well. On several occasions my fourth grader, the one busy obeying all the rules they didn't have, was given writing assignments that took the form of answering a series of questions to build up a paragraph. These questions often asked him to identify with the interests of those in power over him — parents, teachers, doctors, public authorities. He invariably sought ways to resist or subvert these assignments. One assignment, for instance, called for imagining "a helpful invention." The students were asked to write single-sentence responses to the following questions:

> What kind of invention would help you?
> How would it help you?
> Why would you need it?
> What would it look like?
> Would other people be able to use it also?
> What would be an invention to help your teacher?
> What would be an invention to help your parents?

Manuel's reply read as follows:

> A grate adventchin
>
> Some inventchins are GRATE!!!!!!!!!!! My inventchin would be a shot that would put every thing you learn at school in your brain. It would help me by letting me graduate right now!! I would need it because it would let me play with my friends, go on vacachin and, do fun a lot more. It would look like a regular shot. Ather peaple would use to. This inventchin would help my teacher parents get away from a lot of work. I think a shot like this would be GRATE!

Despite the spelling, the assignment received the usual star to indicate the task had been fulfilled in an acceptable way. No recognition was available, however, of the humor, the attempt to be critical or contestatory, to parody the structures of authority. On that score, Manuel's luck was only slightly better than Guaman Poma's. What is the place of unsolicited oppositional discourse, parody, resistance, critique in the imagined classroom community? Are teachers supposed to feel that their teaching has been most successful when they have eliminated such things and unified the social world, probably in their own image? Who wins when we do that? Who loses?

Such questions may be hypothetical, because in the United States in the 1990s, many teachers find themselves less and less able to do that even if they want to. The composition of the national collectivity is changing and so are the styles, as Anderson put it, in which it is being imagined. In the 1980s in many nation-states, imagined national syntheses that had retained hegemonic force began to dissolve. Internal social groups with histories and lifeways different from the official ones began insisting on those histories and lifeways *as part of their citizenship*, as the very mode of their membership in the national collectivity. In their dialogues with dominant institutions, many groups began asserting a rhetoric of belonging that made demands beyond those of representation and basic rights granted from above. In universities we started to hear, "I don't just want you to let me be here, I want to belong here; this institution should belong to me as much as it does to anyone else." Institutions have responded with, among other things, rhetorics of diversity and multiculturalism whose import at this moment is up for grabs across the ideological spectrum.

These shifts are being lived out by everyone working in education today, and everyone is challenged by them in one way or another. Those of us committed to educational democracy are particularly challenged as that notion finds itself besieged on the public agenda. Many of those who govern us display, openly, their interest in a quiescent, ignorant, manipulable electorate. Even as an ideal, the concept of an enlightened citizenry seems to have disappeared from the national imagination. A couple of years ago the university where I work went through an intense and wrenching debate over a narrowly defined Western-culture requirement that had been instituted there in 1980. It kept boiling down to a debate over the ideas of national patrimony, cultural citizenship, and imagined community. In the end, the requirement was transformed into a much more broadly defined course called Cultures, Ideas, Values.[4] In the context of the change, a new course was designed that centered on the Americas and the multiple cultural histories (including European ones) that have intersected here. As you can imagine, the course attracted a very diverse student body. The classroom functioned not like a homogeneous community or a horizontal alliance but like a contact zone. Every single text we read stood in specific historical relationships to the students in the class, but the range and variety of historical relationships in play were enormous. Everybody had a stake in nearly everything we read, but the range and kind of stakes varied widely.

THE VERY NATURE OF THE COURSE PUT IDEAS AND IDENTITIES ON THE LINE.

It was the most exciting teaching we had ever done, and also the hardest. We were struck, for example, at how anomalous the formal lecture became in a contact zone (who can forget Atahuallpa throwing down the Bible because it would not speak to him?). The lecturer's traditional (imagined) task — unifying the world in the class's eyes by means of a monologue that rings equally coherent, revealing, and true for all, forging an ad hoc community, homogeneous with respect to one's own words — this task became not only impossible but anomalous and unimaginable. Instead, one had to work in the knowledge that whatever one said was going to be systematically received in radically heterogeneous ways that we were neither able nor entitled to prescribe.

The very nature of the course put ideas and identities on the line. All the students in the class had the experience, for example, of hearing their culture discussed and objectified in ways that horrified them; all the students saw their roots traced back to legacies of both glory and shame; all the students experienced face-to-face the ignorance and incomprehension, and occasionally the hostility, of others. In the absence of community values and the hope of synthesis, it was easy to forget the positives; the fact, for instance, that kinds of marginalization once taken for granted were gone. Virtually every student was having the experience of seeing the world described with him or her in it. Along with rage, incomprehension, and pain, there were exhilarating moments of wonder and revelation, mutual understanding, and new wisdom — the joys of the contact zone. The sufferings and revelations were, at different moments to be sure, experienced by every student. No one was excluded, and no one was safe.

The fact that no one was safe made all of us involved in the course appreciate the importance of what we came to call "safe houses." We used the term to refer to social and intellectual spaces where groups can constitute themselves as horizontal, homogeneous, sovereign communities with high degrees of trust, shared understandings, temporary protection from legacies of oppression. This is why, as we realized, multicultural curricula should not seek to replace ethnic or women's studies, for example. Where there are legacies of subordination, groups need places for healing and mutual recognition, safe houses in which to construct shared understandings, knowledges, claims on the world that they can then bring into the contact zone.

Meanwhile, our job in the Americas course remains to figure out how to make that crossroads the best site for learning that it can be. We are looking for the pedagogical arts of the contact zone. These will include, we are sure, exercises in storytelling and in identifying with the ideas, interests, histories, and attitudes of others; experiments in transculturation and collaborative work and in the arts of critique, parody, and comparison (including unseemly comparisons between elite and vernacular cultural forms); the redemption of the oral; ways for people to engage with suppressed aspects of history (including their own histories), ways to move *into and out of* rhetorics of authenticity; ground rules for communication across lines of difference and hierarchy that go beyond politeness but maintain mutual respect; a systematic approach to the all-important concept of *cultural mediation*. These arts were in play in every room at the extraordinary Pittsburgh conference on literacy. I learned a lot about them there, and I am thankful.

NOTES

[1] For an introduction in English to these and other aspects of Guaman Poma's work, see Rolena Adorno. Adorno and Mercedes Lopez-Baralt pioneered the study of Andean symbolic systems in Guaman Poma.

[2] It is far from clear that the *Royal Commentaries* was as benign as the Spanish seemed to assume. The book certainly played a role in maintaining the identity and aspirations of indigenous elites in the Andes. In the mid-eighteenth century, a new edition of the *Royal Commentaries* was suppressed by Spanish authorities because its preface included a prophecy by Sir Walter Raleigh that the English would invade Peru and restore the Inca monarchy.

[3] The discussion of community here is summarized from my essay "Linguistic Utopias."
[4] For information about this program and the contents of courses taught in it, write Program in Cultures, Ideas, Values (CIV), Stanford Univ., Stanford, CA 94305.

BIBLIOGRAPHY

Adorno, Rolena. *Guaman Poma de Ayala: Writing and Resistance in Colonial Peru*. Austin: U of Texas P, 1986.
Anderson, Benedict. *Imagined Communities: Reflections on the Origins and Spread of Nationalism*. London: Verso, 1984.
Garcilaso de la Vega, El Inca. *Royal Commentaries of the Incas*. 1613. Austin: U of Texas P, 1966.
Guaman Poma de Ayala, Felipe. *El primer nueva corónica y buen gobierno*. Manuscript. Ed. John Murra and Rolena Adorno. Mexico: Siglo XXI, 1980.
Pratt, Mary Louise. "Linguistic Utopias." *The Linguistics of Writing*. Ed. Nigel Fabb et al. Manchester: Manchester UP, 1987. 48–66.
Treviño, Gloria. "Cultural Ambivalence in Early Chicano Prose Fiction." Diss. Stanford U, 1985.

QUESTIONS FOR A SECOND READING

1. Perhaps the most interesting question "Arts of the Contact Zone" raises for its readers is how to put together the pieces: the examples from Pratt's children, the discussion of Guaman Poma and the *New Chronicle and Good Government*, the brief history of European literacy, and the discussion of curriculum reform at Stanford. The terms that run through the sections are, among others, these: "contact," "community," "autoethnography," "transculturation." As you reread, mark those passages you might use to trace the general argument that cuts across these examples.

2. This essay was originally delivered as a lecture. Before you read Pratt's essay again, create a set of notes on what you remember as important, relevant, or worthwhile. Imagine yourself as part of her audience. Then reread the essay. Where would you want to interrupt her? What questions could you ask her that might make "Arts of the Contact Zone" more accessible to you?

3. This is an essay about reading and writing and teaching and learning, about the "literate arts" and the "pedagogical arts" of the contact zone. Surely the composition class, the first-year college English class, can be imagined as a contact zone. And it seems in the spirit of Pratt's essay to identify (as a student) with Guaman Poma. As you reread, think about how and where this essay might be said to speak directly to you about your education as a reader and writer in a contact zone.

4. There are some difficult terms in this essay: "autochthonous," "autoethnography," "transculturation." The last two are defined in the text; the first you will have to look up. (We did.) In some ways, the slipperiest of the key words in the essay is "culture." At one point Pratt says,

> If one thinks of cultures, or literatures, as discrete, coherently structured, monolingual edifices, Guaman Poma's text, and indeed any

> autoethnographic work, appears anomalous or chaotic — as it apparently did to the European scholars Pietschmann spoke to in 1912. If one does not think of cultures this way, then Guaman Poma's text is simply heterogeneous, as the Andean region was itself and remains today. Such a text is heterogeneous on the reception end as well as the production end: it will read very differently to people in different positions in the contact zone. (p. 324)

If one thinks of cultures as "coherently structured, monolingual edifices," the text appears one way; if one thinks otherwise, the text is "simply heterogeneous." What might it mean to make this shift in the way one thinks of culture? Can you do it — that is, can you read the *New Chronicle* from both points of view, make the two points of view work in your own imagining? Can you, for example, think of a group that you participate in as a "community"? Then can you think of it as a "contact zone"? Which one seems "natural" to you? What does Pratt assume to be the dominant point of view now, for *her* readers?

As you reread, not only do you want to get a sense of how to explain these two attitudes toward culture, but you also need to practice shifting your point of view from one to the other. Think, from inside the position of each, of the things you would be expected to say about Poma's text, Manuel's invention, and your classroom.

ASSIGNMENTS FOR WRITING

Here, briefly, are two descriptions of the writing one might find or expect in the "contact zone." They serve as an introduction to the three writing assignments.

> Autoethnography, transculturation, critique, collaboration, bilingualism, mediation, parody, denunciation, imaginary dialogue, vernacular expression — these are some of the literate arts of the contact zone. Miscomprehension, incomprehension, dead letters, unread masterpieces, absolute heterogeneity of meaning — these are some of the perils of writing in the contact zone. They all live among us today in the transnationalized metropolis of the United States and are becoming more widely visible, more pressing, and, like Guaman Poma's text, more decipherable to those who once would have ignored them in defense of a stable, centered sense of knowledge and reality. (pp. 324–25)

> We are looking for the pedagogical arts of the contact zone. These will include, we are sure, exercises in storytelling and in identifying with the ideas, interests, histories, and attitudes of others; experiments in transculturation and collaborative work and in the arts of critique, parody, and comparison (including unseemly comparisons between elite and vernacular cultural forms); the redemption of the oral; ways for people to engage with suppressed aspects of history (including their own histories), ways

to move *into and out of* rhetorics of authenticity; ground rules for communication across lines of difference and hierarchy that go beyond politeness but maintain mutual respect; a systematic approach to the all-important concept of ***cultural mediation***. (p. 329)

1. One way of working with Pratt's essay, of extending its project, would be to conduct your own local inventory of writing from the contact zone. You might do this on your own or in teams with others from your class. You will want to gather several similar documents, your "archive," before you make your final selection. Think about how to make that choice. What makes one document stand out as representative? Here are two ways you might organize your search:

   a. You could look for historical documents. A local historical society might have documents written by Native Americans ("Indians") to the white settlers. There may be documents written by slaves to masters or to northern whites explaining their experience with slavery. There may be documents by women (like suffragists) trying to negotiate for public positions and rights. There may be documents from any of a number of racial or ethnic groups—Hispanic, Jewish, Irish, Italian, Polish, Swedish—trying to explain their positions to the mainstream culture. There may, perhaps at union halls, be documents written by workers to owners. Your own sense of the heritage of your area should direct your search.

   b. Or you could look for contemporary documents in the print that is around you, things that you might otherwise overlook. Pratt refers to one of the characteristic genres of the Hispanic community, the *"testimonio."* You could look at the writing of any marginalized group, particularly writing intended, at least in part, to represent the experience of outsiders to the dominant culture (or to be in dialogue with that culture or to respond to that culture). These documents, if we follow Pratt's example, would encompass the work of young children or students, including college students.

   Once you have completed your inventory, choose a document you would like to work with and present it carefully and in detail (perhaps in even greater detail than Pratt's presentation of the *New Chronicle*). You might imagine that you are presenting this to someone who would not have seen it and would not know how to read it, at least not as an example of the literate arts of the contact zone.

2. Another way of extending the project of Pratt's essay would be to write your own autoethnography. It should not be too hard to locate a setting or context in which you are the "other"—the one who speaks from outside rather than inside the dominant discourse. Pratt says that the position of the outsider is marked not only by differences of language and ways of thinking and speaking but also by differences in power, authority, status. In a sense, she argues, the only way those in power can understand you is in *their* terms.

These are terms you will need to use to tell your story, but your goal is to describe your position in ways that "engage with representations others have made of [you]" without giving in or giving up or disappearing in their already formed sense of who you are.

This is an interesting challenge. One of the things that will make the writing difficult is that the autoethnographic or transcultural text calls upon skills not usually valued in American classrooms: bilingualism, parody, denunciation, imaginary dialogue, vernacular expression, storytelling, unseemly comparisons of high and low cultural forms — these are some of the terms Pratt offers. These do not fit easily with the traditional genres of the writing class (essay, term paper, summary, report) or its traditional values (unity, consistency, sincerity, clarity, correctness, decorum).

You will probably need to take this essay (or whatever it should be called) through several drafts. It might be best to begin as Pratt's student, using her description as a preliminary guide. Once you get a sense of your own project, you may find that you have terms or examples to add to her list of the literate arts of the contact zone.

3. Citing Benedict Anderson and what he calls "imagined communities," Pratt argues that our idea of community is "strongly utopian, embodying values like equality, fraternity, liberty, which the societies often profess but systematically fail to realize." Against this utopian vision of community, Pratt argues that we need to develop ways of understanding (even noticing) social and intellectual spaces that are not homogeneous, unified; we need to develop ways of understanding and valuing difference.

   Think of a community of which you are a member, a community that is important to you. And think about the utopian terms you are given to name and describe this community. Think, then, about this group in Pratt's terms — as a "contact zone." How would you name and describe this social space? Write an essay in which you present these alternate points of view on a single social group. You will need to present this discussion fully, so that someone who is not part of your group can follow what you say, and you should take time to think about the consequences (for you, for your group) of this shift in point of view, in terms.

MAKING CONNECTIONS

1. Here, from "Arts of the Contact Zone," is Mary Louise Pratt on the "autoethnographic" text:

   > Guaman Poma's *New Chronicle* is an instance of what I have proposed to call an *autoethnographic* text, by which I mean a text in which people undertake to describe themselves in ways that engage with representations others have made of them. Thus if ethnographic texts are those in which European metropolitan subjects represent to themselves their others (usually their conquered others),

> autoethnographic texts are representations that the so-defined others construct *in response to* or in dialogue with those texts. . . . They involve a selective collaboration with and appropriation of idioms of the metropolis or the conqueror. These are merged or infiltrated to varying degrees with indigenous idioms to create self-representations intended to intervene in metropolitan modes of understanding. . . . Such texts often constitute a marginalized group's point of entry into the dominant circuits of print culture. It is interesting to think, for example, of American slave autobiography in its autoethnographic dimensions, which in some respects distinguish it from Euramerican autobiographical tradition. (pp. 319–20)

John Edgar Wideman's "Our Time" (p. 422) and the excerpts from Gloria Anzaldúa's "How to Tame a Wild Tongue" (p. 26) could serve as twentieth-century examples of autoethnographic texts. Choose one of these selections and reread it with "Arts of the Contact Zone" in mind. Write an essay that presents the selection as an example of autoethnographic and/or transcultural texts. You should imagine that you are working to put Pratt's ideas to the test (*do* they do what she says such texts must do?), but also add what you have to say concerning this text as a literate effort to be present in the context of difference.

e 2. In the selection titled "States," Edward Said says,

> All cultures spin out a dialectic of self and other, the subject "I" who is native, authentic, at home, and the object "it" or "you," who is foreign, perhaps threatening, different, out there. From this dialectic comes the series of heroes and monsters, founding fathers and barbarians, prized masterpieces and despised opponents that express a culture from its deepest sense of national self-identity to its refined patriotism, and finally to its coarse jingoism, xenophobia, and exclusivist bias. (e-Pages)

This is as true of the Palestinians as it is of the Israelis — although, he adds, "For Palestinian culture, the odd thing is that its own identity is more frequently than not perceived as 'other.'"

Citing Benedict Anderson and what he refers to as "imagined communities," Mary Louise Pratt in "Arts of the Contact Zone" argues that our idea of community is "strongly utopian, embodying values like equality, fraternity, liberty, which the societies often profess but systematically fail to realize." Against this utopian vision of community, Pratt argues that we need to develop ways of understanding (noticing or creating) social and intellectual spaces that are not homogeneous or unified — contact zones. She argues that we need to develop ways of understanding and valuing difference.

There are similar goals and objects to these projects. Reread Pratt's essay with Said's "States" in mind. As she defines what she refers to as the "literate

---

e See the e-Pages at bedfordstmartins.com/waysofreading.

arts of the contact zone," can you find points of reference in Said's text? Said's thinking always attended to the importance and the conditions of writing, including his own. There are ways that "States" could be imagined as both "autoethnographic" and "transcultural." How might Said's work allow you to understand the "literate arts of the contact zone" in practice? How might his work allow you to understand the problems and possibilities of such writing beyond what Pratt has imagined, presented, and predicted?

3. Mary Louise Pratt, in her essay "The Arts of the Contact Zone," describes the writing that one might find in a contact zone as such:

> Autoethnography, transculturation, critique, collaboration, bilingualism, mediation, parody, denunciation, imaginary dialogue, vernacular expression — these are some of the literate arts of the contact zone. Miscomprehension, incomprehension, dead letters, unread masterpieces, absolute heterogeneity of meaning — these are some of the perils of writing in the contact zone. (p. 324)

She then goes on to define the pedagogical arts of the contact zone:

> These will include, we are sure, exercises in storytelling and in identifying with the ideas, interests, histories, and attitudes of others; experiments in transculturation and collaborative work in the arts of critique, parody, and comparison (including unseemly comparisons between elite and vernacular cultural forms); the redemption of the oral; ways for people to engage with suppressed aspects of history (including their own histories), ways to move into and out of rhetorics of authenticity; ground rules for communication across lines of difference and hierarchy that go beyond politeness but maintain mutal respect; a systematic approach to the all-important concept of *cultural mediation*. (p. 329)

Jamie's "Shia Girls" could be seen as an example of the kinds of writing and pedagogy that Pratt believes typify contact zones. Reread "Shia Girls" alongside "The Arts of the Contact Zone." Then, write an essay that presents "Shia Girls" through the lens of Pratt's essay. How would you describe the particular contact zone evoked in Jamie's essay? What moments from "Shia Girls" might best serve as examples of the writing and pedagogy Pratt describes as hallmarks of the contact zone? How could you explain them as such? e

e See the e-Pages at bedfordstmartins.com/waysofreading.

RICHARD
Rodriguez

Richard Rodriguez, the son of Mexican immigrants, was born in San Francisco in 1944. He grew up in Sacramento, where he attended Catholic schools before going on to Stanford University, Columbia University, the Warburg Institute in London, and the University of California at Berkeley, eventually pursuing a PhD in English Renaissance literature. His essays have been published in *Saturday Review*, *The American Scholar*, *Change*, and elsewhere. He now lives in San Francisco and works as a lecturer, an educational consultant, and a freelance writer. He has published several books: *Hunger of Memory: The Education of Richard Rodriguez* (1981), *Days of Obligation: An Argument with My Mexican Father* (1992), and *Brown: The Last Discovery of America* (2002).

In *Hunger of Memory*, a book of autobiographical essays that the *Christian Science Monitor* called "beautifully written, wrung from a sore heart," Rodriguez tells the story of his education, paying particular attention to both the meaning of his success as a student and, as he says, "its consequent price — the loss." Rodriguez's loss is represented most powerfully by his increased alienation from his parents and the decrease of intimate exchanges in family life. His parents' primary language was Spanish; his, once he became eager for success in school, was English. But the barrier was not only a language barrier. Rodriguez discovered that the interests he developed at school and through his reading were interests he did not share with those at home — in fact, his desire to speak of them tended to threaten and humiliate his mother and father.

This separation, Rodriguez argues, is a necessary part of every person's development, even though not everyone experiences it so dramatically. We must leave home and familiar ways of speaking and understanding in order to participate in public life. On these grounds, Rodriguez has been a strong voice against bilingual education, arguing that classes conducted in Spanish will only reinforce Spanish-speaking students' separateness from mainstream American life. Rodriguez's book caused a great deal of controversy upon publication, particularly in the Hispanic community. As one critic argued, "It is indeed painful that Mr. Rodriguez has come to identify himself so completely with the majority culture that he must propagandize for a system of education which can only produce other deprived and impoverished souls like himself." In his second book, *Days of Obligation: An Argument with My Mexican Father*, Rodriguez continues to explore his relationship with his family and with his Mexican heritage; here, however, he also writes of his life as a gay male and the forms of alienation entailed by his sexuality, including his sense of distance from gay lifestyles and culture, both popular and academic.

The selection that follows, Chapter 2 of *Hunger of Memory*, deals with Rodriguez's experiences in school. "If," he says, "because of my schooling I had grown culturally separated from my parents, my education finally had given me ways of speaking and caring about that fact." This essay is a record of how he came to understand the changes in his life. A reviewer writing in the *Atlantic Monthly* concluded that *Hunger of Memory* will survive in our literature "not because of some forgotten public issues that once bisected Richard Rodriguez's life, but because his history of that life has something to say about what it means to be American . . . and what it means to be human."

The Achievement of Desire

I stand in the ghetto classroom — "the guest speaker" — attempting to lecture on the mystery of the sounds of our words to rows of diffident students. "Don't you hear it? Listen! The music of our words. *'Sumer is icumen in. . . .'* And songs on the car radio. We need Aretha Franklin's voice to fill plain words with music — her life." In the face of their empty stares, I try to create an enthusiasm. But the girls in the back row turn to watch some boy passing outside. There are flutters of smiles, waves. And someone's mouth elongates heavy, silent words through the barrier of glass. Silent words — the lips straining to shape each voiceless syllable: *"Meet meee late errr."* By the door, the instructor smiles at me, apparently hoping that I will be able to spark some enthusiasm in the class. But only one student seems to be listening. A girl, maybe fourteen. In this gray room her eyes shine with ambition. She keeps nodding and nodding at all that I say; she even takes notes. And each time I ask a question, she jerks up and down in her desk like a marionette, while her hand waves over the bowed heads of her classmates. It is myself (as a boy) I see as she faces me now (a man in my thirties).

THE BOY WHO FIRST ENTERED A CLASSROOM BARELY ABLE TO SPEAK ENGLISH, TWENTY YEARS LATER CONCLUDED HIS STUDIES IN THE STATELY QUIET OF THE READING ROOM IN THE BRITISH MUSEUM.

The boy who first entered a classroom barely able to speak English, twenty years later concluded his studies in the stately quiet of the reading room in the British Museum. Thus with one sentence I can summarize my academic career. It will be harder to summarize what sort of life connects the boy to the man.

With every award, each graduation from one level of education to the next, people I'd meet would congratulate me. Their refrain [was] always the same: "Your parents must be very proud." Sometimes then they'd ask me how I managed it — my "success." (How?) After a while, I had several quick answers to give in reply. I'd admit, for one thing, that I went to an excellent grammar school. (My earliest teachers, the nuns, made my success their ambition.) And my brother and both my sisters were very good students. (They often brought home the shiny school trophies I came to want.) And my mother and father always encouraged me. (At every graduation they were behind the stunning flash of the camera when I turned to look at the crowd.)

As important as these factors were, however, they account inadequately for my academic advance. Nor do they suggest what an odd success I managed. For although I was a very good student, I was also a very bad student. I was a "scholarship boy," a certain kind of scholarship boy. Always successful, I was always unconfident. Exhilarated by my progress. Sad. I became the prized student — anxious and eager to learn. Too eager, too anxious — an imitative and unoriginal pupil. My brother and two sisters enjoyed the advantages I did, and they grew to be as successful as I, but none of them ever seemed so anxious about their schooling. A second-grade student, I was the one who came home and corrected the "simple" grammatical mistakes of our parents. ("Two negatives make a positive.") Proudly I announced — to my family's startled silence — that a teacher had said I was losing all trace of a Spanish accent. I was oddly annoyed when I was unable to get parental help with a homework assignment. The night my father tried to help me with an arithmetic exercise, he kept reading the instructions, each time more deliberately, until I pried the textbook out of his hands, saying, "I'll try to figure it out some more by myself."

When I reached the third grade, I outgrew such behavior. I became more tactful, careful to keep separate the two very different worlds of my day. But then, with ever-increasing intensity, I devoted myself to my studies. I became bookish, puzzling to all my family. Ambition set me apart. When my brother saw me struggling home with stacks of library books, he would laugh, shouting: "Hey, Four Eyes!" My father opened a closet one day and was startled to find me inside, reading a novel. My mother would find me reading when I was supposed to be asleep or helping around the house or playing outside. In a voice angry or worried or just curious, she'd ask: "What do you see in your books?" It became the family's joke. When I was called and wouldn't reply, someone would say I must be hiding under my bed with a book.

(How did I manage my success?)

What I am about to say to you has taken me more than twenty years to admit: *A primary reason for my success in the classroom was that I couldn't forget that schooling was changing me and separating me from the life I enjoyed before becoming a student.* That simple realization! For years I never spoke to anyone about it. Never mentioned a thing to my family or my teachers or classmates. From a very early age, I understood enough, just enough about my classroom experiences to keep what I knew repressed, hidden beneath layers of embarrassment. Not until my last months as a graduate student, nearly thirty years old, was it possible for me to think much about the reasons for my academic success. Only then. At the end of my schooling, I needed to determine how far I had moved from my past. The adult finally confronted, and now must publicly say, what the child shuddered from knowing and could never admit to himself or to those many faces that smiled at his every success. ("Your parents must be very proud....")

I

At the end, in the British Museum (too distracted to finish my dissertation) for weeks I read, speed-read, books by modern educational theorists, only to find infrequent and slight mention of students like me. (Much more is written about the more typical case, the lower-class student who barely is helped by his schooling.) Then one day, leafing through Richard Hoggart's *The Uses of Literacy*, I found, in his description of the scholarship boy, myself. For the first time I realized that there were other students like me, and so I was able to frame the meaning of my academic success, its consequent price — the loss.

Hoggart's description is distinguished, at least initially, by deep understanding. What he grasps very well is that the scholarship boy must move between environments, his home and the classroom, which are at cultural extremes, opposed. With his family, the boy has the intense pleasure of intimacy, the family's consolation in feeling public alienation. Lavish emotions texture home life. *Then*, at school, the instruction bids him to trust lonely reason primarily. Immediate needs set the pace of his parents' lives. From his mother and father the boy learns to trust spontaneity and nonrational ways of knowing. *Then*, at school, there is mental calm. Teachers emphasize the value of a reflectiveness that opens a space between thinking and immediate action.

Years of schooling must pass before the boy will be able to sketch the cultural differences in his day as abstractly as this. But he senses those differences early. Perhaps as early as the night he brings home an assignment from school and finds the house too noisy for study.

> He has to be more and more alone, if he is going to "get on." He will have, probably unconsciously, to oppose the ethos of the hearth, the intense gregariousness of the working-class family group. Since everything centres upon the living-room, there is unlikely to be a room of his own; the bedrooms are cold and inhospitable, and to warm them or the front room, if there is one, would not only be expensive, but would require an imaginative leap — out of the tradition — which most families are not capable of making. There is a corner of the living-room table. On the other side Mother is ironing, the wireless is on, someone is singing a snatch of song or Father says intermittently whatever comes into his head. The boy has to cut himself off mentally, so as to do his homework, as well as he can.[1]

The next day, the lesson is as apparent at school. There are even rows of desks. Discussion is ordered. The boy must rehearse his thoughts and raise his hand before speaking out in a loud voice to an audience of classmates. And there is time enough, and silence, to think about ideas (big ideas) never considered at home by his parents.

Not for the working-class child alone is adjustment to the classroom difficult. Good schooling requires that any student alter early childhood habits. But the working-class child is usually least prepared for the change. And, unlike many middle-class children, he goes home and sees in his parents a way of life not only different but starkly opposed to that of the classroom. (He enters the house and hears his parents talking in ways his teachers discourage.)

Without extraordinary determination and the great assistance of others — at home and at school — there is little chance for success. Typically most working-class children are barely changed by the classroom. The exception succeeds. The relative few become scholarship students. Of these, Richard Hoggart estimates, most manage a fairly graceful transition. Somehow they learn to live in the two very different worlds of their day. There are some others, however, those Hoggart pejoratively terms "scholarship boys," for whom success comes with special anxiety. Scholarship boy: good student, troubled son. The child is "moderately endowed," intellectually mediocre, Hoggart supposes — though it may be more pertinent to note the special qualities of temperament in the child. High-strung child. Brooding. Sensitive. Haunted by the knowledge that one *chooses* to become a student. (Education is not an inevitable or natural step in growing up.) Here is a child who cannot forget that his academic success distances him from a life he loved, even from his own memory of himself.

Initially, he wavers, balances allegiance. ("The boy is himself [until he reaches, say, the upper forms] very much of *both* the worlds of home and school. He is enormously obedient to the dictates of the world of school, but emotionally still strongly wants to continue as part of the family circle.") Gradually, necessarily, the balance is lost. The boy needs to spend more and more time studying, each night enclosing himself in the silence permitted and required by intense concentration. He takes his first step toward academic success, away from his family.

From the very first days, through the years following, it will be with his parents — the figures of lost authority, the persons toward whom he feels deepest love — that the change will be most powerfully measured. A separation will unravel between them. Advancing in his studies, the boy notices that his mother and father have not changed as much as he. Rather, when he sees them, they often remind him of the person he once was and the life he earlier shared with them. He realizes what some Romantics also know when they praise the working class for the capacity for human closeness, qualities of passion and spontaneity, that the rest of us experience in like measure only in the earliest part of our youth. For the Romantic, this doesn't make working-class life childish. Working-class life challenges precisely because it is an *adult* way of life.

The scholarship boy reaches a different conclusion. He cannot afford to admire his parents. (How could he and still pursue such a contrary life?) He permits himself embarrassment at their lack of education. And to evade nostalgia for the life he has lost, he concentrates on the benefits education will bestow upon him. He becomes especially ambitious. Without the support of old certainties and consolations, almost mechanically, he assumes the procedures and doctrines of the classroom. The kind of allegiance the young student might have given his mother and father only days earlier, he transfers to the teacher, the new figure of authority. "[The scholarship boy] tends to make a father-figure of his form-master," Hoggart observes.

But Hoggart's calm prose only makes me recall the urgency with which I came to idolize my grammar school teachers. I began by imitating their accents, using their diction, trusting their every direction. The very first facts they dispensed, I grasped with awe. Any book they told me to read, I read — then waited for them to tell me which books I enjoyed. Their every casual opinion I came to adopt and to trumpet when I returned home. I stayed after school "to help" — to get my teacher's undivided attention. It was the nun's encouragement that mattered most to me. (She understood exactly what — my parents never seemed to appraise so well — all my achievements entailed.) Memory gently caressed each word of praise bestowed in the classroom so that compliments teachers paid me years ago come quickly to mind even today.

The enthusiasm I felt in second-grade classes I flaunted before both my parents. The docile, obedient student came home a shrill and precocious son who insisted on correcting and teaching his parents with the remark: "My teacher told us. . . ."

I intended to hurt my mother and father. I was still angry at them for having encouraged me toward classroom English. But gradually this anger was exhausted, replaced by guilt as school grew more and more attractive to me. I grew increasingly successful, a talkative student. My hand was raised in the classroom; I yearned to answer any question. At home, life was less noisy than it had been. (I spoke to classmates and teachers more often each day than to family members.) Quiet at home, I sat with my papers for hours each night. I never forgot that schooling had irretrievably changed my family's life. That knowledge, however, did not weaken ambition. Instead, it strengthened resolve. Those times I remembered the loss of my past with regret, I quickly reminded myself of all the things my teachers could give me. (They could make me an educated man.) I tightened my grip on pencil and books. I evaded nostalgia. Tried hard to forget. But one does not forget by trying to forget. One only remembers. I remembered too well that education had changed my family's life. I would not have become a scholarship boy had I not so often remembered.

Once she was sure that her children knew English, my mother would tell us, "You should keep up your Spanish." Voices playfully groaned in response. *"¡Pochos!"* my mother would tease. I listened silently.

After a while, I grew more calm at home. I developed tact. A fourth-grade student, I was no longer the show-off in front of my parents. I became a conventionally dutiful son, politely affectionate, cheerful enough, even — for reasons beyond choosing — my father's favorite. And much about my family life was easy then, comfortable, happy in the rhythm of our living together: hearing my father getting ready for work; eating the breakfast my mother had made me; looking up from a novel to hear my brother or one of my sisters playing with friends in the backyard; in winter, coming upon the house all lighted up after dark.

But withheld from my mother and father was any mention of what most mattered to me: the extraordinary experience of first-learning. Late afternoon: in the midst of preparing dinner, my mother would come up behind me while I was trying to read. Her head just over mine, her breath warmly scented with food. "What are you reading?" Or, "Tell me all about your new courses." I would barely respond, "Just the usual things, nothing special." (A half smile, then silence. Her head moving

Habitual action

back in the silence. Silence! Instead of the flood of intimate sounds that had once flowed smoothly between us, there was this silence.) After dinner, I would rush to a bedroom with papers and books. As often as possible, I resisted parental pleas to "save lights" by coming to the kitchen to work. I kept so much, so often, to myself. Sad. Enthusiastic. Troubled by the excitement of coming upon new ideas. Eager. Fascinated by the promising texture of a brand-new book. I hoarded the pleasures of learning. Alone for hours. Enthralled. Nervous. I rarely looked away from my books — or back on my memories. Nights when relatives visited and the front rooms were warmed by Spanish sounds, I slipped quietly out of the house.

It mattered that education was changing me. It never ceased to matter. My brother and sisters would giggle at our mother's mispronounced words. They'd correct her gently. My mother laughed girlishly one night, trying not to pronounce *sheep* as *ship*. From a distance I listened sullenly. From that distance, pretending not to notice on another occasion, I saw my father looking at the title pages of my library books. That was the scene on my mind when I walked home with a fourth-grade companion and heard him say that his parents read to him every night. (A strange-sounding book — *Winnie the Pooh*.) Immediately, I wanted to know, "What is it like?" My companion, however, thought I wanted to know about the plot of the book. Another day, my mother surprised me by asking for a "nice" book to read. "Something not too hard you think I might like." Carefully I chose one, Willa Cather's *My Ántonia*. But when, several weeks later, I happened to see it next to her bed unread except for the first few pages, I was furious and suddenly wanted to cry. I grabbed up the book and took it back to my room and placed it in its place, alphabetically on my shelf.

"Your parents must be very proud of you." People began to say that to me about the time I was in sixth grade. To answer affirmatively, I'd smile. Shyly I'd smile, never betraying my sense of the irony: I was not proud of my mother and father. I was embarrassed by their lack of education. It was not that I ever thought they were stupid, though stupidly I took for granted their enormous native intelligence. Simply, what mattered to me was that they were not like my teachers.

But, "Why didn't you tell us about the award?" my mother demanded, her frown weakened by pride. At the grammar school ceremony several weeks after, her eyes were brighter than the trophy I'd won. Pushing back the hair from my forehead, she whispered that I had "shown" the *gringos*. A few minutes later, I heard my father speak to my teacher and felt ashamed of his labored, accented words. Then guilty for the shame. I felt such contrary feelings. (There is no simple road-map through the heart of the scholarship boy.) My teacher was so soft-spoken and her words were edged sharp and clean. I admired her until it seemed to me that she spoke too carefully. Sensing that she was condescending to them, I became nervous. Resentful. Protective. I tried to move my parents away. "You both must be very proud of Richard," the nun said. They responded quickly. (They were proud.) "We are proud of all our children." Then this afterthought: "They sure didn't get their brains from us." They all laughed. I smiled.

Tightening the irony into a knot was the knowledge that my parents were always behind me. They made success possible. They evened the path. They sent their children to parochial schools because the nuns "teach better." They paid a tuition they couldn't afford. They spoke English to us.

For their children my parents wanted chances they never had — an easier way. It saddened my mother to learn that some relatives forced their children to start working right after high school. To *her* children she would say, "Get all the education you can." In schooling she recognized the key to job advancement. And with the remark she remembered her past.

As a girl new to America my mother had been awarded a high school diploma by teachers too careless or busy to notice that she hardly spoke English. On her own, she determined to learn how to type. That skill got her jobs typing envelopes in letter shops, and it encouraged in her an optimism about the possibility of advancement. (Each morning when her sisters put on uniforms, she chose a bright-colored dress.) The years of young womanhood passed, and her typing speed increased. She also became an excellent speller of words she mispronounced. "And I've never been to college," she'd say, smiling, when her children asked her to spell words they were too lazy to look up in a dictionary.

Typing, however, was dead-end work. Finally frustrating. When her youngest child started high school, my mother got a full-time office job once again. (Her paycheck combined with my father's to make us — in fact — what we had already become in our imagination of ourselves — middle class.) She worked then for the (California) state government in numbered civil service positions secured by examinations. The old ambition of her youth was rekindled. During the lunch hour, she consulted bulletin boards for announcements of openings. One day she saw mention of something called an "anti-poverty agency." A typing job. A glamorous job, part of the governor's staff. "A knowledge of Spanish required." Without hesitation she applied and became nervous only when the job was suddenly hers.

"Everyone comes to work all dressed up," she reported at night. And didn't need to say more than that her co-workers wouldn't let her answer the phones. She was only a typist, after all, albeit a very fast typist. And an excellent speller. One morning there was a letter to be sent to a Washington cabinet officer. On the dictating tape, a voice referred to urban guerrillas. My mother typed (the wrong word, correctly): "gorillas." The mistake horrified the anti-poverty bureaucrats who shortly after arranged to have her returned to her previous position. She would go no further. So she willed her ambition to their children. "Get all the education you can; with an education you can do anything." (With a good education *she* could have done anything.)

When I was in high school, I admitted to my mother that I planned to become a teacher someday. That seemed to please her. But I never tried to explain that it was not the occupation of teaching I yearned for as much as it was something more elusive: I wanted to *be* like my teachers, to possess their knowledge, to assume their authority, their confidence, even to assume a teacher's persona.

In contrast to my mother, my father never verbally encouraged his children's academic success. Nor did he often praise us. My mother had to remind him to "say something" to one of his children who scored some academic success. But whereas my mother saw in education the opportunity for job advancement, my father recognized that education provided an even more startling possibility: it could enable a person to escape from a life of mere labor.

In Mexico, orphaned when he was eight, my father left school to work as an "apprentice" for an uncle. Twelve years later, he left Mexico in frustration and arrived in America. He had great expectations then of becoming an engineer. ("Work for my hands and my head.") He knew a Catholic priest who promised to get him money enough to study full time for a high school diploma. But the promises came to nothing. Instead there was a dark succession of warehouse, cannery, and factory jobs. After work he went to night school along with my mother. A year, two passed. Nothing much changed, except that fatigue worked its way into the bone; then everything changed. He didn't talk anymore of becoming an engineer. He stayed outside on the steps of the school while my mother went inside to learn typing and shorthand.

IT WAS MY FATHER WHO LAUGHED WHEN I CLAIMED TO BE TIRED BY READING AND WRITING.

By the time I was born, my father worked at "clean" jobs. For a time he was a janitor at a fancy department store. ("Easy work; the machines do it all.") Later he became a dental technician. ("Simple.") But by then he was pessimistic about the ultimate meaning of work and the possibility of ever escaping its claims. In some of my earliest memories of him, my father already seems aged by fatigue. (He has never really grown old like my mother.) From boyhood to manhood, I have remembered him in a single image: seated, asleep on the sofa, his head thrown back in a hideous corpselike grin, the evening newspaper spread out before him. "But look at all you've accomplished," his best friend said to him once. My father said nothing. Only smiled.

It was my father who laughed when I claimed to be tired by reading and writing. It was he who teased me for having soft hands. (He seemed to sense that some great achievement of leisure was implied by my papers and books.) It was my father who became angry while watching on television some woman at the Miss America contest tell the announcer that she was going to college. ("Majoring in fine arts.") "College!" he snarled. He despised the trivialization of higher education, the inflated grades and cheapened diplomas, the half education that so often passed as mass education in my generation.

It was my father again who wondered why I didn't display my awards on the wall of my bedroom. He said he liked to go to doctors' offices and see their certificates and degrees on the wall. ("Nice.") My citations from school got left in closets at home. The gleaming figure astride one of my trophies was broken, wingless, after hitting the ground. My medals were placed in a jar of loose change. And when I lost my high school diploma, my father found it as it was about to be thrown out with the trash. Without telling me, he put it away with his own things for safe-keeping.

These memories slammed together at the instant of hearing that refrain familiar to all scholarship students: "Your parents must be proud. . . ." Yes, my parents were proud. I knew it. But my parents regarded my progress with more than mere pride. They endured my early precocious behavior — but with what private anger and humiliation? As their children got older and would come home to challenge ideas both of them held, they argued before submitting to the force of logic or superior factual evidence with the disclaimer, "It's what we were taught in our time to believe." These discussions ended abruptly, though my mother remembered them on other occasions when she complained that our "big ideas" were going to our heads. More acute was her complaint that the family wasn't close anymore, like some others she knew. Why weren't we close, "more in the Mexican style"? Everyone is so private, she added. And she mimicked the yes and no answers she got in reply to her questions. Why didn't we talk more? (My father never asked.) I never said.

I was the first in my family who asked to leave home when it came time to go to college. I had been admitted to Stanford, one hundred miles away. My departure would only make physically apparent the separation that had occurred long before. But it was going too far. In the months preceding my leaving, I heard the question my mother never asked except indirectly. In the hot kitchen, tired at the end of her workday, she demanded to know, "Why aren't the colleges here in Sacramento good enough for you? They are for your brother and sister." In the middle of a car ride, not turning to face me, she wondered, "Why do you need to go so far away?" Late at night, ironing, she said with disgust, "Why do you have to put us through this big expense? You know your scholarship will never cover it all." But when September came there was a rush to get everything ready. In a bedroom that last night I packed the big brown valise, and my mother sat nearby sewing initials onto the clothes I would take. And she said no more about my leaving.

Months later, two weeks of Christmas vacation: the first hours home were the hardest. ("What's new?") My parents and I sat in the kitchen for a conversation. (But, lacking the same words to develop our sentences and to shape our interests, what was there to say? What could I tell them of the term paper I had just finished on the "universality of Shakespeare's appeal"?) I mentioned only small, obvious things: my dormitory life; weekend trips I had taken; random events. They responded with news of their own. (One was almost grateful for a family crisis about which there was much to discuss.) We tried to make our conversation seem like more than an interview.

II

From an early age I knew that my mother and father could read and write both Spanish and English. I had observed my father making his way through what, I now suppose, must have been income tax forms. On other occasions I waited apprehensively while my mother read onion-paper letters airmailed from Mexico with news of a relative's illness or death. For both my parents, however, reading was something done out of necessity and as quickly as possible. Never did I see either of them read an entire book. Nor did I see them read for pleasure. Their reading consisted of work manuals, prayer books, newspaper, recipes.

Richard Hoggart imagines how, at home,

> [the scholarship boy] sees strewn around, and reads regularly himself, magazines which are never mentioned at school, which seem not to belong to the world to which the school introduces him; at school he hears about and reads books never mentioned at home. When he brings those books into the house they do not take their place with other books which the family are reading, for often there are none or almost none; his books look, rather, like strange tools.

In our house each school year would begin with my mother's careful instruction: "Don't write in your books so we can sell them at the end of the year." The remark was echoed in public by my teachers, but only in part: "Boys and girls, don't write in your books. You must learn to treat them with great care and respect."

OPEN THE DOORS OF YOUR MIND WITH BOOKS, read the red and white poster over the nun's desk in early September. It soon was apparent to me that reading was the classroom's central activity. Each course had its own book. And the information gathered from a book was unquestioned. READ TO LEARN, the sign on the wall advised in December. I privately wondered: What was the connection between reading and learning? Did one learn something only by reading it? Was an idea only an idea if it could be written down? In June, CONSIDER BOOKS YOUR BEST FRIENDS. Friends? Reading was, at best, only a chore. I needed to look up whole paragraphs of words in a dictionary. Lines of type were dizzying, the eye having to move slowly across the page, then down, and across. . . . The sentences of the first books I read were coolly impersonal. Toned hard. What most bothered me, however, was the isolation reading required. To console myself for the loneliness I'd feel when I read, I tried reading in a very soft voice. Until: "Who is doing all that talking to his neighbor?" Shortly after, remedial reading classes were arranged for me with a very old nun.

At the end of each school day, for nearly six months, I would meet with her in the tiny room that served as the school's library but was actually only a storeroom for used textbooks and a vast collection of *National Geographics*. Everything about our sessions pleased me: the smallness of the room; the noise of the janitor's broom hitting the edge of the long hallway outside the door; the green of the sun, lighting the wall; and the old woman's face blurred white with a beard. Most of the time we took turns. I began with my elementary text. Sentences of astonishing simplicity seemed to me lifeless and drab: "The boys ran from the rain.... She wanted to sing.... The kite rose in the blue." Then the old nun would read from her favorite books, usually biographies of early American presidents. Playfully she ran through complex sentences, calling the words alive with her voice, making it seem that the author somehow was speaking directly to me. I smiled just to listen to her. I sat there and sensed for the very first time some possibility of fellowship between a reader and a writer, a communication, never *intimate* like that I heard spoken words at home convey, but one nonetheless *personal*.

One day the nun concluded a session by asking me why I was so reluctant to read by myself. I tried to explain; said something about the way written words made me feel all alone — almost, I wanted to add but didn't, as when I spoke to myself in a room just emptied of furniture. She studied my face as I spoke; she seemed to be watching more than listening. In an uneventful voice she replied that I had nothing to fear. Didn't I realize that reading would open up whole new worlds? A book could open doors for me. It could introduce me to people and show me places I never imagined existed. She gestured toward the bookshelves. (Bare-breasted African women danced, and the shiny hubcaps of automobiles on the back covers of the *Geographic* gleamed in my mind.) I listened with respect. But her words were not very influential. I was thinking then of another consequence of literacy, one I was too shy to admit but nonetheless trusted. Books were going to make me "educated." *That* confidence enabled me, several months later, to overcome my fear of the silence.

In fourth grade I embarked upon a grandiose reading program. "Give me the names of important books," I would say to startled teachers. They soon found out that I had in mind "adult books." I ignored their suggestion of anything I suspected was written for children. (Not until I was in college, as a result, did I read *Huckleberry Finn* or *Alice's Adventures in Wonderland*.) Instead, I read *The Scarlet Letter* and Franklin's *Autobiography*. And whatever I read I read for extra credit. Each time I finished a book, I reported the achievement to a teacher and basked in the praise my effort earned. Despite my best efforts, however, there seemed to be more and more books I needed to read. At the library I would literally tremble as I came upon whole shelves of books I hadn't read. So I read and I read and I read: *Great Expectations*; all the short stories of Kipling; *The Babe Ruth Story*; the entire first volume of the *Encyclopedia Britannica* (A–ANSTEY); the *Iliad*; *Moby Dick*; *Gone with the Wind*; *The Good Earth*; *Ramona*; *Forever Amber*; *The Lives of the Saints*; *Crime and Punishment*; *The Pearl*.... Librarians who initially frowned when I checked out the maximum ten books at a time started saving books they thought I might like. Teachers would say to the rest of the class, "I only wish the rest of you took reading as seriously as Richard obviously does."

But at home I would hear my mother wondering, "What do you see in your books?" (Was reading a hobby like her knitting? Was so much reading even healthy for a boy? Was it the sign of "brains"? Or was it just a convenient excuse for not helping about the house on Saturday mornings?) Always, "What do you see . . . ?"

What *did* I see in my books? I had the idea that they were crucial for my academic success, though I couldn't have said exactly how or why. In the sixth grade I simply concluded that what gave a book its value was some major idea or theme it contained. If that core essence could be mined and memorized, I would become learned like my teachers. I decided to record in a notebook the themes of the books that I read. After reading *Robinson Crusoe*, I wrote that its theme was "the value of learning to live by oneself." When I completed *Wuthering Heights*, I noted the danger of "letting emotions get out of control." Rereading these brief moralistic appraisals usually left me disheartened. I couldn't believe that they were really the source of reading's value. But for many more years, they constituted the only means I had of describing to myself the educational value of books.

In spite of my earnestness, I found reading a pleasurable activity. I came to enjoy the lonely good company of books. Early on weekday mornings, I'd read in my bed. I'd feel a mysterious comfort then, reading in the dawn quiet — the blue-gray silence interrupted by the occasional churning of the refrigerator motor a few rooms away or the more distant sounds of a city bus beginning its run. On weekends I'd go to the public library to read, surrounded by old men and women. Or, if the weather was fine, I would take my books to the park and read in the shade of a tree. A warm summer evening was my favorite reading time. Neighbors would leave for vacation and I would water their lawns. I would sit through the twilight on the front porches or in backyards, reading to the cool, whirling sounds of the sprinklers.

I also had favorite writers. But often those writers I enjoyed most I was least able to value. When I read William Saroyan's *The Human Comedy*, I was immediately pleased by the narrator's warmth and the charm of his story. But as quickly I became suspicious. A book so enjoyable to read couldn't be very "important." Another summer I determined to read all the novels of Dickens. Reading his fat novels, I loved the feeling I got — after the first hundred pages — of being at home in a fictional world where I knew the names of the characters and cared about what was going to happen to them. And it bothered me that I was forced away at the conclusion, when the fiction closed tight, like a fortune-teller's fist — the futures of all the major characters neatly resolved. I never knew how to take such feelings seriously, however. Nor did I suspect that these experiences could be part of a novel's meaning. Still, there were pleasures to sustain me after I'd finish my books. Carrying a volume back to the library, I would be pleased by its weight. I'd run my fingers along the edge of the pages and marvel at the breadth of my achievement. Around my room, growing stacks of paperback books reenforced my assurance.

I entered high school having read hundreds of books. My habit of reading made me a confident speaker and writer of English. Reading also enabled me to sense something of the shape, the major concerns, of Western thought. (I was able to say something about Dante and Descartes and Engels and James Baldwin in my high school term papers.) In these various ways, books brought me academic success as I hoped that they would. But I was not a good reader. Merely bookish, I lacked a point of view when I read. Rather, I read in order to acquire a point of view. I vacuumed books for epigrams, scraps of information, ideas, themes — anything to fill the hollow within me and make me feel educated. When one of my teachers suggested to his drowsy tenth-grade English class that a person could not have a "complicated idea" until he had read at least two thousand books, I heard the remark without detecting either its irony or its very complicated truth. I merely determined to compile a list of all the books I had ever read. Harsh with myself, I included only once a title I might have read several times. (How, after all, could one read a book more than once?) And I included only those books over a hundred pages in length. (Could anything shorter be a book?)

There was yet another high school list I compiled. One day I came across a newspaper article about the retirement of an English professor at a nearby state college. The article was accompanied by a list of the "hundred most important books of Western Civilization." "More than anything else in my life," the professor told the reporter with finality, "these books have made me all that I am." That was the kind of remark I couldn't ignore. I clipped out the list and kept it for the several months it took me to read all of the titles. Most books, of course, I barely understood. While reading Plato's *Republic*, for instance, I needed to keep looking at the book jacket comments to remind myself what the text was about. Nevertheless, with the special patience and superstition of a scholarship boy, I looked at every word of the text. And by the time I reached the last word, relieved, I convinced myself that I had read *The Republic*. In a ceremony of great pride, I solemnly crossed Plato off my list.

THE SCHOLARSHIP BOY PLEASES MOST WHEN HE IS YOUNG — THE WORKING-CLASS CHILD STRUGGLING FOR ACADEMIC SUCCESS.

III

The scholarship boy pleases most when he is young — the working-class child struggling for academic success. To his teachers, he offers great satisfaction; his success is their proudest achievement. Many other persons offer to help him. A businessman learns the boy's story and promises to underwrite part of the cost of his college education. A woman leaves him her entire library of several hundred books when she moves. His progress is featured in a newspaper article. Many people seem happy for him. They marvel. "How did you manage so fast?" From all sides, there is lavish praise and encouragement.

In his grammar school classroom, however, the boy already makes students around him uneasy. They scorn his desire to succeed. They scorn him for constantly wanting the teacher's attention and praise. "Kiss Ass," they call him when his hand swings up in response to every question he hears. Later, when he makes it to college, no one will mock him aloud. But he detects annoyance on the faces of some students and even some teachers who watch him. It puzzles him often. In college, then in graduate school, he behaves much as he always has. If anything is different about him it is that he dares to anticipate the successful conclusion of his studies. At last he feels that he belongs in the classroom, and this is exactly the source of the dissatisfaction he causes. To many persons around him, he appears too much the academic. There may be some things about him that recall his beginnings — his shabby clothes; his persistent poverty; or his dark skin (in those cases when it symbolizes his parents' disadvantaged condition) — but they only make clear how far he has moved from his past. He has used education to remake himself.

It bothers his fellow academics to face this. They will not say why exactly. (They sneer.) But their expectations become obvious when they are disappointed. They expect — they want — a student less changed by his schooling. If the scholarship boy, from a past so distant from the classroom, could remain in some basic way unchanged, he would be able to prove that it is possible for anyone to become educated without basically changing from the person one was.

Here is no fabulous hero, no idealized scholar-worker. The scholarship boy does not straddle, cannot reconcile, the two great opposing cultures of his life. His success is unromantic and plain. He sits in the classroom and offers those sitting beside him no calming reassurance about their own lives. He sits in the seminar room — a man with brown skin, the son of working-class Mexican immigrant parents. (Addressing the professor at the head of the table, his voice catches with nervousness.) There is no trace of his parents in his speech. Instead he approximates the accents of teachers and classmates. Coming from *him* those sounds seem suddenly odd. Odd too is the effect produced when *he* uses academic jargon — bubbles at the tip of his tongue: "*Topos* ... negative capability ... vegetation imagery in Shakespearean comedy." He lifts an opinion from Coleridge, takes something else from Frye or Empson or Leavis. He even repeats exactly his professor's earlier comment. All his ideas are clearly borrowed. He seems to have no thought of his own. He chatters while his listeners smile — their look one of disdain.

When he is older and thus when so little of the person he was survives, the scholarship boy makes only too apparent his profound lack of *self*-confidence. This is the conventional assessment that even Richard Hoggart repeats:

> [The scholarship boy] tends to over-stress the importance of examinations, of the piling-up of knowledge and of received opinions. He discovers

> a technique of apparent learning, of the acquiring of facts rather than of the handling and use of facts. He learns how to receive a purely literate education, one using only a small part of the personality and challenging only a limited area of his being. He begins to see life as a ladder, as permanent examination with some praise and some further exhortation at each stage. He becomes an expert imbiber and doler-out; his competence will vary, but will rarely be accompanied by genuine enthusiasms. He rarely feels the reality of knowledge, of other men's thoughts and imaginings, on his own pulses.... He has something of the blinkered pony about him....

But this is criticism more accurate than fair. The scholarship boy is a very bad student. He is the great mimic; a collector of thoughts, not a thinker; the very last person in class who ever feels obliged to have an opinion of his own. In large part, however, the reason he is such a bad student is because he realizes more often and more acutely than most other students — than Hoggart himself — that education requires radical self-reformation. As a very young boy, regarding his parents, as he struggles with an early homework assignment, he knows this too well. That is why he lacks self-assurance. He does not forget that the classroom is responsible for remaking him. He relies on his teacher, depends on all that he hears in the classroom and reads in his books. He becomes in every obvious way the worst student, a dummy mouthing the opinions of others. But he would not be so bad — nor would he become so successful, a *scholarship* boy — if he did not accurately perceive that the best synonym for primary "education" is "imitation."

Those who would take seriously the boy's success — and his failure — would be forced to realize how great is the change any academic undergoes, how far one must move from one's past. It is easiest to ignore such considerations. So little is said about the scholarship boy in pages and pages of educational literature. Nothing is said of the silence that comes to separate the boy from his parents. Instead, one hears proposals for increasing the self-esteem of students and encouraging early intellectual independence. Paragraphs glitter with a constellation of terms like *creativity* and *originality*. (Ignored altogether is the function of imitation in a student's life.) Radical educationalists meanwhile complain that ghetto schools "oppress" students by trying to mold them, stifling native characteristics. The truer critique would be just the reverse: not that schools change ghetto students too much, but that while they might promote the occasional scholarship student, they change most students barely at all.

From the story of the scholarship boy there is no specific pedagogy to glean. There is, however, a much larger lesson. His story makes clear that education is a long, unglamorous, even demeaning process — *a nurturing never natural to the person one was before one entered a classroom*. At once different from most other students, the scholarship boy is also the archetypal "good student." He exaggerates the difficulty of being a student, but his exaggeration reveals a general predicament. Others are changed by their schooling as much as he. They too must re-form themselves. They must develop the skill of memory long before they become truly critical thinkers. And when they read Plato for the first several times, it will be with awe more than deep comprehension.

The impact of schooling on the scholarship boy is only more apparent to the boy himself and to others. Finally, although he may be laughable — a blinkered pony — the boy will not let his critics forget their own change. He ends up too much like them. When he speaks, they hear themselves echoed. In his pedantry, they trace their own. His ambitions are theirs. If his failure were singular, they might readily pity him. But he is more troubling than that. They would not scorn him if this were not so.

IV

Like me, Hoggart's imagined scholarship boy spends most of his years in the classroom afraid to long for his past. Only at the very end of his schooling does the boy-man become nostalgic. In this sudden change of heart, Richard Hoggart notes:

> He longs for the membership he lost, "he pines for some Nameless Eden where he never was." The nostalgia is the stronger and the more ambiguous because he is really "in quest of his own absconded self yet scared to find it." He both wants to go back and yet thinks he has gone beyond his class, feels himself weighted with knowledge of his own and their situation, which hereafter forbids him the simpler pleasures of his father and mother. . . .

According to Hoggart, the scholarship boy grows nostalgic because he remains the uncertain scholar, bright enough to have moved from his past, yet unable to feel easy, a part of a community of academics.

This analysis, however, only partially suggests what happened to me in my last year as a graduate student. When I traveled to London to write a dissertation on English Renaissance literature, I was finally confident of membership in a "community of scholars." But the pleasure that confidence gave me faded rapidly. After only two or three months in the reading room of the British Museum, it became clear that I had joined a lonely community. Around me each day were dour faces eclipsed by large piles of books. There were the regulars, like the old couple who arrived every morning, each holding a loop of the shopping bag which contained all their notes. And there was the historian who chattered madly to herself. ("Oh dear! Oh! Now, what's this? What? Oh, my!") There were also the faces of young men and women worn by long study. And everywhere eyes turned away the moment our glance accidentally met. Some persons I sat beside day after day, yet we passed silently at the end of the day, strangers. Still, we were united by a common respect for the written word and for scholarship. We did form a union, though one in which we remained distant from one another.

More profound and unsettling was the bond I recognized with those writers whose books I consulted. Whenever I opened a text that hadn't been used for years, I realized that my special interests and skills united me to a mere handful of academics. We formed an exclusive — eccentric! — society, separated from others who would never care or be able to share our concerns. (The pages I turned were stiff like layers of dead skin.) I began to wonder: Who, beside my dissertation director and a few faculty members, would ever read what I wrote? And: Was my dissertation much more than an act of social withdrawal? These questions went unanswered in the silence of the Museum reading room. They remained to trouble me after I'd leave the library each afternoon and feel myself shy — unsteady, speaking simple sentences at the grocer's or the butcher's on my way back to my bed-sitter.

Meanwhile my file cards accumulated. A professional, I knew exactly how to search a book for pertinent information. I could quickly assess and summarize the usability of the many books I consulted. But whenever I started to write, I knew too much (and not enough) to be able to write anything but sentences that were overly cautious, timid, strained brittle under the heavy weight of footnotes and qualifications. I seemed unable to dare a passionate statement. I felt drawn by professionalism to the edge of sterility, capable of no more than pedantic, lifeless, unassailable prose.

Then nostalgia began.

After years spent unwilling to admit its attractions, I gestured nostalgically toward the past. I yearned for that time when I had not been so alone. I became impatient with books. I wanted experience more immediate. I feared the library's silence. I silently scorned the gray, timid faces around me. I grew to hate the growing pages of my dissertation on genre and Renaissance literature. (In my mind I heard relatives laughing as they tried to make sense of its title.) I wanted something — I couldn't say exactly what. I told myself that I wanted a more passionate life. And a life less thoughtful. And above all, I wanted to be less alone. One day I heard some Spanish academics whispering back and forth to each other, and their sounds seemed ghostly voices recalling my life. Yearning became preoccupation then. Boyhood memories beckoned, flooded my mind. (Laughing intimate voices. Bounding up the front steps of the porch. A sudden embrace inside the door.)

For weeks after, I turned to books by educational experts. I needed to learn how far I had moved from my past — to determine how fast I would be able to recover something of it once again. But I found little. Only a chapter in a book by Richard Hoggart. . . . I left the reading room and the circle of faces.

I came home. After the year in England, I spent three summer months living with my mother and father, relieved by how easy it was to be home. It no longer seemed very important to me that we had little to say. I felt easy sitting and eating and walking with them. I watched them, nevertheless, looking for evidence of those elastic, sturdy strands that bind generations in a web of inheritance. I thought as I watched my mother one night: of course a friend had been right when she told me that I gestured and laughed just like my mother. Another time I saw for myself: my father's eyes were much like my own, constantly watchful.

But after the early relief, this return, came suspicion, nagging until I realized that I had not neatly sidestepped the impact of schooling. My desire to do so was precisely the measure of how much I remained an academic. *Negatively* (for that is how this idea first occurred to me): my need to think so much and so abstractly about my parents and our relationship was in itself an indication of my long education. My father and mother did not pass their time thinking about the cultural meanings of their experience. It was I who described their daily lives with airy ideas. And yet, *positively*: the ability to consider experience so abstractly allowed me to shape into desire what would otherwise have remained indefinite, meaningless longing in the British Museum. If, because of my schooling, I had grown culturally separated from my parents, my education finally had given me ways of speaking and caring about that fact.

My best teachers in college and graduate school, years before, had tried to prepare me for this conclusion, I think, when they discussed texts of aristocratic pastoral literature. Faithfully, I wrote down all that they said. I memorized it: "The praise of the unlettered by the highly educated is one of the primary themes of 'elitist' literature." But, "the importance of the praise given the unsolitary, richly passionate and spontaneous life is that it simultaneously reflects the value of a reflective life." I heard it all. But there was no way for any of it to mean very much to me. I was a scholarship boy at the time, busily laddering my way up the rungs of education. To pass an examination, I copied down exactly what my teachers told me. It would require many more years of schooling (an inevitable miseducation) in which I came to trust the silence of reading and the habit of abstracting from immediate experience — moving away from a life of closeness and immediacy I remembered with my parents, growing older — before I turned unafraid to desire the past, and thereby achieved what had eluded me for so long — the end of education.

NOTE

[1] All quotations in this essay are from Richard Hoggart, *The Uses of Literacy* (London: Chatto and Windus, 1957), chapter 10. [Author's note]

QUESTIONS FOR A SECOND READING

1. In *Hunger of Memory*, the book from which "The Achievement of Desire" is drawn, Rodriguez says several times that the story he tells, although it is very much his story, is also a story of our common experience — growing up, leaving home, becoming educated, entering the world. When you reread this essay, look particularly for sections or passages you might bring forward as evidence that this is, in fact, an essay which can give you a way of looking at your own life, and not just his. And look for sections that defy universal

application. To what degree *is* his story the story of our common experience? Why might he (or his readers) want to insist that his story is everyone's story?

2. At the end of the essay, Rodriguez says:

> It would require many more years of schooling (an inevitable miseducation) in which I came to trust the silence of reading and the habit of abstracting from immediate experience — moving away from a life of closeness and immediacy I remembered with my parents, growing older — before I turned unafraid to desire the past, and thereby achieved what had eluded me for so long — the end of education. (p. 355)

What do you think, as you reread this essay, is the "end of education"? And what does that end (that goal? stopping point?) have to do with "miseducation," "the silence of reading," "the habit of abstracting from immediate experience," and "desir[ing] the past"?

ASSIGNMENTS FOR WRITING

1. You could look at the relationship between Richard Rodriguez and Richard Hoggart as a case study of the relation of a reader to a writer or a student to a teacher. Look closely at Rodriguez's references to Hoggart's book, *The Uses of Literacy*, and at the way Rodriguez made use of that book to name and describe his own experience as a student. (An extended selection of *The Uses of Literacy* can be found in the e-Pages.) What did he find in the book? How did he use it? How does he use it in his own writing?

   Write an essay in which you discuss Rodriguez's use of Hoggart's *The Uses of Literacy*. How, for example, would you compare Rodriguez's version of the "scholarship boy" with Hoggart's? (At one point, Rodriguez says that Hoggart's account is "more accurate than fair." What might he have meant by that?) And what kind of reader is the Rodriguez who is writing "The Achievement of Desire" — is he still a "scholarship boy," or is that description no longer appropriate?

   Note: You might begin your research with what may seem to be a purely technical matter, examining how Rodriguez handles quotations and works Hoggart's words into paragraphs of his own. On the basis of Rodriguez's use of quoted passages, how would you describe the relationship between Hoggart's words and Rodriguez's? Who has the greater authority? Who is the expert, and under what conditions? What "rules" might Rodriguez be said to follow or to break? Do you see any change in the course of the essay in how Rodriguez uses block quotations? in how he comments on them?

See the e-Pages at bedfordstmartins.com/waysofreading.

2. Rodriguez insists that his story is also everyone's story. Take an episode from your life, one that seems in some way similar to one of the episodes in "The Achievement of Desire," and cast it into a shorter version of Rodriguez's essay. Your job here is to look at your experience in Rodriguez's terms, which means thinking the way he does, noticing what he would notice, interpreting details in a similar fashion, using his key terms, seeing through his point of view; it could also mean imitating his style of writing, working with quotations from other writers, doing whatever it is you see him doing characteristically while he writes. Imitation, Rodriguez argues, is not necessarily a bad thing; it can, in fact, be one of the powerful ways in which a person learns.

   Note: This assignment can also be used to read against "The Achievement of Desire." Rodriguez insists on the universality of his experience leaving home and community and joining the larger public life. You could highlight the differences between your experience and his. You should begin by imitating Rodriguez's method; you do not have to arrive at his conclusions, however.

3.
> What I am about to say to you has taken me more than twenty years to admit: *A primary reason for my success in the classroom was that I couldn't forget that schooling was changing me and separating me from the life I enjoyed before becoming a student.* (p. 339)
>
> If, because of my schooling, I had grown culturally separated from my parents, my education finally had given me ways of speaking and caring about that fact. (p. 355)

   As you reread Rodriguez's essay, what would you say are his "ways of speaking and caring"? One way to think about this question is to trace how the lessons he learned about reading, education, language, family, culture, and class shifted as he moved from elementary school through college and graduate school to his career as a teacher and a writer. What scholarly abilities did he learn that provided him with "ways of speaking and caring" valued in the academic community? Where and how do you see him using them in his essay?

   Write an essay in which you discuss how Rodriguez reads (reviews, summarizes, interprets) his family, his teachers, his schooling, himself, and his books. What differences can you say such reading makes to those ways of speaking and caring that you locate in the text?

MAKING CONNECTIONS

1. Paulo Freire, in "The 'Banking' Concept of Education" (p. 216), discusses the political implications of the relations between teachers and students. Some forms of schooling, he says, can give students control over their lives, but most schooling teaches students only to submit to domination by others. If

you look closely at the history of Rodriguez's schooling from the perspective of Freire's essay, what do you see? Write an essay describing how Freire might analyze Rodriguez's education. How would he see the process as it unfolds throughout Rodriguez's experience, as a student, from his early schooling (including the study he did on his own at home), through his college and graduate studies, to the position he takes, finally, as the writer of "The Achievement of Desire"?

2. Here, from "Arts of the Contact Zone" (p. 317), is Mary Louise Pratt on the "autoethnographic" text:

> Guaman Poma's *New Chronicle* is an instance of what I have proposed to call an *autoethnographic* text, by which I mean a text in which people undertake to describe themselves in ways that engage with representations others have made of them. Thus if ethnographic texts are those in which European metropolitan subjects represent to themselves their others (usually their conquered others), autoethnographic texts are representations that the so-defined others construct *in response to* or in dialogue with those texts. . . . They involve a selective collaboration with and appropriation of idioms of the metropolis or the conqueror. These are merged or infiltrated to varying degrees with indigenous idioms to create self-representations intended to intervene in metropolitan modes of understanding. . . . Such texts often constitute a marginalized group's point of entry into the dominant circuits of print culture. (pp. 319–20)

Richard Rodriguez's "The Achievement of Desire" could be considered "autoethnography." He is clearly working to explain himself, to account for who he is and who he has become. But to whom? Who is identified as his audience? Can you talk here about "indigenous idioms" or the "idioms of the metropolis"?

Reread "The Achievement of Desire" with Pratt's essay in mind. And write an essay in which you discuss "The Achievement of Desire" as an example of an autoethnographic and/or a transcultural text. You should imagine that you are working to put Pratt's ideas to the test (does it present itself as a convenient example?), but also add what you have to say about the ways this autobiography defines its audience, speaker, and purpose.

3. Richard Rodriguez in "The Achievement of Desire," Susan Griffin in "Our Secret" (p. 233), and John Edgar Wideman in "Our Time" (p. 422) use a life story to think about and to represent forces beyond the individual that shape life and possibility—family, war, race, and ethnicity. Susan Griffin explains her motive this way: "One can find traces of every life in each life." Perhaps. It is a bold step to think that this is true and to believe that one can, or should, use autobiography as a way to understand the national or international narrative. Write an essay in which you read "The Achievement of Desire" alongside one of the other two essays. Your goal is not only to discuss how these writers do what they do, and to what conclusions and to what ends, but also to discuss your sense of what is at stake in such a project. How are their ac-

counts of family different? How do they connect the structure of the family to larger structural concerns? What are the key differences, and how might you explain them?

4. After years spent unwilling to admit its attractions, I gestured nostalgically toward the past. I yearned for that time when I had not been so alone. I became impatient with books. I wanted experience more immediate. I feared the library's silence. I silently scorned the gray, timid faces around me. I grew to hate the growing pages of my dissertation on genre and Renaissance literature. (In my mind I heard relatives laughing as they tried to make sense of its title.) I wanted something — couldn't say exactly what. (p. 354)

— RICHARD RODRIGUEZ
The Achievement of Desire

For some, it will hardly come as a surprise to learn that reading and writing have no magically transformative powers. But for those of us who have been raised into the teaching and publishing professions, it can be quite a shock to confront the possibility that reading and writing and talking exercise almost *none* of the powers we regularly attribute to them in our favorite stories. The dark night of the soul for literacy workers comes with the realization that training students to read, write, and talk in more critical and self-reflective ways cannot protect them from the violent changes our culture is undergoing. (e-Pages)

— RICHARD E. MILLER
The Dark Night of the Soul

Both Richard E. Miller and Richard Rodriguez are concerned with the limits (and the failures) of education, with particular attention to the humanities and to the supposed benefits to be found in reading and writing. "I have these doubts, you see," Miller writes of academic work, "doubts silently shared by many who spend their days teaching others the literate arts. Aside from gathering and organizing information, aside from generating critiques and analyses that forever fall on deaf ears, what might the literate arts be said to be good for?"

Write an essay that takes up this question — "what might the literate arts be said to be good for?" — and that takes it up with these two essays, Miller's "The Dark Night of the Soul" and Rodriguez's "The Achievement of Desire," as your initial points of reference. What does each say? How might they be said to speak to each other? And, finally, where are you in this? Where are you, and people like you, the group for whom you feel prepared to speak? You, too, have been and will continue to be expected to take courses in reading and writing, to read, write, and talk in "critical and self-reflective ways." Where are you in this conversation?

e

e See the e-Pages at bedfordstmartins.com/waysofreading.

KATHRYN Schulz

Kathryn Schulz is a journalist whose writing can be found in leading U.S. magazines and newspapers including the *New York Times,* the *Boston Globe, Rolling Stone, The Nation, Foreign Policy,* and *Slate.*

Schulz is a graduate of Brown University. She began her career writing for *Feed*, one of the earliest online magazines. For several years, she worked as a reporter and editor in Santiago, Chile, writing on environmental and human rights issues for the *Santiago Times.* As a freelance writer, she has traveled to and written about Central and South America, Japan, and the Middle East. In 2004, she received a Pew Fellowship in International Journalism. *Being Wrong: Adventures in the Margin of Error* (2010) is her first book. It has been widely read, widely reviewed, and widely praised. In an interview with the *New York Times,* Harvard President Drew Gilpin Faust was asked if there was any book she wished all incoming freshmen at Harvard would read. Her choice was *Being Wrong* because, she said, it advocates "doubt as a skill and praises error as the foundation of wisdom."

In the first chapter of *Being Wrong*, Schulz says,

> . . . we are wrong about what it means to be wrong. Far from being a sign of intellectual inferiority, the capacity to err is crucial to human cognition. Far from being a moral flaw, it is inextricable from some of our most humane and honorable qualities: empathy, optimism, imagination, conviction, and courage. And far from being the mark of indifference or intolerance, wrongness is a vital part of how we learn and change. Thanks to error, we can revise our understanding of ourselves and amend our ideas about the world. (5)

You'll find in the following pages a chapter from *Being Wrong* in which Schulz considers evidence—that is, what we take as the grounding of knowledge and belief. At one point in this selection, Schulz alludes to "naïve realism." By this she means our assumption that experience provides us with direct, unmediated access to the world, that the world and the mind enjoy an exact correspondence. (If I see it, it is there, and I can tell its truth—even though the person next to me sees and understands the same scene differently.) To be a generous reader, you'll need to put your preconceptions aside and follow her line of reasoning—even if, in the end, you want to argue with it.

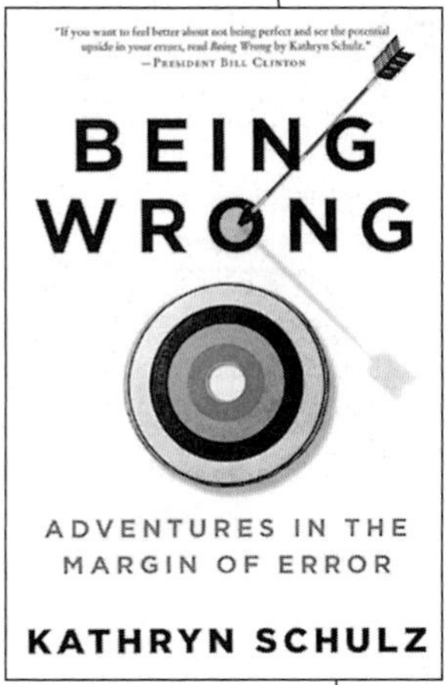
"If you want to feel better about not being perfect and see the potential upside in your errors, read Being Wrong by Kathryn Schulz."
—President Bill Clinton
BEING WRONG
ADVENTURES IN THE MARGIN OF ERROR
KATHRYN SCHULZ

Bottom
top logic — Inductive Reasoning - 367 definition and example

Top
Bottom
Deductive Reasoning - Calculated guess from knowing all the rules.

Confirmation Bias 372 - Believing something is incorrect because it is new are different from how you think.

Error - 263 definition and example

Self - Submersive thinking - more flexible - more open
can be open to new things.
Confidence Bulldozer - more rigidity -
not easily [illegible]

Evidence

> ROSENCRANTZ: That must be east, then. I think we can assume that.
>
> GUILDENSTERN: I'm assuming nothing.
>
> ROSENCRANTZ: No, it's all right. That's the sun. East.
>
> GUILDENSTERN *(looks up)*: Where?
>
> ROSENCRANTZ: I watched it come up.
>
> GUILDENSTERN: No . . . it was light all the time, you see, and you opened your eyes very, very slowly. If you'd been facing back there, you'd be swearing *that* was east.
>
> —TOM STOPPARD, *ROSENCRANTZ AND GUILDENSTERN ARE DEAD*

In 1692, Judge William Stoughton, one of the most venerable lawmakers in Colonial America, found himself facing an unusual procedural question: Should visitations by evil spirits be admitted as evidence in a court of law? Stoughton was presiding over the Salem witch trials and—unfortunately for the 150 people who were imprisoned and the nineteen who were hanged by the end of the ordeal—he determined that such evidence was permissible. If you had been alive at the time, and dreamed one night that the ill-fated Goody Proctor was in your bedroom attempting to throttle you, you could have presented your dream as evidence before the court—"as though there was no real difference between G.Proctor and the shape of G. Proctor," in the disapproving words of a contemporary observer.

It is a testament to how far the legal profession has come that few things seem more antithetical to the spirit of justice today than the admission of so-called spectral evidence. Yet the questions Stoughton faced remain central to the practice of law. What counts as evidence? How must it be gathered? Under what circumstances is it admissible? How do certain kinds of evidence compare to other kinds? How much weight should be given to each? How we answer these questions goes a long way toward determining whether justice will be served. Indeed, the fair and consistent practice of law hinges, to a huge degree, on developing a fair and consistent relationship to evidence. (We have names for situations where that relationship doesn't exist or is disregarded, and one of them is "witch trial.")

What is true within the law is also true far beyond it. Although we seldom think of it this way, evidence is immensely central to our lives. We rely on it in science to expand our technological capacity and advance our understanding of the world. We rely on it in journalism to keep us accurately informed and to hold individuals and institutions accountable for their actions. We rely on it in politics to determine which laws to pass, which policies to implement, and which wars to fight. And we rely on it in medicine to sustain our health and save our lives.

These are all public institutions, and, like the law, they have all developed specific and formal ideas about evidence — what kind of information qualifies, how to gather it, how to evaluate it. But evidence is also central to the private, non-institutional entity that is each of us. We know from the last chapter that we can't function without our beliefs, that they tell us where we are, who we are, and what to do next. But these beliefs don't come to us willy-nilly. We form them, as judges form their opinions and juries reach their decisions, based on the evidence. Of course, we don't necessarily form *accurate* beliefs based on *good* evidence. I'm perfectly capable of forming very iffy notions about string theory based on very scanty secondhand information, and Hannah was perfectly capable of concluding that she could see based on faulty signals from her own brain. In other words, the same goes for us as for the law: how well we gather and evaluate evidence determines how fair or unfair, right or wrong our theories will be. An article in the paper, a weird smell in the basement, the look on your mother's face, your own gut intuition — everything that registers on the sensitive machinery of your brain must be counted in favor of or against your beliefs.

OF COURSE, WE DON'T NECESSARILY FORM *ACCURATE* BELIEFS BASED ON *GOOD* EVIDENCE.

In a perfect world, how would we go about evaluating all this evidence? As it turns out, we have fairly strong and uniform opinions about this. By rough consensus, the ideal thinker approaches a subject with a neutral mind, gathers as much evidence as possible, assesses it coolly, and draws conclusions accordingly. By a further rough consensus, this is not only how *we should* form our beliefs, but how we actually do so. To quote Rebecca Saxe, the neuroscientist from the previous chapter, "we share the conviction that, in general, beliefs follow from relatively dispassionate assessment of facts-of-the-matter and logical reasoning."

This model of how our minds work is a significant step up from naïve realism. Instead of thinking, as toddlers do, that the world is exactly as we perceive it, we recognize that we only perceive certain bits of it — pieces of evidence — and that therefore our understanding might be incomplete or misleading. Unlike naïve realism, then, this model of cognition makes room for error. At the same time, it contains an implicit corrective: the more evidence we compile, and the more thoroughly and objectively we evaluate it, the more accurate our beliefs will be. In this vein, Descartes defined error not as believing something that isn't true, but as believing something based on insufficient evidence.

That definition of error has, at first glance, the virtue of being practical. You can't very well caution people against believing things that aren't true, since, as we've seen, all of us necessarily think our beliefs are true. By comparison, it seems both easy and advisable to caution people against believing things without sufficient evidence. But this idea quickly runs into trouble. First, how are we supposed to know when a body of evidence crosses the threshold from "insufficient" to "sufficient"? Second, what are we supposed to do in situations where additional evidence is not necessarily forthcoming? Augustine, who arrived at Descartes' idea of error some 1,200 years earlier, rejected it when he perceived these problems, and in particular their theological implications. If you encourage people to withhold assent from any proposition that lacks sufficient evidence, he realized, you are inevitably encouraging them to withhold assent from God.*

Augustine needn't have worried. You can urge people not to believe anything based on meager evidence until you are blue in the face, but you will never succeed—because, as it turns out, believing things based on meager evidence is what people *do*. I don't mean that we do this occasionally: only when we are thinking sloppily, say, or only if we don't know any better, or only en route to screwing up. I mean that believing things based on paltry evidence is the engine that drives the entire miraculous machinery of human cognition.

BELIEVING THINGS BASED ON PALTRY EVIDENCE IS THE ENGINE THAT DRIVES THE ENTIRE MIRACULOUS MACHINERY OF HUMAN COGNITION.

Descartes was right to fear that this way of thinking would cause us to make mistakes; it does. Since he was interested in knowing the truth, and knowing that he knew it, he tried to develop a model of thinking that could curtail the possibility of error . . . In fact, curtailing error was the goal of most models of optimal human cognition proposed by most thinkers throughout most of history, and it is the goal behind our own broadly shared image of the ideal thinker. Some of these models, like Descartes', sought to curtail error through radical doubt. Others sought to curtail it through formal logic—using valid premises to derive necessarily valid conclusions. Others, including our shared one of the ideal thinker, seek to curtail it through a kind of general due diligence: careful attention to evidence and counterevidence, coupled with a prudent avoidance of preconceived notions.

By these standards, the cognitive operating system we actually come with is suboptimal. It has no use for radical doubt. It does not rely on formal logic. It isn't diligent about amassing evidence, still less so about counterevidence, and it couldn't function without preconceived notions. It

*Monotheistic religions have a particularly interesting and troubled relationship to the idea of evidence. Belief in God is explicitly supposed to be based on faith, not proof: "Blessed are they who have not seen and yet have believed," Jesus says to doubting Thomas in John 20:29. Yet the devout have tried to muster evidence for their beliefs since time immemorial. The shroud of Turin is cited as proof of Jesus' crucifixion, weeping statues of the Virgin Mary serve to substantiate her holiness, the Catholic Church has a formal process for verifying miracles as evidence of God's work, and—before modern science made the claim untenable—volcanoes, hot springs, and geothermal vents were cited as evidence of the existence of hell. More generally, the whole remarkable sweep of creation, from the human eye to the shells on a beach, is often cited as evidence of God the creator. This religious relationship to evidence might be inconsistent, but it isn't surprising. As I suggest at the end of this chapter, we all recognize the value of evidence in grounding our beliefs, and we'd all just as soon have it on our side.

is eminently capable of getting things wrong. In short, our mind, in its default mode, doesn't work anything like any of these models. And yet — not despite but *because* of its aptitude for error — it works better than them all.

Here, I'm going to prove it to you. Actually, I'm going to *get you* to prove it to *me*. Below you will find a very brief multiple-choice test. Please take it. If you still have that four-year-old handy from the last chapter, have her take it, too. You can reassure her that these aren't meant to be trick questions, so neither of you should overthink anything. Here goes:

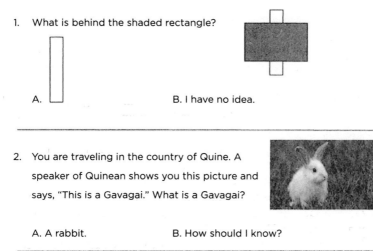

1. What is behind the shaded rectangle?

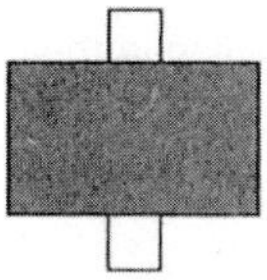

A. 

B. I have no idea.

2. You are traveling in the country of Quine. A speaker of Quinean shows you this picture and says, "This is a Gavagai." What is a Gavagai?

A. A rabbit.

B. How should I know?

3. Complete the following sentence: "The giraffe had a very long ______."

A. Neck

B. I'm stumped.

Congratulations; you got all three answers right. You also found this quiz so easy that you don't think congratulations are called for. But here's the thing: this quiz is not easy. At least, it is not *intrinsically* easy. True, you could do it, and so can I, and so can any reasonably attentive four-year-old. Yet computers — which can calculate pi out to a thousand digits while you sneeze — are completely stymied by problems like these. So here is a non-easy question for you: Why is something that is so effortless for a person all but impossible for a machine?

To get a sense of the answer, consider just a tiny fraction of the possibilities a computer has to contemplate when taking this quiz*:

*The overall concept of this quiz and its second question come from the philosopher Willard Van Orman Quine, who worked on, among other things, language and epistemology. Imagine that a field linguist who is trying to translate an unknown language watches as a native speaker points to a rabbit and says "gavagai." The natural conclusion would be that "gavagai" means "rabbit" — but, Quine pointed out, it could also mean, "let's go hunting" or "there's a storm coming" or any number of other things. Quine called this problem "the indeterminacy of translation."

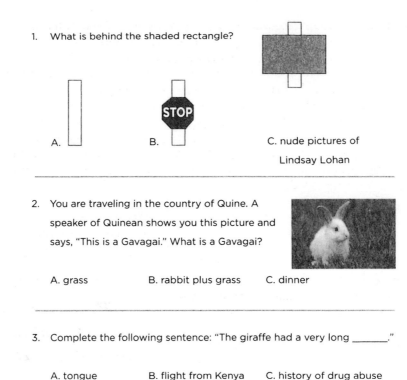

1. What is behind the shaded rectangle?

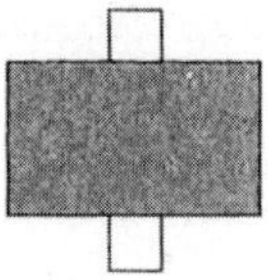

A. 

B. 

C. nude pictures of Lindsay Lohan

---

2. You are traveling in the country of Quine. A speaker of Quinean shows you this picture and says, "This is a Gavagai." What is a Gavagai?

A. grass B. rabbit plus grass C. dinner

---

3. Complete the following sentence: "The giraffe had a very long _______."

A. tongue B. flight from Kenya C. history of drug abuse

These answers strike us as patently absurd. But computers don't have a patent-absurdity monitoring function; they can't rule out these answers (or millions of others like them) because nothing in logic prevents such answers from being right. For that matter, nothing in *life* prevents such answers from being right, either. It is perfectly possible that someone, somewhere — a zookeeper, a veterinarian, a children's book author, someone enjoying a long history of drug abuse — has uttered a sentence about a giraffe's long flight from Kenya. Likewise, it is perfectly possible (although perhaps less probable than some readers would like) that there are naked pictures of Lindsay Lohan behind that shaded rectangle. For that matter, it's perfectly possible that there is a naked picture of *you* behind that rectangle — or of one of the other 7 billion people on the planet, or two pictures of three people, or ten pictures of seven people, or . . . you get the point: there are an infinite number of logically valid, theoretically possible answers to all these questions. Computers recognize this, and therefore can't answer the questions at all.

Human beings, on the other hand, have no trouble answering these questions, because we don't care about what is logically valid and theoretically possible. We care about what is *probable*. We determine what is probable based on our prior experience of the world, which is where evidence comes in: we choose the most likely answer to any given question based on the kinds of things we have (and haven't) experienced in comparable situations before. Over the course of our lifetimes, we've observed somethings about giraffes, sentences, and sentences about giraffes, and based on those observations, we make an educated guess about this particular sentence concerning this particular giraffe. Significantly, it doesn't matter how *much* we've observed about sentences and giraffes. Unlike Descartes, we aren't interested in whether we have ample evidence to support a given conclusion — which is just as well, since, as the computer's conundrum shows, we almost certainly do not. All we're interested in is whether whatever evidence we *do* have supports one conclusion better than another. That's why four-year-olds can answer this question, despite their comparatively limited experience with sentences and (one assumes) even more limited experience with giraffes.

This strategy of guessing based on past experience is known as inductive reasoning. As we've seen, inductive reasoning makes us vastly better than computers at solving problems like the ones in this quiz. But it also makes people like Descartes nervous, because it means that our beliefs are not necessarily true. Instead, they are *probabilistically* true. This point was made (and made famous) by the philosopher David Hume, who was arguably the first thinker to fully grasp both the import and the limitation of inductive reasoning. To borrow his much-cited example: How can I be sure that all swans are white if I myself have seen only a tiny fraction of all the swans that have ever existed? If the world were always uniform, consistent, and predictable, I could trust that I am right about this induction (and about all inductions). Unfortunately, as Hume noted, nothing in logic requires the world to be that way, and we know from experience that it isn't always so. I can keep my eyes open for more white swans, but no matter how many I spot, I'll only be adding to my body of evidence, rather than actually proving something about the necessary color scheme of swans. In other words, inductions are necessarily impossible to substantiate. We can know that they are wrong — as Hume's example turned out to be, when a species of black swan was discovered in Australia after his death — but we can't know that they are right. All we know is that they are at least somewhat more likely to be right than the next best guess we could make.

HOW CAN I BE SURE THAT ALL SWANS ARE WHITE IF I MYSELF HAVE SEEN ONLY A TINY FRACTION OF ALL THE SWANS THAT HAVE EVER EXISTED?

When it comes to multiple-choice quizzes, we are all comfortable with the idea that we make the best guess we can based on whatever evidence we already have. We ought to be, since we've been doing so since grade school. But our use of inductive reasoning isn't limited to that kind of low-stakes situation. On the contrary: psychologists and neuroscientists increasingly think that inductive reasoning undergirds virtually all of human cognition. You make best guesses based on your cumulative exposure to the evidence every day, both unconsciously (as when the motor fibers in your arm estimate where to swing for a baseball) and consciously (as when you bet against the Red Sox, and on the best time to tell your partner how much you lost on that bet).

This kind of guesswork is also how you learned almost everything you know about the world. Take language. Your parents didn't teach you to talk by sitting you down and explaining that English is a subject-verb-object language, that most verbs are converted to the past tense by adding the suffix "-ed," that adjectives generally go before the nouns they modify, and so forth. Mercifully for everyone involved, they didn't have to. All they had to do was keep on chatting about how Mommy poured the milk and Laura painted a pretty picture, and you figured it out by yourself — where "it" is, amazingly, the entire complex grammatical infrastructure of the English language. Not only that, but you did the bulk of this work between birth and four years of age, and you did it despite having heard only the tiniest fraction of all the possible words and combinations of words our language permits.* If there is a better rebuttal to Descartes' claim that we should avoid drawing sweeping conclusions from scanty evidence, I'm not sure what it is.

There are certainly other rebuttals, though, because language isn't the only crucial skill you learned this way. You also used inductive reasoning to learn how to divide the world into categories and kinds — which is why you were somehow able to grasp the concept of "dog" based on a sample population consisting solely of, say, a golden retriever, a shih tzu, and Scooby Doo. Likewise, you used inductive reasoning to learn about the relationships between causes and effects. Just as no one had to teach you the general principles of grammar or the general principles of dogginess, no one had to teach you that, say, lights are usually turned on by flipping switches. You just saw it happen a few times, and in very short order, the relationship between switches and lights was cemented in your mind. (As an adult, if you're standing around indoors and a light suddenly goes on, you'll immediately look around to see who flipped the switch.)

What is true of physical causes and effects is also true of biological and emotional causation. Thanks to inductive reasoning, we are able to determine very quickly that experiencing a strange itchy sensation in our nose means that we are about to sneeze, and that using the F word makes Mom angry. As the latter example suggests, induction is central to how we learn about people, including ourselves. Indeed, much of psychoanalytic theory is based on the belief that our earliest interactions with a tiny number of people permanently shape our theories about who we are,

*One reason the great linguist Noam Chomsky thought language learning must be innate is that the entire corpus of spoken language (never mind the subset spoken to children under four) doesn't seem to contain enough evidence to learn all of grammar. He called this problem "the poverty of the stimulus." In particular, he pointed out, children never hear examples of grammatical structures that aren't permissible in their language, such as "Mommy milk poured" or "picture pretty painted Laura." This raises the question of how kids *know* such structures aren't permissible, since, in formal logic, never hearing such sentences wouldn't mean that they don't exist. (As logicians say, lack of evidence is not evidence of a lack.) But if we learn language inductively, the poverty of the stimulus might not be a problem after all. It's good bet that if you've been paying attention to language for four years and you've never heard a certain grammatical form before, you are never going to hear it. Inductively, lack of evidence actually *is* evidence of a lack.

what other people are like, and what kind of treatment we can expect to receive throughout our lives.

Language, categorization, causality, psychology: without expertise in these domains, we would be sunk. And without inductive reasoning — the capacity to reach very big conclusions based on very little data — we would never gain that expertise. However slapdash it might initially seem, this best-guess style of reasoning is critical to human intelligence. In fact, these days, inductive reasoning is the leading candidate for actually *being* human intelligence.

THESE DAYS, INDUCTIVE REASONING IS THE LEADING CANDIDATE FOR ACTUALLY *BEING* HUMAN INTELLIGENCE.

But score a point for Descartes: inductive reasoning also makes us fundamentally, unavoidably fallible. As I said, the distinctive thing about the conclusions we draw through induction is that they are probabilistically true — which means that they are possibly false. The theory that you should add the suffix "-ed" in order to form a past-tense verb is a brilliant inductive inference. It is largely correct, it teaches you a huge number of words in one fell swoop, and it's a lot less painful (not to mention a lot more possible) than separately memorizing the past tense of every single verb in the English language. But it also means that sooner or later you are going to say things like drinked and thinked and bringed and runned. Those are trivial errors, and eventually overcome. As we are about to see, however, inductive reasoning is also responsible for some very non-trivial, deeply entrenched mistakes.

Before we look at those specific errors, I want to return briefly to error in general. If the goal of this book is to urge us to rethink our relationship to wrongness, inductive reasoning makes it plain why we should do so. We tend to think of mistakes as the consequence of cognitive sloppiness — of taking shortcuts, cutting corners, jumping to conclusions. And, in fact, we *do* take shortcuts, cut corners, and jump to conclusions. But thinking of these tendencies as problems suggests that there are solutions: a better way to evaluate the evidence, some viable method for reaching airtight verdicts about the world. Yet we've already seen what it takes to thoroughly evaluate evidence and reach airtight verdicts. It takes memorizing tens of thousands of separate past-tense verbs. It takes sitting around wondering about the giraffe's long something-or-other until you've run out of time on the test — and on all of life's other, figurative tests, too. So, yes, there are other ways to reason about the world, but those other ways aren't better. The system we have *is* better. The system we have is astonishing.

This is the lesson we learned with optical illusions, and it is the fundamental lesson of inductive reasoning as well: our mistakes are part and parcel of our brilliance, not the regrettable consequences of a separate and deplorable process. Our options in life are not careful logical reasoning, through which we get things right, versus shoddy inductive reasoning, through which we get things wrong. Our options are inductive reasoning,

BELIEVING SOMETHING ON THE BASIS OF MESSY, SPARSE, LIMITED INFORMATION REALLY IS HOW WE ERR. BUT IT IS ALSO HOW WE THINK. WHAT MAKES US RIGHT IS WHAT MAKES US WRONG.

which probably gets things right, and inductive reasoning, which — *because* it probably gets things right — sometimes gets things wrong. In other words, and appropriately enough, Descartes was half right. Believing something on the basis of messy, sparse, limited information really is how we err. But it is also how we think. What makes us right is what makes us wrong.

That's the good news. The bad news is that inductive reasoning doesn't just sometimes make us wrong. It makes us wrong in ways that are a complete embarrassment to our self-image as clear-eyed, fair-minded, conscientious, reasonable thinkers.

Take a story that was told to me by a man named Donald Leka. Back in 1978, when his two children were in elementary school, Don volunteered to help out at a PTA fundraiser. In the interest of earning a laugh as well as some money, he set up a booth advertising legal advice for 25 cents — a sort of lawyerly version of Lucy's advice booth in *Peanuts*. The booth was obviously something of a jest, but as a responsible lawyer, Don was careful to staff it with practicing members of the bar. So he was alarmed to learn that a guest had gotten legal advice about a healthcare issue not from a colleague who was among those appointed to give such advice, a man named Jim, but from Jim's wife. "I grew quite concerned," Don recollected, "because even though this was lighthearted, I didn't want people's wives just going around giving advice. As soon as I could, I located Jim and told him what his wife was doing" — at which point, Jim informed Don that his wife was general counsel of the largest HMO in the city.

Needless to say, this story is cringe inducing. Also needless to say, the person who has cringed the most is Don, who chalked up his mistake to "ignorant sexism" and still winces about it today. But the reason we make mistakes like this isn't *just* ignorant sexism. It is also because of the pitfalls of inductive reasoning. Even in 2007, when Don told me this story, only a quarter of the lawyers in the United States were women. In the 1970s, the figure was in the low single digits, and Don's experiences bore that out. When he graduated from Harvard Law in 1967, twenty-six of his 525 classmates were women — just over 5 percent. When he took his first job, he had one female colleague out of twenty-three lawyers — just under 5 percent. In Don's experience, 95 percent of lawyers were male. Most of us would be willing to put some money on 95 percent odds, and in essence that's what happened at the PTA event. Unbeknownst to Don, his brain crunched the numbers and made a bet. As it happened, that bet bit him in the butt. But, for good or for ill, it wasn't a bad bet — just a wrong one.

This is the problem with the guesswork that underlies our cognitive system. When it works well (and, as we've seen, overall it works better than anything else around), it makes us fast, efficient thinkers capable of remarkable intellectual feats. But, as with so many systems, the strengths of inductive reasoning are also its weaknesses. For every way that induction serves us admirably, it also creates a series of predictable biases in the way we think.

It was Donald Leka's misfortune to illustrate one of these inductive biases: leaping to conclusions. Actually, as I noted above, leaping to conclusions is what we always do in inductive reasoning, but we generally only call it that when the process fails us — that is, when we leap to *wrong* conclusions. In those instances, our habit of relying on meager evidence, normally so clever, suddenly looks foolish (and makes us look foolish, too). That's bad enough, but Don's story also showcases a more specific and disturbing aspect of this bias. Since the whole point of inductive reasoning is to draw sweeping assumptions based on limited evidence, it is an outstanding machine for generating stereotypes. Think about the magnitude of the extrapolation involved in going from "This swan is white" to "All swans are white." In context, it seems unproblematic, but now try this: "This Muslim is a terrorist"; "All Muslims are terrorists." Suddenly, induction doesn't seem so benign.

If the stereotypes we generate based on small amounts of evidence could be overturned by equally small amounts of counterevidence, this particular feature of inductive reasoning wouldn't be terribly worrisome. A counterexample or two would give the lie to false and pernicious generalizations, and we would amend or reject our beliefs accordingly. But this is the paradox of inductive reasoning: although small amounts of evidence are sufficient to make us draw conclusions, they are seldom sufficient to make us revise them.

ALTHOUGH SMALL AMOUNTS OF EVIDENCE ARE SUFFICIENT TO MAKE US DRAW CONCLUSIONS, THEY ARE SELDOM SUFFICIENT TO MAKE US REVISE THEM.

Consider, for instance, a second story, this one told to me by a woman named Elizabeth O'Donovan. Once, many years ago, Elizabeth got into an argument with a friend about whether Orion is a winter constellation. (Because of the annual rotation of the earth around the sun, most constellations are visible only at certain times of the year.) Elizabeth emphatically insisted that it was not. "The embarrassing part," she told me, "is that at the time that I was doing all this insisting, my friend and I were standing in a parking lot in December and I had just pointed to the sky and said, "That's weird. Orion shouldn't be out now; it's a *summer* constellation.'"

You might think that gazing directly at evidence that contradicted her claim would have given Elizabeth pause, but it did not. Instead, the argument escalated until she bet her friend that he was wrong. The loser, they agreed, would take the winner out to dinner once a week for four weeks. "I was so damn determined," she recalled, "that I figured it was some sort of crazy astronomical phenomenon. My logic was something like, 'Well, everyone knows that every fifty-two years, Orion appears for eighteen months straight.'" As we'll see later, this kind of tortured theorizing is typical of the crisis that ensues when new evidence challenges an entrenched theory. It's also a decent indicator that you are about to lose a bet. (For the record, Orion is visible in the night sky from roughly October through March, in both the northern and southern hemispheres. Elizabeth treated her friend to four weeks of fried chicken.)

Elizabeth's story illustrates another of our inductive biases. This one is famous enough to have earned its own separate name in the psychological literature: confirmation bias. As you might guess, confirmation bias is the tendency to give more weight to evidence that confirms our beliefs than to evidence that challenges them. On the face of it, this sounds irrational (and sometimes looks it, as Elizabeth unwittingly demonstrated). In fact, though, confirmation bias is often entirely sensible. We hold our beliefs for a reason, after all—specifically, because we've already encountered other, earlier evidence that suggests that they are true. And, although this, too, can seem pigheaded, it's smart to put more stock in that earlier evidence than in whatever counterevidence we come across later. Remember how our beliefs are probabilistic? Probability theory tells us that the more common something is—long-necked giraffes, white swans, subject-verb-object sentences—the earlier and more often we will encounter it. As a result, it makes sense to treat early evidence preferentially.

Still, however defensible confirmation bias might be, it deals another blow to our ideal thinker. That's the admirable soul we met earlier in this chapter, the one who gathers as much evidence as possible and assesses it neutrally before reaching a conclusion. We already saw inductive reasoning upend the first half of this ideal. We don't gather the maximum possible evidence in order to reach a conclusion; we reach the maximum possible conclusion based on the barest minimum of evidence. Now it turns out that inductive reasoning upends the second half as well. We don't assess evidence neutrally; we assess it in light of whatever theories we've already formed on the basis of whatever other, earlier evidence we have encountered.

This idea was given its most influential treatment by Thomas Kuhn, the historian and philosopher of science, in his 1962 work *The Structure of Scientific Revolutions.* Before Kuhn, scientists were generally regarded as the apotheosis of the above-mentioned ideal thinker. These epistemologically prudent souls were thought to opt for logic over guesswork, reject verification (looking for white swans) in favor of falsification (looking for black swans), test their hypotheses extensively, collect and analyze evidence neutrally, and only then arrive at their theories. Kuhn challenged this notion, arguing that—among other problems with this model—it is impossible to do science in the absence of a preexisting theory.

Kuhn didn't mean this as a criticism, or at least not only as a criticism. Without some kind of belief system in place, he posited, we wouldn't even know what kinds of questions to ask, let alone how to make sense of the answers. Far from freeing us up to regard the evidence neutrally, the absence of theories would render us unable to figure out what even counted as evidence, or what it should be counted as evidence *for.* Kuhn's great insight was that preexisting theories are necessary to the kind of inquiry that is the very essence of science. And the history of the field bears this out: science is full of examples of how faith in a theory has led people to the evidence, rather than evidence leading them to the theory. In the early nineteenth century, for instance, astronomers were puzzled by perturbations in the orbit of Uranus that seemed to contradict Newtonian mechanics. Because they weren't prepared to jettison Newton, they posited the existence of an unknown planet whose gravitational pull was affecting Uranus's path, and calculated that planet's necessary orbit around the sun. Guided by this work, later astronomers with better telescopes took a second look at the sky and, sure enough, discovered Neptune — less than one degree away from where the theorists had predicted it would be.*

The discovery of Neptune is a crystalline illustration of Kuhn's point that theories represent the beginning of science as much as its endpoint. Theories tell us what questions to ask ("Why is Uranus's orbit out of whack?"), what kind of answers to look for ("Something really big must be exerting a gravitational pull on it.") and where to find them ("According to Newtonian calculations, that big thing must be over there."). They also tell us what *not* to look for and what questions *not* to ask, which is why those astronomers didn't bother looking for a giant intergalactic battleship warping Uranus's orbit instead. These are invaluable directives, prerequisite to doing science — or, for that matter, to doing much of anything. As Alan Greenspan pointed out, during a moment in his congressional testimony when he seemed to be coming under fire for merely possessing a political ideology, "An ideology is a conceptual framework, the way people deal with reality. Everyone has one. You have to. To exist, you need an ideology."

TO EXIST, TO DEAL WITH REALITY, WE NEED A CONCEPTUAL FRAMEWORK: THEORIES THAT TELL US WHICH QUESTIONS TO ASK AND WHICH ONES NOT TO, WHERE TO LOOK AND WHERE NOT TO BOTHER.

Greenspan was right. To exist, to deal with reality, we need a conceptual framework: theories that tell us which questions to ask and which ones not to, where to look and where not to bother. When that framework serves us well — when, say, it spares us

*This story about Neptune presents something of a challenge to my earlier claim that tortured theorizing is often a sign of being on the losing end of a bet. Specifically, it suggests that tortured theories only seem tortured when they turn out to be wrong. If Neptune didn't exist, explaining away deviations in Uranus's orbit by positing a giant undiscovered planet in the outer reaches of the solar system would seem like a pretty desperate move. Or consider a still unresolved example: physicists currently think that 96 percent of all the matter and energy in the universe is invisible — so-called dark matter and dark energy. The virtue of this highly counterintuitive (not to say cockamamie) proposal is that it makes sense of scientific findings that would otherwise call into question the theory of gravity. This is a classic example of extremely strong prior beliefs (we *really* believe in gravity) trumping extremely strong counterevidence. It remains to be seen whether the dark-matter theory will ultimately seem as foolish as proposing that Orion loiters in the sky every fifty-two years or as prescient as predicting the existence of Neptune.

the effort of asking what other kinds of long things a giraffe might possess, or taking seriously the proposition that behind a certain shaded rectangle we might encounter a certain naked movie star — we call it brilliant, and call it inductive reasoning. When it serves us poorly, we call it idiotic, and call it confirmation bias. As Elizabeth O'Donovan demonstrated, the effect of that bias — of viewing all evidence in light of the theories we already hold — is that we sometimes view the evidence very strangely indeed.

Actually, Elizabeth showed us only one of the many faces of confirmation bias. To see another one in action, consider a different story about astronomy, this one borrowed from Kuhn. In the West, until the midfifteenth century, the heavens were thought to be immutable. This theory was part of a belief system that reigned far beyond the borders of science; the idea that the heavens were eternal and unchanging (in contrast to the inconsistency and impermanence of life on earth) was a cornerstone of pre-modern Christianity. But then Copernicus came along with his idea about the earth revolving around the sun, and the Church went reeling, and suddenly much of astronomy was up for grabs. In the fifty years immediately following the Copernican revolution, Western astronomers began to observe changes in the heavens they had failed to notice for centuries: new stars appearing, others disappearing, sunspots flaring and fading out. In China, meanwhile, where the sky overhead was identical but the ideology on the ground was different, astronomers had been recording such phenomena for at least 500 years. These early Western astronomers did Elizabeth O'Donovan one better. Instead of failing to believe the counter-evidence, they literally failed to see it.

Sometimes, by contrast, we see the counterevidence just fine — but, thanks to confirmation bias, we decide that it has no bearing on the validity of our beliefs. In logic, this tendency is known, rather charmingly, as the No True Scotsman fallacy. Let's say you believe that no Scotsman puts sugar in his porridge. I protest that my uncle, Angus McGregor of Glasgow, puts sugar in his porridge every day. "Aye," you reply, "but no *true* Scotsman puts sugar in his porridge." So much for my counterevidence — and so much the better for your belief. This is an evergreen rhetorical trick, especially in religion and politics. As everyone knows, no true Christian supports legalized abortion (or opposes it), no true follower of the Qur'an supports suicide bombings (or opposes them), no true Democrat supported the Iraq War (or opposed it) . . . et cetera.

The Iraq War also provides a nice example of another form of confirmation bias. At a point when conditions on the ground were plainly deteriorating, then-President George W. Bush argued otherwise by, in the words of the journalist George Packer, "interpreting increased violence in Iraq as a token of the enemy's frustration with American success." Sometimes, as Bush showed, we look straight at the counterevidence yet conclude that it supports our beliefs instead. The NASA higher-ups responsible for the space shuttle *Columbia* — which disintegrated upon reentry in 2003, killing all seven astronauts onboard — demonstrated this as well:

before the disaster, they consistently claimed that previous damage to the space shuttle was proof of the aircraft's strength rather than evidence of a fatal design flaw. More generally, we all demonstrate it every time we insist that "the exception proves the rule." Think about the claim this adage is making: that a piece of *acknowledged* counterevidence weighs in favor of the hypothesis it appears to weigh against.

The final form of confirmation bias I want to introduce is by far the most pervasive — and, partly for that reason, by far the most troubling. On the face of it, though, it seems like the most benign, because it requires no active shenanigans on our part — no refusal to believe the evidence, like Elizabeth O'Donovan, no dismissal of its relevance, like the stubborn Scotsman, no co-opting of it, like George Bush. Instead, this form of confirmation bias is entirely passive: we simply fail to look for any information that could contradict our beliefs. The sixteenth-century scientist, philosopher, and statesman Francis Bacon called this failure "the greatest impediment and aberration of the human understanding," and it's easy to see why. As we know, only the black swans can tell us anything definitive about our beliefs — and yet, we persistently fail to seek them out.

Two of my favorite examples of this form of confirmation bias come from the wonderfully evidence-resistant realm of early anatomy and physiology. The first is the traditional Judeo-Christian belief that women had one more rib than men (Adam having furnished one for the making of Eve). This belief somehow survived until 1543, when the Flemish anatomist Andreas Vesalius finally showed otherwise — by, you know, counting. The second includes just about every claim ever made by Pliny the Elder, a Roman scientist and author who lived in the first century AD. Pliny was, arguably, the most influential misinformed man in history, a veritable Johnny Appleseed of bad ideas. Consider his thoughts on menstruation, as recorded in his supposed masterpiece, the scientific omnibus *Naturalis Historia:*

> On the approach of a woman in this state, milk will become sour, seeds which are touched by her become sterile, grafts wither away, garden plants are parched up, and the fruit will fall from the tree beneath which she sits. Her very look, even, will dim the brightness of mirrors, blunt the edge of steel, and take away the polish from ivory. A swarm of bees, if looked upon by her, will die immediately; . . . while dogs which may have tasted of the matter so discharged are seized with madness, and their bite is venomous and incurable.

Surely it wouldn't have been hard to run a quick experiment on that one. And yet, until the stirrings of the Scientific Revolution, no one thought to go looking for evidence that might contradict the prevailing medical beliefs of 1,500 years.

As perverse as they may seem, these many forms of creatively dodging the counterevidence represent a backhanded tribute to its importance. However much we ignore, deny, distort, or misconstrue it, evidence continues to matter to us, enormously. In fact, we ignore, deny, distort, and nstrue evidence *because* it matters to us. We know that it is the coin e epistemological realm: that if we expect our beliefs to seem credi- ve will have to furnish their grounds. In a sense, this is the positive of the 'Cuz It's True Constraint. If we think we hold our beliefs be- e they comport with the evidence, we must also think that we will revise them when new evidence arises. As a consequence, every proposition, no matter how much we might initially resist it, must have an evidentiary threshold somewhere, a line beyond which disbelief passes over into belief. If you show up on my doorstep with a spaceship and a small green friend and we all fly off to Pluto together, I will commence believing in UFOs. Closer to home, we see evidentiary thresholds being crossed all the time. That's how belief in geocentrism — once the most radical of conjectures — came to be taken for granted, and how a global consensus is emerging on climate change, and how Elizabeth O'Donovan eventually accepted that Orion is a winter constellation.

IF YOU SHOW UP ON MY DOORSTEP WITH A SPACESHIP AND A SMALL GREEN FRIEND AND WE ALL FLY OFF TO PLUTO TOGETHER, I WILL COMMENCE BELIEVING IN UFOS.

But we also see evidentiary thresholds *not* being crossed — sometimes for centuries, as in the case of Pliny's medical theories. As powerful as confirmation bias is, it cannot fully account for this: for the persistence and duration with which we sometimes fail to accept evidence that could alter our theories. Another factor is the claim, implicit or explicit in many belief systems, that attending to counterevidence can be dangerous — to your health or family or nation, to your moral fiber or your mortal soul. (As a European Communist once said in response to the question of whether he had read any of the criticisms of Communism, "A man does not sip a bottle of cyanide just to find out what it tastes like.") Confirmation bias is also bolstered by the fact that looking for counterevidence often requires time, energy, learning, liberty, and sufficient social capital to weather the suspicion and derision of defenders of the status quo. If the dominant theory works to your detriment, odds are those are resources you don't possess. (Imagine the average medieval woman trying to take on Pliny.) And if the dominant theory works to your advantage, or at least leaves you unscathed — well, why bother challenging it?

As all this suggests, our relationship to evidence is seldom purely a cognitive one. Vilifying menstruating women, bolstering anti-Muslim stereotypes, murdering innocent citizens of Salem: plainly, evidence is almost invariably a political, social, and moral issue as well. To take a particularly stark example, consider the case of Albert Speer, minister of armaments and war production during the Third Reich, close friend to Adolf Hitler, and the highest-ranking Nazi official ever to express remorse for his actions. In his memoir, *Inside the Third Reich,* Speer candidly addressed his failure to look for evidence of what was happening around him. "I did not query [a friend who told him not to visit Auschwitz], I did not query Himmler, I did not query Hitler," he wrote. "I did not speak with personal friends. I did not investigate — for I did not want to know what was happening there . . . for fear of discovering something which might have made me turn away from my course. I had closed my eyes."

Judge William Stoughton of Salem, Massachusetts, became complicit in injustice and murder by accepting evidence he should have ignored. Albert Speer became complicit by ignoring evidence he should have accepted. Together, they show us some of the gravest possible consequences of mismanaging the data around us — and the vital importance of learning to manage it better. It is possible to do this: like the U.S. legal system, we as individuals can develop a fairer and more consistent relationship to evidence over time. By indirection, Speer himself shows us how to begin. *I did not query,* he wrote. *I did not speak. I did not investigate. I closed my eyes.* These are sins of omission, sins of passivity; and they suggest, correctly, that if we want to improve our relationship to evidence, we must take a more active role in how we think — must, in a sense, take the reins of our own minds.

To do this, we must query and speak and investigate and open our eyes. Specifically, and crucially, we must learn to actively combat our inductive biases: to deliberately seek out evidence that challenges our beliefs, and to take seriously such evidence when we come across it. One person who recognized the value of doing this was Charles Darwin. In his autobiography, he recalled that, "I had, during many years, followed a golden rule, namely, that whenever a published fact, a new observation or thought came across me, which was opposed to my general results, to make a memorandum of it without fail and at once; for I had found by experience that such facts and thoughts were far more apt to escape from the memory than favorable ones."

You don't need to be one of history's greatest scientists to combat your inductive biases. Remembering to attend to counterevidence isn't difficult; it is simply a habit of mind. But, like all habits of mind, it requires conscious cultivation. Without that, the first evidence we encounter will remain the last word on the truth. That's why . . . so many of our strongest beliefs are determined by mere accidents of fate: where we were born, what our parents believed, what other information shaped us from our earliest days. Once that initial evidence takes hold, we are off and running. No matter how skewed or scanty it may be, it will form the basis for all our future beliefs. Inductive reasoning guarantees as much. And it guarantees, too, that we will find plenty of data to support us, and precious little to contradict us. And that, in turn, all but guarantees that our theories will be very, very difficult to fell.

Below you will find Schulz's endnotes for this chapter, prefaced by a brief introduction in which she discusses her use of Wikipedia. As you attempt the questions and assignments that follow, you may find it helpful to consult these endnotes.

NOTES

A vast number and variety of sources — comments from friends, conversations with strangers, formal and informal interviews, news items, radio broadcasts, journal articles, websites, books — helped shape this book in ways both subtle and profound. Many of these do not appear in the final text in any explicit way, and it isn't practical to cite them all here. Still, wherever possible I have tried to attribute not just specific facts and quotations but also background sources and influences. More generally, I would like to acknowledge my deep debt to the many thinkers who have grappled with the idea of error, and whose work has made possible my own. Where appropriate, I have prefaced the notes to a given chapter with a brief description of particularly valuable sources. Specific citations then follow. I have sourced my footnotes in the order in which they appear in the book; they are distinguished from the main text by the indication (FN).

A note on Wikipedia: I don't know any writer working today who doesn't regard it as 1) a pretty questionable source; and 2) surpassingly useful. To the second point, I offer my gratitude for the remarkable and largely anonymous collaborative effort it represents. I made use of it regularly to look up passing facts (was Rousseau born before Laplace, or vice versa?) or to get an initial overview of an unfamiliar subject (the proto-Indo-European language). In these cases, either I or my fact checker cross-referenced such information with other, more conventional resources to try to ensure accuracy. To the first point: as grateful as I am for its existence, I have avoided using Wikipedia as the definitive source for any information in this book, let alone for the substantive philosophical, psychological, scientific, and historical ideas I present. Accordingly, I have not cited it.

I am indebted to my sister, Laura Schulz, a cognitive scientist at MIT, whose own work on the double-edged sword of human cognition has been invaluable to me here, and who fundamentally altered and dramatically deepened my understanding of inductive reasoning. I could not have written this chapter without her assistance — or, rather, I could not have written it accurately and well. Among many other things, she supplied me with the idea of the inductive reasoning quiz and pointed me in the direction of Willard Van Orman Quine, whose work on the indeterminacy of translation was originally presented in his *Word and Object* (The MIT Press, 1964). She also supplied the connection between inductive reasoning and Noam Chomsky's "poverty of the stimulus" problem, as well as the example of Neptune and Uranus.

I first learned of Judge William Stoughton upon driving through his namesake town, Stoughton, Massachusetts. The information about him and about spectral evidence in this chapter comes from biographical information provided by the town (available at http://www.stoughtonhistory.com/williamstoughton.htm), and from Francis Hill, *Tbe Salem Witch Trials Reader* (De Capo Press, 2000), 90. Interestingly, the dispute over the use of spectral evidence was as much theological as judicial, since it centered on the question of whether or not the devil required permission from people to use their image to torment the (ostensible) victims of witchcraft. People who believed that the devil could do whatever he pleased were opposed to the use of spectral evidence, on the theory that the Goody Proctors of the world were not merely blameless but, themselves, victims. By contrast, people who believed that the devil needed permission from mortals in order to use their image supported spectral evidence, since anyone who appeared as an evildoer in dreams or visitations had clearly made a pact with Satan. See David Levin's "Shadows of Doubt: Specter Evidence in Hawthorne's 'In Young Goodman Brown,'" *American Literature,* Vol. 34, No. 3 (1962): 344-352.

Donald Leka and Elizabeth O'Donovan are both strangers who responded to a general request I made for stories about wrongness. The quotations in those passages are from direct communication with the two of them.

113 **"beliefs follow from relatively dispassionate assessment."** "Against Simulation: The Argument From Error," Rebecca Saxe, *Trends in Cognitive Sciences,* Vol. 9, No. 4 (April 2005): 174-179.

113 **Descartes defined error.** See Keeler, 161: "where it is not perfectly evident, there is no true knowledge; and if I assent to something that is really so, without full and firm certitude that it is so, I commit an error. Error does not consist precisely in judging that to be, which is not, but in rashly venturing to pronounce in the absence of evidence." Some readers will note that this was the position William James argued against in *The Will to Believe.* James, however, took as his intellectual opposition not Descartes but the philosopher William Clifford (James calls him "that delicious *enfant terrible*"), who wrote, "Belief is desecrated when given to unproved and unquestioned statements for the solace and private pleasure of the believer. . . . If [a] belief has been accepted on insufficient evidence . . . [i]t is sinful because it is stolen in defiance of our duty to mankind. That duty is to guard ourselves from such beliefs as from a pestilence which may shortly master our own body and then spread to the rest of the town. . . . It is wrong always, everywhere, and for every one, to believe anything upon insufficient evidence." (James, *The Will to Believe,* 8.)

114 **Augustine, who arrived at Descartes' idea of error.** Keeler, 74-75.

114 **Monotheistic religions have a particularly interesting and troubled relationship to the idea of evidence (FN).** The writer Sam Harris made a similar point in *The End of Faith: Religion, Terror, and the Future of Reason* (W. W. Norton, 2005). See for instance p. 66: "But faith is an imposter. This can be readily seen in the way that all the extraordinary phenomena of the religious life – a statue of the Virgin weeps, a child casts his crutches to the ground – are seized upon by the faithful as *confirmation* of their faith. At these moments, religious believers appear like men and women in the desert of uncertainty given a cool drink of data. There is no way around the fact that we crave justification for our core beliefs and believe them only because we think such justification is, at the very least, in the offing."

118 **David Hume.** Hume lays out the problem of induction in his *Enquiry Concerning Human Understanding* (Oxford University Press, 2006).

119 **"the poverty of the stimulus" (FN).** Chomsky describes this problem in his *Rules and Representations* (Columbia University Press, 2005).

125 **Thomas Kuhn.** Thomas Kuhn, *The Structure of Scientific Revolutions* (The University of Chicago Press, 1996). The anecdote about Chinese and Western astronomers appears on p. 116.

126 **As Alan Greenspan pointed out.** http://oversight.house.gov/documents/20081024163819.pdf

128 **"interpreting increased violence in Iraq."** George Packer, "History Boys," the *New Yorker,* June 11, 2007.

128 **The NASA higher-ups responsible for the . . . *Columbia*.** Henry Petroski, *Success through Failure: The Paradox of Design* (Princeton University Press, 2006), 166.

129 **"The greatest impediment and aberration of the human understanding."** I first stumbled on this quotation in Daniel Gilbert's *Stumbling on Happiness* (Alfred A. Knopf, 2006), 99. The line originally appears in Bacon's *Novum Organum,* Peter Urbach and John Gibson, ed. and trans. (Open Court, 1994), 60.

129 **Vesalius finally showed otherwise.** Jastrow, 15.

129 **Pliny the Elder.** Howard M. Parshley, "Error in Zoology," in Jastrow, 203-204.

130 **(As a European Communist once said).** Whittaker Chambers, *Witness* (Regnery Publishing, Inc., 1952), 79.

131 **Albert Speer.** Albert Speer, *Inside the Third Reich: Memoirs* (Simon and Schuster, 1997), 376.

131 **"I had, during many years, followed a golden rule."** Quoted in Larry R. Squire, "Biological Foundations of Accuracy and Inaccuracy in Memory," in Schacter, ed., 197.

QUESTIONS FOR A SECOND READING

1. Here is a characteristic passage from *Being Wrong*:

> No wonder we gravitate toward certainty.... It's not that we are oblivious to its intellectual and moral dangers; it's that those dangers seem pretty abstract when compared with the immediate practical, emotional, and existential perils of doubt. In fact, just as our love of being right is best understood as a fear of being wrong, our attraction to certainty is best understood as an aversion to uncertainty. To explore that aversion, I want to turn now to three representatives of the domain of chronic doubt: Hamlet, the famously indecisive prince of the Danes; John Kerry, the Democratic presidential candidate who rescued the term "waffle" from the breakfast table; and that most baffling and maddening figure of modern American politics, the Undecided Voter. (170)

One thing to notice in this passage is Schulz's easy use of "we." Do you include yourself in this "we"? How does she earn the right to speak so easily for all of us?

Another thing to notice here is Schulz's sense of what it means to conduct an "exploration" in a work of nonfiction prose. She says, "To explore that aversion [the aversion to uncertainty], I want now to turn to three representatives of the domain of chronic doubt: Hamlet . . . , John Kerry . . . , and . . . the Undecided Voter." How would you characterize this kind of intellectual project? Have you encountered such an "exploration" in previous coursework?

As you reread, find a passage that you might present as characteristic of Schulz's style and method. What would you have us notice in this passage?

2. One of the pleasures of Schulz's book is its broad range of reference and the easy passage from anecdote and journalistic account to her reading in various fields of academic research — from philosophy to cognitive science to the history of ideas to current events. There are several key figures in this chapter, and among them are Rene Descartes, St. Augustine, Willard Van Orman Quine, Karl Popper, and Thomas Kuhn.

Using the library as well as the Internet (so that you can put your hands on books and scholarly journals) and, perhaps working with a group, create a brief presentation on one of these writers and his or her work. Who are these people? Where do (or did) they work? What are their methods and concerns? Why would they be useful or interesting or important to Schulz?

3. Later in *Being Wrong*, Schulz considers the consequences of her argument. (Keep your eye out for the phrase "that is." This move is a standard device in Schulz's prose.)

> Awareness of one's own qualms, attention to contradiction, acceptance of the possibility of error: these strike me as signs of sophisti-

> cated thinking, far preferable in many contexts to the confident bulldozer of unmodified assertions. Philip Tetlock, too, defends these and similar speech patterns (or rather, the mental habits they reflect), describing them, admiringly, as 'self-subversive thinking.' That is, they let us function as our own intellectual sparring partner, thereby honing — or puncturing — our beliefs. They also help us do greater justice to complex topics and make it possible to have riskier thoughts. At the same time, by moving away from decree and toward inquiry, they set the stage for more open and interesting conversations. (309)

Although Schulz refers to "speech patterns" and the kinds of "conversations" they can inspire, there is a writing lesson here. Writers, too, can demonstrate "self-subversive thinking." They can move away from decree and toward inquiry; they can do "justice to complex topics and make it possible to have riskier thoughts." They can avoid being the "confident bulldozer of unmodified assertions," the writer who never steps back to question or reconsider that for which they've argued.

We know you have had teachers who have celebrated these "bulldozers," and it would be wrong to assume that everyone values "inquiry" over "decree." The point is that there are competing ways to describe a successful piece of writing.

As you reread, look to see where and how and if Schulz, as a writer, practices a form of "self-subversive thinking." Or is she more like a "confident bulldozer"? Be prepared to point to passages and to translate a passage back and forth from one style to the other.

ASSIGNMENTS FOR WRITING

1. Here is a characteristic moment in Schulz's book (note the "we," note the repeated phrase "is best understood," and note the term "explore"):

> No wonder we gravitate toward certainty. . . . It's not that we are oblivious to its intellectual and moral dangers; it's that those dangers seem pretty abstract when compared with the immediate practical, emotional, and existential perils of doubt. In fact, just as our love of being right is best understood as a fear of being wrong, our attraction to certainty is best understood as an aversion to uncertainty. To explore that aversion, I want to turn now to three representatives of the domain of chronic doubt: Hamlet, the famously indecisive prince of the Danes; John Kerry, the Democratic presidential candidate who rescued the term "waffle" from the breakfast table; and that most baffling and maddening figure of modern American politics, the Undecided Voter. (170)

For this assignment, we'd like you to carry out the kind of Schulzian exploration referenced here. You have read her chapter "Evidence." In this chapter

Schulz has presented a number of representative examples—from the Salem witch trials to Elizabeth O'Donovan to Philip Tetlock and Charles Darwin. If you were to engage this chapter and its argument, what extended example might you bring to the conversation?

Take time to think about what you might bring to the table to advance this discussion—some text or experience or event or object. Bring something that matters to you. You will use it to test Schulz's terms and extend or challenge her argument. You won't have time for three representative examples; spend your time with one that is rich and suggestive.

You should imagine that you are writing for people who are smart and interesting, but who have not yet read *Being Wrong.* At some point, then, you will need to present the chapter and what it says. Do this quickly and efficiently, by means of paraphrase, summary, and block quotation, as the primary point of the essay is for you to develop your response to the chapter.

2. Here is Schulz on evidence:

> Descartes was right to fear that this way of thinking ["believing things based on paltry evidence"] would cause us to make mistakes; it does. Since he was interested in knowing the truth, and knowing that he knew it, he tried to develop a model for thinking that could curtail the possibility of error. . . . In fact, curtailing error was the goal of most models of optimal human cognition proposed by most thinkers throughout most of history, and it is the goal behind our own broadly shared image of the ideal thinker. Some of these models, like Descartes', sought to curtail error through radical doubt. Others sought to curtail it through formal logic—using valued premises to derive necessarily valid conclusions. Others, including our shared one of the ideal thinker, seek to curtail it through a kind of general due diligence: careful attention to evidence and counterevidence, coupled with a prudent avoidance of preconceived notions. (364)

"Due diligence," "a model for thinking," and the "ideal thinker." Over time, writing has been one of the ways human beings have tried to find forms and methods to represent (and preserve and transmit) models for thinking. You've received these models through instruction. Topic sentence, example, conclusion—these comprise a model for thinking. And every time you have been assigned something to read (and every time you have chosen something to read), you were presented with a "model for thinking," a model in practice.

For this assignment, we'd like you to find a piece of prose (somewhere in length from a paragraph to a page or two, no more). It can be ancient or it can be recent; it can be academic or it can be from outside the academy. We'd like you to use it to think about writing and belief and evidence. We'd like you to think about it as a model for thinking and we'd like you to think about it, at least for a brief period, through the lens of this chapter in *Being Wrong.*

Remember—you need to present your example to readers who are not familiar with it. And you'll need to present Schulz's chapter to people who have not yet read it. There will be some work you will need to do to prepare your reader for what you want to say. The most important part of your essay, however, will be the sections where you take the stage and present what you have to add to the conversation.

3. Here is Kathryn Schulz on the consequences of her argument:

> Awareness of one's own qualms, attention to contradiction, acceptance of the possibility of error: these strike me as signs of sophisticated thinking, far preferable in many contexts to the confident bulldozer of unmodified assertions. Philip Tetlock, too, defends these and similar speech patterns (or rather, the mental habits they reflect), describing them, admiringly, as 'self-subversive thinking.' That is, they let us function as our own intellectual sparring partner, thereby honing — or puncturing — our beliefs. They also help us do greater justice to complex topics and make it possible to have riskier thoughts. At the same time, by moving away from decree and toward inquiry, they set the stage for more open and interesting conversations. (309)

Although Schulz refers to "speech patterns" and the kinds of "conversations" they can inspire, we think there is a writing lesson here. Writers, too, can demonstrate "self-subversive thinking." They can move away from decree and toward inquiry; they can do "justice to complex topics and make it possible to have riskier thoughts."

We know. We know you have had teachers who have celebrated the "confident bulldozer of unmodified assertions." And it would be wrong to assume that everyone values "inquiry" over "decree." The point is that there are competing ways to describe a successful piece of writing.

For this assignment, we would like you to take something you have written, ideally something you have written for this course. We would like you to revise it, paying particular attention to the representations of evidence and belief. Revise it with Schulz in mind. She values counter-evidence, self-subversive thinking, inquiry (over decree), attention to contradiction, sophistication, an "open and interesting conversation." She says, "if we want to improve our relation to evidence, we must take a more active role in how we think — we must, in a sense, take the reins of our own minds" (377). She continues, "To do this, we must query and speak and investigate and open our eyes. Specifically, and crucially, we must learn to actively combat our inductive biases: to deliberately seek out evidence that challenges our beliefs, and to take seriously such evidence when we come across it. (377)

Revision is one way of taking the "reins of our own minds." Approach this revision as an experiment, as a way of doing something over again, but this time doing it differently.

When you are done, write a brief coda assessing the two drafts. What you were able to do in each, which draft do you prefer, and which would you offer as a model of thinking?

4. Here is Kathryn Schulz on the consequences of her argument:

> Awareness of one's own qualms, attention to contradiction, acceptance of the possibility of error: these strike me as signs of sophisticated thinking, far preferable in many contexts to the confident bulldozer of unmodified assertions. Philip Tetlock, too, defends these and similar speech patterns (or rather, the mental habits they reflect), describing them, admiringly, as 'self-subversive thinking.' That is, they let us function as our own intellectual sparring partner, thereby honing — or puncturing — our beliefs. They also help us do greater justice to complex topics and make it possible to have riskier thoughts. At the same time, by moving away from decree and toward inquiry, they set the stage for more open and interesting conversations. (309)

This assignment begins with a research project. For a week, pay close attention to the people around you — in class and out of class. Keep a notebook where you tally and record examples of "unmodified assertions" and examples of "self-subversive" thinking.

At the end of the week, prepare a report on what you have found. Use your findings to test Schulz's assumption that the latter form of thinking is sophisticated (if risky) and that the former is unsophisticated (and timid).

MAKING CONNECTIONS

1. For this assignment we'd like you to work with another of the selections in *Ways of Reading*. You might look at Judith Butler's "Beside Oneself" (p. 114) or at Susan Griffin's "Our Secret." (p. 233) Work with a section of the prose (somewhere in length from a paragraph to a page or two, no more). We'd like you to think about this section as a model for thinking and we'd like you to think about it, at least for a brief period, through the lens of this chapter in *Being Wrong*.

   Remember — you need to present your example to readers who are not familiar with the text from which it comes. And you'll need to present Schulz's chapter to people who have not yet read it. There will be some work you will need to do to prepare your reader for what you want to say. The most important part of your essay, however, will be the sections where you take the stage and present what you have to add to the conversation.

2. Kathryn Schulz offers herself as an expert on error, as a "wrongologist," as she puts it. She offers a hopeful theory of error. As she says in her conclusion, we have no choice but to rely on our imperfect representations of the world:

> That is why error, even though it sometimes feels like despair, is actually much closer in spirit to hope. We get things wrong because we have an enduring confidence in the faith that, having learned some-

> thing, we will get it right the next time. In this optimistic vein, embracing our fallibility is simply a way of paying homage to, in the words of the late philosophy Richard Rorty, "the permanent possibility of someone having a better idea." The great advantage of realizing that we have told a story about the world is realizing that we can tell a better one: rich with better ideas, better possibilities — even, perhaps, better people. (338-339)

There are several writers in this anthology who are deeply and fundamentally concerned with human error. Here are a few of them: Kwame Anthony Appiah in "Racial Identities" (p. 42); John Berger in "Ways of Seeing" (e-Pages); Judith Butler in "Beside Oneself" (p. 114); Michel Foucault in "Panopticism" (p. 181); Errol Morris in "Will the Real Hooded Man Please Stand Up?"; Mary Louise Pratt in "Arts of the Contact Zone" (p. 317); and Walker Percy in "The Loss of the Creature" (p. 299).

Choose one of these essays and read it through the lens of Kathryn Schulz's chapter "Evidence." What, for each writer, are the sources of human error? What, for each, are the consequences and the cures? And what sort of hope (or despair) do they suggest to you as you think about life, about education, and about the future?

DAVID FOSTER Wallace

David Foster Wallace (1962–2008) wrote big books and big essays, books and essays with long sentences and long footnotes, and yet, for most readers, his prose was like riding a roller coaster—scary, fun, compelling, exuberant, impossible to resist. In Wallace's *New York Times* obituary, Bruce Weber described Wallace as a "versatile writer of seemingly bottomless energy, . . . a maximalist, exhibiting in his work a huge, even manic curiosity—about the physical world, about the much larger universe of human feelings and about the complexity of living in America at the end of the 20th century." Wallace's sentences, he said, show the "playfulness of a master punctuater and the inventiveness of a genius grammarian."

Wallace grew up in Illinois, in an academic family (his father was a philosopher; his mother was an English teacher—and a teacher of composition); he graduated from Amherst College in 1985 with a double honors degree in English and philosophy. His philosophy thesis won the Gail Kennedy Memorial Prize; his English thesis became his first novel, *The Broom of the System* (1987). He took graduate courses in philosophy at Harvard; he received a master of fine arts degree in fiction from the University of Arizona in 1987. He taught creative writing at Illinois State University. In 2002, he became the Roy E. Disney Professor of Creative Writing at Pomona College, of the Claremont Colleges in California. He won a Whiting Writers' Award (1987), a Lannan Literary Award (1996), a Salon Book Award (1996), the Aga Kahn Prize for Fiction (1997), and a John D. and Catherine T. MacArthur Foundation Fellowship (1997), commonly known as the "Genius Award."

Wallace wrote novels, short stories, and essays. His second novel, *Infinite Jest* (1996), placed him as one of the most important, innovative, and influential writers of his generation. At more than 1,000 pages, it was, as the *New York Times* said, "a whopper." Sven Birketts, in a review for the *Atlantic Monthly,* called it "resourceful, hilarious, intelligent, and unique." Wallace published three collections of short stories—*Girl with Curious Hair* (1989), *Brief Interviews with Hideous Men* (1999), and *Oblivion: Stories* (2004). He was also a prolific and much-admired essayist. In fact, although his fiction sparked controversy among the critics, his nonfiction was almost universally praised. In a lovely *Rolling Stone* essay (October 30, 2008) celebrating Wallace's life and work, David Lipsky said:

> When people tell you they're fans of David Foster Wallace, what they're often telling you is that they've read the cruise-ship piece [an essay written for *Harper's Magazine*]; Wallace would make it the title essay in his first collection of journalism, *A Supposedly Fun Thing I'll Never Do Again*. In a way, the difference between the fiction and the nonfiction reads as the difference between Wallace's social self and his private self. The essays were endlessly charming, they were the best friend you'd ever have, spotting everything, whispering jokes, sweeping you past what was irritating or boring or awful in humane style. Wallace's fiction, especially after *Infinite Jest*, would turn chilly, dark, abstract. You could imagine the author of the fiction sinking into a depression. The nonfiction writer was an impervious sun.

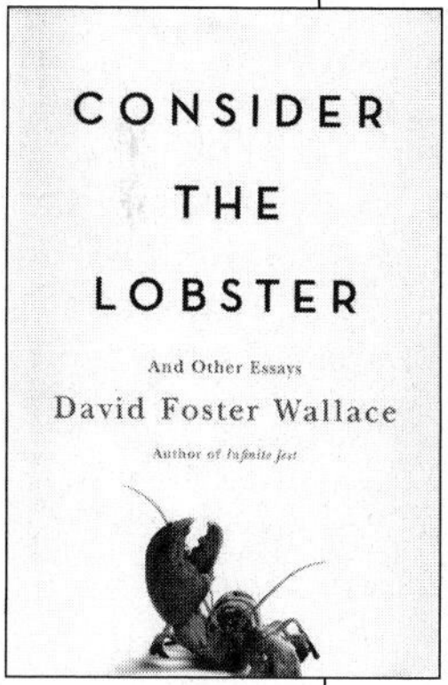

Wallace's nonfiction books include *Signifying Rappers: Rap and Race in the Urban Present* (1990, with Mark Costello); *A Supposedly Fun Thing I'll Never Do Again* (1990); *Everything and More: A Compact History of Infinity* (2003); *Consider the Lobster: And Other Essays* (2005); and *McCain's Promise: Aboard the Straight Talk Express with John McCain and a Whole Bunch of Actual Reporters, Thinking about Hope* (2008). The transcript of a commencement speech Wallace delivered at Kenyon College was published posthumously as *This Is Water: Some Thoughts, Delivered on a Significant Occasion, about Living a Compassionate Life* (2009). Also published posthumously were an unfinished novel, *The Pale King*, (2011), and a collection of essays, *Both Flesh and Not* (2012).

The essay that follows, "Authority and American Usage," was originally published in *Harper's Magazine* (April 2001) under the title "Tense Present: Democracy, English, and the Wars over Usage." It was republished with the current title in *Consider the Lobster*.

Authority and American Usage*

Dilige et quod vis fac.
—AUGUSTINE

Did you know that probing the seamy underbelly of US lexicography reveals ideological strife and controversy and intrigue and nastiness and fervor on a near-Lewinskian scale?

For instance, did you know that some modern dictionaries are notoriously liberal and others notoriously conservative, and that certain conservative dictionaries were actually conceived and designed as corrective responses to the "corruption" and "permissiveness" of certain liberal dictionaries? That the oligarchic device of having a special "Distinguished Usage Panel . . . of outstanding professional speakers and writers" is some dictionaries' attempt at a compromise between the forces of egalitarianism and traditionalism in English, but that most linguistic liberals dismiss the Usage Panel device as mere sham-populism, as in e.g. "Calling upon the opinions of the elite, it claims to be a democratic guide"?

Did you know that US lexicography even *had* a seamy underbelly?

The occasion for this article is Oxford University Press's recent release of Mr. Bryan A. Garner's *A Dictionary of Modern American Usage,* a book that Oxford is marketing aggressively and that it is my assigned function to review. It turns out to be a complicated assignment. In today's US, a typical book review is driven by market logic and implicitly casts the reader in the role of consumer. Rhetorically, its whole project is informed by a question that's too crass ever to mention up front: "Should you buy this book?" And because Bryan A. Garner's usage dictionary belongs to a particular subgenre of a reference genre that is itself highly specialized and particular, and because at least a dozen major usage guides have been published in the last couple years and some of them have been quite good indeed,[1] the central unmentionable question here appends the prepositional comparative ". . . rather than *that* book?" to the main clause and so entails a discussion of whether and how *ADMAU* is different from other recent specialty-products of its kind.

---

* (or, "Politics and the English Language" Is Redundant)

[1] (the best and most substantial of these being *The American Heritage Book of English Usage,* Jean Eggenschwiler's *Writing: Grammar, Usage, and Style,* and Oxford/Clarendon's' own *The New Fowler's Modern English Usage*)

The fact of the matter is that Garner's dictionary is extremely good, certainly the most comprehensive usage guide since E. W. Gilman's *Webster's Dictionary of English Usage,* now a decade out of date.[2] But the really salient and ingenious features of *A Dictionary of Modern American Usage* involve issues of rhetoric and ideology and style, and it is impossible to describe why these issues are important and why Garner's management of them borders on genius without talking about the historical context[3] in which *ADMAU* appears, and this context turns out to be a veritable hurricane of controversies involving everything from technical linguistics and public education to political ideology,[4] and these controversies take a certain amount of time to unpack before their relation to what makes Garner's dictionary so eminently worth your hard-earned reference-book dollar can even be established; and in fact there's no way even to begin the whole harrowing polymeric discussion without first taking a moment to establish and define the highly colloquial term *SNOOT.*

From one perspective, a certain irony attends the publication of any good new book on American usage. It is that the people who are going to be interested in such a book are also the people who are least going to need it – i.e., that offering counsel on the finer points of US English is preaching to the choir. The relevant choir here comprises that small percentage of American citizens who actually care about the current status of double modals and ergative verbs. The same sorts of people who watched *The Story of English* on PBS (twice) and read Safire's column with their half-caff every Sunday. The sorts of people who feel that special blend of wincing despair and sneering superiority when they see EXPRESS LANE – 10 ITEMS OR LESS or hear *dialogue* used as a verb or realize that the founders of the Super 8 Motel chain must surely have been ignorant of the meaning of *suppurate.* There are lots of epithets for people like

---

[2] *The New Fowler's* is also extremely comprehensive and fine, but its emphasis is on British usage.

[3] Sorry about this phrase; I hate this phrase, too. This happens to be one of those very rare times when "historical context" is the phrase to use and there is no equivalent phrase that isn't even worse (I actually tried "lexico-temporal backdrop" in one of the middle drafts, which I think you'll agree is not preferable).

INTERPOLATION

The above ¶ is motivated by the fact that this reviewer nearly always sneers and/or winces when he sees a phrase like "historical context" deployed in a piece of writing and thus hopes to head off any potential sneers/winces from the reader here, especially in an article about felicitous usage. One of the little personal lessons I've learned in working on this essay is that being chronically inclined to sneer/wince at other people's usage tends to make me chronically anxious about other people's sneering/wincing at my usage. It is, of course, possible that this bivalence is news to nobody but me; it may be just a straightforward instance of Matt 7:1's thing about "Judge not lest ye be judged." In any case, the anxiety seems worth acknowledging up front.

[4] One of the claim-clusters I'm going to spend a lot of both our time arguing for is that issues of English usage are fundamentally and inescapably political, and that putatively disinterested linguistic authorities like dictionaries are always the products of certain ideologies, and that as authorities they are accountable to the same basic standards of sanity and honesty and fairness as our political authorities.

this – Grammar Nazis, Usage Nerds, Syntax Snobs, the Grammar Battalion, the Language Police. The term I was raised with is *SNOOT*.[5] The word might be slightly self-mocking, but those other terms are outright dysphemisms. A SNOOT can be loosely defined as somebody who knows what *dysphemism* means and doesn't mind letting you know it.

I submit that we SNOOTs are just about the last remaining kind of truly elitist nerd. There are, granted, plenty of nerd-species in today's America, and some of these are elitist within their own nerdy purview (e.g., the skinny, carbuncular, semi-autistic Computer Nerd moves instantly up on the totem pole of status when your screen freezes and now you need his help, and the bland condescension with which he performs the two occult keystrokes that unfreeze your screen is both elitist and situationally valid). But the SNOOT's purview is interhuman life itself. You don't, after all (despite withering cultural pressure), have to use a computer, but you can't escape language: language is everything and everywhere; it's what lets us have anything to do with one another; it's what separates us from animals; Genesis 11:7–10 and so on. And we SNOOTs know when and how to hyphenate phrasal adjectives and to keep participles from dangling, and we know that we know, and we know how very few other Americans know this stuff or even care, and we judge them accordingly.

I SUBMIT THAT WE SNOOTS ARE JUST ABOUT THE LAST REMAINING KIND OF TRULY ELITIST NERD.

In ways that certain of us are uncomfortable with, SNOOTs' attitudes about contemporary usage resemble religious/political conservatives' attitudes about contemporary culture.[6] We combine a missionary zeal and a near-neural faith in our beliefs' importance with a curmudgeonly hell-in-a-handbasket despair at the way English is routinely defiled by supposedly literate adults.[7] Plus a dash of the elitism of, say, Billy Zane

---

[5] SNOOT (*n*) (*highly colloq*) is this reviewer's nuclear family's nickname à clef for a really extreme usage fanatic, the sort of person whose idea of Sunday fun is to hunt for mistakes in the very prose of Safire's column. This reviewer's family is roughly 70 percent SNOOT, which term itself derives from an acronym, with the big historical family joke being that whether S.N.O.O.T. stood for "Sprachgefühl Necessitates Our Ongoing Tendance" or "Syntax Nudniks Of Our Time" depended on whether or not you were one.

[6] This is true in my own case, at any rate – plus also the "uncomfortable" part. I teach college English part-time. Mostly Lit, not Composition. But I am so pathologically obsessed with usage that every semester the same thing happens: once I've had to read my students' first set of papers, we immediately abandon the regular Lit syllabus and have a three-week Emergency Remedial Usage and Grammar Unit, during which my demeanor is basically that of somebody teaching HIV prevention to intravenous-drug users. When it emerges (as it does, every term) that 95 percent of these intelligent upscale college students have never been taught, e.g., what a clause is or why a misplaced *only* can make a sentence confusing or why you don't just automatically stick in a comma after a long noun phrase, I all but pound my head on the blackboard; I get angry and self-righteous; I tell them they should sue their hometown school boards, and mean it. The kids end up scared, both of me and for me. Every August I vow silently to *chill about usage* this year, and then by Labor Day there's foam on my chin. I can't seem to help it. The truth is that I'm not even an especially good or dedicated teacher; I don't have this kind of fervor in class about anything else, and I know it's not a very productive fervor, nor a healthy one – it's got elements of fanaticism and rage to it, plus a snobbishness that I know I'd be mortified to display about anything else.

in *Titanic* — a fellow SNOOT I know likes to say that listening to most people's public English feels like watching somebody use a Stradivarius to pound nails. We[8] are the Few, the Proud, the More or Less Constantly Appalled at Everyone Else.

THESIS STATEMENT FOR WHOLE ARTICLE

Issues of tradition vs. egalitarianism in US English are at root political issues and can be effectively addressed only in what this article hereby terms a "Democratic Spirit." A Democratic Spirit is one that combines rigor and humility, i.e., passionate conviction plus a sedulous respect for the convictions of others. As any American knows, this is a difficult spirit to cultivate and maintain, particularly when it comes to issues you feel strongly about. Equally tough is a DS's criterion of 100 percent intellectual integrity — you have to be willing to look honestly at yourself and at your motives for believing what you believe, and to do it more or less continually.

This kind of stuff is advanced US citizenship. A true Democratic Spirit is up there with religious faith and emotional maturity and all those other top-of-the-Maslow-Pyramid-type qualities that people spend their whole lives working on. A Democratic Spirit's constituent rigor and humility and self-honesty are, in fact, so hard to maintain on certain issues that it's almost irresistibly tempting to fall in with some established dogmatic camp and to follow that camp's line on the issue and to let your position harden within the camp and become inflexible and to believe that the other camps[9] are either evil or insane and to spend all your time and energy trying to shout over them.

I submit, then, that it is indisputably easier to be Dogmatic than Democratic, especially about issues that are both vexed and highly

---

[7] N.B. that this article's own title page features blocks of the typical sorts of contemporary boners and clunkers and oxymorons and solecistic howlers and bursts of voguish linguistic methane that tend to make a SNOOT's cheek twitch and forehead darken. (N.B. further that it took only about a week of semi-attentive listening and note-taking to assemble these blocks — the Evil is all around us.)

[8] Please note that the strategically repeated I-P pronoun is meant to iterate and emphasize that this reviewer is very much one too, a SNOOT, plus to connote the nuclear family mentioned *supra*. SNOOTitude runs in families. In *ADMAU*'s preface, Bryan Garner mentions both his father and grandfather and actually uses the word *genetic,* and it's probably true: 90 percent of the SNOOTs I know have at least one parent who is, by profession or temperament or both, a SNOOT. In my own case, my mom is a Comp teacher and has written remedial usage books and is a SNOOT of the most rabid and intractable sort. At least part of the reason I am a SNOOT is that for years my mom brainwashed us in all sorts of subtle ways. Here's an example. Family suppers often involved a game: if one of us children made a usage error, Mom would pretend to have a coughing fit that would go on and on until the relevant child had identified the relevant error and corrected it. It was all very self-ironic and lighthearted; but still, looking back, it seems a bit excessive to pretend that your small child is actually *denying you oxygen* by speaking incorrectly. The really chilling thing, though, is that I now sometimes find myself playing this same "game" with my own students, complete with pretend pertussion.

[9] (It seems to be a natural law that camps form only in opposition to other camps and that there are always at least two w/r/t any difficult issue.)

charged. I submit further that the issues surrounding "correctness" in contemporary American usage are both vexed and highly charged, and that the fundamental questions they involve are ones whose answers have to be literally *worked out* instead of merely found.

A distinctive feature of *ADMAU* is that its author is willing to acknowledge that a usage dictionary is not a bible or even a textbook but rather just the record of one bright person's attempts to work out answers to certain very difficult questions. This willingness appears to me to be informed by a Democratic Spirit. The big question is whether such a spirit compromises Bryan Garner's ability to present himself as a genuine "authority" on issues of usage. Assessing Garner's book, then, requires us to trace out the very weird and complicated relationship between Authority and Democracy in what we as a culture have decided is English. That relationship is, as many educated Americans would say, still in process at this time.

A Dictionary of Modern American Usage has no Editorial Staff or Distinguished Panel. It's been conceived, researched, and written *ab ovo usque ad mala* by Mr. Bryan A. Garner. This Garner is an interesting guy. He's both a lawyer and a usage expert (which seems a bit like being both a narcotics wholesaler and a DEA agent). His 1987 *A Dictionary of Modern Legal Usage* is already a minor classic; and now, instead of practicing law anymore, he goes around conducting writing seminars for JDs and doing prose-consulting for various judicial bodies. Garner's also the founder of something called the H. W. Fowler Society,[10] a worldwide group of usage Trekkies who like to send one another linguistic boners clipped from different periodicals. You get the idea. This Garner is one serious and very hard-core SNOOT.

The lucid, engaging, and extremely sneaky preface to *ADMAU* serves to confirm Garner's SNOOTitude in fact while undercutting it in tone. For one thing, whereas the traditional usage pundit cultivates a remote and imperial persona — the kind who uses *one* or *we* to refer to himself — Garner gives us an almost Waltonishly endearing sketch of his own background:

> I realized early — at the age of 15[[11]] — that my primary intellectual interest was the use of the English language.... It became an all-consuming passion.... I read everything I could find on the subject. Then, on a wintry evening while visiting New Mexico at the age of 16, I discovered Eric Partridge's *Usage and Abusage*. I was enthralled. Never had I held a more exciting book.... Suffice it to say that by the time I was 18, I had committed to memory most of Fowler, Partridge, and their successors.

---

10 If Samuel Johnson is the Shakespeare of English usage, think of Henry Watson Fowler as the Eliot or Joyce. His 1926 *A Dictionary of Modern English Usage* is the granddaddy of modern usage guides, and its dust-dry wit and blushless imperiousness have been models for every subsequent classic in the field, from Eric Partridge's *Usage and Abusage* to Theodore Bernstein's *The Careful Writer* to Wilson Follett's *Modern American Usage* to Gilman's '89 *Webster's*.

11 (Garner prescribes spelling out only numbers under ten. I was taught that this rule applies just to Business Writing and that in all other modes you spell out one through nineteen and start using cardinals at 20. *De gustibus non est disputandum*.)

Although this reviewer regrets the bio-sketch's failure to mention the rather significant social costs of being an adolescent whose overriding passion is English usage,[12] the critical hat is off to yet another personable preface-section, one that Garner entitles "First Principles": "Before going any further, I should explain my approach. That's an unusual thing for the author of a usage dictionary to do — unprecedented, as far as I know. But a guide to good writing is only as good as the principles on which it's based. And users should be naturally interested in those principles. So, in the interests of full disclosure . . ."[13]

The "unprecedented" and "full disclosure" here are actually good-natured digs at Garner's Fowlerite predecessors, and a slight nod to one camp in the wars that have raged in both lexicography and education ever since the notoriously liberal *Webster's Third New International Dictionary* came out in 1961 and included terms like *heighth* and *irregardless* without any monitory labels on them. You can think of *Webster's Third* as sort of the Fort Sumter of the contemporary Usage Wars. These wars are both the context and the target of a very subtle rhetorical strategy in *A Dictionary of Modern American Usage,* and without talking about them it's impossible to explain why Garner's book is both so good and so sneaky.

We regular citizens tend to go to The Dictionary for authoritative guidance.[14] Rarely, however, do we ask ourselves who exactly decides what gets in The Dictionary or what words or spellings or pronunciations get deemed substandard or incorrect. Whence the authority of dictionary-makers to decide what's OK and what isn't? Nobody elected them, after all. And simply appealing to precedent or tradition won't work, because what's considered correct changes over time. In the 1600s, for instance, the second-singular took a singular conjugation — "You is." Earlier still, the standard 2-S pronoun wasn't *you* but *thou*. Huge numbers of now-acceptable words like *clever, fun, banter,* and *prestigious* entered English as what usage authorities considered errors or egregious slang. And not just usage conventions but English itself changes over time; if it didn't, we'd all still be talking like Chaucer. Who's to say which changes are natural and good and which are corruptions? And when Bryan Garner or E. Ward Gilman do in fact presume to say, why should we believe them?

---

[12] From personal experience, I can assure you that any kid like this is going to be at best marginalized and at worst savagely and repeatedly Wedgied — see *sub.*

[13] What follow in the preface are "the ten critical points that, after years of working on usage problems, I've settled on." These points are too involved to treat separately, but a couple of them are slippery in the extreme — e.g., "10. **Actual Usage.** In the end, the actual usage of educated speakers and writers is the overarching criterion for correctness," of which both "educated" and "actual" would really require several pages of abstract clarification and qualification to shore up against Usage Wars–related attacks, but which Garner rather ingeniously elects to define and defend via their application in his dictionary itself. Garner's ability not only to stay out of certain arguments but to render them irrelevant ends up being very important — see much *sub.*

[14] There's no better indication of The Dictionary's authority than that we use it to settle wagers. My own father is still to this day living down the outcome of a high-stakes bet on the correct spelling of *meringue,* a bet made on 14 September 1978.

These sorts of questions are not new, but they do now have a certain urgency. America is in the midst of a protracted Crisis of Authority in matters of language. In brief, the same sorts of political upheavals that produced everything from Kent State to Independent Counsels have produced an influential contra-SNOOT school for whom normative standards of English grammar and usage are functions of nothing but custom and the ovine docility of a populace that lets self-appointed language experts boss them around. See for example MIT's Steven Pinker in a famous *New Republic* article — "Once introduced, a prescriptive rule is very hard to eradicate, no matter how ridiculous. Inside the writing establishment, the rules survive by the same dynamic that perpetuates ritual genital mutilations" — or, at a somewhat lower emotional pitch, Bill Bryson in *Mother Tongue: English and How It Got That Way*:

> Who sets down all those rules that we know about from childhood — the idea that we must never end a sentence with a preposition or begin one with a conjunction, that we must use *each other* for two things and *one another* for more than two . . . ? The answer, surprisingly often, is that no one does, that when you look into the background of these "rules" there is often little basis for them.

In *ADMAU*'s preface, Garner himself addresses the Authority question with a Trumanesque simplicity and candor that simultaneously disguise the author's cunning and exemplify it:

> As you might already suspect, I don't shy away from making judgments. I can't imagine that most readers would want me to. Linguists don't like it, of course, because judgment involves subjectivity.[15] It isn't scientific. But rhetoric and usage, in the view of most professional writers,[16]

---

[15] This is a clever half-truth. Linguists compose only one part of the anti-judgment camp, and their objections to usage judgments involve way more than just "subjectivity."

[16] Notice, please, the subtle appeal here to the same "writing establishment" that Steven Pinker scorns. This isn't accidental; it's rhetorical.* What's crafty is that this is one of several places where Garner uses professional writers and editors as support for his claims, but in the preface he also treats these language pros as the primary *audience* for *ADMAU*, as in e.g. "The problem for professional writers and editors is that they can't wait idly to see what direction the language takes. Writers and editors, in fact, influence that direction: they must make decisions. . . . That has traditionally been the job of the usage dictionary: to help writers and editors solve editorial predicaments."

This is the same basic rhetorical move that President R. W. Reagan perfected in his televised Going-Over-Congress's-Head-to-the-People addresses, one that smart politicians ever since have imitated. It consists in citing the very audience you're addressing as the source of support for your proposals: "I'm pleased to announce tonight that we are taking the first steps toward implementing the policies that you elected me to implement," etc. The tactic is crafty because it (1) flatters the audience, (2) disguises the fact that the rhetor's purpose here is actually to persuade and rally support, not to inform or celebrate, and (3) preempts charges from the loyal opposition that the actual policy proposed is in any way contrary to the interests of the audience. I'm not suggesting that Bryan Garner has any particular political agenda. I'm simply pointing out that *ADMAU*'s preface is fundamentally rhetorical in the same way that Reagan's little Chats With America were.

* (In case it's not totally obvious, be advised that this article is using the word *rhetoric* in its strict traditional sense, something like "the persuasive use of language to influence the thoughts and actions of an audience.")

aren't scientific endeavors. You[17] don't want dispassionate descriptions; you want sound guidance. And that requires judgment.

Whole monographs could be written just on the masterful rhetoric of this passage. Besides the FN 16 stuff, note for example the ingenious equivocation of *judgment,* which in "I don't shy away from making judgments" means actual rulings (and thus invites questions about Authority), but in "And that requires judgment" refers instead to perspicacity, discernment, reason. As the body of *ADMAU* makes clear, part of Garner's overall strategy is to collapse these two different senses of *judgment,* or rather to use the second sense as a justification for the first. The big things to recognize here are (1) that Garner wouldn't be doing any of this if he weren't *keenly* aware of the Authority Crisis in modern usage, and (2) that his response to this crisis is — in the best Democratic Spirit — rhetorical.

So . . .

COROLLARY TO THESIS STATEMENT FOR WHOLE ARTICLE

The most salient and timely feature of Bryan A. Garner's dictionary is that its project is both lexicographical and rhetorical. Its main strategy involves what is known in classical rhetoric as the Ethical Appeal. Here the adjective, derived from the Greek *ēthos,* doesn't mean quite what we usually mean by *ethical.* But there are affinities. What the Ethical Appeal amounts to is a complex and sophisticated "Trust me." It's the boldest, most ambitious, and also most democratic of rhetorical Appeals because it requires the rhetor to convince us not just of his intellectual acuity or technical competence but of his basic decency and fairness and sensitivity to the audience's own hopes and fears.[18]

These latter are not qualities one associates with the traditional SNOOT usage-authority, a figure who for many Americans exemplifies snobbishness and anality, and one whose modern image is not helped by stuff like *The American Heritage Dictionary*'s Distinguished Usage Panelist Morris Bishop's "The arrant solecisms of the ignoramus are here often omitted entirely, 'irregardless' of how he may feel about this neglect" or critic John Simon's "The English language is being treated nowadays exactly as slave traders once handled their merchandise." Compare those lines' authorial personas with Garner's in, e.g., "English usage is so challenging that even experienced writers need guidance now and then."

The thrust here is going to be that *A Dictionary of Modern American Usage* earns Garner pretty much all the trust his Ethical Appeal asks us

[17] See?

[18] In this last respect, recall for example W. J. Clinton's "I feel your pain," which was a blatant if not especially deft Ethical Appeal.

for. What's interesting is that this trust derives not so much from the book's lexicographical quality as from the authorial persona and spirit it cultivates. *ADMAU* is a feel-good usage dictionary in the very best sense of *feel-good*. The book's spirit marries rigor and humility in such a way as to let Garner be extremely prescriptive without any appearance of evangelism or elitist put-down. This is an extraordinary accomplishment. Understanding why it's basically a *rhetorical* accomplishment, and why this is both historically significant and (in this reviewer's opinion) politically redemptive, requires a more detailed look at the Usage Wars.

You'd definitely know that lexicography had an underbelly if you read the different little introductory essays in modern dictionaries—pieces like *Webster's DEU*'s "A Brief History of English Usage" or *Webster's Third*'s "Linguistic Advances and Lexicography" or *AHD-2*'s "Good Usage, Bad Usage, and Usage" or *AHD-3*'s "Usage in the Dictionary: The Place of Criticism." But almost nobody ever bothers with these little intros, and it's not just their six-point type or the fact that dictionaries tend to be hard on the lap. It's that these intros aren't actually written for you or me or the average citizen who goes to The Dictionary just to see how to spell (for instance) *meringue*. They're written for other lexicographers and critics; and in fact they're not really introductory at all, but polemical. They're salvos in the Usage Wars that have been under way ever since editor Philip Gove first sought to apply the value-neutral principles of structural linguistics to lexicography in *Webster's Third*. Gove's now-famous response to conservatives who howled[19] when *W3* endorsed *OK* and described *ain't* as "used colloquially by educated speakers in many regions of the United States" was this: "A dictionary should have no truck with artificial notions of correctness or superiority. It should be descriptive and not prescriptive." Gove's terms stuck and turned epithetic, and linguistic conservatives are now formally known as Prescriptivists and linguistic liberals as Descriptivists.

The former are better known, though not because of dictionaries' prologues or scholarly Fowlerites. When you read the columns of William Safire or Morton Freeman or books like Edwin Newman's *Strictly Speaking* or John Simon's *Paradigms Lost*, you're actually reading Popular Prescriptivism, a genre sideline of certain journalists (mostly older males, the majority of whom actually do wear bow ties[20]) whose bemused irony often masks a Colonel Blimp's rage at the way the beloved English of their

---

[19] Really, *howled:* Blistering reviews and outraged editorials from across the country—from the *Times* and *The New Yorker* and the *National Review* and good old *Life*, or see e.g. this from the January '62 *Atlantic Monthly*: "We have seen a novel dictionary formula improvised, in great part, out of snap judgments and the sort of theoretical improvement that in practice impairs; and we have seen the gates propped wide open in enthusiastic hospitality to miscellaneous confusions and corruptions. In fine, the anxiously awaited* work that was to have crowned cisatlantic linguistic scholarship with a particular glory turns out to be a scandal and a disaster."

* (*Sic*—should obviously be "eagerly awaited." *Nemo mortalium omnibus horis sapit.*)

[20] It's true: Newman, Simon, Freeman, James J. Kilpatrick . . . can George F. Will's best-seller on usage be long in coming?

youth is being trashed in the decadent present. Some Pop Prescriptivism is funny and smart, though much of it just sounds like old men grumbling about the vulgarity of modern mores.[21] And some PP is offensively small-minded and knuckle-dragging, such as *Paradigms Lost*'s simplistic dismissal of Standard Black English: "As for 'I be,' 'you be,' 'he be,' etc., which should give us all the heebie-jeebies, these may indeed be comprehensible, but they go against all accepted classical and modern grammars and are the product not of a language with its roots in history but of ignorance of how a language works." But what's really interesting is that the plutocratic tone and styptic wit of Newman and Safire and the best of the Pop Prescriptivists are modeled after the mandarin-Brit personas of Eric Partridge and H. W. Fowler, the same twin towers of scholarly Prescriptivism whom Garner talks about revering as a kid.[22]

Descriptivists, on the other hand, don't have weekly columns in the *Times*. These guys tend to be hard-core academics, mostly linguists or Comp theorists. Loosely organized under the banner of structural (or "descriptive") linguistics, they are doctrinaire positivists who have their intellectual roots in Comte and Saussure and L. Bloomfield[23] and their ideological roots firmly in the US Sixties. The brief explicit mention Garner's preface gives this crew—

> Somewhere along the line, though, usage dictionaries got hijacked by the descriptive linguists,[[24]] who observe language scientifically. For the pure descriptivist, it's impermissible to say that one form of language is any better than another: as long as a native speaker says it, it's OK—and anyone who takes a contrary stand is a dunderhead. . . . Essentially, descriptivists and prescriptivists are approaching different problems. Descriptivists want to record language as it's actually used, and they perform a useful

---

[21] Even Edwin Newman, the most thoughtful and least hemorrhoidal of the pop SNOOTs, sometimes lets his Colonel B. poke out, as in e.g. "I have no wish to dress as many younger people do nowadays. . . . I have no wish to impair my hearing by listening to their music, and a communication gap between an electronic rock group and me is something I devotedly cherish and would hate to see disappear."

[22] Note for instance the mordant pith (and royal *we*) of this random snippet from Partridge's *Usage and Abusage:*

> **anxious of.** 'I am not hopeless of our future. But I am profoundly anxious of it,' Beverley Nichols, *News of England,* 1938: which made us profoundly anxious *for* (or *about*)—not *of*—Mr. Nichols's literary future.

Or observe the near-Himalayan condescension of Fowler, here on some people's habit of using words like *viable* or *verbal* to mean things the words don't really mean:

> **slipshod extension . . .** is especially likely to occur when some accident gives currency among the uneducated to words of learned origin, & the more if they are isolated or have few relatives in the vernacular. . . . The original meaning of *feasible* is simply doable (L. *facere* do); but to the unlearned it is a mere token, of which he has to infer the value from the contexts in which he hears it used, because such relatives as it has in English—*feat, feature, faction,* &c.—either fail to show the obvious family likeness to which he is accustomed among families of indigenous words, or are (like *malfeasance*) outside his range.

[23] FYI, Leonard Bloomfield's 1933 *Language* pretty much founded descriptive linguistics by claiming that the proper object of study was not language but something called "language behavior."

[24] Utter bushwa: As *ADMAU*'s body makes clear, Garner knows precisely where along the line the Descriptivists started influencing usage guides.

function — although their audience is generally limited to those willing to pore through vast tomes of dry-as-dust research.[25]

— is disingenuous in the extreme, especially the "approaching different problems" part, because it vastly underplays the Descriptivists' influence on US culture. For one thing, Descriptivism so quickly and thoroughly took over English education in this country that just about everybody who started junior high after c. 1970 has been taught to write Descriptively — via "freewriting," "brainstorming," "journaling" — a view of writing as self-exploratory and expressive rather than as communicative, an abandonment of systematic grammar, usage, semantics, rhetoric, etymology. For another thing, the very language in which today's socialist, feminist, minority, gay, and environmental movements frame their sides of political debates is informed by the Descriptivist belief that traditional English is conceived and perpetuated by Privileged WASP Males[26] and is thus inherently capitalist, sexist, racist, xenophobic, homophobic, elitist: unfair. Think Ebonics. Think Proposition 227. Think of the involved contortions people undergo to avoid using *he* as a generic pronoun, or of the tense, deliberate way white males now adjust their vocabularies around non-w.m.'s. Think of the modern ubiquity of spin or of today's endless rows over just the *names* of things — "Affirmative Action" vs. "Reverse Discrimination," "Pro-Life" vs. "Pro-Choice," "Undocumented Worker" vs. "Illegal Alien," "Perjury" vs. "Peccadillo," and so on.

DESCRIPTIVISM SO QUICKLY AND THOROUGHLY TOOK OVER ENGLISH EDUCATION IN THIS COUNTRY THAT JUST ABOUT EVERYBODY WHO STARTED JUNIOR HIGH AFTER C. 1970 HAS BEEN TAUGHT TO WRITE DESCRIPTIVELY.

The Descriptivist revolution takes a little time to unpack, but it's worth it. The structural linguists' rejection of conventional usage rules in English depends on two main kinds of argument. The first is academic and methodological. In this age of technology, some Descriptivists contend, it's the scientific method — clinically objective, value-neutral, based on direct observation and demonstrable hypothesis — that should determine both the content of dictionaries and the standards of "correct" English. Because language is constantly evolving, such standards will always be fluid. Philip

---

25 His SNOOTier sentiments about linguists' prose emerge in Garner's preface via his recollection of studying under certain eminent Descriptivists in college: "The most bothersome thing was that they didn't write well: their offerings were dreary gruel. If you doubt this, go pick up any journal of linguistics. Ask yourself whether the articles are well-written. If you haven't looked at one in a while, you'll be shocked."

INTERPOLATION

Garner's aside about linguists' writing has wider applications, though *ADMAU* mostly keeps them implicit. The truth is that most US academic prose is appalling — pompous, abstruse, claustral, inflated, euphuistic, pleonastic, solecistic, sesquipidelian, Heliogabaline, occluded, obscure, jargon-ridden, empty: resplendently dead. . . .

26 (which is in fact true)

Gove's now-classic introduction to *Webster's Third* outlines this type of Descriptivism's five basic edicts: "1 — Language changes constantly; 2 — Change is normal; 3 — Spoken language *is* the language; 4 — Correctness rests upon usage; 5 — All usage is relative."

These principles look prima facie OK — simple, commonsensical, and couched in the bland s.-v.-o. prose of dispassionate science — but in fact they're vague and muddled and it takes about three seconds to think of reasonable replies to each one of them, viz.:

1 — All right, but how much and how fast?

2 — Same thing. Is Hericlitean flux as normal or desirable as gradual change? Do some changes serve the language's overall pizzazz better than others? And how many people have to deviate from how many conventions before we say the language has actually changed? Fifty percent? Ten percent? Where do you draw the line? Who draws the line?

3 — This is an old claim, at least as old as Plato's *Phaedrus*. And it's specious. If Derrida and the infamous Deconstructionists have done nothing else, they've successfully debunked the idea that speech is language's primary instantiation.[27] Plus consider the weird arrogance of Gove's (3) with respect to correctness. Only the most mullah-like Prescriptivists care all that much about spoken English; most Prescriptive usage guides concern Standard *Written* English.[28]

4 — Fine, but whose usage? Gove's (4) begs the whole question. What he wants to suggest here, I think, is a reversal of the traditional entailment-relation between abstract rules and concrete usage: instead of usage's ideally corresponding to a rigid set of regulations, the regulations ought to correspond to the way real people are actually using the language. Again, fine, but which people? Urban Latinos? Boston Brahmins? Rural Midwesterners? Appalachian Neogaelics?

5 — *Huh?* If this means what it seems to mean, then it ends up biting Gove's whole argument in the ass. Principle (5) appears to imply that the correct answer to the above "which people?" is: All of them. And it's easy to show why this will not stand up as a lexicographical principle. The most obvious problem with it is that not everything can go in The Dictionary. Why not? Well, because you can't actually observe and record every last bit of every last native speaker's "language behavior," and even if you

---

[27] (Q.v. the "Pharmakon" stuff in Derrida's *La dissémination* — but you'd probably be better off just trusting me.)

[28] Standard Written English (SWE) is sometimes called Standard English (SE) or Educated English, but the basic inditement-emphasis is the same. See for example *The Little, Brown Handbook*'s definition of Standard English as "the English normally expected and used by educated readers and writers."

SEMI-INTERPOLATION

Plus let's note that Garner's preface explicitly characterizes his dictionary's intended audience as "writers and editors." And even the recent ads for *ADMAU* in organs like the *New York Review of Books* are built around the slogan "If you like to WRITE . . . **Refer to us.**"*

* Your SNOOT reviewer cannot help observing, w/r/t this ad, that the opening ***r*** in its **Refer** shouldn't be capitalized after a dependent clause + ellipsis. (*Quandoque bonus dormitat Homerus.*)

could, the resultant dictionary would weigh four million pounds and need to be updated hourly.[29] The fact is that any real lexicographer is going to have to make choices about what gets in and what doesn't. And these choices are based on . . . what? And so we're right back where we started.

It is true that, as a SNOOT, I am naturally predisposed to look for flaws in Gove et al.'s methodological argument. But these flaws still seem awfully easy to find. Probably the biggest one is that the Descriptivists' "scientific lexicography" — under which, keep in mind, the ideal English dictionary is basically number-crunching: you somehow observe every linguistic act by every native/naturalized speaker of English and put the sum of all these acts between two covers and call it The Dictionary — involves an incredibly crude and outdated understanding of what *scientific* means. It requires a naive belief in scientific Objectivity, for one thing. Even in the physical sciences, everything from quantum mechanics to Information Theory has shown that an act of observation is itself part of the phenomenon observed and is analytically inseparable from it.

If you remember your old college English classes, there's an analogy here that points up the trouble scholars get into when they confuse observation with interpretation. It's the New Critics.[30] Recall their belief that literary criticism was best conceived as a "scientific" endeavor: the critic was a neutral, careful, unbiased, highly trained observer whose job was to find and objectively describe meanings that were right there, literally inside pieces of literature. Whether you know what happened to New Criticism's reputation depends on whether you took college English after c. 1975; suffice it to say that its star has dimmed. The New Critics had the same basic problem as Gove's Methodological Descriptivists: they believed that there was such a thing as unbiased observation. And that linguistic meanings could exist "Objectively," separate from any interpretive act.

The point of the analogy is that claims to Objectivity in language study are now the stuff of jokes and shudders. The positivist assumptions that underlie Methodological Descriptivism have been thoroughly confuted and displaced — in Lit by the rise of post-structuralism, Reader-Response Criticism, and Jaussian Reception Theory, in linguistics by the rise of Pragmatics — and it's now pretty much universally accepted that (a) meaning is inseparable from some act of interpretation and (b) an act of interpretation is always somewhat biased, i.e., informed by the interpreter's particular ideology. And the consequence of (a) + (b) is that there's no way around it — decisions about what to put in The Dictionary and what to exclude are going to be based on a lexicographer's ideology. And every lexicographer's got one. To presume that dictionary-making

---

[29] Granted, some sort of 100 percent compendious real-time Megadictionary might conceivably be possible online, though it would take a small army of lexical webmasters and a much larger army of *in situ* actual-use reporters and surveillance techs; plus it'd be GNP-level expensive (. . . plus what would be the point?).

[30] *New Criticism* refers to T. S. Eliot and I. A. Richards and F. R. Leavis and Cleanth Brooks and Wimsatt & Beardsley and the whole autotelic Close Reading school that dominated literary criticism from the Thirties to well into the Seventies.

can somehow avoid or transcend ideology is simply to subscribe to a particular ideology, one that might aptly be called Unbelievably Naive Positivism.

There's an even more important way Descriptivists are wrong in thinking that the scientific method developed for use in chemistry and physics is equally appropriate to the study of language. This one doesn't depend on stuff about quantum uncertainty or any kind of postmodern relativism. Even if, as a thought experiment, we assume a kind of 19th-century scientific realism — in which, even though some scientists' interpretations of natural phenomena might be biased,[31] the natural phenomena themselves can be supposed to exist wholly independent of either observation or interpretation — it's still true that no such realist supposition can be made about "language behavior," because such behavior is both *human* and fundamentally *normative*.

To understand why this is important, you have only to accept the proposition that language is by its very nature public — i.e., that there is no such thing as a private language[32] — and then to observe the way Descriptivists seem either ignorant of this fact or oblivious to its consequences, as in for example one Dr. Charles Fries's introduction to an epigone of *Webster's Third* called *The American College Dictionary*:

> A dictionary can be an "authority" only in the sense in which a book of chemistry or physics or of botany can be an "authority" — by the accuracy and the completeness of its record of the observed facts of the field examined, in accord with the latest principles and techniques of the particular science.

This is so stupid it practically drools. An "authoritative" physics text presents the results of *physicists'* observations and *physicists'* theories about those observations. If a physics textbook operated on Descriptivist principles, the fact that some Americans believe electricity flows better downhill (based on the observed fact that power lines tend to run high above the homes they serve) would require the Electricity Flows Better Downhill Hypothesis to be included as a "valid" theory in the textbook — just as, for Dr. Fries, if some Americans use *infer* for *imply* or *aspect* for *perspective,* these usages become *ipso facto* "valid" parts of the language. The truth is that structural linguists like Gove and Fries are not scientists at all; they're pollsters who misconstrue the importance of the "facts" they are recording. It isn't scientific phenomena they're observing and tabulating, but rather a set of human behaviors, and a lot of human behaviors are — to be blunt — moronic. Try, for instance, to imagine an "authoritative" ethics textbook whose principles were based on what most people actually *do*.

---

[31] ("EVIDENCE OF CANCER LINK REFUTED BY TOBACCO INSTITUTE RESEARCHERS")

[32] This proposition is in fact true, . . . and although the demonstration is persuasive it is also . . . lengthy and involved and rather, umm, dense, so that once again you'd maybe be better off simply granting the truth of the proposition and forging on with the main text.

Grammar and usage conventions are, as it happens, a lot more like ethical principles than like scientific theories. The reason the Descriptivists can't see this is the same reason they choose to regard the English language as the sum of all English utterances: they confuse mere regularities with *norms*.

Norms aren't quite the same as rules, but they're close. A norm can be defined here simply as something that people have agreed on as the optimal way to do things for certain purposes. Let's keep in mind that language didn't come into being because our hairy ancestors were sitting around the veldt with nothing better to do. Language was invented to serve certain very specific purposes — "That mushroom is poisonous"; "Knock these two rocks together and you can start a fire"; "This shelter is mine!" and so on. Clearly, as linguistic communities evolve over time, they discover that some ways of using language are better than others — not better *a priori*, but better with respect to the community's purposes. If we assume that one such purpose might be communicating which kinds of food are safe to eat, then we can see how, for example, a misplaced modifier could violate an important norm: "People who eat that kind of mushroom often get sick" confuses the message's recipient about whether he'll get sick only if he eats the mushroom frequently or whether he stands a good chance of getting sick the very first time he eats it. In other words, the fungiphagic community has a vested practical interest in excluding this kind of misplaced modifier from acceptable usage; and, given the purposes the community uses language for, the fact that a certain percentage of tribesmen screw up and use misplaced modifiers to talk about food safety does not *eo ipso* make m.m.'s a good idea.

Maybe now the analogy between usage and ethics is clearer. Just because people sometimes lie, cheat on their taxes, or scream at their kids, this doesn't mean that they think those things are "good."[33] The whole point of establishing norms is to help us evaluate our actions (including utterances) according to what we as a community have decided our real interests and purposes are. Granted, this analysis is oversimplified; in practice it's incredibly hard to arrive at norms and to keep them at least minimally fair or sometimes even to agree on what they are (see e.g. today's Culture Wars). But the Descriptivists' assumption that all usage norms are arbitrary and dispensable leads to — well, have a mushroom.

The different connotations of *arbitrary* here are tricky, though — and this sort of segues into the second main kind of Descriptivist argument. There is a sense in which specific linguistic conventions really *are* arbitrary. For instance, there's no particular metaphysical reason why our word for a four-legged mammal that gives milk and goes moo is *cow* and

---

[33] In fact, the Methodological Descriptivists' reasoning is known in social philosophy as the "Well, Everybody Does It" fallacy — i.e., if a lot of people cheat on their taxes, that means it's somehow morally OK to cheat on your taxes. Ethics-wise, it takes only two or three deductive steps to get from there to the sort of State of Nature where everybody's hitting each other over the head and stealing their groceries.

not, say, *prtlmpf*. The uptown term for this is "the arbitrariness of the linguistic sign,"[34] and it's used, along with certain principles of cognitive science and generative grammar, in a more philosophically sophisticated version of Descriptivism that holds the conventions of SWE to be more like the niceties of fashion than like actual norms. This "Philosophical Descriptivism" doesn't care much about dictionaries or method; its target is the standard SNOOT claim that prescriptive rules have their ultimate justification in the community's need to make its language meaningful and clear.

Steven Pinker's 1994 *The Language Instinct* is a good and fairly literate example of this second kind of Descriptivist argument, which, like the Gove-et-al. version, tends to deploy a jr.-high-filmstrip SCIENCE: POINTING THE WAY TO A BRIGHTER TOMORROW–type tone:

> [T]he words "rule" and "grammar" have very different meanings to a scientist and a layperson. The rules people learn (or, more likely, fail to learn) in school are called "prescriptive" rules, prescribing how one *ought* to talk. Scientists studying language propose "descriptive" rules, describing how people *do* talk. Prescriptive and descriptive grammar are simply different things.[35]

The point of this version of Descriptivism is to show that the descriptive rules are more fundamental and way more important than the prescriptive rules. The argument goes like this. An English sentence's being *meaningful* is not the same as its being *grammatical*. That is, such clearly ill-formed constructions as "Did you seen the car keys of me?" or "The show was looked by many people" are nevertheless comprehensible; the sentences do, more or less, communicate the information they're trying to get across. Add to this the fact that nobody who isn't damaged in some profound Oliver Sacksish way actually ever makes these sorts of very deep syntactic errors[36] and you get the basic proposition of N. Chomsky's generative linguistics, which is that there exists a Universal Grammar beneath and common to all languages, plus that there is probably an actual

---

[34] This phrase is attributable to Ferdinand de Saussure, the Swiss philologist who more or less invented modern technical linguistics, separating the study of language as an abstract formal system from the historical and comparative emphases of 19th-century philology. Suffice it to say that the Descriptivists like Saussure a *lot*. Suffice it also to say that they tend to misread him and take him out of context and distort his theories in all kinds of embarrassing ways — e.g., Saussure's "arbitrariness of the linguistic sign" means something other and far more complicated than just "There's no ultimate necessity to English speakers' saying *cow*." (Similarly, the structural linguists' distinction between "language behavior" and "language" is based on a simplistic misreading of Saussure's distinction between *"parole"* and *"langue."*)

[35] (If that last line of Pinker's pourparler reminds you of Garner's "Essentially, descriptivists and prescriptivists are approaching different problems," be advised that the similarity is neither coincidence nor plagiarism. One of the many cunning things about *ADMAU*'s preface is that Garner likes to take bits of Descriptivist rhetoric and use them for very different ends.)

[36] Pinker puts it this way: "No one, not even a valley girl, has to be told not to say *Apples the eat boy* or *The child seems sleeping* or *Who did you meet John and?* or the vast, vast majority of the millions of trillions of mathematically possible combinations of words."

part of the human brain that's imprinted with this Universal Grammar the same way birds' brains are imprinted with Fly South and dogs' with Sniff Genitals. There's all kinds of compelling evidence and support for these ideas, not least of which are the advances that linguists and cognitive scientists and AI researchers have been able to make with them, and the theories have a lot of credibility, and they are adduced by the Philosophical Descriptivists to show that since the really *important* rules of language are at birth already hardwired into people's neocortex, SWE prescriptions against dangling participles or mixed metaphors are basically the linguistic equivalent of whalebone corsets and short forks for salad. As Steven Pinker puts it, "When a scientist considers all the high-tech mental machinery needed to order words into everyday sentences, prescriptive rules are, at best, inconsequential decorations."

"SWE" PRESCRIPTIONS AGAINST DANGLING PARTICIPLES OR MIXED METAPHORS ARE BASICALLY THE LINGUISTIC EQUIVALENT OF WHALEBONE CORSETS AND SHORT FORKS FOR SALAD.

This argument is not the barrel of drugged trout that Methodological Descriptivism was, but it's still vulnerable to objections. The first one is easy. Even if it's true that we're all wired with a Universal Grammar, it doesn't follow that *all* prescriptive rules are superfluous. Some of these rules really do seem to serve clarity and precision. The injunction against two-way adverbs ("People who eat this often get sick") is an obvious example, as are rules about other kinds of misplaced modifiers ("There are many reasons why lawyers lie, some better than others") and about relative pronouns' proximity to the nouns they modify ("She's the mother of an infant daughter who works twelve hours a day").

Granted, the Philosophical Descriptivist can question just how absolutely necessary these rules are: it's quite likely that a recipient of clauses like the above could figure out what they mean from the sentences on either side or from the overall context or whatever.[37] A listener can usually figure out what I really mean when I misuse *infer* for *imply* or say *indicate* for *say,* too. But many of these solecisms — or even just clunky redundancies like "The door was rectangular in shape" — require at least a couple extra nanoseconds of cognitive effort, a kind of rapid sift-and-discard process, before the recipient gets it. Extra work. It's debatable just how much extra work, but it seems indisputable that we put *some* extra interpretive burden on the recipient when we fail to honor certain conventions. W/r/t confusing clauses like the above, it simply seems more "considerate" to follow the rules of correct English . . . just as it's more "considerate" to de-slob your home before entertaining guests or to brush your teeth before picking up a date. Not just more considerate but more

---

[37] (FYI, there happens to be a whole subdiscipline of linguistics called Pragmatics that essentially studies the way statements' meanings are created by various contexts.)

respectful somehow — both of your listener/reader and of what you're trying to get across. As we sometimes also say about elements of fashion and etiquette, the way you use English "makes a statement" or "sends a message" — even though these statements/messages often have nothing to do with the actual information you're trying to communicate.

We've now sort of bled into a more serious rejoinder to Philosophical Descriptivism: from the fact that linguistic communication is not strictly dependent on usage and grammar it does *not* necessarily follow that the traditional rules of usage and grammar are nothing but "inconsequential decorations." Another way to state this objection is that something's being "decorative" does not necessarily make it "inconsequential." Rhetoric-wise, Pinker's flip dismissal is very bad tactics, for it invites precisely the question it's begging: inconsequential *to whom*?

A key point here is that the resemblance between usage rules and certain conventions of etiquette or fashion is closer than the Philosophical Descriptivists know and far more important than they understand. Take, for example, the Descriptivist claim that so-called correct English usages like *brought* rather than *brung* and *felt* rather than *feeled* are arbitrary and restrictive and unfair and are supported only by custom and are (like irregular verbs in general) archaic and incommodious and an all-around pain in the ass. Let us concede for the moment that these claims are 100 percent reasonable. Then let's talk about pants. Trousers, slacks. I suggest to you that having the so-called correct subthoracic clothing for US males be pants instead of skirts is arbitrary (lots of other cultures let men wear skirts), restrictive and unfair (US females get to wear either skirts or pants), based solely on archaic custom (I think it's got to do with certain traditions about gender and leg-position, the same reasons women were supposed to ride sidesaddle and girls' bikes don't have a crossbar), and in certain ways not only incommodious but illogical (skirts are more comfortable than pants;[38] pants ride up; pants are hot; pants can squish the 'nads and reduce fertility; over time pants chafe and erode irregular sections of men's leg-hair and give older men hideous half-denuded legs; etc. etc.). Let us grant — as a thought experiment if nothing else — that these are all sensible and compelling objections to pants as an androsartorial norm. Let us, in fact, in our minds and hearts say yes — *shout* yes — to the skirt, the kilt, the toga, the sarong, the jupe. Let us dream of or even in our spare time work toward an America where nobody lays any arbitrary sumptuary prescriptions on anyone else and we can all go around as comfortable and aerated and unchafed and motile as we want.

And yet the fact remains that in the broad cultural mainstream of millennial America, men do not wear skirts. If you, the reader, are a US male, and even if you share my personal objections to pants and dream as I do of a cool and genitally unsquishy American Tomorrow, the odds are still 99.9 percent that in 100 percent of public situations you wear

[38] (presumably)

pants/slacks/shorts/trunks. More to the point, if you are a US male and also have a US male child, and if that child might happen to come to you one evening and announce his desire/intention to wear a skirt rather than pants to school the next day, I am 100 percent confident that you are going to discourage him from doing so. *Strongly* discourage him. You could be a Molotov-tossing anti-pants radical or a kilt manufacturer or Dr. Steven Pinker himself—you're going to stand over your kid and be prescriptive about an arbitrary, archaic, uncomfortable, and inconsequentially decorative piece of clothing. Why? Well, because in modern America any little boy who comes to school in a skirt (even, say, a modest all-season midi) is going to get stared at and shunned and beaten up and called a total geekoid by a whole lot of people whose approval and acceptance are important to him.[39] In our present culture, in other words, a boy who wears a skirt is "making a statement" that is going to have all kinds of gruesome social and emotional consequences for him.

You can probably see where this is headed. I'm going to describe the intended point of the pants analogy in terms that I'm sure are simplistic—doubtless there are whole books in Pragmatics or psycholinguistics or something devoted to unpacking this point. The weird thing is that I've seen neither Descriptivists nor SNOOTs deploy it in the Wars.[40,41]

When I say or write something, there are actually a whole lot of different things I am communicating. The propositional content (i.e., the verbal information I'm trying to convey) is only one part of it. Another part is stuff about me, the communicator. Everyone knows this. It's a function of the fact that there are so many different well-formed ways to say the same basic thing, from e.g. "I was attacked by a bear!" to "Goddamn bear tried to kill me!" to "That ursine juggernaut did essay to sup upon my person!" and so on. Add the Saussurian/Chomskian consideration that many grammatically ill-formed sentences can also get the propositional content across—"Bear attack Tonto, Tonto heap scared!"—and the number of subliminal options we're scanning/sorting/interpreting as we communicate with one another goes transfinite very quickly. And different levels of diction and formality are only the simplest kinds of distinction; things get way more complicated in the sorts of interpersonal

---

[39] In the case of little Steve Pinker Jr., these people are the boy's peers and teachers and crossing guards. In the case of adult cross-dressers and drag queens who have jobs in the straight world and wear pants to those jobs, it's bosses and coworkers and customers and people on the subway. For the die-hard slob who nevertheless wears a coat and tie to work, it's mostly his boss, who doesn't want his employees' clothes to send clients "the wrong message." But it's all basically the same thing.

[40] Even Garner scarcely mentions it, and just once in his dictionary's miniessay on CLASS DISTINCTIONS: "[M]any linguistic pratfalls can be seen as class indicators—even in a so-called classless society such as the United States." And when Bryan A. Garner uses a clunky passive like "can be seen" as to distance himself from an issue, you know something's in the air.

[41] In fact, pretty much the only time one ever hears the issue made wholly explicit is in radio ads for tapes that promise to improve people's vocabularies. These ads tend to be extremely ominous and intimidating and always start out with "DID YOU KNOW PEOPLE JUDGE YOU BY THE WORDS YOU USE?"

communication where social relations and feelings and moods come into play. Here's a familiar kind of example. Suppose that you and I are acquaintances and we're in my apartment having a conversation and that at some point I want to terminate the conversation and not have you be in my apartment anymore. Very delicate social moment. Think of all the different ways I can try to handle it: "Wow, look at the time"; "Could we finish this up later?"; "Could you please leave now?"; "Go"; "Get out"; "Get the hell out of here"; "Didn't you say you had to be someplace?"; "Time for you to hit the dusty trail, my friend"; "Off you go then, love"; or that sly old telephone-conversation-ender: "Well, I'm going to let you go now"; etc. etc.*[n]* And then think of all the different factors and implications of each option.[42]

The point here is obvious. It concerns a phenomenon that SNOOTs blindly reinforce and that Descriptivists badly underestimate and that scary vocab-tape ads try to exploit. People really do judge one another according to their use of language. Constantly. Of course, people are constantly judging one another on the basis of all kinds of things — height, weight, scent, physiognomy, accent, occupation, make of vehicle[43] — and, again, doubtless it's all terribly complicated and occupies whole battalions of sociolinguists. But it's clear that at least one component of all this interpersonal semantic judging involves *acceptance,* meaning not some touchy-feely emotional affirmation but actual acceptance or rejection of someone's bid to be regarded as a peer, a member of somebody else's collective or community or Group. Another way to come at this is to acknowledge something that in the Usage Wars gets mentioned only in very abstract terms: "correct" English usage is, as a practical matter, a function of whom you're talking to and of how you want that person to respond — not just to your utterance but also to *you*. In other words, a large part of the project of any communication is rhetorical and depends on what some rhet-scholars call "Audience" or "Discourse Community."[44] It is the present existence in the United States of an enormous number

---

[42] To be honest, the example here has a special personal resonance for this reviewer because in real life I always seem to have a hard time winding up a conversation or asking somebody to leave, and sometimes the moment becomes so delicate and fraught with social complexity that I'll get overwhelmed trying to sort out all the different possible ways of saying it and all the different implications of each option and will just sort of blank out and do it totally straight — "I want to terminate the conversation and not have you be in my apartment anymore" — which evidently makes me look either as if I'm very rude and abrupt or as if I'm semi-autistic and have no sense of how to wind up a conversation gracefully. Somehow, in other words, my reducing the statement to its bare propositional content "sends a message" that is itself scanned, sifted, interpreted, and judged by my auditor, who then sometimes never comes back. I've actually lost friends this way.

[43] (. . . not to mention color, gender, ethnicity — you can see how fraught and charged all this is going to get)

[44] *Discourse Community* is a rare example of academic jargon that's actually a valuable addition to SWE because it captures something at once very complex and very specific that no other English term quite can.*

* (The above, while true, is an obvious attempt to preempt readerly sneers/winces at the term's continued deployment in this article.)

of different Discourse Communities, plus the fact that both people's use of English and their interpretations of others' use are influenced by rhetorical assumptions, that are central to understanding why the Usage Wars are so politically charged and to appreciating why Bryan Garner's *ADMAU* is so totally sneaky and brilliant and modern.

Fact: There are all sorts of cultural/geographical dialects of American English — Black English, Latino English, Rural Southern, Urban Southern, Standard Upper-Midwest, Maine Yankee, East-Texas Bayou, Boston Blue-Collar, on and on. Everybody knows this. What not everyone knows — especially not certain Prescriptivists — is that many of these non-SWE-type dialects have their own highly developed and internally consistent grammars, and that some of these dialects' usage norms actually make more linguistic/aesthetic sense than do their Standard counterparts.* Plus, of course, there are also innumerable sub- and subsubdialects[45] based on all sorts of things that have nothing to do with locale or ethnicity — Medical-School English, Twelve-Year-Old-Males-Whose-Worldview-Is-Deeply-Informed-by-*South-Park* English — that are nearly incomprehensible to anyone who isn't inside their very tight and specific Discourse Community (which of course is part of their function[46]).

***INTERPOLATION**
POTENTIALLY DESCRIPTIVIST-LOOKING EXAMPLE OF SOME GRAMMATICAL ADVANTAGES OF A NON-STANDARD DIALECT THAT THIS REVIEWER ACTUALLY KNOWS ABOUT FIRSTHAND

I happen to have two native English dialects — the SWE of my hypereducated parents and the hard-earned Rural Midwestern of most of my peers. When I'm talking to RMs, I tend to use constructions like "Where's it at?" for "Where is it?" and sometimes "He don't" instead of "He doesn't." Part of this is a naked desire to fit in and not get rejected as an egghead or fag (see *sub*). But another part is that I, SNOOT or no, believe that these RMisms are in certain ways superior to their Standard equivalents.

---

45 Just how tiny and restricted a subdialect can get and still be called a subdialect isn't clear; there might be very firm linguistic definitions of what's a dialect and what's a subdialect and what's a subsub-, etc. Because I don't know any better and am betting you don't either, I'm going to use *subdialect* in a loose inclusive way that covers idiolects as distinctive as Peorians-Who-Follow-Pro-Wrestling-Closely or Geneticists-Who-Specialize-in-Hardy-Weinberg-Equilibrium. *Dialect* should probably be reserved for major players like Standard Black English et al.

46 (Plus it's true that whether something gets called a "subdialect" or "jargon" seems to depend on how much it annoys people outside its Discourse Community. Garner himself has miniessays on AIRPLANESE, COMPUTERESE, LEGALESE, and BUREAUCRATESE, and he more or less calls all of them jargon. There is no *ADMAU* miniessay on DIALECTS, but there is one on JARGON, in which such is Garner's self-restraint that you can almost hear his tendons straining, as in "[Jargon] arises from the urge to save time and space — and occasionally to conceal meaning from the uninitiated.")

For a dogmatic Prescriptivist, "Where's it at?" is double-damned as a sentence that not only ends with a preposition but whose final preposition forms a redundancy with *where* that's similar to the redundancy in "the reason is because" (which latter usage I'll admit makes me dig my nails into my palms). Rejoinder: First off, the avoid-terminal-prepositions rule is the invention of one Fr. R. Lowth, an 18th-century British preacher and indurate pedant who did things like spend scores of pages arguing for *hath* over the trendy and degenerate *has*. The a.-t.-p. rule is antiquated and stupid and only the most ayotolloid SNOOT takes it seriously. Garner himself calls the rule "stuffy" and lists all kinds of useful constructions like "a person I have great respect for" and "the man I was listening to" that we'd have to discard or distort if we really enforced it.

Plus, the apparent redundancy of "Where's it at?"[47] is offset by its metrical logic: what the *at* really does is license the contraction of *is* after the interrogative adverb. You can't say "Where's it?" So the choice is between "Where is it?" and "Where's it at?", and the latter, a strong anapest, is prettier and trips off the tongue better than "Where is it?", whose meter is either a clunky monosyllabic-foot + trochee or it's nothing at all.

Using "He don't" makes me a little more uncomfortable; I admit that its logic isn't quite as compelling. Nevertheless, a clear trend in the evolution of English from Middle to Modern has been the gradual regularizing of irregular present-tense verbs,[48] a trend justified by the fact that irregulars are hard to learn and to keep straight and have nothing but history going for them. By this reasoning, Standard Black English is way out on the cutting edge of English with its abandonment of the 3-S present in *to do* and *to go* and *to say* and its marvelously streamlined six identical present-tense inflections of *to be*. (Granted, the conjugation "he be" always sounds odd to me, but then SBE is not one of my dialects.)

This is probably the place for your SNOOT reviewer openly to concede that a certain number of traditional prescriptive rules really are stupid and that people who insist on them (like the legendary assistant to Margaret Thatcher who refused to read any memo with a split infinitive in it, or the jr.-high teacher I had who automatically graded you down if you started a sentence with *Hopefully*) are that very most contemptible and dangerous kind of SNOOT, the SNOOT Who Is Wrong. The injunction against split infinitives, for instance, is a consequence of the weird fact that English grammar is modeled on Latin even though Latin is a synthetic language and English is an analytic

---

[47] (a redundancy that's a bit arbitrary, since "Where's it *from*?" isn't redundant [mainly because *whence* has receded into semi-archaism])

[48] E.g., for a long time English had a special 2-S present conjugation — "thou lovest," "thou sayest" — that now survives only in certain past tenses (and in the present of *to be*, where it consists simply in giving the 2-S a plural inflection).

language.[49] Latin infinitives consist of one word and are impossible to as it were split, and the earliest English Prescriptivists — so enthralled with Latin that their English usage guides were actually *written* in Latin[50] — decided that English infinitives shouldn't be split either. Garner himself takes out after the s.i. rule in his miniessays on both SPLIT INFINITIVES and SUPERSTITIONS.[51] And *Hopefully* at the beginning of a sentence, as a certain cheeky eighth-grader once (to his everlasting social cost) pointed out in class, actually functions not as a misplaced modal auxiliary or as a manner adverb like *quickly* or *angrily* but as a sentence adverb (i.e., as a special kind of "veiled reflexive that indicates the speaker's attitude about the state of affairs described by the rest of the sentence — examples of perfectly OK sentence adverbs are *clearly, basically, luckily*), and only SNOOTs educated in the high-pedantic years 1940–1960 blindly proscribe it or grade it down.

WHETHER WE'RE CONSCIOUS OF IT OR NOT, MOST OF US ARE FLUENT IN MORE THAN ONE MAJOR ENGLISH DIALECT.

The cases of split infinitives and *Hopefully* are in fact often trotted out by dogmatic Descriptivists as evidence that all SWE usage rules are arbitrary and dumb (which is a bit like pointing to Pat Buchanan as evidence that all Republicans are maniacs). FYI, Garner rejects *Hopefully*'s knee-jerk proscription, too, albeit grudgingly, saying "the battle is lost" and including the adverb in his miniessay on SKUNKED TERMS, which is his phrase for a usage that is "hotly disputed . . . any use of it is likely to distract some readers." (Garner also points out something I'd never quite realized, which is that *hopefully*, if misplaced/mispunctuated in the body of a sentence, can create some of the same two-way ambiguities as other adverbs, as in e.g. "I will borrow your book and hopefully read it soon."

Whether we're conscious of it or not, most of us are fluent in more than one major English dialect and in several subdialects and are probably at least passable in countless others. Which dialect you choose to use depends, of course, on whom you're addressing. More to the point, I submit that the

---

[49] A synthetic language uses grammatical inflections to dictate syntax, whereas an analytic languages uses word order. Latin, German, and Russian are synthetic; English and Chinese are analytic.

[50] (Q.v. for example Sir Thomas Smith's cortex-withering *De Recta et Emendata Linguae Anglicae Scriptione Dialogus* of 1568.)

[51] N.B., though, that he's sane about it. Some split infinitives really are clunky and hard to parse, especially when there are a lot of words between *to* and the verb ("We will attempt to swiftly and to the best of our ability respond to these charges"), which Garner calls "wide splits" and sensibly discourages. His overall verdict on split infinitives — which is that some are "perfectly proper" and some iffy and some just totally bad news, and that no one wide tidy dogmatic ukase can handle all s.i. cases, and thus that "knowing when to split an infinitive requires a good ear and a keen eye" — is a fine example of the way Garner distinguishes sound and helpful Descriptivist objections from wacko or dogmatic objections and then incorporates the sound objections into a smarter and more flexible Prescriptivism.

dialect you use depends mostly on what sort of Group your listener is part of and on whether you wish to present yourself as a fellow member of that Group. An obvious example is that traditional upper-class English has certain dialectal differences from lower-class English and that schools used to have courses in elocution whose whole *raison* was to teach people how to speak in an upper-class way. But usage-as-inclusion is about much more than class. Try another sort of thought experiment: A bunch of US teenagers in clothes that look several sizes too large for them are sitting together in the local mall's food court, and imagine that a 53-year-old man with jowls, a comb-over, and clothes that fit perfectly comes over to them and says he was scoping them and thinks they're totally rad and/or phat and asks is it cool if he just kicks it and chills with them here at their table. The kids' reaction is going to be either scorn or embarrassment for the guy — most likely a mix of both. Q: Why? Or imagine that two hard-core young urban black guys are standing there talking and I, who am resoundingly and in all ways white, come up and greet them with "Yo" and address one or both as "Brother" and ask "s'up, s'goin' on," pronouncing *on* with that NYCish o͞o-ŏ diphthong that Young Urban Black English deploys for a standard o. Either these guys are going to think that I am mocking them and be offended or they are going to think I am simply out of my mind. No other reaction is remotely foreseeable. Q: Why?

Why: A dialect of English is learned and used either because it's your native vernacular or because it's the dialect of a Group by which you wish (with some degree of plausibility) to be accepted. And although it is a major and vitally important one, SWE is only one dialect. And it is never, or at least hardly ever,[52] anybody's only dialect. This is because there are — as you and I both know and yet no one in the Usage Wars ever seems to mention — situations in which faultlessly correct SWE is *not* the appropriate dialect.

Childhood is full of such situations. This is one reason why SNOOTlets tend to have such a hard social time of it in school. A SNOOTlet is a little kid who's wildly, precociously fluent in SWE (he is often, recall, the offspring of SNOOTs). Just about every class has a SNOOTlet, so I know you've seen them — these are the sorts of six-to-twelve-year-olds who use *whom* correctly and whose response to striking out in T-ball is to shout "How incalculably dreadful!" The elementary-school SNOOTlet is one of the earliest identifiable species of academic geekoid and is duly despised by his peers and praised by his teachers. These teachers usually don't see the incredible amounts of punishment the SNOOTlet is receiving from his classmates, or if they do see it they blame the classmates and shake their heads sadly at the vicious and arbitrary cruelty of which children are capable.

---

[52] (It is, admittedly, difficult to imagine William F. Buckley using or perhaps even being aware of anything besides SWE.)

Teachers who do this are dumb. The truth is that his peers' punishment of the SNOOTlet is not arbitrary at all. There are important things at stake. Little kids in school are learning about Group-inclusion and -exclusion and about the respective rewards and penalties of same and about the use of dialect and syntax and slang as signals of affinity and inclusion. They're learning about Discourse Communities. Little kids learn this stuff not in Language Arts or Social Studies but on the playground and the bus and at lunch. When his peers are ostracizing the SNOOTlet or giving him monstrous quadruple Wedgies or holding him down and taking turns spitting on him, there's serious learning going on. Everybody here is learning except the little SNOOT[53] — in fact, what the SNOOTlet is being punished for is precisely his *failure* to learn. And his Language Arts teacher — whose own Elementary Education training prizes "linguistic facility" as one of the "social skills" that ensure children's "developmentally appropriate peer rapport,"[54] but who does not or cannot consider the possibility that linguistic facility might involve more than lapidary SWE — is unable to see that her beloved SNOOTlet is actually *deficient* in Language Arts. He has only one dialect. He cannot alter his vocabulary, usage, or grammar, cannot use slang or vulgarity; and it's these abilities that are really required for "peer rapport," which is just a fancy academic term for being accepted by the second-most-important Group in the little kid's

---

53 AMATEUR DEVELOPMENTAL-SOCIOLINGUISTIC INTERPOLATION #1

The SNOOTlet is, as it happens, an indispensable part of the other children's playground education. School and peers are kids' first socialization outside the family. In learning about Groups and Group tectonics, the kids are naturally learning that a Group's identity depends as much on exclusion as inclusion. They are, in other words, starting to learn about Us and Them, and about how an Us always needs a Them because being not-Them is essential to being Us. Because they're little children and it's school, the obvious Them is the teachers and all the values and appurtenances of the teacher-world.* This teacher-Them helps the kids see how to start to be an Us, but the SNOOTlet completes the puzzle by providing a kind of missing link: he is the traitor, the Us who is in fact not Us but *Them*. The SNOOTlet, who at first appears to be one of Us because like Us he's three feet tall and runny-nosed and eats paste, nevertheless speaks an erudite SWE that signals membership not in Us but in Them, which since Us is defined as not-Them is equivalent to a rejection of Us that is also a *betrayal* of Us precisely because the SNOOTlet is a kid, i.e., one of Us.

Point: The SNOOTlet is teaching his peers that the criteria for membership in Us are not just age, height, paste-ingestion, etc., that in fact Us is primarily a state of mind and a set of sensibilities. An ideology. The SNOOTlet is also teaching the kids that Us has to be *extremely vigilant* about persons who may at first appear to be Us but are in truth *not* Us and may need to be identified and excluded *at a moment's notice*. The SNOOTlet is not the only type of child who can serve as traitor: the Teacher's Pet, the Tattletale, the Brown-Noser, and the Mama's Boy can also do nicely . . . just as the Damaged and Deformed and Fat and Generally Troubled children all help the nascent mainstream Us-Groups refine the criteria for in- and exclusion.

In these crude and fluid formations of ideological Groupthink lies American kids' real socialization. We all learn early that community and Discourse Community are the same thing, and a fearsome thing indeed. It helps to know where We come from.

* (Plus, because the teacher-Them are tall humorless punishers/rewarders, they come to stand for all adults and — in a shadowy, inchoate way — for the Parents, whose gradual shift from composing Us to defining Them is probably the biggest ideological adjustment of childhood.)

54 (Elementary Ed professors really do talk this way.)

life.[55] If he is sufficiently in thrall to his teachers and those teachers are sufficiently clueless, it may take years and unbelievable amounts of punishment before the SNOOTlet learns that you need more than one dialect to get along in school.

This reviewer acknowledges that there seems to be some, umm, personal stuff getting dredged up and worked out here;[56] but the stuff is germane. The point is that the little A+ SNOOTlet is actually in the same dialectal position as the class's "slow" kid who can't learn to stop using *ain't* or *bringed.* Exactly the same position. One is punished in class, the other on the playground, but both are deficient in the same linguistic skill — viz., the ability to move between various dialects and levels of "correctness," the ability to communicate one way with peers and another way with teachers and another with family and another with T-ball coaches and so on. Most of these dialectal adjustments are made below the level of conscious awareness, and our ability to make them seems part psychological and part something else — perhaps something hardwired into the same motherboard as Universal Grammar — and in truth this ability is a much better indicator of a kid's raw "verbal IQ" than test scores or grades, since US English classes do far more to retard dialectal talent than to cultivate it.

---

55 AMATEUR DEVELOPMENTAL-SOCIOLINGUISTIC INTERPOLATION #2

And by the time the SNOOTlet hits adolescence it'll have supplanted the family to become the *most* important Group. And it will be a Group that depends for its definition on a rejection of traditional Authority.* And because it is the recognized dialect of mainstream adult society, there is no better symbol of traditional Authority than SWE. It is not an accident that adolescence is the time when slang and code and subdialects of subdialects explode all over the place and parents begin to complain that they can hardly even understand their kids' language. Nor are lyrics like "I can't get no / Satisfaction" an accident or any kind of sad commentary on the British educational system. Jagger et al. aren't stupid; they're rhetoricians, and they know their audience.

* (That is, the teacher- / parent-Them becomes the Establishment, Society — Them becomes THEM.)

56 (The skirt-in-school scenario was not personal stuff, though, FYI.)

A NOTE TO READERS FROM THE AUTHORS OF *WAYS OF READING*: For reasons we struggle to understand, David Foster Wallace's publisher would give us permission to reprint only about two-thirds of the essay "Authority and American Usage." As we made the cuts, we made sure that the essay retained a shape and a conclusion. Still, we thought you might be interested in a quick, summary account of what comes *after* the section you just read.

1. *The Teaching of Writing*. Wallace argues that teachers need to develop "overt, honest, and compelling arguments for why SWE is a dialect worth learning." And these arguments are hard to make because they are elitist. He says, "The real truth, of course, is that SWE is the dialect of the American elite." Wallace concludes this discussion by turning specifically to the problems this argument presents to those whose ways of speaking and writing place them outside the

circle of the elite, including "students of color." In his own teaching, Wallace says the following to his students (and he says it in his "official teacher-voice"):

> I don't know whether anybody's told you this or not, but when you're in a college English class you're basically studying a foreign dialect. This dialect is Standard Written English. . . . In my class, you have to learn and write in SWE. If you want to study your own primary dialect and its rules and history and how it's different from SWE, fine — there are some great books by scholars of Black English, and I'll help you find some and talk about them with you if you want. But that will be outside class. In class — in my English class — you will have to master and write in Standard Written English, which we might just as well call "Standard White English" because it was developed by white people and is used by white people, especially educated, powerful white people. . . . (p. 108)

He adds: "I should note here that a couple of the students I've said this stuff to were offended — one lodged an Official Complaint — and that I have had more than one colleague profess to find my spiel 'racially insensitive.' Perhaps you do too." And he concludes: "This reviewer's own humble opinion is that some of the cultural and political realities of American life are themselves racially insensitive and elitist and offensive and unfair, and that pussyfooting around these realities with euphemistic doublespeak is not only hypocritical but toxic to the project of ever really changing them."

2. *Why Bryan A. Garner Is a Genius.* Wallace concludes that Garner is a genius. And his genius is present in the quality of his writing. Although Garner is making judgments throughout *A Dictionary of Modern American Usage*, the persona that emerges is "disinterested," "reasonable," "objective," and compelling. It is neither elitist nor fussy (like a SNOOT). Garner appears not as "a cop or a judge" but more as an interested and passionate professional, like a doctor or a lawyer. Wallace says, "[Garner's] argumentative strategy is totally brilliant and totally sneaky, and part of both qualities is that it usually doesn't seem like there's an argument going on at all."

   Bryan Garner understood something that made his dictionary of American usage different from those that came before it: "the lexicographer's challenge now is to be not just accurate and comprehensive but *credible*. . . . [I]n the absence of capital-A Authority in language, the reader must now be moved or persuaded to grant a dictionary its authority, freely and for what appear to be good reasons." The autobiographical moments in Garner's introduction are part of the ethical appeal of his writing — a reader is asked to identify with this person, to trust him, and to admire him. And Wallace concludes:

   > Probably the most ingenious and attractive thing about his dictionary's Ethical Appeal . . . is Garner's scrupulousness about considering the reader's own hopes and fears and reasons for caring enough about usage to bother with something like *ADMAU* at all. These reasons, as Garner makes clear, tend to derive from a reader's concern

about his/her *own* linguistic authority and rhetorical persona and ability to convince an audience that he/she cares. Again and again, Garner frames his prescriptions in rhetorical terms: "To the writer or speakers for whom credibility is important, it's a good idea to avoid distracting *any* readers or listeners"; "Whatever you do, if you use *data* in a context in which its number becomes known, you'll bother some of your readers." *A Dictionary of Modern Usage*'s real thesis, in other words, is that the purposes of the expert authority and the purposes of the lay reader are identical, and identically rhetorical — which is about as Democratic these days as you're going to get. (p. 124)

QUESTIONS FOR A SECOND READING

1. It is common to talk about punctuation in relation to the sentence. Writers use marks of punctuation (commas, dashes, colons, semicolons, parentheses) to organize a sentence and to help readers locate themselves in relation to what they are reading. Writers also, however, punctuate essays or chapters — longer units of text. Wallace provides an excellent — and distinctive — example of this practice. You can notice immediately, for example, how he uses white space and subheadings to organize the essay into sections. There are also italics, "interpolations," enumerations, footnotes, footnotes to footnotes, all deployed to shape a reader's encounter with the text. Some are designed to be helpful; some, you might say, are deliberately designed to get in a reader's way.

   As you reread, take note of the places where Wallace could be said to be "punctuating" this essay. (You can do this in the margins.) When you are done, go back over your notes to see if there are distinct strategies, to see if your examples cluster into types. What, as a writer, is Wallace doing in each case? Why? What are the consequences for a reader? What attracts you as a writer?

2. Wallace's essay is purportedly a book review of Bryan A. Garner's *A Dictionary of Modern American Usage*. It is a long review. It provides an account of Garner's book while also placing it in relation to current issues, writers, and texts concerning the making of dictionaries and the correct and incorrect uses of words. It participates in a genre common in academic circles, a "review of the literature," and yet it has a different feel or sound than most academic writing. It has "style," you might say. You might say that there is a surprising, interesting, and distinctive character speaking in this text.

   As you reread, think about the speaker as a character, as an invention of David Foster Wallace, the writer (who could, at least hypothetically, have written about dictionaries in a different voice and in a different form). And mark moments when this character seems most distinctively present or alive. This character (whom we might also call Wallace) is a figure who reads in the field, who thinks about these issues, and who speaks with authority. He has a distinctive personality, way of thinking, view of the world. (Students are often invited, for example, to think of the "Thoreau" in *Walden* in just these terms, to think of him as a great American character.) When you are done, be prepared to talk about this as a strategy. Why would Wallace, the writer, present himself (or enter the conversation) in just these ways? What was at stake for him?

3. At several places in his essay, Wallace applauds Bryan Garner for being "rhetorical" and "totally sneaky." These seem unusual terms with which to signal praise. Indeed, "rhetoric" is often associated with being sneaky, as in the politician who sneakily avoids a question or converts an opponent's strength into a weakness. As you reread, look again at Wallace's uses of the term *rhetoric*. What does it come to mean? What work does it do for him? With what terms is it paired or opposed?

   When you are done, and as an exercise in understanding, prepare a paraphrase, one long paragraph, to explain what "rhetoric" comes to mean for Wallace. As you do this (and again as an exercise in understanding), include a passage in block quotation — that is, an extended passage that you will introduce, include (following the appropriate conventions), and then discuss.

4. The structure of Wallace's text is complex, with its footnotes, interpolations, digressions, numbered lists, and assorted oddities. Though he mentions a "thesis" at several points, he doesn't announce a thesis in the opening paragraph and then dutifully follow it with examples and the way to a conclusion. As you reread, pay attention to the argument (or arguments) that are developed in this essay. What are the key terms? Where does Wallace begin, and where does he move thereafter? What are his major contentions? How does he support them? Where does he end?

   When you are done, and as an exercise in understanding, prepare a paraphrase, one long paragraph, to explain what you take to be the key argument in this essay. As you do this (and again as an exercise in understanding), include a passage in block quotation — that is, an extended passage that you will introduce, include (following the appropriate conventions), and then discuss.

5. The Latin phrase by Augustine — *Dilige et quod vis fac* — that Wallace uses as his epigraph means "Love, and do what thou wilt." Wallace doesn't offer any explanation of this epigraph in his text. As you reread, reflect on how it might relate to his arguments about language use.

6. According to Bruce Weber, writing for the *New York Times,* Wallace's sentences showed the "playfulness of a master punctuator and the inventiveness of a genius grammarian." As you reread, choose a sentence that might fit this description. Type it out; and then create a sentence of your own in direct imitation — the same length, punctuation, grammar, and rhythm, but with new words and a different topic. When you are done, be prepared to talk about what a sentence like this *does* — not what it says but what it *does* — the sentence as a gesture, an action, a deed in words.

7. If you are interested in reading this essay in its entirety, you'll likely find it at your college or university library in a collection titled *Consider the Lobster: And Other Essays* (2005), by David Foster Wallace. It is also interesting to read this essay, and to think about its style, in relationship to other essays in that collection. Those we would recommend as starters would be the title essay, "Consider the Lobster," on the Maine Lobster Festival, and "Some Remarks on Kafka's Funniness from Which Probably Not Enough Has Been Removed," about the difficulty of teaching the novelist and short story writer Franz Kafka in college literature courses.

ASSIGNMENTS FOR WRITING

1. At certain moments in his essay, Wallace describes his approach as a teacher of college students. He tells us in footnote 6, for instance, that while he teaches literature courses, he usually abandons the syllabus after he reads his students' first papers in order to hold "a three-week Emergency Remedial Usage and Grammar Unit, during which my demeanor is basically that of somebody teaching HIV prevention to intravenous-drug users." And later he provides a representation of a lengthy speech he gives to individual college students who struggle with Standard Written English. He says,

> I'm not trying to suggest here that an effective SWE pedagogy would require teachers to wear sunglasses and call students Dude. What I am suggesting is that the rhetorical situation of a US English class — a class composed wholly of young people whose Group identity is rooted in defiance of Adult Establishment values, plus also composed partly of minorities whose primary dialects are different from SWE — requires a teacher to come up with overt, honest, and compelling arguments for why SWE is a dialect worth learning. (p. 107)

But Wallace also teaches writing by example — that is, by what he says in this essay about effective writing and by the way he chooses to write. In this sense, "Authority and American Usage" offers a writing lesson.

Write an essay in which you take up the invitation to engage Wallace's argument about U.S. English, about SWE, about rhetoric, and about the function and importance of a writing class. You will need to work directly in reference to what Wallace says in the text. In other words, you'll need to work with sentences and examples. But you also bring experience to the table. From your point of view, and from the point of view of students like you, what is at stake? How and where might you enter this conversation? Where are you in the settings Wallace invokes? in his arguments?

2. A character emerges in this essay, a figure representing one version of a well-schooled, learned, and articulate adult, an intellectual, someone who reads widely, who thinks closely and freshly and methodically about big questions, someone with ideas and with style, someone who is defined in relation to sources—to books and to other writers. (The second of the "Questions for a Second Reading" is designed to help you locate this character as a figure in a text, as a writer's invention.)

   Write an essay in which you discuss the figure of the intellectual represented in the essay "Authority and American Usage." You'll need to work closely with a few key and representative moments in the text. And write an essay in which you assess this figure in relation to your own education—better yet, in relation to the figure you intend to cut as a well-schooled adult, as an intellectual, as a person with ideas and knowledge and something to say.

3. Wallace's essay is purportedly a book review of Bryan A. Garner's *A Dictionary of Modern American Usage*. It is a long review. It provides an account of Garner's book while also placing it in relation to current issues, writers, and texts concerning the making of dictionaries and the correct and incorrect uses of words. It participates in a genre common in academic circles, a "review of the literature," and yet it has a different feel or sound than most academic writing. It has "style," you might say. And it has a method. (The first and fourth of the "Questions for a Second Reading" are designed to help you locate key features of this method.)

   Write something *like* this essay, something Wallace-like, in relation to a book (or an essay) you have read. The subject or topic does not have to be related to dictionaries or to usage. This could well be something you have read for this class or for another class, something you may have already written about, but differently, not in a Wallace-like way. Your range of reference may not be as great as Wallace's, but you should bring one or two other writers into play, others who have thought and written about the topic. The most important thing, however, is to make this an exercise in adopting and experimenting with Wallace's method and style.

MAKING CONNECTIONS

1. In his essay "The Dark Night of the Soul", Richard E. Miller notes that, at times, Eric Harris, one of two teens who killed thirteen people at Columbine High School in 1999,

> had the affectation of an English teacher, declaring on his Web site that one of the many habits he found unforgivable in his peers was the tendency to pronounce the "t" in "often": "Learn to speak correctly, you morons," he commands. . . .

See the e-Pages at bedfordstmartins.com/waysofreading.

Reading this passage, we might recall the discussion of "SNOOTs" and other "Prescriptivists" in "Authority and American Usage" by David Foster Wallace, who confesses he finds it difficult to tolerate usage that departs from Standard Written English. Both Foster and Miller are concerned with the future of print-based literacy — with the ways in which the reading and writing of books will (or won't) matter to our culture in the years to come. Wallace worries that schools will quit teaching standard conventions for communication in writing, while Miller worries that "training students to read and write in more critical and self-reflective ways cannot protect them from the violent changes our culture is undergoing."

Write an essay in which you discuss your own sense of the future of American literacy and its relationship to cultural change, paying particular attention to the language habits of your generation. Based on what you've observed among your peers, do you find Foster's and Miller's anxieties well founded? overwrought? reflective of something they don't examine? How do you respond to their concern that books and teachers are losing their authority? Focus your essay on a moment or a series of moments in your experience or observation that speaks to Foster's and Miller's fears about the fate of reading and writing in the twenty-first century.

2. Both Kwame Anthony Appiah's "Racial Identities" (p. 42) and David Foster Wallace's "Authority and American Usage" have a distinctive style, voice, and method. A character emerges in each essay, a figure representing one version of a well-schooled, learned, and articulate adult, an intellectual, someone who reads widely, who thinks closely and freshly and methodically about big questions, someone with ideas and with style, someone who is defined in relation to sources — to books and to other writers — and someone who takes pains to address his readers. This is an intellectual, then, with a desire to reach others, to engage them, and to bring them into his point of view.

   Write an essay in which you discuss the figure of the intellectual represented in these two essays. You'll need to work closely with a few key and representative moments in the texts. And write an essay in which you assess this figure in relation to your own education — better yet, in relation to the figure you intend to cut as a well-schooled adult, as an intellectual, as a person with ideas and knowledge and something to say.

JOHN EDGAR Wideman

John Edgar Wideman was born in 1941 in Washington, D.C., but spent most of his youth in Homewood, a neighborhood in Pittsburgh. He earned a BA from the University of Pennsylvania and taught at the University of Wyoming and the University of Massachusetts at Amherst. He is currently Asa Messer Professor and Professor of Africana Studies and English at Brown University and sits on the board of the literary journal *Conjunctions*. In addition to the nonfiction work *Brothers and Keepers* (1984), from which this selection is drawn, Wideman has published a number of critically acclaimed works of fiction, including *The Lynchers* (1986); *Reuben* (1989); *Fever: Twelve Stories* (1989); *Philadelphia Fire: A Novel* (1991); and a series of novels set in Homewood: *Damballah* (1981), *Hiding Place* (1982), and *Sent for You Yesterday* (which won the 1984 PEN/Faulkner Award). The latter novels have been reissued as a set, titled *The Homewood Trilogy*. His most recent books include *The Cattle Killing* (1996), *Two Cities* (1998), *Hoop Roots* (2001), *The Island, Martinique* (2003), *God's Gym* (2005), *Fanon* (2008), and *Briefs* (2010). In 1994, Wideman published another work of nonfiction, *Fatheralong: A Meditation on Fathers and Sons, Race and Society*.

In the preface to *The Homewood Trilogy*, Wideman writes,

> The value of black life in America is judged, as life generally in this country is judged, by external, material signs of success. Urban ghettoes are dangerous, broken-down, economically marginal pockets of real estate infected with drugs, poverty, violence, crime, and since black life is seen as rooted in the ghetto, black people are identified with the ugliness, danger, and deterioration surrounding them. This logic is simpleminded and devastating, its hold on the American imagination as old as slavery; in fact, it recycles the classic justification for slavery, blaming the cause and consequences of oppression on the oppressed. Instead of launching a preemptive strike at the flawed assumptions that perpetuate racist thinking, blacks and whites are doomed to battle endlessly with the symptoms of racism.
>
> In these three books again bound as one I have set myself to the task of making concrete those invisible planes of existence that bear witness to the fact that black life, for all its material impoverishment,

continues to thrive, to generate alternative styles, redemptive strategies, people who hope and cope. But more than attempting to prove a "humanity," which should be self-evident anyway to those not blinded by racism, my goal is to celebrate and affirm. *Where did I come from? Who am I? Where am I going?*

Brothers and Keepers is a family story; it is about Wideman and his brother Robby. John went to Oxford as a Rhodes scholar, and Robby went to prison for his role in a robbery and a murder. In the section that follows, "Our Time," Wideman tries to understand his brother, their relationship, where they came from, where they are going. In this account, you will hear the voices of Robby, John, and people from the neighborhood, but also the voice of the writer, speaking about the difficulty of writing and the dangers of explaining away Robby's life.

Brothers and Keepers is not the first time Wideman has written to or about his brother. The first of the Homewood series, *Damballah*, is dedicated to Robby. The dedication reads:

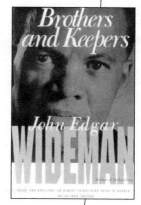

> Stories are letters. Letters sent to anybody or everybody. But the best kind are meant to be read by a specific somebody. When you read that kind you know you are eavesdropping. You know a real person somewhere will read the same words you are reading and the story is that person's business and you are a ghost listening in.
>
> Remember. I think it was Geral I first heard call a watermelon a letter from home. After all these years I understand a little better what she meant. She was saying the melon is a letter addressed to us. A story for us from down home. Down Home being everywhere we've never been, the rural South, the old days, slavery, Africa. That juicy, striped message with red meat and seeds, which always looked like roaches to me, was blackness as cross and celebration, a history we could taste and chew. And it was meant for us. Addressed to us. We were meant to slit it open and take care of business.
>
> Consider all these stories as letters from home. I never liked watermelon as a kid. I think I remember you did. You weren't afraid of becoming instant nigger, of sitting barefoot and goggle-eyed and Day-Glo black and drippy-lipped on massa's fence if you took one bite of the forbidden fruit. I was too scared to enjoy watermelon. Too self-conscious. I let people rob me of a simple pleasure. Watermelon's still tainted for me. But I know better now. I can play with the idea even if I can't get down and have a natural ball eating a real one.
>
> Anyway . . . these stories are letters. Long overdue letters from me to you. I wish they could tear down the walls. I wish they could snatch you away from where you are.

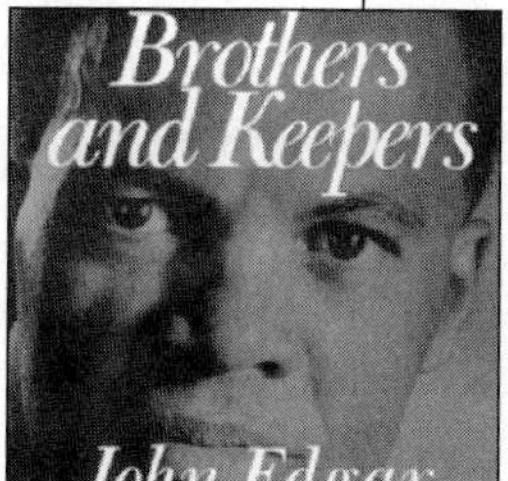

Our Time

You remember what we were saying about young black men in the street-world life. And trying to understand why the "square world" becomes completely unattractive to them. It has to do with the fact that their world is the GHETTO and in that world all the glamour, all the praise and attention is given to the slick guy, the gangster especially, the ones that get over in the "life." And it's because we can't help but feel some satisfaction seeing a brother, a black man, get over on these people, on their system without playing by their rules. No matter how much we have incorporated these rules as our own, we know that they were forced on us by people who did not have our best interests at heart. So this hip guy, this gangster or player or whatever label you give these brothers that we like to shun because of the poison that they spread, we, black people, still look at them with some sense of pride and admiration, our children openly, us adults somewhere deep inside. We know they represent rebellion — what little is left in us. Well, having lived in the "life," it becomes very hard — almost impossible — to find any contentment in joining the status quo. Too hard to go back to being nobody in a world that hates you. Even if I had struck it rich in the life, I would have managed to throw it down the fast lane. Or have lost it on a revolutionary whim. Hopefully the latter.

I have always burned up in my fervent passions of desire and want. My senses at times tingle and itch with my romantic, idealistic outlook on life, which has always made me keep my distance from reality, reality that was a constant insult to my world, to my dream of happiness and peace, to my people-for-people kind of world, my easy-cars-for-a-nickel-or-a-dime sorta world. And these driving passions, this sensitivity to the love and good in people, also turned on me because I used it to play on people and their feelings. These aspirations of love and desire turned on me when I wasn't able to live up to this sweet-self morality, so I began to self-destruct, burning up in my sensitivity, losing direction, because nowhere could I find this world of truth and love and harmony.

In the real world, the world left for me, it was unacceptable to be "good," it was square to be smart in school, it was jive to show respect to people outside the street world, it was cool to be cold to your woman and the people that loved you. The things we liked we called "bad." "Man, that was a bad girl." The world of the angry black kid growing up in the sixties was a world in which to be in was to be out — out of touch with the square world and all of its rules on what's right and wrong. The thing was to make your own rules, do your own thing, but make sure it's contrary to what society says or is.

I SHALL ALWAYS PRAY

I

Garth looked bad. Real bad. Ichabod Crane anyway, but now he was a skeleton. Lying there in the bed with his bones poking through his skin, it made you want to cry. Garth's barely able to talk, his smooth, medium-brown skin yellow as pee. Ichabod legs and long hands and long feet, Garth could make you laugh just walking down the street. On the set you'd see him coming a far way off. Three-quarters leg so you knew it had to be Garth the way he was split up higher in the crotch than anybody else. Wilt the Stilt with a lean bird body perched on top his high waist. Size-fifteen shoes. Hands could palm a basketball easy as holding a pool cue. Fingers long enough to wrap round a basketball, but Garth couldn't play a lick. Never could get all that lankiness together on the court. You'd look at him sometimes as he was trucking down Homewood Avenue and think that nigger ain't walking, he's trying to remember how to walk. Awkward as a pigeon on roller skates. Knobby joints out of whack, arms and legs flailing, going their separate ways, his body jerking to keep them from going too far. Moving down the street like that wouldn't work, didn't make sense if you stood back and watched, if you pretended you hadn't seen Garth get where he was going a million times before. Nothing funny now, though. White hospital sheets pulled to his chest. Garth's head always looked small as a tennis ball way up there on his shoulders. Now it's a yellow, shrunken skull.

Ever since Robby had entered the ward, he'd wanted to reach over and hide his friend's arm under the covers. For two weeks Gar had been wasting away in the bed. Bad enough knowing Gar was dying. Didn't need that pitiful stick arm reminding him how close to nothing his main man had fallen. So fast. It could happen so fast. If Robby tried to raise that arm it would come off in his hand. As gentle as he could would not be gentle enough. The arm would disintegrate, like a long ash off the end of a cigarette.

Time to leave. No sense in sitting any longer. Garth not talking, no way of telling whether he was listening either. And Robby has nothing more to say. Choked up the way he gets inside hospitals. Hospital smell and quiet, the bare halls and bare floors, the echoes, something about all that he can't name, wouldn't try to name, rises in him and chills him. Like his teeth are chattering the whole time he's inside a hospital. Like his entire body is trembling uncontrollably, only nobody can see it or hear it but him. Shaking because he can't breathe the stuffy air. Hot and cold at the same time. He's been aching to leave since he entered the ward. Aching to get up and bust through the big glass front doors. Aching to pounce on that spidery arm flung back behind Gar's head. The arm too wasted to belong to his friend. He wants to grab it and hurl it away.

Robby pulls on tight white gloves the undertaker had dealt out to him and the rest of the pallbearers. His brown skin shows through the thin material, turns the white dingy. He's remembering that last time in Garth's ward. The hospital stink. Hot, chilly air. A bare arm protruding from the sleeve of the hospital gown, more dried-up toothpick than arm, a withered twig, with Garth's fingers like a bunch of skinny brown bananas drooping from the knobby tip.

Robby had studied the metal guts of the hospital bed, the black scuff marks swirling around the chair's legs. When he'd finally risen to go, his chair scraping against the vinyl floor broke a long silence. The noise must have roused Garth's attention. He'd spoken again.

You're good, man. Don't ever forget, Rob. You're the best.

Garth's first words since the little banter back and forth when Robby had entered the ward and dragged a chair to the side of Gar's bed. A whisper scarcely audible now that Robby was standing. Garth had tried to grin. The best he could manage was a pained adjustment of the bones of his face, no more than a shadow scudding across the yellow skull, but Robby had seen the famous smile. He hesitated, stopped rushing toward the door long enough to smile back. Because that was Gar. That was the way Gar was. He always had a smile and a good word for his cut buddies. Garth's grin was money in the bank. You could count on it like you could count on a good word from him. Something in his face would tell you you were alright, better than alright, that he believed in you, that you were, as he'd just whispered, "the best." You could depend on Garth to say something to make you feel good, even though you knew he was lying. With that grin greasing the lie you had to believe it, even though you knew better. Garth was the gang's dreamer. When he talked, you could see his dreams. That's why Robby had believed it, seen the grin, the bright shadow lighting Garth's face an instant. Out of nothing, out of pain, fear, the certainty of death gripping them both, Garth's voice had manufactured the grin.

Now they had to bury Garth. A few days after the visit to the hospital the phone rang and it was Garth's mother with the news of her son's death. Not really news. Robby had known it was just a matter of time. Of waiting for the moment when somebody else's voice would pronounce the words he'd said to himself a hundred times. *He's gone. Gar's dead.* Long gone before the telephone rang. Gar was gone when they stuck him up in the hospital bed. By the time they'd figured out what ailed him and admitted him to the hospital, it was too late. The disease had turned him to a skeleton. Nothing left of Garth to treat. They hid his messy death under white sheets, perfumed it with disinfectant, pumped him full of drugs so he wouldn't disturb his neighbors.

The others had squeezed into their pallbearers' gloves. Cheap white cotton gloves so you could use them once and throw them away like the rubber ones doctors wear when they stick their fingers up your ass. Michael, Cecil, and Sowell were pallbearers, too. With Robby and two men from Garth's family they would carry the coffin from Gaines Funeral Parlor to the hearse. Garth had been the dreamer for the gang. Robby counted four black fingers in the white glove. Garth was the thumb. The hand would be clumsy, wouldn't work right without him. Garth was different. But everybody else was different, too. Mike, the ice man, supercool. Cecil indifferent, ready to do most anything or nothing and couldn't care less which it was. Sowell wasn't really part of the gang; he didn't hang with them, didn't like to take the risks that were part of the "life." Sowell kept a good job. The "life" for him was just a way to make quick money. He didn't shoot up; he thought of himself as a businessman, an investor not a partner in their schemes. They knew Sowell mostly through Garth. Perhaps things would change now. The four survivors closer after they shared the burden of Gar's coffin, after they hoisted it and slid it on steel rollers into the back of Gaines's Cadillac hearse.

Robby was grateful for the gloves. He'd never been able to touch anything dead. He'd taken a beating once from his father rather than touch the bloody mousetrap his mother had nudged to the back door with her toe and ordered him to empty. The brass handle of the coffin felt damp through the glove. He gripped tighter to stop the flow of blood or sweat, whatever it was leaking from him or seeping from the metal. Garth had melted down to nothing by the end so it couldn't be him nearly yanking off Robby's shoulder when the box shifted and its weight shot forward. Felt like a coffin full of bricks. Robby stared across at Mike but Mike was a soldier, eyes front, riveted to the yawning rear door of the hearse. Mike's eyes wouldn't admit it, but they'd almost lost the coffin. They were rookie pallbearers and maneuvering down the carpeted front steps of Gaines Funeral Parlor they'd almost let Garth fly out their hands. They needed somebody who knew what he was doing. An old, steady head to show them the way. They needed Garth. But Garth was long gone. Ashes inside the steel box.

They began drinking later that afternoon in Garth's people's house. Women and food in one room, men hitting the whiskey hard in another. It was a typical project apartment. The kind everybody had stayed in or visited one time or another. Small, shabby, featureless. Not a place to live. No matter what you did to it, how clean you kept it or what kind of furniture you loaded it with, the walls and ceilings were not meant to be home for anybody. A place you passed through. Not yours, because the people who'd been there before you left their indelible marks everywhere and you couldn't help adding your bruises and knots for the next tenants. You could rent a kitchen and bedroom and a bathroom and a living room, the project flats were laid out so you had a room for each of the things people did in houses. Problem was, every corner was cut. Living cramped is one thing and people can get cozy in the closest quarters. It's another thing to live in a place designed to be just a little less than adequate. No slack, no space to personalize, to stamp the flat with what's peculiar to your style. Like a man sitting on a toilet seat that's too small and the toilet too close to the bathtub so his knees shove against the enamel edge. He can move his bowels that way and plenty of people in the world have a lot less but he'll never enjoy sitting there, never feel the deep down comfort of belonging where he must squat.

Anyway, the whiskey started flowing in that little project apartment. Robby listened, for Garth's sake, as long as he could to old people reminiscing about funerals they'd attended, about all the friends and relatives they'd escorted to the edge of Jordan, old folks sipping good whiskey and moaning and groaning till it seemed a sin to be left behind on this side of the river after so many saints had crossed over. He listened to people express their grief, tell sad, familiar stories. As he got high he listened less closely to the words. Faces and gestures revealed more than enough. When he split with Mike and Cecil and their ladies, Sowell tagged along. By then the tacky, low-ceilinged rooms of the flat were packed. Loud talk, laughter, storytellers competing for audiences. Robby half expected the door he pushed shut behind himself to pop open again, waited for bottled-up noise to explode into the funky hallway.

Nobody thinking about cemeteries now. Nobody else needs to be buried today, so it was time to get it on. Some people had been getting close to rowdy. Some people had been getting mad. Mad at one of the guests in the apartment, mad at doctors and hospitals and whites in general who had the whole world in their hands but didn't have the slightest idea what to do with it. A short, dark man, bubble-eyed, immaculately dressed in a three-piece, wool, herringbone suit, had railed about the callousness, the ignorance of white witch doctors who, by misdiagnosing Garth's illness, had sealed his doom. His harangue had drawn a crowd. He wasn't just talking, he was testifying, and a hush had fallen over half the room as he dissected the dirty tricks of white folks. If somebody ran to the hospital and snatched a white-coated doctor and threw him into the circle surrounding the little fish-eyed man, the mourners would tear the pale-faced devil apart. Robby wished he could feed them one. Remembered Garth weak and helpless in the bed and the doctors and nurses flitting around in the halls, jiving the other patients, ignoring Gar like he wasn't there. Garth was dead because he had believed them. Dead because he had nowhere else to turn when the pain in his gut and the headaches grew worse and worse. Not that he trusted the doctors or believed they gave a flying fuck about him. He'd just run out of choices and had to put himself in their hands. They told him jaundice was his problem, and while his liver rotted away and pain cooked him dizzy Garth assured anyone who asked that it was just a matter of giving the medicine time to work. To kill the pain he blew weed as long as he had strength to hold a joint between his lips. Take a whole bunch of smoke to cool me out these days. Puffing like a chimney till he lost it and fell back and Robby scrambling to grab the joint before Garth torched hisself.

When you thought about it, Garth's dying made no sense. And the more you thought the more you dug that nothing else did neither. The world's a stone bitch. Nothing true if that's not true. The man had you coming and going. He owned everything worth owning and all you'd ever get was what he didn't want anymore, what he'd chewed and spit out and left in the gutter for niggers to fight over. Garth had pointed to the street and said, If we ever make it, it got to come from there, from the curb. We got to melt that rock till we get us some money. He grinned then, Ain't no big thing. We'll make it, brother man. We got what it takes. It's our time.

Something had crawled in Garth's belly. The man said it wasn't nothing. Sold him some aspirins and said he'd be alright in no time. The man killed Garth. Couldn't kill him no deader with a .357 magnum slug, but ain't no crime been committed. Just one those things. You know, everybody makes mistakes. And a dead nigger ain't really such a big mistake when you think about it. Matter of fact you mize well forget the whole thing. Nigger wasn't going nowhere, nohow. I mean he wasn't no brain surgeon or astronaut, no movie star or big-time athlete. Probably a dope fiend or gangster. Wind up killing some innocent person or wasting another nigger. Shucks. That doctor ought to get a medal.

Hey, man. Robby caught Mike's eye. Then Cecil and Sowell turned to him. They knew he was speaking to everybody. Late now. Ten, eleven, because it had been dark outside for hours. Quiet now. Too quiet in his pad. And too much smoke and drink since the funeral. From a bare bulb in the kitchen ceiling light seeped down the hallway and hovered dimly in the doorway of the room where they sat. Robby wondered if the others felt as bad as he did. If the cemetery clothes itched their skin. If they could smell grave dust on their shoes. He hoped they'd finish this last jug of wine and let the day be over. He needed sleep, downtime to get the terrible weight of Garth's death off his mind. He'd been grateful for the darkness. For the company of his cut buddies after the funeral. For the Sun Ra tape until it ended and plunged them into a deeper silence than any he'd ever known. Garth was gone. In a few days people would stop talking about him. He was in the ground. Stone-cold dead. Robby had held a chunk of crumbly ground in his white-gloved fingers and mashed it and dropped the dust into the hole. Now the ground had closed over Garth and what did it mean? Here one day and gone the next and that was that. They'd bury somebody else out of Gaines tomorrow. People would dress up and cry and get drunk and tell lies and next day it'd be somebody else's turn to die. Which one of the shadows in this black room would go first? What did it matter? Who cared? Who would remember their names; they were ghosts already. Dead as Garth already. Only difference was, Garth didn't have it to worry about no more. Garth didn't have to pretend he was going anywhere cause he was there. He'd made it to the place they all were headed fast as their legs could carry them. Every step was a step closer to the stone-cold ground, the pitch-black hole where they'd dropped Garth's body.

Hey, youall. We got to drink to Garth one last time.

They clinked glasses in the darkness. Robby searched for something to say. The right words wouldn't come. He knew there was something proper and precise that needed to be said. Because the exact words eluded him, because only the right words would do, he swallowed his gulp of heavy, sweet wine in silence.

He knew he'd let Garth down. If it had been one of the others dead, Michael or Cecil or Sowell or him, Garth wouldn't let it slide by like this, wouldn't let it end like so many other nights had ended, the fellows nodding off one by one, stupefied by smoke and drink, each one beginning to shop around in his mind, trying to figure whether or not he should turn in or if there was a lady somewhere who'd welcome him in her bed. No. Garth would have figured a way to make it special. They wouldn't be hiding in the bushes. They'd be knights in shining armor around a big table. They'd raise their giant, silver cups to honor the fallen comrade. Like in the olden days. Clean, brave dudes with gold rings and gold chains. They'd draw their blades. Razor-edged swords that gleam in the light with jewels sparkling in the handles. They'd make a roof over the table when they stood and raised their swords and the points touched in the sky. A silver dagger on a satin pillow in the middle of the table. Everybody roll up their sleeves and prick a vein and go round, each one touching everybody else so the blood runs together and we're brothers forever, brothers as long as blood flows in anybody's arm. We'd ride off and do unbelievable shit. The dead one always with us cause we'd do it all for him. Swear we'd never let him down.

It's our time now. We can't let Garth down. Let's drink this last one for him and promise him we'll do what he said we could. We'll be the best. We'll make it to the top for him. We'll do it for Garth.

Glasses rattled together again. Robby empties his and thinks about smashing it against a wall. He'd seen it done that way in movies but it was late at night and these crazy niggers might not know when to stop throwing things. A battlefield of broken glass for him to creep through when he gets out of bed in the morning. He doesn't toss the empty glass. Can't see a solid place anyway where it would strike clean and shatter to a million points of light.

My brother had said something about a guy named Garth during one of my visits to the prison. Just a name mentioned in passing. *Garth* or *Gar*. I'd asked Robby to spell it for me. Garth had been a friend of Robby's, about Robby's age, who died one summer of a mysterious disease. Later when Robby chose to begin the story of the robbery and killing by saying, "It all started with Gar dying," I remembered that first casual mention and remembered a conversation with my mother. My mom and I were in the kitchen of the house on Tokay Street. My recollection of details was vague at first but something about the conversation had made a lasting impression because, six years later, hearing Robby say the name *Garth* brought back my mother's words.

My mother worried about Robby all the time. Whenever I visited home, sooner or later I'd find myself alone with Mom and she'd pour out her fears about Robby's *wildness,* the deep trouble he was bound for, the web of entanglements and intrigues and bad company he was weaving around himself with a maddening disregard for the inevitable consequences.

Mom

I don't know. I just don't know how to reach him. He won't listen. He's doing wrong and he knows it but nothing I say makes any difference. He's not like the rest of youall. You'd misbehave but I could talk to you or smack you if I had to and you'd straighten up. With Robby it's like talking to a wall.

I'd listen and get angry at my brother because I registered not so much the danger he was bringing on himself, but the effect of his escapades on the woman who'd brought us both into the world. After all, Robby was no baby. If he wanted to mess up, nobody could stop him. Also Robby was my brother, meaning that his wildness was just a stage, a chaotic phase of his life that would only last till he got his head together and decided to start doing right. Doing as the rest of us did. He was my brother. He couldn't fall too far. His brushes with the law (I'd had some, too), the time he'd spent in jail, were serious but temporary setbacks. I viewed his troubles, when I thought about them at all, as a form of protracted juvenile delinquency, and fully expected Robby would learn his lesson sooner or later and return to the fold, the prodigal son, chastened, perhaps a better person for the experience. In the meantime the most serious consequence of his wildness was Mom's devastating unhappiness. She couldn't sustain the detachment, the laissez-faire optimism I had talked myself into. Because I was two thousand miles away, in Wyoming, I didn't have to deal with the day-to-day evidence of Robby's trouble. The syringe Mom found under his bed. The twenty-dollar bill missing from her purse. The times he'd cruise in higher than a kite, his pupils reduced to pinpricks, with his crew and they'd raid the refrigerator and make a loud, sloppy feast, all of them feeling so good they couldn't imagine anybody not up there on cloud nine with them enjoying the time of their lives. Cruising in, then disappearing just as abruptly, leaving their dishes and pans and mess behind. Robby covering Mom with kisses and smiles and drowning her in babytalk hootchey-coo as he staggers through the front door. Her alone in the ravaged, silent kitchen, listening as doors slam and a car squeals off on the cobblestones of Tokay, wondering where they're headed next, wishing, praying Robby will return and eat and eat and eat till he falls asleep at the table so she can carry him upstairs and tuck him in and kiss his forehead and shut the door gently on his sleep.

I WASN'T AROUND FOR ALL THAT. DIDN'T WANT TO KNOW HOW BAD THINGS WERE FOR HIM.

I wasn't around for all that. Didn't want to know how bad things were for him. Worrying about my mother was tough enough. I could identify with her grief, I could blame my brother. An awful situation, but simple too. My role, my responsibilities and loyalties were clear. The *wildness* was to blame, and it was a passing thing, so I just had to help my mother survive the worst of it, then everything would be alright. I'd steel myself for the moments alone with her when she'd tell me the worst. In the kitchen, usually, over a cup of coffee with the radio playing. When my mother was alone in the house on Tokay, either the TV or a radio or both were always on. Atop the kitchen table a small clock radio turned to WAMO, one of Pittsburgh's soul stations, would background with scratchy gospel music whatever we said in the morning in the kitchen. On a morning like that in 1975, while I drank a cup of coffee and part of me, still half-asleep, hidden, swayed to the soft beat of gospel, my mother had explained how upset Robby was over the death of his friend, Garth.

It was a terrible thing. I've known Garth's mother for years. He was a good boy. No saint for sure, but deep down a good boy. Like your brother. Not a mean bone in his body. Out there in the street doing wrong, but that's where most of them are. What else can they do, John? Sometimes I can't blame them. No jobs, no money in their pockets. How they supposed to feel like men? Garth did better than most. Whatever else he was into, he kept that little job over at Westinghouse and helped out his mother. A big, playful kid. Always smiling. I think that's why him and Robby were so tight. Neither one had good sense. Giggled and acted like fools. Garth no wider than my finger. Straight up and down. A stringbean if I ever saw one. When Robby lived here in the house with me, Garth was always around. I know how bad Robby feels. He hasn't said a word but I know. When Robby's quiet, you know something's wrong. Soon as his eyes pop open in the morning he's looking for the party. First thing in the morning he's chipper and chattering. Looking for the party. That's your brother. He had a match in Garth.

Shame the way they did that boy. He'd been down to the clinic two or three times but they sent him home. Said he had an infection and it would take care of itself. Something like that anyway. You know how they are down there. Have to be spitting blood to get attention. Then all they give you is a Band-Aid. He went back two times, but they kept telling him the same dumb thing. Anybody who knew Garth could see something awful was wrong. Circles under his eyes. Sallow look to his skin. Losing weight. And the poor thing didn't have any weight to lose. Last time I saw him I was shocked. Just about shocked out my shoes. Wasn't Garth standing in front of me. Not the boy I knew.

Well, to make a long story short, they finally took him in the hospital but it was too late. They let him walk the streets till he was dead. It was wrong. Worse than wrong how they did him, but that's how those dogs do us every day God sends here. Garth's gone, so nothing nobody can say will do any good. I feel so sorry for his mother. She lived for that boy. I called her and tried to talk but what can you say? I prayed for her and prayed for Garth and prayed for Robby. A thing like that tears people up. It's worse if you keep it inside. And that's your brother's way. He'll let it eat him up and then go out and do something crazy.

Until she told me Garth's story I guess I hadn't realized how much my mother had begun to change. She had always seemed to me to exemplify the tolerance, the patience, the long view epitomized in her father. John French's favorite saying was, Give 'em the benefit of the doubt. She could get as ruffled, as evil as the rest of us, cry and scream or tear around the house fit to be tied. She had her grudges and quarrels. Mom could let it all hang out, yet most of the time she radiated a deep calm. She reacted strongly to things but at the same time held judgment in abeyance. Events, personalities always deserved a second, slower appraisal, an evaluation outside the sphere of everyday hassles and vexations. You gave people the benefit of the doubt. You attempted to remove your ego, acknowledge the limitations of your individual view of things. You consulted as far as you were equipped by temperament and intelligence a broader, more abiding set of relationships and connections.

You tried on the other person's point of view. You sought the other, better person in yourself who might talk you into relinquishing for a moment your selfish interest in whatever was at issue. You stopped and considered the long view, possibilities other than the one that momentarily was leading you by the nose. You gave yourself and other people the benefit of the doubt.

My mother had that capacity. I'd admired, envied, and benefited infinitely from its presence. As she related the story of Garth's death and my brother's anger and remorse, her tone was uncompromisingly bitter. No slack, no margin of doubt was being granted to the forces that destroyed Garth and still pursued her son. She had exhausted her reserves of understanding and compassion. The long view supplied the same ugly picture as the short. She had an enemy now. It was that revealed truth that had given the conversation its edge, its impact. *They* had killed Garth, and his dying had killed part of her son; so the battle lines were drawn. Irreconcilably. Absolutely. The backside of John French's motto had come into play. Giving someone the benefit of the doubt was also giving him enough rope to hang himself. If a person takes advantage of the benefit of the doubt and keeps on taking and taking, one day the rope plays out. The piper must be paid. If you've been the one giving, it becomes incumbent on you to grip your end tight and take away. You turn the other cheek, but slowly, cautiously, and keep your fist balled up at your side. If your antagonist decides to smack rather than kiss you or leave you alone, you make sure you get in the first blow. And make sure it's hard enough to knock him down.

Before she told Garth's story, my mother had already changed, but it took years for me to realize how profoundly she hated what had been done to Garth and then Robby. The gentleness of my grandfather, like his fair skin and good French hair, had been passed down to my mother. Gentleness styled the way she thought, spoke, and moved in the world. Her easy disposition and sociability masked the intensity of her feelings. Her attitude to authority of any kind, doctors, clerks, police, bill collectors, newscasters, whites in general partook of her constitutional gentleness. She wasn't docile or cowed. The power other people possessed or believed they possessed didn't frighten her; she accommodated herself, offered something they could accept as deference but that was in fact the same resigned, alert attention she paid to roaches or weather or poverty, any of the givens outside herself that she couldn't do much about. She never engaged in public tests of will, never pushed herself or her point of view on people she didn't know. Social awkwardness embarrassed her. Like most Americans she didn't like paying taxes, was suspicious of politicians, resented the disparity between big and little people in our society and the double standard that allowed big shots to get away with murder. She paid particular attention to news stories that reinforced her basic political assumption that power corrupts. On the other hand she knew the world was a vale of tears and one's strength, granted by God to deal with life's inevitable calamities, should not be squandered on small stuff.

In spite of all her temperamental and philosophic resistance to extremes, my mother would be radicalized. What the demonstrations, protest marches, and slogans of the sixties had not effected would be accomplished by Garth's death and my brother's troubles. She would become an aggressive, acid critic of the status quo in all its forms: from the President ("If it wasn't for that rat I'd have a storm door to go with the storm windows but he cut the program") on down to bank tellers ("I go there every Friday and I'm one of the few black faces she sees all day and she knows me as well as she knows that wart on her cheek but she'll still make me show my license before she'll cash my check"). A son she loved would be pursued, captured, tried, and imprisoned by the forces of law and order. Throughout the ordeal her love for him wouldn't change, couldn't change. His crime tested her love and also tested the nature, the intent of the forces arrayed against her son. She had to make a choice. On one side were the stark facts of his crime: robbery, murder, flight; her son an outlaw, a fugitive; then a prisoner. On the other side the guardians of society, the laws, courts, police, judges, and keepers who were responsible for punishing her son's transgression.

She didn't invent the two sides and initially didn't believe there couldn't be a middle ground. She extended the benefit of the doubt. Tried to situate herself somewhere in between, acknowledging the evil of her son's crime while simultaneously holding on to the fact that he existed as a human being before, after, and during the crime he'd committed. He'd done wrong but he was still Robby and she'd always be his mother. Strangely, on the dark side, the side of the crime and its terrible consequences, she would find room to exercise her love. As negative as the elements were, a life taken, the grief of the survivors, suffering, waste, guilt, remorse, the scale was human; she could apply her sense of right and wrong. Her life to that point had equipped her with values, with tools for sorting out and coping with disaster. So she would choose to make her fight there, on treacherous yet familiar ground — familiar since her son was there — and she could place herself, a woman, a mother, a grieving, bereaved human being, there beside him.

Nothing like that was possible on the other side. The legitimacy of the other side was grounded not in her experience of life, but in a set of rules seemingly framed to sidestep, ignore, or replace her sense of reality. Accepting the version of reality encoded in *their* rules would be like stepping into a cage and locking herself in. Definitions of her son, herself, of need and frailty and mercy, of blackness and redemption and justice had all been neatly formulated. No need here for her questions, her uncertainty, her fear, her love. Everything was clean and clear. No room for her sense that things like good and evil, right and wrong bleed into each other and create a dreadful margin of ambiguity no one could name but could only enter, enter at the risk of everything because everything is at stake and no one on earth knows what it means to enter or what will happen if and when the testing of the margin is over.

She could love her son, accept his guilt, accept the necessity of punishment, suffer with him, grow with him past the stage of blaming everyone but himself for his troubles, grieve with him when true penitence began to exact its toll. Though she might wish penance and absolution could be achieved in private, without the intervention of a prison sentence, she understood dues must be paid. He was her son but he was also a man who had committed a robbery in the course of which another woman's son had been killed. What would appall her and what finally turned her against the forces of law and order was the incapacity of the legal system to grant her son's humanity. "Fair" was the word she used — a John French word. She expected them to treat Robby fair. Fairness was what made her willing to give him up to punishment even though her love screamed no and her hands clung to his shoulders. Fairness was what she expected from the other side in their dealings with her and her son.

She could see their side, but they steadfastly refused to see hers. And when she realized fairness was not forthcoming, she began to hate. In the lack of reciprocity, in the failure to grant that Robby was first a man, then a man who had done wrong, the institutions and individuals who took over control of his life denied not only his humanity but the very existence of the world that had nurtured him and nurtured her — the world of touching, laughing, suffering black people that established Robby's claim to something more than a number.

Mom expects the worst now. She's peeped their hole card. She understands they have a master plan that leaves little to accident, that most of the ugliest things happening to black people are not accidental but the predictable results of the working of the plan. What she learned about authority, about law and order didn't make sense at first. It went against her instincts, what she wanted to believe, against the generosity she'd observed in her father's interactions with other Homewood people. He was fair. He'd pick up the egg rolls he loved from the back kitchen door of Mr. Wong's restaurant and not blame Wong, his old talking buddy and card-playing crony, for not serving black people in his restaurant. Wong had a family and depended on white folks to feed them, so Wong didn't have any choice and neither did John French if he wanted those incredible egg rolls. He treated everyone, high and low, the same. He said what he meant and meant what he said. John French expected no more from other people than he expected from himself. And he'd been known to mess up many a time, but that was him, that was John French, no better, no worse than any man who pulls on his britches one leg at a time. He needed a little slack, needed the benefit of that blind eye people who love, or people who want to get along with other people, must learn to cast. John French was grateful for the slack, so was quick to extend it to others. Till they crossed him.

My mother had been raised in Homewood. The old Homewood. Her relations with people in that close-knit, homogeneous community were based on trust, mutual respect, common spiritual and material concerns. Face-to-face contact, shared language and values, a large fund of communal experience rendered individual lives extremely visible in Homewood. Both a person's self-identity ("You know who you are") and accountability ("Other people know who you are") were firmly established.

If one of the Homewood people said, "That's the French girl" or, "There goes John French's daughter," a portrait with subtle shading and complex resonance was painted by the words. If the listener addressed was also a Homewood resident, the speaker's voice located the young woman passing innocently down Tioga Street in a world invisible to outsiders. A French girl was somebody who lived in Cassina Way, somebody you didn't fool with or talk nasty to. Didn't speak to at all except in certain places or on certain occasions. French girls were church girls, Homewood African Methodist Episcopal Zion Sunday-school-picnic and social-event young ladies. You wouldn't find them hanging around anywhere without escorts or chaperones. French girls had that fair, light, bright, almost white redbone complexion and fine blown hair and nice big legs but all that was to be appreciated from a distance because they were nice girls and because they had this crazy daddy who wore a big brown country hat and gambled and drank wine and once ran a man out of town, ran him away without ever laying a hand on him or making a bad-mouthed threat, just cut his eyes a certain way when he said the man's name and the word went out and the man who had cheated a drunk John French with loaded dice was gone. Just like that. And there was the time Elias Brown was cleaning his shotgun in his backyard. Brown had his double-barreled shotgun across his knees and a jug of Dago Red on the ground beside him and it was a Saturday and hot and Brown was sweating through his BVD undershirt and paying more attention to the wine than he was to the gun. Next thing you know, *Boom!* Off it goes and buckshot sprayed down Cassina Way, and it's Saturday and summer like I said, so chillens playing everywhere but God watches over fools and babies so nobody hit bad. Nobody hit at all except the little French girl, Geraldine, playing out there in the alley and she got nicked in her knee. Barely drew blood. A sliver of that buckshot musta ricocheted off the cobblestones and cut her knee. Thank Jesus she the only one hit and she ain't hit bad. Poor Elias Brown don't quite know what done happened till some the mens run over in his yard and snatch the gun and shake the wine out his head. What you doing, fool? Don't you know no better all those children running round here? Coulda killed one these babies. Elias stone drunk and don't hear nothing, see nothing till one the men say French girl. Nicked the little French girl, Geraldine. Then Elias woke up real quick. His knees, his dusty butt, everything he got starts to trembling and his eyes get big as dinner plates. Then he's gone like a turkey through the corn. Nobody seen Elias for a week. He's in Ohio at his sister's next time anybody hear anything about Elias. He's cross there in Ohio and still shaking till he git word John French ain't after him. It took three men gon over there telling the same story to get Elias back to Homewood. John French ain't mad. He *was* mad but he ain't mad now. Little girl just nicked is all and French ain't studying you, Brown.

You heard things like that in Homewood names. Rules of etiquette, thumbnail character sketches, a history of the community. A dire warning to get back could be coded into the saying of a person's name, and a further inflection of the speaker's voice could tell you to ignore the facts, forget what he's just reminded you to remember and go on. Try your luck.

Because Homewood was self-contained and possessed such a strong personality, because its people depended less on outsiders than they did on each other for so many of their most basic satisfactions, they didn't notice the net settling over their community until it was already firmly in place. Even though the strands of the net — racial discrimination, economic exploitation, white hate and fear — had existed time out of mind, what people didn't notice or chose not to notice was that the net was being drawn tighter, that ruthless people outside the community had the power to choke the life out of Homewood, and as soon as it served their interests would do just that. During the final stages, as the net closed like a fist around Homewood, my mother couldn't pretend it wasn't there. But instead of setting her free, the truth trapped her in a cage as tangible as the iron bars of Robby's cell.

Some signs were subtle, gradual. The A & P started to die. Nobody mopped filth from the floors. Nobody bothered to restock empty shelves. Fewer and fewer white faces among the shoppers. A plate-glass display window gets broken and stays broken. When they finally close the store, they paste the going-out-of-business notice over the jagged, taped crack. Other signs as blatant, as sudden as fire engines and patrol cars breaking your sleep, screaming through the dark Homewood streets. First Garth's death, then Robby's troubles brought it all home. My mother realized her personal unhappiness and grief were inseparable from what was happening *out there*. Out there had never been further away than the thousand insults and humiliations she had disciplined herself to ignore. What she had deemed petty, not worth bothering about, were strings of the net just as necessary, as effective as the most dramatic intrusions into her life. She decided to stop letting things go by. No more benefit of the doubt. Doubt had been cruelly excised. She decided to train herself to be as wary, as unforgiving as she'd once been ready to live and let live. My mother wouldn't become paranoid, not even overtly prickly or bristling. That would have been too contrary to her style, to what her blood and upbringing had instilled. The change was inside. What she thought of people. How she judged situations. Things she'd say or do startled me, set me back on my heels because I didn't recognize my mother in them. I couldn't account for the stare of pure unadulterated hatred she directed at the prison guard when he turned away from her to answer the phone before handing her the rest-room key she'd requested, the vehemence with which she had cussed Richard Nixon for paying no taxes when she, scraping by on an income of less than four thousand dollars a year, owed the IRS three hundred dollars.

Garth's death and Robby's troubles were at the center of her new vision. Like a prism, they caught the light, transformed it so she could trace the seemingly random inconveniences and impositions coloring her life to their source in a master plan.

I first heard Garth's story in the summer of 1975, the summer my wife carried our daughter Jamila in her belly, the summer before the robbery and killing. The story contained all the clues I'm trying to decipher now. Sitting in the kitchen vaguely distracted by gospel music from the little clock radio atop the table, listening as my mother expressed her sorrow, her indignation at the way Garth was treated, her fears for my brother, I was hearing a new voice. Something about the voice struck me then, but I missed what was novel and crucial. I'd lost my Homewood ear. Missed all the things unsaid that invested her words with special urgency. People in Homewood often ask: You said that to say what? The impacted quality of an utterance either buries a point too obscurely or insists on a point so strongly that the listener wants the meat of the message repeated, wants it restated clearly so it stands alone on its own two feet. If I'd been alert enough to ask that question, to dig down to the root and core of Garth's story after my mother told it, I might have understood sooner how desperate and dangerous Homewood had become. Six years later my brother was in prison, and when he began the story of his troubles with Garth's death, a circle completed itself; Robby was talking to me, but I was still on the outside, looking in.

I WAS HEARING A NEW VOICE. SOMETHING ABOUT THE VOICE STRUCK ME THEN, BUT I MISSED WHAT WAS NOVEL AND CRUCIAL. I'D LOST MY HOMEWOOD EAR.

That day six years later, I talked with Robby three hours, the maximum allotted for weekday visits with a prisoner. It was the first time in life we'd ever talked that long. Probably two and a half hours longer than the longest, unbroken, private conversation we'd ever had. And it had taken guards, locks, and bars to bring us together. The ironies of the situation, the irony of that fact, escaped neither of us.

I listened mostly, interrupting my brother's story a few times to clarify dates or names. Much of what he related was familiar. The people, the places. Even the voice, the words he chose were mine in a way. We're so alike, I kept thinking, anticipating what he would say next, how he would say it, filling in naturally, easily with my words what he left unsaid. Trouble was our minds weren't interchangeable. No more than our bodies. The guards wouldn't have allowed me to stay in my brother's place. He was the criminal. I was the visitor from outside. Different as night and day. As Robby talked I let myself forget that difference. Paid too much attention to myself listening and lost some of what he was saying. What I missed would have helped define the difference. But I missed it. It was easy to half listen. For both of us to pretend to be closer than we were. We needed the closeness. We were brothers. In the prison visiting lounge I acted toward my brother the way I'd been acting toward him all my life, heard what I wanted to hear, rejected the rest.

When Robby talked, the similarity of his Homewood and mine was a trap. I could believe I knew exactly what he was describing. I could relax into his story, walk down Dunfermline or Tioga, see my crippled grandmother sitting on the porch of the house on Finance, all the color her pale face had lost blooming in the rosebush beneath her in the yard, see Robby in the downstairs hall of the house on Marchand, rapping with his girl on the phone, which sat on a three-legged stand just inside the front door. I'd slip unaware out of his story into one of my own. I'd be following him, an obedient shadow, then a cloud would blot the sun and I'd be gone, unchained, a dark form still skulking behind him but no longer in tow.

The hardest habit to break, since it was the habit of a lifetime, would be listening to myself listen to him. That habit would destroy any chance of seeing my brother on his terms; and seeing him in his terms, learning his terms, seemed the whole point of learning his story. However numerous and comforting the similarities, we were different. The world had seized on the difference, allowed me room to thrive, while he'd been forced into a cage. Why did it work out that way? What was the nature of the difference? Why did it haunt me? Temporarily at least, to answer these questions, I had to root my fiction-writing self out of our exchanges. I had to teach myself to listen. Start fresh, clear the pipes, resist too facile an identification, tame the urge to take off with Robby's story and make it my own.

I understood all that, but could I break the habit? And even if I did learn to listen, wouldn't there be a point at which I'd have to take over the telling? Wasn't there something fundamental in my writing, in my capacity to function, that depended on flight, on escape? Wasn't another person's skin a hiding place, a place to work out anxiety, to face threats too intimidating to handle in any other fashion? Wasn't writing about people a way of exploiting them?

A stranger's gait, or eyes, or a piece of clothing can rivet my attention. Then it's like falling down to the center of the earth. Not exactly fear or panic but an uneasy, uncontrollable momentum, a sense of being swallowed, engulfed in blackness that has no dimensions, no fixed points. That boundless, incarcerating black hole is another person. The detail grabbing me functions as a door and it swings open and I'm drawn, sucked, pulled in head over heels till suddenly I'm righted again, on track again and the peculiarity, the ordinariness of the detail that usurped my attention becomes a window, a way of seeing out of another person's eyes, just as for a second it had been my way in. I'm scooting along on short, stubby legs and the legs are not anybody else's and certainly not mine, but I feel for a second what it's like to motor through the world atop these peculiar duck thighs and foreshortened calves and I know how wobbly the earth feels under those run-over-at-the-heel, split-seamed penny loafers. Then just as suddenly I'm back. I'm me again, slightly embarrassed, guilty because I've been trespassing and don't know how long I've been gone or if anybody noticed me violating somebody else's turf.

Do I write to escape, to make a fiction of my life? If I can't be trusted with the story of my own life, how could I ask my brother to trust me with his?

The business of making a book together was new for both of us. Difficult. Awkward. Another book could be constructed about a writer who goes to a prison to interview his brother but comes away with his own story. The conversations with his brother would provide a stage for dramatizing the writer's tortured relationship to other people, himself, his craft. The writer's motives, the issue of exploitation, the inevitable conflict between his role as detached observer and his responsibility as a brother would be at the center of such a book. When I stopped hearing Robby and listened to myself listening, that kind of book shouldered its way into my consciousness. I didn't like the feeling. That book compromised the intimacy I wanted to achieve with my brother. It was as obtrusive as the Wearever pen in my hand, the little yellow sheets of Yard Count paper begged from the pad of the guard in charge of overseeing the visiting lounge. The borrowed pen and paper (I was not permitted into the lounge with my own) were necessary props. I couldn't rely on memory to get my brother's story down and the keepers had refused my request to use a tape recorder, so there I was. Jimmy Olson, cub reporter, poised on the edge of my seat, pen and paper at ready, asking to be treated as a brother.

We were both rookies. Neither of us had learned very much about sharing our feelings with other family members. At home it had been assumed that each family member possessed deep, powerful feelings and that very little or nothing at all needed to be said about these feelings because we all were stuck with them and talk wouldn't change them. Your particular feelings were a private matter and family was a protective fence around everybody's privacy. Inside the perimeter of the fence each family member resided in his or her own quarters. What transpired in each dwelling was mainly the business of its inhabitant as long as nothing generated within an individual unit threatened the peace or safety of the whole. None of us knew how traditional West African families were organized or what values the circular shape of their villages embodied, but the living arrangements we had worked out among ourselves resembled the ancient African patterns. You were granted emotional privacy, independence, and space to commune with your feelings. You were encouraged to deal with as much as you could on your own, yet you never felt alone. The high wall of the family, the collective, communal reality of other souls, other huts like yours eliminated some of the dread, the isolation experienced when you turned inside and tried to make sense out of the chaos of your individual feelings. No matter how grown you thought you were or how far you believed you'd strayed, you knew you could cry *Mama* in the depths of the night and somebody would tend to you. Arms would wrap round you, a soft soothing voice lend its support. If not a flesh-and-blood mother then a mother in the form of song or story or a surrogate, Aunt Geral, Aunt Martha, drawn from the network of family numbers.

Privacy was a bridge between you and the rest of the family. But you had to learn to control the traffic. You had to keep it uncluttered, resist the temptation to cry wolf. Privacy in our family was a birthright, a union card granted with family membership. The card said you're one of us but also certified your separateness, your obligation to keep much of what defined your separateness to yourself.

An almost aesthetic consideration's involved. Okay, let's live together. Let's each build a hut and for security we'll arrange the individual dwellings in a circle and then build an outer ring to enclose the whole village. Now your hut is your own business, but let's in general agree on certain outward forms. Since we all benefit from the larger pattern, let's compromise, conform to some degree on the materials, the shape of each unit. Because symmetry and harmony please the eye. Let's adopt a style, one that won't crimp anybody's individuality, one that will buttress and enhance each member's image of what a living place should be.

So Robby and I faced each other in the prison visiting lounge as familiar strangers, linked by blood and time. But how do you begin talking about blood, about time? He's been inside his privacy and I've been inside mine, and neither of us in thirty-odd years had felt the need to exchange more than social calls. We shared the common history, values, and style developed within the tall stockade of family, and that was enough to make us care about each other, enough to insure a profound depth of mutual regard, but the feelings were undifferentiated. They'd seldom been tested specifically, concretely. His privacy and mine had been exclusive, sanctioned by family traditions. Don't get too close. Don't ask too many questions or give too many answers. Don't pry. Don't let what's inside slop out on the people around you.

The stories I'd sent to Robby were an attempt to reveal what I thought about certain matters crucial to us both. Our shared roots and destinies. I wanted him to know what I'd been thinking and how that thinking was drawing me closer to him. I was banging on the door of his privacy. I believed I'd shed some of my own.

We were ready to talk. It was easy to begin. Impossible. We were neophytes, rookies. I was a double rookie. A beginner at this kind of intimacy, a beginner at trying to record it. My double awkwardness kept getting in the way. I'd hidden the borrowed pen by dropping my hand below the level of the table where we sat. Now when in hell would be the right moment to raise it? To use it? I had to depend on my brother's instincts, his generosity. I had to listen, listen.

Luckily there was catching up to do. He asked me about my kids, about his son, Omar, about the new nieces and nephews he'd never seen. That helped. Reminded us we were brothers. We got on with it. Conditions in the prisons. Robby's state of mind. The atmosphere behind the prison walls had been particularly tense for over a year. A group of new, younger guards had instituted a get-tough policy. More strip searches, cell shakedowns, strict enforcement of penny-ante rules and regulations. Grown men treated like children by other grown men. Inmates yanked out of line and punished because a button is undone or hair uncombed. What politicians demanded in the free world was being acted out inside the prison. A crusade, a war on crime waged by a gang of gung-ho guards against men who were already certified casualties, prisoners of war. The walking wounded being beaten and shot up again because they're easy targets. Robby's closest friends, including Cecil and Mike, are in the hole. Others who were considered potential troublemakers had been transferred to harsher prisons. Robby was warned by a guard. We ain't caught you in the shit yet, but we will. We know what you're thinking and we'll catch you in it. Or put you in it. Got your buddies and we'll get you.

The previous summer, 1980, a prisoner, Leon Patterson, had been asphyxiated in his cell. He was an asthma sufferer, a convicted murderer who depended on medication to survive the most severe attacks of his illness. On a hot August afternoon when the pollution index had reached its highest count of the summer, Patterson was locked in his cell in a cell block without windows and little air. At four o'clock, two hours after he'd been confined to the range, he began to call for help. Other prisoners raised the traditional distress signal, rattling tin cups against the bars of their cells. Patterson's cries for help became screams, and his fellow inmates beat on the bars and shouted with him. Over an hour passed before any guards arrived. They carted away Patterson's limp body. He never revived and was pronounced dead at 10:45 that evening. His death epitomized the polarization in the prison. Patterson was seen as one more victim of the guards' inhumanity. A series of incidents followed in the ensuing year, hunger strikes, melees between guards and prisoners, culminating in a near massacre when the dog days of August hung once more over the prison.

One of the favorite tactics of the militant guards was grabbing a man from the line as the prisoners moved single-file through an archway dividing the recreation yard from the main cell blocks. No reason was given or needed. It was a simple show of force, a reminder of the guards' absolute power, their right to treat the inmates any way they chose, and do it with impunity. A sit-down strike in the prison auditorium followed one of the more violent attacks on an inmate. The prisoner who had resisted an arbitrary seizure and strip search was smacked in the face. He punched back and the guards jumped him, knocked him to the ground with their fists and sticks. The incident took place in plain view of over a hundred prisoners and it was the last straw. The victim had been provoked, assaulted, and surely would be punished for attempting to protect himself, for doing what any man would and should do in similar circumstances. The prisoner would suffer again. In addition to the physical beating they'd administered, the guards would attack the man's record. He'd be written up. A kangaroo court would take away his *good time*, thereby lengthening the period he'd have to wait before becoming eligible for probation or parole. Finally, on the basis of the guards' testimony he'd probably get a sixty-day sojourn in the hole. The prisoners realized it was time to take a stand. What had happened to one could happen to any of them. They rushed into the auditorium and locked themselves in. The prisoners held out till armed state troopers and prison guards in riot gear surrounded the building. Given the mood of that past year and the unmistakable threat in the new warden's voice as he repeated through a loudspeaker his refusal to meet with the prisoners and discuss their grievances, everybody inside the building knew that the authorities meant business, that the forces of law and order would love nothing better than an excuse to turn the auditorium into a shooting gallery. The strike was broken. The men filed out. A point was driven home again. Prisoners have no rights the keepers are bound to respect.

That was how the summer had gone. Summer was bad enough in the penitentiary in the best of times. Warm weather stirred the prisoners' blood. The siren call of the streets intensified. Circus time. The street blooming again after the long, cold winter. People outdoors. On their stoops. On the corners. In bright summer clothes or hardly any clothes at all. The free-world sounds and sights more real as the weather heats up. Confinement a torture. Each cell a hotbox. The keepers take advantage of every excuse to keep you out of the yard, to deprive you of the simple pleasure of a breeze, the blue sky. Why? So that the pleasant weather can be used as a tool, a boon to be withheld. So punishment has a sharper edge. By a perverse turn of the screw something good becomes something bad. Summer a bitch at best, but this past summer as the young turks among the guards ran roughshod over the prisoners, the prison had come close to blowing, to exploding like a piece of rotten fruit in the sun. And if the lid blew, my brother knew he'd be one of the first to die. During any large-scale uprising, in the first violent, chaotic seconds no board of inquiry would ever be able to reconstruct, scores would be settled. A bullet in the back of the brain would get rid of troublemakers, remove potential leaders, uncontrollable prisoners the guards hated and feared. You were supremely eligible for a bullet if the guards couldn't press your button. If they hadn't learned how to manipulate you, if you couldn't be bought or sold, if you weren't into drug and sex games, if you weren't cowed or depraved, then you were a threat.

Robby understood that he was sentenced to die. That all sentences were death sentences. If he didn't buckle under, the guards would do everything in their power to kill him. If he succumbed to the pressure to surrender dignity, self-respect, control over his own mind and body, then he'd become a beast, and what was good in him would die. The death sentence was unambiguous. The question for him became: How long could he survive in spite of the death sentence? Nothing he did would guarantee his safety. A disturbance in a cell block halfway across the prison could provide an excuse for shooting him and dumping him with the other victims. Anytime he was ordered to go with guards out of sight of other prisoners, his escorts could claim he attacked them, or attempted to escape. Since the flimsiest pretext would make murdering him acceptable, he had no means of protecting himself. Yet to maintain sanity, to minimize their opportunities to destroy him, he had to be constantly vigilant. He had to discipline himself to avoid confrontations, he had to weigh in terms of life and death every decision he made; he had to listen and obey his keepers' orders, but he also had to determine in certain threatening situations whether it was better to say no and keep himself out of a trap or take his chances that this particular summons was not the one inviting him to his doom. Of course to say no perpetuated his reputation as one who couldn't be controlled, a bad guy, a guy you never turn your back on, one of the prisoners out to get the guards. That rap made you more dangerous in the keepers' eyes and therefore increased the likelihood they'd be frightened into striking first. Saying no put you in no less jeopardy than going along with the program. Because the program was contrived to kill you. Directly or indirectly, you knew where you were headed. What you didn't know was the schedule. Tomorrow. Next week. A month. A minute. When would one of them get itchy, get beyond waiting a second longer? Would there be a plan, a contrived incident, a conspiracy they'd talk about and set up as they drank coffee in the guards' room or would it be the hair-trigger impulse of one of them who held a grudge, harbored an antipathy so elemental, so irrational that it could express itself only in a burst of pure, unrestrained violence?

If you're Robby and have the will to survive, these are the possibilities you must constantly entertain. Vigilance is the price of survival. Beneath the vigilance, however, is a gnawing awareness boiling in the pit of your stomach. You can be as vigilant as you're able, you can keep fighting the good fight to survive, and still your fate is out of your hands. If they decide to come for you in the morning, that's it. Your ass is grass and those minutes, and hours, days and years you painfully stitched together to put off the final reckoning won't matter at all. So the choice, difficult beyond words, to say yes or say no is made in light of the knowledge that in the end neither your yes nor your no matters. Your life is not in your hands.

The events, the atmosphere of the summer had brought home to Robby the futility of resistance. Power was absurdly apportioned all on one side. To pretend you could control your own destiny was a joke. You learned to laugh at your puniness, as you laughed at the stink of your farts lighting up your cell. Like you laughed at the seriousness of the masturbation ritual that romanticized, cloaked in darkness and secrecy, the simple, hungry shaking of your penis in your fist. You had no choice, but you always had to decide to go on or stop. It had been a stuttering, stop, start, maybe, fuck it, bitch of a summer, and now, for better or worse, we were starting up something else. Robby backtracks his story from Garth to another beginning, the house on Copeland Street in Shadyside where we lived when he was born.

I know that had something to do with it. Living in Shadyside with only white people around. You remember how it was. Except for us and them couple other families it was a all-white neighborhood. I got a thing about black. See, black was like the forbidden fruit. Even when we went to Freed's in Homewood, Geraldine and them never let me go no farther than the end of the block. All them times I stayed over there I didn't go past Mr. Conrad's house by the vacant lot or the other corner where Billy Shields and them stayed. Started to wondering what was so different about a black neighborhood. I was just a little kid and I was curious.

I really wanted to know why they didn't want me finding out what was over there. Be playing with the kids next door to Freed, you know, Sonny and Gumpy and them, but all the time I'm wondering what's round the corner, what's up the street. Didn't care if it was *bad* or good or dangerous or what, I had to find out. If it's something bad I figured they would have told me, tried to scare me off. But nobody said nothing except, No. Don't you go no farther than the corner. Then back home in Shadyside nothing but white people so I couldn't ask nobody what was special about black. Black was a mystery and in my mind I decided I'd find out what it was all about. Didn't care if it killed me, I was going to find out.

One time, it was later, I was close to starting high school, I overheard Mommy and Geraldine and Sissy talking in Freed's kitchen. They was talking about us moving from Shadyside back to Homewood. The biggest thing they was worried about was me. How would it be for me being in Homewood and going to Westinghouse? I could tell they was scared. Specially Mom. You know how she is. She didn't want to move. Homewood scared her. Not so much the place but how I'd act if I got out there in the middle of it. She already knew I was wild, hard to handle. There'd be too much mess for me to get into in Homewood. She could see trouble coming.

And she was right. Me and trouble hooked up. See, it was a question of being somebody. Being my own person. Like youns had sports and good grades sewed up. Wasn't nothing I could do in school or sports that youns hadn't done already. People said, Here comes another Wideman. He's gon be a good student like his brothers and sister. That's the way it was spozed to be. I was another Wideman, the last one, the baby, and everybody knew how I was spozed to act. But something inside me said no. Didn't want to be like the rest of youns. Me, I had to be a rebel. Had to get out from under youns' good grades and do. Way back then I decided I wanted to be a star. I wanted to make it big. My way. I wanted the glamour. I wanted to sit high up.

Figured out school and sports wasn't the way. I got to thinking my brothers and sister was squares. Loved youall but wasn't no room left for me. Had to figure out a new territory. I had to be a rebel.

Along about junior high I discovered Garfield. I started hanging out up on Garfield Hill. You know, partying and stuff in Garfield cause that's where the niggers was. Garfield was black, and I finally found what I'd been looking for. That place they was trying to hide from me. It was heaven. You know. Hanging out with the fellows. Drinking wine and trying anything else we could get our hands on. And the ladies. Always a party on the weekends. Had me plenty sweet little soft-leg Garfield ladies. Niggers run my butt off that hill more than a couple times behind messing with somebody's piece but I'd be back next weekend. Cause I'd found heaven. Looking back now, wasn't much to Garfield. Just a rinky-dink ghetto up on a hill, but it was the street. I'd found my place.

Having a little bit of a taste behind me I couldn't wait to get to Homewood. In a way I got mad with Mommy and the rest of them. Seemed to me like they was trying to hold me back from a good time. Seemed like they just didn't want me to have no fun. That's when I decided I'd go on about my own business. Do it my way. Cause I wasn't getting no slack at home. They still expected me to be like my sister and brothers. They didn't know I thought youns was squares. Yeah. I knew I was hipper and groovier than youns ever thought of being. Streetwise, into something. Had my own territory and I was bad. I was a rebel. Wasn't following in nobody's footsteps but my own. And I was a hip cookie, you better believe it. Wasn't a hipper thing out there than your brother, Rob. I couldn't wait for them to turn me loose in Homewood.

Me being the youngest and all, the baby in the family, people always said, ain't he cute. That Robby gon be a ladykiller. Been hearing that mess since day one so ain't no surprise I started to believing it. Youns had me pegged as a lady's man so that's what I was. The girls be talking the same trash everybody else did. Ain't he cute. Be petting me and spoiling me like I'm still the baby of the family and I sure ain't gon tell them stop. Thought I was cute as the girls be telling me. Thought sure enough, I'm gon be a star. I loved to get up and show my behind. Must have been good at it too cause the teacher used to call me up in front of the class to perform. The kids'd get real quiet. That's probably why the teacher got me up. Keep the class quiet while she nods off. Cause they'd listen to me. Sure nuff pay attention.

Performing always come natural to me. Wasn't nervous or nothing. Just get up and do my thing. They liked for me to do impressions. I could mimic anybody. You remember how I'd do that silly stuff around the house. Anybody I'd see on TV or hear on a record I could mimic to a T. Bob Hope, Nixon, Smokey Robinson, Ed Sullivan. White or black. I could talk just like them or sing a song just like they did. The class yell out a famous name and I'd do the one they wanted to hear. If things had gone another way I've always believed I could have made it big in show business. If you could keep them little frisky kids in Liberty School quiet you could handle any audience. Always could sing and do impressions. You remember Mom asking me to do them for you when you came home from college.

I still be performing. Read poetry in the hole. The other fellows get real quiet and listen. Sing down in there too. Nothing else to do, so we entertain each other. They always asking me to sing or read. "Hey, Wideman. C'mon man and do something." Then it gets quiet while they waiting for me to start. Quiet and it's already dark. You in your own cell and can't see nobody else. Barely enough light to read by. The other fellows can hear you but it's just you and them walls so it feels like being alone much as it feels like you're singing or reading to somebody else.

Yeah. I read my own poems sometimes. Other times I just start in on whatever book I happen to be reading. One the books you sent me, maybe. Fellows like my poems. They say I write about the things they be thinking. Say it's like listening to their own self thinking. That's cause we all down there together. What else you gonna do but think of the people on the outside. Your woman. Your kids or folks, if you got any. Just the same old sad shit we all be thinking all the time. That's what I write and the fellows like to hear it.

Funny how things go around like that. Go round and round and keep coming back to the same place. Teacher used to get me up to pacify the class and I'm doing the same thing in prison. You said your teachers called on you to tell stories, didn't they? Yeah. It's funny how much we're alike. In spite of everything I always believed that. Inside. The feeling side. I always believed we was the most alike out of all the kids. I see stuff in your books. The kinds of things I be thinking or feeling.

Your teachers got you up, too. To tell stories. That's funny, ain't it.

I listen to my brother Robby. He unravels my voice. I sit with him in the darkness of the Behavioral Adjustment Unit. My imagination creates something like a giant seashell, enfolding, enclosing us. Its inner surface is velvet-soft and black. A curving mirror doubling the darkness. Poems are Jean Toomer's petals of dusk, petals of dawn. I want to stop. Savor the sweet, solitary pleasure, the time stolen from time in the hole. But the image I'm creating is a trick of the glass. The mirror that would swallow Robby and then chime to me: You're the fairest of them all. The voice I hear issues from a crack in the glass. I'm two or three steps ahead of my brother, making fiction out of his words. Somebody needs to snatch me by the neck and say, Stop. Stop and listen, listen to him.

The Behavioral Adjustment Unit is, as one guard put it, "a maximum-security prison within a maximum-security prison." The "Restricted Housing Unit" or "hole" or "Home Block" is a squat, two-story cement building containing thirty-five six-by-eight-foot cells. The governor of Pennsylvania closed the area in 1972 because of "inhumane conditions," but within a year the hole was reopened. For at least twenty-three hours a day the prisoners are confined to their cells. An hour of outdoor exercise is permitted only on days the guards choose to supervise it. Two meals are served three hours apart, then nothing except coffee and bread for the next twenty-one. The regulation that limits the time an inmate can serve in the BAU for a single offense is routinely sidestepped by the keepers. "Administrative custody" is a provision allowing officials to cage men in the BAU indefinitely. Hunger strikes are one means the prisoners have employed to protest the harsh conditions of the penal unit. Hearings prompted by the strikes have produced no major changes in the way the hole operates. Law, due process, the rights of the prisoners are irrelevant to the functioning of this prison within a prison. Robby was sentenced to six months in the BAU because a guard suspected he was involved in an attempted escape. The fact that a hearing, held six months later, established Robby's innocence, was small consolation since he'd already served his time in the hole.

I LISTEN TO MY BROTHER ROBBY. HE UNRAVELS MY VOICE.

Robby tells me about the other side of being the youngest: Okay, you're everybody's pet and that's boss, but on the other hand you sometimes feel you're the least important. Always last. Always bringing up the rear. You learn to do stuff on your own because the older kids are always busy, off doing their things, and you're too young, left behind because you don't fit, or just because they forget you're back here, at the end, bringing up the rear. But when orders are given out, you sure get your share. "John's coming home this weekend. Clean up your room." Robby remembers being forced to get a haircut on the occasion of one of my visits. Honor thy brother. Get your hair cut, your room rid up, and put on clean clothes. He'll be here with his family and I don't want the house looking like a pigpen.

I have to laugh at the image of myself as somebody to get a haircut for. Robby must have been fit to be tied.

Yeah, I was hot. I mean, you was doing well and all that, but shit, you were my brother. And it was my head. What's my head got to do with you? But you know how Mommy is. Ain't no talking to her when her mind gets set. Anything I tried to say was "talking *back*," so I just went ahead to the man and got my ears lowered.

I was trying to be a rebel but back then the most important thing still was what the grown-ups thought about me. How they felt meant everything. Everything. Me and Tish and Dave were the ones at home then. You was gone and Gene was gone so it was the three of us fighting for attention. And we fought. Every crumb, everytime something got cut up or parceled out or it was Christmas or Easter, we so busy checking out what the other one got wasn't hardly no time to enjoy our own. Like a dogfight or cat fight all the time. And being the youngest I'm steady losing ground most the time. Seemed like to me, Tish and Dave the ones everybody talked about. Seemed like my time would never come. That ain't the way it really was, I know. I had my share cause I was the baby and ain't he cute and lots of times I know I got away with outrageous stuff or got my way cause I could play that baby mess to the hilt. Still it seemed like Dave and Tish was the ones really mattered. Mommy and Daddy and Sis and Geral and Big Otie and Ernie always slipping some change in their pockets or taking them to the store or letting them stay over all night in Homewood. I was a jealous little rascal. Sometimes I thought everybody thought I was just a spoiled brat. I'd say damn all youall. I'd think, Go on and love those square turkeys, but one day I'll be the one coming back with a suitcase full of money and a Cadillac. Go on and love them good grades. Robby gon do it his own way.

See, in my mind I was Superfly. I'd drive up slow to the curb. My hog be half a block long and these fine foxes in the back. Everybody looking when I ease out the door clean and mean. Got a check in my pocket to give to Mom. Buy her a new house with everything in it new. Pay her back for the hard times. I could see that happening as real as I can see your face right now. Wasn't no way it wasn't gon happen. Rob was gon make it big. I'd be at the door, smiling with the check in my hand and Mommy'd be so happy she'd be crying.

Well, it's a different story ain't it. Turned out different from how I used to think it would. The worst thing I did, the thing I feel most guilty behind is stealing Mom's life. It's like I stole her youth. Can't nothing change that.

I can't give back what's gone. Robbing white people didn't cause me to lose no sleep back then. Couldn't feel but so bad about that. How you gon feel sorry when society's so corrupt, when everybody got their hand out or got their hand in somebody else's pocket and ain't no rules nobody listens to if they can get away with breaking them? How you gon apply the rules? It was dog eat dog out there, so how was I spozed to feel sorry if I was doing what everybody else doing. I just got caught is all. I'm sorry about that, and damned sorry that guy Stavros got killed, but as far as what I did, as far as robbing white people, ain't no way I was gon torture myself over that one.

I tried to write Mom a letter. Not too long ago. Should say I did write the letter and put it in a envelope and sent it cause that's what I did, but I be crying so much trying to write it I don't know what wound up in that letter. I wanted Mom to know I knew what I'd done. In a way I wanted to say I was sorry for spoiling her life. After all she did for me I turned around and made her life miserable. That's the wrongest thing I've done and I wanted to say I was sorry but I kept seeing her face while I was writing the letter. I'd see her face and it would get older while I was looking. She'd get this old woman's face all lined and wrinkled and tired about the eyes. Wasn't nothing I could do but watch. Cause I'd done it and knew I done it and all the letters in the world ain't gon change her face. I sit and think about stuff like that all the time. It's better now. I think about other things too. You know like trying to figure what's really right and wrong, but there be days the guilt don't never go away.

I'm the one made her tired, John. And that's my greatest sorrow. All the love that's in me she created. Then I went and let her down.

When you in prison you got plenty of time to think, that's for damned sure. Too much time. I've gone over and over my life. Every moment. Every little thing again and again. I lay down on my bed and watch it happening over and over. Like a movie. I get it all broke down in pieces then I break up the pieces then I take the pieces of the pieces and run them through my hands so I remember every word a person said to me or what I said to them and weigh the words till I think I know what each and every one meant. Then I try to put it back together. Try to understand where I been. Why I did what I did. You got time for that in here. Time's all you got in here.

Going over and over things sometimes you can make sense. You know. Like the chinky-chinky Chinaman sittin' on the fence. You put it together and you think, yes. That's why I did thus and so. Yeah. That's why I lost that job or lost that woman or broke that one's heart. You stop thinking in terms of something being good or being evil, you just try to say this happened because that happened because something else came first. You can spend days trying to figure out just one little thing you did. People out there in the world walk around in a daze cause they ain't got time to think. When I was out there, I wasn't no different. Had this Superfly thing and that was the whole bit. Nobody could tell me nothing.

Seems like I should start the story back in Shadyside. In the house on Copeland Street. Nothing but white kids around. Them little white kids had everything, too. That's what I thought, anyway. Nice houses, nice clothes. They could buy pop and comic books and candy when they wanted to. We wasn't that bad off, but compared to what them little white kids had I always felt like I didn't have nothing. It made me kinda quiet and shy around them. Me knowing all the time I wanted what they had. Wanted it bad. There was them white kids with everything and there was the black world Mommy and them was holding back from me. No place to turn, in a way. I guess you could say I was stuck in the middle. Couldn't have what the white kids in Shadyside had, and I wasn't allowed to look around the corner for something else. So I'd start the story with Shadyside, the house on Copeland.

Another place to start could be December 29, 1950 — the date of Robby's birth. For some reason — maybe my mother and father were feuding, maybe we just happened to be visiting my grandmother's house when my mother's time came — the trip to the hospital to have Robby began from Finance Street, from the house beside the railroad tracks in Homewood. What I remember is the bustle, people rushing around, yelling up and down the stairwell, doors slammed, drawers being opened and shut. A cold winter day so lots of coats and scarves and galoshes. My mother's face was very pale above the dark cloth coat that made her look even bigger than she was, carrying Robby the ninth month. On the way out the front door she stopped and stared back over her shoulder like she'd forgotten something. People just about shoving her out the house. Lots of bustle and noise getting her through the crowded hallway into the vestibule. Somebody opened the front door and December rattled the glass panes. Wind gusting and whistling, everybody calling out last-minute instructions, arrangements, goodbyes, blessings, prayers. My mother's white face calm, hovering a moment above it all as she turned back toward the hall, the stairs where I was planted, halfway to the top. She didn't find me, wasn't looking for me. A thought had crossed her mind and carried her far away. She didn't know why so many hands were rushing her out the door. She didn't hear the swirl of words, the icy blast of wind. Wrapped in a navy-blue coat, either Aunt Aida's or an old one of my grandmother's, which didn't have all its black buttons but stretched double over her big belly, my mother was wondering whether or not she'd turned off the water in the bathroom sink and deciding whether or not she should return up the stairs to check. Something like that crossing her mind, freeing her an instant before she got down to the business of pushing my brother into the world.

Both my grandfathers died on December 28. My grandmother died just after dawn on December 29. My sister lost a baby early in January. The end of the year has become associated with mournings, funerals; New Year's Day arrives burdened by a sense of loss, bereavement. Robby's birthday became tainted. To be born close to Christmas is bad enough in and of itself. Your birthday celebration gets upstaged by the orgy of gift giving on Christmas Day. No matter how many presents you receive on

December 29, they seem a trickle after the Christmas flood. Plus there's too much excitement in too brief a period. Parents and relatives are exhausted, broke, still hung over from the Christmas rush, so there just isn't very much left to work with if your birthday comes four short days after Jesus'. Almost like not having a birthday. Or even worse, like sharing it with your brothers and sister instead of having the private oasis of your very own special day. So Robby cried a lot on his birthdays. And it certainly wasn't a happy time for my mother. Her father, John French, died the year after Robby was born, one day before Robby's birthday. Fifteen years and a day later Mom would lose her mother. The death of the baby my sister was carrying was a final, cruel blow, scaring my mother, jinxing the end of the year eternally. She dreaded the holiday season, expected it to bring dire tidings. She had attempted at one point to consecrate the sad days, employ them as a period of reflection, quietly, privately memorialize the passing of the two people who'd loved her most in the world. But the death of my father's father, then the miscarriage within this jinxed span of days burst the fragile truce my mother had effected with the year's end. She withdraws into herself, anticipates the worst as soon as Christmas decorations begin appearing. In 1975, the year of the robbery and murder, Robby was on the run when his birthday fell. My mother was sure he wouldn't survive the deadly close of the year.

Robby's birthday is smack dab in the middle of the hard time. Planted like a flag to let you know the bad time's arrived. His adult life, the manhood of my mother's last child, begins as she is orphaned, as she starts to become nobody's child.

I named Robby. Before the women hustled my mother out the door into a taxi, I jumped down the stairs, tugged on her coattail, and reminded her she'd promised it'd be Robby. No doubt in my mind she'd bring me home a baby brother. Don't ask me why I was certain. I just was. I hadn't even considered names for a girl. Robby it would be. Robert Douglas. Where the Douglas came from is another story, but the Robert came from me because I liked the sound. Robert was formal, dignified, important. Robert. And that was nearly as nice as the chance I'd have to call my little brother Rob and Robby.

He weighed seven pounds, fourteen ounces. He was born in Allegheny Hospital at 6:30 in the evening, December 29, 1950. His fingers and toes were intact and quite long. He was a plump baby. My grandfather, high on Dago Red, tramped into the maternity ward just minutes after Robby was delivered. John French was delighted with the new baby. Called him Red. A big fat little red nigger.

December always been a bad month for me. One the worst days of my life was in December. It's still one the worst days in my life even after all this other mess. Jail. Running. The whole bit. Been waiting to tell you this a long time. Ain't no reason to hold it back no longer. We into this telling-the-truth thing so mize well tell it all. I'm still shamed, but there it is. You know that TV of youall's got stolen from Mommy's. Well, I did it. Was me and Henry took youall's TV that time and set the house up to look like a robbery. We did it. Took my own brother's TV. Couldn't hardly look you in the face for a long time after we done it. Was pretty sure youall never knowed it was me, but I felt real bad round youns anyway. No way I was gon confess though. Too shamed. A junkie stealing from his own family. See. Used to bullshit myself. Say I ain't like them other guys. They stone junkies, they hooked. Do anything for a hit. But me, I'm Robby. I'm cool. I be believing that shit, too. Fooling myself. You got to bullshit yourself when you falling. Got to do it to live wit yourself. See but where it's at is you be doing any goddam thing for dope. You hooked and that's all's to it. You a stone junkie just like the rest.

Always wondered if you knew I took it.

Mom was suspicious. She knew more than we did then. About the dope. The seriousness of it. Money disappearing from her purse when nobody in the house but the two of you. Finding a syringe on the third floor. Stuff like that she hadn't talked about to us yet. So your stealing the TV was a possibility that came up. But to me it was just one of many. One of the things that could have happened along with a whole lot of other possibilities we sat around talking about. An unlikely possibility as far as I was concerned. Nobody wanted to believe it was you. Mom tried to tell us how it *could* be but in my mind you weren't the one. Haven't thought about it much since then. Except as one of those things that make me worry about Mom living in the house alone. One of those things making Homewood dangerous, tearing it down.

I'm glad I'm finally getting to tell you. I never could get it out. Didn't want you to think I'd steal from my own brother. Specially since all youall done to help me out. You and Judy and the kids. Stealing youall's TV. Don't make no sense, does it? But if we gon get the story down mize well get it all down.

It was a while ago. Do you remember the year?

Nineteen seventy-one was Greens. When we robbed Greens and got in big trouble so it had to be the year before that, 1970. That's when it had to be. Youns was home for Christmas. Mommy and them was having a big party. A reunion kinda cause all the family was together. Everybody home for the first time in a long time. Tish in from Detroit. David back from Philly. Youns in town. My birthday, too. Party spozed to celebrate my birthday too, since it came right along in there after Christmas. Maybe that's why I was feeling so bad. Knowing I had a birthday coming and knowing at the same time how fucked up I was.

Sat in a chair all day. I was hooked for the first time. Good and hooked. Didn't know how low you could feel till that day. Cold and snowing outside. And I got the stone miseries inside. Couldn't move. Weak and sick. Henry too. He was wit me in the house feeling bad as I was. We was two desperate dudes. Didn't have no money and that Jones down on us.

Mommy kept asking, What's wrong with you two? She was on my case all day. What ails you, Robby? Got to be about three o'clock. She come in the room again: You better get up and get some decent clothes on. We're leaving for Geral's soon. See cause it was the day of the big Christmas party. Geral had baked a cake for me. Everybody was together and they'd be singing Happy Birthday Robby and do. The whole bit an I'm spozed to be guest of honor and can't even move out the chair. Here I go again disappointing everybody. Everybody be at Geral's looking for me and Geral had a cake and everything. Where's Robby? He's home dying cause he can't get no dope.

Feeling real sorry for myself but I'm hating me too. Wrapped up in a blanket like some damned Indin. Shivering and wondering how the hell Ima go out in this cold and hustle up some money. Wind be howling. Snow pitching a bitch. There we is. Stuck in the house. Two pitiful junkies. Scheming how we gon get over. Some sorry-assed dudes. But it's comical in a way too, when you look back. To get well we need to get money. And no way we gon get money less we go outside and get sicker than we already is. Mom peeking in the room, getting on my case. Get up out that chair, boy. What are you waiting for? We're leaving in two minutes.

So I says, Go on. I ain't ready. Youns go on. I'll catch up with youns at Geral's.

Mommy standing in the doorway. She can't say too much, cause youns is home and you ain't hip to what's happening. C'mon now. We can't wait any longer for you. Please get up. Geral baked a cake for you. Everybody's looking forward to seeing you.

Seem like she stands there a hour begging me to come. She ain't mad no more. She's begging. Just about ready to cry. Youall in the other room. You can hear what she's saying but you can't see her eyes and they tearing me up. Her eyes begging me to get out the chair and it's tearing me up to see her hurting so bad, but ain't nothing I can do. Jones sitting on my chest and ain't no getup in me.

Youns go head, Mommy. I'll be over in a little while. Be there to blow them candles out and cut the cake.

She knew better. Knew if I didn't come right then, chances was I wasn't coming at all. She knew but wasn't nothing she could do. Guess I knew I was lying too. Nothing in my mind cept copping that dope. Yeah, Mom. Be there to light them candles. I'm grinning but she ain't smiling back. She knows I'm in trouble, deep trouble. I can see her today standing in the doorway begging me to come with youns.

But it ain't meant to be. Me and Henry thought we come up with a idea. Henry's old man had some pistols. We was gon steal em and hock em. Take the money and score. Then we be better. Wouldn't be no big thing to hustle some money, get the guns outa hock. Sneak the pistols back in Henry's house, everything be alright. Wouldn't even exactly be stealing from his old man. Like we just borrowing the pistols till we score and take care business. Henry's old man wouldn't even know his pistols missing. Slick. Sick as we was, thinking we slick.

A hundred times. Mom musta poked her head in the room a hundred times.

What's wrong with you?

Like a drum beating in my head. What's wrong with you? But the other thing is stronger. The dope talking to me louder. It says get you some. It says you ain't never gon get better less you cop.

We waited long as we could but it didn't turn no better outside. Still snowing. Wind shaking the whole house. How we gon walk to Henry's and steal them pistols? Henry live way up on the hill. And the way up Tokay then you still got a long way to go over into the projects. Can't make it. No way we gon climb Tokay. So then what? Everybody's left for Geral's. Then I remembers the TV youns brought. A little portable Sony black-and-white, right? You and Judy sleeping in Mom's room and she has her TV already in there, so the Sony ain't unpacked. Saw it sitting with youall's suitcases over by the dresser. On top the dresser in a box. Remembered it and soon's I did I knew we had to have it. Sick as I was that TV had to go. Wouldn't really be stealing. Borrow it instead of borrowing the pistols. Pawn it. Get straight. Steal some money and buy it back. Just borrowing youall's TV.

Won't take me and Henry no time to rob something and buy back the TV. We stone thieves. Just had to get well first so we could operate. So we took youns TV and set the house up to look like a robbery.

I'm remembering the day. Wondering why it had slipped completely from my mind. I feel like a stranger. Yet as Robby talks, my memory confirms details of his recollection. I admit, yes. I was there. That's the way it was. But *where* was I? Who was I? How did I miss so much?

His confessions make me uncomfortable. Instead of concentrating on what he's revealing, I'm pushed into considering all the things I could be confessing, should be confessing but haven't and probably won't ever. I feel hypocritical. Why should I allow my brother to repose a confidence in me when it's beyond my power to reciprocate? Shouldn't I confess that first? My embarrassment, my uneasiness, the clinical, analytic coldness settling over me when I catch on to what's about to happen.

I have a lot to hide. Places inside myself where truth hurts, where incriminating secrets are hidden, places I avoid, or deny most of the time. Pulling one piece of that debris to the surface, airing it in the light of day doesn't accomplish much, doesn't clarify the rest of what's buried down there. What I feel when I delve deeply into myself is chaos. Chaos and contradiction. So how up front can I get? I'm moved by Robby's secrets. The heart I have is breaking. But what that heart is and where it is I can't say. I can't depend on it, so he shouldn't. Part of me goes out to him. Heartbreak is the sound of ice cracking. Deep. Layers and layers muffling the sound.

I listen but I can't trust myself. I have no desire to tell everything about myself so I resist his attempt to be up front with me. The chaos at my core must be in his. His confession pushes me to think of all the stuff I should lay on him. And that scares the shit out of me. I don't like to feel dirty, but that's how I feel when people try to come clean with me.

Very complicated and very simple too. The fact is I don't believe in clean. What I know best is myself and, knowing what I know about myself, clean seems impossible. A dream. One of those better selves occasionally in the driver's seat but nothing more. Nothing to be depended upon. A self no more or less in control than the countless other selves who each, for a time, seem to be running things.

Chaos is what he's addressing. What his candor, his frankness, his confession echo against. Chaos and time and circumstances and the old news, the bad news that we still walk in circles, each of us trapped in his own little world. Behind bars. Locked in our cells.

But my heart can break, does break listening to my brother's pain. I just remember differently. Different parts of the incident he's describing come back. Strange thing is my recollections return through the door he opened. My memories needed his. Maybe the fact that we recall different things is crucial. Maybe they are foreground and background, propping each other up. He holds on to this or that scrap of the past and I listen to what he's saved and it's not mine, not what I saw or heard or felt. The pressure's on me then. If his version of the past is real, then what's mine? Where does it fit? As he stitches his memories together they bridge a vast emptiness. The time lost enveloping us all. Everything. And hearing him talk, listening to him try to make something of the nothing, challenges me. My sense of the emptiness playing around his words, any words, is intensified. Words are nothing and everything. If I don't speak I have no past. Except the nothing, the emptiness. My brother's memories are not mine, so I have to break into the silence with my own version of the past. My words. My whistling in the dark. His story freeing me, because it forces me to tell my own.

I'm sorry you took so long to forgive yourself. I forgave you a long time ago, in advance for a sin I didn't even know you'd committed. You lied to me. You stole from me. I'm in prison now listening because we committed those sins against each other countless times. I want your forgiveness. Talking about debts you owe me makes me awkward, uneasy. We remember different things. They set us apart. They bring us together searching for what is lost, for the meaning of difference, of distance.

For instance, the Sony TV. It was a present from Mort, Judy's dad. When we told him about the break-in and robbery at Mom's house, he bought us another Sony. Later we discovered the stolen TV was covered by our homeowner's policy even though we'd lost it in Pittsburgh. A claim was filed and eventually we collected around a hundred bucks. Not enough to buy a new Sony but a good portion of the purchase price. Seemed a lark when the check arrived. Pennies from heaven. One hundred dollars free and clear since we already had the new TV Mort had surprised us with. About a year later one of us, Judy or I, was telling the story of the robbery and how well we came out of it. Not until that very moment when I caught a glimpse of Mort's face out of the corner of my eye did I realize what we'd done. Judy remembers urging me to send Mort that insurance check and she probably did, but I have no recollection of an argument. In my mind there had never been an issue. Why shouldn't we keep the money? But when I saw the look of surprise and hurt flash across Mort's face, I knew the insurance check should have gone directly to him. He's a generous man and probably would have refused to accept it, but we'd taken advantage of his generosity by not offering the check as soon as we received it. Clearly the money belonged to him. Unasked, he'd replaced the lost TV. I had treated him like an institution, one of those faceless corporate entities like the gas company or IRS. By then, by the time I saw the surprise in Mort's face and understood how selfishly, thoughtlessly, even corruptly I'd behaved, it was too late. Offering Mort a hundred dollars at that point would have been insulting. Anything I could think of saying sounded hopelessly lame, inept. I'd fucked up. I'd injured someone who'd been nothing but kind and generous to me. Not intentionally, consciously, but that only made the whole business worse in a way because I'd failed him instinctively. The failure was a measure of who I was. What I'd unthinkingly done revealed something about my relationship to Mort I'm sure he'd rather not have discovered. No way I could take my action back, make it up. It reflected a truth about who I was.

That memory pops right up. Compromising, ugly. Ironically, it's also about stealing from a relative. Not to buy dope, but to feed a habit just as self-destructive. The habit of taking good fortune for granted, the habit of blind self-absorption that allows us to believe the world owes us everything and we are not responsible for giving anything in return. Spoiled children. The good coming our way taken as our due. No strings attached.

Lots of other recollections were triggered as Robby spoke of that winter and the lost TV. The shock of walking into a burgled house. How it makes you feel unclean. How quickly you lose the sense of privacy and security a house, any place you call home, is supposed to provide. It's a form of rape. Forced entry, violation, brutal hands defiling what's personal, and precious. The aftershock of seeing your possessions strewn about, broken. Fear gnawing at you because what you thought was safe isn't safe at all. The worst has happened and can happen again. Your sanctuary has been destroyed. Any time you walk in your door you may be greeted by the same scene. Or worse. You may stumble upon the thieves themselves. The symbolic rape of your dwelling place enacted on your actual body. Real screams. Real blood. A knife at your throat. A stranger's weight bearing down.

Mom put it in different words but she was as shaken as I was when we walked into her house after Geral's party. Given what I know now, she must have been even more profoundly disturbed than I imagined. A double bind. Bad enough to be ripped off by anonymous thieves. How much worse if the thief is your son? For Mom the robbery was proof Robby was gone. Somebody else walking round in his skin. Mom was wounded in ways I hadn't begun to guess at. At the root of her pain were your troubles, the troubles stealing you away from her, from all of us. The troubles thick in the air as that snow you are remembering, the troubles falling on your head and mine, troubles I refused to see. . . .

Snowing and the hawk kicking my ass but I got to have it. TV's in a box under my arm and me and Henry walking down Bennett to Homewood Avenue. Need thirty dollars. Thirty dollars buy us two spoons. Looking for One-Arm Ralph, the fence. Looking for him or that big white Cadillac he drives.

Wind blowing snow all up in my face. Thought I's bout to die out there. Nobody on the avenue. Even the junkies and dealers inside today. Wouldn't put no dog out in weather like that. So cold my teeth is chattering, talking to me. No feeling in my hands but I got to hold on to that TV. Henry took it for a little while so's I could put both my hands in my pockets. Henry lookin bad as I'm feeling. Thought I was gon puke. But it's too goddamn cold to puke.

Nobody in sight. Shit and double shit's what I'm thinking. They got to be somewhere. Twenty-four hours a day, seven days a week somebody doing business. Finally we seen One-Arm Ralph come out the Hi Hat.

This TV, man, Lemme hold thirty dollars on it.

Ralph ain't goin for it. Twenty-five the best he say he can do. Twenty-five don't do us no good. It's fifteen each for a spoon. One spoon ain't enough. We begging the dude now. We got to have it, man. Got to get well. We good for the money. Need thirty dollars for two hits. You get your money back.

Too cold to be standing around arguing. The dude go in his pocket and give us the thirty. He been knowing us. He know we good for it. I'm telling him don't sell the TV right away. Hold it till tomorrow we have his money. He say, You don't come back tonight you blow it. Ralph a hard motherfucker and don't want him changing his mind again about the thirty so I say, We'll have the money tonight. Hold the TV till tonight, you get your money.

Now all we got to do is find Goose. Goose always be hanging on the set. Ain't nobody else dealing, Goose be out there for his people. Goose an alright dude, but even Goose ain't out in the street on no day like this. I know the cat stays over the barbershop on Homewood Avenue. Across from Murphy's five-and-ten. I goes round to the side entrance, the alleyway tween Homewood and Kelly. That's how you get to his place. Goose lets me in and I cop. For some reason I turn up the alley and go toward Kelly instead of back to Homewood the way I came in. Don't know why I did it. Being slick. Being scared. Henry's waiting on the avenue for me so I go round the long way just in case somebody pinned him. I can check out the scene before I come back up the avenue. That's probably what I'm thinking. But soon's I turn the corner of Kelly, Bam. Up pops the devil.

Up against the wall, Squirrel.

It's Simon and Garfunkel, two jive undercover cops. We call them that, you dig. Lemme tell you what kind of undercover cops these niggers was. Both of em wearing Big Apple hats and jackets like people be wearing then but they both got on police shoes. Police brogans you could spot a mile away. But they think they slick. They disguised, see. Apple hats and hippy-dip jackets. Everybody knew them chumps was cops. Ride around in a big Continental. Going for bad. Everybody hated them cause everybody knew they in the dope business. They bust a junkie, take his shit and sell it. One them had a cousin. Biggest dealer on the Hill. You know where he getting half his dope. Be selling again what Simon and Garfunkel stole from junkies. Some rotten dudes. Liked to beat on people too. Wasn't bad enough they robbing people. They whipped heads too.

Soon's I turn the corner they got me. Bams me up against the wall. They so lame they think they got Squirrel. Think I'm Squirrel and they gon make a big bust. We got you, Squirrel. They happy, see, cause Squirrel dealing heavy then. Thought they caught them a whole shopping bag of dope.

Wearing my double-breasted pea coat. Used to be sharp but it's raggedy now. Ain't worth shit in cold weather like that. Pockets got holes and the dope dropped down in the lining so they don't find nothing the first time they search me. Can tell they mad. Thought they into something big and don't find shit. Looking at each other like, What the fuck's going on here? We big-time undercover supercops. This ain't spozed to be happening to us. They roughing me up too. Pulling my clothes off and shit. Hands all down in my pockets again. It's freezing and I'm shivering but these fools don't give a fuck. Rip my goddamn pea coat off me. Shaking it. Tearing it up. Find the two packs of dope inside the lining this time. Ain't what they wanted but they pissed off now. Take what they can get now.

What's this, Squirrel? Got your ass now.

Slinging me down the alley. I'm stone sick now. Begging these cats for mercy. Youall got me. You got your bust. Lemme snort some the dope, man. Little bit out each bag. You still got your bust. I'm dying. Little taste fore you lock me up.

Rotten motherfuckers ain't going for it. They see I'm sick as a dog. They know what's happening. Cold as it is, the sweat pouring out me. It's sweat but it's like ice. Like knives cutting me. They ain't give back my coat. Snowing on me and I'm shaking and sweating and sick. They can see all this. They know what's happening but ain't no mercy in these dudes. Henry's cross the street watching them bust me. Tears in his eyes. Ain't nothing he can do. The street's empty. Henry's bout froze too. Watching them sling my ass in their Continental. Never forget how Henry looked that day. All alone on the avenue. Tears froze in his eyes. Seeing him like that was a sad thing. Last thing I saw was him standing there across Homewood Avenue before they slammed me up in the car. Like I was in two places. That's me standing there in the snow. That's me so sick and cold I'm crying in the empty street and ain't a damn thing I can do about it.

By the time they get me down to the Police Station, down to No. 5 in East Liberty, I ain't no more good, sure nuff. Puking. Begging them punks not to bust me. Just bout out my mind. Must have been a pitiful sight. Then's when Henry went to Geral's house and scratched on the window and called David out on the porch. That's when youall found out I was in trouble and had to come down and get me. Right in the middle of the party and everything. Henry's sick too and he been walking round Homewood in the cold didn't know what to do. But he's my man. He got to Geral's so youall could come down and help me. Shamed to go in so he scratched on the window to get Dave on the porch.

Party's over and youns go to Mommy's and on top everything else find the house broke in and the TV gone. All the stuff's going through my mind. I'm on the bottom now. Low as you can go. Had me in a cell and I was lying cross the cot staring at the ceiling. Bars all round. Up cross the ceiling too. Like in a cage in the zoo. Miserable as I could be. All the shit staring me in the face. You're a dope fiend. You stole your brother's TV. You're hurting Mommy again. Hurting everybody. You're sick. You're nothing. Looking up at the bars on the ceiling and wondering if I could tie my belt there. Stick my neck in it. I wanted to be dead.

Tied my belt to the ceiling. Then this guard checking on me he starts to hollering.

What you doing? Hey, Joe. This guy's trying to commit suicide.

They take my clothes. Leave me nothing but my shorts. I'm lying there shivering in my underwear and that's the end. In a cage naked like some goddamn animal. Shaking like a leaf. Thinking maybe I can beat my head against the bars or maybe jump down off the bed head first on the concrete and bust my brains open. Dead already. Nothing already. Low as I can go.

Must have passed out or gone to sleep or something, cause it gets blurry round in here. Don't remember much but they gave back my clothes and took me Downtown and there was a arraignment next morning.

Mommy told me later, one the cops advised her not to pay my bond. Said the best thing for him be to stay in jail awhile. Let him see how it is inside. Scare im. But I be steady beggin. Please, please get me out here. Youns got soft-hearted. Got the money together and paid the bond.

What would have happened if you left me to rot in there till my hearing? Damned if I know. I probably woulda went crazy, for one thing. I do know that. Know I was sick and scared and cried like a baby for Mommy and them to get me out. Don't think it really do no good letting them keep me in there. I mean the jail's a terrible place. You can get everything in jail you get in the street. No different. Cept in jail it's more dangerous cause you got a whole bunch of crazies locked up in one little space. Worse than the street. Less you got buddies in there they tear you up. Got to learn to survive quick. Cause jail be the stone jungle. Call prison the House of Knowledge cause you learns how to be a sure nuff criminal. Come in lame you leave knowing all kinds of evil shit. You learn quick or they eats you up. That's where it's at. So you leave a person in there, chances are they gets worse. Or gets wasted.

But Mom has that soft heart anyway and she ain't leaving her baby boy in no miserable jail. Right or wrong, she ain't leaving me in no place like that. Daddy been talking to Simon and Garfunkel. Daddy's hip, see. He been out there in the street all his life and he knows what's to it. Knows those guys and knows how rotten they is. Ain't no big thing they catch one pitiful little junkie holding two spoons. They wants dealers. They wants to look good Downtown. They wants to bust dealers and cop beaucoup dope so's they can steal it and get rich. Daddy makes a deal with them rats. Says if they drop the charges he'll make me set up Goose. Finger Goose and then stay off Homewood Avenue. Daddy says I'll do that so they let me go.

No way Ima squeal on Goose but I said okay, it's a deal. Soon's I was loose I warned Goose. Pretend like I'm trying to set him up so the cops get off my ass but Goose see me coming know the cops is watching. Helped him, really. Like a lookout. Them dumb motherfuckers got tired playing me. Simon got greedy. Somebody set him up. He got busted for drugs. Still see Garfunkel riding round in his Continental but they took him off the avenue. Too dangerous. Everybody hated them guys.

My lowest day. Didn't know till then I was strung out. That's the first time I was hooked. Started shooting up with Squirrel and Bugs Johnson when Squirrel be coming over to Mom's sometimes. Get up in the morning, go up to the third floor, and shoot up. They was like my teachers. Bugs goes way back. He started with Uncle Carl. Been shooting ever since. Dude's old now. Call him King of the Junkies, he been round so long. Bugs seen it all. You know junkies don't hardly be getting old. Have their day then they gone. Don't see em no more. They in jail or dead. Junkie just don't have no long life. Fast life but your average dopehead ain't round long. Bugs different. He was a pal of Uncle Carl's back in the fifties. Shot up together way back then. Now here he is wit Squirrel and me, still doing this thing. Everybody knows Bugs. He the King.

Let me shoot up wit em but they wouldn't let me go out in the street and hustle wit em. Said I was too young. Too green.

Learning from the King, see. That's how I started the heavy stuff. Me and Squirrel and Bugs first thing in the morning when I got out of bed. Mom was gone to work. They getting themselves ready to hit the street. Make that money. Just like a job. Wasn't no time before I was out there, too. On my own learning to get money for dope. Me and my little mob. We was ready. Didn't take us no time fore we was gangsters. Gon be the next Bugs Johnson. Gon make it to the top.

Don't take long. One day you the King. Next day dope got you and it's the King. You ain't nothing. You lying there naked bout to die and it don't take but a minute. You fall and you gone in a minute. That's the life. That's how it is. And I was out there. I know. Now they got me jammed up in the slammer. That's the way it is. But nobody could tell me nothing then. Hard head. You know. Got to find out for myself. Nobody could tell me nothing. Just out of high school and my life's over and I didn't even know it. Too dumb. Too hardheaded. I was gon do it my way. Youns was square. Youns didn't know nothing. Me, I was gon make mine from the curb. Hammer that rock till I was a supergangster. Be the one dealing the shit. Be the one running the junkies. That's all I knew. Street smarts. Stop being a chump. Forget that nickel-dime hoodlum bag. Be a star. Rise to the top.

You know where that got me. You heard that story. Here I sit today behind that story. Nobody to blame but my ownself. I know that now. But things was fucked up in the streets. You could fall in them streets, Brother. Low. Them streets could snatch you bald-headed and turn you around and wring you inside out. Streets was a bitch. Wake up some mornings and you think you in hell. Think you died and went straight to hell. I know cause I been there. Be days I wished I was dead. Be days worser than that.

QUESTIONS FOR A SECOND READING

1. Wideman frequently interrupts this narrative to talk about the problems he is having as a writer. He says, for example, "The hardest habit to break, since it was the habit of a lifetime, would be listening to myself listen to him. That habit would destroy any chance of seeing my brother on his terms; and seeing him in his terms, learning his terms, seemed the whole point of learning his story" (p. 437). What might Wideman mean by this — listening to himself listen? As you reread "Our Time," note the sections in which Wideman speaks to you directly as a writer. What is he saying? Where and how are you surprised by what he says?

   Wideman calls attention to the problems he faces. How does he try to solve them? Are you sympathetic? Do the solutions work, so far as you are concerned?

2. Wideman says that his mother had a remarkable capacity for "[trying] on the other person's point of view." Wideman tries on another point of view himself, speaking to us in the voice of his brother Robby. As you reread this selection, note the passages spoken in Robby's voice and try to infer Robby's point of view from them. If you look at the differences between John and Robby as evidenced by the ways they use language to understand and represent the world, what do you notice?

3. Wideman talks about three ways he could start Robby's story: with Garth's death, with the house in Shadyside, and with the day of Robby's birth. What difference would it make in each case if he chose one and not the others? What's the point of presenting all three?

ASSIGNMENTS FOR WRITING

1. At several points in the essay, Wideman discusses his position as a writer, telling Robby's story, and he describes the problems he faces in writing this piece (or in "reading" the text of his brother's life). You could read this selection, in other words, as an essay about reading and writing.

   Why do you think Wideman talks about these problems here? Why not keep quiet and hope that no one notices? Choose three or four passages in which Wideman refers directly or indirectly to his work as a writer, and write an essay defining the problems Wideman faces and explaining why you think he raises them as he does. Finally, what might this have to do with your work as a writer — or as a student in this writing class?

2. Wideman tells Robby's story in this excerpt, but he also tells the story of his neighborhood, Homewood; of his mother; and of his grandfather John French. Write an essay retelling one of these stories and explaining what it might have to do with Robby and John's.

3. "Our Time" is a family history, but it is also a meditation on the problems of writing family histories — or, more generally, the problems of writing about the "real" world. There are sections in "Our Time" where Wideman speaks directly about the problems he faces as a writer. And the unusual features in the prose stand as examples of how he tried to solve these problems — at certain points Wideman writes as an essayist, at others like a storyteller; at certain points he switches voices; the piece breaks up into sections, it doesn't move from introduction to conclusion. Think of these as part of Wideman's method, as his way of working on the problems of writing as practical problems, where he is trying to figure out how to do justice to his brother and his story.

   As you prepare to write this assignment, read back through the selection to think about it as a way of doing one's work, as a project, as a way of writing. What are the selection's key features? What is its shape or design? How does Wideman, the writer, do what he does? And you might ask: What would it take to learn to write like this? How is this writing related to the writing taught in school? Where and how might it serve you as a student?

   Once you have developed a sense of Wideman's method, write a Wideman-like piece of your own, one that has the rhythm and the moves, the shape and the design of "Our Time." As far as subject matter is concerned, let Wideman's text stand as an invitation (inviting you to write about family and neighborhood), but don't feel compelled to follow his lead. You can write about anything you want. The key is to follow the essay as an example of a *way* of writing — moving slowly, turning this way and that, combining stories and reflection, working outside of a rigid structure of thesis and proof.

MAKING CONNECTIONS

1. Various selections in this textbook can be said to be "experimental" in their use of nonfiction prose. These are essays that don't do what essays are supposed to do. They break the rules. They surprise. The writers work differently than most writers. They imagine a different project (or they imagine their project differently).

   Although any number of the selections in *Ways of Reading* might be read alongside "Our Time," here are some that have seemed interesting to our students: Gloria Anzaldúa, "How to Tame a Wild Tongue" (p. 26); Susan Griffin, "Our Secret" (p. 233); and Richard E. Miller, "The Dark Night of the Soul."

Choose one selection to compare with Wideman's and write an essay in which you both explain and explore the projects represented by the two pieces of writing. How do they address a reader's expectations? How do they manipulate the genre? How do they reimagine the features we take for granted in the genre of the essay — sentences and paragraphs; introductions and conclusions; argument, narrative, and exposition? And what is to be gained (or what is at stake) in writing this way? (Would you, for example, argue that these forms of writing should be taught in college?) You should assume that you are writing for someone who is a sophisticated reader but who is not familiar with these particular essays. You will need, that is, to be careful in choosing and presenting examples.

2. Both John Edgar Wideman's "Our Time," and Kwame Anthony Appiah's "Racial Identities" (p. 42), call attention to the difficulties of representing and understanding the experience of those whom we call "African Americans" — the difficulty of telling their story, of getting it right, of recovering experience from the representations of others.

   Write an essay in which you represent these two texts as examples of writers working on a problem that has a particular urgency for all Americans, not just black Americans. How might you name this problem? What do you find compelling in each of these approaches to the problem? And what might this problem have to do with you — as a writer, a thinker, a person, and a citizen?

3. In his essay "Our Time," John Edgar Wideman worries over the problems of representation, of telling his brother's story. He speaks directly to the fundamental problem writers face when they try to represent the lives of others: "I'd slip unaware out of his story and into one of my own. I'd be following him, an obedient shadow, then a cloud would blot the sun and I'd be gone, unchained, a dark form still skulking behind him but no longer in tow" (p. 437). Wideman goes on to say:

   > The hardest habit to break . . . would be listening to myself listen to him. That habit would destroy any chance of seeing my brother on his terms; and seeing him in his terms, learning his terms, seemed the whole point of learning his story. . . . I had to teach myself to listen. Start fresh, clear the pipes, resist too facile an identification, tame the urge to take off with Robby's story and make it my own. (p. 437)

   Richard E. Miller, in "The Dark Night of the Soul", is also concerned with the problems of representation. He provides readings of the lives of others — from Eric Harris to Chris McCandless to Martin Amis to René Descartes and

See the e-Pages at bedfordstmartins.com/waysofreading.

Mary Karr — who are also engaged with the problems of representation and understanding. Write an essay about writing and representation, about the real world and the world of texts, with Wideman and Miller as your primary points of reference. How do they understand representation as a problem for writers and readers? How is that understanding represented (or enacted) in their own work? Which writer might have something to learn from the example of the other?

Assignment
SEQUENCES

Working with Assignment Sequences

Six assignment sequences follow. Another six sequences are located in the e-Pages and an additional nine are located in *Resources for Teaching Ways of Reading*. These assignment sequences are different from the single writing assignments at the end of each essay. The single writing assignments are designed to give you a way back into the works you have read. They define the way you, the reader, can work on an essay by writing about it—testing its assumptions, probing its examples, applying its way of thinking to a new setting or to new material. A single assignment might ask you to read what Paulo Freire has to say about education and then, as a writer, to use Freire's terms and methods to analyze a moment from your own schooling. The single assignments are designed to demonstrate how a student might work on an essay, particularly an essay that is long or complex, and they are designed to show how pieces that might seem daunting are open, manageable, and managed best by writing.

The assignment sequences have a similar function, but with one important difference. Instead of writing one paper, or working on one or two selections from the book, you will be writing several essays and reading several selections. Your work will be sequential as well as cumulative. The work you do on Freire, for example, will give you a way of beginning with Mary Louise Pratt or Judith Butler. It will give you an angle of vision. You won't be a newcomer to such discussions. Your previous reading will make the new essay rich with association. Passages or examples will jump out, as if magnetized, and demand your attention. And by

e See the e-Pages at bedfordstmartins.com/waysofreading.

reading these essays in context, you will see each writer as a single voice in a larger discussion. Neither Freire, nor Pratt, nor Butler, after all, has had the last word on the subject of education. It is not as though, by working on one of the essays, you have wrapped the subject up, ready to be put on the shelf.

The sequences are designed, then, so that you will be working not only on essays but on a subject, like education (or history, or culture, or the autobiography), a subject that can be examined, probed, and understood through the various frames provided by your reading. Each essay becomes a way of seeing a problem or a subject; it becomes a tool for thinking, an example of how a mind might work, a way of using language to make a subject rich and alive. In the assignment sequences, your reading is not random. Each sequence provides a set of readings that can be pulled together into a single project.

The sequences allow you to participate in an extended academic project, one with several texts and several weeks' worth of writing. You are not just adding one essay to another (Freire + Pratt = ?) but trying out an approach to a subject by revising it, looking at new examples, hearing what someone else has to say, and beginning again to take a position of your own. Projects like these take time. It is not at all uncommon for professional writers to devote weeks or even months to a single essay, and the essay they write marks not the end of their thinking on the subject, but only one stage. Similarly, when readers are working on a project, the pieces they read accumulate on their desks and in their minds and become part of an extended conversation with several speakers, each voice offering a point of view on a subject, a new set of examples, or a new way of talking that resonates with echoes from earlier reading.

A student may read many books, take several courses, write many papers; ideally each experience becomes part of something larger, an education. The work of understanding, in other words, requires time and repeated effort. The power that comes from understanding cannot be acquired quickly — by reading one essay or working for a few hours. A student, finally, is a person who choreographs such experiences, not someone who passes one test only to move on to another. And the assignment sequences are designed to reproduce, although in a condensed period of time, the rhythm and texture of academic life. They invite you to try on its characteristic ways of seeing, thinking, and writing. The work you do in one week will not be lost when it has bearing on the work you do in the next. If an essay by Susan Griffin has value for you, it is not because you proved to a teacher that you read it, but because you have put it to work and made it a part of your vocabulary as a student.

WORKING WITH A SEQUENCE

Here is what you can expect as you work with a sequence. You begin by working with a single story or essay. You will need to read each piece twice, the second time with the "Questions for a Second Reading" and the assignment sequence in mind. Before rereading the selection, in other words, you should read through the assignments to get a sense of where you will be headed. And you should read the questions at the end of each selection. (You can use those questions to help frame questions of your own.) The purpose of all these questions, in a sense, is to prepare the text to speak—to bring it to life and insist that it respond to your attention, answer your questions. If you think of the authors as people you can talk to, if you think of their pages as occasions for dialogue (as places where you get to ask questions and insist on responses)—if you prepare your return to those pages in these ways, you are opening up the essays or stories (not closing them down or finishing them off) and creating a scene where you get to step forward as a performer.

While each sequence moves from selection to selection in *Ways of Reading*, the most significant movement in the sequence is defined by the essays you write. Your essays provide the other major texts for the course. In fact, when we teach these sequences, we seldom have any discussion of the assigned readings before our students have had a chance to write. When we talk as a group about Anne Carson's "Short Talks," for example, we begin by reproducing one or two student essays, handing them out to the class, and using them as the basis for discussion. We want to start, in other words, by looking at ways of reading Carson's essay—not at his essay alone.

The essays you write for each assignment in a sequence might be thought of as works-in-progress. Your instructor will tell you the degree to which each essay should be finished—that is, the degree to which it should be revised and copy-edited and worked into a finished performance. In our classes, most writing assignments go through at least one revision. After we have had a chance to see a draft (or after a draft has been seen by others in the class), and after we have had some discussion of sample student essays, we ask students to read the assigned essay or story one more time and to rework their essays to bring their work one step further—not necessarily to finish the essays (as though there would be nothing else to say) but to finish up this stage in their work and to feel their achievement in a way a writer simply cannot the first time through. Each assignment, then, really functions as two assignments in the schedule for the course. As a consequence, we don't "cover" as many essays in a semester as students might in another class. But coverage is not our goal. In a sense, we are teaching our students how to read slowly and closely, to return to a text rather than set it aside, to take the time to reread and rewrite and to reflect on what these activities entail. Some of these sequences, then, contain more readings or more writing assignments than you can address in a quarter or semester. Different courses work at different paces. It is important, however, to preserve time for rereading and rewriting. The sequences were written with the assumption that they would be revised to meet the needs of teachers, students, and programs. As you look at your syllabus, you may find, then, that reading or writing assignments have been changed, added, or dropped. There are alternative selections and assignments at the end of most of these sequences so that the sequences can be customized. Your instructor may wish to replace some of the selections and assignments in the sequence with alternatives.

You will be writing papers that can be thought of as single essays. But you will also be working on a project, something bigger than its individual parts. From the perspective of the project, each piece you write is part of a larger body of work that evolves over the term. You might think of each sequence as a revision exercise, where the revision looks forward to what comes next as well as backward to what you have done. This form of revision asks you to do more than complete a single paper; it invites you to resee a subject or reimagine what you might say about it from a new point of view. You should feel free, then, to draw on your earlier essays when you work on one of the later assignments. There is every reason for you to reuse ideas, phrases, sentences, even paragraphs as your work builds from one week to the next. The advantage of works-in-progress is that you are not starting over completely every time you sit down to write. You've been over this territory before. You've developed some expertise in your subject. There is a body of work behind you.

Most of the sequences bring together several essays from the text and ask you to imagine them as an extended conversation, one with several speakers. The assignments are designed to give you a voice in the conversation as well, to allow you to speak in turn and to take your place in the company of other writers. This is the final purpose of the assignment sequence: after several weeks' work on the essays and on the subject that draws them together, you will begin to establish your own point of view. You will develop a position from which you can speak with authority, drawing strength from the work you have done as well as from your familiarity with the people who surround you.

This book brings together some of the most powerful voices of our culture. They speak in a manner that asks for response. The assignments at the end of each selection and, with a wider range of reference, the assignment sequences here at the end of the book demonstrate that there is no reason for a student, in such company, to remain silent.

SEQUENCE ONE

Exploring Identity, Exploring the Self

Kwame Anthony Appiah
Edward Said
Judith Butler
Susan Griffin

ALTERNATIVES:

Richard Miller
John Edgar Wideman
Kathleen Jamie

This sequence invites you to explore some complicated questions about identity—questions about who we are as human beings, about our relationships to others, and about the narratives we tell about ourselves and others. The sequence is particularly challenging because it asks you to be self-reflexive and to think critically about representations of race, sexuality, gender, and class. These categories are ways of characterizing identity, but as with all categories, the characterizations they produce are partial, flawed, and incomplete. Each of these authors asks you to think about different aspects of identity, and the questions in this sequence ask you to draw from the readings and from your own experience, at times, to explore the question: who are we?

In the first two assignments, you'll get the chance to think about two ways identity might be said to be expressed or enacted: narrative and representation. We tell stories about who we are. Inevitably, we also tell stories about others. In those narratives, we find representations. You might think of the sequence as moving from those specific examples of narrative and representation to more philosophical and political questions about what it means to be human, and how the concept of the human is employed to make some identities seem more legitimate or compelling than others. To work with this sequence, you have to be willing to imagine other ways of being outside whatever your own ways of being might be; you have to be able to look closely at the texts at hand to raise questions about what they reveal and how their assertions might be connected to your own life. The final assignment asks you to respond to Susan Griffin's assertion that we are part of a complex web of connections. If Griffin is right that "all the lives that surround us are in us," this would suggest that we might have some responsibility to think about lives other than our own as a way of thinking about ourselves.

ASSIGNMENT 1

Narrative and Identity

KWAME ANTHONY APPIAH

Consider this passage from "Racial Identities":

> Collective identities, in short, provide what we might call scripts: narratives that people can use in shaping their life plans and in telling their life stories. In our society (though not, perhaps, in the England of Addison and Steele) being witty does not in this way suggest the life script of "the wit." And that is why what I called the personal dimensions of identity work differently from the collective ones.
>
> This is not just a point about modern Westerners: cross-culturally it matters to people that their lives have a certain narrative unity; they want to be able to tell a story of their lives that makes sense. The story — my story — should cohere in the way appropriate by the standards made available in my culture to a person of my identity. In telling that story, how I fit into the wider story of various collectivities is, for most of us, important. (p. 57)

Your project in this assignment is to consider the terms, the stages, the conclusions, and the consequences of Appiah's argument in his essay, "Racial Identities." If, as a mental exercise (or because you are convinced), you accept Appiah's notion that "Collective identities, in short, provide what we might call scripts: narratives that people can use in shaping their life plans and in telling their life stories," (p. ooo) how might you tell a story that places yourself in relation to the available scripts, to the life stories available to a person like you — a person of your culture (or collectivity), a person of your age, now, in the second decade of the twenty-first century?

You are not required to write in the genre of the memoir (as though you were writing a chapter of your autobiography), but many find that an inviting way to begin. What a reader wants is a view of you and your world, not in the pen-pal sense of what you look like or what you prefer in music, but with the goal of understanding something more general, something about people like you, something about what it is that shapes and defines a person or an identity in this place and at this point in time. In Appiah's terms, your writing will negotiate the competing demands of a life and a "script," of the personal and the collective, of individual freedom and the politics of identity.

We are trying to avoid the word "essay" in describing this project, since that word carries certain generic restrictions. Our advice is for you to begin not with a generalization but with some specific scene or scenes. Begin with a story (or stories) rather than with an argument. If people are speaking, you may choose to let them speak as characters speak in fiction. You may write in the first person if you find it helpful to do so.

ASSIGNMENT 2
Identity and Representation
EDWARD SAID

The final chapter of *After the Last Sky* ends with this:

> I would like to think, though, that such a book not only tells the reader about us, but in some way also reads the reader. I would like to think that we are not just the people seen or looked at in these photographs: We are also looking at our observers.

e

Read back through Said's essay "States" by looking at the photos with this reversal in mind—looking in order to see yourself as the one who is being looked at, as the one observed. How are you positioned by the photographer, Jean Mohr? How are you positioned by the person in the scene, always acknowledging your presence? What are you being told?

Once you have read through the photographs, reread the essay with a similar question in mind. This time, however, look for evidence of how Said positions you, defines you, invents you as a presence in the scene.

ASSIGNMENT 3
The Concept of Human
JUDITH BUTLER

The opening lines of Butler's essay might be understood as an invitation to participate with her in one of the traditions of philosophy. She writes:

---

e See the e-Pages at bedfordstmartins.com/waysofreading.

> What makes for a livable world is no idle question. It is not merely a question for philosophers. It is posed in various idioms all the time by people in various walks of life. If that makes them all philosophers, then that is a conclusion I am happy to embrace. It becomes a question for ethics, I think, not only when we ask the personal question, what makes my own life bearable, but when we ask, from a position of power, and from the point of view of distributive justice, what makes, or ought to make, the lives of others bearable? Somewhere in the answer we find ourselves not only committed to a certain view of what life is, and what it should be, but also of what constitutes the human, the distinctively human life, and what does not. (p. 114)

Write an essay that takes up this invitation—and that takes it up in specific reference to what Butler has offered in "Beside Oneself: On the Limits of Sexual Autonomy." You will need, then, to take some time to represent her essay—both what it says and what it does. The "Questions for a Second Reading" should be helpful in preparing for this. Imagine an audience of smart people, people who may even know something about Butler, but who have not read this essay. You have read it, and you want to give them a sense of how and why you find it interesting and important. You'll also need to take time to address her questions in your own terms: What makes for a livable world? What constitutes the human? Don't slight this part of your essay. Give yourself as many pages as you gave Butler. You should, however, make it clear that you are writing in response to what you have read. You'll want to indicate, both directly and indirectly, how your thoughts are shaped by, indebted to, or in response to hers.

ASSIGNMENT 4

The Politics of Dehumanization

JUDITH BUTLER, EDWARD SAID

In his essay "States," Edward Said theorizes about the notion of exile in relation to Palestinian identity, offering a study of exile and dislocation through his analysis of photographs taken by Jean Mohr. Consider the following passage:

> We turn ourselves into objects not for sale, but for scrutiny. People ask us, as if looking into an exhibit case, "What is it you Palestinians want?"—as if we can put our demands into a single neat phrase. All of us speak of *awdah*, "return," but do we mean that literally, or do we mean "we must restore ourselves to ourselves"?

When Said talks about being looked at as though in an exhibit case, we might understand him as being concerned with the problem of dehumanization. After

e See the e-Pages at bedfordstmartins.com/waysofreading.

all, to be in an exhibit case is to be captured, trapped, even dead. We might understand Butler as also wrestling with the problem of dehumanization. She writes: "I would like to start, and to end, with the question of the human, of who counts as the human, and the related question of whose lives count as lives, and with a question that has preoccupied many of us for years: what makes for a grievable life?"

Write an essay in which you consider the ways Said and Butler might be said to be speaking with each other. How might the condition of exile be like the condition of being *beside oneself*? What kind of connections — whether you see them as productive or problematic, or both at once — can be made between the ways Said talks about nation, identity, and home, and the ways Butler talks about gender and sexuality? What passages from each seem to have the other in mind? How does each struggle with reference, with pronouns like "we" and "our"?

ASSIGNMENT 5

Interconnectedness and Identity

SUSAN GRIFFIN

Griffin argues that we — all of us, especially all of us who have read her essay — are part of a complex web of connections. At one point she says,

> Who are we? The question is not simple. What we call the self is part of a larger matrix of relationship and society. Had we been born to a different family, in a different time, to a different world, we would not be the same. All the lives that surround us are in us. (p. 263)

At another point she asks, "Is there any one of us who can count ourselves outside the circle circumscribed by our common past?" She speaks of a "field,"

> . . . like a field of gravity that is created by the movements of many bodies. Each life is influenced and it in turn becomes an influence. Whatever is a cause is also an effect. Childhood experience is just one element in the determining field. (p. 238)

One way of thinking about this concept of the self and of interrelatedness, at least under Griffin's guidance, is to work on the connections that she implies and asserts. As you reread the selection, look for powerful and surprising juxtapositions, fragments that stand together in interesting and suggestive ways. Think about the arguments represented by the blank space between those sections. (And look for Griffin's written statements about "relatedness.")

Look for connections that seem important to the text (and to you) and representative of Griffin's thinking (and yours). Then, write an essay in which you use these examples to think through your understanding of Griffin's claims for this "larger matrix," the "determining field," or our "common past."

ALTERNATIVE ASSIGNMENT

A Writer's Identity, A Writer's Position

JOHN EDGAR WIDEMAN

At several points in the essay ("Our Time," p. 422), Wideman discusses his position as a writer, telling Robby's story, and he describes the problems he faces in writing this piece (or in "reading" the text of his brother's life). You could read this selection, in other words, as an essay about reading and writing.

Why do you think Wideman talks about these problems here? Why not keep quiet and hope no one notices? Choose three or four passages in which Wideman refers directly or indirectly to his work as a writer, and write an essay defining the problems Wideman faces and explaining why you think he raises them as he does. Finally, what might this have to do with your work as a writer — or as a student in this writing class?

ALTERNATIVE ASSIGNMENT

What We Read and Its Connection to Who We Are

RICHARD MILLER

Consider the following passage from Miller's "The Dark Night of the Soul":

> What makes *Into the Wild* remarkable is Krakauer's ability to get some purchase on McCandless's actual reading practice, which, in turn, enables him to get inside McCandless's head and speculate with considerable authority about what ultimately led the young man to abandon the comforts of home and purposefully seek out mortal danger. Krakauer is able to do this, in part, because he has access to the books that McCandless read, with all their underlinings and marginalia, as well as to his journals and the postcards and letters McCandless sent to friends during his journey. Working with these materials and his interviews with McCandless's family and friends, Krakauer develops a sense of McCandless's inner life and eventually comes to some understanding of why the young man was so susceptible to being seduced by the writings of London, Thoreau, Muir, and Tolstoy. Who McCandless is and what becomes of him are, it turns out, intimately connected to the young man's approach to reading — both what he chose to read and how he chose to read it.

e

e See the e-Pages at bedfordstmartins.com/waysofreading.

When Miller is writing about Krakauer's *Into the Wild*, he seems to suggest that what we read and how we read can say something about who we are and about what we might become. This is a bold claim.

Think of a book that made a difference to you, that captured you, maybe one you have read more than once, maybe one that you've made marks in, or one that still sits on your bookshelf. Or, if not a book, think of your favorite song, album, movie, or TV show, something that engaged you at least potentially as McCandless was engaged by London, Thoreau, Muir, and Tolstoy. What was it that you found there? What kind of reader were you? And what makes this a story in the past tense? How and why did you move on? (Or if it is not a story in the past tense, where are you now, and are you, like McCandless, in any danger?)

ALTERNATIVE ASSIGNMENT

Representing Others

JOHN EDGAR WIDEMAN

In his essay "Our Time," John Edgar Wideman worries over the problems of representation, of telling his brother's story. He speaks directly to the fundamental problem writers face when they try to represent the lives of others: "I'd slip unaware out of his story and into one of my own. I'd be following him, an obedient shadow, then a cloud would blot the sun and I'd be gone, unchained, a dark form still skulking behind him but no longer in tow" (p. 437). Wideman goes on to say:

> The hardest habit to break . . . would be listening to myself listen to him. That habit would destroy any chance of seeing my brother on his terms; and seeing him in his terms, learning his terms, seemed the whole point of learning his story. . . . I had to teach myself to listen. Start fresh, clear the pipes, resist too facile an identification, tame the urge to take off with Robby's story and make it my own. (p. 437)

Richard E. Miller, in "The Dark Night of the Soul," is also concerned with the problems of representation. He provides readings of the lives of others — from Eric Harris to Chris McCandless to Martin Amis to René Descartes and Mary Karr — who are also engaged with the problems of representation and understanding. Write an essay about writing and representation, about the real world and the world of texts, with Wideman and Miller as your primary points of reference. How do they understand representation as a problem for writers and readers? How is that understanding represented (or enacted) in their own work? Which writer might have something to learn from the example of the other? e

---

e See the e-Pages at bedfordstmartins.com/waysofreading.

ALTERNATIVE ASSIGNMENT

Who is Talking?

KATHLEEN JAMIE

Jamie recreates numerous conversations with others throughout her essay. For this assignment, mark those conversations in some way so that you can read them in succession. When you've done that, identify one or two conversations that you can use for an essay. Why are these exchanges so prominent in Jamie's essay? What does she accomplish with them? Why would she choose to recreate conversations such as these rather than to report on them? What do these conversations tell us about the people engaging in them? How does Jamie want those conversations to reflect the identities of those speaking?

Write an essay in which you draw conclusions about how these particular conversations allow Jamie to position, complicate, or represent those she writes about. What does conversation demonstrate about who we are? Or, put another way, how do conversations reflect selves?

See the e-Pages at bedfordstmartins.com/waysofreading.

SEQUENCE TWO

The Aims of Education

Paulo Freire
Mary Louise Pratt
Richard Rodriguez
Richard E. Miller

ALTERNATIVE:

Susan Griffin

You have been in school for many years, long enough for your experiences in the classroom to seem natural, inevitable. The purpose of this sequence is to invite you to step outside a world you may have begun to take for granted, to look at the ways you have been taught and at the unspoken assumptions behind your education. The seven assignments that follow bring together four essays that discuss how people (and particularly students) become trapped inside habits of thought. These habits of thought become invisible (or seem natural) because of the ways our schools work or because of the ways we have traditionally learned to use language when we speak, read, or write.

ASSIGNMENT 1

Applying Freire to Your Own Experience as a Student

PAULO FREIRE

The teacher talks about reality as if it were motionless, static, compartmentalized, and predictable. Or else he expounds on a topic completely alien to the existential experience of the students. His task is to "fill" the students with the contents of his narration—

> contents which are detached from reality, disconnected from the totality that engendered them and could give them significance. Words are emptied of their concreteness and become a hollow, alienated, and alienating verbosity. (p. 216)
>
> — PAULO FREIRE
> *The "Banking" Concept of Education*

Surely, anyone who has made it through twelve years of formal education can think of a class, or an occasion outside of class, to serve as a quick example of what Freire calls the "banking" concept of education, where students are turned into "containers" to be "filled" by their teachers. If Freire is to be useful to you, however, he must do more than call up quick examples. He should allow you to say more than that a teacher once treated you like a container (or that a teacher once gave you your freedom).

Write an essay that focuses on a rich and illustrative incident from your own educational experience and read it (that is, interpret it) as Freire would. You will need to provide careful detail: things that were said and done, perhaps the exact wording of an assignment, a textbook, or a teacher's comments. And you will need to turn to the language of Freire's argument, to take key phrases and passages from his argument and see how they might be used to investigate your case.

To do this, you will need to read your account as not simply the story of you and your teacher, since Freire is not writing about individual personalities (an innocent student and a mean teacher, a rude teacher, or a thoughtless teacher) but about the roles we are cast in, whether we choose to be or not, by our culture and its institutions. The key question, then, is not who you were or who your teacher was but what roles you played and how those roles can lead you to better understand the larger narrative or drama of Education (an organized attempt to "regulate the way the world 'enters into' the students").

Note: Freire would not want you to work passively or mechanically, as though you were merely following orders. He would want you to make your own mark on the work he has begun. Use your example, in other words, as a way of testing and examining what Freire says, particularly those passages that you find difficult or obscure.

– Major part should be your story
– Freire
– what you think of this & why

4 pages by Tues 3 copies
Paragraphs 3 sentences – 3/4 page

– Relate to different institutions just your experience.
ex) politics
– Bigger than
– General readers
what Freire read

ASSIGNMENT 2

The Contact Zone

MARY LOUISE PRATT

> The idea of the contact zone is intended in part to contrast with ideas of community that underlie much of the thinking about language, communication, and culture that gets done in the academy. (p. 325)
>
> — MARY LOUISE PRATT
> *Arts of the Contact Zone*

Citing Benedict Anderson and what he calls "imagined communities," Pratt argues that our idea of community is "strongly utopian, embodying values like equality, fraternity, liberty, which the societies often profess but systematically fail to realize." Against this utopian vision of community, Pratt argues that we need to develop ways of understanding (even noticing) social and intellectual spaces that are not homogeneous, unified; we need to develop ways of understanding and valuing difference. And, for Pratt, the argument extends to schooling. "What is the place," she asks,

> of unsolicited oppositional discourse, parody, resistance, critique in the imagined classroom community? Are teachers supposed to feel that their teaching has been most successful when they have eliminated such things and unified the social world, probably in their own image? Who wins when we do that? Who loses? (p. 327)

Such questions, she says, "may be hypothetical, because in the United States in the 1990s, many teachers find themselves less and less able to do that even if they want to."

"In the United States in the 1990s." "The imagined classroom community." From your experience, what scenes might be used to represent schooling in the 1990s and beyond? How are they usually imagined (idealized, represented, interpreted, valued)? What are the implications of Pratt's argument?

Write an essay in which you use Pratt's terms to examine a representative scene from your own experience with schools and schooling. What examples, stories, or images best represent your experience? How might they be interpreted as examples of community? as examples of "contact zones"? As you prepare your essay, you will want to set the scene as carefully as you can, so that someone who was not there can see it fully. Think about how someone who has not read Pratt might interpret the scene. And think through the various ways *you* might interpret your example. And you should also think about your position in an argument about school as a contact zone. What do you (or people like you) stand to gain or lose when you adopt Pratt's point of view?

ASSIGNMENT 3

The Pedagogical Arts of the Contact Zone

MARY LOUISE PRATT

> Meanwhile, our job in the Americas course remains to figure out how to make that crossroads the best site for learning that it can be. We are looking for the pedagogical arts of the contact zone. These will include, we are sure, exercises in storytelling and in identifying with the ideas, interests, histories, and attitudes of others; experiments in transculturation and collaborative work and in the arts of critique, parody, and

> comparison (including unseemly comparisons between elite and vernacular cultural forms); the redemption of the oral; ways for people to engage with suppressed aspects of history (including their own histories), ways to move *into and out of* rhetorics of authenticity; ground rules for communication across lines of difference and hierarchy that go beyond politeness but maintain mutual respect; a systematic approach to the all-important concept of *cultural mediation*. (p. 329)
>
> — MARY LOUISE PRATT
> *Arts of the Contact Zone*

Pratt writes generally about culture and history, but also about reading and writing and teaching and learning, about the "literate" and "pedagogical" arts of this place she calls the contact zone. Think about the class you are in — its position in the curriculum, in the institution. Think about its official goals (and its unofficial goals). Think about the positions represented by the students, the teacher. Think about how to think about the class, in Pratt's terms, as a contact zone.

And think about the unusual exercises represented by her list: "storytelling," "experiments in transculturation," "critique," "parody," "unseemly comparisons," moving into and out of "rhetorics of authenticity" — these are some of them. Take one of these suggested exercises, explain what you take it to mean, and then go on to discuss how it might be put into practice in a writing class. What would students do? to what end? How would their work be evaluated? What place would the exercise have in the larger sequence of assignments over the term, quarter, or semester? In your terms, and from your point of view, what might you learn from such an exercise?

Or you could think of the question this way: What comments would a teacher make on one of the papers you have written so far in order that its revision might stand as one of these exercises? How would the revision be different from what you are used to doing?

Write an essay in which you present and discuss an exercise designed to serve the writing class as a contact zone.

ASSIGNMENT 4

Ways of Reading, Ways of Speaking, Ways of Caring

RICHARD RODRIGUEZ

> What I am about to say to you has taken me more than twenty years to admit: *A primary reason for my success in the classroom was that I couldn't forget that schooling was changing me and separating me from the life I enjoyed before becoming a student.* (p. 339)

> If, because of my schooling, I had grown culturally separated from my parents, my education finally had given me ways of speaking and caring about that fact. (p. 355)
>
> — RICHARD RODRIGUEZ
> *The Achievement of Desire*

As you reread Rodriguez's essay, what would you say are his "ways of speaking and caring"? One way to think about this question is to trace how the lessons he learned about reading, education, language, family, culture, and class shifted as he moved from elementary school through college and graduate school to his career as a teacher and a writer. What scholarly abilities did he learn that provided him with "ways of speaking and caring" valued in the academic community? Where and how do you see him using them in his essay?

Write an essay in which you discuss how Rodriguez reads (reviews, summarizes, interprets) his family, his teachers, his schooling, himself, and his books. What differences can you say such reading makes to those ways of speaking and caring that you locate in the text?

ASSIGNMENT 5

A Story of Schooling

RICHARD RODRIGUEZ

Rodriguez insists that his story is also everyone's story. Take an episode from your life, one that seems in some way similar to one of the episodes in "The Achievement of Desire," and cast it into a shorter version of Rodriguez's essay. Your job here is to look at your experience in Rodriguez's terms, which means thinking the way he does, noticing what he would notice, interpreting details in a similar fashion, using his key terms, seeing through his point of view; it could also mean imitating his style of writing, working with quotations from other writers, doing whatever it is you see him doing characteristically while he writes. Imitation, Rodriguez argues, is not necessarily a bad thing; it can, in fact, be one of the powerful ways in which a person learns.

Note: This assignment can also be used to read against "The Achievement of Desire." Rodriguez insists on the universality of his experience leaving home and community and joining the larger public life. You could highlight the differences between your experience and his. You should begin by imitating Rodriguez's method; you do not have to arrive at his conclusions, however.

ASSIGNMENT 6

The Literate Arts

RICHARD E. MILLER

Miller's essay opens with a list of fatal shootings in school—troublingly, an incomplete list. As the essay builds to questions—questions for educators and for students—the specters of violence and alienation remain, changing how we think about the reading and writing school endeavors to teach us. "I have these doubts, you see," Miller writes of academic work, "doubts silently shared by many who spend their days teaching others the literate arts. Aside from gathering and organizing information, aside from generating critiques and analyses that forever fall on deaf ears, what might the literate arts be said to be good for?".

Write an essay that takes up this question—"what might the literate arts be said to be good for?"—and that takes it up from your range of reference and from your point of view—or, more properly, from the point of view of you and people like you, the group you feel prepared to speak for. As an exercise in understanding, your essay should be modeled on one (or more) of the sections in "The Dark Night of the Soul." You can choose the text—and the text can be anything that might serve as an example of the literate arts, things in print but also including songs, films, and TV shows. But your presentation and discussion of the text should be in conversation with Miller—with his concerns, his key terms, his examples, and his conclusions.

ASSIGNMENT 7

Making Connections

PAULO FREIRE, MARY LOUISE PRATT,
RICHARD RODRIGUEZ, RICHARD E. MILLER

> After years spent unwilling to admit its attractions, I gestured nostalgically toward the past. I yearned for that time when I had not been so alone. I became impatient with books. I wanted experience more immediate. I feared the library's silence. I silently scorned the gray, timid faces around me. I grew to hate the growing pages of my dissertation on genre and Renaissance literature. (In my mind I heard relatives laughing as they tried to make sense of its title.) I wanted something – I couldn't say exactly what. (p. 354)
>
> —RICHARD RODRIGUEZ
> *The Achievement of Desire*

See the e-Pages at bedfordstmartins.com/waysofreading.

> For some, it will hardly come as a surprise to learn that reading and writing have no magically transformative powers. But for those of us who have been raised into the teaching and publishing professions, it can be quite a shock to confront the possibility that reading and writing and talking exercise almost ***none*** of the powers we regularly attribute to them in our favorite stories. The dark night of the soul for literacy workers comes with the realization that training students to read, write, and talk in more critical and self-reflective ways cannot protect them from the violent changes our culture is undergoing.
>
> — RICHARD MILLER
> *The Dark Night of the Soul*

"I have these doubts, you see," Miller writes of academic work, "doubts silently shared by many who spend their days teaching others the literate arts. Aside from gathering and organizing information, aside from generating critiques and analyses that forever fall on deaf ears, what might the literate arts be said to be good for?"

These questions are repeated, in different contexts and with different inflections, by all of the writers you have been reading: Freire, Pratt, Rodriguez, and Miller. All are concerned with the limits (and the failures) of education, with particular attention to the humanities and to the supposed benefits to be found in reading and writing.

Write an essay that takes up this question — "what might the literate arts be said to be good for?" — and that takes it up with these writers and these essays as your initial point of reference. What do they say? How might they be said to speak to one another? And, finally, where are you in this? Where are you, and people like you, the group for whom you feel prepared to speak? You, too, have been and will continue to be expected to take courses in reading and writing, to read, write, and talk in critical and self-reflective ways. Where are you in this conversation?

- Adress question
- Good for anything
- Support
- development
- Naysayer
- own experiences
- observations
  - own exp
  - schools
  - Mag, online, media

- Make a case for controlling Idea
- Criticing
- evaluations
- Judgements

ALTERNATIVE ASSIGNMENT

Writing Against the Grain

SUSAN GRIFFIN

As you reread "Our Secret," think of Griffin's prose as experimental, as deliberate and crafted. She is trying to do something that she can't do in the "usual" essay form. She wants to make a different kind of argument and engage her reader in a different manner. And so she mixes personal and academic writing. She assembles fragments and juxtaposes seemingly unrelated material in surprising and suggestive relationships. She breaks the "plane" of the page with italicized intersections. She organizes her material, that is, but not in the usual mode of thesis-

---

See the e-Pages at bedfordstmartins.com/waysofreading

example-conclusion. The arrangement is not nearly so linear. At one point, when she seems to be prepared to argue that German child-rearing practices produced the Holocaust, she quickly says:

> Of course there cannot be one answer to such a monumental riddle, nor does any event in history have a single cause. Rather a field exists, like a field of gravity that is created by the movements of many bodies. Each life is influenced and it in turn becomes an influence. Whatever is a cause is also an effect. Childhood experience is just one element in the determining field. (p. 238)

Her prose serves to create a "field," one where many bodies are set in relationship.

It is useful, then, to think about Griffin's prose as the enactment of a method, as a way of doing a certain kind of intellectual work. One way to study this, to feel its effects, is to imitate it, to take it as a model. For this assignment, write a Griffin-like essay, one similar in its methods or organization and argument. You will need to think about the stories you might tell, about the stories and texts you might gather (stories and texts not your own). As you write, you will want to think carefully about arrangement and about commentary (about where, that is, you will speak to your reader as the writer of the piece). You should not feel bound to Griffin's subject matter, but you should feel that you are working in her spirit.

ALTERNATIVE ASSIGNMENT

The Task of Attention

SUSAN GRIFFIN

> I am looking now at the etching called *Poverty*, made in 1897. Near the center, calling my attention, a woman holds her head in her hands. (p. 242)
>
> — SUSAN GRIFFIN
> *Our Secret*

This is one of the many moments when Griffin speaks to us as though in the midst of her work. The point of this assignment is to think about that work — what it is, how she does it, and what it might have to do with schools and schooling. She is, after all, doing much of the traditional work of scholars — going to the archive, studying old materials, traveling and interviewing subjects, learning and writing history.

And yet this is not the kind of prose you would expect to find in a textbook for a history course. Even if the project is not what we usually think of as a research project, Griffin is a careful researcher. Griffin knows what she is doing. Go back to look again (this time with a writer's eye) at both the features of Griffin's prose and the way she characterizes her work as a scholar, gathering and studying her materials.

Write an essay in which you present an account of *how* Griffin does her work. You should use her words and examples from the text, but you should also feel that it is your job to explain what you present and to comment on it from the point of view of a student. As you reread, look to those sections where Griffin seems to be speaking to her readers about her work—about how she reads and how she writes, about how she gathers her materials and how she studies them. What is she doing? What is at stake in adopting such methods? How might they be taught? Where in the curriculum might (should?) such lessons be featured?

SEQUENCE THREE

The Arts of the Contact Zone

Mary Louise Pratt
Gloria Anzaldúa
John Edgar Wideman
Edward Said

ALTERNATIVES:

Kathleen Jamie

This sequence allows you to work closely with the argument of Mary Louise Pratt's "Arts of the Contact Zone," not so much through summary (repeating the argument) as through extension (working under its influence, applying its terms and protocols). In particular, you are asked to try your hand at those ways of reading and writing Pratt defines as part of the "literate arts of the contact zone," ways of reading and writing that have not historically been taught or valued in American schools.

Pratt is one of the country's most influential cultural critics. In "Arts of the Contact Zone," she makes the argument that our usual ways of reading and writing assume identification—that is, we learn to read and write the texts that express our own position and point of view. As a result, texts that reproduce different ways of thinking, texts that allude to different cultural systems, seem flawed, wrong, or inscrutable. As a counterposition, Pratt asks us to imagine scenes of reading, writing, teaching, and learning as "contact zones," places of contact between people who can't or don't or won't necessarily identify with one another.

In the first assignment, you are asked to search for or produce a document to exemplify the arts of the contact zone, working in library archives, searching the streets, surfing the Internet, or writing an "autoethnography." This is a big job, and probably new to most students; it is a project you will want to come back to and revise. The remaining assignments outline a project in which you examine other selections from *Ways of Reading* that exemplify or present moments of cultural contact.

ASSIGNMENT 1

The Literate Arts of the Contact Zone

MARY LOUISE PRATT

Here, briefly, are two descriptions of the writing one might find or expect in the contact zone:

> Autoethnography, transculturation, critique, collaboration, bilingualism, mediation, parody, denunciation, imaginary dialogue, vernacular expression — these are some of the literate arts of the contact zone. Miscomprehension, incomprehension, dead letters, unread masterpieces, absolute heterogeneity of meaning — these are some of the perils of writing in the contact zone. They all live among us today in the transnationalized metropolis of the United States and are becoming more widely visible, more pressing, and, like Guaman Poma's text, more decipherable to those who once would have ignored them in defense of a stable, centered sense of knowledge and reality. (p. 324)

> We are looking for the pedagogical arts of the contact zone. These will include, we are sure, exercises in storytelling and in identifying with the ideas, interests, histories, and attitudes of others; experiments in transculturation and collaborative work and in the arts of critique, parody, and comparison (including unseemly comparisons between elite and vernacular cultural forms); the redemption of the oral; ways for people to engage with suppressed aspects of history (including their own histories), ways to move ***into and out of*** rhetorics of authenticity; ground rules for communication across lines of difference and hierarchy that go beyond politeness but maintain mutual respect; a systematic approach to the all-important concept of ***cultural mediation***. (p. 329)

Here are two ways of working on Pratt's idea of the contact zone. Choose one.

1. One way of working with Pratt's essay, of extending its project, would be to conduct your own local inventory of writing from the contact zone. You might do this on your own or in teams, with others from your class. You will want to gather several similar documents, your "archive," before you make a final selection. Think about how to make that choice. What makes one document stand out as representative? Here are two ways you might organize your search:

   a. You could look for historical documents. A local historical society might have documents written by Native Americans ("Indians") to the white settlers. There may be documents written by slaves to masters or to northern whites explaining their experience. There may be documents written by women (suffragists, for example) trying to negotiate for public positions or rights. There may be documents from any of a number of racial or ethnic groups—Hispanic, Jewish, Irish, Italian, Polish, Swedish—trying to explain their positions to the mainstream culture. There may, perhaps at union halls, be documents written by workers to owners. Your own sense of the heritage of your area should direct your search.

b. Or you could look at contemporary documents in the print that is around you, texts that you might otherwise overlook. Pratt refers to one of the characteristic genres of the Hispanic community, the "*testimonio*." You could look for songs, testimonies, manifestos, statements by groups on campus, stories, autobiographies, interviews, letters to the editor, Web pages. You could look at the writing of any marginalized group, particularly writing intended, at least in part, to represent the experience of outsiders to the dominant culture (or to be in dialogue with that culture or to respond to that culture). These documents, if we follow Pratt's example, would encompass the work of young children or students, including college students.

Once you have completed your inventory, choose a document you would like to work with and write an essay that presents it carefully and in detail (perhaps in even greater detail than Pratt's presentation of the *New Chronicle*). You will, in other words, need to set the scene, summarize, explain, and work block quotations into your essay. You might imagine that you are presenting this to someone who would not have seen it and would not know how to read it, at least not as an example of the literate arts of the contact zone.

2. Another way of extending the project of Pratt's essay would be to write your autoethnography. It should not be too hard to locate a setting or context in which you are the "other"—the one who speaks from outside rather than inside the dominant discourse. Pratt says that the position of the outsider is marked not only by differences of language and ways of thinking and speaking but also by differences in power, authority, status. In a sense, she argues, the only way those in power can understand you is in *their* terms. These are terms you will need to use to tell your story, but your goal is to describe your position in ways that "engage with representations others have made of [you]" without giving in or giving up or disappearing in their already formed sense of who you are.

   This is an interesting challenge. One of the things that will make the writing difficult is that the autoethnographic or transcultural text calls upon skills not usually valued in American classrooms: bilingualism, parody, denunciation, imaginary dialogue, vernacular expression, storytelling, unseemly comparisons of high and low cultural forms—these are some of the terms Pratt offers. These do not fit easily with the traditional genres of the writing class (essay, term paper, summary, report) or its traditional values (unity, consistency, sincerity, clarity, correctness, decorum).

   You will probably need to take this essay (or whatever it should be called) through several drafts. (In fact, you might revise this essay after you have completed assignments 2 and 3.) It might be best to begin as Pratt's student, using her description as a preliminary guide. Once you get a sense of your own project, you may find that you have terms or examples to add to her list of the literate arts of the contact zone.

ASSIGNMENT 2

Borderlands

MARY LOUISE PRATT, GLORIA ANZALDÚA

In "Arts of the Contact Zone," Pratt talks about the "autoethnographic" text, "a text in which people undertake to describe themselves in ways that engage with representations others have made of them," and about "transculturation," the "processes whereby members of subordinated or marginal groups select and invent from the materials transmitted by a dominant or metropolitan culture."

Write an essay in which you present a reading of "How to Tame a Wild Tongue" as an example of an autoethnographic and/or transcultural text. You should imagine that you are writing to someone who is not familiar with either Pratt's argument or Anzaldúa's thinking. Part of your work, then, is to present Anzaldúa's text to readers who don't have it in front of them. You have the example of Pratt's reading of Guaman Poma's *New Chronicle and Good Government*. And you have her discussion of the literate arts of the contact zone. Think about how Anzaldúa's text might be similarly read and about how her text does and doesn't fit Pratt's description. Your goal should be to add an example to Pratt's discussion and to qualify it, to alter or reframe what she has said now that you have had a chance to look at an additional example.

ASSIGNMENT 3

Counterparts

JOHN EDGAR WIDEMAN

Here, from "Arts of the Contact Zone," is Mary Louise Pratt on the autoethnographic text:

> Guaman Poma's *New Chronicle* is an instance of what I have proposed to call an *autoethnographic* text, by which I mean a text in which people undertake to describe themselves in ways that engage with representations others have made of them. Thus if ethnographic texts are those in which European metropolitan subjects represent to themselves their others (usually their conquered others), autoethnographic texts are representations that the so-defined others construct *in response to* or in dialogue with those texts.... [T]hey involve a selective collaboration with and appropriation of idioms of

> the metropolis or the conqueror. These are merged or infiltrated to varying degrees with indigenous idioms to create self-representations intended to intervene in metropolitan modes of understanding. . . . Such texts often constitute a marginalized group's point of entry into the dominant circuits of print culture. It is interesting to think, for example, of American slave autobiography in its autoethnographic dimensions, which in some respects distinguish it from Euramerican autobiographical tradition. (p. 319)

John Edgar Wideman's "Our Time" (p. 422) could serve as a twentieth-century counterpart to the *New Chronicle*. Reread it with "Arts of the Contact Zone" in mind. Write an essay that presents "Our Time" as an example of autoethnographic and/or transcultural text. You should imagine that you are working to put Pratt's ideas to the test (*does* it do what she says such texts must do?), but also add what you have to say concerning this text as a literate effort to be present in the context of difference.

ASSIGNMENT 4

A Dialectic of Self and Other

MARY LOUISE PRATT, EDWARD SAID

In "States," an account of Palestinian life written by a Palestinian in exile, Edward Said says,

> All cultures spin out a dialectic of self and other, the subject "I" who is native, authentic, at home, and the object "it" or "you," who is foreign, perhaps threatening, different, out there. From this dialectic comes the series of heroes and monsters, founding fathers and barbarians, prized masterpieces and despised opponents that express a culture from its deepest sense of national self-identity to its refined patriotism, and finally to its coarse jingoism, xenophobia, and exclusivist bias.

e

This is as true of the Palestinians as it is of the Israelis — although, he adds, "For Palestinian culture, the odd thing is that its own identity is more frequently than not perceived as 'other.'"

Pratt argues that our idea of community is "strongly utopian, embodying values like equality, fraternity, liberty, which the societies often profess but systematically fail to realize." Against this utopian vision of community, Pratt argues that we need to develop ways of understanding (noticing or creating) social and intellectual spaces that are not homogeneous or unified — contact zones. She argues that we need to develop ways of understanding and valuing difference.

---

e See the e-Pages at bedfordstmartins.com/waysofreading.

There are similar goals and objects to these projects. Reread Pratt's essay with Said's "States" in mind. As she defines what she refers to as the "literate arts of the contact zone," can you find points of reference in Said's text? Said's thinking always attended to the importance and the conditions of writing, including his own. There are ways that "States" could be imagined as both autoethnographic and transcultural. How might his work allow you to understand the literate arts of the contact zone in practice? How might his work allow you to understand the problems and possibilities of such writing beyond what Pratt has imagined, presented, and predicted?

ASSIGNMENT 5

On Culture

MARY LOUISE PRATT, GLORIA ANZALDÚA,
JOHN EDGAR WIDEMAN, EDWARD SAID

In some ways, the slipperiest of the key words in Pratt's essay "Arts of the Contact Zone" is "culture." At one point Pratt says,

> If one thinks of cultures, or literatures, as discrete, coherently structured, monolingual edifices, Guaman Poma's text, and indeed any autoethnographic work, appears anomalous or chaotic — as it apparently did to the European scholars Pietschmann spoke to in 1912. If one does not think of cultures this way, then Guaman Poma's text is simply heterogeneous, as the Andean region was itself and remains today. Such a text is heterogeneous on the reception end as well as the production end: it will read very differently to people in different positions in the contact zone. (p. 324)

If one thinks of cultures as "coherently structured, monolingual edifices," the text appears one way; if one thinks otherwise, the text is "simply heterogeneous." What might it mean to make this shift in the way one thinks of culture? Can you do it — that is, can you read the *New Chronicle* (or its excerpts) from both points of view? Better yet — what about your own culture and its key texts? Can you, for example, think of a group that you participate in as a "community"? Where and how does it represent itself to others? Where and how does it do this in writing? What are its "literate arts"?

The assignments in this sequence are an exercise in reading texts as heterogeneous, as contact zones. As a way of reflecting on your work in this sequence, write an essay in which you explain the work you have been doing to someone not in the course, someone who is interested in reading, writing, and learning, but who has not read Pratt, Anzaldúa, Wideman, or Said.

ALTERNATIVE ASSIGNMENT

Producing Place

KATHLEEN JAMIE

Kathleen Jamie is Scottish-born and calls Scotland home. Some would characterize her writing in *Among Muslims* as "travel writing"—writing aimed to chronicle one's experiences traveling or living somewhere other than his or her home. While Pratt talks about the "autoethnographic" text whereby people describe *themselves* in ways that engage with what others have made of them, Jamie is not describing herself. She is, in many ways, describing others. As we discuss in our introduction to Pratt's "Arts of the Contact Zone" (p. 315), Pratt's piece was meant to serve as an introduction to *Imperial Eyes,* which examines European travel writing in the eighteenth and nineteenth centuries and explores the idea that travel writing was "producing" more than "reporting" those places and people it seeks to describe. What do you suppose Pratt would think of Jamie's travel writing? How do you see Jamie grappling with the problem of "producing" and "reporting"? If you imagine Jamie as producing Pakistan rather than reporting on it, what kind of Pakistan does she produce, and why?

See the e-Pages at bedfordstmartins.com/waysofreading.

SEQUENCE FOUR

Autobiographical Explorations

Richard Rodriguez
Edward Said
Susan Griffin
Richard E. Miller

ALTERNATIVES:

John Edgar Wideman
Alison Bechdel

Autobiographical writing has been a regular feature of writing courses since the nineteenth century. There are a variety of reasons for the prevalence of autobiography, not the least of which is the pleasure students take in thinking about and writing about their lives and their world. There is also a long tradition of published autobiographical writing, particularly in the United States. The title of this sequence puts a particular spin on that tradition, since it points to a more specialized use of autobiography, phrased here as "exploration." What is suggested by the title is a use of writing (and the example of one's experience, including intellectual experience) to investigate, question, explore, inquire. Often the genre is not used for these purposes at all. Autobiographical writing is often used for purposes of display or self-promotion, or to further (rather than question) an argument (about success, about how to live a good or proper or fulfilling life).

There are two threads to this sequence. The first is to invite you to experiment with the genre of "autobiographical exploration." The second is to foreground the relationship between your work and the work of others, to think about how and why and where you are prepared to write autobiographically (prepared not only by the lessons you've learned in school but also by the culture and the way it invites you to tell — and live — the story of your life). And, if you are working inside a conventional field, a predictable way of writing, the sequence asks where and how you might make your mark or assert your position—your identity as a person (a character in a life story) and as a writer (someone working with the conventions of life-writing).

The alternative assignments that follow provide similar assignments but with different readings. They can be substituted for or added to the assignments in this sequence.

ASSIGNMENT 1

Desire, Reading, and the Past

RICHARD RODRIGUEZ

In "The Achievement of Desire," Richard Rodriguez tells stories of home but also stories of reading, of moments when things he read allowed him a way of reconsidering or revising ("framing," he calls it) the stories he would tell himself about himself. It is a very particular account of neighborhood, family, ethnicity, and schooling.

At the same time, Rodriguez insists that his story is also everyone's story—that his experience is universal. Take an episode from your life, one that seems in some ways similar to one of the episodes in "The Achievement of Desire," and cast it into a shorter version of Rodriguez's essay. Try to make use of your reading in ways similar to his. Think about what you have read lately in school, perhaps in this anthology.

In general, however, your job in this assignment is to look at your experience in Rodriguez's terms, which means thinking the way he does, noticing what he would notice, interpreting details in a similar fashion, using his key terms, seeing through his point of view; it could mean imitating his style of writing, doing whatever it is you see him doing characteristically when he writes. Imitation, Rodriguez argues, is not necessarily a bad thing; it can, he argues, be one of the powerful ways a person learns. Let this assignment serve as an exercise.

ASSIGNMENT 2

A Photographic Essay

EDWARD SAID

Edward Said, in the introduction to *After the Last Sky*, says of his method in "States":

> Its style and method—the interplay of text and photos, the mixture of genres, modes, styles—do not tell a consecutive story, nor do they constitute a political essay. Since the main features of our present existence are dispossession, dispersion, and yet also a kind of power

> incommensurate with our stateless exile, I believe that essentially unconventional, hybrid, and fragmentary forms of expression should be used to represent us. What I have quite consciously designed, then, is an alternative mode of expression to the one usually encountered in the media, in works of social science, in popular fiction.

And later:

> The multifaceted vision is essential to any representation of us. Stateless, dispossessed, de-centered, we are frequently unable either to speak the "truth" of our experience or to make it heard. We do not usually control the images that represent us; we have been confined to spaces designed to reduce or stunt us; and we have often been distorted by pressures and powers that have been too much for us. An additional problem is that our language, Arabic, is unfamiliar in the West and belongs to a tradition and civilization usually both misunderstood and maligned. Everything we write about ourselves, therefore, is an interpretive translation — of our language, our experience, our senses of self and others.

Reread "States," paying particular attention to the relationship of text and photograph, and paying attention to form. What *is* the order of the writing in this essay? (We will call it an essay for lack of a better term.) How might you diagram or explain its organization? By what principle(s) is it ordered and arranged? The essay shifts genres — memoir, history, argument. It is, as Said comments, "hybrid." What surprises are there? or disappointments? How might you describe the writer's strategy as he works on his audience, on readers? And, finally, do you find Said's explanation sufficient or useful — does the experience of exile produce its own inevitable style of report and representation? e

For this assignment, compose a similar project, a Said-like reading of a set of photos. These can be photos prepared for the occasion (by you or a colleague); they could also be photos already available. Whatever their source, they should represent people and places, a history and/or geography that you know well, that you know to be complex and contradictory, and that you know will not be easily or readily understood by others, both the group for whom you will be writing (most usefully the members of your class) and readers more generally. You must begin with a sense that the photos cannot speak for themselves; you must speak for them.

In preparation, you should reread closely to come to a careful understanding of Said's project. (The first and second "Questions for a Second Reading" should be useful for this.) e

---

e See the e-Pages at bedfordstmartins.com/waysofreading.

ASSIGNMENT 3

The Matrix

SUSAN GRIFFIN

At several points in her essay "Our Secret," Susan Griffin argues that we—all of us—are part of a complex web of connections. We live in history, and history is determining. At one point she says:

> Who are we? The question is not simple. What we call the self is part of a larger matrix of relationship and society. Had we been born to a different family, in a different time, to a different world, we would not be the same. All the lives that surround us are in us. (p. 263)

At another point she asks, "Is there any one of us who can count ourselves outside the circle circumscribed by our common past?" She speaks of a "field"

> like a field of gravity that is created by the movements of many bodies. Each life is influenced and it in turn becomes an influence. Whatever is a cause is also an effect. Childhood experience is just one element in the determining field. (p. 238)

One way of thinking about this concept of the self (and of interrelatedness), at least under Griffin's guidance, is to work on the connections that she implies and asserts. As you reread the selection, look for powerful and surprising juxtapositions, fragments that stand together in interesting and suggestive ways. Think about the arguments represented by the blank spaces on the page or the jumps from section to section. (And look for Griffin's written statements about relatedness.) Look for connections that seem important to the text (and to you) and to be representative of Griffin's thinking (and useful to yours).

Write an essay in which you use these examples to think through the ways Griffin answers the question she raises: Who are we?

ASSIGNMENT 4

The Experience of Thought

RICHARD E. MILLER

In the final chapter of *Writing at the End of the World*, Richard E. Miller says the following about his own writing:

> While the assessments, evaluations, proposals, reports, commentaries, and critiques I produce help to keep the bureaucracy of higher education going, there is another kind of writing I turn to in order to sustain the ongoing search for meaning in a world no one controls. This writing asks the reader to make imaginative connections be-

> tween disparate elements; it tracks one path among many possible ones across the glistening water.

We can assume that this is the kind of writing present in "The Dark Night of the Soul."

Reread "The Dark Night of the Soul" with particular attention to Miller's method, which is, in simplest terms, putting one thing next to another. Pay attention to the connections Miller makes, to the ways he makes them, and to the ways as a reader you are (or are not) invited into this process. And write a Miller-like essay. To give the project some shape and limit, let's say that it should bring together at least three "disparate elements," three examples you can use to think about whatever it is you want to think about. You don't need to be constrained to Miller's subject — writing, reading, and schooling — although this subject might be exactly the right one for you. Your writing should, however, be like Miller's in its sense of urgency. In other words, write about something that matters to you, that you care about, that touches you personally and deeply.

ASSIGNMENT 5

The "I" of the Personal Essay

RICHARD RODRIGUEZ, EDWARD SAID, RICHARD E. MILLER

The assignments in this sequence have been designed to prompt autobiographical writing. They have been invitations for you to tell your story and to think about the ways stories represent a person and a life. They have also, of course, been exercises in imitation, in writing like Rodriguez, Said, and Miller, in casting your story in their terms. These exercises highlight the ways in which your story is never just your own but also written through our culture's sense of what it means to be a person, to live, grow, change, learn, experience. No writer simply gets to invent childhood. Childhood, like adulthood, is a category already determined by hundreds of thousands of representations of life — in books, in songs, on TV, in paintings, in the stories we tell ourselves about ourselves. As you have written these four personal narratives, you have, of course, been telling the truth, just as you have also, of course, been creating a character, setting scenes, providing certain representations that provide a version of (but that don't begin to sum up) your life.

Read back over the essays you have written (and perhaps revised). As you read, look for examples of where you feel you were doing your best work, where you are proud of the writing and interested in what it allows you to see or to think (where the "investigations" seem most worthwhile).

And think about what is *not* contained in these essays. What experiences are missing? what point of view? what ways of speaking or thinking or writing? If you were to go back to assemble these pieces into a longer essay, what would

---

e See the e-Pages at bedfordstmartins.com/waysofreading.

you keep, and what would you add or change? What are the problems facing a writer, like you, trying to write a life, to take experience and represent it in sentences?

With these questions in mind, reread the essays you have written and write a preface, a short piece introducing a reader to what you have written (to your work—and perhaps work you may do on these essays in the future).

ALTERNATIVE ASSIGNMENT

Old Habits

JOHN EDGAR WIDEMAN

Wideman frequently interrupts the narrative in "Our Time" to talk about the problems he is having as a writer. He says, for example, "The hardest habit to break, since it was the habit of a lifetime, would be listening to myself listen to him. That habit would destroy any chance of seeing my brother on his terms; and seeing him in his terms, learning his terms, seemed the whole point of learning his story" (p. 437).

Wideman gives you the sense of a writer who is aware from the inside, while writing, of the problems inherent in the personal narrative. This genre always shades and deflects; it is always partial and biased; in its very attempts to be complete, to understand totally, it reduces its subject in ways that are unacceptable. And so you can see Wideman's efforts to overcome these problems—he writes in Robby's voice; he starts his story three different times, first with Garth, later with the neighborhood, hoping that a variety of perspectives will overcome the limits inherent in each; he stops and speaks to us not as the storyteller but as the writer, thinking about what he is doing and not doing.

Let Wideman's essay provide a kind of writing lesson. It highlights problems; it suggests alternatives. Using Wideman, then, as your writing teacher, write a family history of your own. Yours will most likely be shorter than Wideman's, but let its writing be the occasion for you also to work on a personal narrative as a writing problem, an interesting problem that forces a writer to think about the limits of representation and point of view (about who gets to speak and in whose terms, about who sums things up and what is left out in this accounting).

ALTERNATIVE ASSIGNMENT

Graphic Autobiography

ALISON BECHDEL

Bechdel writes, "Of course the point at which I began to write the story is not the same as the point at which the story begins." (p. 79) We might read this statement as a commentary on the work of composing autobiography or memoir. She remarks later, "Another difficulty is the fact that the story of my mother and me is unfolding even as I write it." (p. 82)

Consider Bechdel's comments about writing this book and about herself. What does she seem to be suggesting about the difficulties of writing autobiographical work? How would it be different if her work were composed of only words, or if it were a more conventional memoir of mother and daughter? How does her chosen form of graphic memoir enable and limit what she is able to do in writing about herself and her family?

Think of an autobiographical narrative you are familiar with, perhaps in literature or film. You might want to think of a story that involves a mother and daughter, like Bechdel's does. Write an essay in which you discuss the differences between this familiar narrative and Bechdel's work. In your discussion, you'll want to provide particular sets of frames or clusters from Bechdel's work and specific moments in the narrative as examples. What is the relationship between the two autobiographical approaches? What does Bechdel's graphic work do that the other narrative does not do? What can you say about Bechdel's approach from looking at it alongside this other example?

SEQUENCE FIVE

Experts and Expertise

Kwame Anthony Appiah
Judith Butler
Edward Said
Walker Percy

ALTERNATIVES:

Richard E. Miller
Kathryn Schulz
Anne Carson

The first three assignments in this sequence give you the chance to think about familiar settings or experiences through the work of writers who have had a significant effect on contemporary thought: Kwame Anthony Appiah, Judith Butler, and Edward Said.

In each case, you will be given the opportunity to work alongside these thinkers as an apprentice, carrying out work they have begun. The final assignment in the sequence will ask you to look back on what you have done, to take stock, and, with Walker Percy's account of the oppressive nature of expertise in mind, to draw some conclusions about the potential and consequences of this kind of intellectual apprenticeship. There are three alternative assignments following the sequence. Any of these could be used in place of the assignments in the sequence.

ASSIGNMENT 1

Depicting the Intellectual

KWAME ANTHONY APPIAH, DAVID FOSTER WALLACE

Both Kwame Anthony Appiah's "Racial Identities" (p. 42) and David Foster Wallace's "Authority and American Usage" (p. 388) have distinctive styles, voices, and methods.

A character emerges in each essay, a figure representing one version of a well-schooled, learned and articulate adult, an intellectual—someone who reads widely, who thinks closely, freshly, and methodically about big questions, someone with ideas and style, someone who is defined in relation to sources, books, and other writers, and someone who takes pains to engage his readers. This is an intellectual who has a desire to reach others, to address them, to bring them into his point of view.

Write an essay in which you discuss the figure of the intellectual represented in these two essays. You'll need to work closely with a few key ideas and representative moments in the texts. Your essay should assess this figure in relation to your own education—better yet, in relation to the kind of figure you yourself intend to be as a well-schooled adult, as an intellectual, as a person with ideas, knowledge, and something to say.

ASSIGNMENT 2

A Question for Philosophers

JUDITH BUTLER

The opening lines of Judith Butler's essay "Beside Oneself: On the Limits of Sexual Autonomy" might be understood as an invitation to participate with her in one of the traditions of philosophy. She writes:

> What makes for a livable world is no idle question. It is not merely a question for philosophers. It is posed in various idioms all the time by people in various walks of life. If that makes them all philosophers, then that is a conclusion I am happy to embrace. It becomes a question for ethics, I think, not only when we ask the personal question, what makes my own life bearable, but when we ask, from a position of power, and from the point of view of distributive justice, what makes, or ought to make, the lives of others bearable? Somewhere in the answer we find ourselves not only committed to a certain view of what life is, and what it should be, but also of what constitutes the human, the distinctively human life, and what does not. (p. 114)

Write an essay that takes up this invitation—and that takes it up in specific reference to what Butler has offered in "Beside Oneself: On the Limits of Sexual Autonomy." You will need, then, to take some time to represent her essay—both what it says and what it does. The "Questions for a Second Reading" (p. 132) should be helpful in preparing for this. Imagine an audience of smart people, people who may even know something about Butler, but who have not read this essay. You have read it, and you want to give them a sense of how and why you find it interesting and important.

But you'll also need to take time to address her questions in your own terms: What makes for a livable world? What constitutes the human? Don't slight this part of your essay. Give yourself as many pages as you gave Butler. You should, however, make it clear that you are writing in response to what you have read. You'll want to indicate, both directly and indirectly, how your thoughts are shaped by, indebted to, or in response to hers.

ASSIGNMENT 3

On Representation

EDWARD SAID

In his essay "States," Edward Said insists on our recognizing the contemporary social, political, and historical context for intimate scenes he (and Jean Mohr) present of people going about their everyday lives. The Palestinian people are still much in the news — photographs of scenes from their lives are featured regularly in newspapers, in magazines, and on the Internet. Collect a series of these images from a particular and defined recent period of time — a week or a month, say, when the Palestinians have been in the news. Using these images, and putting them in conversation with some of the passages and images in "States," write an essay in the manner of Said's essay, with text and image in productive relationship. The goal of your essay should be to examine how Said's work in "States" can speak to us (or might speak to us) today.

ASSIGNMENT 4

On Experts and Expertise

KWAME ANTHONY APPIAH, JUDITH BUTLER, EDWARD SAID, WALKER PERCY

> The whole horizon of being is staked out by "them," the experts. The highest satisfaction of the sightseer (not merely the tourist but any layman seer of sights) is that his sight should be certified as genuine. The worst of this impoverishment is that there is no sense of impoverishment. (p. 304)

> I refer to the general situation in which sovereignty is surrendered to a class of privileged knowers, whether these be theorists or artists. A reader may surrender sovereignty over that which has been written about, just as a consumer may surrender sovereignty over a thing which has been theorized about. The consumer is content to receive an experience just as it has been presented to him by theorists and planners.

---

e See the e-Pages at bedfordstmartins.com/waysofreading.

> The reader may also be content to judge life by whether it has or has not been formulated by those who know and write about life. (p. 305)
>
> — WALKER PERCY
> *The Loss of the Creature*

In the last three assignments you were asked to try on other writers' ways of seeing the world. You looked at what you had read or done, and at scenes from your own life, casting your experience in the terms of others.

Percy, in "The Loss of the Creature," offers what might be taken as a critique of such activity. "A reader," he says, "may surrender sovereignty over that which has been written about, just as a consumer may surrender sovereignty over a thing which has been theorized about." Appiah, Butler, and Said have all been presented to you as, in a sense, "privileged knowers." You have been asked to model your own work on their examples.

It seems safe to say that, at least so far as Percy is concerned, surrendering sovereignty is not a good thing to do. If Percy were to read over your work in these assignments, how do you think he would describe what you have done? If he were to take your work as an example in his essay, where might he place it? And how would his reading of your work fit with your sense of what you have done? Would Percy's assessment be accurate, or is there something he would be missing, something he would fail to see?

Write an essay in which you describe and comment on your work in this sequence, looking at it both from Percy's point of view and from your own, but viewing that work as an example of an educational practice, a way of reading (and writing) that may or may not have benefits for the reader.

Note: You will need to review carefully those earlier papers and mark sections that you feel might serve as interesting examples in your discussion. You want to base your conclusions on the best evidence you can. When you begin writing, it might be useful to refer to the writer of those earlier papers as a "he" or a "she" who played certain roles and performed his or her work in certain characteristic ways. You can save the first person, the "I," for the person who is writing this assignment and looking back on those texts.

ALTERNATIVE ASSIGNMENT

A Story of Reading

RICHARD E. MILLER

Consider the following passage from Richard E. Miller's "The Dark Night of the Soul":

> What makes *Into the Wild* remarkable is Krakauer's ability to get some purchase on McCandless's actual reading practice, which, in turn, enables him to get inside McCandless's head and speculate with

> considerable authority about what ultimately led the young man to abandon the comforts of home and purposefully seek out mortal danger. Krakauer is able to do this, in part, because he has access to the books that McCandless read, with all their underlinings and marginalia, as well as to his journals and the postcards and letters McCandless sent to friends along his journey. Working with these materials and his interviews with McCandless's family and friends, Krakauer develops a sense of McCandless's inner life and eventually comes to some understanding of why the young man was so susceptible to being seduced by the writings of London, Thoreau, Muir, and Tolstoy. Who McCandless is and what becomes of him are, it turns out, intimately connected to the young man's approach to reading — both what he chose to read and how he chose to read it.

When Miller is writing about Krakauer's *Into the Wild*, he seems to suggest that what we read, and how we read, can say something about who we are and about what we might become. This is a very bold claim.

Think of a book that made a difference to you, that captured you, maybe one you have read more than once, maybe one that you've made marks in or that still sits on your bookshelf. Or, if not a book, think of your favorite song or album or movie or TV show, something that engaged you at least potentially as McCandless was engaged by London, Thoreau, Muir, and Tolstoy. What was it that you found there? What kind of reader were you? And what makes this a story in the past tense? How and why did you move on? (Or, if it is not a story in the past tense, where are you now, and are you, like McCandless, in any danger?)

ALTERNATIVE ASSIGNMENT

Models for Thinking

KATHRYN SCHULZ

Schulz says the following about evidence in the chapter you have just read:

> Descartes was right to fear that this way of thinking ["believing things based on paltry evidence"] would cause us to make mistakes; it does. Since he was interested in knowing the truth, and knowing that he knew it, he tried to develop a model for thinking that could curtail the possibility of error. . . . In fact, curtailing error was the goal of most models of optimal human cognition proposed by most thinkers throughout most of history, and it is the goal behind our own broadly shared image of the ideal thinker. Some of these models, like Descartes', sought to curtail error through radical doubt. Others sought to curtail it through formal logic — using valued premises to

See the e-Pages at bedfordstmartins.com/waysofreading.

> derive necessarily valid conclusions. Others, including our shared one of the ideal thinker, seek to curtail it through a kind of general due diligence: careful attention to evidence and counterevidence, coupled with a prudent avoidance of preconceived notions. (364)

"Due diligence," "a model for thinking," and the "ideal thinker": Over time, writing has been one of the ways human beings have tried to find forms and methods to represent, preserve, and transmit models for thinking. You've received these models through instruction. Topic sentence, example, conclusion—these comprise a model for thinking. And every time you have been assigned something to read, and every time you have chosen something to read, you were presented with a "model for thinking," a model in practice.

For this assignment, find a piece of prose (somewhere in length from a paragraph to a page or two, no more). It can be ancient or it can be recent; it can be academic or it can be from outside the academy. We'd like you to use it to think about writing, belief, and evidence. We'd like you to think about it as a model for thinking, and think about it, at least for a brief period, through the lens of this chapter in *Being Wrong*.

Remember—you need to present your example to readers who are not familiar with it. And you'll need to present Schulz's chapter to people who have not yet read it. You will need to do some work to prepare your reader for what you want to say. The most important part of your essay, however, will be the sections where you take the stage and present what you have to add to the conversation.

ALTERNATIVE ASSIGNMENT

Short Talks

ANNE CARSON

The form of Carson's "Short Talks" presents challenges, but it also presents opportunities. As you reread, think about this text as a type of experimental essay. How does it draw upon the conventions of the essay? How does it defy or revise those conventions? How would you describe its formal features in relation to what you understand to be conventional essay form? How does "Short Talks" satisfy or challenge a reader's expectations?

Prepare an essay that is Carson-like. It should be, at minimum, as long as hers. It should be similar in style and intent. Her work is your model and inspiration, and yet this project is also yours. A reader should be able to see where and how your work is in conversation with hers; a reader should also be able to see what you bring to the table. Be sure that your essay has an introduction, something to orient a reader to what follows. ("Introductions" are often either written last or seriously revised once the project is complete.)

SEQUENCE SIX

Reading Culture

John Berger
Susan Bordo
Judith Halberstam
Kathryn Schulz
Michel Foucault

ALTERNATIVES:

Richard E. Miller
David Foster Wallace
James Baldwin

In this sequence, you will be reading and writing about culture. Not "Culture," something you get if you go to the museum or a concert on Sunday, but culture—the images, words, and sounds that pervade our lives and organize and represent our common experience. This sequence invites your reflection on the ways culture "works" in and through the lives of individual consumers.

The difficulty of this sequence lies in the way it asks you to imagine that you are not a sovereign individual, making your own choices and charting the course of your life. This is conceptually difficult, but it can also be distasteful, since we learn at an early age to put great stock in imagining our own freedom. Most of the readings that follow ask you to imagine that you are the product of your culture; that your ideas, feelings, and actions, your ways of thinking and being, are constructed for you by a large, organized, pervasive force (sometimes called history, sometimes called culture, sometimes called ideology). You don't feel this to be the case, but that is part of the power of culture, or so the argument goes. These forces hide themselves. They lead you to believe that their constructions are naturally, inevitably there, that things are the way they are because that is just "the way things are." The assignments in this sequence ask you to read against your common sense. You will be expected to try on the role of the critic—to see how and where it might be useful to recognize complex motives in ordinary expressions.

The authors in this sequence all write as though, through great effort, they could step outside culture to see and criticize its workings. The assignments in this sequence will ask you both to reflect on this type of criticism and to participate in it.

ASSIGNMENT 1

Looking at Pictures

JOHN BERGER

> Original paintings are silent and still in a sense that information never is. Even a reproduction hung on a wall is not comparable in this respect for in the original the silence and stillness permeate the actual material, the paint, in which one follows the traces of the painter's immediate gestures. This has the effect of closing the distance in time between the painting of the picture and one's own act of looking at it. . . . What we make of that painted moment when it is before our eyes depends upon what we expect of art, and that in turn depends today upon how we have already experienced the meaning of paintings through reproductions.
>
> —JOHN BERGER
> *Ways of Seeing*

e

While Berger describes original paintings as silent in this passage, it is clear that these paintings begin to speak if one approaches them properly, if one learns to ask "the right questions of the past." Berger demonstrates one route of approach, for example, in his reading of the Hals paintings, where he asks questions about the people and objects and their relationship to the painter and the viewer. What the paintings might be made to say, however, depends on the viewer's expectations, his or her sense of the questions that seem appropriate or possible. Berger argues that because of the way art is currently displayed, discussed, and reproduced, the viewer expects only to be mystified.

For this assignment, imagine that you are working against the silence and mystification Berger describes. Go to a museum—or, if that is not possible, to a large-format book of reproductions in the library (or, if that is not possible, to the Internet)—and select a painting that seems silent and still, yet invites conversation. Your job is to figure out what sorts of questions to ask, to interrogate the painting, to get it to speak, to engage with the past in some form of dialogue. Write an essay in which you record this process and what you have learned from it. Somewhere in your essay, perhaps at the end, turn back to Berger's chapter to talk about how this process has or hasn't confirmed what you take to be Berger's expectations.

---

e See the e-Pages at bedfordstmartins.com/waysofreading.

Note: If possible, include with your essay a reproduction of the painting you select. (Check the postcards at the museum gift shop.) In any event, you want to make sure that you describe the painting in sufficient detail for your readers to follow what you say.

ASSIGNMENT 2

Berger and After

JOHN BERGER, SUSAN BORDO

In "Beauty (Re)discovers the Male Body," Bordo refers to John Berger and his work in *Ways of Seeing*, although she refers to a different chapter than the one included here. In general, however, both Berger and Bordo are concerned with how we see and read images; both are concerned to correct the ways images are used and read; both trace the ways images serve the interests of money and power; both are written to teach readers how and why they should pay a different kind of attention to the images around them.

For this assignment, use Bordo's work to reconsider Berger's. Write an essay in which you consider the two chapters as examples of an ongoing project. Berger's essay precedes Bordo's by about a quarter of a century. If you look closely at one or two of their examples, and if you look at the larger concerns of their arguments, are they saying the same things? doing the same work? If so, how? And why is such work still necessary? If not, how do their projects differ? And how might you explain those differences?

ASSIGNMENT 3

Reading the Body

SUSAN BORDO

In "Beauty (Re)discovers the Male Body," Bordo looks back to the history of advertising (the "cultural genealogy of the ads I've been discussing") and works directly with the ads that prompted and served this chapter in her book. These images are a key part of the writing.

Bordo also speaks directly to you and invites you into her project: "So the next time you see a Dockers or a Haggar ad, think of it not only as an advertisement for khakis but also as an advertisement for a certain notion of what it means to be a man." You don't have to be limited to Dockers, Haggar, or khaki, but as you reread the essay and prepare for this writing assignment, keep your eye out for advertisements that come your way, advertisements that seem perfect for think-

See the e-Pages at bedfordstmartins.com/waysofreading.

ing along with Bordo (or advertisements that seem like interesting counterexamples). Clip these or copy them so that you can use them, as she does, as material for writing.

Write an essay in which you take up Bordo's invitation. You should assume an audience that has not read Bordo (or not read her work recently), so you will need to take time to present the terms and direction of her argument. Your goal, however, is to extend her project to your moment in time, when advertising may very well have moved on to different images of men and strategies of presentation. Bordo is quite specific about her age and experience, her point of view. You should be equally specific. You, too, should establish your point of view. You are placed at a different moment in time; your experience is different; your exposure to images has prepared you differently. You write from a different subject position. Your job, then, is not simply to reproduce Bordo's project but to extend it, to refine it, to put it to the test.

ASSIGNMENT 4

Animating Revolt

JUDITH HALBERSTAM

Part of the intellectual work Halberstam does in this piece is taking a film we might recognize as familiar (films like *Finding Nemo* or *March of the Penguins*) and inviting us to see something new about that film. Think about an animated film you've seen recently. Watch this film again with Halberstam's writing in mind. Then, write an essay in which you consider the film's potential for what Halberstam calls "animating revolt."

To begin your essay, you may have to explain to your reader what Halberstam means by "animating revolt" (which is one half of her title for this piece of writing). To write an essay that takes up Halberstam's method of looking, you'll want to ask yourself: What would Halberstam notice about this film? What passages from her essay would guide someone to read this film in a particular way? How does the film illuminate, complicate, or extend Halberstam's central questions?

ASSIGNMENT 5

Combating Biases

KATHRYN SCHULZ, JUDITH HALBERSTAM

In "Evidence," (p. 362) Kathryn Schulz tell us that:

> . . . if we want to improve our relationship to evidence, we must take a more active role in how we think — must, in a sense, take the reins of our own minds. To do this, we must query and speak and

> investigate and open our eyes. Specifically, and crucially, we must learn to actively combat our inductive biases: to deliberately seek out evidence that challenges our beliefs, and to take seriously such evidence when we come across it. (p. 377)

Schulz suggests here that looking for evidence and ideas that go against what we already believe to be true is to "take the reins of our own minds." One might see Judith Halberstam's work on animation as seeking out evidence that goes against dominant or accepted truths.

Write an essay in which you explore Halberstam's work through the lens of Schulz's claims about improving "our relationship with evidence." What is Halberstam's relationship to evidence? How does she "combat our inductive biases"? If you think of yourself as taking on Schulz's view of evidence, and seeking out evidence that challenges your own beliefs, how might Halberstam's work be a way of doing that? What, in Halberstam's writing, challenges your beliefs about the culture in which you live? If you take Schulz's project seriously, what might be productive about the perhaps contrarian evidence Halberstam offers? How do both authors invite you to reread culture — or to reconsider the methods you use when you do so?

ALTERNATIVE ASSIGNMENT

What Is It Good For?

RICHARD E. MILLER

Richard E. Miller's essay "The Dark Night of the Soul" opens with a list of fatal shootings in school — troublingly, an incomplete list. As the essay builds to questions — questions for educators and for students — the specters of violence and alienation remain, changing how we think about the reading and writing that school endeavors to teach us. "I have these doubts, you see," Miller writes of academic work, "doubts silently shared by many who spend their days teaching others the literate arts. Aside from gathering and organizing information, aside from generating critiques and analyses that forever fall on deaf ears, what might the literate arts be said to be good for?".

Write an essay that takes up this question — "what might the literate arts be said to be good for?" — and that takes it up from your range of reference and from your point of view — or, more properly, from the point of view of you and people like you, the group you feel prepared to speak for. As an exercise in understanding, your essay should be modeled on one (or more) of the sections in "The Dark Night of the Soul." You can choose the text — and the text can be anything that might serve as an example of the literate arts, things in print but also including songs, films, and TV shows. But your presentation and discussion of the text

---

e See the e-Pages at bedfordstmartins.com/waysofreading.

should be in conversation with Miller—with his concerns, his key terms, his examples, and his conclusions.

ALTERNATIVE ASSIGNMENT

Standard English in a Democratic Culture

DAVID FOSTER WALLACE

At certain moments in his essay "Authority and American Usage," David Foster Wallace describes his approach as a teacher of college students. He tells us in footnote 6, for instance, that while he teaches literature courses, he usually abandons the syllabus after he reads his students' first papers in order to hold "a three-week Emergency Remedial Usage and Grammar Unit, during which my demeanor is basically that of somebody teaching HIV prevention to intravenous-drug users." And later he provides a representation of a lengthy speech he gives to individual college students who struggle with Standard Written English. He says,

> I'm not trying to suggest here that an effective SWE pedagogy would require teachers to wear sunglasses and call students Dude. What I am suggesting is that the rhetorical situation of a US English class — a class composed wholly of young people whose Group identity is rooted in defiance of Adult Establishment values, plus also composed partly of minorities whose primary dialects are different from SWE — requires a teacher to come up with overt, honest, and compelling arguments for why SWE is a dialect worth learning. (p. 417)

But Wallace also teaches writing by example—that is, by what he says in this essay about effective writing and by the way he chooses to write. In this sense, "Authority and American Usage" offers a writing lesson.

Write an essay in which you take up the invitation to engage Wallace's argument about U.S. English, about SWE, about rhetoric, and about the function and importance of a writing class. You will need to work directly in reference to what Wallace says in the text. In other words, you'll need to work with sentences and examples. But you also bring experience to the table. From your point of view, and from the point of view of students like you, what is at stake? How and where might you enter this conversation? Where are you in the settings Wallace invokes? in his arguments?

ALTERNATIVE ASSIGNMENT

Representing Race

JAMES BALDWIN

Toward the end of his essay, after talking about the riot in Harlem in 1943, Baldwin says,

> If ever, indeed, the violence which fills Harlem's churches, pool halls, and bars erupts outward in a more direct fashion, Harlem and its citizens are likely to vanish in an apocalyptic flood. That this is not likely to happen is due to a great many reasons, most hidden and powerful among them the Negro's real relation to the white American. This relation prohibits, simply, anything as uncomplicated and satisfactory as pure hatred.

We are still, as a country and as a culture, trying to explain to ourselves the real relationship between white Americans and people we refer to as "African Americans." Choose any contemporary example that is available to you—writing, music, film, TV—something that you could offer as a parallel attempt to represent the relationship of black to white Americans. Write an essay in which you compare "Notes" with whatever example you have chosen.

Assume that your reader is familiar with neither of your selections. You will need to introduce and present "Notes of a Native Son" (present through summary, paraphrase, and quotation), and you will need to do the same for the example you bring to this project. The point of the comparison (or one of its points) should be to think about the history of the representation of race.

See the e-Pages at bedfordstmartins.com/waysofreading.

Text Credits

Gloria Anzaldúa. "How to Tame a Wild Tongue." From *Borderlands/La Frontera: The New Mestiza.* Copyright © 1987, 1999, 2007 by Gloria Anzaldúa. Reprinted by permission of Aunt Lute Books.

Kwame Anthony Appiah. "Race, Culture, Identity: Misunderstood Connections." (Presented as "Racial Identities" in this textbook.) Appiah, K. Anthony: *Color Conscious.* © 1996 Princeton University Press. 1998 paperback edition. Reprinted by permissions of Princeton University Press.

James Baldwin. "Notes of a Native Son" by James Baldwin. Copyright © 1955, renewed 1983, by James Baldwin. Reprinted by permission of Beacon Press, Boston.

Alison Bechdel. "The Ordinary Devoted Mother" from *Are You My Mother?: A Comic Drama* by Alison Bechdel. Copyright © 2012 by Alison Bechdel. Reprinted by permission of Houghton Mifflin Harcourt Publishing Company. All rights reserved.

John Berger. "Chapter 1" from *Ways of Seeing* by John Berger. Copyright © 1972 by Penguin Books Ltd. Used by permission of Viking Penguin, a division of Penguin Group (USA) Inc.

John Berger. "Ways of Seeing." Excerpt from *And Our Faces, My Heart, Brief As Photos* by John Berger, copyright © 1984 by John Berger. Used by permission of Pantheon Books, an imprint of the Knopf Doubleday Publishing Group, a division of Random House LLC. All rights reserved.

Susan Bordo. "Beauty (Re)Discovers the Male Body" from *The Male Body: A new look at men in public and in private* by Susan Bordo. Copyright © 1999 by Susan Bordo. Used by permission of Farrar, Straus and Giroux, LLC. All rights reserved. CAUTION: Users are warned that this work is protected under copyright laws and downloading is strictly prohibited. The right to reproduce or transfer the work via any medium must be secured with Farrar, Straus and Giroux, LLC.

Judith Butler. "Beside Oneself: On the Limits of Sexual Autonomy." From *Undoing Gender* by Butler, Judith P. Copyright © 2004. Reproduced with permission of Taylor & Francis Group LLC – Books in the format Other Book via Copyright Clearance Center.

Anne Carson. "Short Talks." From *Plainwater: Essays and Poetry* by Anne Carson, copyright © 1995 by Anne Carson. Used by permission of Alfred A. Knopf, a division of Random House, Inc. Any third party use of this material, outside of this publication, is prohibited. Interested parties must apply directly to Random House, Inc. for permission.

Brian Doyle. "Joyas Voladoras." From *The American Scholar,* Volume 73, No. 4, Autumn 2004. Used by permission of The American Scholar.

Joshua Foer. "The End of Remembering" from *Moonwalking with Einstein: The Art and Science of Remembering Everything* by Joshua Foer, copyright © 2011 by Joshua Foer. Used by permission of The Penguin Press, a division of Penguin Group (USA) Inc.

Michel Foucault. "Panopticism." From *Discipline and Punish* by Michel Foucault. English Translation copyright © 1977 by Alan Sheridan (New York: Pantheon). Originally published in French as Surveiller et Punir. Copyright © 1975 by Editions Gallimard. Reprinted by permission of Georges Borchardt, Inc., for Editions Gallimard.

Paulo Freire. "The 'Banking' Concept of Education." Excerpt from *Pedagogy of the Oppressed,* by Paulo Freire, © 1970, 1993. Reprinted by permission of the Continuum, an imprint of Bloomsbury Publishing Plc.

Susan Griffin. Excerpt from "Our Secret." From *Chorus of Stones* by Susan Griffin, copyright © 1992 by Susan Griffin. Used by permission of Doubleday, a division of Random House, Inc. Any third party use of this material, outside of this publication, is prohibited. Interested parties must apply directly to Random House, Inc. for permission.

Judith Halberstam. "Animating Revolt and Revolting Animation," in *The Queer Art of Failure,* Judith Halberstam, pp. 27–52. Copyright, 2011, Duke University Press.

All rights reserved. Republished by permission of the copyright holder. www .dukeupress.edu.

Richard Hoggart. "A Scholarship Boy." From *The Uses of Literacy* by Richard Hoggart, published by Chatto & Windus. Reprinted by permission of The Random House Group Ltd.

Kathleen Jamie. "Shia Girls" from *Among Muslims*. Copyright 2002 Kathleen Jamie, *Among Muslims*. Reprinted by permission of Seal Press, a member of the Perseus Books Group.

Jonathan Lethem. "The Ecstasy of Influence: A Plagiarism." Excerpt from *The Ecstasy of Influence: Nonfictions, Etc.* by Jonathan Lethem, copyright © 2011 by Jonathan Lethem. Used by permission of Doubleday, an imprint of the Knopf Doubleday Publishing Group, a division of Random House LLC. All rights reserved.

Richard E. Miller. "The Dark Night of the Soul" from *Writing at the End of the World*, by Richard E. Miller, © 2005. All rights are controlled by the University of Pittsburgh Press, Pittsburgh, PA 15260. Used by permission of the University of Pittsburgh Press.

Errol Morris. "Will the Real Hooded Man Please Stand Up?" From *Believing is Seeing: Observations on the Mysteries of Photography* by Errol Morris, copyright © 2011 by Errol Morris. Used by permission of The Penguin Press, a division of Penguin Group (USA) LLC.

Walker Percy. "The Loss of the Creature" from *The Message in the Bottle* by Walker Percy. Copyright © 1975 by Walker Percy. Reprinted by permission of Farrar, Straus and Giroux, LLC.

Mary Louise Pratt. "Arts of the Contact Zone" from Profession 91. Copyright © 1991. Reprinted by permission of copyright owner, the Modern Language Association of America.

Richard Rodriguez. "The Achievement of Desire." From *Hunger of Memory: The Education of Richard Rodriguez* by Richard Rodriguez. Reprinted by permission of David R. Godine, Publisher, Inc. Copyright © 1982 by Richard Rodriguez.

Edward Said. "States" from *After the Last Sky*. Copyright © 1999 by Columbia University Press.

Kathryn Schulz. "Evidence" (from *Being Wrong: Adventures in the Margins of Error*). Pages 111–32 from Being Wrong by Kathryn Schulz. Excerpts from pp. 170, 309, 338–39, 345, 361–64 [336 words total] from Being Wrong by Kathryn Schulz. Copyright © 2010 by Kathryn Schulz. Reprinted by permission of HarperCollins Publishers.

David Foster Wallace. "Authority and American Usage." From *Consider the Lobster* by David Foster Wallace. Copyright © 2005 by David Foster Wallace. By permission of Little, Brown and Company. All rights reserved.

John Edgar Wideman. "Our Time" from *Brothers and Keepers* by John Edgar Wideman. Copyright © 1984 by John Edgar Wideman, reprinted with permission of The Wylie Agency LLC.

Photo Credits

Gloria Anzaldúa photograph courtesy of © Jean Weisinger. Cover design from *Borderlands/La Frontera: The New Mestiza*. Copyright © 1987, 1999, 2007, 2012 by Gloria Anzaldúa. Reproduced by permission of Aunt Lute Books. 25th anniversary edition published in 2012.

Kwame Anthony Appiah photograph courtesy of Office of Communications/ Princeton University. Cover design from Appiah, K. Anthony: *Color Conscious* ©1996 Princeton University Press, 1998 paperback edition. Reprinted by permission of Princeton University Press.

James Baldwin photograph courtesy of Mary Evans Picture Library/Alamy. Cover design for James Baldwin: *Notes of a Native Son*, © 1955. Reproduced by permission of the publisher, Beacon Press.

Alison Bechdel photograph courtesy of © Greg Ruffing/Redux Pictures. Cover from *Are You My Mother?: A Comic Drama* by Alison Bechdel. Reprinted by permission of Houghton Mifflin Harcourt Publishing Company. All rights reserved.

John Berger photograph courtesy of © Henri Cartier-Bresson/Magnum Photos. "Jacket Cover" copyright © 1994 by Pantheon Books, a division of Random House, Inc., from *And Our Faces, My Heart, Brief as Photos* by John Berger. Used by permission of Pantheon Books, a division of Random House, Inc. Any third party use of this material, outside of this publication, is prohibited. Interested parties must apply directly to Random House, Inc. for permission. *Key of Dreams* photograph courtesy of Pinakothek der Moderne, Bayerische Staatsgemaeldesammlungen, Munich Germany. Photo: bpk, Berlin. Art Resource, NY. Rene Magritte, *The Key of Dreams* © 2013 C. Herscovici, London / Artists Rights Society (ARS), New York. *Regents of Old Men's Alm's* house photograph courtesy of *The Regents of the Old Men's Almhouse,* Haarlem, 1664 (oil on canvas), Hals, Frans (1582/3–1666) / Frans Hals Museum, Haarlem, The Netherlands / Peter Willi / The Bridgeman Art Library. *Regentesses of Old Men's Alm's House* photographs courtesy of *The Regentesses of the Old Men's Almhouse,* Haarlem, 1664 (oil on canvas), Frans Halls / Frans Hals Museum, Haarlem, The Netherlands. Album/Art Resource, NY. *Still Life with Wicker Chair* photograph courtesy of Pablo Picasso, *Still Life with a Wicker Chair* © RMN-Grand Palais/Art Resource, NY. *Still Life with a Wicker Chair* © 2013 Estate of Pablo Picasso / Artists Rights Society (ARS), New York. *Virgin of the Rocks* photograph courtesy of Leonardo da Vinci, *The Virgin of the Rocks* ©National Gallery, London/Art Resource, NY. *Virgin of the Rocks* (Louvre) photograph courtesy of Leonardo da Vinci, *The Madonna of the Rocks, c. 1483* Louvre Museum, Paris, © RMN-Grand Palais/ Art Resource, NY. *Virgin & Child w. St. Anne & St. John Baptist* photograph courtesy of Leonardo da Vinci, *The Virgin of the Rocks* © National Gallery, London/Art Resource, NY. *Venus and Mars* ART374857 photograph courtesy of Sandro Botticelli, *Venus and Mars* © National Gallery, London/Art Resource, NY. *Procession to Calvary* photograph courtesy of Pieter Brueghel the Elder, *Jesus Carrying the Cross, or the Way to Calvary*, 1564. Photo Credit: Erich Lessing / Art Resource, NY. *Wheatfield with Crows* photograph courtesy of Vincent van Gogh, *Wheatfield with Crows* Van Gogh Museum Foundation, Amsterdam, The Netherlands, Art Resource, N.Y. Walter Benjamin photograph courtesy of © J. LL. Banús/age footstock. *Woman Pouring Milk* photograph courtesy of Jan Vermeer, *The Kitchenmaid* Rijkmuseum, Amsterdam, The Netherlands. Erich Lessing/Art Resource, NY. *Woman in Bed* photograph courtesy of Rembrandt, *Woman in Bed* National Galleries of Scotland, Dist. RMN-Grand Palais/Art Resource, NY. *Calling of St. Matthew* photograph courtesy of Michaelangelo Merisi daCaravaggio, " Photo Credit: Scala / Art Resource, NY. *Ways of Seeing* [BBC]: Episode One courtesy of *Ways of Seeing*, Episode One. © 2014 BBC Worldwide. Used by permission. All rights reserved.

Susan Bordo photograph courtesy of the University of Kentucky. Jacket design by Susan Mitchell from *The Male Body* by Susan Bordo. Copyright © 1999 by Susan Mitchell. Jacket art © The Special Photographer Co./Photonica. Used by permission of Farrar, Straus and Giroux, LLC. All rights reserved. The following caution notice will also appear on-screen with the work: CAUTION: Users are warned that this work is protected under copyright laws and downloading is strictly prohibited. The right to reproduce or transfer the work via any medium must be secured with Farrar, Straus and Giroux, LLC.

Judith Butler photograph courtesy of © Markus Kirchgessner/Redux Pictures. Copyright 2004 from *Undoing Gender* by Judith Butler. Reproduced by permission of Taylor and Francis Group, LLC, a division of Informa plc. *Your Behavior Creates Your Gender* video courtesy of Judith Butler: *Your Behavior Creates Your Gender* [video interview] http://bigthink.com/ideas/30766. Used by permission of The Big Think, Inc.

Anne Carson photograph courtesy of © Peter Smith Photography. Cover of *Short Talks* by Anne Carson. Reprinted by permission of United Talent Agency.

Brian Doyle photograph courtesy of © Jerry Hart. Jacket cover from *The American Scholar*, Volume 73, No.4, Autumn 2004. Copyright © 2004 by The Phi Beta Kappa Society.

Ralph Waldo Emerson photograph courtesy of George Eastman House/Archive Photos/Getty Images.

Joshua Foer photograph courtesy of © Leo van Velzen/Hollandse Hoogte/Redux Pictures. Cover design for *Moonwalking With Einstein: The Art and Science of Remembering Everything* by Joshua Foer, reprinted by permission of Penguin Group USA.

Michel Foucault photograph courtesy of © AFP/Getty Images. "Jacket Cover" copyright © 1977 by Vintage Books, a division of Random House, Inc., from *Discipline and Punish* by Michel Foucault, translated by Alan Sheridan, translation copyright © 1977 by Alan Sheridan. Used by permission of Pantheon Books, a division of Random House, Inc. Any third party use of this material, outside of this publication, is prohibited. Interested parties must apply directly to Random House, Inc. for permission. *Panopticon* photograph courtesy of ©Mansell/Time & Life Pictures/Getty Images. *Handwriting model* photograph courtesy of ©The Granger Collection, New York. *Stateville penitentiary* photograph courtesy of © Bettmann/CORBIS. *Evils of alcoholism* photograph courtesy of Mary Evans Picture Library/Alamy.

Paulo Freire author photo from *Pedagogy of the Oppressed* by Paulo Freire ©1970, 2000. Reprinted with the permission of the publisher, The Continuum International Publishing Group, an imprint of Bloomsbury Publishing Inc. Cover design from *Pedagogy of the Oppressed* by Paulo Freire ©1970, 2000. Reprinted with the permission of the publisher, The Continuum International Publishing Group, an imprint of Bloomsbury Publishing Inc.

Susan Griffin photograph courtesy of © Irene Young. Jacket Cover copyright © 1992 by Doubleday, a division of Random House, Inc., from *Chorus of Stones* by Susan Griffin. Used by permission of Doubleday, a division of Random House, Inc. Any third party use of this material, outside of this publication, is prohibited. Interested parties must apply directly to Random House, Inc. for permission.

Judith Halberstam photograph courtesy of J. Jack Halberstam, author of *Lady Gaga Feminism* (2012) and *The Queer Art of Failure* (2011). *"I'll Give You Something to Cry About" (Dead Baby Finch)*, 1990, detail. Courtesy of the artist, Judie Bamber, and Angles Gallery, Los Angeles. Book jacket for *The Queer Art of Failure*, published by Duke University Press.

Kathleen Jamie photograph courtesy of © Eamonn McCabe/Camera Press/Redux Pictures. Book cover from Kathleen Jamie, *Among Muslims*, courtesy Sort of Books, UK.

Jonathan Lethem photograph courtesy of © John Lucas. Jacket Cover copyright © 2011 by Doubleday, a division of Random House, Inc., from *The Ecstasy of Influence* by Jonathan Lethem. Used by permission of Doubleday, a division of Random House, Inc. Any third party use of this material, outside of this publication, is prohibited. Interested parties must apply directly to Random House, Inc. for permission.

Richard Miller photograph courtesy of Photo © Anannya Dasgupta. Cover from *Writing at the End of the World*, by Richard E. Miller, ©2005. Reprinted by permission of the University of Pittsburgh Press.

Errol Morris photograph courtesy of © Sean Gallup/Getty Images. Jacket cover courtesy of *Believing Is Seeing: Observations on the Mysteries of Photography* by Errol Morris. Reprinted by permission of Penguin Group USA. *Hooded Man* photograph by Sgt. Ivan Frederick, Abu Ghraib Prison, November 5, 2003. Rabbit/duck profile illustration from Joseph Jastrow, "The Mind's Eye," *Appleton's Popular Science Monthly*, January 1899, vol. 54, p. 312, fig. 20. Ali Shalal Quassi photograph courtesy of © Shawn Baldwin/The New York Times/Redux Pictures. "The claw" (various views) photographs by U.S. military personnel, Abu Ghraib Prison, Iraq, 2003. Exif file photo D-20 & D-21 courtesy of detail of timeline of Abu Ghraib photographs created by Brent Pack, special agent, US Army Criminal Investigation Division. Wide-angle by Harman & hooded man photographs by U.S. military personnel, Abu Ghraib Prison, Iraq, 2003. *We've Forgotten that Photographs are Connected to the Physical World* photograph courtesy of Oliver Laughland, Andy

Gallagher, Richard Sprenger, www.guardian.co.uk. Reproduced by permission of Guardian News and Media Limited. All rights reserved.

Walker Percy photograph courtesy of © Rhoda K. Faust, New Orleans, LA. Jacket design by Janet Halverson from *The Message in the Bottle* by Walker Percy. Jacket design copyright © 1975 by Janet Halverson. Reprinted by permission of Farrar, Straus and Giroux, LLC.

Mary Louise Pratt photograph courtesy of © Linda A. Cicero/ Stanford News Service. Cover design for Profession 91. Reprinted by permission of the Modern Language Association of America. Adam and Eve photograph courtesy of *Adam and Eve*, Guaman Poma de Ayala manuscript. Original in the archives of the State Library of Denmark. Used by permission. All rights reserved. Conquista, Meeting of Spaniards and Inca photograph courtesy of *Conquista, Meeting of Spaniards and Inca*. Guaman Poma de Ayala manuscript. Original in the archives of the State Library of Denmark. Used by permission. All rights reserved. Corregidor de Minas photograph courtesy of *Corregidor de Minas*, Guaman Poma de Ayala manuscript. Original in the archives of the State Library of Denmark. Used by permission. All rights reserved.

Richard Rodriguez photograph courtesy of © 2001 Christine Alicino. Jacket cover from *Hunger of Memory: The Education of Richard Rodgriguez* by Richard Rodriguez. Reprinted by permission of David R. Godine, Publisher, Inc. Copyright © 1982 by Richard Rodriguez.

Edward Said photograph courtesy of © Ulf Andersen/Getty Images. Cover image from *After the Last Sky* designed by Benjamin Shin Farber and photographs by Jean Mohr, reprinted by permission of Columbia University Press. Photographs accompanying Edward Said's *After the Last Sky* © Jean Mohr, Geneva. Palestine photos from *After the Last Sky* courtesy of © Jean Mohr.

Kathryn Schulz photograph courtesy of Photography by Michael Polito. Kathryn Schultz book cover from *Being Wrong* by Kathryn Schulz. Copyright © 2010 by Kathryn Schulz. Reprinted by permission of Harper Collins Publishers.

David Foster Wallace photograph courtesy of © Gary Hannabarger/Corbis. Cover reprint from *Consider the Lobster* by David Foster Wallace, used by permission of Little Brown and company, a division of the Hachette Book Group.

Edgar Wideman photograph courtesy of the University of Massachusetts, Amherst. Jacket Cover copyright © 1995 by Vintage Books, a division of Random House, Inc., from *Brothers and Keepers* by John Edgar Wideman. Used by permission of Vintage Books, a division of Random House, Inc. Any third party use of this material, outside of this publication, is prohibited. Interested parties must apply directly to Random House, Inc. for permission.

Missing something? To access the online material that accompanies this text, visit **bedfordstmartins.com/waysofreading**. Students who do not buy a new book can purchase access at this site.

Inside Bedford Integrated Media for *Ways of Reading*

James Baldwin

Notes of a Native Son [text essay]
Questions

John Berger

Ways of Seeing [text essay + images]
On Rembrandt's Woman in Bed [text essay + images]
On Caravaggio's The Calling of St. Matthew [text essay + images]
Questions
Ways of Seeing: Episode One [video]

Susan Bordo

Beauty (Re)discovers the Male Body [text essay]
Questions

Judith Butler

Your Behavior Creates Your Gender [video]

Ralph Waldo Emerson

The American Scholar [text essay]
Questions

Kathleen Jamie

Shia Girls [text essay]
Questions

Jonathan Lethem

The Ecstasy of Influence: A Plagiarism [text essay]
Questions

Richard E. Miller

The Dark Night of the Soul [text essay]
Questions

Errol Morris

Will the Real Hooded Man Please Stand Up? [text essay + images]
Questions
We've Forgotten That Photographs are Connected to the Physical World [video]

Edward Said

States [text essay + images]
Questions

Additional Assignment Sequences

Additional Assignment Sequence One: Deliberate Acts of Discovery
Additional Assignment Sequence Two: On Difficulty
Additional Assignment Sequence Three: The Uses of Reading (I)
Additional Assignment Sequence Four: The Uses of Reading (II)
Additional Assignment Sequence Five: The Art of Argument
Additional Assignment Sequence Six: Working with Metaphor